Gay, Lesbian, Bisexual, and Transgender Civil Rights

A Public Policy Agenda for Uniting a Divided America

Gay, Lesbian, Bisexual, and Transgender Civil Rights

A Public Policy Agenda for Uniting a Divided America

Edited by
Wallace Swan

Routledge
Taylor & Francis Group
NEW YORK AND LONDON

First published 2015 by CRC Press

Published 2019 by Routledge
605 Third Avenue, New York, NY 10017
2 Park Square, Milton Park, Abingdon, Oxon OX14 4RN

International Standard Book Number-13: 978-1-4665-6730-6 (Hardback)

Contents

Foreword

The passage of time is one of the great divides in the movement for greater equality and opportunity for lesbian, gay, bisexual, and transgender (LGBT) citizens of the United States. Ask any LGBT person who is "chronologically advantaged" (older than 40), and they will exclaim with wonder and delight, "I never thought I'd live to see this day …." It is incredible to contemplate the difference between then and now. "Then" was our formative years, growing up in public and private schools of the suburbs, small towns, and big cities across our country. Most of us who are LGBT were not even able to fully understand what or who, exactly, we were. There was no frame of reference for the difference we felt inside. No images of people like us appeared anywhere. No adults were open about themselves. To the extent we had an inkling, derision from peers, condemnation from religious and political leaders, and being defined as pathological by health care professionals created great suffering. "Now" is this time in which we live, where we can stand up and state publicly who the person we love is and form a family with that person, because full marriage equality is the law in 18 states and the District of Columbia. The emerging generation of young people looks at the LGBT struggle for social acceptance and civil rights as one of the defining moral questions of the day and as an argument that is in their minds settled—in favor of equality and freedom.

It has been said that the advances experienced by LGBT people in social acceptance and the corresponding public policy gains arising from political advances have come faster than any other similar movement in our country's history, especially when compared to the civil and human rights movements that benefited African Americans and women. Without taking anything away from those incredibly brave early LGBT pioneers from the early parts of the 20th century on whose shoulders we stand, the movement really got rolling with the Stonewall riots, sparked by unchecked brutality and persecution by police against LGBT people in late June of 1969 in New York City. A mere 43 years passed from that day to 2012, which witnessed a sitting president of the United States announce, during his reelection year, his support of full marriage for same sex couples—well within the lifetimes of many who count themselves among the leaders and frontline activists in this movement. In 1974, Senator Allan Spear, my predecessor and mentor, became the first out legislator in the country. He was treated horribly by some of his colleagues. During his final eight years in office, he served as president of the Senate and successfully amended Minnesota's Human Rights Act to include LGBT Minnesotans. Twenty years later, as the caretaker of his seat and legacy, I was able to serve as chief author of the bill, opening up marriage for families like mine. Historians and social scientists will render the verdict on why a community, so universally feared, despised, and marginalized at one time, was able to make such strides at a pace that, though halting and seemingly hopeless at times, only seemed to accelerate. It is a safe bet that the impetus of previous movements, the social upheaval of the 1960s, a growing sense of an LGBT identity and corresponding idea of an LGBT "community," the dynamic of the HIV/AIDS epidemic, the settling of philosophical arguments inside the movement, incredible advances in communications technology and popular culture, and the willingness of individuals to take incredible personal and professional risks were of great importance.

Our country is founded on the very principles that underlie the strivings and yearnings of this movement. In the United States, regardless of the circumstances of one's birth, be it wealth, race, beliefs, physical ability, gender, culture, and so on, we are all equal to one another in the eyes of the law. This is a democracy, a government of, for, and by the people where everyone has an equal say—one person, one vote. Those were the ideals articulated at the founding and formation of our country and system of government—though the practice fell far short. Those founding principles are rooted in a larger belief of the dignity and inherent worth of humanity and every single person. So it has never been acceptable to treat anyone in the manner in which our country has seen fit to treat some of its citizens (even denying their citizenship) of African descent, women, people who didn't own land, Japanese Americans, Native Americans, religious minorities, and so many others. These movements have not sought to change our system, but to hold it accountable to its very own inspiring and lofty ideals. And when there is success, no scarcity dynamic plays out. Just as is the case with love, when freedom and opportunity expand for others, it expands for everyone. It is the domain of "the commons," where we all partake and benefit. No zero sum game, no loss for any other stakeholder—expansion of opportunity and prosperity for everyone.

Some like to separate ideas of economic policy from so-called social issues. What is the extension of social tolerance and acceptance but a way in which those who had been previously barred can gain admittance to a host of practical opportunities: unfettered access to education, employment, social institutions, and economic arrangements; public services that give rise to one's ability to pursue dreams, start families, raise children, and begin businesses; and offer one's talents to provide services, leadership, and new ideas. Individuals and families benefit, communities are stronger, and economies become more resilient and competitive.

There remain places in our country where time has passed by and life remains very difficult for LGBT people. Two ideals we value greatly—full equality for every individual and majority rule—are inherently in tension when an unpopular minority community's rights are in flux. Many places have refused to resolve that tension. Exacerbating this circumstance is the fact that those places that prosper and thrive and attract the best and brightest minds, thus creating even greater opportunity for even more people, are those that exhibit an openness to diversity and difference among its citizens. Ours is a mobile society, and people will not stay where they're not welcome. That is not confined to mobility among LGBT people. Young professionals of all stripes and orientations are looking for those kinds of places.

This book analyzes the disparities across numerous locales, fields, and endeavors. Ours is a political system where power is diffuse. The institutions that are charged with leadership—whether one is looking at jurisdiction, economic sector, or type of public service—by and large will need to extend the franchise of full equality, fair treatment, dignity, and inclusion to LGBT people on their own. In very few instances will a larger external force bring about change. Advances can come about through enlightened and courageous leadership from the top down or be propelled at the grassroots by their key constituencies. Those that fail will falter, become regarded as irrelevant, incompetent, obsolete, and be left behind. Hopefully this book will provide an impetus for a better future that will be more broadly shared. As a senator from Minnesota, Paul Wellstone, was fond of saying, "We all do better when we all do better."

Scott Dibble
Minnesota State Senator

Preface

These are monumental times for the lesbian, gay, bisexual, and transgender (LGBT) community. We are seeing changes now that would have been unimaginable only a few years ago. The U.S. Supreme Court decisions on same-sex marriage, the elimination of prohibitions against LGBT people serving in the armed forces, a dramatic shift in the way that the United States governmental bureaucracy deals with the issues of the LGBT community—all of these are changes that many of the writers in this book could only have dreamed about as they coped with the stresses of being part of a community under siege. The stresses of the AIDS epidemic (where I lost 35 of my friends and acquaintances), the attacks upon our family structure by many politicians in both major parties, and the desire to silence our community have led in turn to a more resilient LGBT community, which in many cases has been reflected in the writings of those who have prepared chapters for this book. We have perhaps been misled by the great successes of our efforts to legalize marriage as a basic human right. The problem is that our country is still divided into those states where most if not all rights are granted to LGBT people, and those states where no rights have been granted and protected. I was born in Nebraska and lived much of my early life in Idaho: in neither of those states do LGBT people have anywhere near the rights that I have as a resident of Minnesota. Unless they live in a few of the larger cities in those and well over a majority of the remaining disempowered states, they will have few if any rights at all. Thus it is that I have titled the book *Gay, Lesbian, Bisexual, and Transgender Civil Rights: A Public Policy Agenda for Uniting a Divided America*. The idea of the "great divide" comes from my experience of living in the mountain state of Idaho, where part of my family still lives within a few miles of the Aryan Nations and neo-Nazi encampments. And it comes from being born in the state of Nebraska, which has only a few urban centers with protection for LGBT people. It has taken me some time to view LGBT struggles as "civil rights," but when the United Nations Universal Declaration of Human Rights tells us that all people should be equal under the law, that all people should have the right to found a family, that no one (including undocumented people) should be subject to unnecessary detention, that everyone has the right to serve their country, and that everyone has a right to a reasonable standard of living (including a right to health services)—should I conclude that the United Nations decided to make an exclusion for LGBT people who live in the Southern United States, the Rust Belt states, the Central Plains states, and the Mountain states? Clearly this should not, and will not, be the case.

A few thanks are due to the people who have lived through experiences that made them resilient enough to edit and write this book. First on this list is Dallas Drake, who has labored for months ensuring that this book meets the esoteric requirements of the *Chicago Manual of Style*. His work at the Minneapolis-based Center for Homicide Research (the only research center on this topic in the entire United States) ensures that police forces throughout the world have the knowledge base to identify hate crimes against LGBT people. Second is Timothy Bonham, who served as my campaign manager while I was the only openly gay elected official in the city of Minneapolis. Tim made sure that I saw the way that the United States is divided into two "empowered" and "disempowered" countries. Third is my Hmong partner, who let me see firsthand the way in which low-income people in racial and ethnic minorities suffer treatment in the workplace that would be unimaginable for Caucasian people. Fourth, my roommate while I was writing this book showed me that even in the moneyed and "liberal" reaches of higher education at the graduate-school level (at the same school where I received my MPA), extremely talented racial and ethnic minority people are treated with disdain, causing them to have to work twice as hard as Caucasian people to gain less than the same rewards. Then there are the writers who used their talents to allow all of us to see the inequities of our society as they apply to LGBT people. Denise Burke, who gave a powerful sermon that I heard at our Metropolitan Community Church in Minneapolis, worked tirelessly on a very tight timeline to come up with a chapter that tells the incredible suffering that has been levied against the transgender community, and how to change that situation. Christopher Thomason lays out the way in which massive configurations of resources are gathered both by opponents and proponents of LGBT civil rights. Beth Bibus, a tireless fighter and competent administrator, provides us with a picture of why it was that Minnesota was able to turn the tide against the powerful forces that attempted to enshrine discriminatory practice into the marriage law of Minnesota, and Elizabeth Swanzy-Parker provided me with the raw documents to see how such practices were actually incorporated into the law of the state of North Carolina. Sid Guthrie defines for us the way in which health care for LGBT people has changed in the 10 years since our previous volume, the *Handbook of Gay, Lesbian, Bisexual, and Transgender Administration and Policy*, was published in 2004. The nationally recognized demographer Gary Gates (whom I on occasion watch on CNN and public television) has given to us in this volume an incredibly meticulous picture of the demographics of the LGBT community, as well as our resilient family structure, which has grown in the past few years. Sam McClure, in her tireless work around the country documented every day on my Facebook page, shows us how the LGBT business community has helped to pave the way for the rights revolution that we are now experiencing. The work of the Gay and Lesbian

Victory Fund, and many of the openly LGBT elected officials who provided role models for the citizenry of this country, is described in great detail by Jane Laine, who discusses the admirable work of so many open elected officials in many of the states and the difficult struggles they face. The great divide between the empowered and disempowered states in the field of K–12 through higher education is discussed by Tracy Phariss, one of the nation's leaders in K–12 LGBT issues, and by a talented university-level LGBT leader, Michael Grewe at Augsburg University in Minneapolis. The issues of the bisexual movement, and the ways in which the gay and lesbian community (not to mention the heterosexual community) conspire to accomplish "bisexual erasure" are carefully delineated by Victor Raymond, a nationally recognized figure in the field. Jean Quam and Abel Knochel skillfully discuss the newly emerging research on LGBT senior issues and some of the aspects of "transgender erasure." Stephanie Kimble provides an incredibly detailed picture of the way in which the blight of LGBT youth homelessness has evolved and how it might be remedied: We also become aware of the fact that the percentage (out of the total homeless population) of LGBT youth (20%–40%) and LGBT adult/senior homeless people (29%) are not that much different. Kristen Norman-Major, who has made me feel at home at Hamline University, provides us with an insight into how the very limited infrastructure protecting LGBT rights is actually enforced by some of the state and local bureaucracies around the country, and suggests areas of research that are needed. And finally, Heather Posthumus provides us with a matrix of the protections that are made available to LGBT people around the country. She also allows us to see where our deficiencies exist.

I think that you will find this book incredibly imaginative in the way in which it identifies the two Americas in which we as LGBT people live. It should help us identify the truth of our existence, and in the words of the Bible, John 8:32, "... you will know the truth, and the truth will make you free."

Wallace Swan
Minneapolis, Minnesota

Editor

Wallace Swan is a contributing faculty member at Walden University in Minneapolis, Minnesota, and an adjunct instructor in the College of Business Masters of Public Administration program at Hamline University in St. Paul, Minnesota. He has published 8 books, 11 articles, 3 chapters, 6 proceedings, 2 book reviews, and has chaired or participated in 23 public administration conference sessions or presentations. Swan is a member and regular presenter at the American Society for Public Administration as well as the International Conference on Public Administration.

Contributors

Beth Bibus is a long-time advocate of equality and civil rights who worked in civil rights enforcement for more than a decade. Short but fierce, Bibus dedicated many hours in the early 1990s to volunteering with the Queer Street Patrol in Minneapolis. Bibus is currently a management consultant with the State of Minnesota, providing research, writing, advice, and project management for a variety of government clients. She earned a master's degree in public administration from Hamline University in St. Paul. Bibus and her (now) spouse Anne took immediate advantage of Minnesota's marriage equality law, and she is grateful to the many dedicated LGBT people and allies who made marriage equality possible in Minnesota.

Denise Burke is a trans-activist and former pastor. She is a graduate of the State University of New York–Albany and Bangor Theological Seminary in Bangor, Maine, and plans to return to active ministry in the Metropolitan Community Churches, a denomination noted as a spiritual home for LGBT people. Burke also contributes to LGBT film screenings through the Out Twin Cities Film Festival and plans to start filming a project soon. She is currently writing a memoir of transition and addiction recovery titled *To Know the Difference—A Transwoman Discovers the Serenity Prayer*. She has lived in numerous places, from the Virgin Islands to Fairbanks, Alaska, and now resides in the Minneapolis area.

Minnesota Senator Scott Dibble first became involved in politics in the mid-1980s, working on issues concerning the civil rights of LGBT communities, including HIV/AIDS. His involvement led to organizing on issues of social and economic justice—especially in the areas of neighborhood livability, transportation, housing, energy, and the environment. After working for a Minneapolis City Council member, Dibble ran for a seat in the Minnesota House of Representatives, becoming the third openly gay legislator to serve in the Minnesota Legislature. After serving one term in the House, Dibble ran for State Senate in 2002 where he is now serving in his fourth term. He chairs the Transportation and Public Safety Committee and serves on the Environment and Energy Committee; Environment, Economic Development, and Agriculture Finance Division; and Finance Committee. The focus of his legislative work is civil and human rights, housing and homelessness, transportation, public health, energy, and environment. Dibble has helped lead the charge defending against numerous attacks on human rights, especially directed against the LGBT community. He helped defeat a proposed anti-marriage constitutional amendment successfully for a number of years, and helped lead the campaign for its defeat on the ballot in November 2012. Dibble was the chief author of legislation to give same-sex couples the freedom to marry. The bill was passed and signed into law in May 2013, making Minnesota the 12th state to legalize same-sex marriage.

Dallas S. Drake is principal researcher at the Center for Homicide Research in Minneapolis, Minnesota, where he conducts original research on homicide prevention and case solvability, as well as supervises a large academy of undergraduate and graduate student interns. He holds a bachelor of science degree in sociology, law crime, and deviance from the University of Minnesota where he graduated magna cum laude in 2005. Currently Drake is secretary of the International Homicide Research Working Group and the recipient of the 2013 Carolyn Rebecca Block Award for outstanding homicide research by a practitioner. He is a member of the American Society of Criminology and the International Association of Homicide Investigators Association. In addition to research, Drake conducts reviews of active and cold-case homicides nationwide.

Gary J. Gates, PhD, is a recognized expert on the demography of the lesbian, gay, bisexual, and transgender (LGBT) population. He coauthored *The Gay and Lesbian Atlas* and publishes extensively on the demographic, geographic, and economic characteristics of the LGBT population. Many national and international media outlets regularly feature his work. He holds a PhD in public policy from the Heinz College of Public Policy and Management at Carnegie Mellon University along with a master of divinity from St. Vincent College and a BS in computer science from the University of Pittsburgh at Johnstown.

Michael Grewe is currently the coordinator of LGBTQIA (lesbian, gay, bisexual, transgender, questioning, intersex, and asexual) Services at Augsburg College, working with students, staff, faculty, and administrators to create a welcoming campus climate for students of all gender and sexual identities. He has run educational workshops and training at a number of nonprofits, businesses, and institutions of higher education across the Upper Midwest focusing on issues of gender and sexuality, as well as around dismantling systems of institutional homophobia, biphobia, and transphobia within organizations. He holds a master of social work from Augsburg College. He is also the recipient of the 2009 Val DuMontier New Professional Award from the American College Personnel Association for his work around fostering positive change for LGBTQIA students as a student affairs professional.

Sid Guthrie, MSN, CNS, RN-C, is a clinical nurse specialist in adult health and also holds an American Nurses Credentialing Center (ANCC) certification in pain management. Currently he works as a clinical nurse specialist in the Department of Practice and Education, Medical–Surgical Division at the HealthPartners, Regions Hospital in St. Paul, Minnesota. His past work in the LGBT community includes serving as a nurse in the AIDS Evaluation and Treatment Unit at the University of Minnesota Hospital and Clinics, and starting a prostate cancer support group for gay men and their partners. In 2004 Guthrie authored two health care–related chapters in the *Handbook of Gay, Lesbian, Bisexual, and Transgender Administration and Policy.*

Andrea Jenkins is an award-winning poet and writer. Most recently she was awarded a Bush Fellowship and a Fellowship in the Cultural Community Leadership Institute at Intermedia Arts, sponsored by the Bush Foundation, and named a fellow in the Many Voices Fellowship at the Playwrights Center. Jenkins earned her master's of science in community economic development from Southern New Hampshire University, Manchester; a certificate from the University of St. Thomas, Community Leadership Institute; a bachelor's of science in human services/interpersonal communications from Metropolitan State University; and an MFA in creative writing from Hamline University. Jenkins currently works as a policy aide for the 8th Ward City Council member Elizabeth Glidden in Minneapolis, Minnesota.

Stephanie Kimble earned a bachelor's of science in broadcast journalism from the University of Wisconsin–River Falls. She is currently working on her master's in nonprofit management at Hamline University, St. Paul, Minnesota. She is a volunteer coordinator with Bolder Options (a Minneapolis–St. Paul-based one-to-one mentorship organization).

K. Abel Knochel, PhD, MSW, a former community organizer, teaches social work in the Twin Cities. Dr. Knochel has published and presented both locally and nationally on aging among transgender and LGB older adults, including the preparation of providers of aging services to serve these populations. Dr. Knochel serves on the Council on Social Work Education's Commission on Sexual Orientation, Gender Identity and Expression.

Jane Laine has a bachelor's of arts in philosophy from the University of St. Thomas in St. Paul and is pursuing two master's of arts at Hamline University in nonprofit management and public administration.

Sam McClure is a longtime leader in the LGBT economic equality movement. Prior to her current national appointment as director of affiliate relations and external affairs with the National Gay & Lesbian Chamber (NGLCC), she served as the Midwest Regional Chair and then the National Chair of the NGLCC's Council of Chambers and Business Organizations (CCBO) leadership council. McClure also served as the executive director of Quorum, the Twin Cities LGBT and Allied Business Community, recognized as the NGLCC 2009 Chamber of the Year. She also worked with the University of Minnesota's Department of Equity and Diversity as a member of the President's Intercultural Advisory Council. McClure is frequently sought for public speaking with local chambers of commerce and national diversity and inclusion conferences, and received the 2013 Disability Leader of the Year award from the World Institute on Disability. Driven by entrepreneurial spirit and passion for community and economic development, she is a passionate advocate for a fully inclusive economy.

Kristen Norman-Major, PhD, is a professor and director of Public Administration programs in the School of Business at Hamline University in St. Paul, Minnesota. She holds a doctorate in political science from Vanderbilt University and a master's in public affairs from the Humphrey School at the University of Minnesota. Her research focuses on issues of social equity, diversity and cultural competency. She is coeditor with Susan Gooden of *Cultural Competency for Public Administrators* (M.E. Sharpe).

Tracy Phariss is a high school educator for Jefferson County Public Schools in Golden, Colorado. As a teacher and educational counselor, he is deeply involved in LGBT educational issues. He has written extensively and presented seminars on LGBT equity and privilege issues in education. He is cochairperson of the Colorado chapter of the Gay, Lesbian, and Straight Education Network (GLSEN), a national organization that works to make schools safe and equitable for all, regardless of sexual orientation or gender identity/expression. In the 1980s, Phariss served on the first ever Gay and Lesbian Youth Advisory Board within the Colorado Department of Education. As a member of the Gay and Lesbian Teacher's Group in 1987, he was instrumental in establishing the first scholarship for LGBT students in the nation, and in the 1990s, he organized the Colorado Gay/Straight Student Leadership Conference and maintains a massive website. He has presented at state high school diversity conferences and served on the Jefferson County Diversity Advisory Council for numerous years. His work is used throughout the United States to save the lives of our youth and to create safer schools.

Heather Posthumus is currently finishing a dual master's in the nonprofit management and business administration programs at Hamline University in St. Paul, Minnesota.

Jean K. Quam, PhD, is currently the dean of the College of Education and Human Development at the University of Minnesota where she has been a faculty member since 1980. For 16 years, she was the director of the School of Social Work. She earned a PhD from the University of Wisconsin–Madison and an MSW from the

University of Nebraska–Lincoln. Dr. Quam is the author of an edited volume on social services for gay and lesbian elders, and has written many articles, chapters, and short pieces on LGBT aging. She was a consultant on two large-scale surveys completed by the MetLife Mature Market Institute.

Victor J. Raymond, PhD, is a sociology instructor at Madison College. A member of the Rosebud Sioux tribe, he earned a PhD in sociology from Iowa State University with a graduate minor in women's studies. Currently he is a board member of the Carl Brandon Society and Wisconsin 521. Dr. Raymond was a founding member of the BECAUSE Conference, a former national coordinator for BiNet USA, and a vice chair for the Minnesota American Indian AIDS Task Force (now the Indigenous People's Task Force). He lives in Madison with his two partners.

Elizabeth Swanzy-Parker is employed by Carolinas HealthCare System. She has industry experience in health care, retail, financial services, public accounting, and nonprofits. She was educated at the University of Connecticut (BA) and Case Western Reserve University (MBA). She has expertise in the following areas: providing information security best practices to improve the information technology culture; conducting strategic consulting for information security, information management services, IT strategy and management, and risk assurance focused on technology delivery, solutions enablement, and operations improvement for health care, retail, and financial services entities, evaluating enterprise risk, analyzing data, developing and evaluating options, and presenting recommendations to clients to identify complex financial business and IT operational process gaps; exposing operational risk silos, utilizing issue identification skills, valuing chain analysis and related assumption, documenting to educate stakeholders to build enterprise awareness; and collaborating with management and leading cross-functional teams to reveal enterprise risk transparency, defining key controls to manage key performance indicators, and ensuring business and IT processes meet corporate goals as well as risk-tolerance levels.

Christopher A. Thomason is a graduate student at Hamline University, St. Paul, Minnesota, where he is pursuing a master's in public administration. He has a bachelor of science from the University of Wisconsin–Stout in vocational rehabilitation. Thomason has been a civil rights advocate for several years in a variety of areas, and this is his first published written work.

Introduction

Wallace Swan

Perhaps it seems a bit unusual to start a book on human rights by taking a trip into the issue of American competitiveness in an increasingly globalized marketplace. But the increased polarization of the United States on lesbian, gay, bisexual, and transgender (LGBT) and other related issues (what I like to call the "Great Divide") is increasingly making large areas of our country a place that corporations may not want to invest in and that many individuals may not wish to work in.

As the United States evolves into a more multicultural environment, there are a variety of factors that may make it more or less competitive in an extremely competitive world. These factors may include the need for employees who are well trained, a political system that is responsive to the needs of business as well as the citizens, a relatively simple tax code that meets the needs of business as well as all citizens, and recognition of the human rights of all of the citizens of the country.

The United States is increasingly facing a multiplicity of issues as it attempts to compete in world markets and provide opportunities for its people. First, employers want potential employees with sufficient skills to perform the increasingly difficult jobs necessitated by our high-tech global society, but the United States is not doing well in producing workers with those skills. Second, we see that "as recently as April (2012), median household incomes, adjusted for inflation, were still 5.9% lower than in June 2009, when the recession ended … and 8.3% lower than in late 2007" (Mullaney 2012, 1). Third, the relationship between employee and top management salaries has changed dramatically in the past 20 years. "In 2010, the average annual wage for U.S. workers in production operations was $33,770 while the average CEO pay in S&P 500 companies was $11,358,445. CEO pay was 336 times more than the average employee" (Hicks 2011, 1). Fourth, "the median family's net worth dropped to $77,300 (2012) from $126,400 in 2007" (Mullaney 2012, 1). Wealthy families, by contrast, have done so much better. Fifth, and more generally, the Harvard competitiveness study surveyed many decision-makers and discussed the decisions they were planning to make in terms of investment of resources. "[The] United States competed with virtually the entire world and fared poorly, losing two-thirds of the decisions that were resolved ... [The] greatest current or emerging weaknesses [were perceived] to be in America's tax code, political system, K–12 education system, macroeconomic policies, legal framework regulations, infrastructure, and workforce skills ..." (Ausick 2012, 1). It is the issues of our *political system, legal framework regulations, K–12 education system, human rights,* and the *tax code* that we will be discussing in this introduction.

Political System

The American political system was designed to have multiple power centers and to ensure that one person or group did not have absolute power. Why was this? Because King George III was seen as tyrannical by American colonists, and when they declared independence, they did not want a form of government that would reinstate the possibility of having another such ruler. Of course this system had its complexities. It had both separation of powers (executive, legislative, judicial) as well as division of powers (federal and state). A number of safeguards were included to ensure that there was a set of checks and balances to prevent accumulation of power. Originally there were no political parties, and the idea of having them was frowned on by the framers of the Constitution. The negative term "faction" was used by James Madison to describe them. Gradually, however, different outlooks led to different ways of politically organizing; the Federalists (based in Northern cities) supported a stronger presidency while the Democratic Republicans (the party of Thomas Jefferson and James Madison) were a bit more populist and centered in the South. After the party of the Federalists fell apart, it evolved into the National Republican and then the Whig party. Later, Southern Whigs became the Democratic Party and Northern Whigs became the Republican Party. For many years, this system worked well, until the issue of slavery, which had been papered over by a variety of compromises, finally broke the union apart, with the Republican Party, led by Abraham Lincoln, and the Confederacy dividing into two different systems of government. Although the Civil War was fought and the Confederacy was defeated, the aftermath of eliminating slavery led to a situation where "separate but equal" gradually became the prevailing norm, but it was not until *Brown v. Board of Education** that this system began to unravel. The rights revolution that began for African Americans was followed by the women's rights revolution, and finally by the gay rights revolution with the advent of the Stonewall riots in June 1969.

Legal Framework Regulations

Although there was considerable organizational work before Stonewall, the gay rights revolution began in earnest with the Stonewall riots. It gradually translated itself into a political sea of change. At first, there were only a few jurisdictions that

* *Brown v. Board of Education,* 347 U.S. 483 (1954).

allowed for the protection of rights of LGBT people. The usual protections were for housing, education, and employment. The number of jurisdictions grew and began to include not only cities, but also counties, and then executive orders for state employees, followed by human rights laws that would encompass entire states. The pattern was often the same: Large cities would include a few new rights, and then those rights would be expanded to other jurisdictions in reasonably supportive states. Typically, though, the jurisdictions that adopted such rights were the same metropolitan areas. The cities of San Francisco, New York City, Minneapolis, Los Angeles (and occasionally a small college town, like Marshall, Minnesota) would "preview" the regulation, often accompanied by loud protestations from church groups and organizations representing families. Then, some entrepreneurial spirits would introduce the idea in a county or a state, and the effort would be beaten back. But later, more effective coalitions would be developed, and a legislature here or there might ensure the provision of human rights for all people in a state. The other avenue for adoption of human rights would involve increasingly effective appeals to a relatively small group of state and federal courts. Organizations such as Lambda Legal Defense would bring cases challenging archaic laws (e.g., sodomy laws) and would occasionally win major cases that would broaden the rights of LGBT people. At first, these cases would be designed to protect the most elemental rights; for example, the right to mail LGBT materials through the U.S. Post Office, but later, organizations took on more major issues, such as the issues of sodomy, human rights, domestic partnerships, and then marriage itself. During and after the 1990s, the Gay and Lesbian Victory Fund would increasingly play a role by strategically choosing LGBT candidates to run for office, thereby ensuring that people in the jurisdictions became more comfortable with LGBT people.

The existence of this pattern has continued through each of the stages of development of the LGBT movement. A new right would be introduced in a major jurisdiction, then an advocacy group in another jurisdiction would pick up on this particular entitlement, and would organize to obtain that right in its jurisdiction. Particularly difficult situations, where the rights were not easily attainable, would be dealt with by bringing court cases. This same pattern was used as LGBT people began to want recognition of their rights as family members. The author documented the gradual approval of domestic partners rights in 4 school districts, 29 cities, 10 counties, 4 states, 10 unions, 64 corporations, 32 universities, and 26 nonprofits in *Businesses, Non-Profits and Unions with Domestic Partners Benefits* (Verschraegen 1994, 233–240), then watched the movement evolve in governmental units around the country, and thence into corporations where the gains soon surpassed those of government agencies. Workplace alliances within governments, corporations, and nonprofits began to ask their managements for recognition of human rights and then family rights. Corporations especially wanted to ensure standardized rights for their employees rather than develop the kind of patchwork approach utilized by governmental units, where strong political opposition prevented their adoption in many localities and states. In essence, the division and separation of powers that had previously prevented *concentrated power* by a tyrant (and which also allowed governmental innovation) simply led to *fragmented public policy* on gay and lesbian issues. The lack of equivalent rights for all citizens meant that people in 29 states are denied protection of health care coverage, educational opportunities, and the right to equal opportunity in housing; while in 15 or more states those rights are routinely protected.

The movement to grant marital rights to same-sex couples has highlighted the fault line that exists in American politics. Who in the LGBT community can forget the day that President Obama announced that he was in support of gay and lesbian same-sex relationships? The news media was alive with stories about ministers supporting or opposing this position (Cauchon 2012; Hagerty 2012), about racial and ethnic minorities dividing in support or against the president's position (Newsmax 2012; Williams 2012), and ministers telling their parishes that it was just fine to hit a son who was acting differently than the other boys (Signorile 2012). The same states that have human rights for LGBT people often also provide protection from hate crimes, have laws that address bullying enumerated against specific groups, have provisions allowing foster care and adoption, and have laws that grant rights to partners. By contrast, states that have provisions preventing same-sex relationships often do not have human rights laws, have no hate crime laws for LGBT people, and sometimes even prevent adoptions and foster care for LGBT people. But behind this division between 21 "empowered" states and 29 "disempowered" states is a huge infrastructure of organizations pro and con, which do not think anything of spending tens of millions of dollars in each of the "battleground" states to ensure that laws are enacted in their favor. Organizations like the Human Rights Campaign, the National Organization for Marriage, the National Gay and Lesbian Task Force, Concerned Women of America, and Lambda Legal Defense put together television ads, newspaper and Internet campaigns, garden parties and events, all of which are designed to raise money and persuade a small percentage of independent voters that they should vote for their "side" of the issue, thereby ensuring victory. On the LGBT side, the voters' decisions to prohibit marital rights by either legislation or constitutional amendment have led to documented declines in aggregate mental health (Haas 2011). Conversely, in the state of Massachusetts when marital rights were given, there is documentation that usage of medical facilities by LGBT people went down substantially (Weaver 2012). "A Massachusetts study done the year after legalization of same-sex civil marriages in that state demonstrated a 13 percent drop in health care visits and a 14 percent reduction in health care costs among gay men" (Ehlinger 2012, 1). The one side wants to ensure that their dream of having a gay marriage is protected (losing the battle in 32 states, but winning it in 18 other states), while the other side feels that somehow heterosexual marriage is endangered by having a new model of marriage wherein otherwise similarly situated individuals in the country are treated equally. A strange set of circumstances indeed, on both sides—especially considering the amount of money being spent for both idealistic and ideological purposes.

Some states that adopt a law or constitutional amendment prohibiting same-sex marriage increasingly include provisions prohibiting any domestic partnerships, or any legal relationships that approximate marriage, foster care, or adoptions arrangements. The example of the passage of the North Carolina constitutional amendment is a good one: Not only gay and lesbian couples, but also heterosexual couples, were immediately denied use of domestic partner benefits in several large cities (e.g., Charlotte and Asheville) where they had previously been granted. Those states that do not have such provisions ("empowered states") have a distinct advantage in recruiting talented professionals compared with the states that do have them ("disempowered states"). There are a variety of reasons for this. First, there is the simple fact that there are hundreds of rights that LGBT couples do not have as a result of such laws. In Minnesota, for instance, there were 515 rights that married heterosexuals had that same-sex couples did not have until the recent same-sex marriage law was passed. Why would a talented gay or lesbian couple want to move to a state where they are deprived of basic human relationship rights? In the United States, the General Accountability Office found 1138 rights that married heterosexuals may exercise that similarly situated gay and lesbian people may not utilize. A fair number of these are embedded in the U.S. Tax Code. As only one of many examples, domestic partner benefits are taxed differently for gay and lesbian couples than for heterosexual married couples. The same rule applies conversely in regard to couples who want to live in countries with all marital benefits, including Argentina, Belgium, Canada, Iceland, Netherlands, Norway, Portugal, South Africa, Spain, and Sweden (*The Daily Beast* 2012). Argentina, Britain, Denmark, France, Luxembourg, New Zealand, and Uruguay have been added to the list of countries that have marriage. If a talented gay or lesbian couple had a choice of being situated in a country with same-sex marriage or in a country that did not have this option, where would they want to settle? For example, the author is aware of a case where one member of a gay couple was a citizen of the United States but another was not because of citizenship in another country (Belgium), and as a result, they moved to another country (France). In another case, a talented gay man from Peru with two master's degrees and a doctorate met a physician in the United States. The Peruvian member of the couple has had to move to Britain to be in a country that will accept him, and the physician has decided to move there as well. Second, Richard Florida in his book (2009) used advanced statistical *path* models to show the effect of having bohemian and gay populations in one's city: "Regions in which artists and gays have integrated and settled are more likely than others to place high premiums on innovation, entrepreneurship, and new firm formation … They make areas that were already ripe for growth even more desirable, and to a greater number of people" (p. 139). Third, a recent study in Minnesota highlighted the nature of the problem when applied to a particular state. A Knight Foundation study "the 'Soul of the Community' … found that fewer than 2 in 10 people say the Twin Cities is a good place for young, talented college graduates looking for work, in part because of a growing perception that the area is not open to differences in race and sexual orientation" (Zelle 2012). This is now changing because of passage of the marriage law in Minnesota. Fourth, we need to think through the implications of the three major points made earlier. Increasingly, younger people support gay people, and especially gay marriage. "[Support] for gay marriage reaches 69 percent among adults under age 30 (with 51 percent "strong" support), compared with just 38 percent of seniors (half of seniors are strongly opposed). Support is also 14 points higher among college graduates than among non-graduates, 63 to 49 percent" (Ergun and Damla 2012). When one has a culture that excludes difference, one will not only discourage gay and lesbian people from settling but will also prevent younger racial and ethnic minorities from settling there, as well as sending a message to a high percentage of younger talented and supportive people that the location is not a good place to work and live. One can safely say that the jurisdiction will just become a nice place for homogeneous heterosexual seniors to live.

Perhaps another illustration will assist the reader: "Of all the states with constitutional amendments prohibiting marriage equality, Virginia became the most strident and mean-spirited. During our 10 years in Virginia, we've watched this great state turn against its gay and lesbian residents" (White 2012). As a result of this change in atmospherics, Mel White and his partner moved to California.

K–12 System

The K–12 system has been a challenge for LGBT children for a number of years. The case of Jamie Nabozny (systematically abused by fellow students) highlighted the way in which school systems were blind to the needs of LGBT youth (*Nabozny v. Podlesny* 1996).* And, more recently, we have the issue of bullying, which has increasingly been a focus of efforts around the country to provide not only protections for LGBT youth but also for many heterosexual youth who, for one reason or another, have been singled out for abusive treatment by some of their peers. This type of treatment means that a whole class of children is not allowed to learn in a safe and secure environment. Reduced funding of K–12 education has been a major deficiency as well (Eisele-Dyrli 2010). And this contributes to an educational environment that does not fully develop the capabilities of all children. We also need to note the way in which the educational system has been changed by the use of online, charter, home schools, and private schools: A number of these schools use a religious-based approach for education, which does not leave room for LGBT

* *Nabozny v. Podlesny,* 92F.3d446. 7th Circuit (1996).

perspectives or resources. The "tone" of a country's educational system, not to mention its allocation of resources, is what will ensure that talented people are trained and nurtured.

Human Rights

The Universal Declaration of Human Rights (1948) includes a number of human rights that are of particular interest to LGBT people.

"Human rights are international norms that help to protect all people everywhere from severe political, legal and social abuses." Especially important to the LGBT movement are "*liberty rights* that protect freedoms in areas such as belief, expression, association, assembly and movement … [and] … *equality rights* that guarantee equal citizenship, equality before the law, and nondiscrimination."* In the past, in the United States we have seen abridgement of liberty rights in the form of limits upon *expression* (e.g., the U.S. Postal System rules in the 1950s prohibiting transmission of LGBT materials in the mail) (Marcus 2002) as well as right to *assemble* (Carpenter 2001). This author had experienced continuing battles in Minneapolis in the 1970s between the Minneapolis City Council and the LGBT community (Smith 2012) about location and even designation of gay pride parades—the City Council at one point decided to rename "Gay Pride Day" by calling it something else (Roth 2004). Of course, the current emphasis is upon equality rights. The battle for protection of educational access, employment rights, and housing is a key one today.

The example of a teacher in Texas (a state lacking human rights protection for LGBT persons) perfectly illustrates the employment rights issue. Jackie Gill and her partner both earned college degrees, and then Jackie decided to get her doctoral degree in English. In 2009, Tarrant County College in Hurst, Texas was hiring new English professors. She was hired as a full-time temporary instructor. "My department posted seven permanent positions … But one student in my class, whom I'd reported for stealing an exam, filed a complaint claiming that I had flirted with female students in class." Jackie was subsequently told by her chair that the college and the state were adverse to LGBT people, and that she would not be allowed to interview for a permanent position, resulting in unemployment for her since 2010 (Gill 2012, 7). This story has repeatedly occurred in state and local jurisdictions in the United States that do not have human rights protections for LGBT persons (Keys 2000).

And the Universal Declaration of Human Rights also states in Article 12 that "no one shall be subjected to arbitrary interference with his privacy, family, home or correspondence." It also says in Article 16 that "the family is the natural and

* "Human Rights." 2010. *Stanford Encyclopedia of Philosophy*, September 28, pp. 1–2. http://plato.stanford.edu/entries/rightsd-human/.

fundamental group unit of society and is entitled to protection by society and the State" (Universal Declaration of Human Rights 1948, 1).

Former Secretary of State Hillary Clinton recently said:

> I want to talk about the work we have left to do to protect one group of people whose human rights are still denied in too many parts of the world today. In many ways they are an invisible minority. They are arrested, beaten, terrorized, even executed. Many are treated with contempt and violence by their fellow citizens while authorities empowered to protect them look the other way, or, too often, even join in the abuse. They are denied opportunities to work and learn, driven from their homes and countries, and forced to suppress or deny who they are to protect themselves from harm. I am talking about gay, lesbian, bisexual, and transgender people, human beings born free and given equality and dignity, who have a right to claim that, which is one of the remaining human rights challenges of our time. (Clinton 2011, 1)

Conclusion

By any standard, the fragmented approach to LGBT human rights in the United States leads to lack of standardization of education, employment, and housing; and it contributes substantially to a situation in which the United States increasingly lags in relation to other countries in the race for global resources, not to mention human rights; and in which a number of states are even less competitive in the race for intellectual capability.

References

Ausick, Paul. 2012. "Harvard Study Says U.S. Competitiveness Will Decline." *24/7 Wall Street.com*. Accessed January 18, 2013, http://247wallst.com/2012/01/18/harvard-study-says-us-competitiveness-will-decline/.

Carpenter, Dale. 2001. Expressive Association and Anti-Discrimination Law after Dale: A Tripartite Approach, *Minnesota Law Review, 85*, 1525–33.

Cauchon, Dennis. 2012. Obama Gay Marriage Support Leaves Black Churches Conflicted. *Huffington Post: Religion,* May 15. Accessed August 5, 2013, http://www.huffingtonpost.com/2012/05/15/obama-gay-marriage-black-church_n_1516272.html.

Clinton, Hillary Rodham. 2011. "Remarks in Recognition of International Human Rights Day." U.S. Department of State. Accessed December 6, 2011, http://www.state.gov/secretary/rm/2011/12/178368.htm.

Daily Beast. 2012. Countries Where Gay Marriage Is Legal: Netherlands, Argentina, and More. May 9. Accessed from http://www.thedailybeast.com/articles/2012/05/09/countries-where-gay-marriage-is-legal-netherlands-argentina-more.html.

Ehlinger, Edward. 2012. "Marriage Is a Matter of Public Health." *Star Tribune* (Minneapolis), September 23. Accessed September 23, 2012, http://www.startribune.com/opinion/commentaries/170760996.html?refer=y.

Eisele-Dyrli, Kurt. 2010, July. School Safety Gets the Ax: Districts Are Struggling to Maintain Safety and Security When Budgets Are Cut. *District Administration*. Accessed August 5, 2013, http://www.districtadministration.com/article/school-safety-gets-ax.

Ergun, Damla. 2012. "Strong Support for Gay Marriage Now Exceeds Strong Opposition." *ABC News*. Accessed May 23, 2013, http://abcnews.go.com/blogs/politics/2012/05/strong-support-for-gay-marriage-now-exceeds-strong-opposition/.

Florida, Richard. 2009. *Who's Your City? How the Creative Economy Is Making Where to Live the Most Important Decision of Your Life*. New York, NY: Basic Books.

Gill, Jackie. 2012. "A Dream Derailed." *Impact Magazine*, 29(2), 7. Accessed August 2, 2013, http://www.lambdalegal.org/sites/default/files/publications/downloads/impact_201206_in-my-own-words.pdf.

Haas, Anne. 2011. Editor's notes from panel presentation on "LGBTQ Mental Health: A Priority Issue," National Gay and Lesbian Task Force Conference, Minneapolis, February 5.

Hagerty, Barbara Bradley. 2012. Same Bible, Different Verdict on Gay Marriage. *NPR*. May 11. Accessed August 5, 2013, http://www.npr.org/2012/05/11/152466134/same-bible-different-verdict-on-gay-marriage.

Hicks, Jennifer. 2011. "Does CEO-to-Worker Pay Ratio Matter?" *SmartBlog*, June 1. Accessed August 2, 2013, http://smartblogs.com/leadership/2011/06/01/does-ceo-to-worker-pay-ratio-matter/.

Keys, Carol (ed.). 2000. *Hostile Climate: Report on Anti-Gay Activity*. Washington, DC: People for the American Way Foundation

Marcus, Eric. 2002. *Making Gay History*. New York, NY: Harper Collins, pp. 47–48.

Mullaney, Tim. 2012. "Families' Wealth Dives 39% in 3 Years." *USA Today*, June 12. Accessed August 2, 2013, http://usatoday30.usatoday.com/NEWS/usaedition/2012-06-12-Recessionconsumer-finances_ST_U.htm.

Newsmax. 2012. Voters Divided between Obama, Romney along Widening Racial Lines. May 25. Accessed August 5, 2013, http://www.newsmax.com/Newsfront/obama-romney-racial-lines/2012/05/25/id/440305.

Roth, Carol. 2004. "Twin Cities Pride Festival—32 Years Notable Changes." [Blog]. Men Talk Articles—June/July. Accessed August 2, 2013, http://www.tcmc.org/mentalk2/mt040601.html.

Signorile, Michelangelo. 2012. "Pastor Sean Harris, Who Advocated Parents 'Punch' Effeminate Children, Defends Sermon, Compares Himself to Jesus." *Huffington Post*. May 3. Accessed August 5, 2013, http://www.huffingtonpost.com/2012/05/03/pastor-sean-harris-beat-gay-children-sermon_n_1474510.html.

Smith, Jason. 2012. *Gay Pride vs. The City of Minneapolis: The Gay Pride Block Party Case*. Minneapolis, MN: Friends of the Bill of Rights Foundation.

Universal Declaration of Human Rights, 1948. Article 12, Article 16. Accessed August 2, 2013, http://www.un.org/en/documents/udhr/.

Verschraegen, Bea. 1994. *Gleichgesctliche "Ehen."* Vienna: Medien und Recht Verlags GmbH.

Weaver, Tom. 2012. "Climate Change for Gay Marriage and Equal Rights in the US of A." *Men Talk*, 36(3).

White, Mel. 2012. "Community Viewpoint: The Sweet Sorrow of Parting." *NewsAdvance.com*. Accessed June 20, http://www2.newsadvance.com/news/2012/apr/15/community-viewpoint-sweet-sorrow-parting-ar-1840742/.
Williams, Joseph. 2012. "Gay Marriage: Black Voters Remain Divided." *Politico*, May 9. Accessed August 5, 2013, http://www.politico.com/news/stories/0512/76133.html.
Zelle, Charlie. 2012. "Marriage Ban Is Bad for Business." *Star Tribune* (Minneapolis), June 18. Accessed June 18, 2013, http://www.startribune.com/opinion/commentaries/159478415.html.

Chapter 1

Lesbian, Gay, Bisexual, and Transgender Demographics

Gary J. Gates

Contents

Introduction

The concept of sexual orientation as a demographic characteristic is a relatively new idea. Academic scholarship focusing on the distinct demographic, economic, and geographic characteristics of the lesbian, gay, bisexual, and transgender (LGBT) community is relatively recent and tends to rely on limited data resources.

This chapter will summarize existing literature that describes the demographic, economic, and geographic characteristics of the LGBT population. It will primarily present analyses using population-based data sources including data on same-sex couples from the 2010 U.S. Census and the U.S. Census Bureau's American Community Survey, along with data from the General Social Survey (Smith et al. 2013),* the Gallup Daily tracking survey, and the Pew Research LGBT Survey.

The chapter begins with a discussion of some of the data and methodological challenges associated with studying sexual orientation as a demographic characteristic. Analyses are then presented to describe estimates of the size of the LGBT population as well as information about coming out. The remainder of the chapter considers how the LGBT population compares to the heterosexual population with regard to a variety of demographic characteristics, including geographic distribution, age, race/ethnicity, educational attainment, socioeconomic status, immigration, and military service.

Data Resources and Methodological Challenges

It remains relatively rare that large-scale population-based surveys include questions about sexual orientation or gender identity (Institute of Medicine 2011). In the United States, the decennial census tabulations and the Census Bureau's annual American Community Survey constitute the most widely used data for analyses of the demographic characteristics of the U.S. population. Unfortunately, the two Census Bureau surveys do not include questions that directly assess sexual orientation or gender identity. As a result, researchers must often rely on relatively small and usually non-population-based surveys to provide information about the characteristics of the LGBT population.

Small sample sizes are a common issue in LGBT research and can create serious methodological challenges for demographic analyses. For example, the General Social Survey (GSS), a national population-based survey conducted by NORC at the University of Chicago, surveys approximately 2,000 Americans every two years. Since 1988, the GSS has included questions about the sex of respondent sex partners and, in 2008, added a sexual orientation identity question. In most years, the number of respondents who report having same-sex sexual behaviors or an LGB identity is less than a hundred. These small samples limit the ability to explore differences between LGB and non-LGB individuals as well as differences within the LGB population based on characteristics such as geography, age, race/ethnicity, or socioeconomic status. Sample size limitations constitute an ongoing challenge in demographic research on lesbian, gay, bisexual, and transgender populations.

* All GSS findings reported in this chapter are based on the author's analyses of the data using the Survey Documentation and Analysis (SDA) Web-based analyses tool developed and maintained by the Computer-assisted Survey Methods Program (CSM) at the University of California, Berkeley, available at http://sda.berkeley.edu/cgi-bin/hsda?harcsda+gss12.

While population-based data on the LGB population is limited, similar data that assesses gender identity is virtually nonexistent. As a result, nearly all research on the transgender population has relied on relatively small purposive samples that cannot be generalized to the broader population. Though not population-based, the National Transgender Discrimination Survey (Grant et al. 2011) marks one of the largest surveys of the transgender population in the United States with a sample size of nearly 6,500 respondents.

The 1990 Decennial Census marked the first time that census data could be used to identify same-sex couples in cohabiting relationships. In that year, the response options for the "relationship to householder" question (which asks how all individuals in the household are related to the person filling out the form) included the category of "unmarried partner" in addition to options including "husband/wife" and "roommate." The "unmarried partner" option, combined with information about the age and sex of all residents of a household, allows for identification of same-sex cohabiting couples who are not simply roommates.

Beginning with Census 2000, same-sex couples who identified one partner as a "husband" or "wife" were also tabulated among same-sex couples, but were combined with same-sex "unmarried partner" couples. Regardless of whether a couple identified as spouses or unmarried partners, all same-sex couples were reported in public data as "unmarried partners." This procedure has also been used in the Census Bureau's annual American Community Survey, which has been collected annually since 2005 and surveys several million U.S. households each year. In Census 2010, the Census Bureau released separate tabulations for same-sex couples who identified as spouses along with those who identified as unmarried partners. However, the Bureau cautioned not to interpret the same-sex spouse tabulations as an indication that a couple is legally married. Using a national survey of same-sex couples conducted immediately after Census 2010, Gates (2010a) estimates that 29% of same-sex couples who identified one partner as a "husband" or "wife" in Census 2010 reported that there were not legally married. Further, 4% of same-sex couples who identified as "unmarried partner" reported that they were, in fact, legally married but thought that the unmarried partner response was more accurate since either their state or the federal government did not recognize their marriage. Census Bureau data on same-sex couples have sufficient sample sizes to allow consideration of geographic variation and differences across demographic subgroups between same-sex and different-sex couples. An obvious limitation of same-sex couple data is that LGBT individuals who are not in a same-sex couple are not identified and characteristics of individuals in same-sex couples may be different from the broader LGBT population.

Beginning in June 2012, Gallup added an LGBT-identity question to its Daily Tracking survey, which interviews a thousand Americans each day. The Gallup data represent one of the largest population-based samples of LGBT-identified adults. Data used in these analyses combine responses collected from June to December 2012 and include more than 6,000 LGBT-identified adults. One limitation of the Gallup data is that the question used does not allow for separate analyses of lesbians, gay men, bisexual, or transgender individuals. LGBT respondents are those who answered yes when asked if they "identify as lesbian, gay, bisexual, or transgender."

In June 2013, Pew Research Center (2013a) conducted a national survey of LGBT adults with a sample of nearly 1,200 respondents. Unlike the Gallup data, respondents can be separately identified as lesbian, gay, bisexual, or transgender. Further, the Pew survey was designed for LGBT individuals and includes questions about LGBT-specific experiences including, discrimination, coming out, and sense of affiliation with the LGBT community.

What Is the Number of People Who Are Bisexual, Lesbian, Gay, or Transgender?

A variety of challenges are inherent in any effort to estimate the size of the LGBT community. These challenges include differences in the perceptions about who is or should be included in the LGBT population, social stigma, and variation in estimates depending on survey methods. Sexual orientation is generally considered to have three components:

- Self-identification as lesbian, gay, bisexual, or heterosexual
- Sexual behaviors with same- or different-sex partners
- Sexual or emotional attraction to same- or different-sex partners

Identity, behavior, and attraction all capture related dimensions of sexual orientation, but individually these constructs do not fully measure an individual's sexual orientation. Further, measures of sexual behavior or attraction raise questions about the extent of the behaviors or attraction that constitute inclusion as lesbian, gay, or bisexual. Consider two 40-year-old women. One reports having had one same-sex sexual experience at age 20 while the other has had several dozen same-sex sexual experiences in the last five years. Should both be considered lesbian or bisexual? Similarly, are those who say they are "mostly" attracted to different-sex partners actually LGB? There are not necessarily "correct" answers to these questions, but decisions about who is included in estimates of the LGBT population can affect the size of the estimates and the demographic composition of those included.

Measuring gender identity can also be challenging. Measuring the size of the transgender community includes consideration of current gender identity in relation to the sex that an individual was assigned at birth along with assessing how individuals may express their gender and the degree to which that expression may be seen as conforming or not conforming to gender norms. Similar to sexual orientation, one way to measure the transgender community is through self-identity. Individuals may identify using terms like transgender, queer, or genderqueer. The latter two identities actually capture aspects of both sexual orientation and gender identity. Questions may also be devised that consider gender expression and nonconformity regardless of the terms individuals may use to describe themselves. These types of questions would assess the relationship between the sex that individuals are assigned at birth and the degree to which that assignment conforms to how they express their gender through their outward appearance or behavior. Like the measurement of sexual orientation, these various approaches to measuring gender identity capture related dimensions of who might be classified as transgender but may not individually address all aspects of assessing gender identity and expression.

As a result of social stigma, some LGBT individuals may be reluctant to identify as such on surveys. Further, the propensity to identify may also be related to survey methodology. Turner et al. (1998) showed that surveys that utilize computer technology to decrease human interaction in providing responses increased the reporting of a variety of stigmatizing behaviors, including same-sex sexual experiences. Feelings of confidentiality and anonymity increase the likelihood that respondents will be more accurate in reporting sensitive information. Survey methods that include face-to-face interviews may underestimate the size of the LGBT community, whereas those that include methods that allow respondents to complete questions on a computer or via the Internet may increase the likelihood of LGBT respondents identifying themselves.

The Gallup Daily tracking survey is a phone survey of adults age 18 and older. Respondents speak directly to an interviewer. The General Social Survey (GSS) is an in-person interview with respondents, who are age 18 and older. Another large population-based survey, the National Survey of Family Growth (NSFG), conducted by the U.S. Department of Health and Human Services, asks questions about sexual orientation, sexual behavior, and sexual attraction questions, but the sample is limited to adults age 18 to 44 (Chandra et al. 2011). The NSFG is administered using a computer-assisted personal interview where respondents are provided with a computer by an in-person interviewer and answers are entered into the computer directly by the respondent.

Across these three surveys, there is general consistency in the percentage of respondents who identify as LGB, from 3.5% to 3.7% (see Figure 1.1). This would represent between 8.2 and 8.7 million Americans. There is also consistency between the GSS and the NSFG in estimates of those who have had a same-sex sexual experience since age 18. The estimate is 8.7% in the GSS and 8.6% in the NSFG. That would constitute 20.2 to 20.4 million adults. The NSFG is the only one of the three surveys to ask about sexual attraction and 11.1% of respondents reported at least some same-sex sexual attraction. If that figure is applied to all adults, it would imply that more than 26 million Americans have a same-sex attraction.

Although calculating the extent of underreporting of LGBT status is difficult, evidence of substantial variation across age cohorts in the percent of those who identify as lesbian, gay, or bisexual suggests that underreporting may be decreasing as younger age cohorts feel more comfortable in being open about their sexual orientation identity. For example, in the Gallup data, adults under age 30 are twice as likely as those older than 30 to identify as LGBT (Gates and Newport 2012). Although underreporting may be declining over time, it remains a factor

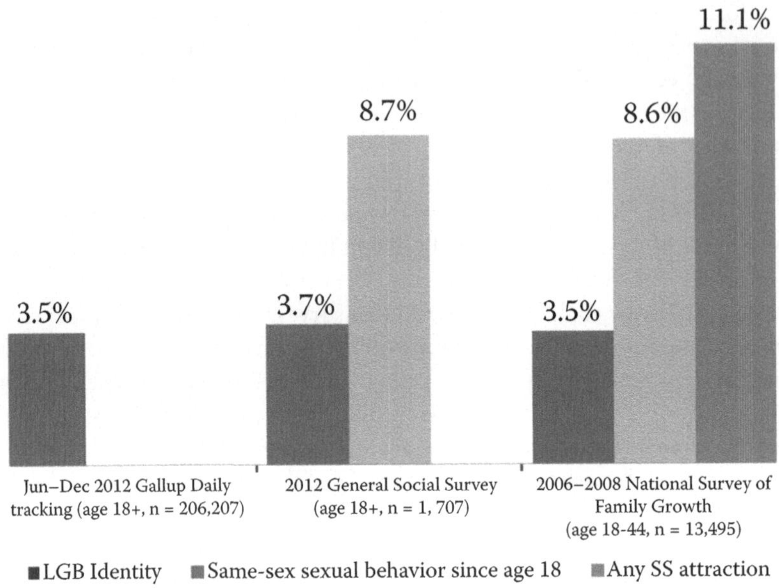

Figure 1.1 Measures of lesbian, gay, or bisexual sexual orientation, by various surveys.

in interpreting findings from population-based surveys that include lesbian, gay, bisexual, or transgender populations.

One caution with regard to same-sex sexual behaviors and attractions is that the results are substantially different if a more recent time period for sexual behavior is used and if same-sex attraction measures exclude those who say they are "mostly" attracted to different-sex partners. In the GSS, only 3.5% of adults report that they have had a same-sex partner in the last year. That figure is substantially higher in the NSFG at 8% (Chandra et al. 2011). However, in both cases, the portion of adults who have had same-sex partners in the recent past is lower than the portion who has ever had a same-sex sexual experience. In the NSFG, just 3.3% of respondents say that they are equally, mostly, or exclusively attracted to different-sex partners. The bulk of those with any same-sex attraction are those who say they are "mostly" attracted to different-sex partners.

Surveys suggest varied results regarding the portion of the LGB-identified adults who are female and the portions who are lesbian/gay versus bisexual (see Figure 1.2). Analyses of the GSS using data from 2008, 2010, and 2012 (in order to increase sample sizes of LGB respondents), suggest that the majority of LGB respondents (59%) are female, and bisexual women constitute the largest grouping when considering both sexual orientation identity and sex (37%). Bisexual men are the smallest group (15%). In analyses that average findings across a range of surveys, bisexual women also represent the largest group (33%), however, lesbians represent the smallest group

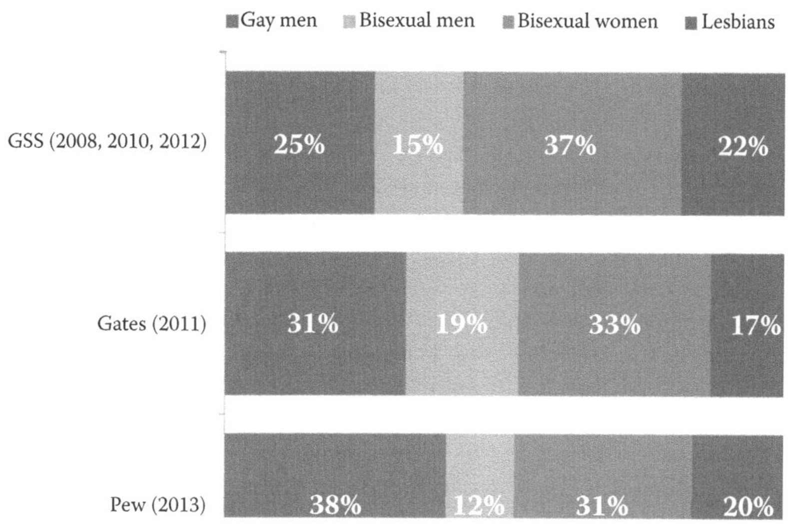

Figure 1.2 Sexual orientation by sex, among various surveys.

at 17% (Gates 2011). Overall, men and women are evenly divided within the LGB population. The Pew survey (Pew Research Center 2013a) and the Gates (2011) analyses suggest that gay men are the largest group and bisexual men are the smallest.

One common finding in all of these data is that women are more likely to identify as bisexual than lesbian, whereas men are more likely to identify as gay than bisexual. In all of these data, more than 7 in 10 bisexuals are women. Conversely, among gay men and lesbians, the majority are men. These data also show that bisexuals are a very large portion of the LGB community; in most surveys, nearly half of LGB adults identify as bisexual.

National population-based data on the transgender community is not available. The Pew data found that 4.3% of its LGBT sample primarily identified as transgender (Pew Research Center 2013a). That would represent 0.15% of the adult population (assuming the Gallup finding that 3.5% of adults are LGBT). A survey in Massachusetts (Conron et al. 2012) found that 0.5% of adults identify as transgender. Applying those figures to the U.S. population would suggest that from 360,000 to 1.2 million adults identify as transgender.

Coming Out

Coming out can be a complicated emotional experience for many LGBT people. Coming out has both private and public dimensions. Most LGBT individuals report a period of time in which they question themselves privately about and eventually come to terms with their sexual orientation or gender identity. At some point, most LGBT individuals also engage in a process of being more public about their sexual orientation or gender identity by sharing that information with friends, family, and work colleagues. These private and public dimensions of coming out are part of what, for many, can be a lifelong process.

The Pew survey of LGBT adults provides some of the most comprehensive information available about the coming out process for LGBT Americans (Pew Research Center 2013a). Findings show that 46% of LGBT-identified individuals report that they are not out to all of the most important people in their lives. Nearly a quarter (23%) indicate that they are out to only a few or none of those important people. The data reveal substantial differences between bisexual versus gay- and lesbian-identified individuals in this regard. For bisexual women and men, 28% are out to all of the major people in their lives, whereas 77% of gay men and 71% of lesbians are out to the major people in their lives (Pew Research Center 2013b).

LGB individuals report that they first thought they might not be heterosexual at relatively young ages. The Pew data found that the median age for this awareness was 12. While awareness started at a young age, LGB individuals were much older when they first told a close friend or family member. For most, this occurred when they were young adults, over age 18. The survey also suggests that the age of coming out is declining. For example, the median age when lesbian and gay respondents aged 18 to 29 report first telling someone about their sexual orientation was 17. For 30 to 49 year olds the median age was 20, and for those aged 50 and older it was 21. The Pew data also considered the specific circumstance of coming out to one's parents. About a third (34%) of LGBT individuals had not come out to their mother, and even more, 39%, had not come out to their father.

These revealing data on the coming out process offer some evidence that as social acceptance grows toward LGBT people, the age of coming out will be younger and more will be out to friends and family. But the data also reveal that there are still many LGBT individuals, particularly bisexual men and women, who are not out to many of their friends and family. This could, in part, explain the interesting Pew finding that the general population in the United States is substantially more likely to report being "very happy" (30%) than are LGBT Americans (17%).

Geographic Distribution of the LGBT Community

Any assessment of geographic patterns within the LGBT community must consider why there might be variation in the portion of LGBT individuals by region, state, or locality. Some geographic variation is likely a result of preferences of LGBT individuals to live in areas with greater levels of social acceptance or LGBT-supportive laws, however Pew data suggest that few LGBT individuals actually take this into account when deciding where to live. Fully two-thirds of LGBT respondents (67%) said that LGBT social acceptance was not a factor in their decision about where to live (Pew Research Center 2013a). Analyses of GSS data suggest that LGB mobility may not be that much different from heterosexual mobility. In the 2012 data, an estimated 44% of LGB respondents reported that they live in the same city where they lived when they were 16 years old. This compares to 39% of heterosexual respondents. A large portion of geographic variation in LGBT identity may simply be associated with the willingness of individuals to identify as such. High proportions of LGBT individuals in an area are likely more an indication of greater willingness of those living there to self-identify due to higher levels of social acceptance than a greater tendency of LGBT individuals to migrate to that area.

The map in Figure 1.3 shows the percentage of adults who identify as LGBT by state based on the Gallup Daily tracking survey data (Gates and Newport 2013). In general, states in New England and along the West Coast have the highest proportions of LGBT individuals. Among states, Hawaii reported the highest percentage at 5.1%, followed by Vermont and Oregon at 4.9%, Maine at 4.8%, and Rhode Island at 4.5%. The figure in the District of Columbia was 10%, perhaps not surprising since DC is entirely urban and evidence does suggest that LGBT identity is higher in urban areas. For example, the Gallup data show that among respondents who live in a metropolitan area, 3.6% identify as LGBT compared to 2.9% of those who live outside of those areas.

The Census 2010 same-sex couple data allow for the consideration of geographic variation below the state level. The map in Figure 1.4 shows the number of same-sex couples per 1,000 households by county. Notably, same-sex couples were present in 93% of all U.S. counties (Gates and Cooke 2011). Similar to the state-level map of LGBT concentration, counties in New England and the West Coast are

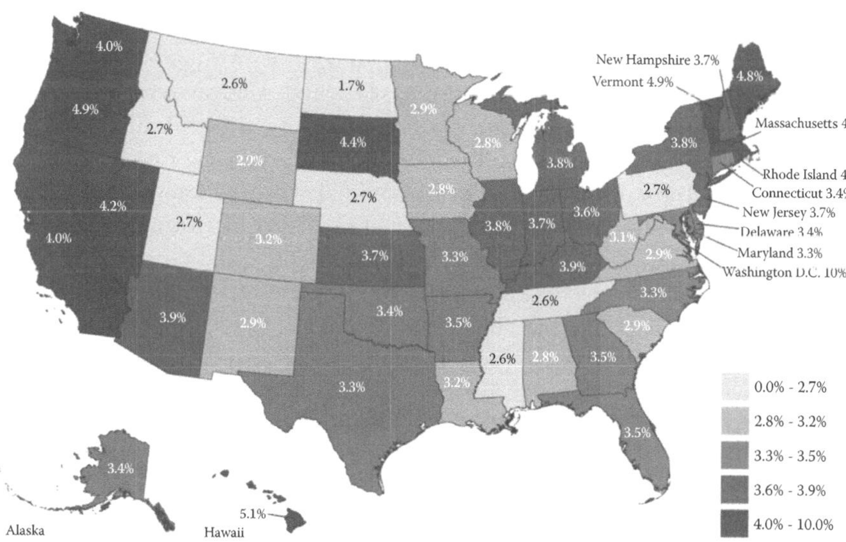

Figure 1.3 Percent of adults age 18 and older who identify as LGBT, by state.

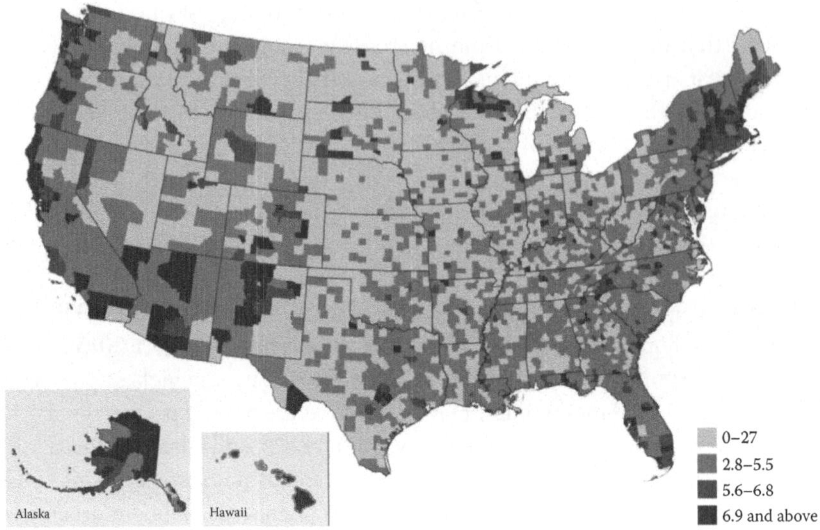

Figure 1.4 Same-sex couples per 1,000 households. (From Census 2010.)

among those with the highest proportions of same-sex couples. San Francisco and Hampshire County in western Massachusetts are the two top-ranking counties in this regard and Multnomah County in Oregon ranks fifth. The other counties in the top ten are spread throughout the country. The ten counties with the highest concentration of same-sex couples are shown in Table 1.1.

Cities with the highest concentrations of same-sex couples are also spread throughout the country (see Table 1.2). Among large cities with populations above 500,000, San Francisco (CA), Seattle (WA), Portland (OR), Washington (DC), and Denver (CO) are ranked as the top five. Midsize cities with high rankings include Oakland (CA), Minneapolis (MN), Atlanta (GA), Long Beach (CA), and St. Louis (MO). Top-ranked small cities are dominated by well-known LGBT tourist destinations and retirement communities including Provincetown (MA), Wilton Manors (FL), Palm Springs (CA), Rehoboth Beach (DE), and Guerneville (CA). These relatively small towns have concentrations of same-sex couples that are from 2.7 to 4.9 times higher than that of San Francisco.

Demographic Characteristics: Age, Race, and Ethnicity

The propensity to identify as LGBT declines with age. Older LGBT Americans likely have experienced levels of discrimination and stigma that exceed those experienced by younger generations and may be more reluctant to identify as LGBT in surveys. Analyses of the Gallup data show that 6.5% of adults age 18 to 29 identify as LGBT compared to less than 2% of those age 65 and older (Gates and Newport 2012).

Table 1.1 Counties Ranked by Number of Same-Sex Couples per 1,000 Households, Census 2010

County	*Same-Sex Couples per 1,000 Households*
1. San Francisco County, CA	30.2
2. Hampshire County, MA	19.7
3. Monroe County, FL	18.8
4. District of Columbia, DC	18.1
5. Multnomah County, OR	16.8
6. Manhattan, NY	16.7
7. Santa Fe County, NM	15.5
8. Denver County, CO	15.4
9. Sussex County, DE	15.4
10. DeKalb County, GA	15.1

Table 1.2 Cities Ranked by Number of Same-Sex Couples per 1,000 Households, by City Size, Census 2010

Large, Population >500K		*Midsize, Population 250K–500K*		*Small, Population <250K*	
1. San Francisco, CA	30.2	Oakland, CA	21.8	Provincetown, MA	148.1
2. Seattle, WA	23.1	Minneapolis, MN	21.7	Wilton Manors, FL	125.3
3. Portland, OR	19.2	Atlanta, GA	19.7	Palm Springs, CA	107.3
4. Washington, DC	18.1	Long Beach, CA	19.1	Rehoboth Beach, DE	100.0
5. Denver, CO	15.6	St. Louis, MO	14.1	Guerneville, CA	80.4
6. Boston, MA	14.7	Sacramento, CA	13.0	West Hollywood, CA	62.1
7. Dallas, TX	12.2	New Orleans, LA	10.7	Pleasant Ridge, MI	54.8
8. San Diego, CA	12.2	St. Paul, MN	10.6	Rancho Mirage, CA	52.3
9. Austin, TX	11.8	Tampa, FL	10.4	New Hope, PA	50.0
10. Columbus, OH	11.4	Kansas City, MO	10.2	Oakland Park, FL	49.4

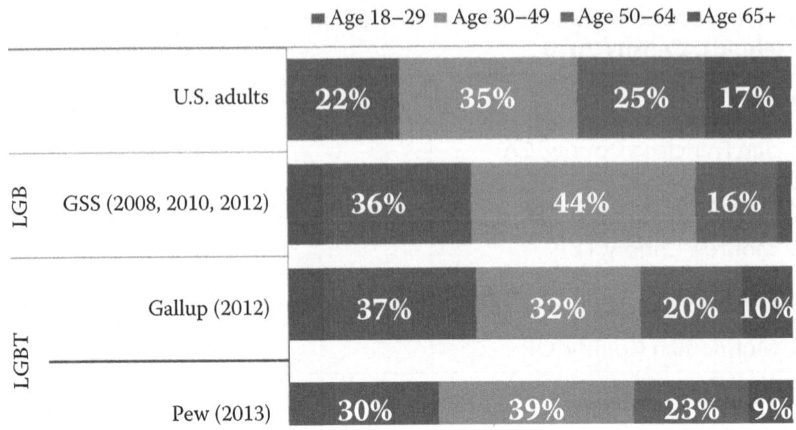

Figure 1.5 Age distribution of LGBT adults and U.S. adults (various surveys).

The 2012 GSS data show a similar pattern with 5.2% of those aged 18 to 29 identifying as LGB compared to less than 1% of seniors age 65 and older.

As a result of these patterns, LGBT individuals tend to be younger than the general population. Figure 1.5 shows results from various surveys. While less than a quarter of adults in the United States are under age 30, the three surveys of LGBT adults suggest that the figure is closer to a third for LGBT Americans. At the other end of the age spectrum, 17% of adults in the United States are age 65 or older compared to less than 10% of LGBT adults.

Several surveys find that non-white Americans are as likely, if not more likely, than their white counterparts to identify as LGBT. In the Gallup data, 3.1% of white adults identified as LGBT compared to 3.7% of African-Americans and 4.5% of Latinos and Latinas (Gates and Newport 2012). In the GSS, LGB identification figures are 2.9% among whites, 3.3% among African-Americans, and 3.6% among Latinos and Latinas.

The distribution of LGBT adults across racial and ethnic characteristics in various surveys is shown in Figure 1.6. The surveys clearly show that the racial and ethnic characteristics of the LGBT population are essentially the same as the U.S. population: about two-thirds are white, from 10% to 15% are African-American, and 14% to 17% are Latino or Latina. The U.S. adult population figures are 66% white, 12% African-American, and 15% Latino or Latina.

Educational Attainment and Socioeconomic Status

LGBT individuals report education levels that are similar to or, in some surveys, somewhat higher than that of the general population of adults. Education tends to be associated with economic advantage. Despite some evidence of higher levels of education, data do not suggest that LGBT adults have any substantial economic advantages.

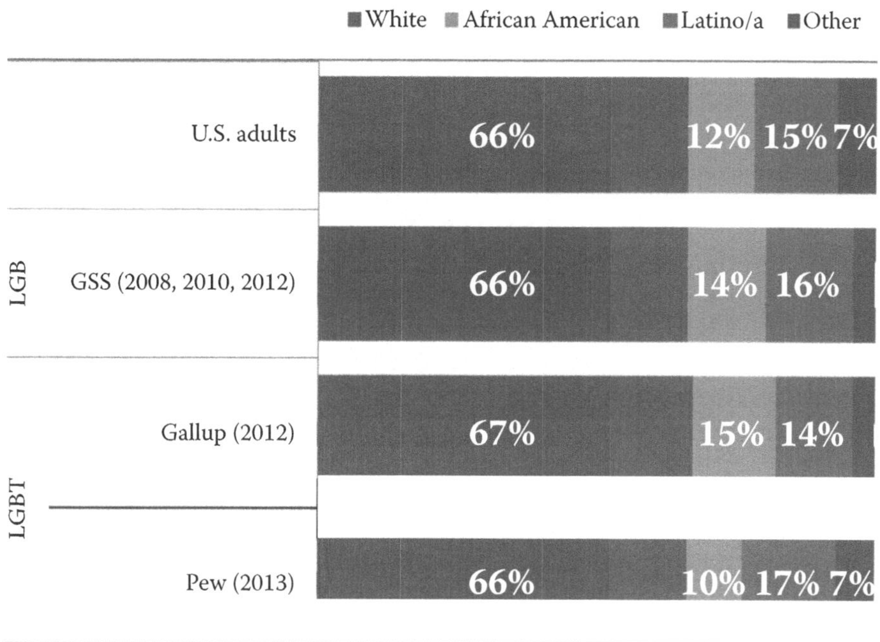

Figure 1.6 Race and ethnicity of LGBT adults and the U.S. adult population (various surveys).

The education levels of LGBT individuals compared to adults in the United States are shown in Figure 1.7. GSS and Pew data suggest that, relative to all adults, LGB/LGBT individuals are more likely to have a college degree and less likely to have a high school education or less. The Gallup data suggests that LGBT adults have very similar levels of education when compared to all adults in the United States.

The American Community Survey of 2011 shows that 32% of different-sex couples have a college degree, whereas same-sex couples analysis from the same study indicates that 46% of them have college degrees (Gates 2013a, 1).

Unfortunately, the GSS, Gallup, and Pew data on LGBT individuals do not include information about individual income and instead only include information about the incomes of the households where LGBT people live. This can be difficult to interpret with regard to the individual economic well-being of LGBT individuals. Relative to the U.S. population, LGBT individuals in the Pew data are more likely to live in households with family income of less than $30,000 per year (28% versus 39%, respectively). They are also less likely to live in households with family incomes that exceed $75,000 per year (Pew Research Center 2013a).

Data from the ACS provides information about individual incomes for men and women in same-sex couples. It is interesting to note that in 2011 the median

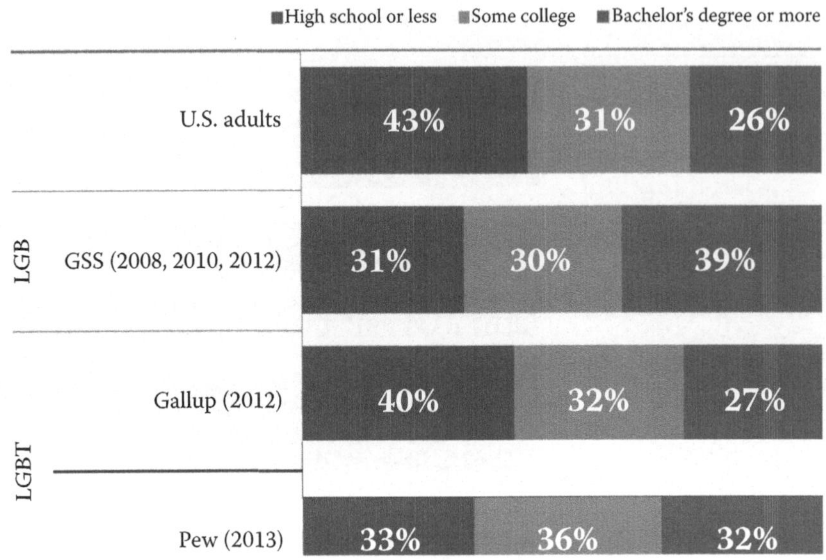

Figure 1.7 Educational attainment of LGBT adults and the U.S. adult population (various surveys).

annual personal income for men in same-sex couples ($47,000) is lower than that for men in different sex couples ($48,000); whereas the median annual personal income for women in different-sex couples is $30,000, and for same-sex couples, the amount is $38,000 (Gates 2013a).

Work force involvement of partners/spouses leads to some variation in median annual household income. If both individuals in a couple are in the workforce, same-sex couples have a higher median household income ($94,000) than different-sex couples ($86,000) (Gates 2013a). This is consistent with the fact that those in same-sex couples have higher levels of education. If couples have no spouses/partners or one spouse/partner in the workforce, the median incomes for different and same-sex couples are very close to identical (Gates 2013a). Notably, these patterns are different for couples raising children. The median annual household income of same-sex couples with children under age 18 in the home is lower than comparable different-sex couples ($63,900 vs. $74,000, respectively).

Badgett et al. (2013) show that same-sex couples are, in general, more vulnerable to poverty than their different-sex married counterparts when a range of demographic characteristics are taken into account in comparisons between the two groups. This is particularly true for same-sex couples with children. Children living in same-sex couple households are nearly twice as likely as children living with different-sex married couples to be in poverty. LGB individuals are as likely as their non-LGB counterparts to be living in poverty.

Immigration

Like other data on the LGBT community, information about the LGBT immigrant community in the United States is sparse. Using several data sources to estimate the size of the LGBT foreign-born population as well for some of their demographic characteristics, Gates's (2013b) analyses suggest that there are more than 900,000 LGBT foreign-born adults living in the United States. Of that group, an estimated 267,000 are part of the undocumented, immigrant population, representing approximately 2.7% of undocumented adults in the United States. About 2.4% of the documented immigrants who are adults are LGBT-identified, or approximately 637,000 individuals. (Gates 2013b). Compared to their documented and undocumented counterparts, LGBT immigrants are more likely to be male and are younger.

The same-sex couple data from the ACS provide information about the citizenship status and country of birth for this segment of the LGBT community. Unfortunately, the data provide no information about the visa status of individuals that would allow for a determination of what portion might be undocumented.

When we look at people born in other countries who are either noncitizens or naturalized citizens while also being part of a same-sex couple, we find 113,000 individuals, of whom 54,600 are not U.S. citizens (Gates 2013b). An estimated 54,600 of these individuals are not U.S. citizens. Approximately 32,300 same-sex couples are binational (one a U.S. citizen and one a noncitizen) and 11,700 same-sex couples are comprised of two noncitizens. Approximately 12,400 children under age 18 are being raised by almost 7,000 same-sex couples (which include two non-citizens) (Gates 2013b).

The majority of noncitizens in same-sex couples are male (59%). They are also younger than their foreign-born counterparts in different-sex couples. Nearly a quarter of foreign born individuals in same-sex couples (23%) are under age 30 compared to just 15% of their counterparts in different-sex couples.

Military Service

During the era of the U.S. military's so-called Don't Ask/Don't Tell (DADT) policy, data that would directly assess the sexual orientation or gender identity of those in military service were not available. Providing one's sexual orientation or gender identity to a survey taker came with risks of disclosure for service members that could have resulted in damaging effects on their military careers. During the era of DADT, an analysis of data regarding the military service of individuals in same-sex couples was conducted to derive estimates for the broader LGB population that was on active duty or in the Guard or Ready Reserve (Gates 2010b). The findings suggested that approximately 2.2% of that group were LGB. The proportion was estimated to be higher in the Guard and Ready Reserve (3.4%) as compared to those on active duty (0.9%). The findings also suggested higher rates of military service among lesbian and bisexual women than among gay and bisexual men, showing that an estimated 6.2% of women in the military were lesbian or bisexual, whereas just 1.5% of men were gay or bisexual.

The Gallup Daily tracking data provide a more recent and direct measure of LGBT military service, though the sample is limited to military personnel currently residing in the United States.* Analyses of these data suggest that an estimated 2% of those on active duty and 3.2% of those in the Guard and Ready Reserve are LGBT. This would imply that there are nearly 29,000 LGBT individuals on active duty in the U.S. military along with approximately 27,000 in Guard and Reserve units.†

These data are also consistent with the findings of the earlier analyses based on same-sex couples with regard to differences in military service patterns of LGBT men and women. Among women on active duty, the Gallup data suggest that 7.7% identify as LGBT. For men, the figure is just 1%. Among women in the Guard and Ready Reserve, 5.8% identify as LGBT compared to 2.8% among men.

Relative to non-LGBT individuals, LGBT individuals are less likely to report being currently on active duty. Nearly 1% of adults in the Gallup survey were on active duty compared to approximately 0.5% of LGBT-identified respondents. However, this pattern is only true for men. Non-LGBT men are approximately 3.4 times more likely than their LGBT counterparts to report being on active duty. Women who are LGBT are twice as likely to report that they are on active duty as non-LGBT women.

There are fewer differences between LGBT and non-LGBT individuals with regard to service in the Guard or Ready Reserve. For both groups, approximately 0.8% report serving in that capacity. Non-LGBT men are slightly more likely than LGBT men to report Guard or Reserve service (1.5% versus 1.2%, respectively). Conversely, LGBT women are more likely to report service than non-LGBT women (0.4% versus 0.2%, respectively).

Gallup data suggest that an estimated 2.5% of veterans identify as LGBT. Among LGBT individuals, approximately 7.4% are veterans compared to 10.4% of non-LGBT individuals. This would imply that there are more than 600,000 LGBT veterans in the United States. More than 12% of LGBT men and 3% of LGBT women are veterans compared to nearly 20% of non-LGBT men and 1.6% of non-LGBT women. Among men in same-sex couples, 9.3% report being veterans. For women in same-sex couples, the figure is 5%. Approximately 1.1% of same-sex

* Findings presented here are author analyses of Gallup Daily tracking survey data collected from June to December 2012.

† Based on U.S. Department of Defense estimates of active duty, Guard, and Ready Reserve forces found at http://prhome.defense.gov/RFM/MPP/ACCESSION%20POLICY/PopRep2010/contents/contents.html.

couples include at least one spouse or partner who is a veteran, meaning that more than 7,100 same-sex couples include a veteran.

Conclusion

Although population-based demographic data on the LGBT population remains relatively rare, recent data collection efforts by large survey organizations like Gallup and Pew Research have significantly enhanced our ability to understand similarities and differences between LGBT and non-LGBT populations. The analyses described in this chapter show high levels of concordance across surveys regarding demographic patterns in the LGBT community. Major findings of these surveys and accompanying analyses include the following:

- Approximately 3.5% of adults in the Unite States identify as LGBT but substantially more acknowledge having had same-sex sexual relationships and attractions.
- Bisexuals represent approximately half of the LGB community and women are more likely to identify as bisexual than men.
- LGBT identity tends to be higher in areas with more LGBT supportive social and legal climates.
- LGBT identity is higher within younger populations.
- There are few differences in the racial and ethnic composition of LGBT and non-LGBT populations.
- Although LGBT individuals report relatively high levels of education, they do not necessarily evidence the economic advantage that would normally be associated with that education.
- The immigrant community in the United States includes an estimated 257,000 undocumented LGBT adults, 637,000 documented LGBT adults, and more than 32,000 binational couples.
- There are an estimated 600,000 LGBT veterans in the United States and at least 56,000 LGBT individuals on active duty or in the Guard or Ready Reserve. A higher proportion of LGBT women report serving in the military when compared to non-LGBT women and LGBT men.

These findings demonstrate that LGBT individuals are part of communities in every region of the United States. They are also present within the nation's racial and ethnic communities, the immigrant community, and within the armed forces. In short, they are a clear part of the cultural and demographic diversity of the country. As social acceptance grows and struggles for legal equality progress, an increasing number of LGBT individuals will likely become more comfortable with identifying themselves on surveys and in their families and communities. As a result, the demographic similarities between LGBT and non-LGBT populations, already evident in existing data, will likely increase.

References

Badgett, M. V. Lee, Laura E. Durso, and Alyssa Schneebaum. 2013. "New Patterns of Poverty in the Lesbian, Gay, and Bisexual Community." Williams Institute, UCLA School of Law. http://williamsinstitute.law.ucla.edu/wp-content/uploads/LGB-Poverty-Update-Jun-2013.pdf.

Chandra, Anjani, William D. Mosher, Casey Copen, and Catlainn Sionean. 2011. "Sexual Behavior, Sexual Attraction, and Sexual Identity in the United States: Data from the 2006–2008 National Survey of Family Growth." Hyattsville, MD: National Health Statistics Reports, Number 36, US Department of Health and Human Services, Centers for Disease Control and Prevention, National Center for Health Statistics. http://www.cdc.gov/nchs/data/nhsr/nhsr036.pdf.

Conron, K. J., G. Scott, G. S. Stowell, and S. Landers. 2012. "Transgender Health in Massachusetts: Results from a Household Probability Sample of Adults." *American Journal of Public Health, 102*(1), 118-122.

Gates, Gary J. 2010a. "Same-Sex Couples in US Census Bureau Data: Who Gets Counted and Why." Williams Institute, UCLA School of Law. http://williamsinstitute.law.ucla.edu/wp-content/uploads/Gates-Who-Gets-Counted-Aug-2010.pdf.

Gates, Gary J. 2010b. "Lesbian, Gay, and Bisexual Men and Women in the US Military: Updated Estimates." Williams Institute, UCLA School of Law. http://williamsinstitute.law.ucla.edu/wp-content/uploads/Gates-GLBmilitaryUpdate-May-20101.pdf.

Gates, Gary J. 2011. "How Many People are Gay, Lesbian, Bisexual, and Transgender?" Williams Institute, UCLA School of Law. http://williamsinstitute.law.ucla.edu/research/census-lgbt-demographics-studies/how-many-people-are-lesbian-gay-bisexual-and-transgender/.

Gates, Gary J. 2013a. "Sex and Different Sex Couples in the American Community Survey: 2005–2011." Williams Institute, UCLA School of Law. http://williamsinstitute.law.ucla.edu/wp-content/uploads/ACS-2013.pdf.

Gates, Gary J. 2013b. "LGBT Adult Immigrants in the United States." Williams Institute, UCLA School of Law. http://williamsinstitute.law.ucla.edu/wp-content/uploads/LGBTImmigrants-Gates-Mar-2013.pdf.

Gates, Gary J., and Abigail M. Cooke. 2011. "United States Census Snapshot: 2010." Williams Institute, UCLA School of Law. http://williamsinstitute.law.ucla.edu/wp-content/uploads/Census2010Snapshot-U.S.-v2.pdf?r=1.

Gates, Gary J., and Frank Newport. 2012. "Special Report: 3.4% of U.S. Adults Identify as LGBT." Princeton, NJ: Gallup. http://www.gallup.com/poll/158066/special-report-adults-identify-lgbt.aspx.

Gates, Gary J., and Frank Newport. 2013. "LGBT Percentage Highest in D.C., Lowest in North Dakota." Princeton, NJ: Gallup. http://www.gallup.com/poll/160517/lgbt-percentage-highest-lowest-north-dakota.aspx.

Grant, Jaime M., Lisa A. Mottet, Justin Tanis, Jack Harrison, Jody L. Herman, and Mara Keisling. 2011. "Injustice at Every Turn: A Report of the National Transgender Discrimination Survey." Washington, D.C.: National Center for Transgender Equality and National Gay and Lesbian Task Force. http://www.thetaskforce.org/downloads/reports/reports/ntds_full.pdf.

Institute of Medicine. 2011. *The Health of Lesbian, Gay, Bisexual, and Transgender People: Building a Foundation for Better Understanding.* Washington, DC: The National Academies Press.

Pew Research Center. 2013a. "A Survey of LGBT Americans: Attitudes, Experiences and Values in Changing Times." Washington D.C.: Pew Research Center. http://www.pewsocialtrends.org/files/2013/06/SDT_LGBT-Americans_06-2013.pdf.

Pew Research Center. 2013b. "A Survey of LGBT Americans: Overview." http://www.pewsocialtrends.org/2013/06/13/a-survey-of-lgbt-americans/.

Smith, Tom W., Peter Marsden, Michael Hout, and Jibum Kim. 2013. "General Social Survey 2008, 2010, 2012." National Opinion Research Center, University of Chicago.

Turner, C. F., B. H. Forsyth, J. O'Reilly, P. C. Cooley, T. K. Smith, S. M. Rogers, and H. G. Miller. 1998. "Automated Self-interviewing and the Survey Measurement of Sensitive Behaviors." In *Computer-Assisted Survey Information Collection*, edited by Mick P. Couper, Reginald P. Baler, Jelke Bethlehem, Cynthia Z, Clark, Jean Martin, William Nicholls II, and James M. O'Reilly. New York: Wiley and Sons.

Chapter 2

Lesbian, Gay, Bisexual, and Transgender Family Formation and Demographics

Gary J. Gates

Contents

Introduction

In a review of the academic literature on same-sex parenting, Biblarz and Stacey (2010) observe that contemporary studies of parenting by same-sex couples have focused largely on parents who tend to be disproportionately white with relatively high levels of income and education. Most of this research has focused on same-sex couples who had their children as openly lesbian or gay couples and through adoption or some form of assisted-reproduction technology. Our understanding of transgender parents, single LGBT (lesbian, gay, bisexual, and transgender) parents, and same-sex couples who have children from prior different-sex relationships is much more limited.

As data on the LGBT population improves, we now understand that LGBT families are more geographically, racially, ethnically, and socioeconomically diverse than much of the academic literature might suggest. Although adoption has been increasing among LGBT individuals, evidence continues to suggest that the majority of LGBT parents have a biological relationship with their children, likely born as a result of a different-sex relationship that the LGBT parent had when he or she was relatively young. This chapter will provide analyses from several population-based data sources that offer a wider demographic portrait of LGBT parents and families. The analyses will conclude with a discussion of the policy implications associated with improving the ability of LGBT individuals to parent and raise their children in safe and nurturing environments.

How Common Is Parenting among LGBT People?

Population-based data that measures parenting in the LGBT community, particularly data that include transgender individuals, remain relatively rare. The General Social Survey (GSS), a population-based survey of the U.S. adult population conducted every two years by NORC at the University of Chicago, includes a question about sexual orientation identity and parenting in the 2008, 2010, and 2012 surveys (Smith et al. 2012).

Analyses of those data suggest that approximately 37% of LGB adults indicate that they have ever had a child. Data from the National Transgender Discrimination Survey, though not population based, find that a similar proportion of transgender adults (38%) report that they have had a child. Assuming that there are approximately 8.2 million LGBT-identified adults in the United States (based on data from the Gallup Daily tracking survey), the GSS figures imply that approximately 3 million LGBT adults in the United States have had a child. On average,

LGB respondents in the GSS who say they have had a child report having had two children. This implies that there may be as many as 6 million children and adults in the United States who have an LGB parent (Gates 2013a). The vast majority of LGB parents in the United States are bisexual. Nearly three-quarters of LGB parents in the GSS identify as bisexual.*

Further analyses of the GSS data suggest that approximately 28% of LGB-identified respondents are currently raising a child under age 18 in their home. This suggests that there are approximately 2.25 million LGB individuals (approximately three-quarters of LGB parents) in the United States who are parenting children under age 18. A substantial majority of these LGB parents are bisexual. Less than 15% of lesbian- or gay-identified individuals in the GSS report raising a child under age 18 compared to more than 40% of bisexual individuals. This implies that, like those who have ever had a child, nearly three-quarters of LGB-identified individuals raising young children are bisexual.†

Data from the U.S. Census Bureau provide information about same-sex couples raising children. Analyses of the 2011 American Community Survey data show that approximately 19% of the nearly 650,000 same-sex couples in the United States are raising children under age 18. Approximately 125,000 same-sex couples are raising nearly 220,000 children (Gates 2013b).

The percentage of same-sex couples raising children under age 18 has declined between 2005 and 2011. In 2005, nearly 25% of same-sex couples were raising children, compared to the 2011 figure of 19% (Gates 2013b). This is likely due in large part to changes in how individuals in same-sex couples likely become parents.

How Do LGBT People Come to Be Parents?

Relationship to Children

Population-based data that directly consider how LGBT individuals become parents is not available. However, U.S. Census Bureau data do provide some information about the relationship between parents and children being raised by same-sex couples. Among children under age 18 being raised by same-sex couples, approximately 59% are identified as the biological child of the "householder," who is usually the person in the household who owns or rents the home (see Figure 2.1). Approximately 7% are stepchildren (presumably children of the partner), 10% are adopted children,

---

* Author analyses of 2008–2012 GSS using University of California, Berkeley Survey Data and Analysis (SDA) web-based analysis tool, available at http://sda.berkeley.edu/cgi-bin/hsda?harcsda+gss12.

† Author analyses of 2008–2012 GSS using University of California, Berkeley Survey Data and Analysis (SDA) web-based analysis tool, available at http://sda.berkeley.edu/cgi-bin/hsda?harcsda+gss12.

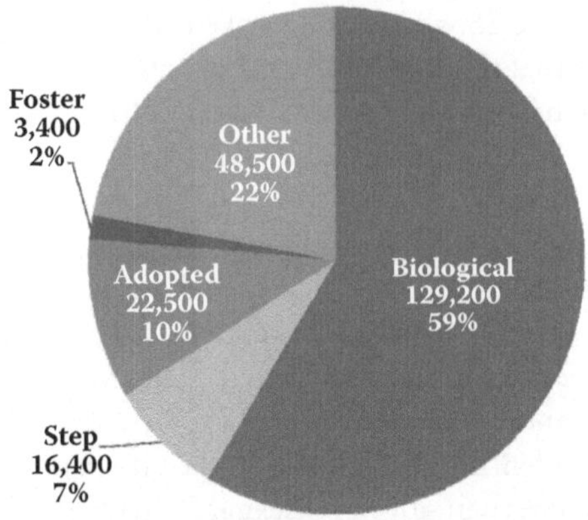

Figure 2.1 Relationship of children under age 18 to householder (Person 1) in same-sex couples. (From American Community Survey, 2011.)

2% are foster children, and 22% are identified as related (e.g., sibilings, cousins) and unrelated children (Gates 2013a).

Geographic Distribution

Analyses of the demographic characteristics of LGB-identified parents offers evidence that the majority of children being raised by same-sex couples are likely the product of different-sex relationships that occurred while LGB individuals were relatively young and before they were open about their sexual orientation. As initial evidence of this, consider where same-sex couples in the United States are most likely to be raising a child. Table 2.1 shows states ranked by the number of same-sex couples per 1,000 households along with states ranked by the fraction of same-sex couples who are raising biological, adopted, or stepchildren under age 18. Among the top-ten states with the highest proportion of same-sex couples per 1,000 households, all had percentages of same-sex couples raising children that were below the national average. Among the states with the highest percentage of same-sex couples raising children, all were below the national average in the number of same-sex couples per 1,000 households.

States with higher proportions of same-sex couples in the population are areas where broader LGBT visibility is generally higher. The rankings in Table 2.1 demonstrate that same-sex couples are more likely to be raising children in parts of the country where LGBT visibility is lower, likely in part due to stigma in more socially conservative states like Mississippi, Wyoming, Alaska, Idaho, and Montana.

The map in Figure 2.2 shows counties in the United States where same-sex couples are most likely to be raising children under age 18. Consistent with the state rankings from Table 2.1, the map shows that same-sex couples are most likely to be parents in the socially conservative South, Midwest, and Mountain regions of the country.

Table 2.1 Top 10 States Ranked by Same-Sex Couples per 1,000 Households and Percentage of Same-Sex Couples Raising Biological, Adopted, or Stepchildren under Age 18

Rank	*State*	*Same-Sex Couples per 1,000 Households*	*% Same-Sex Couples with Children under Age 18*	*State*	*% Same-Sex Couples with Children under Age 18*	*Same-Sex Couples per 1,000 Households*
	United States	5.5	17.2%	United States	17.2%	5.5
1	District of Columbia	18.1	7.4%	Mississippi	25.7%	3.1
2	Vermont	8.4	15.6%	Wyoming	24.7%	2.9
3	Massachusetts	8.0	10.3%	Alaska	23.1%	4.8
4	California	7.8	11.5%	Idaho	22.3%	3.5
5	Oregon	7.8	13.7%	Montana	22.0%	3.3
6	Delaware	7.7	12.2%	Kansas	21.8%	3.6
7	New Mexico	7.4	15.0%	North Dakota	21.6%	2.0
8	Washington	7.3	13.2%	Arkansas	21.2%	3.7
9	Hawaii	7.1	12.5%	South Dakota	21.1%	2.2
10	Maine	7.1	12.8%	Oklahoma	20.9%	4.2

Source: Census 2010.

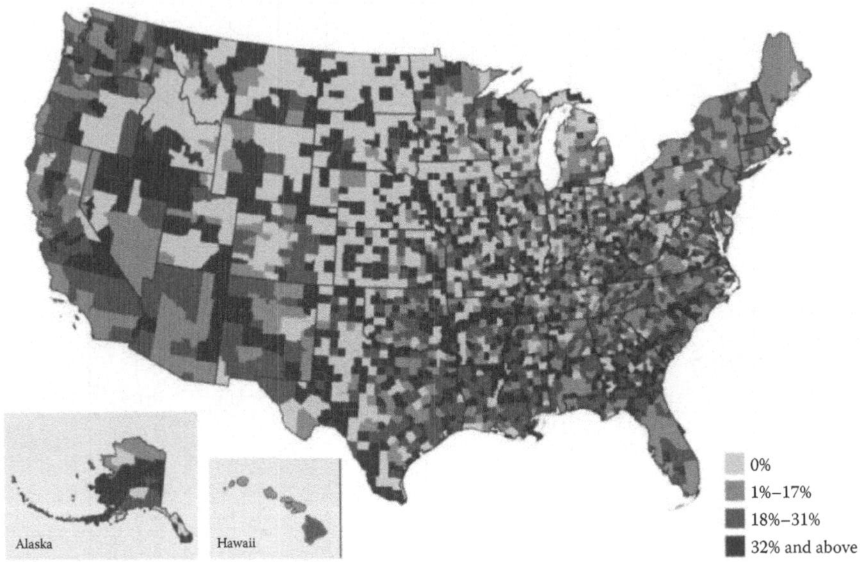

Figure 2.2 Percent of same-sex couples raising biological, adopted, or foster children, by county. (Census 2010.)

Geographically, same-sex parenting is more common in socially conservative parts of the country where LGBT individuals likely come out later in life and are more likely to have had different-sex relationships earlier in life.

Age of Parents

Another demographic characteristic of LGB parents that supports this concept is the age when LGB parents have their first child. Analyses of the GSS data suggest that LGB individuals who report ever having a child had their first child at a median age that is two years younger than their heterosexual counterparts, 21 years old versus 23 years old, respectively (Gates 2013a).

While most biological children born to LGBT parents may be as a result of different-sex relationships at relatively young ages, evidence suggests that adoptive LGBT parents are more likely comprised of individuals who adopt as openly LGBT individuals. Adoptive parents among same-sex couples are, on average, more than 5 years older than same-sex parents with biological or stepchildren, 37.4 years old versus 42.5 years old, respectively.* U.S. Census Bureau data suggest that adoption (and likely other forms of intentional LGBT parenting like surrogacy, sperm donation, and other assisted-reproduction technology) among

* Author analyses of 2011 American Community Survey Public Use Microdata Sample.

same-sex couples has increased substantially in the last decade. In Census 2000, there were approximately 6,400 adopted children being raised by same-sex couples.* Data from the 2011 American Community Survey suggest that this figure has more than tripled to an estimated 22,000 adopted children (Gates 2013a).

The recent declines in the percentage of same-sex couples raising children are likely a product of two trends. As LGBT individuals come out earlier in life, they are less likely to have children with different-sex partners and this form of parenting is declining. Intentional LGBT parenting through adoption and assisted-reproductive technologies can be very expensive and the legal accessibility of these forms of parenting for LGBT individuals and those in same-sex couples can vary by location. This creates constraints on these types of parenting as not all LGBT individuals who want to parent can afford to do so or may be unable to do so because of legal difficulties where they live. So increases in intentional LGBT parenting are not yet sufficient to offset the broader declines in LGBT individuals having biological children with different-sex partners.

Demographic Characteristics of LGBT Families

Sex of Parents

Little data are available to explore the demographic characteristics of transgender parents; however LGB-identified parents and those in same-sex couples raising children are disproportionately female, and are more racially and ethnically diverse when compared to their heterosexual and different-sex coupled counterparts. In the GSS data, among those who have ever had a child, 74% of LGB-identified parents are female compared to 57% of heterosexual parents. Approximately 49% of lesbian and bisexual women report having had a child compared to 25% of gay and bisexual men.† Data from the 2011 American Community Survey show that 73% of same-sex couples raising children under age 18 are female. Among female same-sex couples, 28% are raising children compared to 11% of male couples.‡

Race and Ethnicity

LGB-identified individuals who have ever had a child are less likely to be white than their heterosexual counterparts, 58% to 70%, respectively (see Figure 2.3). LGB male parents are substantially more likely than LGB women or heterosexuals to be a racial or ethnic minority. Just 45% of LGB male parents are white compared

* Author analyses of Census 2000 Public Use Microdata Samples (5% and 1%).

† Author analyses of 2008–2012 GSS using University of California, Berkeley Survey Data and Analysis (SDA) web-based analysis tool, available at http://sda.berkeley.edu/cgi-bin/hsda?harcsda+gss12.

‡ Author analyses of 2011 American Community Survey Public Use Microdata Sample.

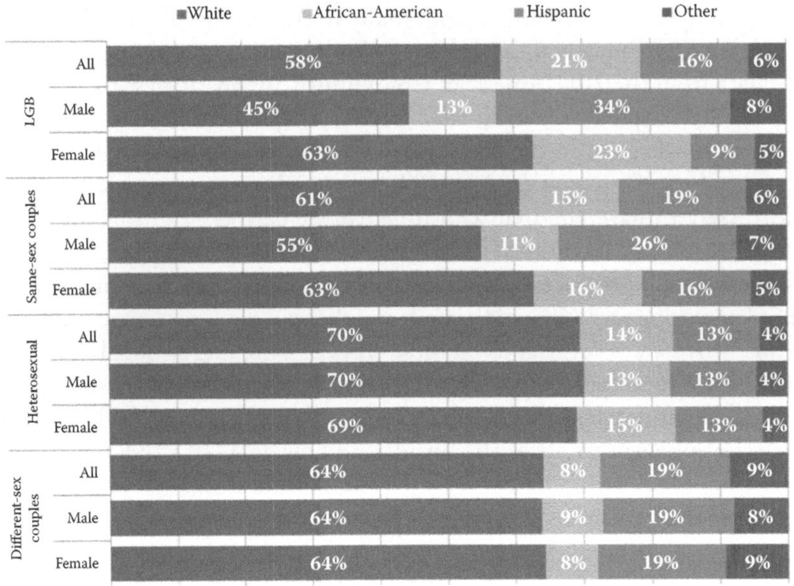

Figure 2.3 Race/ethnicity of individuals who have ever had a child and individuals in couples raising children under age 18, by sexual orientation and couple type. (From General Social Survey, 2008–2012; American Community Survey, 2011.)

to 63% of LGB female parents and 70% of heterosexual parents. More than a third of LGB male parents (34%) are Hispanic, compared to 9% of LGB female parents and 13% of heterosexual parents. Nearly a quarter of LGB female parents (23%) are African-American compared to 13% of LGB male parents and 14% of heterosexual parents.*

These broad patterns are similar when comparing those in same-sex couples raising children under age 18 with their different-sex couple counterparts. Individuals in same-sex couples raising children are less likely to be white than those in different-sex couples, 61% versus 64%, respectively. Men in same-sex couples raising children are the least likely to be white (55%) and most likely to be Hispanic (26%). Women in same-sex couples raising children are twice as likely as comparable women in different-sex couples to be African-American (16% versus 8%, respectively). Approximately 1 in 10 men in same-sex couples raising children (11%) are African-American.†

* Author analyses of 2008–2012 GSS using University of California, Berkeley Survey Data and Analysis (SDA) web-based analysis tool, available at http://sda.berkeley.edu/cgi-bin/hsda?harcsda+gss12.

† Author analyses of 2011 American Community Survey Public Use Microdata Sample.

Given the racial and ethnic diversity of same-sex couples raising children, it is not surprising that children being raised by same-sex couples are more likely to be racial and ethnic minorities when compared to children in different-sex couples. Fully half of children being raised by same-sex couples are non-white compared to 41% of children being raised by different-sex couples. The children of same-sex couples are twice as likely as children of different-sex couples to be African-American, 16% versus 8%, respectively, and about as likely to be Hispanic, 25% versus 23%, respectively (Gates 2013a).

Educational Attainment and Socioeconomic Status

Data from the GSS suggest that LGB individuals who have ever had a child report higher levels of educational attainment when compared to their heterosexual counterparts. Approximately 31% of LGB parents report having a college degree compared to 27% of heterosexual parents.* The pattern is different when comparing individuals in same-sex and different-sex couples raising children under age 18. An estimated 30% of those in same-sex couples raising children have a college degree compared to 34% of their different-sex counterparts.†

Same-sex couples raising children evidence some economic disadvantage when compared to different-sex couples. This is perhaps not surprising given that same-sex couples raising children show demographic characteristics that are associated with relatively lower incomes. Same-sex couple parents are more likely to be female, tend to be younger, and are more likely to be racial/ethnic minorities when compared to those in different-sex couples.

The median annual household income of same-sex couples with children under age 18 in the home is lower than comparable different-sex couples ($63,900 versus $74,000, respectively). Children being raised by same-sex couples are twice as likely as those being raised by married different-sex couples to be poor. Similarly, same-sex couples with children are more likely to be in poverty than their different-sex married counterparts. Among men in same-sex couples with children, 19.2% are in poverty. For women in same-sex couples with children, the figure is 15.4%. The poverty rate among different-sex married couples with children is just 9.3% (Badgett, Durso, and Schneebaum 2013).

These lower incomes may be in part a result of higher rates of unemployment among same-sex couple parents. More than 8 in 10 (81%) individuals in both same-sex and different-sex couples with children indicate that they are in the labor force. However, those in same-sex couples are less likely to be employed, 72% versus 76%, respectively. While same-sex and different-sex couples with children

---

* Author analyses of 2008–2012 GSS using University of California, Berkeley Survey Data and Analysis (SDA) web-based analysis tool, available at http://sda.berkeley.edu/cgi-bin/hsda?harcsda+gss12.

† Author analyses of 2011 American Community Survey Public Use Microdata Sample.

are just as likely to have both spouses or partners employed (56%), same-sex couples are more likely to have neither partner employed, 14% versus 5%, respectively (Gates 2013a).

Differences between Same-Sex and Different-Sex Couple Families Raising Adopted Children versus Biological or Stepchildren

It has already been observed that adoptive parents among same-sex couples are, on average, older than those who are raising biological or stepchildren. Demographically, these two groups of parents are very different. There are distinctive patterns regarding where same-sex couples are most likely to have adopted children and adoptive parents evidence substantial economic advantage.

Geographic Patterns

Among same-sex couples with biological, step-, and adopted children, the portion with adopted children tends to be higher in areas of the country with more accepting legal climates for same-sex parents, particularly New England and the Pacific Coast states (see Figure 2.4). All states in New England allow same-sex couples to petition jointly for adoption statewide. In these states, 23% of same-sex couples with biological or stepchildren include adopted children. Among Pacific states, all but Alaska permit statewide joint adoption petitions for same-sex couples and the figure is 20%. Conversely, in the Deep South states of Alabama, Kentucky, Mississippi, and Tennessee, none of which provide state-level access to joint adoption for same-sex couples, just 5% of these couples include adopted children.

Race and Ethnicity

Nearly 9 in 10 adoptive parents among same-sex couples are white (88%) compared to just 56% of comparable couples with biological stepchildren. This difference in the racial/ethnic makeup of parents is larger in same-sex couples than in different-sex couples, among whom 75% of adoptive parents are white along with 64% of those with biological or stepchildren.*

The racial and ethnic composition of the adopted versus biological or stepchildren of same-sex couples does not vary as much as the differences observed in their parents. An estimated 53% of adopted children of same-sex couples are white compared to 49% of biological and stepchildren. Biological and stepchildren are more

* Author analyses of 2011 American Community Survey Public Use Microdata Sample.

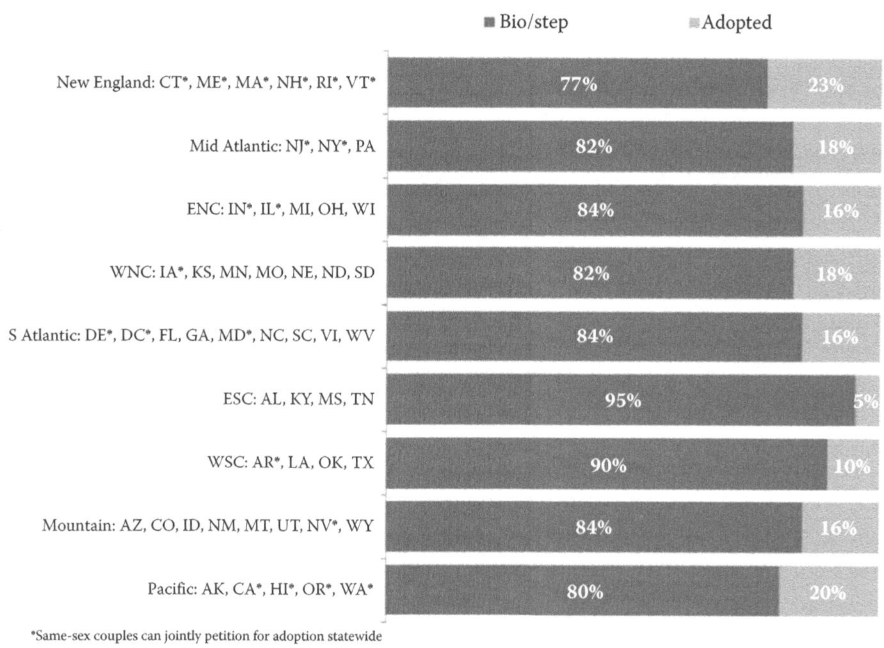

Figure 2.4 Portion of couples with biological or step versus adopted children among same-sex couples with biological, step, and adopted children, by region of the country. (From American Community Survey, 2008–2011.)

likely to be African-American than adopted children, 16% versus 11%, respectively. More than a quarter of children in both groups are Hispanic (28% of adopted and 26% of biological or stepchildren).*

One notable difference in the racial and ethnic characteristics of adopted children between those with same-sex or different-sex parents is the presence of Asian/Pacific Islander children. They comprise less than 3% of adopted children in same-sex couple families and 11% of those in different-sex couple households. That difference is not as pronounced among biological and stepchildren where 5% of those with different-sex parents are Asian/Pacific Islander compared to 2.5% among those with same-sex parents.†

Educational Attainment and Socioeconomic Status

Same-sex couples raising adopted children evidence very high levels of education. Fully 70% have a college degree compared to 27% of those raising biological or

* Author analyses of 2011 American Community Survey Public Use Microdata Sample.

† Author analyses of 2011 American Community Survey Public Use Microdata Sample.

stepchildren. While different-sex couples with adopted children also show higher levels of education, the difference between those with adopted versus biological or stepchildren is not nearly as large, 39% and 35%, respectively.*

These differences in educational attainment are likely a significant factor in why same-sex couples with adopted children have high incomes. Median household income for same-sex couples with adopted children is $125,100 compared to $58,000 for same-sex couples with biological or stepchildren. Again, this pattern is not as pronounced among different-sex couples. Those with adopted children have median household income of $82,730 compared to $74,400 among those with biological or stepchildren.†

Marriage and Childrearing

Evidence from Census 2010 data suggests that as same-sex couples gain more access to legal marriage, childrearing may become more common. Census data do not actually assess legal marital status, but do consider how members of a couple describe their relationship. Both same-sex and different-sex couples can be identified as spouses or unmarried partners. Data from a Williams Institute survey of same-sex couples conducted just after Census 2010 show that 71% of same-sex couples who identified themselves as spouses were legally married (though 22% lived in states that did not recognize the marriage), 15% were in civil unions or registered domestic partnerships, and 13% were not in a legally recognized relationship. Among those who identified as unmarried partners, 4% were legally married, 17% were in a civil union or registered domestic partnership, and 79% were not in a legal relationship (Gates 2010).

Given this understanding of the relationship question in the Census, it is interesting to note that same-sex couples who identify as spouses are much more likely to be raising children than those who identify as unmarried partners. This is particularly true among male couples (see Figure 2.5). Among all same-sex couples, 17% are raising a biological, adopted, or stepchild. Among couples who identified as spouses, the figure is 24% compared to just 10% of those who identified as unmarried partners. Among male couples, those who identified as spouses are five times more likely than their unmarried partner counterparts to be raising children, 28% versus 5%, respectively. For female couples, the difference is 35% versus 21%, respectively.‡

---

* Author analyses of 2011 American Community Survey Public Use Microdata Sample.

† Author analyses of 2011 American Community Survey Public Use Microdata Sample.

‡ Author analyses of Census 2010 preferred estimates of same-sex couples raising children as reported in O'Connell and Feliz (2011).

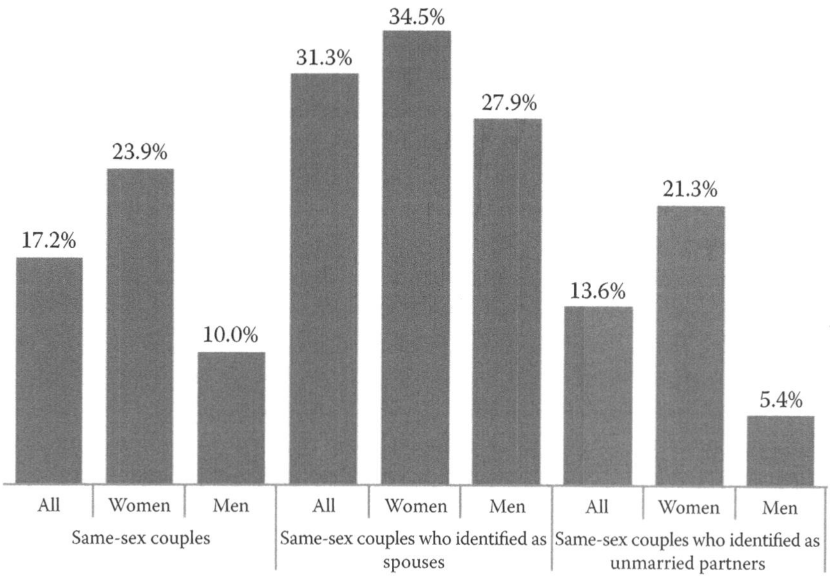

Figure 2.5 Percent raising biological, adopted, or foster children among same-sex couples, by relationship to householder and sex. (From Census 2010.)

Discussion and Conclusion

The analyses presented in this chapter demonstrate the rich diversity of LGBT parents and families. Unfortunately, this diversity is not always reflected in scholarly research on LGBT parenting and in the policy priorities that would likely best meet all of their needs. Although relationship recognition through marriage equality and access to second-parent and joint adoption are important legal rights that can help LGBT families gain greater economic stability and legal protections, they are not the only issues that can make a difference for these families.

LGBT families evidence broad economic disadvantage, and often live in parts of the country still struggling with a high level of stigma toward LGBT people along with racial and ethnic minorities. This likely means that LGBT families also struggle with access to quality schools and affordable health care. Policy debates regarding poverty alleviation, racism, social stigma, education reform, and health care reform all have particular salience and perhaps heightened influence in the lives of LGBT parents and their children.

The findings regarding the rather substantial differences between same-sex couple adoptive parents versus those with biological and stepchildren raise important concerns about the emergence of a two-tiered hierarchy of same-sex parenting. At the moment, adoptive parenting is the purview of a relatively small minority of same-sex couples who evidence substantial economic advantage and likely accompanying social privilege for them and their children.

Better and more universal access to public adoption agencies for LGBT people and same-sex couples could help in allowing less economically advantaged individuals to parent since public adoption is much less expensive than private adoption. Health insurance plans that provide coverage for assisted-reproductive technology to LGBT individuals and same-sex couples would also make it more financially viable for them to become parents.

More than three decades of scholarly research shows that LGBT individuals and same-sex couple parents are as loving and supportive of their children as any other parents. Their children are as healthy and successful in life as any other children (American Sociological Association 2013). But social stigma and hostile legal climates can add burdens to LGBT parents and their children. These analyses highlight some of the ways that burden can be evidenced in economic and social disadvantage. Such disadvantage can only be remedied if policy makers focused on LGBT equality take a broad view beyond marriage equality and adoption rights. They must integrate LGBT concerns into the array of social policies and debates that affect the ability of American families to achieve economic stability and give all children access to high-quality education, health care, and a society free of prejudice and stigma.

References

American Sociological Association. 2013. Brief of Amicus Curiae, American Sociological Association in Support of Respondent Kristin M. Perry and Respondent Edith Schlain Windsor. In the United States Supreme Court, NOS. 12-144, 12-307.

Badgett, M. V. Lee, Laura E. Durso, and Alyssa Schneebaum. 2013. "New Patterns of Poverty in the Lesbian, Gay, and Bisexual Community." Williams Institute, UCLA School of Law.

Biblarz, Timothy J., and Judith Stacey. 2010. "How Does the Gender of Parents Matter?" *Journal of Marriage and Family,* 72(1), 3–22.

Gates, Gary J. 2010. "Same-Sex Couples in US Census Bureau Data: Who Gets Counted and Why." Williams Institute, UCLA School of Law.

Gates, Gary J. 2013a. "LGBT Parenting in the United States." Williams Institute, UCLA School of Law.

Gates, Gary J. 2013b. "Same-Sex and Different-sex Couples in the American Community Survey: 2005–2011." Williams Institute, UCLA School of Law.

O'Connell, Martin, and Sarah Feliz. 2011. "Same-Sex Couple Household Statistics From the 2010 Census." US Bureau of the Census, Fertility and Family Statistics Branch, Social, Economic and Housing Statistics Division.

Smith, Tom W., Peter Marsden, Michael Hout, and Jibum Kim. 2012. General Social Surveys, 1972–2012. National Opinion Research Center, University of Chicago.

Chapter 3

The Great Divide: Two Nations and Its Battlegrounds

Wallace Swan

Contents

In order to understand the argument of this book, it is first necessary to understand the numbers of states that have or do not have protections for gay, lesbian, bisexual, and transgender (LGBT) persons. Consider Table 3.1. Some of the most important facts to notice based upon this table are (1) of the total of 50 states, many still allow discrimination based upon sexual orientation; (2) 30 states prosecute hate crimes that are based upon sexual orientation and/or gender identity/expression, while five states have no prohibitions at all upon hate crimes; (3) 2 states offer broad-gauge domestic partnerships, 1 state offers broad-gauge civil unions, 18 states allow for full marital equality, and 1 state offers limited domestic partnerships for same-sex couples. A number of states have bans on legalization of same-sex relationships that are now being overturned by court rulings (Freedom to Marry 2013).

Table 3.1 The Status of LGBT Rights in the United States

Description	*Number*
Ban discrimination based on sexual orientation or gender identity/ expression (1)	17
Ban discrimination based on sexual orientation only (1)	4
Ban hate crimes based on sexual orientation or gender identity/ expression (2)	15
Ban hate crimes based upon sexual orientation (2)	15
Ban hate crimes but do not include sexual orientation and gender identity (2)	15
Do not have hate crime laws (2)	5
Offer full marital equality (3)	18
Broad Relationship Recognition	
Civil unions (Colorado) (3)	1
Domestic partnerships (Oregon and Nevada) (3)	2
Limited Relationship Recognition	
Domestic partnerships (Wisconsin) (3)	1

Sources: (1) National Gay and Lesbian Task Force (NGLTF), "State Nondiscrimination Laws in the U.S.," May 21, 2014, http://www.thetaskforce.org/downloads/reports/issue_maps/non_discrimination_5_14color.pdf; (2) National Gay and Lesbian Task Force (NGLTF), "Hate Crime Laws in the U.S.," June 21, 2013, http://www.thetaskforce.org/downloads/reports/issue_maps/hate_crimes_06_13_color.pdf; and (3) National Gay and Lesbian Task Force, "Relationship Recognition for Same-Sex Couples in the United States," November 21, 2013, http://www.thetaskforce.org/downloads/reports/issue_maps/rel_recog_1_16_14_color.pdf.

What is the basis for this difference in provisions of human rights? One issue that this author believes is key would be that of technological and economic change. Each era of change has brought a different family structure. There are a number of factors that condition change in the development of public policy. These may include religious, scientific, social, cultural, technological, environmental, economic, political, and ideological factors. The *agricultural* era brought us a family with husband, wife, and children who were employed on the family farm or a small business. The *industrial* era brought us a family where the husband might work in one factory, the wife in another factory, and even young children working in an industrial setting (until the passage of laws prohibiting child labor and requiring mandatory education).

The *service* era brought us the husband working, the wife staying at home with the children who were attending elementary and secondary school. But the current *high-tech/low-tech* era (along with a relatively recent economic near-collapse, and a "rights revolution") has brought us families that are doing their work increasingly on the computer, at home, in an office, or wherever they may be at a given time. And these families have been reconfigured to allow for substantial increases in single-family headed households, decreases in traditional male–female households with children, and the development of same-sex households, sometimes with children.

In the case of the LGBT subculture, this includes a variety of beliefs that run counter to the values of the broader U.S. culture. For instance, traditional religious values in the United States treat homosexuality as sin, and see homosexuals as people who are to be rejected. "Love the sinner, but not the sin" is the watchword of this particular culture. But within the more accepting elements of this culture, one also finds some religions that are accepting of LGBT people, affirming congregations of many mainstream churches and gay churches, such as Metropolitan Community Church. There is also an antiscientific element to the movement in opposition to acceptance of homosexuality (Alexakos 2009). For instance, on the basis of scientific study, the American Psychiatric Association in 1973 declared that homosexuality was no longer a mental health category, and the American Psychological Association essentially did the same in 1975. However, those in opposition to homosexuality reacted by continuing to diagnose this as a disease and moved in the direction of reparative therapy, the purpose of which was to change the behavior of homosexuals. Of course, the efficacy of this approach has been clearly disproven (Drescher 1998; Haldeman 1991; Shidlo and Schroeder 2002). This concept of reparative therapy has recently been challenged in some states, but a California case ran into first amendment problems (Smart Brief 2012b), but the final decision was to ban this therapy.

Social and cultural factors are also important in understanding how homosexuality is viewed in the United States. There are a variety of characteristics that are viewed as male and female in the society, and any subculture that violates these norms is seen by some as nonexistent or abnormal. For instance, the concept of bisexuality is viewed as problematic by both "straight" society as well as "gay" culture; despite the fact the scale developed by Kinsey described human sexual behavior on a continuum from 0 (totally heterosexual) to 6 (exclusively homosexual). The result of this is what Kenji Yoshino (2000) calls "bisexual erasure"—the tendency to not recognize the existence of bisexual people, despite the fact that there are tens of millions of them. Similarly, the experience of people with gender orientation and identity issues within the American Psychological Association has not been positive either, because of problems in the *Diagnostic and Statistical Manual of Mental Disorders: DSM-IV* (American Psychiatric Association 1994) that had characterized them as a problem rather than an orientation with which a person is born. Transgender status is no longer, however, included as a mental disorder (SmartBrief 2012a). And, electoral politics in 2012 has yielded the country its first bisexual elected to Congress, Kyrsten Sinema, of Arizona (SmartBrief 2012c).

Technological change is another issue that underlies many of the problems that face people in society today. People are losing their jobs and having to make major changes in their work lives because of technological change.

Similarly, the economic dislocation resulting from the relatively recent Great Recession may be causing some people to project their fears onto the LGBT minority in our society, just as was the case during the Great Depression in Germany.

Political factors include some of the major issues from which divisiveness derives. The Republican Party in particular has placed a great deal of emphasis upon mobilizing both traditional religious as well as Tea Party factions using a strategy of passage of Constitutional Amendments (voter ID, anti–same-sex marriage, elimination of the union workshop, among others); and the Republican Party presidential candidates in 2012 all made known their opposition to same-sex marriage. Similarly, the Democratic Party has made major efforts to ensure that LGBT people are emphasized in their outreach and White House summits have been held on LGBT topics (including the 2012 White House LGBT Conference on Aging; the White House LGBT Conference on HIV/AIDS; the LGBT Conference on Safe Schools and Communities; the White House Anti-Bullying Conference; and the White House LGBT Conference on Health). The positions of both President Barack Obama and the Vice President Joe Biden have also been highly supportive of many LGBT issues, including same-sex marriage (Lynsen 2008).

Ideological factors have also been extremely important in the battle between the Republican Party and the Democratic Party on LGBT issues. Both parties have developed their own ideology as it relates to LGBT issues. The Republicans build their ideology upon the rapidly diminishing numbers of traditional family households, whereas the Democrats increasingly focus their interests upon single-family households, single women, LGBT families, and racial/ethnic minorities.

Throw into this unstable situation the fact that gay and lesbian families are interested in changing the traditional definition of marriage. And, within the gay, lesbian, bisexual, and transgender communities there is also a fault line between those gays and lesbians who are in couples and those who are single. Although gays and lesbians may be discriminated against in certain ways, gay and lesbian couples do constitute a formidable political force. In the first place, they have a considerable amount of money available that they can jointly spend (particularly male couples). Second, it is gay and lesbian *couples* who are recognized (and counted) by the U.S. Census Bureau. Single gay, lesbian, bisexual, and transgender people are not counted. Instead, it is only gay and lesbian couples who are counted and for whom we have data. Third, and very important, the effect of this is that gay and lesbian couples constitute the driving force for the same-sex marriage movement. Fourth, we also see the development of family-based organizations in the gay and lesbian community. Essentially, in addition to gay and lesbian couples as an economic force, there are numerous families within this subset that are raising children. On April 28, 2012, the author attended the White House LGBT Conference on Families in Minneapolis. A series of panels at this daylong conference highlighted, among other things, the issues facing LGBT couples who have children: "the 2 million children raised by 1 million LGBT families." These couples are expecting to have benefits for themselves and their children that are equal to those of heterosexual couples. A recent *New York Times* article highlights the way in which college-educated people have increasingly seen it as advantageous to marry each other, and have children who are much more likely than children of single parents to have all kinds of social and economic advantages (Deparle 2012). The same is most likely true of some gay and lesbian couples.

A major economic gulf is thus arising between the married heterosexual couples with children and single individuals with children. In the gay and lesbian community, the same kind of gulf is arising, but in this case it is arising between gay and lesbian couples (including those who have children) and those who are single. The gulf is both economic as well as social. People who are college-educated want to meet "Mr. or Ms. Right": They look for a person who is also college-educated, and then possibly they may wish to have children. The differences between these LGBT couples and singles can be extreme. For example, let us take a gay couple (ages 30 and 40) who are both working jobs with benefits with an income well over $100,000 per year: They both have new cars, are *out* at work, and have lots of skills. They have saved $30,000 and used $22,000 of that amount to buy a home. Then contrast them with a gay individual from a minority group who has a high school degree and works in a manufacturing firm, making $20,800 per year: This person has no chance of buying a house, has a car that is many years old, lives with relatives, and is not *out*. If he is in a couple with a child, he is one in four of gay male couples who live in poverty.

The situation is even more difficult for people with differing gender identity and orientation. Their economic status and the way in which they are discriminated against is very much more severe than that experienced by the gay and lesbian community. The simple fact of extremely severe discrimination against them is perhaps more interesting to them than the higher level goal (qua Maslow) of marriage. And finally, the bisexual movement is severely limited by the fact of bisexual erasure: Bisexuals may be single or they may be in couples who have a heterosexual member, or in couples with a gay or lesbian member. This puts them into a difficult and occasionally conflicted role, which does not easily lend itself into support for same-sex marriage. And they experience extremely low socioeconomic status.

What effect does all of this discussion of LGBT people have in the empowered, disempowered, and battleground states? It has made the relatively more well-to-do people in gay and lesbian same-sex couples (some of whom have children as well) insistent upon receiving benefits, based upon their belief that they are in loving families, and they cannot miss the fact that they receive less in the way of salaries and benefits than do similarly situated heterosexual couples. Following are some of the ways in which those factors shape the opinions of LGBT people about benefits,

Increasingly, public, nonprofit, university, and business managers and citizens need to be aware of these factors as their clients and customers attempt to navigate efforts to serve and be served by government agencies, and especially LGBT employees of these organizations. Why is this true? A manager may well have LGBT employees, some of whom are single and others who are in coupled relationships. For the single employees, there are numerous workplace issues that one needs to be cognizant of. For example, one needs to think about whether the employee is being held to the same work standards as other employees. A Human Rights Campaign study indicated that many LGBT people (51%) do not want to come out at work for a wide variety of reasons, including fear of how other people will treat them (Human Rights Foundation 2009, 13).

People who are in a coupled relationship may be more likely to be interested in the fact that although they are two people situated in a couple, they are held to a different standard than married people who are heterosexuals. In the following examples, we see ways in which LGBT issues impact gay, lesbian, and transgender people. Glaringly obvious is lack of reference to bisexual members of couples.

In one case, with which the author is familiar, one of the gay partners in a couple died by suicide. The other partner was left to the task of (1) sorting out the financial affairs of a nonprofit and (2) trying to ensure usage of assets that the two had both used during the course of the relationship. This is the story of this gay couple:

> Dallas Drake was a trusted and familiar face in his community after dedicating his career to protecting his neighbors. He was the first openly gay firefighter in Minnesota. But when he tried to retrieve his car from the impound lot after the death of his long-time partner, Joe Shulka, the clerk at the suburban Twin Cities impound lot said, "the police department told me not to release it to you because you're not the next of kin." Dallas and Joe began their partnership in 1991 after meeting at a local event. Through the years they bought a house, started a non-profit organization and … They understood that Minnesota laws did not recognize their same-sex relationship, so they made sure to list each other as the power of attorney and executor in their wills. Joe took his own life in September 2008. He could no longer take the daily insults hurled at him about his sexuality and the discrimination he faced as a gay man. In the early 1990s he was nearly beaten to death by a group of men who suspected he was gay. These pressures, along with recent financial trouble, were too much for Joe to bear. He ended his life in a local hotel room. Dallas waited more than a day-and-a-half for any word about Joe's whereabouts. Finally, Joe's sister called to say Joe was gone. The medical examiner refused to call Dallas directly even though instructions for who should be notified were in Joe's wallet. When Dallas tried to withdraw money from Joe's bank account, he was denied access. Six weeks after Joe's death, armed with a death certificate

> and the help of a judge's order, Dallas finally accessed his account to pay his bills. Dallas had no recourse with financial institutions, insurance companies and other companies even though both Dallas and Joe were both listed on the accounts. "The most difficult part is that I lost half of me the day Joe died," Dallas said. "But I also lost my income, my companionship, and understanding. I can't do this without my partner ... The fact is, if our relationship was legally recognized I would not have had to wait so long. No one would have questioned my access to my bank account, my car, or Joe's social security or paycheck," he said. Dallas and Joe spent their lives working to solve unnecessary deaths through their work at the Center for Homicide Research. Ironically, the journey of Dallas and Joe was interrupted by death. They participated fully in the collective human story, but their relationship wasn't recognized in life or in death. (Project 515 2013b)

This next story is about a lesbian in a relationship:

> Dave Engstrom wants what any parent desires for their children—equality and fairness. But he's frustrated that his 29-year-old lesbian daughter can't count on receiving the equal and fair treatment his married daughter or his 17-year-old son may take for granted. "I'm very protective of all of my kids," Dave said. "You'd like them to get a fair shot and equal treatment on everything, and I know she doesn't." Recently, Dave's daughter began working for a company that offers health benefits to domestic partners. His daughter, who is in a committed relationship, was thrilled to find an employer that considers her as valuable as its other employees "It's not so much the benefits, but the acceptance," Dave said. "I'm happy she has a good, stable relationship. She needs someone just as everyone does. It's difficult to go through life alone." Dave has been married for 31 years and currently lives in Afton, Minn., with his wife and son. He has served as City of Afton mayor and was a two-term Washington County commissioner. As commissioner, he served on the county's social services advisory committee. "Over and over again, you'd see that preventative funding is always the best," Dave said. "When you can support stable relationships and families, it benefits everybody long-term. But when you go through life alone or you're being discriminated against, there are more problems and you need more help, but you can't get it because state law may prohibit it." Dave is currently a lobbyist at the state capitol and thinks it is "outrageous" and "shocking" that so many state laws exclude committed and long-term partners. "Just hearing that number has enlightened me and will cause me to consider in my own work how future laws affect people and their relationships," he said. "Hopefully this report will highlight those

> laws that should be straightened out or eliminated. There should be no discrimination, whether people are same-sex or opposite-sex partners," Dave continued. "As a parent of a lesbian daughter, I want what I expect for all three of my children: equality and fairness, whether they're gay, lesbian or straight." (Project 515 2013a)

The issues for the transgender community are markedly worse than those of the gay and lesbian community. For example, despite the fact that transgender people in California have legal protections from discrimination and harassment, the following are the kinds of issues that they face. "Seventy percent of the transgender community reports experiencing workplace discrimination directly related to their gender identity. Transgender respondents are twice as likely to be living below the poverty line of $10,400 when compared to the general population. 1 in 5 respondents have been homeless since they first identified as transgender" (Transgender Law Center 2008, 2). There are also a high percentage of respondents (30%) who indicated prevalence of discrimination in regard to health care.

Developing a Theory about How Change Impacts People in the Empowered and Disempowered States

We are undergoing a period of intense technological and economic change, which is putting a lot of stress on many individuals and families. Those who already are strongly religious and antiscientific, reflect traditional cultural and social values about masculinity and femininity. They are threatened by economic dislocations and easily manipulated by political movements and parties. Similarly, those people who are strongly antireligious, scientific, or analytical; adopting newly emerging social values; dislocated from jobs; and having more liberal views on personal identity are attracted to another party. Each of the political parties has designed an ideology that has an action element to it—to fight gay rights efforts wherever they may be proposed or or to support gay rights. Each of these approaches is used in turn to get votes for each of the political parties in elections. For example, the Tea Party and religious groups work to emphasize their economic and social agenda (which may or may not include antigay values) within the Republican Party. But the same is true of the Democratic Party, which also has its component organizations (unions, progressive religious groups, feminists, Stonewall DFL members) that are pressing it to adopt their economic and social agenda (including pro-gay values). The result is two increasingly polarized political parties that incorporate an ideological framework, wherein each of the opposing parties is viewed as problematic. But there is another way to look at these states, which raises some interesting questions.

Fifty State Data Comparisons and an Economic Description of the Empowered States and Disempowered States

When I was writing a chapter in an earlier book, I prepared a spreadsheet that showed the names of states with and without human rights protections (including basic rights all the way up to marital rights) for LGBT individuals. About six months thereafter, it occurred to me that there was some kind of pattern among those states that had rights and those that did not. The easy way to look at this is to say that this is simply an ideological phenomenon. The Chick-fil-A controversy (Severson 2012) is a perfect example. One side says that this is simply a polarized country (with a Southern company) in which "those bigots in the South and West don't want to give LGBT people their basic human rights," while the other side (while disapprovingly watching kiss-ins at Chick-fil-A restaurants on television) says that "those anti-biblical radicals on the East and the West Coast want to require marital rights for people who do not deserve them." Like all too many ideological arguments, the proponents are like two trains passing in the night, moving in parallel lines without understanding the other side.

It appears to me that our current framework for understanding these empowered and disempowered states may be a bit flawed. As Marx suggested, one could look at the pages of history in terms of economics: In his theory, the "means of production" precedes the derivation of ideas (Marx 1961). What does this mean? It means that the way in which *monetary relationships* are established in both rich and poor states *precede the ideas* (religious ideas that LGBT people are inherently evil; that they should not be given marital benefits; that LGBT people should be the scapegoats in order to raise voter turnout).

It was then that I decided I should take a look some of the basic economic issues underlying behavior. So I began going through 2010 U.S. Census data to analyze the issues in a different way, a way that would emphasize broad demographic trends (U.S. Census Bureau 2010a). What I found in research that I conducted in the summer of 2012 was the states that have granted basic human rights (including but not limited to same-sex partner rights) seem to be considerably different than those that have not granted such rights.

First, most of the states that have granted such rights have a higher percentage of their population with advanced degrees, which is also typically a predictor of high income (U.S. Census Bureau 2010b, Table A-21, 25). Specifically, of the 20 states with the highest percentages of people with advanced degrees, 15 of these states have granted basic human rights to LGBT persons—sometimes including martial rights (U.S. Census Bureau 2010b, Table A-21, 25).

Second, most of the states that have granted such rights have a high percentage of their population with bachelor's degrees. Of the top 20 states with people over 25 having a bachelor's degree, 14 of those states are ones that grant basic human rights, or more advanced marital rights, to LGBT people (U.S. Census Bureau 2010b, Table A-21, 25).

Third, of the 20 states with the highest median incomes (2007), 16 of those states grant basic LGBT human rights (from basic rights such as housing, education, and employment up to same-sex couple benefits), while 4 of the states do not have these rights including Alaska (with major oil income), Virginia, Utah (a state with major religious influence), and Wyoming (another state with major coal and gas reserves) (U.S. Census Bureau 2010b, Table A-33, 39).

Fourth, of the top 20 states that have the highest personal income per capita based upon current dollars (2008), 15 of these states have basic human rights (up to and including marital rights), while 5 (Wyoming, Alaska, Virginia, Pennsylvania, and North Dakota) do not (U.S. Census Bureau 2010b, Table A-41, 51).

Fifth, of the 20 top states with the highest federal adjusted gross income per return (2006), 14 of the states are the ones with the basic LGBT human rights, while 6 of the states (Wyoming, Virginia, Florida, Arizona, Texas, and Utah) do not have such rights (U.S. Census Bureau 2010b, Table A-76, 95).

Sixth, of the 20 states with a rate of relatively high rate of union membership, 15 states granting the LGBT human rights also have relatively high rates of union membership; while 5 of the states (Alaska, Michigan, Pennsylvania, Ohio, and West Virginia) do not grant such rights (U.S. Census Bureau 2010b, Table A-32, 38).

Seventh, of the top 20 states with high home ownership rates (2008), 14 are states that do not grant such rights, while only 6 states with high levels of home ownership do grant such rights (U.S. Census Bureau 2010b, Table A-37, 43).

Eighth, of the top 20 states lacking children's health care coverage, 15 are states that also do not provide basic human rights for LGBT people, while 5 states that do provide children's health care coverage also provide basic up to extensive LGBT human rights (U.S. Census Bureau 2010b, Table A-16, 20).

Ninth, of the top 20 states with the highest percentage of people not covered by health insurance, 16 of those states are also ones that provide no basic up to extensive human rights coverage, while 4 of those states (Colorado, Oregon, California, and Nevada) do provide basic or more advanced forms of human rights for LGBT people (U.S. Census Bureau 2010b, Table A-16, 20). Conversely, of the 20 states with the lowest percentage of people covered by health insurance (2008), 9 of the states are ones that provide no basic LGBT (up to extensive) human rights, while 11 of the states are the ones that do provide such basic rights (U.S. Census Bureau 2010b, Table A-16, 20).

Tenth, of 20 states with the highest level of individuals below poverty level, 18 are states that provide no basic up to extensive LGBT human rights, while only 2 states (Oregon and New York) are ones that actually do provide basic LGBT human rights. Conversely, of the states that have the lowest rate of individuals below the poverty line (2005–2007), 5 are states that provide no basic LGBT human rights, while 15 of these states are ones that also provide basic LGBT human rights (U.S. Census Bureau 2010b, Table A-34, 40).

But most interesting is the way in which 2010 Census data on family households is related to the tabulation of states that have few if any LGBT human rights.

First, 12 of the top 20 states with the highest rank-ordered percentage of "Married Couple Families" have few if any human rights (including marital rights) for LGBT people: And, 20 of the top 30 states with the highest rank-ordered percentage of "Married Couple Families" have few if any human rights (including marital rights) for LGBT people (U.S. Census Bureau 2010b, Table A-5, 9).

Second, 19 of the top 30 states with the highest rank-ordered percentage of "Female Householders, No Husband" have few if any human rights (including marital rights) for LGBT people (U.S. Census Bureau 2010b, Table A-5, 9). Later, we will see that it depends on what kind of female householder we are discussing.

Third, when one combines the "Married Couple Families" and the "Female Householder, No Husband" families into a single category of "Family Households," one finds 14 of the top 20 states with the highest rank-ordered percentage of "Family Households" have few if any human rights (including marital rights) for LGBT people. And, 22 of the top 30 states with the highest rank-ordered percentage of "Family Households" have few if any human rights (including marital rights) for LGBT people. Thus the two categories of "Married Couple Families" and "Female Householder, No Husband" units, when combined into a third more general category of "Family Households" tells us that the more there are of these three categories in a given state, the more likely it is that the state will have no human rights (or marital rights) for LGBT individuals and families (U.S. Census Bureau 2010b, Table A-5, 9).

When we break this information down, we find some interesting results.

Fourth, when we are looking at all males by state who are 15 years old or older who are now married, the percentage of males married in this group ranges from 58.5% married (highest state) down to 54.1% married (lowest state). Of the states that are in this "top 20 states group" (rank ordered from highest to lowest by rate), 15 of these states offer no LGBT rights (including marital rights). The lower the percentage of males married, the more likely the states (12 out of 20) are to be ones that offer LGBT rights (U.S. Census Bureau 2010b, Table A-6, 10).

Fifth, when we are looking at females by state who are 15 years old or older who are now married, the percentage of females married in this group ranges from 56.6% married (highest state) down to 50.6% (lowest state). Of the states that are in this "top 20 states group" (rank ordered from highest to lowest by rate), again 14 of the states (females over age 15 now married) offer no LGBT rights (including marital rights). And again, the lower the percentage of females married, the more likely the states are to be ones that offer LGBT rights: 11 out of 20 offer such rights (U.S. Census Bureau 2010b, Table A-6, 10).

Sixth, intrigued by these findings, I then decided to take a look at males by state who are 15 years old or older who are now divorced. The percentage of these males in the "top 20 states group" ranges from a high of 12.6% to a low of 10.4%. Of the states that are in this "top 20 states group" (rank ordered from highest to lowest by rate), 14 of these states offer no LGBT rights (including marital rights), while 6 do (U.S. Census Bureau 2010b, Table A-6, 10).

Seventh, I looked at females by state who are 15 years old or older who are now divorced. The percentage of these females in the "top 20 states group" ranges from a high of 14.6% to a low of 12.5%. Of the states that are in this "top 20 states group" (rank ordered from highest to lowest by rate of divorce), 13 of these states offer no LGBT rights (including marital rights), while 7 do offer the rights (U.S. Census Bureau 2010b, Table A-6, 10).

Eighth, it is interesting to look at the way the numbers change when the males and females have never married. The percentage of males included in this group ranges from 38.6% never married (highest state) down to 33.2% never married (lowest state). Of the states that are in this "top 20 states group" (rank ordered from highest to lowest by rate), 11 of the states do offer LGBT rights (including marital rights), while 9 do not. Interestingly enough, the states that offer same-sex couple benefits are clustered at or near the top (e.g., New York, California, Massachusetts, Rhode Island, Hawaii, Illinois, Maryland, and New Jersey are among those top 11 states). The higher the percentage of males never married, the more likely the states are to be ones that offer LGBT rights (U.S. Census Bureau 2010b, Table A-6, 10).

Ninth, for females who have never married, the states that offer same-sex couple benefits are clustered at or near the top of the percentage listing. For example, New York, Massachusetts, Rhode Island, California, Maryland, Illinois, New Jersey, Connecticut, and Delaware are among the top 11 states (U.S. Census Bureau 2010b, Table A-6, 10).

Tenth, for males by state who are 15 years old or older who are separated, the rate of separation ranges from 3.0% to 1.8%. The 15 states that do not offer same-sex benefits tend to be clustered at the higher percentages, while the 5 states that do not offer same-sex benefits tend to be clustered near the lower percentages (U.S. Census Bureau 2010b, Table A-6, 10).

Tenth, for females by state who are 15 years old or older who are separated, the rate of separation ranges from 4.0% to 2.4%. The 13 states that do not offer same-sex benefits tend to be clustered at the higher percentages, while the 7 states that do not offer same-sex benefits tend to be clustered near the lower percentages (U.S. Census Bureau 2010b, Table A-6, 10).

Eleventh, for those males who are 15 years old or older and are widowed, the higher the percentage of these widowed persons, the more likely they are to be residents of the 12 states that do not support LGBT rights (U.S. Census Bureau 2010b, Table A-6, 10).

Twelfth, for females by state who are 15 years old or older who are widowed, the rate ranges from 12.6% to 10.4%. Most of the nonsupportive states

(West Virginia, Mississippi, Arkansas, Pennsylvania, Alabama, Florida, Louisiana, Kentucky, North Dakota, South Carolina, Oklahoma, and Tennessee) are clustered at the higher percentages of widowed people, while the 5 states that have human rights laws that are clustered at the lower percentages (U.S. Census Bureau 2010b, Table A-6, 10).

Now we will look at some other information from different sources (also analyzed in the summer of 2012) than the *State and Metropolitan Area Data Book: 2010.* We have the theory incorporated in *Our Patchwork Nation: The Surprising Truth about the "Real" America* by Dante Chinni and James Gimpel. They break the United States into 12 "Community Types": Boom Towns, Immigration Nation, Monied "Burbs," Campus and Careers, Industrial Metropolis, Mormon Outposts, Emptying Nests, Military Bastions, Service Centers, Evangelical Epicenters, Minority Central, and Tractor Country (Patchwork Nation 2011). Looking at the maps of these areas, it is very helpful to look at these community types (and where they fall in relation to the states), because of the way that they help to build constituencies (and also states) that are either Republican or Democratic.

Another study that bears upon this issue is one compiled by the Pew Research Center in 2012. The study analyzes the way in which residential segregation by income is developing. Essentially it uses a Residential Income Segregation Index (RISI) to determine how much residential segregation there is by income. "The analysis finds that 28% of lower-income households in 2010 were located in a majority lower-income census tract, up from 23% in 1980, and that 18% of upper-income households were located in a majority upper-income census tract, up from 9% in 1980" (Fry and Taylor 2012).

The RISI for the 30 largest metro areas in the United States is provided by Fry and Taylor for 2010 in descending order. Of the 16 metro areas with the highest residential segregation scores, there are 11 that are in the states with no LGBT human rights protections or with a Defense of Marriage statute; and there are 2 metro areas that include at least one city that is in a state with no LGBT human rights protections. Keep in mind the *Patchwork Nation* finding that increasingly, there are geographical areas where the people not only have similar demographics, but they also tend to vote for the same political party.

Of the remaining 14 cities with lower RISI scores, there are only four metro areas that are in states with no LGBT human rights protections. One is in what we defined as a battleground state, one is in a metro area in Washington where same-sex marriage has been passed in a part of the metro, while one area metro area includes at least one city that is in a state with no LGBT human rights protections (Fry and Taylor 2012).

Clearly, there is some relationship between the economic status of individuals, states, and their major component jurisdictions and the presence or absence of LGBT human rights laws. Building upon this knowledge, we then might see how those forces are mobilized on both sides of the issue.

Key to anti-gay and pro-gay rights efforts are the national organizations that supply financial and organizational resources in these divisive battles. On the side of those opposing LGBT rights include (among many others) American Family Association, Christian Coalition of America, Exodus International, Family Research Council, Focus on the Family, GodHatesFags.com, Repent America, "Save our Scouts," and the Traditional Values Coalition. On the side of those supporting LGBT rights include the Human Rights Campaign, National Black Justice Coalition, National Gay and Lesbian Task Force, Gay and Lesbian Alliance Against Defamation (GLAAD), the Gay and Lesbian Victory Fund, the Log Cabin Republicans, Metropolitan Community Churches, National Stonewall Democratic Federation, Parents and Friends of Lesbians and Gays, and Lambda Legal Defense. Each of these has a city, state, and national base of donors and supporters that can be called upon whenever needed. In Chapter 4, "Organizations that Keep the Great Divide in Place," we will learn a great deal more about each of these organizations. When a particular statewide issue involving LGBT rights appears, then some of the groups (dependent upon their relative strength in a particular state) will mobilize their supporters and develop operational coalitions.

But of course, these organizations not only use their capabilities in battles opposing or supporting gay rights. They also increasingly throw their resources into state and congressional political races, hurling massive numbers of volunteers and huge amounts of money into these efforts to gain a political advantage by use of coalitions. They are part and parcel of the broader divisive national debate on everything from the right to organize as a union (e.g., the effort to recall Governor Walker in Wisconsin) to dismantling of public pensions and efforts to prevent abortions, as well as eliminate many of the rights gained by minorities. Their capabilities are also increasingly used in presidential elections, along with the political action committees, and the super-PACS whose efforts were initiated as a result of the *Citizens United* v. *Federal Election Commission, 558 U.S. 50 (2010)* case, which was affirmed in 2012 in *American Tradition Partnership Inc. et al.* v. *Steve Bullock, Attorney General of Montana et al. McCutcheon* v. *Federal Election Commission* is yet another court case that will actually strengthen both sides in this battle.

References

Alexakos, Konstantinos. 2009. "Science and Creationism: A Response to Kenneth Tobin." *Cultural Studies of Science Education, 4*(2), 495–504.

American Psychiatric Association (APA). 1994. *Diagnostic and Statistical Manual of Mental Disorders: DSM-IV.* Washington, DC: American Psychiatric Association.

Chinni, Dante, and Gimpel, James. 2010. *Our Patchwork Nation: The Surprising Truth about the "Real" America.* New York: Gotham Books.

Deparle, Jason. 2012. "Economic Inequality and the Changing Family." *New York Times,* July 14, http://economix.blogs.nytimes.com/2012/07/14/economic-inequality-and-the-changing-family/.

Drescher, J. 1998. "I'm Your Handyman: A History of Reparative Therapies." *Journal of Homosexuality, 36*(1), 19–42.
Freedom to Marry. 2013. "Winning the Freedom to Marry: Progress in the States." Accessed May 8, 2014, http://www.freedomtomarry.org/states.
Fry, Richard, and Paul Taylor. 2012. "The Rise of Residential Segregation by Income." Pew Research: Pew Social and Demographic Trends, August 1, http://www.pewsocialtrends.org/2012/08/01/the-rise-of-residential-segregation-by-income/.
Haldeman, Douglas C. 1991. "Sexual Orientation Conversion Therapy for Gay Men and Lesbians: A Scientific Examination." In *Homosexuality: Research Implications for Public Policy*, edited by John C. Gonsiorek and James D. Weinrich, 149–160. Newbury Park, CA: Sage.
Human Rights Campaign Foundation. 2009. *Degrees of Equality: A National Study Examining Workplace Climate for LGBT Employees*. Washington, D.C.: Human Rights Campaign Foundation.
Lynsen, J. 2008. "Obama Renews Commitment to Gay Issues." *Washington Blade* (Window Media LLC Productions). http://www. washblade.com/2008/6-13/news/national/12766.
Marx, Karl. 1961. *Das Kapital: A Critique of Political Economy*. F. Engels (Ed.). Gateway Editions.
National Gay and Lesbian Task Force. 2013a. "Hate Crime Laws in the U.S.," June 21. http://www.thetaskforce.org/downloads/reports/issue_maps/hate_crimes_06_13_color.pdf.
National Gay and Lesbian Task Force. 2013b. "Relationship Recognition for Same-Sex Couples in the United States," November 21. http://www.thetaskforce.org/downloads/reports/issue_maps/rel_recog_1_16_14_color.pdf.
Patchwork Nation. 2011. "Community Types: Map." http://www.patchworknation.org/content/patchwork-nation-map?m=1&set_community_type=in.
Project 515. 2013a. "It's Not About Benefits, but Acceptance." Accessed December 31, 2012, http://project515.org/educate/stories/its-not-about-benefits-but-acceptance/.
Project 515. 2013b. "Unrecognized in Life and Death." Accessed December 31, 2012, http://project515.org/educate/stories/unrecognized-in-life-and-death/.
Severson, Kim. 2012. "Chick-fil-A Thrust Back into Spotlight on Gay Rights." *New York Times*, July 25, A13.
Shidlo, A., and M. Schroeder. 2002. "Changing Sexual Orientation: A Consumers' Report." *Professional Psychology: Research and Practice, 33*(3), 249.
SmartBrief. 2012a. "Being Trans No Longer Classified as Mental Disorder." Dec. 4, http://www.smartbrief.com/servlet/wireless?issueid=DD61044D-E578-4DEA-9557-3F4E959A1E5E&sid=5e32ed3d-1c27-421f-beab-e0e23f037499.
SmartBrief. 2012b. "Judge Blocks California Ban on 'Ex-Gay' Therapy." Dec. 4, http://www.smartbrief.com/news/lgbt/storyDetails.jsp?issueid=DD61044D-E578-4DEA-9557-3F4E959A1E5E&copyid=A01173BF-6C7D-4DBB-994F-09271D7FCFCF&brief=lgbt&sb_code=rss&&campaign=rss.
SmartBrief. 2012c. "Out Bisexual Declared Winner in Ariz. Congressional Race." November 13, http://www.smartbrief.com/news/lgbt/storyDetails.jsp?issueid=AEEDD3AF-EDC0-4ACF-AFB1-9845DE0B981A&copyid=AB21470B-81E4-47CF-875E-65F4DB9EBAD5&brief=lgbt&sb_code=rss&&campaign=rss.
Transgender Law Center. n.d. "The State of Transgender California Report: Reports from the 2008 California Transgender Economic Health Survey." San Francisco, CA: Transgender Law Center.

U.S. Census Bureau. 2010a. "2010 Census Data." http://www.census.gov/2010census/data/.
U.S. Census Bureau. 2010b. *State and Metropolitan Area Data Book: 2010*. http://www.census.gov/compendia/databooks/pdf_version.html. (Open "Tables: States.")
Yoshino, Kenji. 2000. "The Epistemic Contract of Bisexual Erasure." *Stanford Law Review*, 353461. http://www.kenjiyoshino.com/articles/epistemiccontract.pdf.

Chapter 4

Organizations That Keep the Great Divide in Place

Christopher A. Thomason

Contents

This chapter will discuss the combatants in the battle over gay, lesbian, bisexual, and transgender (LGBT) civil rights. We will begin at the ideological level and examine the organizations that play a role in public thought. These are religious and political organizations, which usually have broader agendas than the LGBT civil rights movement, but which also make their stance on the issue clear, one way or the other. These organizations typically do not directly participate in activism, but they provide the rhetoric that incites their members to do so. We will then move to the organizations that fight the battle over LGBT civil rights more directly. These organizations raise funds, have demonstrations, lobby government officials, and advertise their positions to the masses to change public opinion.

Churches and Religious Organizations

It is not hard to make the connection that religion plays a major role in the ideological war of the Great Divide. Generally speaking, major components of Christianity, Islam, and Judaism view the LGBT community as partaking in sinful life choices, though there are exceptions to this view based on differing interpretations of scripture. In Christianity, this conflict is based primarily on eight scriptures: Genesis 19:1-5, Leviticus 18:22, Leviticus 20:13, Deuteronomy 23:17, 1 Corinthians 6:9-10, 1 Timothy 1:9-10, Romans 1:21-32, and Jude 1:6-7. Differing interpretations of these scriptures have yielded a wide variation of beliefs between denominations and individual churches as to whether homosexuality is a sin, how severe this "sin" is viewed, how much "choice" is perceived, the interpretation of scriptures on these matters, and how much of an influence their religious viewpoint should have on secular law. Support for the LGBT community has increased in recent years within many churches, causing them to re-examine their doctrines and viewpoints on LGBT issues. This spectrum of viewpoints will be examined next, starting with the most conservative, then moving to the most progressive.

Conservative Viewpoint

There are a number of churches that believe that members of the LGBT community are actively choosing to commit acts that are great sins. The "active choice" means that in their view, a person's sexual attraction and gender orientation are choices, and that a member of the LGBT community can choose to be heterosexual and oriented to the gender of which they were born, or at least choose to live celibately and deny their LGBT status. The "great sin" means that in their view, homosexuality is an abomination that God condemns. Most of these churches view LGBT members as "spiritually ill" and in need of repentance for salvation. Others, however, view them as beyond salvation, and in some cases, as a spiritual illness that is a threat to spread throughout the community and bring God's wrath down upon them. A number of high-profile religious leaders have taken a strong stance against homosexuality, including Pat Robertson, the late Jerry Falwell Sr., Pope Benedict XVI, and Billy Graham (Billy Graham Evangelistic Association 2013; Kengor 2013; Niebuhr 2001).

Churches in Active Opposition to LGBT Rights

As stated earlier, there are some churches that consider practicing homosexuals to be beyond salvation unless they repent. They do not allow practicing homosexuals to be members of their churches, may excommunicate members who come out of the closet, and are uncomfortable sharing their secular community with LGBT members at all. The Westboro Baptist Church and the extreme conservative elements of many other churches fall within this viewpoint. They believe that homosexuality is a spiritual disease that is allowed to grow and spread by the tolerance of the community. Therefore, in their view, it is their spiritual duty to discourage LGBT "activities" and take a firm stance against the perceived normalization of homosexual behavior in our society (Robinson 2012; Westboro Baptist Church 2012).

Although most conservative churches formally discourage discrimination or persecution of homosexuals, the churches of this viewpoint feel "called" to "guide" LGBT members either to repentance or relocation. This perceived "spiritual call" is of particular danger to the LGBT community. Equal rights are out of the question, but beyond this, people of this viewpoint intentionally make life miserable for members of the LGBT community (Robinson 2012). Many hate crimes stem from this viewpoint, and this will be discussed in Chapter 20, "Understanding Economic Power Dynamics as a Method to Combat Lesbian, Gay, Bisexual, and Transgender (LGBT) Homicides."

Spiritually Ill

A slightly more moderate and popular viewpoint is that members of the LGBT community are spiritually ill in some way; that they need to repent, be delivered from their "illness," and come to salvation. If an individual cannot be delivered from his or her homosexual tendencies, that person is expected to be celibate in order to avoid committing sin. This viewpoint is popular with the majority of mainstream

Christian churches, including Roman Catholics, Seventh Day Adventists, the Wisconsin Evangelical Lutheran Synod and Missouri Synod Lutherans, most Pentecostal denominations, and most Baptist denominations. These churches see homosexual tendencies as unsinful, but they condemn homosexual acts (American Baptist Churches U.S.A. 2012; Barry 2012; General Council of Seventh Day Adventists 2012; Southern Baptist Convention 2012; United Pentecostal Church International 2011; United States Conference of Catholic Bishops 2012; Wisconsin Evangelical Lutheran Synod 2012).

Some of these churches will only allow homosexual people to join their congregations if they have repented of their homosexuality and chosen to live celibate lives. Other churches acknowledge that it may not be possible for a homosexual to be delivered from homosexuality, and that he or she may lack the strength to live a celibate life. Therefore, the least sinful option is to live in a long-term, monogamous, homosexual relationship. These churches typically see it as their responsibility to reach out to "sinners" and show them "God's love." As a whole, the spiritually ill viewpoint could be seen as the shades of gray between churches that completely condemn members of the LGBT community and those churches that are affirming. Some of these churches are much more conservative than others, but they all claim to maintain the stance of "love the sinner, hate the sin." These churches generally do not acknowledge same-sex marriage or allow the ordination of LGBT clergy, but they also do not condone discrimination or the persecution of LGBT members (American Baptist Churches U.S.A. 2012; Barry 2012; General Council of Seventh Day Adventists 2012; Southern Baptist Convention 2012; United Pentecostal Church International 2011; United States Conference of Catholic Bishops 2012; Wisconsin Evangelical Lutheran Synod 2012).

Despite the official stance of the churches, this broad category represents a continuum of nonviolent prejudicial thought. Whether the prejudice manifests consciously or subconsciously, this group considers being a LGBT member to be a negative characteristic associated with perceived "sin." Some people of this category would knowingly, actively discriminate against a LGBT member in employment practices, business, housing, and social endeavors. Many others, on the other hand, discriminate subconsciously, burying their choices in layers of rationalization. These individuals may view other people's discrimination as wrong, not realizing that they have engaged in discrimination themselves. Some may even overcompensate for their biases by actively trying to "help" LGBT members, in an attempt to prove that they are not prejudiced.

This category can be very difficult to understand when it comes to beliefs on LGBT legal matters, activism, and voting. Although many of the churches and individuals in this group take a conservative political stance on LGBT issues, some do not. As opposed to both radical conservatives and those of an affirming viewpoint, this group sees certain "grayness" in LGBT issues, especially when they are placed in the context of other issues, such as religious freedom, separation of church and state, defense of the family, and personal freedom, which they may view as more important. The framing of these issues has been given a tremendous amount of effort by people who wish to radicalize these groups to one side or the other. Depending on which frame an individual adopts, he or she may vote and even give time and money to a side that is the opposite of his or her natural leaning. Conversely, if the frame that the individual accepts agrees with a strong natural leaning to either support or oppose the LGBT community, the person may become an outspoken advocate or opponent of the LGBT community. Therefore, these are the people who are targeted the most in campaigns related to LGBT issues.

The Roman Catholic Church, for instance, has become highly politically active in state marriage amendment contests, because it sees same-sex marriage as not just a sin but also a matter of religious freedom (United States Conference of Catholic Bishops 2012). As a result, several individual Catholic dioceses have made substantial donations to the conservative side in state-level battles over same-sex marriage, and the Knights of Columbus has become one of the primary funders for the conservative side of the campaigns (Helgeson 2012). On the other hand, a recent study by the Public Religion Research Institute found that a majority of Roman Catholic parishioners disagree with the formal positions of the church on LGBT issues. Nearly three-fourths of Catholics support some form of legal recognition for gay and lesbian couples, whether in the form of marriage (43%) or in the form of civil unions (31%). Only 22% oppose all forms of legal recognition for gay couples. Support for full marriage increased dramatically when it was made clear that priests would not be forced to perform a marriage ceremony against their will. About 71% of Catholics supported marriage for gay and lesbian couples when it was framed as "civil marriages like you get at city hall." Furthermore, 73% of Catholics support antidiscrimination employment laws to protect gays and lesbians, and 60% support equal opportunity for same-sex couples that wish to adopt children. Perhaps most important, 56% of Catholics do not believe that sex between two consenting adults of the same gender is a sin, compared to just 46% of the general population who believe the same way (Jones and Cox 2011, 1). Such statistics show that the majority of Roman Catholics follow their own convictions about LGBT issues, rather than church doctrine, and tend to be supportive of the LGBT community. Pope Francis has softened the Roman Catholic position a bit by saying, "Who am I to judge a gay person of good will who seeks the Lord?"

Ex-Gay Movement

If homosexuality is a spiritual or mental illness, then it should reasonably follow that there is a cure. Out of this idea came the ex-gay movement. The basic premise of this movement is that homosexuality can somehow be cured through a process called conversion therapy or reparative therapy. These therapies typically include psychotherapy, prayer, and pastoral counseling. Electroshock therapy, exorcisms, touch therapy, sex therapy, and other methods have also been attempted over the years to deliver gays and lesbians from their homosexual tendencies. The beliefs that homosexuality is a choice and that people can change their sexual orientation are fundamental pillars of conservative Christian thought. Therefore, the ex-gay movement, which began in the 1970s, has received a tremendous amount of support in the Christian community (Herek 1999; Just the Facts Coalition 2008; Truth Wins Out 2012).

A number of organizations have emerged to minister to homosexuals and to provide them with support as they go through reparative therapy. The first ex-gay organization was Love In Action (LIA), now called Restoration Path, which was formed in 1973. Three years later, Love In Action collaborated with other ex-gay organizations to form Exodus International, the largest and most prominent ex-gay organization. Focus on the Family formed a prominent ex-gay ministry called Love Won Out in 1998, but sold it to Exodus International in 2009. A number of other ex-gay organizations cater to a specific religious affiliation, such as Courage International for Catholics, Jews Offering New Alternatives for Healing (JONAH), and Evergreen International for Mormons. The primary secular counterpart to these groups is the National Association for Research and Therapy of Homosexuality (NARTH). In 2002, a huge coalition of ex-gay groups, including most of the ones previously mentioned, united to form Positive Alternatives to Homosexuality (PATH). Exodus International was among these groups, but left PATH in April 2007 (Exodus International 2013a; Positive Alternatives to Homosexuality 2002; Truth Wins Out 2012).

Criticism of the Ex-Gay Movement

The ex-gay movement has been widely criticized in the scientific community. In 1998, a coalition of 13 national organizations published "Just the Facts" in response to information that ex-gay organizations had been propagating in schools. The Just the Facts Coalition includes the American Academy of Pediatrics, American Counseling Association, American Association of School Administrators, American Federation of Teachers, American Psychological Association, American School Counselor Association, American School Health Association, Interfaith Alliance Foundation, National Association of School Psychologists, National Association of Secondary School Principals, National Association of Social Workers, National Education Association, and School Social Work Association of America. The Just the Facts Coalition has continued to be active since that time, releasing a new publication in 2008, titled "Just the Facts About Sexual Orientation and Youth: A Primer for Principals, Educators, and School Personnel" (Just the Facts Coalition 2008).

These organizations came together to dispute the ex-gay movement for several reasons. First is the assumption that homosexuality is mental disorder that can be cured. The *Diagnostic and Statistical Manual of Mental Disorders* (1994), published by the American Psychiatric Association, declassified homosexuality as a mental disorder in 1973. This decision has been supported by all major health professional organizations. Furthermore, the Just the Facts Coalition asserted in its 2008 publication: "The idea that homosexuality is a mental disorder or that the emergence of same-sex attraction and orientation among some adolescents is in any way abnormal or mentally unhealthy has no support among any mainstream health and mental health professional organizations" (p. 5).

Second is the lack of scientific evidence to show that reparative therapies can actually change a person's sexual orientation. In fact, there has been no published, scientific evidence to validate the effectiveness of reparative therapies. The last primary objection of the Just the Facts Coalition is the psychological harm that many people have experienced as a result of reparative therapy, both directly by having gone through the therapy themselves and failing, and indirectly by the discrimination that results from the belief that homosexuality is an illness (Just the Facts Coalition 2008).

Ironically, some of the worst criticism of the ex-gay movement has come from its own leadership, past and present. Many of these individuals had considered themselves to be "ex-gay," but have since realized that getting rid of homosexual attraction is impossible. These leaders have in many cases come to recognize the harm done by their organizations, and some have issued public apologies.

One prominent example of this happened in 1979 when Michael Bussee and Gary Cooper, two of the original cofounders of Exodus, suddenly left both Exodus and their wives to pursue a homosexual relationship with each other. They held a life commitment ceremony and were quiet until 1991, when Cooper was battling AIDS. At that time, they began speaking out and told their story in the documentary *One Nation Under God*. Cooper died before the documentary was completed (Bussee 2007).

On June 27, 2007, Bussee, along two other former Exodus (U.S. and Europe) leaders, Darlene Bogle and Jeremy Marks, issued formal apologies for their roles in the ex-gay movement. All three of these apologies shared similar themes. First, these leaders all testified that reparative therapies had failed to liberate them from their own homosexual tendencies. Second, they had witnessed no evidence of the success of reparative therapies in liberating anyone from their homosexual tendencies during their time with the ex-gay movement. Last, they all expressed remorse for the harm that their programs had done to their participants, including causing some participants to become suicidal (Bogle 2007; Bussee 2007; Marks 2007; "Statement of Apology" 2007).

Since these first apologies came out, several more apologies and formal position changes have followed from ex-gay leaders. In March 2010, John Smid, a former leader of both Exodus and Love In Action, wrote a heartfelt apology, which included these words: "If you have been wounded by me or harmed through the hands of my leadership; please come to me and allow an opportunity for me to personally apologize with the hope that we can both be released from the bondage of unforgiveness" (Smid 2010, 1).

Smid, himself an ex-ex-gay, has since begun leading a new ministry called Grace Rivers, which ministers to people affected by homosexuality without the assumptions of homosexual choice or the possibility of conversion to heterosexuality. Rather, Grace Rivers focuses on acceptance, respect, and empowering all individuals to find their faith in Jesus Christ (Smid 2010).

Perhaps the biggest blow to the ex-gay movement has been a change in the direction of Exodus International itself. Alan Chambers, the current president of Exodus International, has been trying to distance the organization from the ex-gay movement, and especially reparative therapy. Chambers has made a number of public statements in 2012 that could mark a change in viewpoint for Exodus, expressing that reparative therapy cannot provide the absolute cure for homosexuality that it has promised in the past, that Christians should shift from trying to change homosexuals to accepting them, that practicing homosexuals can go to heaven, and that gays who believe in God can know God as intimately as any heterosexual can. Above all else, Chambers views homosexual temptation as a sin equal to any other, and maintains that regardless of a person's ability to change or not change his/her attractions, God will not walk away from those that choose to love Him. Several churches have left the Exodus network as a result of Chambers' statements, and some are accusing Chambers of heresy. However, despite this criticism, it is clear that Exodus now no longer endorses reparative therapy (Eckholm 2012; Exodus International 2013b; Gentry 2012a, 2012b; Hagerty 2012). This is a monumental change for Exodus International and an equally monumental blow to the old assumptions of the ex-gay movement. Yet, this may prove to be an incredible opportunity for healing between the LGBT community and the Christian community.

Newly Supportive Churches in Crisis

In recent years, a number of churches that had traditionally held the spiritually ill viewpoint have begun to reexamine their positions on LGBT spiritual and political issues. In terms of spiritual health, these churches have begun to question how much choice a person has over his or her sexual or gender orientation. This questioning is largely the result of the failure of the ex-gay movement. If psychotherapy cannot alleviate it, is homosexuality really the result of a "bad upbringing" or "traumatic event"? If prayer can't get rid of it, is it really a demon or a spiritual illness? If God won't turn a homosexual person straight, and the person would obviously appear to prefer to be straight, is being homosexual such a problem in His eyes? If a person can't make the choice to not be homosexual, how is it possible for that person to have sinned? These questions have weighed heavily on the minds of many people, congregations, and in some cases, entire denominations. Several major denominations are going through this process, including Anglicanism, the Presbyterian Church (U.S.A.), the United Methodist Church, and the Evangelical Lutheran Church in America (ELCA). Two of these denominations will be discussed next.

Anglicanism

In the last two decades, the issue of homosexuality as related to the blessing of same-sex couples as well as the performance of marriage ceremonies, and the ordination of noncelibate gay priests and bishops, has brought the worldwide Anglican Communion to the brink of schism. The Anglican Communion is made up of 38 national churches, including the Church of England, the Episcopal Church in the U.S., the Anglican Church of Canada, and other affiliated groups around the world. Disagreements within the Anglican Communion are often divided on a regional basis, and this issue is no different. Anglican churches in Africa and Asia tend to be very conservative in their interpretations of scripture related to homosexuality. In comparison, the North American churches tend to be rather liberal in their view. The Church of England falls in the middle between these two extremes (Goodstein 2008; Pearson 2012; The Church of England 2012; Zaimov 2013).

The Episcopal Church in the U.S. brought this issue to a head during its General Convention in 2003. At that time, the Reverend Gene Robinson, who was in a long-term, committed relationship with another man (which has recently ended), was consecrated as the Bishop of New Hampshire. The issue of blessing same-sex couples and performing marriage ceremonies where they are legal was considered directly linked to Robinson's approval, though it took 9 more years before the Episcopal Church approved an official liturgy for blessing same-sex unions. These decisions created uproar in the global Anglican Communion, and there has been much talk about a possible schism. Such a schism has not yet happened in the global community (Goldstein 2008; Pearson 2012; Zaimov 2013).

In 2008, however, disgruntled conservatives who were upset with the liberal teachings of the Episcopal Church in the U.S. and the Anglican Church of Canada formed a new denomination, called the Anglican Church in North America. This church has expressed that it wishes to be accepted as part of the Anglican Communion. Although several national Anglican churches have declared that they are in full communion with the Anglican Church in North America, acceptance in the Anglican Communion has not happened yet (Goodstein 2008; Anglican Church in North America 2012).

Presbyterian Church (U.S.A.)

The Presbyterian Church (U.S.A.) is the largest Presbyterian group in the United States. This church is currently struggling with the interpretation of scripture and faithfulness to the instructions given therein. The Presbyterian Church (U.S.A.) has been slowly removing language from its governing documents that had previously been stumbling blocks to the ordination of partnered gays and lesbians. On May 10, 2011, a narrow majority of Presbyteries voted to permit the ordination of partnered gays and lesbians in ministerial roles (Goldstein 2011). Immediately after this decision, conservative Presbyterians formed a new denomination, called the Evangelical

Covenant Order of Presbyterians, which does not allow the ordination of partnered gays and lesbians (Burke 2012).

On July 6, 2012, the Presbyterian Church (U.S.A.) General Assembly voted down a proposal to change the definition of marriage in the Church's Book of Order to "between two people." The proposal narrowly failed, so at that time, the church's definition of marriage remained as between "a man and a woman." As things currently stand, the Presbyterian Church (U.S.A.) will allow the ordination of partnered gays and lesbians, and ministers are allowed to bless same-sex couples in some states. On June 19, 2014, the church voted to allow its ministers to hold same-sex marriages in states where they are legal.

A subgroup of the Presbyterian Church (U.S.A.), the More Light Presbyterians, is a group of congregations that promote the full inclusion of the LGBT community in all aspects of church life, including marriage and ministry. This group does not believe that homosexuality is a sin, and churches within this group are fully welcoming and affirming in all ways that they hold authority. This group is a staunch advocate for the LGBT community within the larger body of the Presbyterian Church (U.S.A.), and it has had a major influence on the recent decisions of the Presbyterian Church (U.S.A.) General Assembly (More Light Presbyterians 2013).

Affirming Churches

LGBT affirming churches are those that do not view homosexuality or transgender status as sins. To people of this viewpoint, these are innate characteristics that a person cannot change. They also believe that God would not condemn a person for something that is not a choice. There is no eye color or skin color that is better than another, and innate sexuality is seen the same way. Contrary to what conservatives would charge, these groups do not choose what is immoral over the word of God. Rather, they look for an interpretation of the scriptures in question that makes sense within the context of what they know about homosexuality, the compassionate nature of Christ's message, and the whole body of scriptures taken together.

Affirming churches are typically considered to be liberal in their interpretation of scripture, but this is not always the case. To a conservative, following biblical teachings is the number one priority. In the case of homosexuality, many conservatives have realized that there is discord between the scriptures that seem to condemn homosexuality, what has been proven about the nature of homosexuality through the failure of the ex-gay movement, and scriptural teachings on justice, love, compassion, and the nature of sin. Some churches have gone so far as to study biblical scriptures in their original languages, finding that the scriptures that seem to be so clear-cut in opposition of homosexuality hold no such significance when translated directly from the original languages into English. In fact, this examination of scripture has created the first synthesis of conservative and liberal viewpoints, that by following the word of God as it was originally intended without compromising on integrity or rigor, homosexuality is recognized as in every way equal to heterosexuality. These very conservative churches in terms of biblical practice are therefore fully affirming of the LGBT community.

Affirming churches are more politically active than other church groups, as they tend to have social justice and equality for the LGBT community at or near the forefront of their mission. They see it as their job to be the counterpoint against Christian Conservatives in the political arena. A few prominent affirming denominations will be discussed next.

Metropolitan Community Church

The first LGBT-specific denomination in the United States was the Metropolitan Community Church (MCC), also known as the Universal Fellowship of Metropolitan Community Churches, founded in 1968. At that time, members of the LGBT community were experiencing nearly universal rejection and persecution in churches. Reverend Troy Perry, a gay man who had experienced the rejection of the church community personally, recognized that members of the LGBT community needed a place where they could worship without shame. Perry held MCC's first service on October 6, 1968. He led 12 people in worship in his own living room in Los Angeles, California. Word spread through the LGBT community, and MCC quickly expanded, becoming a leading advocate for the LGBT community and other oppressed minorities in the United States and abroad (Metropolitan Community Church 2004). As of 2011, the MCC fellowship had 222 churches in 37 countries, including 50 churches that MCC started (Metropolitan Community Church 2013).

Subdenominations and Schisms

In recent years, many mainstream congregations have independently adopted an affirming viewpoint. As more congregations took this viewpoint, they began to form groups within their existing denominations. These groups often found resistance from the more conservative elements within their denominations, which felt that they were abandoning the truth of scripture in favor of condoning sinful behavior. The resulting conflict has been and is often bitter and divisive in nature.

In some cases, affirming church groups are not allowed to remain within their denomination. This is often the case within denominations that are traditionally very conservative. The affirming viewpoint is viewed as a betrayal of the denomination, against scripture, and against God. As a result, the affirming churches are forced to leave, either becoming independent, or if the group is large enough, form a new affirming denomination. Examples of this include the Affirming Pentecostal

Church International and the Global Alliance of Affirming Apostolic Pentecostals. As discussed earlier, both of these groups base their affirming viewpoint on intense biblical scholarship and translating the passages in question directly from their original languages. Thus, they maintain a conservative viewpoint in most matters while being affirming of the LGBT community (Affirming Pentecostal Church International 2013).

In other cases, the affirming churches are allowed to exist as a sort of subdenomination within their larger denomination. Since the larger group allows their voices to be heard, they advocate for the LGBT community and ultimately cause the larger denomination to become more tolerant of the LGBT community. The More Light Presbyterians, the Association of Welcoming and Affirming Baptists (2013), and the Reconciling Ministries Network in the United Methodist Church (2013) are all examples of groups that function in this manner.

United Church of Christ

On July 4, 2005, the United Church of Christ's General Synod voted overwhelmingly in support of a resolution titled "In Support of Equal Marriage Rights for All." This resolution meant that the United Church of Christ was the first major Christian denomination in the United States to convert to an affirming stance. It also became the largest Christian denomination to support same-sex marriage. This resolution does not require that unwilling congregations adopt an affirming stance, but it does set the standard that the denomination as a whole is affirming (Dewan 2005; United Church of Christ 2005, 1).

Political Parties

LGBT issues have taken center stage in recent politics. Today a majority of Americans support gay marriage, which is the culmination of increasing support for the LGBT community over the past decade. In 2012, Tammy Baldwin became the first openly lesbian U.S. senator, defeating former Wisconsin Governor Tommy Thompson. Also President Barack Obama has given his support to the LGBT community in a number of ways. He pushed for the repeal of Don't Ask, Don't Tell (CNN, Hornick, and Ure 2010), which was repealed and officially ended on September 20, 2011 (Freedom to Marry 2012a). President Obama has also given his support to the Respect for Marriage Act, which would repeal the Defense of Marriage Act and require the U.S. government to recognize the validity of same-sex marriages. Last, President Obama became the first sitting U.S. president to publicly announce that he supports same-sex marriage on May 9, 2012. Democrats generally support the president in these sentiments, while most Republicans vehemently oppose them. These positions will be discussed next (Cooper 2012; Democratic National Committee 2012; Freedom to Marry 2012a; Republican National Committee 2012).

Republican Party

The Republican Party espouses conservative Christian and traditional family values. As such, Republican leaders are generally in opposition to same-sex marriage and other legislation that specifically protects the LGBT community. The 2012 Republican platform included several statements in opposition of same-sex marriage, calling the redefinition of marriage "an assault on the foundations of our society, challenging the institution which, for thousands of years in virtually every civilization, has been entrusted with the rearing of children and the transmission of cultural values" (Republican National Committee 2012, 10). The platform goes on to say:

> We reaffirm our support for a Constitutional amendment defining marriage as the union of one man and one woman. We applaud the citizens of the majority of States which have enshrined in their constitutions the traditional concept of marriage, and we support the campaigns underway in several other States to do so. (Republican National Committee 2012, 10)

Such a platform indicates that the majority of Republican leaders do not support same-sex marriage or the rights of the LGBT community, but this is not true of the entire party.

The Log Cabin Republicans is a group that works within the Republican Party to advocate for equal rights for the LGBT community. The mission statement of the Log Cabin Republicans reads:

> The mission of Log Cabin Republicans shall advance the interests of the gay and lesbian community within the Republican Party of the United States of America. It shall assist in the development and enactment of policies affecting the gay and lesbian community within the Republican Party and by municipal, state and federal governments. Its membership shall advocate and support candidates, activities or initiatives which provide equal rights under law to persons who are gay or lesbian, promote nondiscrimination against or harassment of persons who are gay or lesbian, and encourage participation in the Republican Party by gay and lesbian Americans. (Log Cabin Republicans 2013)

The Log Cabin's mission is a difficult one to accomplish, and this group has come under a great deal of criticism by the Republican establishment. Still, considering recent shifts in public opinion, one might hypothesize that the Republican Party will soon be forced to consider taking a more inclusive approach to politics. The Log Cabin will strive to take a leadership role when this shift occurs.

Democratic Party

The Democratic Party has historically been more supportive of the LGBT community than its Republican counterparts, but it has taken until 2012 for the Democratic Party to add support of same-sex marriage to its national platform. Not all Democrats are supportive of same-sex marriage, but most acknowledge the need to extend legal protections to same-sex couples through legalizing either marriage or civil unions. The 2012 Democratic Party Platform includes this statement:

> We support the right of all families to have equal respect, responsibilities, and protections under the law. We support marriage equality and support the movement to secure equal treatment under law for same-sex couples. We also support the freedom of churches and religious entities to decide how to administer marriage as a religious sacrament without government interference.
>
> We oppose discriminatory federal and state constitutional amendments and other attempts to deny equal protection of the laws to committed same-sex couples who seek the same respect and responsibilities as other married couples. We support the full repeal of the so-called Defense of Marriage Act and the passage of the Respect for Marriage Act. (Democratic National Committee 2012, 53).

The Stonewall Democrats are the Democratic counterpart to the Log Cabin Republicans. They advocate for LGBT rights within the Democratic Party and in American communities. Stonewall Democrats have been active in all levels of government and have helped to lead the Democratic Party to its current position on LGBT issues (Stonewall Democrats 2013).

The Combatants

Now that we have discussed the groups that influence the ideology behind the battle over LGBT issues, it is time to discuss the groups that fight the battle directly. Specifically, we will look at the groups that provide the funding for the massive marriage amendment campaigns, influence who gets elected to political office, and reach the largest audiences. These are groups that have the fight over LGBT issues written into their mission statements, and that measure their success by amendments passed and laws enacted. We will start by looking at conservative organizations that oppose same-sex marriage, and then we will look at organizations that advocate for LGBT rights. It should be noted that while there are many groups on both sides that are noteworthy and have greatly contributed to their respective causes, in order to maintain neutrality and brevity, we have chosen to discuss three major players for each side. Each of these organizations represents a slightly different approach to the battle, and as such, this section is representative more of the strategies of the organizations than of the organizations themselves.

Conservative Organizations

There are a number of organizations that advocate for conservative principles. Among those principles is the stance of opposition to same-sex marriage. The most vocal and powerful groups against LGBT rights are those that specialize in these issues. Naturally, these groups do not frame themselves as promoting discrimination and hatred against the LGBT community or fighting against equal rights. Rather, they frame themselves as defending the sanctity of marriage, traditional family values, and religious freedom. Three of the most prominent national conservative organizations in this fight are the National Organization for Marriage, Focus on the Family, and American Family Association. These groups will be discussed next.

National Organization for Marriage

The National Organization for Marriage (NOM) was formed in 2007 with the intention of organizing and focusing the opposition to same-sex marriage in a single national voice. NOM has two nonprofit arms: the NOM Marriage PAC and the NOM Education Fund. The NOM Marriage PAC operates as a 501(c)(4) nonprofit organization, which has the ability to raise funds to contribute to elections and marriage amendment campaigns. The NOM Marriage PAC has had a major impact on the battle over same-sex marriage through massive political donations and the framing of conservative ideology in large campaigns. This will be discussed further. The NOM Education Fund operates as a 501(c)(3) and can accept tax-deductible donations. However, its scope is limited, so the NOM Education Fund focuses primarily on education and research (National Organization for Marriage 2013a).

The National Organization for Marriage has wielded a tremendous amount of economic power in the fight over same-sex marriage. In 2012, NOM contributed over $5.5 million to the marriage campaigns in Minnesota, Maine, Maryland, and Washington (Lavers 2012). NOM used this money for advertising campaigns that framed their arguments in opposition of same-sex marriage and presented them to the voters (Brown 2012). Additionally, NOM uses its financial prowess to influence elections and motivate lawmakers to vote their way. In a press release on January 3, 2013 regarding the anticipated vote on same-sex marriage in Illinois, NOM illustrated this principle well:

> "Any Republican in Illinois who betrays the cause of marriage will be casting a career-ending vote and will be held accountable to their

> constituents," said Brian Brown, NOM's president. "We will spend whatever it takes—hundreds of thousands of dollars if necessary—to remove them from office, just as we did three of the four turncoat Republican state Senators in New York who were responsible for gay 'marriage' passing there. We will not hesitate to support pro-family Democrats to replace them, as our record in New York proves." (National Organization for Marriage 2013b)

Such a threat makes it very difficult for pro-LGBT Republicans to vote their conscience and is seen by many LGBT supporters as unethical. However, at this point in time, the right of a PAC to make such a statement, and back it up with campaign contributions, is protected under the First Amendment. Ethical or not, such tactics are highly effective in today's political climate.

Focus on the Family

Focus on the Family is a 501(c)(3) nonprofit organization that was founded in 1977 to promote Christian family values. Its scope includes a wide range of social issues beyond the LGBT movement. However, Focus on the Family's actions against the LGBT movement on multiple levels is deserving of mention in this chapter. While Focus on the Family's 501(c)(3) status prevents it from advocating on behalf of individual political candidates, its 501(c)(4) registered affiliate, CitizenLink, formerly known as Focus on the Family Action, has no such restriction (CitizenLink 2013; Focus on the Family 2013).

Focus on the Family is a staunch advocate for the ex-gay movement, maintaining its belief that it is possible for homosexuals to change their sexual identity and become straight. As was previously mentioned in this chapter, Focus on the Family ran a prominent ex-gay ministry called Love Won Out for 11 years before selling it to Exodus International in 2009. Though Focus on the Family no longer has control of this ex-gay ministry, it continues to promote reparative therapy as a possible way to eliminate unwanted same-sex attractions (Exodus International 2013b; Focus on the Family Issue Analysts 2008).

Focus on the Family has done some very high-profile advertising of traditional Christian family values. In February 2010, Focus on the Family bought a 30-second commercial spot during Super Bowl XLIV promoting a pro-life viewpoint on abortion. On January 14, 2011, Focus on the Family aired a second commercial during the New England Patriots–Denver Broncos AFC Divisional Playoff game. This commercial featured children reciting the Bible verse John 3:16 (Focus on the Family 2010, 2011).

Focus on the Family is highly politically active through its affiliate, CitizenLink, formerly known as Focus on the Family Action. CitizenLink has traditionally followed Focus on the Family's model of creating and distributing informational material, though CitizenLink can do so about specific candidates. In the 2008

Presidential Election, for instance, Focus on the Family Action distributed a 16-page booklet, titled "Letter from 2012 in Obama's America," which described an American future in which many freedoms were taken away by the liberals in power. Focus on the Family and CitizenLink have come under a great deal of criticism from LGBT advocacy groups and the scientific community for the inaccuracy of information that they have propagated, particularly regarding the effectiveness of reparative therapy. However, these groups maintain that their information is true and accurate (CitizenLink 2013; Focus on the Family Action 2008).

American Family Association

The American Family Association (AFA), founded in 1977 under the name National Federation for Decency, is a 501(c)(3) nonprofit organization that is committed to being an outspoken advocate for fundamentalist Christian principles and traditional family values. AFA uses technology to its advantage, wielding multiple types of media to spread its message. AFA claims to have over 2 million online viewers and roughly 180,000 subscribers (People for the American Way 2007) to its monthly magazine, *AFA Journal*. AFA maintains two activist websites: OneMillionMoms.com and OneMillionDads.com, which AFA uses to organize boycotts. AFA also has an online news provider, called OneNewsNow.com. Together, these media outlets give the American Family Association the ability to reach and organize a huge niche audience of conservative Christians, giving the AFA tremendous political power (American Family Association 2013).

The American Family Association uses its ability to reach a large audience to wage war on liberalism and LGBT supporters. AFA does this by organizing boycotts and letter-writing campaigns to affect the decisions of companies that do not uphold AFA's values. In 2010 alone, AFA organized boycotts of Home Depot and PepsiCo in response to their support of the LGBT civil rights movement, and launched the iVote campaign, placing hundreds of billboards across the country encouraging people to vote according to conservative values. That same year, AFA also launched two letter-writing campaigns. One was in response to the Fox Network airing an episode of *American Dad* that had a bestiality scene in it. AFA promoted the filing of thousands of indecency complaints with the Federal Communications Commission (FCC) in that campaign (Schatz 2010). The other letter-writing campaign was regarding the President Obama's nomination of Erroll Southers to lead the Transportation Security Administration. The AFA launched this campaign in the wake of allegations that Southers had inappropriately used law enforcement databases to gain information about an ex-boyfriend of his wife. Southers eventually withdrew his name from consideration (American Family Association 2013).

The American Family Association has been widely criticized for its extreme conservative viewpoint. In fact the Southern Poverty Law Center changed its classification of the AFA from a group that uses hate speech to an actual hate group in

November 2010 (Southern Poverty Law Center 2013). Evelyn Schlatter explained that this decision was based on "their propagation of known falsehoods—claims about LGBT people that have been thoroughly discredited by scientific authorities—and repeated, groundless name-calling" (Schlatter 2010, 1). In order to maintain neutrality, the author of this chapter will leave the discussion of the AFA here. The reader does have the option of examining the statements of the Southern Poverty Law Center and comparing them to the actual writings of the American Family Association.

LGBT Advocacy Organizations

The LGBT community also has many advocacy organizations that are fighting on their behalf. These organizations frame their viewpoint as fighting to end discrimination, to promote justice and equality, and to reclaim the civil rights that have been taken away by those who hate and fear them. These groups strongly view their battle as similar those fought by racial minorities and women in this country to get equal rights. As a result, they take a large amount of their strategy from the leaders of past civil rights movements. We will again discuss three of the most prominent national LGBT advocacy organizations: Freedom to Marry, the Gay and Lesbian Victory Fund, and the Human Rights Campaign.

Freedom to Marry

Evan Wolfson, a prominent civil rights attorney, created Freedom to Marry in 2003. Freedom to Marry is composed of two parts: Freedom to Marry, Inc, a 501(c)(3); and Freedom to Marry Action, Inc, a 501(c)(4) nonprofit organization. These two organizations together give Freedom to Marry the legal versatility it needs to accomplish its stated goal, which is to "end the exclusion of same-sex couples from marriage once and for all." In its *Roadmap to Victory*, Freedom to Marry lists three major steps in this process: "win more states," "grow the majority for marriage," and "end federal marriage discrimination." Each step will be discussed next (Freedom to Marry 2012b, 2012d).

Similar to the battle over race discrimination in marriage, Freedom to Marry knows that it needs to reach a certain critical mass of states that support same-sex marriage before federal action will be feasible. Although it is not known how many states this is, it took winning 34 states to end race-based marriage discrimination before the Supreme Court ruled to end such discrimination on the national level in *Loving* v. *Virginia* (1967). In March 2012, Freedom to Marry recognized that there were several battleground states that would be making decisions about same-sex marriage that year. Knowing that organizations like the National Organization for Marriage would be funneling a tremendous amount of money into these states for various ad campaigns, Freedom to Marry created the Win More States Fund. The Win More States Fund was given the goal of raising at least $3 million to funnel into the state campaigns of Minnesota, Washington, New Jersey, Maine, Maryland, and New Hampshire. The fund met this goal in August 2012 (Polaski 2012) and continued to work to raise money for these states (Dallara 2012; Freedom to Marry 2012b, 2012c).

The impact of Win More States Fund was a huge victory for the LGBT community in 2012. Minnesota defeated its marriage amendment proposal. Washington, Minnesota, Maine, Maryland, and New Hampshire have all legalized same-sex marriages. New Jersey also passed legislation to legalize same-sex marriage, but Governor Chris Christie vetoed it. New Jersey, which already had civil unions for same-sex couples, finally passed a same-sex marriage law in October 2013. Due in part to contributions from the Win More States Fund, a number of states, plus the District of Columbia, now offer some sort of legal protection to same-sex couples via marriage, explicit respect for out-of-state marriage, civil union, domestic partnership, or limited domestic partnership (Freedom to Marry 2012c; Polaski 2012).

In addition to winning states, Freedom to Marry knows that there must also be a strong majority of Americans overall who support same-sex marriage before an action like *Loving v. Virginia* (1967) can happen. This needs to not only be a strong majority but also a diverse majority. In August 2010, CNN released the first national poll in history to show that a slim majority of Americans support same-sex marriage. This was corroborated by an Associated Press poll in September 2010. Knowing that it has more support for same-sex marriage than there was for interracial marriage in 1967, Freedom to Marry is still working to expand this majority and make it more diverse. Specifically, it would like to win over more male voters who still are not in favor of same-sex marriage (Associated Press 2010; CNN 2010; Freedom to Marry 2012b).

Freedom to Marry's third goal of ending federal marriage discrimination has experienced initial success as well. The Defense of Marriage Act (DOMA), which was signed in 1996, had made it so that the federal government could not recognize same-sex marriages, but this is no longer the case. Freedom to Marry has been a strong advocate for the Respect for Marriage Act, which would repeal DOMA and ensure that the federal government would recognize the validity of same-sex marriages. The Respect for Marriage Act would not force same-sex marriage on states that do not wish to allow it. Rather, it would give federal validation to the decision of states that do allow same-sex marriage and extend the federal benefits and protections of marriage to same-sex couples that are married (Freedom to Marry 2012a, 2012b).

Freedom to Marry knew that it needed powerful allies in order to win this fight, so it launched two campaigns: one addressed at the president and one addressed at the Democratic Party. In March 2011, Freedom to Marry launched a campaign aimed at the president, called "Say, 'I do' Mr. President." This was essentially an open letter asking President Obama to publicly declare support for same-sex marriage. Over 122,000 people signed this letter (Riley 2011), including many celebrities. President Obama endorsed the Respect for Marriage Act on July 19, 2011, immediately after North Carolina endorsed its marriage amendment, and became the first sitting U.S. president to publicly announce that he supports same-sex marriage on May 9, 2012. In February 2012, Freedom to Marry launched a similar campaign, called "Democrats: Say I Do," which sought to persuade the Democratic Party to include a plank supporting same-sex marriage in its national platform. "Democrats: Say I Do" was able to gain a tremendous amount of support, and in September 2012, the party platform was ratified, including the desired plank in support of same-sex marriage. Now that such powerful allies have supported same-sex marriage, Freedom to Marry and other LGBT advocacy groups have a chance of getting the Respect for Marriage Act passed into law (Democratic National Committee 2012; Freedom to Marry 2012a; Tolle 2012).

Gay and Lesbian Victory Fund

The Gay and Lesbian Victory Fund, also referred to as Victory Fund, is a political action committee that is devoted specifically to increasing the number of LGBT elected officials at all levels of government in the United States. Taking inspiration from another political action committee, EMILY's List (Early Money Is Like Yeast), which supports female, pro-choice, Democratic candidates with strong financial contributions early in their campaigns, gay activist William Waybourn approached former Human Rights Campaign Fund executive director Vic Basile to see if it would be possible to create a similar organization to help LGBT political candidates. The result of this was the creation of the Gay and Lesbian Victory Fund on May 1, 1991 (Gay and Lesbian Victory Fund 2013).

Victory Fund started off small, supporting one candidate in the fall of 1991. That candidate was Seattle City Council candidate Sherry Harris. Victory Fund was able to raise over $14,000 for Harris' campaign, which propelled her to victory over a 24-year incumbent. With her victory, Harris made American history as the first openly lesbian African-American city councilmember. From that point on, Victory Fund drew the attention and support of the LGBT community (Gay and Lesbian Victory Fund 2013).

Increasing support for Victory Fund allowed it to assist more candidates who did what they were supposed to do: win. With each victory came more attention and more donations. Twenty-eight candidates received Victory Fund endorsement in 1994, and 50 in 1996. In 2012, the Victory Fund endorsed 180 candidates, 123 of whom won their elections (Gay and Lesbian Victory Fund 2013, 1). The most notable of these victories happened in Wisconsin with Tammy Baldwin's victory over former Governor Tommy Thompson to become the nation's first openly lesbian U.S. senator (Gay and Lesbian Victory Fund 2013; Dison 2012).

Human Rights Campaign

The Human Rights Campaign (HRC) is the largest LGBT civil rights advocacy organization in the United States. Founded in 1980, the Human Rights Campaign claims to now have over 1.5 million members and supporters nationwide (HRC 2013). In comparison to Freedom to Marry and the Gay and Lesbian Victory Fund, the Human Rights Campaign has been able to have a much broader role in the LGBT civil rights movement due to its enormous size and ability to direct funds. HRC's mission statement is as follows:

> By inspiring and engaging all Americans, HRC strives to end discrimination against LGBT citizens and realize a nation that achieves fundamental fairness and equality for all.
>
> HRC seeks to improve the lives of LGBT Americans by advocating for equal rights and benefits in the workplace, ensuring families are treated equally under the law and increasing public support among all Americans through innovative advocacy, education and outreach programs. HRC works to secure equal rights for LGBT individuals and families at the federal and state levels by lobbying elected officials, mobilizing grassroots supporters, educating Americans, investing strategically to elect fair-minded officials and partnering with other LGBT organizations. (HRC 2013)

This mission is no small undertaking, but HRC appears to be up to the task. The Human Rights Campaign boasts a tremendous number of victories in a variety of initiatives, including political campaigns, state and federal marriage initiatives, lobbying for anti-discriminatory measures, and educational campaigns (HRC 2013).

The Human Rights Campaign's political action committee has experienced a tremendous amount of success in helping LGBT and pro-equality candidates to get elected to public office. HRC boasts that over 90% of its endorsees win their elections (HRC 2013). HRC endorsed Bill Clinton's presidential campaign in 1992, and also endorsed Barack Obama in both 2008 and 2012. In 2012, HRC claims to have raised or contributed over $20 million (HRC 2013), which went to re-elect President Obama; win marriage equality in Maine, Maryland, and Washington; defeat the Minnesota marriage amendment; and elect a Congress with the most openly GLB and straight-allied members in history. The election of supportive leaders has had a tremendous impact on the effectiveness of the HRC's other initiatives (HRC 2013).

On the marriage front, the Human Rights Campaign has worked extensively with Freedom to Marry and other groups to defeat state and federal anti-marriage amendments, and secure same-sex marriage in several locations. In 2004 and 2006, HRC took a leadership role in the fight against the proposed Federal Marriage Amendment. In 2004, HRC used a massive lobbying effort and a $1 million television, print, and online advertising campaign to get its point across (HRC 2013). HRC's efforts in 2006 culminated in sending nearly 250,000 postcards to Capitol Hill offices just before the vote. In 2006, HRC was also active in defeating marriage amendments in Iowa and New Hampshire, and then continued working in those states to elect supportive legislatures. Both states eventually secured marriage for same-sex couples. HRC has continued to be a leader in state-level battles over marriage, contributing funds and expertise that helped to secure marriage for same-sex couples in 18 states so far, plus the District of Columbia (HRC 2013).

The Human Rights Campaign has also had great success in lobbying and providing expert testimony at Congressional hearings. In 2009, President Obama signed the Matthew Shepard and James Byrd, Jr. Hate Crimes Prevention Act into law. HRC spent 11 years advocating for this law, which strengthens existing hate crimes laws and includes violence perpetrated against the LGBT community within the definition of a hate crime. HRC also took a leadership role in lobbying for the repeal of Don't Ask, Don't Tell, which was officially eliminated as of September 20, 2011, and for the lifting of the HIV travel ban, which was officially lifted as of January 4, 2010. In addition, former HRC President Joe Solmonese provided expert testimony in two high-profile Congressional hearings for the LGBT community: the first Congressional hearing to address transgender discrimination on June 26, 2008, and the first hearing regarding the Respect for Marriage Act, in front of the Senate Judiciary Committee on July 20, 2011 (HRC 2013).

Last, the Human Rights Campaign has made great strides in community education and advocacy initiatives. HRC created the Corporate Equality Index in 2002, which rates American businesses on their treatment of LGBT employees, consumers, and investors. That year, 89 companies voluntarily provided their employment policies so that they could be rated on the index. Just 13 companies were rated at 100%. In 2012, 636 companies participated, and of these, 190 companies were rated at 100% on criteria that were more stringent than in 2002 (HRC 2011). Other initiatives include: the LGBT Mentorship program, which nurtures religious scholars and theologians who are interested in LGBT studies; the Clergy Call for Justice and Equality, which brings a diverse array of religious leaders to Washington D.C. to lobby for LGBT equality; the Welcoming Schools program, which addresses the bullying LGBT students in schools; "Growing Up LGBT in America," which is a study that examines the challenges LGBT teenagers face; and NOM Exposed, which is a website they say is devoted to holding the National Organization for Marriage accountable for its financing, ethics, and truthfulness. Such programs seek to finish the task of eliminating LGBT discrimination from the places that have allowed it the most: corporate America, churches, and schools (HRC 2013).

Of course, one cannot discuss LGBT organizations that impact public policy without mentioning those organizations that advance civil rights by means of litigation. Gay and Lesbian Advocates and Defenders (GLAD) and Lambda Legal. They have initiated a large number of cases over the years that have advanced the cause of LGBT civil rights enormously (GLAD 2013).

Financial Resources Invested

Wyatt-Nichol and Naylor (2013), in their article titled "The Policy Landscape of Social Orientation," include "Table 4: State Prohibition of Same-Sex Marriage: Expenditures and Votes" (p. 14). This table provides the amounts spent by proponents and opponents of same sex marriage in each of 32 states as of 2012. When summed, the proponents of same sex marriage in these states have spent $94,939,745; while the opponents of same sex marriage in these states have spent $66,640,309. This table does not include the large amounts spent in Minnesota, Maryland, Washington, and New York, but it does indicate the scale of the battle being waged across this country.

Conclusion

In this chapter, we have discussed the combatants in the battle over LGBT rights. Specifically, we examined the ideologies that cause such passionate division over LGBT issues. Not surprisingly, it is religious interpretation that has been the root cause of much of the division between these groups. It should be noted, however, that religion also holds the key to the acceptance of the LGBT community by the mainstream public. Respect and compassion by both sides has already caused a shift in how many religious groups view the LGBT community. As these newly supportive mainstream religious groups join the fight for LGBT rights, even the most conservative leaders will have to acknowledge that the LGBT community wants what everybody else does: equality, respect, and the ability to have a relationship with God if they so choose. Religion is what maintains the great divide for now, but in time, it is religion that will close the great divide for good.

References

Affirming Pentecostal Church International. 2013. "Our History." Accessed January 2, 2013. http://myapci.xbuild.com/#/history/4555142318.

American Baptist Churches U.S.A. 2012. "American Baptist Churches U.S.A: Responses/Actions Pertaining to Homosexuality." Accessed December 28, 2012. http://www.abc-usa.org/resources/abcusa-resources/abcusa-documents/policy-statements-and-resolutions/.

American Family Association. 2013. "About AFA." Accessed January 5, 2013. http://www.afa.net/Detail.aspx?id = 31.

American Psychiatric Association. 1994. Task Force on DSM-IV. 1994. *Diagnostic and Statistical Manual of Mental Disorders: DSM-IV.* Washington, D.C.: American Psychiatric Association.

Anglican Church in North America. 2012. "About the Anglican Church in North America." Accessed December 30, 2012. http://anglicanchurch.net/?/main/page/about-acna.

Associated Press. 2010. "The AP-National Constitution Center Poll." September. Accessed December 25, 2012. http://www.freedomtomarry.org/page/-/files/pdfs/AP-NCC%20Poll%20August%20topline.pdf.

Association of Welcoming and Affirming Baptists. 2013. "Mission and Vision." Accessed January 2, 2013. http://www.awab.org/mission-and-vision.html.

Barry, A. L. 2012. "What About…Homosexuality." The Lutheran Church- Missouri Synod. Accessed December 28, 2012. http://www.lcms.org/page.aspx?pid = 388.

Billy Graham Evangelistic Association. 2013. "Does the Bible Approve of Some Homosexual Relationships?" Accessed January 5, 2013. http://www.billygraham.org/articlepage.asp?articleid = 1976.

Bogle, Darlene. 2007. "Statement of Apology by Former Ex-Gay Leader." June 27. Beyond Ex-Gay. Accessed December 29, 2012. http://www.beyondexgay.com/article/bogleapology.html.

Brown, Brian. 2012. "National Organization for Marriage: We Are Not Defeated in Our Fight for Traditional Marriage." November 7. Accessed January 5, 2013. http://www.nationformarriage.org/site/apps/nlnet/content2.aspx?c = omL2KeN0LzH&b = 5075189&ct = 12333723.

Burke, Daniel. 2012. "Conservative Presbyterians in U.S. Launch New Denomination." January 21. *The Presbyterian Outlook.* Accessed January 1, 2013. http://www.pres-outlook.com/news-and-analysis/1/12156.html.

Bussee, Michael. 2007. "Statement of Apology by Former Exodus Leaders." June 27. Beyond Ex-Gay. Accessed December 29, 2012. http://www.beyondexgay.com/article/busseeapology.html.

CitizenLink. 2013. "About Us." Accessed January 5, 2013. http://www.citizenlink.com/about-us/.

CNN. 2010. "CNN Opinion Research Poll." Accessed December 25, 2012. http://www.freedomtomarry.org/page/-/files/pdfs/CNN%20Poll.pdf.

CNN, Ed Hornick, and Laurie Ure. 2010. "Obama Calls for 'Don't Ask, Don't Tell' Repeal." *CNN.* Accessed December 18, 2013. http://www.cnn.com/2010/POLITICS/01/27/obama.gays.military/.

Cooper, Michael. 2012. "Party Platforms Are Poles Apart in Their View of the Nation." *New York Times,* September 4. Accessed January 2, 2013. http://www.nytimes.com/2012/09/05/us/politics/how-the-party-platforms-differ.html?_r = 0.

Dallara, Angela. 2012. "Freedom to Marry Announces 'Win More States Fund' for 2012." Freedom to Marry. March 22. Accessed December 25, 2012. http://www.freedomtomarry.org/blog/entry/freedom-to-marry-announces-win-more-states-fund-for-2012.

Democratic National Committee. 2012. "Moving America Forward 2012 Democratic National Platform." Accessed January 2, 2013. http://www.democrats.org/democratic-national-platform.

Dewan, Shalia. 2005. "United Church of Christ Backs Same-Sex Marriage." *New York Times,* July 5. Accessed January 2, 2013. http://www.nytimes.com/2005/07/05/national/05church.html?_r = 0.

Dison, Dennis. 2012. "Victory Fund Celebrates Huge Night for Gay Candidates." Gay Politics, November 7. Accessed January 5, 2013. http://www.gay politics.com/2012/11/07/victory-fund-celebrates-huge-night-for-gay-candidates/.

Eckholm, Erik. 2012. "Rift Forms in Movement as Belief in Gay 'Cure' Is Renounced." *New York Times*, July 6. Accessed December 29, 2012. http://www.nytimes.com/2012/07/07/us/a-leaders-renunciation-of-ex-gay-tenets-causes-a-schism.html?pagewanted = all&_r = 0.

Exodus International. 2013a. "About Love Won Out." Accessed January 5, 2013. http://exodusinternational.org/love-won-out/about-love-won-out/.

Exodus International. 2013b. "Fact Sheet." Accessed January 5, 2013. http://exodusinternational.org/press/fact-sheet/.

Focus on the Family. 2010. "Focus on the Family to Air Super Bowl Ad." January 15. Accessed January 5, 2013. http://www.focusonthefamily.com/about_us/news_room/news-releases/20100115-focus-on-the-family-to-air-super-bowl-ad.aspx.

Focus on the Family. 2011. "Focus on the Family Airs National TV Commercial during Tonight's Broncos-Patriots Playoff Game." January 14. Accessed January 5, 2013. http://www.focusonthefamily.com/about_us/news_room/news-releases/20120114-focus-airs-national-tv-commercial-during-broncos-playoff-game.aspx.

Focus on the Family. 2013. "About Us." Accessed January 5, 2013. http://www.focus onthefamily.com/about_us.aspx.

Focus on the Family Action. 2008. "Letter from 2012 in Obama's America." Accessed January 5, 2013. http://www.wnd.com%2Ffiles%2FFocusletter.pdf.

Focus on the Family Issue Analysts. 2008. "Our Position (Same-Sex Counseling)." Accessed January 5, 2013. http://www.focusonthefamily.com/socialissues/social-issues/counseling-for-unwanted-same-sex-attractions/our-position.aspx.

Freedom to Marry. 2012a. "Federal." Accessed December 25, 2012. http://www.freedomtomarry.org/landscape/entry/c/federal.

Freedom to Marry. 2012b. "Roadmap to Victory." Accessed December 25, 2012. http://www.freedomtomarry.org/pages/roadmap-to-victory.

Freedom to Marry. 2012c. "States." Accessed December 25, 2012. http://www.freedomtomarry.org/states/.

Freedom to Marry. 2012d. "The Two Components of Freedom to Marry." Accessed December 25, 2012. http://www.freedomtomarry.org/pages/the-two-components-of-freedom-to-marry.

Gay and Lesbian Advocates and Defenders (GLAD). 2013. http://www.glad.org/.

Gay and Lesbian Victory Fund. 2013. "The Victory Fund: A Brief History." Accessed January 5, 2013. http://www.victoryfund.org/our_story/history.

General Council of Seventh Day Adventists. 2012. "Seventh Day Adventist Position Statement on Homosexuality." Accessed December 28, 2012. http://www. adventist.org/beliefs/statements/main-stat46.html.

Gentry, Weston. 2012a. "Exodus International Fragments Over Focus." *Christianity Today*, December 4. Accessed December 29, 2012. http://www.christianitytoday.com/ct/2012/december/exodus-from-exodus.html.

Gentry, Weston. 2012b. "Exodus International's Alan Chambers Accused of Antinomian Theology." *Christianity Today*, July 12. Accessed December 29, 2012. http://www.christianitytoday.com/ct/2012/julyweb-only/alan-chambers-accused-of-antinomian-theology.html.

Goodstein, Laurie. 2008. "Episcopal Split as Conservatives Form New Group." *New York Times*, December 3. Accessed December 30, 2012. http://www.nytimes.com/2008/12/04/us/04episcopal.html?pagewanted = all.

Goodstein, Laurie. 2011. "Presbyterians Approve Ordination of Gay People." *New York Times*, May 10. Accessed January 1, 2013. http://www.nytimes.com/2011/05/11/us/11presbyterian.html.

Hagerty, Barbara B. 2012. "Evangelicals Fight Over Therapy to 'Cure' Gays." NPR, July 6. Accessed December 28, 2012. http://www.npr.org/2012/07/06/156367287/evangelicals-fight-over-therapy-to-cure-gays.

Helgeson, Baird 2012. "Minnesota's Marriage Amendment Funded by Catholics Across the U.S." *Star Tribune* (Minneapolis), October 18. Accessed December 15, 2012. http://www.startribune.com/politics/statelocal/174875371.html.

Herek, Gregory. 1999. "'Reparative Therapy' and Other Attempts to Alter Sexual Orientation: A Background Paper." Accessed January 1, 2013. http://psychology. ucdavis.edu/rainbow/html/reptherapy.pdf.

Honan, Edith. 2012. "U.S. Presbyterian Church at Crossroads Over Gay Marriage." Reuters, July 14. Accessed January 1, 2013. http://www.reuters.com/article/2012/07/14/us-usa-religion-gaymarriage-idUSBRE86D0CD20120714.

Human Rights Campaign (HRC). 2011. "Decade of Progress in Workplace Equality Chronicled in HRC's 2012 Corporate Equality Index." Accessed December 18, 2013. http://www.hrc.org/press-releases/entry/decade-of-progress-in-workplace-equality-chronicled-in-hrcs-2012-cei.

Human Rights Campaign (HRC). 2013. "The HRC Story." Accessed January 5, 2013. http://www.hrc.org/the-hrc-story.

Jones, Robert, and Daniel Cox. 2011. "Catholic Attitudes on Gay and Lesbian Issues: A Comprehensive Portrait from Recent Research." Public Religion Research Institute, March. Accessed June 17, 2013. http://publicreligion.org/site/wp-content/uploads/2011/06/Catholics-and-LGBT-Issues-Survey-Report.pdf.

Just the Facts Coalition. 2008. "Just the Facts About Sexual Orientation and Youth: A Primer for Principals, Educators, and School Personnel." American Psychological Association. Accessed January 1, 2013. http://www.apa.org/pi/lgbt/publications/just-thefacts.html.

Kengor, Paul. 2013. "Pope Benedict on Gay Marriage." Catholic Exchange, January 10. Accessed January 13, 2013. http://catholicexchange.com/pope-benedict-on-gay-marriage/.

Lavers, Michael K. 2012. "4 Marriage Ballot Fights and 4 Big Wins." *Washington Blade*, November 7. Accessed December 18, 2013. http://www.washingtonblade.com/2012/11/07/4-marriage-ballot-fights-and-4-big-wins/.

Log Cabin Republicans. 2013. "About Log Cabin Republicans." Accessed September 7, 2013. http://www.logcabin.org/about-us/.

Marks, Jeremy. 2007. "Statement of Apology by Former Exodus Leader." *Beyond Ex-Gay*, June 27. Accessed December 29, 2012. http://www.beyondexgay.com/article/jeremy-apology.html.

Metropolitan Community Churches. 2004. "History of MCC." Accessed January 2, 2013. http://mccchurch.org/overview/history-of-mcc/.

Metropolitan Community Churches. 2013. "Our Churches." Accessed January 2, 2013. http://mccchurch.org/overview/ourchurches/.

More Light Presbyterians. 2013. "About Us." Accessed January 1, 2013. http://www.mlp.org/about-us/.

National Organization for Marriage. 2013a. "NOM Pledges to Defeat Any Republican Legislator in Illinois Who Votes for Gay Marriage." January 2. Accessed January 5, 2013. http://www.nationformarriage.org/site/apps/nlnet/content2. aspx?c = omL2KeN0LzH&b = 5075189&ct = 12703701.

National Organization for Marriage. 2013b. "About NOM." Accessed January 5, 2013. http://www.nationformarriage.org/site/c.omL2KeN0LzH/b.3479573/k.E2D0/About_NOM.htm.

Niebuhr, Gustav. 2001. "After the Attacks: Finding Fault; U.S. 'Secular' Groups Set Tone for Terror Attacks, Falwell Says." *New York Times*, September 14. Accessed January 5, 2013. http://www.nytimes.com/2001/09/14/us/after-attacks-finding-fault-us-secular-groups-set-tone-for-terror-attacks.html?scp = 3&sq = Pat+ Robertson & st = nyt.

Pearson, Michael. 2012. "Episcopal Church Approves Same-Sex Blessing Service." CNN, July 10. Accessed December 30, 2012. http://www.cnn.com/2012/07/10/us/episcopal-same-sex-unions/index.html.

People for the American Way. 2007. "Right Wing Organization: American Family Association." July 4. Accessed December 18, 2013, http://www.rightwingwatch.org/content/american-family-association.

Polaski, Adam. 2012. "Win More States Fund Reaches $3 Million Goal for Investment in State Campaigns." Freedom to Marry, August 13. Accessed December 25, 2012. http://www.freedomtomarry.org/blog/entry/win-more-states-fund-reaches-3-million-goal-for-investment-in-state-campaig.

Positive Alternatives to Homosexuality (P.A.T.H.). 2002. "Diverse Coalition Forms to Support People Seeking 'Non-Gay' Alternatives to Unwanted Homosexuality," news release, July 8. Accessed December 29, 2012. http://www.pathinfo.org/support-coalition-forms.html.

Reconciling Ministries Network. 2013. "About Reconciling Ministries Network." Accessed January 2, 2013. http://www.rmnetwork.org/about-us/.

Republican National Committee. 2012. "Republican Platform." Accessed January 2, 2013. http://www.gop.com/2012-republican-platform_home/.

Riley, Jennifer. 2011. "Natalie Portman, Fiancé Millepied Push President Obama for Gay Marriage." *Christian Post*, June 9. Accessed December 18, 2013. http://www.christianpost.com/news/natalie-portman-fiance benjamin-millepied-push-for-gay-marriage-51008/.

Robinson, B. A. 2012. "Lesbian, Gay, and Bisexual Issues." Ontario Consultants on Religious Tolerance. Accessed December 24, 2012. http://www.religioustolerance.org/homosexu.htm.

Schatz, Amy. 2010. "FCC Proposes Fine against Fox TV over 'American Dad.'" *Wall Street Journal*, June 3. Accessed December 27, 2013, http://online.wsj.com/news/articles/SB10001424052748704025304575284973263018094.

Schlatter, Evelyn. 2010. "18 Anti-Gay Groups and Their Propaganda." *Intelligence Report* (Southern Poverty Law Center), Winter (140). Accessed January 5, 2013. http://splcenter.org/get-informed/intelligence-report/browse-all-issues/2010/winter/the-hard-liners.

Smid, John J. 2010. "A Letter of Apology." Accessed December 29, 2012. http://www.gracerivers.com/apology/.

Southern Baptist Convention. 2012. "Basic Beliefs." Accessed December 28, 2012. http://www.sbc.net/aboutus/basicbeliefs.asp.

Southern Poverty Law Center. 2013. "American Family Association." Accessed January 5, 2013. http://www.splcenter.org/get-informed/intelligence-files/groups/american-family-association.

"Statement of Apology from Former Exodus Leaders Darlene Bogle, Michael Bussee, and Jeremy Marks." 2007. Beyond Ex-Gay, June 27. Accessed December 29, 2012. http://www.beyondexgay.com/article/apology.html.

Stonewall Democrats. 2013. "Who We Are," Accessed January 2, 2013. http://www.stonewalldemocrats.org/about/who.

The Church of England. 2012. "Same-Sex Marriage." Accessed December 30, 2012. http://www.churchofengland.org/our-views/marriage,-family-and-sexuality-issues/same-sex-marriage.aspx.

Tolle, Cameron. 2012. "Democrats: Say I Do." Freedom to Marry, February 13. Accessed December 25, 2012. http://www.freedomtomarry.org/blog/entry/democrats-say-i-do.

Truth Wins Out. 2012. "History of the Ex-Gay Ministries." Accessed December 30, 2012. http://www.truthwinsout.org/history-of-the-ex-gay-ministries/.

United Church of Christ. 2005. "In Support of Equal Marriage Rights for All." July 4. Accessed January 2, 2013. http://www.ucc.org/assets/pdfs/in-support-of-equal-marriage-rights-for-all-with-background.pdf.

United Church of Christ. 2013. "LGBT Ministries." Accessed January 2, 2013. http://www.ucc.org/lgbt/.

United Pentecostal Church International. 2011. "Homosexuality." Accessed December 28, 2012. http://www.upci.org/resources/instructional-devotional-leadership/75-homosexuality.

United States Conference of Catholic Bishops. 2012. Accessed December 28, 2012. http://www.usccb.org/.

Westboro Baptist Church. 2012. Accessed December 28, 2012. http://www.godhates fags.com/.

Wisconsin Evangelical Lutheran Synod. 2012. "Statement On Homosexuality." Accessed December 28, 2012. http://www.wels.net/about-wels/doctrinal-statements/homosexuality.

Wyatt-Nichol, Heather, and Lorenda Ann Naylor. 2013. "The Policy Landscape of Sexual Orientation." *Journal of Public Management and Social Policy* 19(1): 5–18. Accessed August 30, 2013. http://oied.ncsu.edu/selc/wp-content/uploads/2013/03/Policy-Landscape-of-Sexual-Orientation.pdf.

Zaimov, Stoyan. 2013. "African Anglicans Say Gay Bishops Affirmation 'Shatters Hopes of Reconciliation.'" *Christian Post*, January 10. Accessed January 12, 2013. http://www.christianpost.com/news/african-anglicans-say-gay-bishops-affirmation-shatters-hopes-of-reconciliation-88038/.

Chapter 5

An Introduction to the Battleground States

Wallace Swan

When this book was initially visualized, the goal was to contrast a state that could win a ballot measure with one that would most likely not win such a vote. Two states were chosen: Minnesota and North Carolina. Minnesota was chosen because the Minnesota legislature had passed a bill that would put into the state constitution language that would limit marriage to an arrangement that included only a man and a woman. There was no prohibition upon other types of relationships (e.g., civil unions and domestic partnerships). In 1993, Minnesota had included language in its laws that provided human rights protection to lesbian, gay, bisexual, and transgender (LGBT) people. One significant result of the passage of the human rights protection was that the state had had years to develop a supportive statewide infrastructure. The result of this was the immediate development of a coalition called "Minnesotans United for All Families," once the constitutional amendment proposal was passed by the legislature. This coalition included well over 600 signatory organizations from all over the state. It became a fund-raising effort that raised very large amounts of money, and designed innovative internet and television ads that challenged the message that had won elections in other states.

North Carolina was chosen because it was the last state in the South to anticipate having language placed in the state constitution not only limiting marriage to relationships with a man and a woman, but also prohibiting a number of legal relationships that might be designed to circumvent this limitation (e.g., domestic partnerships and civil unions). North Carolina had not gone through the process of statewide recognition of LGBT rights, except in a few progressive enclaves.

U.S. President Barak Obama, had declared his support for same-sex marriage immediately after the North Carolina electorate approved the same-sex marriage (and relationship) limitation.

Three other states (Maine, Washington, and Maryland) also had the issue of same-sex marriage on the docket for consideration at the November 6, 2012 election. Each of them was a bit different:

Washington—This state held a Same Sex Marriage Referendum (Referendum 74), in which voters were asked whether they supported the action of the Washington State legislature (ratified by the governor) to allow same-sex marriages in the state. This referendum received 1,659,915 "Yes" votes and 1,431,285 "No" votes (*Ballotpedia* "Washington" 2012).

Maryland—Same-sex marriage had originally been incorporated in the Civil Marriage Protection Act of 2012, which allowed all couples to receive a civil marriage license; and ensured that clergy would not be required to perform such ceremonies. But then opponents initiated a veto referendum. The vote on this was 1,374,504 "Yes" and 1,246,045 "No" (*Ballotpedia* "Maryland" 2012).

Maine—This state had a considerably different proposal, the Maine Same-Sex Marriage Question, or Question 1, which obviated a 2009 ballot measure prohibiting same-sex marriage. The 2009 ballot measure had been initiated by those who were opposed to a state law allowing it (*Ballotpedia* "Maine" 2012).

In the end, Minnesota disapproved of the proposal to limit marriage to a couple comprised of a man and woman; Washington approved the action of the legislature and the governor; Maryland voters approved of civil marriage for all couples; and Maine approved of same-sex marriage. Only North Carolina limited marriage to a man and a woman (and disapproved of similar legal relationships). As a result, the momentum increased for same-sex marriage. "A rapid shift in public opinion is bolstering their cause" (Eckholm 2012, A1). As is sometimes the case, newspaper accounts miss the more complex context of political decision making. For example, in Minnesota when the newly elected Senate Majority Leader Senator Tom Bakk spoke about priorities for a new Minnesota legislature, he said that "he did not interpret the results of this week's marriage amendment vote as a message from voters that they want same-sex marriage legalized in Minnesota" (Weber and Dunbar 2012). He was perhaps swayed by the fact that of the 87 counties in Minnesota, 75 of them voted to pass the Marriage Amendment. The same care needs to be taken with the assumption that disempowered states will soon have both human rights as well as gay marriage. The 18 states that now have same-sex marriage would seem to represent the "low-hanging fruit"; that is, so-called blue states where sentiment might begin to be ready for this change. But this point especially applies to the remaining constitutional amendments and statutes in states where there is not only no same-sex marriage, but there are also no LGBT human rights laws, enumerated anti-bullying provisions, no LGBT hate crimes laws, or other laws relating to protecting the rights of LGBT citizens. These states are not only Southern, but they are Western, Central, Rust Belt, and Mountain states; and they have somewhat different demographic, social, and political characteristics. Take for instance the example of two Kansas cities that repealed their nondiscrimination regulations regarding LGBT citizens, "after which Secretary of State Kris Kobach said that those who don't like the state's conservative bent can move elsewhere" ("Kansas Secretary of State" 2012).

Similarly the National Organization for Marriage indicated that it plans to initiate such an amendment (and win it) in Indiana within the next few years. And leaders of Evangelical and Catholic churches "are comparing it to the fight against legal abortion" (Eckholm 2012, A15). The battle has only just begun. It will be fought in legislative chambers, state courts, federal district courts, and finally the halls of the United States Supreme Court again in the near future.

References

Ballotpedia. "Maine, Same-Sex Marriage, Question 1 (2012)." http://ballotpedia.org/wiki/index.php/Maine_Same-Sex_Marriage_Question,_Question_1_(2012).

Ballotpedia. "Maryland Same-Sex Civil Marriage Referendum, Question 6 (2012)." http://ballotpedia.org/wiki/index.php/Maryland_Same-Sex_Marriage_Referendum_(2012).

Ballotpedia. "Washington Same-Sex Marriage Veto Referendum, Referendum 74 (2012)." http://ballotpedia.org/wiki/index.php/Washington_Same-Sex_Marriage_Veto_Referendum,_Referendum_74_(2012).

Eckholm, Erik. 2012. "Push Expands for Legalizing Gay Marriage." *New York Times*, November 13.

"Kansas Secretary of State Says Gays Are Free to Leave." 2012. *Gay Politics Report*, November 13.

Weber, Tom, and Elizabeth Dunbar. 2012. "Bakk: Amendment Vote Was Not a Mandate to Legalize Same-Sex Marriage," MPR News, *The Daily Circuit*, November 13.

Chapter 6

Battleground State: Minnesota

Beth Bibus

Contents

Constitutional Amendment 1: Recognition of Marriage Solely Between One Man and One Woman

Ballot Question: "Shall the Minnesota Constitution be amended to provide that only a union of one man and one woman shall be valid or recognized as a marriage in Minnesota?"

At around 1:30 AM on November 7, 2012, the campaign director of Minnesotans United for All Families, Richard Carlbom, addressed a room full of supporters at St. Paul Minnesota's RiverCentre (Demko 2012a). As he began his remarks, the outcome of the election was uncertain: though votes in favor of the ballot measure had been running less than 50% all evening (Demko 2012a), it was still too close to call. A video posted on YouTube shows Carlbom standing at the front of the room, thanking volunteers and employees for all of their work during the campaign, and promising them that there would be news in the morning: "I want you to go to bed tonight, and I want you to be very very proud of the result we have ..." A voice interrupts him: "Hey, Richard! The AP has called it!" "HAH!" a jubilant Richard Carlbom raises his hands above his head, the crowd erupts in a mix of laughter, shouts, and audible crying, and the camera operator forgets he is recording, as evidenced by the recording of sideways and upside-down shots of people's pants (author's summary of video posted by Carpenter 2012). This video, shared widely via social media, captured the emotions of the campaign to defeat Constitutional Amendment #1 in 2012.

As the votes were counted into the early morning hours of November 7, 2012, it became clear that Minnesota voters had become the first in the United States of America to reject a proposed constitutional amendment to define marriage as being between one man and one woman, effectively banning same-sex marriage. In 30 other states, from Alaska to Utah, similar amendments were considered by voters in other years, and the outcomes were the same, time and time again: voters supported constitutional amendments defining marriage as being between one man and one woman.

Indeed, the history of lesbian, gay, bisexual, and transgender (LGBT) rights at the hands of direct democracy had been bleak in general in the United States. In the comprehensive book *Gay Rights at the Ballot Box*, Amy L. Stone writes that from 1974 to 2009, "counting all referendums and initiatives that made it to the ballot box, voters rejected LGBT rights in 70% of all direct legislative measures" (2010, 4). These margins did decrease over time: for example, voters increased their support of initiatives relating to domestic partnerships and marriage from an average of 31% in the 1992 to 2002 period to 46% in the 2008 to 2009 period (Stone 2010, 132).

What made Minnesota different? Certainly, 2012 was a different year for LGBT rights than previous election cycles: Maine, Maryland, and Washington all passed referenda that extended marriage rights to same-sex couples (Demko 2013). Minnesota, a traditionally Democratic-leaning state, was even more blue in 2012, arguably because the Republican Party ceded the territory to the Democrats: aside from ballot measures, the only statewide race was for Senate, and the Republican candidate ran a remarkably weak campaign (Bierschbach 2012a); the national Romney–Ryan campaign did not have a campaign office in Minnesota and paid limited attention to the state until the final week of the presidential campaign (Scheck 2012).

National Organization of Marriage President Brian Brown urged his followers to disregard the 2012 results for LGBT people, saying, "Americans remain strongly in favor of marriage as the union of one man and one woman. The election results reflect the political and funding advantages our opponents enjoyed in these very liberal states" (Brown 2012). In a way, Brown is harkening to the theme of this book, suggesting that there is a significant divide in this country, a divide that plays out in terms of expanded or contracted rights for LGBT people. When we ask why Minnesota is different the short answer could be: Minnesota just fell into the pro-LGBT side of this divide, becoming an empowered state among other empowered states in the northern United States.

In this chapter, however, I argue that Minnesota has been and remains a battleground state, as the term is defined in this book.* Several factors led Minnesota to reject the marriage amendment, and I argue here that among them is a strong LGBT political and social movement that has developed over decades. The actions of LGBT people and their allies can tip the scales of a battleground state in favor of empowerment for LGBT people, and they did so in Minnesota in 2012. Following the work of Amy Stone (2010), who links social movements and ballot campaigns, I trace the growth of Minnesota's LGBT social movement (along with the concurrent growth of the religious right) and credit Minnesotans United for All Families with a strong ballot campaign. In this effort, I hope to point to reasons why the outcome of Minnesota's amendment battle was different than the battle in North Carolina and other states.

In focusing on the connection between the well-developed LGBT social movement in Minnesota and the successful defeat of the constitutional amendment, I am not arguing that there is anything deterministic about the connection between the empowerment generated by a social movement and a campaign victory. A quick recollection of California's Proposition 8 loss would dispel any illusions of determinism. Rather, I argue that Minnesota's amendment campaign success was a combination of good luck, movement and community readiness, and excellent campaign work.

Part of that good luck was a matter of timing: According to research from the Pew Research Center, 2012 marks the point at which the polling percentages reversed, from a historic trend of more people opposing same-sex marriage, to more people in favor of extending marriage rights (48% in favor to 43% opposed) (Pew Research Center, Pew Forum on Religion and Public Life 2012). The Midwest overall, however, remains "more evenly divided" according to Pew Research, with 46% of people surveyed favoring gay and lesbian access to marriage, and 44% opposing; notably, this represents a 14% increase since 2003 (Pew Research Center for the People and the Press 2012). As explored further in a later segment of this chapter, the polling data in Minnesota regarding the amendment was close to 50–50 in the

* Minnesota has not been a battleground in terms of ballot initiatives, as defined by Stone (2010).

weeks leading up to the election, in keeping with this Midwestern trend. So, good timing regarding public opinion alone cannot explain the success of the campaign to defeat the amendment.

Clearly, the presence of LGBT people and organizations in Minnesota played an important part in defeating the amendment. Minnesota has a sizable LGBT community: The Williams Institute estimates that there are more than 175,000 lesbian and gay people living in Minnesota (Romero et al. 2008, using 2005 data), and there are more than 10,000 same-sex couples across the state (Gates and Cooke ca 2011, using 2010 data). The LGBT community in the Twin Cities hosts one of the largest Pride festivals in the country (Friedman 2012; Van Cleve 2012), with weekend activities drawing hundreds of thousands of people.* Minneapolis has been called "the San Francisco of the wheat belt" (a phrase initially meant negatively, but later used as a humorous title) (Hicks 2004).

The existence of same-sex couples, going about their own lives, helps straight people see LGBT people as "normal" (a tendency positively exploited in advertisements used in the campaign, such as Minnesotans United's advertisement showing a heterosexual suburban couple talking about their lesbian neighbors; see Demko 2012c). Although there are certainly other social, political, and demographic factors at play, there is an interesting correlation between the presence of same-sex couples and amendment voting patterns within Minnesota counties. Of the 15 counties with the largest proportion of same-sex couples (with proportions ranging from 1 same-sex couple per 1,000 households to 11 couples per 1,000 households), 8 counties voted against the amendment. This is significant because the amendment prevailed in 75 of 87 Minnesota counties. Of the 12 counties voting against the amendment, the majority of these counties had more than 3 same-sex couples per 1,000 households.† Of course, many Minnesota voters within counties where there are relatively few same-sex couples *also* opposed the amendment, so the mere existence of gay individuals and families does not explain the vote-no campaign's success.

Another notable difference between Minnesota and most other states where amendments have prevailed is that Minnesota has a state-wide Human Rights Act that includes coverage of LGBT people.‡ LGBT people and allies have frequently used the Minnesota Human Rights Act. From July 1993 to June 2012, the Minnesota Department of Human Rights received over 600 charges of sexual orientation discrimination, which represents about 3% of all charges filed during this period.§ The allegations in these cases range from employment cases involving job loss,

* High-end estimates range from 300,000 (Shenoy 2012) to 400,000 people (Hicks 2004).

† County demographic data from The Williams Institute, adjusting data from Census 2010 (Gates and Cooke ca 2011). County voting data from Minnesota Secretary of State (2012b).

‡ A review of maps developed by the Human Rights Campaign (2012) indicates that only five states that have passed marriage restriction amendments have statewide protections in areas such as employment, housing, and education.

§ Data for state fiscal years 1994 through 2012 obtained through public data request to the Minnesota Department of Human Rights, October 2012.

to housing cases involving refusal to rent, to education cases involving harassment (based on actual or perceived LGBT status), to cases involving stigma against people with HIV/AIDS, to cases involving gender identification in the workplace (such as name tags and restroom use). As with other charges investigated by civil rights enforcement agencies, relatively few of these charges result in a finding of discrimination, but the presence of civil law protections helps prevent and address discrimination.

I contend that the social movement that passed this statewide civil rights law two decades ago and fought to keep it in place, along with the safety that this law gave to LGBT people to come out in their workplaces and communities (and the subsequent familiarity and connections that straight people have with LGBT people) contributed to the rejection of the amendment. I therefore spend a large share of this chapter focusing on the development of the LGBT social movement in Minnesota.

Movement alone is not enough to win, of course, so this chapter also focuses on the campaign itself.* As scholar Amy Stone pointed out in a blog post soon after the November 2012 election, some primary reasons for the success of the campaigns in Minnesota and the other three states are "[h]uge [c]ampaigns" (in relatively small population states), "[l]earning from [p]ast [c]ampaigns" (including "sophisticated canvassing models through projects like Vote For Equality"), and "[p]ublic [o]pinion" (Stone 2012).

In the concluding section of this chapter, I outline the future battlegrounds for LGBT people in Minnesota.

Minnesota: North Star State

Minnesota is, both geographically and historically, a "transition zone," (Gilman 2000, 1) with connections ranging from the North Woods' lumber and mining industries, to the shipping and trading facilitated by Lake Superior and the Mississippi River, to the agricultural lands now dominated by corn and soybean production, to banking and finance companies. Minnesota also has long histories of leftist political movements, civil rights movements (including Native American, African American, and Latino movements) and countercultural social movements, as well as socially conservative religious and conservative movements (Gilman 2000).

Minnesota is no stranger to political wrangling and close electoral contests. As one example, in 1962, the gubernatorial race was so close that it took months to determine the victor. The incumbent at the time kept his office until the outcome was known, but he also made space in the capitol for his opponent and kept him informed of state business until all the ballots were counted (Gilman 2000). Decades later, the drawn-out recount process involving senatorial candidates

* Other, more comprehensive studies of the Minnesota campaign will no doubt be published in the future; my aim in this chapter is to hit the high points that appear to have led to the campaign's success.

Norm Coleman (the incumbent) and Al Franken (a comedian who had never held elected office) drew national attention (Carr 2009).

Students of Minnesota politics are familiar with traits that make Minnesota stand out, including an active citizenry, commitment to clean government, and high voter turnout—elements of what Elazar, Gray, and Spano (1999) consider a moralistic political culture. "Minnesota leads the nation in civic engagement when a variety of measures, from voting levels and volunteering to involvement in neighborhood problem-solving and charitable contributions, are taken into account" (Boyt 2012, para. 1). Minnesota historically "has tended to deviate from national voting patterns" (Elazar et al. 1999, 21), which is demonstrated by its third-party predilections including the election of Jesse Ventura in 1998 as just one example (Elazar et al. 1999; also see Carr 2009).

These aspects of Minnesota's political and social culture are evident in the 2012 amendment campaign and outcome: voter turnout was high, and voters bucked the national trend in favor of amendments.

A Brief History of LGBT Social Movements and Civil Rights Initiatives in the North Star State

This section and the next, while focusing on the development of LGBT social movements, will also highlight how anti-LGBT groups changed and modified their tactics and strategies in defensive or offensive ways. As Amy Stone (2010) points out, historically, "As a social movement tries a new tactic, counter movements would neutralize that tactic with 'effective tactical counters' requiring the movement to engage in a new round of tactical innovation" (p. xxiii, quoting Doug McAdam 1983). This section is not at all intended as a thoroughgoing history of LGBT people in Minnesota; rather, I am highlighting significant areas of growth of the LGBT movement and significant conflicts with the movement and countermovements.

Minnesota's early history contains examples of LGBT people (though those terms are of course problematic when discussing historic events and people): from Native American two-spirit people, to a biological woman who lived as a man in Meeker County, to a possibly gay governor, to visits from gay literary icons in the state's early history (Van Cleve 2012).

By the mid-20th century, gay people had established forms of community, especially in the Twin Cities, where a few bars welcomed or tolerated the presence of queer people—mostly men (Van Cleve 2012). As Amy Tyson's (2010) examination of oral histories reveals, perspectives of local residents differed regarding police attention toward gay bars in the 1950s; the overall theme, however, was that police rarely raided gay bars, and certainly not at the scale seen in other communities in the United States. Local law enforcement did take action (some overt, some negotiated) to curb the presence of cross-dressing cabaret acts in Minneapolis and St. Paul (Tyson 2010). During this period, public debate (in the form of letters to the editor of a local newspaper) indicates that some Minnesotans, consistent with the liberalism forming at the time, were viewing gays and lesbians as minorities, not to be ridiculed but perhaps tolerated (Tyson 2010).

By the late 1960s—and before Stonewall—the Twin Cities had an established (and sometimes relatively out) gay and lesbian community, as collected oral histories reveal (Murphy 2010). In 1967, the Minneapolis-based publishing company Directory Services Incorporated (which distributed gay-oriented periodicals and merchandise) fought charges brought under the anti-obscenity Comstock laws and won, leading the path to the repeal of these types of laws (Van Cleve 2012). The University of Minnesota-based group FREE (Fight Repression of Erotic Expression) formed in spring 1969 and gained prominence, and one of its members—Jack Baker—was later elected student body president (Murphy 2010; Van Cleve 2012; Hanson 2009).*

Jack Baker and his partner Michael McConnell went on to file the landmark case for marriage equality after their application for a marriage license was denied by county officials in 1970. Their case, *Baker v Nelson*, was rejected by the Minnesota courts, and the United States Supreme Court refused to hear the case (Hanson 2009; Minnesota Legislative Reference Library [MLRL] 2012). In what was to be a harbinger of community divisions to come, some gay rights supporters of the time opposed the couple's actions, fearing that the traction gay rights had been gaining with the mainstream community would be lost by the actions of the "lunatic fringe" (Van Cleve 2012, 86, quoting then-closeted state politician Allan Spear). Baker and McConnell both experienced repercussions from the mainstream community for their actions: Baker had to fight to take the bar examination in Minnesota, and the University of Minnesota rescinded an employment offer to McConnell (Hanson 2009). In 1971, a bill was introduced in the Minnesota legislature to define marriage as being between a man and woman; the bill did not pass (MLRL 2012).

In the early and mid-1970s, the LGBT movement developed both politically and socially. The first proposal at the state legislature to include protection for gays and lesbians in the Human Rights Act was introduced in 1972 (Van Cleve 2012). In 1974, state Senator Allan Spear became one of the first elected officials in the United States to come out of the closet. Along with Spear, Steve Endean, who later founded the national Human Rights Campaign, and Jean-Nickolas Tretter, who serves as the Twin Cities' gay community's archivist and historian, founded what later became the Minnesota Committee for Gay and Lesbian Rights and advanced grassroots organizing of gays and lesbians at a statewide level (Van Cleve 2012).

Also in 1974, both Minneapolis and St. Paul (the largest cities at the time) passed civil rights ordinances without much fanfare or initial opposition (Hanson 2009; Van Cleve 2012). In Minneapolis, the Minnesota Civil Liberties Union helped lobby for the ordinance, and grassroots organizing of LGBT people convinced

* Hanson (2009) notes that this was possibly the first time in the United States that an out gay person was elected president of the student body.

the City Council to adopt the ordinance (Hanson 2009). Similarly, in St. Paul, grassroots organizing and lobbying from LGBT people helped move the ordinance (Hanson 2009); the City Council vote was 5–1 (Van Cleve 2012).

Social movement gains during this period also included developments outside of the overtly political sphere. As one example, the annual Pride festival and march became more established, and the 1973 pride guide even invited non-gays to attend the festival (Van Cleve 2012). Faith communities also developed: Dignity Twin Cities, an organization dedicated to challenging the Catholic Church's teaching that homosexuality is a sin and to provide support to gay and lesbian Catholics, formed in 1974 (Van Cleve 2012). Minnesota's first gay church was established in 1974 as a congregation of the Metropolitan Community Church (Van Cleve 2012).

Gains during this period were not confined to the Twin Cities metropolitan area. Also in the mid-1970s, Mankato State College (a school located in southern Minnesota, now known as Minnesota State University, Mankato) housed the efforts of Jim Chalgren, an advocate for gay consciousness raising and community building (Van Cleve 2012). Statewide efforts were complimented by local organizations, such as the Lesbian Feminist Organizing Committee, which gained ground in Minneapolis neighborhoods and in parts of Greater Minnesota (Van Cleve 2012).

Early tensions in the LGBT community involved whether the movement should be mainstream and work for political and social inclusion, or whether gay power and gay pride should be aligned with counterculture movements of the time (Hicks 2004).

On a national level, progress on gay rights was triggering a backlash among social conservatives; the most prominent example of which is the infamous Miami-Dade County referendum fight in 1977. After her success in Florida, Anita Bryant served as the spokesperson (and her ministries a funding source) for several other initiatives, including ones in Kansas, Oregon, and St. Paul, Minnesota (Stone 2010). Bryant's Save Our Children campaign visited Minnesota to urge repeal of the St. Paul civil rights ordinance (Murphy and Urquart 2010). Bryant's visit to Minnesota was ostensibly to mark the opening of a fruit plant in Minneapolis; local gay activists marked the occasion by calling a National Fruit Day and holding the largest gay and lesbian rally of the time (Van Cleve 2012).

Local social conservatives were also developing a strong social movement during this period. In 1977, Catholic diocese lobbyists were a significant factor in the defeat of a gay rights bill proposed at the state legislature (Van Cleve 2012). During that same session, the Minnesota legislature added a provision to the civil law definition of marriage to specify that marriage is between a man and a woman (MLRL 2012).

In 1978, an organization called Citizens Alert for Morality effectively collected enough signatures to put the St. Paul civil rights ordinance to a vote (Van Cleve 2012).*

* The Minneapolis ordinance was saved from this type of ballot initiative backlash because the Minneapolis charter did not allow for referenda (Hanson 2009).

A Baptist minister, the leader of the campaign, organized leaders in other congregations (Catholic, Protestant, and Jewish) to support overturning the ordinance (Hanson 2009). The gay reaction to this effort, though significant (Hanson 2009), was hindered by the organizational challenges and infighting of the three primary organizations involved in the campaign: Target City Coalition, St. Paul Citizens for Human Rights, and the Minnesota Committee for Gay Rights (Van Cleve 2012). The April 1978 vote to repeal surprised local activists (Van Cleve 2012); the margin of victory for repeal was 2 to 1 (Hanson 2009). This repeal was one of the first public referendums to overturn a civil rights law that extended protection to gay people (Stone 2010). Though advocates appealed the legitimacy of this referendum, the Minnesota Supreme Court upheld the election results (Hanson 2009).

The social conservative movement continued to grow into the early 1980s. In 1982–1983, the Berean League was formed as a coalition of a number of prominent fundamentalist Christian ministers and activists. In its early years, the group focused on preventing the expansion of rights to LGBT people, maintaining the state's sodomy law, and combating pornography (Birkey 2008; Van Cleve 2012; also Diaz 1991).

As Stuart Van Cleve notes, many of Minnesota's first gay and lesbian organizations struggled in the late 1970s, and "[b]y 1982, few of the pioneering community organizations remained" (2012, 234). By 1985–86, the social services organization Lesbian and Gay Community services had ceased operations (Hanson 2009; Van Cleve 2012). It was not until the community coalesced around the AIDS crisis that momentum in the movement gathered strength again (Hicks 2004; Van Cleve 2012).

By the early 1980s, existing tensions in the gay community were becoming more apparent, particularly between some lesbians and gay men who saw themselves on contradictory sides in public protests and debates about pornography: some lesbian feminists supported anti-pornography ordinances and crackdowns on adult bookstores and theaters, while many gay men saw these efforts as contributing to their oppression by police (Butler 2010). For example, tensions in the Minnesota Gay and Lesbian Legal Assistance organization ranged from backlash against a lesbian leader's insistence on setting higher event ticket prices for white men because of their relative higher income, to disagreements about using funds for a guardianship case involving a lesbian couple versus using funds to defend gay men who had been arrested in police raids (Hanson 2009). These tensions in the community were most publicly displayed in organizing of 1982 Pride celebrations, when the organizing committee voted to exclude the word "lesbian" from festival materials; in response, lesbians organized a separate festival in another part of Minneapolis (Butler 2010). Though these tensions did not go away entirely, gays and lesbians came together in coalitions to respond to the HIV/AIDS crisis and growing social conservative backlash against LGBT people (Butler 2010).

During this same time period (the late 1970s into the mid-'80s), over 40 members of the Twin Cities gay community were homicide victims, and some crimes had overt connections to anti-gay sentiments (Murphy and Urquart 2010). As Murphy and Urquart (2010) point out, the police directed more attention to raiding bathhouses than investigating anti-gay violence; between 1979 and 1985, 5,000 people were arrested, mostly for alleged violations of indecency laws (also see Hanson, 2009, for more details on these arrests).

There were some advances in the early 1980s. For example, the organization Minnesota Gay and Lesbian Legal Assistance worked to draw attention to the unfairness of police raids on bathhouses, offered legal representation to gay men who had been arrested during these raids or in bookstores, and drew attention to media representations of gays and lesbians (Hanson 2009). In 1981, efforts to repeal the state's sodomy law were stalled at the legislature, but these efforts continued the conversation about the harmful aspects of these kinds of laws (Hanson 2009). In 1981, local activists successfully sued the City of Minneapolis to allow a permit to hold a block party in downtown Minneapolis during the Pride festival (Hanson 2009). In 1983, the LGBT community and its allies promoted legislation to add protections for gays and lesbians in the state's human rights law and to increase penalties against vandals if they were motivated by bias against gays or other minorities; again, though the legislation did not pass, the conversations continued (Hanson 2009). Also in 1983, the Minnesota AIDS Project formed and went on to become a significant force in the development of the LGBT social and political movements (Hanson 2009).

Much of the LGBT community's work in the mid- and late 1980s involved HIV/AIDS, including successful efforts to block Department of Health legislation that would have allowed quarantining of people with AIDS (Hanson 2009). Work continued, however, on passing legislation that would help LGBT people. Advocates for LGBT people formed the Gay and Lesbian Community Action Council (GLCAC) in 1987, joining the existing, but struggling, Minnesota Gay and Lesbian Legal Assistance and the Minnesota Civil Liberties Union as active organizations working to promote gay rights (Hanson 2009). The GLCAC was founded with funding from Hennepin County and the United Way to provide community services (OutFront ca 2007). GLCAC provided a helpline for LGBT people in crisis, provided services for crime victims, offered a referral list for services (such as housing and medical services), and led public policy advocacy (OutFront ca 2007).

In 1987, two LGBT lawmakers introduced a bill (which did not become law) that would at the same time decriminalize sodomy and add to the criminal code a prohibition on "public sex" (Murphy and Urquart 2010, 74). Attempts to pass the law included a coalition of civil liberties and gay rights advocates (Bently 1998).* This same year, the Minnesota Supreme Court rejected the argument that the sodomy law violated constitutional privacy principles (Hanson 2009); the case hinged on

* Metro Edition.

the conduct of a young male prostitute, and there were indications that the court might have held differently if the case involved consenting adults in private (Diaz 1991). Work to pass domestic partner benefits in the city of Minneapolis began and then stalled during this period. In 1989, a City Council candidate suggested that domestic partner benefits for city workers could be tied to a ban on cruising in a major city park; that effort also failed, in part due to the work of queer activists opposed to the cruising ban (Murphy and Urquart 2010).

Work also continued in Greater Minnesota. For example, in 1987, efforts to add protections for LGBT people in city ordinance in Mankato (a relatively small college town in southern Minnesota) were unsuccessful (Van Cleve 2012). In the early 1990s, the LGBT community in northeast Minnesota established the Northland Gay Men's Center in Duluth, a complement to the existing Aurora Northland Lesbian Center (Van Cleve 2012).

In 1990, St. Paul's City Council again passed an ordinance adding sexual orientation to civil rights protections (Van Cleve 2012). The 1991 ballot campaign in St. Paul was viewed as a test of the LGBT community's strength. This was the third ballot initiative the LGBT community had faced in St. Paul, and it won (Stone 2010). The campaign chair credited the get-out-the-vote efforts, including voter identification and phone banks (Stone 2010).

Members of the LGBT community saw the success in St. Paul as an indication of a possible opportunity for statewide civil rights legislation (Milton 2010). In 1990, Governor Rudy Perpich authorized a task force on gay rights, which met in communities across the state to hear from gays and lesbians; one of the recommendations in the final report was to amend the state's laws to include protections for gays and lesbians (Milton 2010) and to repeal the state's sodomy law (Diaz 1991). In 1991, Governor Arne Carlson* extended the work of the group with a second task force, which concluded that there should be explicit protection for bisexual and transgender people in the law as well (Milton 2010). Governor Carlson also signed executive orders prohibiting discrimination against state workers who were lesbian or gay (Diaz 1991).

The year 1991 also marked the end of the Sharon Kowalski case, which was a protracted legal battle involving partnership rights for a lesbian couple, one of whom was significantly injured in a car accident (Hanson 2009). Ultimately, the Minnesota Court of Appeals held that Kowalski's partner Karen Thompson was her legal guardian, despite Kowalski's parents' objections. In the context of the time, when "partners of ailing gay men [with AIDS] were struggling to secure visitation rights from homophobic parents," this was a significant victory (Van Cleve 2012, 105).

---

* Republican Governor Arne Carlson was among the cohort of moderate Republicans in state politics who "struck an uneasy balance between fiscal conservatism and a relatively liberal stand on social issues" (Gilman 2000, 22).

Work of LGBT organizers and lobbyists finally culminated in 1993, with the landmark passage of a bill to include "sexual orientation" in the state's Human Rights Act, extending antidiscrimination provisions in all areas of the law, from employment, to housing, to public accommodations. Compared to previous efforts in Minnesota, proponents of gay rights consciously sought to broaden the campaign across the state, "especially beyond the Twin Cities where there were less visible clusters of support, as well as building a coalition of human rights groups, women's and minority organizations, major religious denominations, labor unions and student groups" (Milton 2010, para. 6). The Gay Lesbian Community Action Council coordinated a strong statewide campaign, "It's Time Minnesota" (OutFront ca 2007).

During debate on the bill, Senator Allan Spear argued that the civil rights protections would not affect the definition of marriage in Minnesota, nor would the law extend any types of benefits to same-sex couples (see excerpts from debate transcript in *Lilly v. City of Minneapolis* 1995). The final version of the legislation included explicit direction for the courts in interpreting the law:

> Nothing in this chapter shall be construed to: (1) mean the state of Minnesota condones homosexuality or bisexuality or any equivalent lifestyle; (2) authorize or permit the promotion of homosexuality or bisexuality in education institutions or require the teaching in education institutions of homosexuality or bisexuality as an acceptable lifestyle; (3) authorize or permit the use of numerical goals or quotas, or other types of affirmative action programs, with respect to homosexuality or bisexuality in the administration or enforcement of the provisions of this chapter; or (4) authorize the recognition of or the right of marriage between persons of the same sex. (Minnesota Human Rights Act, 2012 Minnesota Statutes §363A.27)

Notably, across the country, the anti-gay right was increasing its activism from the 1988 to 1992 period. As Amy Stone identifies, much of this organizing was "concentrated in a few states" like Oregon and California, and there was a "growing anti-gay industry" leading efforts nationally (2010, 18–19).

In Minnesota, the Berean League changed its name to the Minnesota Family Council in 1992, "in order to align itself with two other prominent religious right organizations, James Dobson's Focus on the Family and Gary Bauer's Family Research Council" (Birkey 2008, para. 7). The group strengthened its focus in opposition to gay civil rights (Birkey 2008; Van Cleve 2012). In 1994, for example, the Minnesota Family Council supported litigation against the City of Minneapolis' extension of domestic partner benefits, which led to case law (*Lilly v. City of Minneapolis* 1995) barring any Minnesota municipality from providing this type of benefit (Birkey 2008). Also in 1994, St. Paul Mayor Norm Coleman refused to sign a gay pride proclamation and refused to approve financial support for a showing of *Angels in America,* although such financial support was common for other productions (Van Cleve 2012).

In the mid-1990s, K–12 education also became a battleground for LGBT rights in Minnesota. Both Minneapolis and St. Paul school districts launched programs for gay students, and the Minnesota Department of Education issued a pamphlet for educators on gay and lesbian issues called "Alone No More" (Rossman 1997). The Minneapolis School Board agreed to offer domestic partner benefits to public school employees and began advertising for employees in the local gay press (Rossman 1997). As with other successes, these initiatives led to push-back from social conservatives and religious right organizations, including efforts to elect religious conservatives to school board seats (Rossman 1997).

Throughout the 1990s, the LGBT movement expanded in Minnesota, and the mainstream community increasingly accepted LGBT people. As one example of this trend, in the early and mid-1990s corporations began sponsoring the Twin Cities Pride Festival at the request of organizers (Van Cleve 2012). This change sparked controversy among some LGBT activists, with one activist noting that the change in the Pride festival to a "corporate theme park" highlights the change in the LGBT movement to a more conservative, less political movement (Hicks 2004, under section 4, quoting Bob Halfhill). In the Twin Cities in the mid-1990s, gay activists were sometimes at odds with each other about whether to push for mainstream equality and assimilation into the larger community, or to continue connections with more countercultural aspects of the idealistic left (Hicks 2004).

LGBT organizations developed during this period to address pressing issues in the community. For example, to address the ongoing violence against LGBT people in downtown Minneapolis, the Queer Street Patrol modified strategies used in other cities and mobilized trained antiviolence volunteers to patrol the downtown bar scene in Minneapolis (Van Cleve 2012). The Minnesota Lavender Bar Association formed as an outgrowth of the Gay Lesbian Community Action Council in 1996, and later became a separate organization (Hanson 2009). The late 1990s also saw the continuation of the development of the LGBT social movement in Minnesota, with the 10th anniversary Two Spirit Gathering of Native Americans (hosted in Onamia, Minnesota), the growth of Black LGBT organizations and pride celebrations, expansion of bisexual organizations, and the continued success of Gays and Lesbian Elders Active in Minnesota (Van Cleve 2012).

In another setback for gay rights, in 1996, the federal government passed the Defense of Marriage Act (DOMA). This law spurred a significant amount of state-level legislation to prevent same-sex marriage. Only four states had such laws prior to DOMA; within a few years, the majority of states had passed laws to define marriage as between a man and a woman (Damore, Jelen, and Bowers 2007). Minnesota passed a version of DOMA in 1997, which defined marriage as being between a man and a woman and which prohibited marriage between people of the same sex (MLRL 2012). As noted by Amy Stone, these types of state-level antimarriage initiatives became common in the late 1990s, and they became a "winning tactic" for anti-gay activists (2010, 33).

In the late 1990s, social conservatives in Minnesota, organized by the Minnesota Family Council, focused on transgender people using public restrooms, claiming that "men" were using "women's" bathrooms. For example, in 1998, a Minneapolis Public School employee alleged that her privacy rights were violated when she saw a transgender woman in the women's restroom (Minnesota Family Council 1999). The woman filed a complaint with the Minnesota Department of Human Rights, alleging sex discrimination; her complaint was dismissed (Minnesota Family Council 1999). The rights of trans people were again questioned in *Goins* v. *West Group* (2001), in which the Minnesota Supreme Court ultimately held that it was lawful for an employer to discriminate on the basis of sex with regard to bathroom use (though the court's decision left open the possibility that a trans person could prevail in other kinds of harassment or discrimination claims under the Minnesota Human Rights Act).

In the latter part of the decade, the LGBT political movement continued to press for equality. OutFront Minnesota (the renamed GLCAC) worked during the late 1990s to expand and coordinate statewide community development (OutFront ca 2007). In 1998, several lawmakers introduced a bill to authorize same-sex marriages; the bill did not move out of a House committee, and no Senate version was offered (MLRL 2012).

Minnesota's progress on gay rights drew the attention of national social conservatives during this period. For example, as part of a nationwide strategy against LGBT candidates, anti-gay minister Fred Phelps threatened to picket the state Democratic Farmer Labor party campaign headquarters because of the candidacy of an openly gay man for state treasurer in 1997–1998 (Swan 1998). Minnesota was a stop on Phelps's "God Hate Fags" national campaign in 1998; he was met by a significant counterdemonstration (Van Cleve 2012).

In the late 1990s and into the early 2000s, there was increasing debate within the LGBT movement about whether resources and efforts should be expended in pursuing more mainstream relationship status, like same-sex marriage (Stone 2010; also see Shaiko 2007).

A Decade of Division: 2000–2010

The new century began with some good news for LGBT Minnesotans at the state level. In 2001, a group of plaintiffs (gay and straight) prevailed in a Hennepin County district court case when a judge declared the state's sodomy law to be unconstitutional (Louwagie 2001a). The plaintiffs successfully sought class action status so that the ruling would extend to all Minnesotans, and the state's attorney general refused to appeal the decision (Louwagie 2001b). Social conservatives unsuccessfully sought to recall the attorney general for his actions (Louwagie 2001b).

In state employee contracts negotiated in 2001, Governor Jesse Ventura's administration proposed including domestic partner benefits for state workers (Whereatt 2001). Though labor and management differed on other aspects of the contracts (so much so that the negotiations led to a two-week strike in October 2001) the only difference of opinion regarding including domestic partner benefits was whether to extend the coverage to opposite-sex couples as well as same-sex couples (Whereatt 2001). About 75 to 80 state workers took advantage of the benefits (Phelps 2003). This victory was short-lived: in 2003, Republican lawmakers introduced legislation ratifying the negotiated contracts but removing references to domestic partners (Phelps 2003). The legislation was signed by newly elected Republican Governor Tim Pawlenty, who had been a vocal opponent of domestic partner benefits (Phelps 2003). Notably, Pawlenty had voted in favor of the Human Rights Act a decade earlier; he later said he regretted that vote (Smith 2006b).

Also in 2003, conservative lawmakers attempted to remove protections for LGBT people from state law, striking the phrase "sexual orientation" from every part of Minnesota Statutes, including state's bias crime statute and human rights act (Minnesota Legislature 2003, House File 341/Senate File 545); the efforts were defeated after lobbying from OutFront Minnesota (OutFront ca 2007).

Among these victories, however, and similarly to events in previous years, the expansion of rights for LGBT people prompted reaction among social conservatives. As Amy Stone showed in her research on ballot initiatives across the country, "the largest wave of anti-marriage activity ever [was launched] in 2004," and this period was also the religious right's most successful, with constitutional amendments and more restrictive DOMAs passing in many states (2010, 34–35).

Researchers Damore, Jelen, and Bowers describe the 2003–2004 period in the United States as one of "reactionary preemption" from social conservatives: in response to states that had extended marriage or partnership rights to same-sex couples, religious social movements opposed to these unions mobilized in force to block further extension of rights to LGBT people (2007, 53). In Minnesota, the Minnesota Family Council was very active during this period, using its connections with Republican elected officials and its grassroots organizing to block sex education initiatives and to block anti-bullying legislation (Birkey 2008). The Family Council established a side project, known as Minnesota for Marriage, which aligned with the more confrontational Minnesota Citizens in Defense of Marriage to push for a constitutional amendment to ban same-sex marriage (Smith 2006a).*

In the 2000s, debate on LGBT issues in Minnesota's legislature revolved around attempts to establish a constitutional amendment to define marriage as between one man and one woman, as social conservatives attempted to block feared judicial actions that would recognize marriages from other states or allow a constitutional challenge to the Minnesota version of DOMA. In each year from 2004 to 2011, bills were introduced to create a constitutional amendment defining marriage as

* Metro Edition.

between one man and one woman (MLRL 2012). A list of these bills helps to illustrate the point that Minnesota truly became a battleground during this period (list modified from MLRL 2012, section "Legislative History"):

- 2004—Bills introduced in the House and Senate to amend the Minnesota constitution to define marriage as between a man and a woman; bill introduced in the Senate to amend the constitution to restrict the judicial branch from defining marriage.
- 2005–2006—Multiple bills introduced in the House and Senate during both sessions to amend the Minnesota constitution to define marriage as between a man and a woman; bill introduced in the Senate to amend the constitution to restrict the judicial branch from defining marriage.*
- 2007–2008—Multiple bills introduced in the House and Senate during both sessions to amend the Minnesota constitution to define marriage as between a man and a woman; bills introduced in the House and Senate to make marriage laws gender neutral.
- 2009–2010—Bills introduced in the House and Senate to make marriage laws gender neutral; bill introduced in the house to create civil union contracts; bills introduced in the House and Senate to create a marriage evaluation study group; bills introduced in the House and Senate to allow recognition of same-sex marriages from other states; multiple bills introduced in the House and Senate to amend the Minnesota constitution to define marriage as between a man and a woman.†
- 2011–2012—Multiple bills introduced in the House and Senate to amend the Minnesota constitution to define marriage as between a man and a woman (Senate File 1308 passed, and a ballot question was set for the November 2012 general election); bills introduced in the House and Senate to make marriage laws gender neutral; bills introduced to repeal the constitutional amendment bill.

The political strength of the LGBT community in Minnesota was demonstrated by its success at beating back most anti-gay efforts during this period. One measure of political growth is annual legislative citizen lobby days at the state capitol, organized by OutFront Minnesota. According to OutFront, attendance at these lobby

---

* Michelle Bachman, who gained prominence in Minnesota politics because of her efforts on these bills and other social conservative causes, drew extra attention during the 2005 legislative session because of a photograph of her apparently hiding in the bushes during an OutFront rally at the capitol and because she fled a bathroom after two lesbian constituents tried to speak with her (see Goldberg 2011).

† Though the first group of bills promoting equity or evaluation of marriage was heard in committee in 2010, the sponsors of the marriage amendment bill decided not to ask the committee chair to hold hearings on these bills that year, citing other pressing concerns (Cook 2010).

days grew from 200 in 2002 to 5,000 in 2006, making the event one of the largest such events in the country (OutFront ca 2007).

In the latter half of the decade, the LGBT community took a multipronged approach to advancing LGBT equity. While urging caution in pushing for marriage equality through litigation, groups like OutFront Minnesota and Project 515 (named after the number of Minnesota statutes that provide benefits to officially married couples) worked to expose the unfairness of existing laws (Grow 2008). OutFront pushed for local cities to establish domestic partner registries. These registries do not actually provide domestic partner benefits, but they do send a message of inclusion. There are now 19 Minnesota cities with these registries (OutFront ca. 2012). Project 515 worked to gather bipartisan support of legislation addressing inequality in Minnesota statutes, including legislation that would ensure that partners have the same rights to enact the final wishes of a deceased partner or sue in cases of wrongful death; though these bills did not pass, the group's efforts increased public awareness (Project 515 2010).

OutFront Minnesota took a leadership role in working toward protections for LGBT students during the 2000s, including working for bipartisan legislation to strengthen antiharassment laws and offering assistance to students, schools, and families who support LGBT youth (OutFront 2013). In the mid-2000s, a suburban school in Maple Grove refused to allow a gay–straight alliance group to meet on campus; the school district was forced to allow the group to meet after a protracted legal battle (Van Cleve 2012). In the late 2000s and early 2010s, the state's largest school district (Anoka-Hennepin, covering a large section of the Twin cities suburbs) came under increasing scrutiny for its policy requiring "neutrality" regarding sexual orientation, a high-profile case involving teachers who allegedly harassed a student by suggesting he was gay, and after an alarming number of students committed suicide (some of whom had been harassed for being gay) (Van Cleve 2012).

As the LGBT community grew and developed as a political and social movement during this period, tensions among community members also expanded. Marginalized groups within the LGBT community pushed back against large (corporate) LGBT events, like the Twin Cities Pride Festival. For example, in 2007, Twin Cities trans people and allies organized a march in downtown Minneapolis, highlighting differences in treatment among gays and lesbians and trans people (Van Cleve 2012).

2010–2011: Momentum for the Religious Right

The elections of 2010 surprised many local political experts: Republicans took control of both the state House and Senate, while Democrat Mark Dayton narrowly prevailed in the governor's race. Same-sex marriage played a role in that election. The National Organization of Marriage (NOM) launched a statewide television campaign in Minnesota in May 2010, spending $200,000 on television ads; NOM's president identified Minnesota as "the next key battleground state in the fight to preserve marriage" and noted that a lawsuit and legislative efforts to "redefine" marriage were already underway in Minnesota (NOM 2010b). During the gubernatorial campaign, the Archdiocese of Minneapolis and St. Paul sent 400,000 people a copy of a DVD urging Catholics to vote for Republican gubernatorial candidate Tom Emmer because of his opposition to same-sex marriage (Hawkins 2012a). NOM and the Minnesota Family Council jointly produced a radio advertisement that used audio of Martin Luther King to argue that marriage should be determined by a vote of the people, listing the dangers of gay marriage (e.g., lawsuits against people and organizations who oppose it), and advising voters that Republican gubernatorial candidate Tom Emmer supported the idea that marriage is between one man and one woman (NOM 2010c). Though its efforts to elect a conservative governor were unsuccessful, NOM took credit for conservative trends in Minnesota and other states, boasting that it spent over $2.5 million on campaigns in what they identified as key states in the 2010 election cycle (NOM 2010a). After the election, NOM noted that "Minnesota and New Hampshire are both poised to put marriage amendments on the ballot" (NOM 2010a, para. 5).

After the election, social conservatives and the LGBT movement began preparations for the next battle. In the fall of 2010, LGBT activists began planning for what they believed would come in the next legislative session: a proposal to amend Minnesota's constitution to ban same-sex marriage (Ringham and Aslanian 2012). Work was already underway on the conservative side: earlier in 2010, NOM retained campaign expert Frank Schubert to conduct polls and focus groups in Minnesota about same-sex marriage, in preparation for a later amendment proposal (Helgeson 2012).

The following legislative session was acrimonious and ultimately led to a shutdown of state government when the Republican-controlled legislature and the Democratic governor could not come to agreement on a state budget (Helgeson, Kaszuba, Roper, and Stassen-Berger 2011). Among the budget proposals rejected by Governor Dayton was the legislature's plan to cut the budget of the Minnesota Human Rights Department by 50% to 65% (Jossi 2012).

One of the most contentious debates was the renewed effort to put a constitutional variation of DOMA on the ballot for 2011. Both the Senate and House passed the bill without significant comment from legislators who supported the bill; as one observer noted, the House debate "actually wasn't a debate at all since supporters generally kept to themselves, just as the Senate did a week ago" (Collins 2011, para. 2). Throughout the House debate and vote on May 21, 2011, protesters outside the chamber rallied in opposition to the legislation; chants were audible within the chamber during the often emotional speeches by representatives opposed to the amendment (Ringham and Aslanian 2012; Van Cleve 2012).

A Republican political operative involved with the legislative effort later asserted that the amendment was an effort to motivate conservatives to get to the polls and vote for Republican candidates in 2012; his admission was not a surprise to political insiders (Boldt and Belden 2012). Minnesota for Marriage staff and Republican leaders denied his allegations (Boldt and Belden 2012).

Constitutional Amendment Campaign

Shortly after the vote in May 2011 LGBT organizers, including leaders of OutFront Minnesota and Project 515, formed the coalition Minnesotans United for All Families (Ringham and Aslanian 2012). The coalition sought to capitalize on ballot campaigns in other states, receiving guidance from an alumnus of many campaigns, David Fleischer (Ringham and Aslanian 2012). Fleischer is a veteran trainer of LGBT activists engaged in ballot initiatives, working with organizations ranging from the Gay and Lesbian Victory Fund, to National Gay and Lesbian Task Force, to the Power Summit (Stone 2010), and now as director of the Leadership Lab at the Los Angeles Gay and Lesbian Center (Ringham and Aslanian 2012). Not surprisingly, then, the ballot campaign successfully steered by Minnesotans United for All Families used many of the campaign tactics developed in successful campaigns. Amy Stone's (2010) research identified key tactics from ballot campaigns, including identifying voters, developing narrow campaign messaging, focusing on persuading voters, and using a large grassroots organizing effort to build the social movement.

On the other side of the debate, the lead organization was Minnesota for Marriage. This was a coalition of the Minnesota Family Council, the Minnesota Catholic Conference, and the National Organization for Marriage (Birkey 2011). The main organizing forces in favor of the amendment included stalwarts such as Frank Schubert, who has orchestrated every statewide marriage ballot initiative since 2008 and who was instrumental in passing California's Proposition 8 (Helgeson 2012). As in other states, Schubert's efforts included working with churches and other like-minded organizations at the grassroots level, with a plan to flood the airwaves with pro-amendment advertisements shortly before the election (Helgeson 2012).

In other similar campaigns, socially conservative religious groups have used "preexisting grassroots networks to coordinate the actions of like-minded individuals and raise the funds necessary to mount aggressive campaigns" (Damore, et al. 2007, 71). The Minnesota for Marriage campaign explicitly relied on this approach. For example, when June 2012 funding reports showed that Minnesotans United had raised about $4.6 million dollars compared to Minnesota for Marriage's $1.4 million, Minnesota for Marriage issued a press release expressing confidence that "the people of Minnesota will come together to raise the resources necessary to win and not let our state's definition of marriage be defined by activist judges or liberal out of state organizations" (Minnesota for Marriage 2012).*

After the close of the campaign, and after the votes from November 6, 2012, were tallied, the final vote showed the majority of Minnesota voters opposed the constituted amendment to ban same-sex marriage: 51.2% voted no, 47.4% voted

* Minnesotans United issued a press release at the same time, noting that 90% of individual donors during the reporting period were Minnesotans (Brickman 2012, para. 1).

yes, and 1.4% left the question blank (effectively voting no*) (Minnesota Secretary of State 2012b). Voters in urban and suburban counties tended to oppose the amendment, while voters in rural counties generally voted in favor of the amendment (Pretangelo 2012).

Over 76% of eligible Minnesota voters voted in the 2012 election (Minnesota Secretary of State 2012a). This is in sharp contrast to recent initiatives that went against LGBT people: in the 2009 Maine election, less than half of eligible voters participated; in North Carolina's May 2012 election, only about 35% of eligible people voted (Demko 2012b).

Again, I return to the question that began this chapter: What made Minnesota different? Participants in the campaign identified key factors that led to the victory: allies, faith, money, and time (Ringham and Aslanian 2012), and I use that framework here.

Allies

Minnesotans United made coalition-building a key component of its campaign effort, and the campaign frequently updated its growing coalition partner list during the months leading up to the election. By the end of the campaign, the campaign's website boasted almost 700 organizations as named coalition partners, with faith organizations, labor union and professional associations, businesses, nonprofits, neighborhood associations, educational institutions, media entities, and local governments included in the list (Minnesotans United for all Families 2012b). Though the Minnesota for Marriage campaign no doubt had many organizations in its coalition beyond the founding members named earlier, that campaign did not publish a list, and efforts by this author to find a publicly available comprehensive list were unsuccessful.

In ballot initiatives nationwide, anti-gay campaigns have used special messaging in communities of color, trying to capitalize on perceptions of white affluent gays and presenting the "Religious Right as supportive of civil rights for 'deserving' minorities" (Stone 2010, 22). Both sides of the campaign in Minnesota attempted to include communities of color in organizing efforts. In the Hmong community, for example, Minnesota for Marriage recruited a prominent Hmong businessman, the president of the Hmong Village Shopping Center, to support the amendment and to distribute literature among vendors in the mall (Aslanian 2012). Another organization, the nonprofit community organization Hmong American Partnership, supported Minnesotans United's efforts against the amendment, and the Hmong LGBT group Shades of Yellow worked with the campaign (Aslanian 2012). Minnesotans United also had a Latino outreach coordinator and used demographically targeted voter lists to focus the efforts of volunteer phone banks (Hawkins 2012d).

* To pass a constitutional amendment in Minnesota, the majority of all people voting in the election must vote in favor of the amendment. If a voter leaves the question blank, that effectively counts as a "no" vote (Demko 2012b).

Key officials took on a visible role in the amendment campaign. Minnesota's elected Secretary of State Mark Ritchie attempted to frame the ballot initiatives by naming them differently on the ballot than the legislature defined in statute (Kimball 2012b). One of the primary roles of the secretary of state is to administer elections, which includes preparing a sample ballot (Minnesota Rules 8250, subpara. 18). The original title of the amendment, as passed by the legislature, was "Recognition of marriage solely between one man and one woman." Ritchie planned to change the title on the printed ballot to "Limiting the status of marriage to opposite sex couples" and Attorney General Lori Swanson approved the change (Kimball 2012b). The Minnesota for Marriage campaign and several Republican legislators initiated a lawsuit to compel Ritchie to use the legislative title (Kimball 2012b). The Minnesota Supreme Court rejected Ritchie's change (McIntee 2012).

A public administrator who took on a visible role was Human Rights Department Commissioner Kevin Lindsey, who spoke out against both the marriage amendment and a voter identification amendment (Pugmire 2012). "Lindsey made public presentations more than 15 times across the state in opposition to both amendments" (Jossi 2012, para. 5). Republican leaders charged that Commissioner Lindsey inappropriately used his office to express political opinion and called on the legislative auditor to investigate (Pugmire 2012). Ultimately, the legislative auditor declined to investigate either Commissioner Lindsey or Secretary of State Ritchie, citing a lack of clear legal standards (Pugmire 2013).

City governments also played active roles in the campaign. Fourteen city councils passed resolutions in opposition to the amendment, including cities in the Twin Cities metropolitan area and in Greater Minnesota (Minnesotans United for All Families 2012a). Among these was Edina, a "traditionally Republican area" (Boldt and Belden 2012, sixth paragraph from the end of article).

Minnesotans United also cultivated allies among Republicans and independents (Demko 2012a). For example, Republican state Representative John Kreisel, who was one of the few Republicans who voted against the legislation to put the amendment on the ballot, lent his support to the campaign, and the campaign used video of his floor speech in one of the final advertisements of the campaign (Demko 2012a).

One somewhat surprising ally in the anti-amendment campaign was Chris Kluwe, the punter for the Minnesota Vikings football team. Kluwe became an active volunteer in the organization Minnesotans for Equality, speaking out in local and national media in favor of marriage equality (Gervino 2012). Kluwe's participation in the debate gained national attention when he responded to a Maryland legislator's call that a Baltimore Ravens linebacker (Brendon Ayanbadejo) should be prohibited (by his employer) from speaking in favor of Maryland's same-sex marriage initiative (Gervino 2012). Kluwe authored an open letter to the Maryland representative, lambasting him for his position against equity and for his attempt to use his political power to silence another person. Kluwe's letter is fairly characterized as a "profanity-laden rant," and it contained a number of "colorful" terms that were later printed on t-shirts, with proceeds going to the campaign to defeat the amendment and to Kluwe's charity for children with muscular dystrophy (Gervino 2012, para. 14 and 24). Kluwe repeated the humorous profanity in a radio advertisement, and Minnesotans for Equality purchased ad time on radio stations focusing on (in the words of an organization spokesperson) "independent, tougher skewing men ... [such as] Rock, Classic Rock, and Sports" (Buzinski 2012, para. 3). Shortly before the election, Kluwe resigned his role as contributing blogger in the local *Pioneer Press* newspaper after the editorial board took a linguistically and argumentatively strained "neutrality" position on the amendment, which Kluwe criticized as "irresponsible" and "hypocritical" (Linkins 2012, second paragraph from the end).

Other celebrities threw weight behind the campaign in Minnesota, including actor Brad Pitt, who donated a $100,000 match to the Human Rights Campaign's fundraising efforts for all four states with marriage initiatives on the ballot (Kimball 2012a).

Faith

Religious groups played a significant role on both sides of the campaign. Minnesotans United made a conscious decision to engage faith communities in the campaign, and about one-fourth of its early coalition partners were faith organizations (Hawkins 2012b). Minnesotans United hired a religious communities coordinator in March 2012, with the goal to engage religious people and organizations in discussions about marriage equality and the amendment (Hawkins 2012b). As Harry Boyte (2012) noted, none of the amendment campaigns in other states had successfully connected with faith communities—Minnesota was the first to make this a priority. The campaign's efforts were rewarded: the coalition ultimately included over 600 religious leaders (Booth 2012) and 120 named faith communities or organizations (Minnesotans United for All Families 2012b).

Although the anti-amendment side was successful in not ceding all the religious ground, many religious groups acted in favor of the amendment. In other state amendment campaigns, socially conservative religious groups overcame doctrinal differences to work in favor of constitutional amendments (Damore et al. 2007). This was no different in Minnesota, where religious leaders of "Pentecostal, Evangelical, African American, Catholic and Orthodox faith traditions" joined together to express their support of the amendment; one African American leader noted that he would have previously thought such a coalition "crazy" because the groups "differ on so many things when it comes to social justice" (Noble 2012, para. 1 and 6, quoting Reverend Jerry McAfee).

Conflict within the Catholic community was particularly visible and well-publicized in Twin Cities media. By mid-July 2012, almost 100 former Catholic priests had signed on to the Minnesotans United coalition list (Hawkins 2102c), and over 100 had signed on by late August (Hawkins 2012a). In response, the Minnesota Catholic Conference issued a statement endorsing the former priests' right to speak, but chastising them for their choice "to separate themselves from the teaching of the Catholic Church regarding marriage" and advising all current priests and deacons of their "responsibility to communicate Catholic teaching on this most fundamental matter" (Hawkins 2012c, second and third paragraphs from end of article). In August, Archbishop Nienstedt authored a letter in support of the amendment and urged involvement in Minnesota for Marriage;* the letter was read at 17 Twin Cities parishes during Sunday services (Hawkins 2012a). As reported by the organization Catholics for Marriage Equality, the letter sparked many Catholics to publicly express their opposition to the amendment (Hawkins 2012a).

On election day, the efforts of pro-equality religious organizations (mobilized by Minnesotans United) bore the hoped-for result: defeat of the amendment at the polls. Pro-amendment campaign leader Frank Schubert attributed his side's loss to the lack of religious participation in the campaign, lamenting that the campaign was unable to get more faith leaders to preach on the issue and to lead voter registration drives ("Hotdish Politics" 2013).

Money

As Amy Stone points out, having a successful ballot campaign costs money, a factor left out of many social movement analyses (2010). Air time and production of advertisements is a significant cost of any campaign, whether the campaign uses traditional media outlets or the Internet. As Stone notes, "the majority of campaign budgets are spent on message development and delivery" (2010, 107).

The amendment campaign was the most expensive in Minnesota history (Demko 2012a). Minnesotans United spent more than $12 million during the campaign, while Minnesota for Marriage spent about $5.7 million (Stassen-Berger 2013).

To give an idea of the consequences of such a funding disparity: A review of 2012 campaign finance reports shows that Minnesotans United spent over $5,400,000 on expenses relating to advertising and media.† This amount exceeds the total amount of cash expended by Minnesota for Marriage in all categories for 2012.

* Notably, the language of the letter endorsed the idea that "all people should be able to visit loved ones in the hospital, pass on their property to whomever they choose and have access to employment, housing and the basic necessities of life" (Hawkins 2012a, para. 13). This tactic of expressing concern for the rights of LGBT people while simultaneously endorsing an exclusionary marriage definition is similar to seemingly tolerant messaging used in other states. "Particularly in liberal states, Religious Right messaging was able to build on heterosexist sentiments, which encourage voters to like their LGBT friends or neighbors but have reservations about same-sex marriage or their children growing up to be gay or lesbian" (Stone 2010, 146).

† Campaign reports for 2012 from Minnesota Campaign and Public Disclosure Board (2013). Calculations of media expenses included categories such as social media expenses, media consulting, media buys, and advertisements. The total is likely an undercount, since I did not include possible media-related assistance from in-kind donors.

Frank Schubert offered an explanation for the funding disparity as he reflected on the loss in Minnesota. Schubert explained that he was able to generate substantial funding in California in the Proposition 8 campaign in 2008 by appealing to donors nationwide. In Minnesota, he was unable to do so because three other states launched campaigns; pro-amendment supporters in Minnesota had to share national resources with other ballot battles ("Hotdish Politics" 2013). A quick review of campaign finance documents points to a different explanation: Minnesotans United's overwhelming fundraising success. Minnesotans United's 2012 report provides over 1,600 pages listing named donors, whereas Minnesota for Marriage's report has only 90 pages of listed contributions (Minnesota Campaign Finance and Public Disclosure Board 2013).

Time

The Minnesotans United campaign employed a campaign tactic that gained prominence after the 2008 losses in California and Maine: one-on-one conversations with voters (Stone 2010). This tactic in particular takes time, and Minnesotans United was able to capitalize on the 18 months between when the legislature acted to put the amendment on the ballot and the election itself. Campaign volunteers were trained to have conversations with potential voters—not to argue, but to listen and engage (Boyte 2012). "Phone canvassers spend two to three times as long as the average campaign canvass" (Boyte 2012, para. 13). Unlike in other amendment campaigns, Minnesotans United focused on hearing from people opposed to gay marriage (Boyte 2012).

Minnesotans United was also able to use its existing coalitions and the gift of time to recruit volunteers and establish a presence across the state. Importantly, Minnesotans United had offices across the state (Boyte 2012). This statewide effort replicated an important aspect of the campaign to pass the Human Rights Act in 1993—advocates intentionally engaged with voters in every part of the state. Minnesotans United boasted over 27,000 volunteers statewide by the end of the campaign (Demko 2013). This grassroots effort paid off: campaign director Richard Carlbom told a group of staff and volunteers that the campaign had called over 900,000 people and knocked on over 400,000 doors in the final week of the campaign (Carpenter 2012).

The strength of the grassroots effort is evidenced by social media usage. Both primary organizations involved in the campaign developed presences on the social media sites Facebook and Twitter. In terms of volume and number of users, Minnesotans United had an overwhelmingly larger presence: by the end of the campaign, Minnesota for Marriage had 8,125 "likes" on Facebook, while Minnesotans United for all Families had 42,496. On Twitter, Minnesota for Marriage had 688 followers and had made 336 tweets, while Minnesotans United had 13,888 followers and had made 2,087 tweets. An informal qualitative review of comments on these groups' Facebook pages show that the pages were forums for people to share information about campaign events, to debate people on the other side of the issue (sometimes civilly, sometimes not), and to encourage supporters across the state.*

If polling data is any indication, the anti-amendment campaign needed every moment of the 18 months to move the majority to a "vote no" opinion. Polling information varied widely during the campaign. In January 2012, Public Policy Polling data indicated that 48% of surveyed voters in Minnesota were in favor of amendment (Public Policy Polling 2012). In June 2012, Public Policy Polling showed that only 43% of people surveyed planned to vote in favor of the amendment, with 49% of people planning to vote against it (Hawkins 2012e). A July poll by Survey USA, however, suggested the opposite trend, with 52% of voters expressing support (Hawkins 2012e). In September, a Survey USA poll indicated that 50% of voters were in favor of the amendment and 43% opposed (Hauser 2012). A Survey USA poll from mid-October showed that 47% of voters surveyed were in favor of the amendment and 46% opposed, and 7% undecided (with a 4.3% sampling error, the race was too close to call), (Hauser 2012).

For campaigners, the polling data was even more difficult to rely on because of a well-documented phenomenon: polls about same-sex marriage often underestimate opposition to same-sex marriage (Demko 2012b). In the weeks leading to the election, Minnesota for Marriage staff expressed reliance on this phenomenon, with the communications director saying "when people get into the voting booth they vote to affirm marriage as between one man and one woman" (Demko 2012b, para. 9, quoting Chuck Darrell).

Of course, the only poll that truly mattered was the one at the ballot box, and Minnesotans United and the LGBT community prevailed. The success of the campaign to defeat the Minnesota marriage amendment was no fluke: a well-developed social movement was ignited to action by a well-developed political campaign, and several factors aligned to the benefit of LGBT people (allies, faith, money, and time). Whether the efforts that led to victory here will result in additional benefits to LGBT Minnesotans remains to be seen of course, and there are a number of issues in upcoming legislative sessions that will test the social movement's muscle. In previous ballot initiatives in other states, LGBT people have spent significant amounts of "time, money, and energy organizing local communities to defeat referendums and initiatives, and many of those campaigns do little to advance gay rights" (Stone 2010, 5). Campaign organizers and participants saw hope in the momentum gained from the campaign, and began work to translate that momentum into tangible progress on marriage equality (Dibblee and Rongitsch 2012).

* Facebook pages captured November 7, 2012. Tweets captured December 9, 2012.

Minnesota: An Active Battleground for LGBT Rights

The defeat of the marriage amendment was not the only cause for celebration on election night for many LGBT people in Minnesota: both the state House and Senate, in Republican hands for the previous two years, switched to Democratic control. The marriage amendment campaign impacted several key races, including tight districts in the Twin Cities suburbs and in Greater Minnesota, where votes against the amendment correlated with victory for Democratic candidates (Bierschbach 2012a). As one Democratic operative noted, the marriage amendment "really came back to bite them [Republican candidates]…, particularly in the suburbs and these college towns, and that's where the fault lines in this election were" (Bierschbach 2012a, para. 17, quoting Mike Kennedy).

Shortly after the close of the 2012 election, LGBT advocates and allies began mobilizing for the 2013 legislative session. OutFront Minnesota organized a community summit attended by over 500 people, 100 of whom attended a workshop on marriage equality legislation (Shenoy and Scheck 2012; also see Dibblee and Rongitsch 2012). As the 2013 legislative session began, Minnesotans United announced plans to lobby for equality legislation, and Minnesota for Marriage claimed readiness for any such initiative (Shenoy and Scheck 2012).

Marriage is not the only legislative initiative affecting the LGBT community in 2013 and beyond. As with previous years, OutFront Minnesota took a leadership role in lobbying for comprehensive legislation to address school bullying (OutFront 2013): The bill subsequently passed.

As these initiatives move forward, the LGBT community can expect opposition from social conservatives, with Minnesota remaining a battleground state for years to come.

Epilogue

In the months since I drafted this chapter, Minnesota has continued to earn its battleground state designation. The 2013 Minnesota legislative session's heated debates about gun control, frac sand mining, and tax increases were overshadowed by efforts to pass a marriage equality bill. HF1054/SF925, which was championed by Senator Scott Dibble and Representative Karen Clark, ultimately passed; Governor Mark Dayton signed the bill into law on May 14, 2013. The law went into effect on August 1, 2013, and same-sex couples acted quickly: over 1,600 same sex couples applied for marriage licenses in August 2013 (this represents over one-third of all licenses issued) (Condon and Bakst, 2013).

Marriage equality was a tremendous victory for LGBT people in Minnesota, but electoral and legislative challenges remain. As one example, anti-bullying legislation was stalled in the Minnesota legislature because of Republican promises to filibuster the bill, but supporters pledged to continue efforts in 2014 (Post 2013), when it passed.

Legislative races in Minnesota in 2014 and 2016 will likely rehash the marriage debate: On the same day the marriage equality statute went into effect, Minnesota for Marriage announced that it was forming the Minnesota Majority Initiative to challenge legislators who had voted in favor of the legislation; NOM President Brian Brown will serve as the group's treasurer (and NOM has pledged $500,000 to the effort) (Helgeson 2013a). (Minnesotans United had already formed a political action committee to support legislators who backed marriage equality [Helgeson 2013b].)

The momentum generated by the 2012 amendment campaign led to tangible benefits for LGBT Minnesotans. Eventually, Minnesota may become an empowered state (as the term is used in this book); given its social history and political climate, however, Minnesota will likely remain a battleground for LGBT rights in the near term.

References

Aslanian, Sasha. 2011. "Campaign Finance Board Dismisses Complaint against Catholic DVD." *Minnesota Public Radio.* December 9. Accessed December 8, 2012, http://minnesota.publicradio.org/display/web/2011/12/09/campaign-finance-catholic-dvd/.

Aslanian, Sasha. 2012. "Hmong American Partnership Opposes Marriage Amendment; Community Divided." Minnesota Public Radio. July 30. Accessed January 26, 2013, http://minnesota.publicradio.org/display/web/2012/07/30/politics/hmong-amendment-stance.

Bentley, Rosalind. 1998. "Activists React to Repeal of Georgia Sodomy Law/In Minnesota, It's Expected to Spark Debate on Fairness and Privacy Issues." *Star Tribune* (Minneapolis). November 25. Accessed February 2, 2013, ProQuest.

Bierschbach, Briana. 2012a. "Marriage Amendment Had Big Impact in Burbs in Minnesota." *The Legal Ledger* (St. Paul, Minnesota). November 9. Accessed January 21, 2013, LexisNexis Academic.

Bierschbach, Briana. 2012b. "MNGOP Debt Shrinks, but Turmoil Persists." *Politics In Minnesota.* December 12. Accessed February 2, 2013, http://politicsinminnesota.com/2012/12/mngop-debt-shrinks-but-turmoil-persists/.

Birkey, Andy. 2008. "Minnesota's Homegrown Christian Right: Meet the Minnesota Family Council." *Minnesota Independent.* August 11. Accessed December 8, 2012, http://minnesotaindependent.com/4227/minnesotas-homegrown-christian-right-meet-the-minnesota-family-council.

Birkey, Andy. 2011. "Anti-Gay Marriage Groups Say They Won't Follow New Campaign Finance Guidelines." *The Minnesota Independent.* October 4. Accessed December 8, 2012, http://minnesotaindependent.com/89205/anti-gay-marriage-groups-say-they-wont-follow-new-campaign-finance-guidelines.

Boldt, Megan, and Doug Beldon. 2012. "Ousted GOP Insider Brodkorb: Marriage Amendment about Votes, Not Values." *Pioneer Press* (St. Paul, Minnesota). October 17. Accessed October 18, 2012, http://www.twincities.com/allheadlines/ci_21785537/gay-marriage-ousted-gop-insider-brodkorb-say-amendment.

Booth, David. 2012. "What Happened Here? Three Observations about Minnesota's Marriage Vote." *MinnPost.* November 26. Accessed December 16, 2012, http://www.minnpost.com/community-voices/2012/11/what-happened-here-three-observations-about-minnesotas-marriage-vote.

Boyte, Harry. 2012. "Citizen Politics: A New Minnesota Miracle. Harry Boyte & Hunter Gordon." *Huffington Post* (blog). August 9. Accessed August 23, 2012, http://www.huffingtonpost.com/harry-boyte/citizen-politics-a-new-mi_b_1756538.html.

Brickman, Kate. 2012. "Minnesotans United Raises $4.6 million to Defeat Freedom-Limiting Marriage Amendment." *Minnesotans United for All Families* (press release). June 19. Accessed October 16, 2012, http://mnunited.org/news/minnesotans-united-raises-4-6-million-to-defeat-freedom-limiting-marriage-amendment/.

Brown, Brian. 2012. "National Organization for Marriage: We Are Not Defeated in Our Fight for Traditional Marriage." National Organization for Marriage. November 7. Accessed November 8, 2012, http://www.nationformarriage.org/site/c.omL2KeN0LzH/b.5075687/apps/s/content.asp?ct=12333723.

Butler, Pam. 2010. "Sex and the Cities: Reevaluating 1980s Feminist Politics in Minneapolis and St. Paul." In *Queer Twin Cities,* Twin Cities GLBT Oral History Project, 203–239. Minneapolis, MN: University of Minnesota Press.

Buzinski, Jim. 2012. "Chris Kluwe's Brilliant Gay Marriage Radio Ad Uses 'Lustful C***monster' to Humorous Effect." Outsports.com (blog). October 24. Accessed October 26, 2012, http://outsports.com/jocktalkblog/2012/10/24/chris-kluwes-brilliant-pro-gay-marriage-radio-ad-uses-lustful-cmonster-to-humorous-effect/.

Carpenter, Dale. 2012. "The Moment of Victory in Minnesota (2012)." Video by Robert Arvid Nelsen posted on YouTube.com. November 7. Accessed November 9, 2012, http://www.youtube.com/watch?feature=player_embedded&v=FQZxF_roWyk.

Carr, David. 2009. "Al Franken and the Odd Politics of Minnesota." *New York Times.* July 4. Accessed January 21, 2013, http://www.nytimes.com/2009/07/05/weekinreview/05franken.html?pagewanted=all&_r=0.

Collins, Bob. 2011. "Roll Call Vote: Same Sex Marriage Ban Amendment." *Minnesota Public Radio: NewsCut.* May 21. Accessed December 1, 2012, http://minnesota.publicradio.org/collections/special/columns/news_cut/archive/2011/05/roll_call_vote_same-sex_ban_am.shtml.

Condon, Patrick, and Brian Bakst. 2013. "Minn. Sees Rush to Same-Sex Marriage." *Minnesota Public Radio.* September 3. Accessed November 11, 2013, http://minnesota.publicradio.org/display/web/2013/09/02/minn-sees-rush-to-same-sex-marriage.

Cook, Mike. 2010. "To Have and to Hold." *Session Weekly* (Publication of the Minnesota House of Representatives). February 25. Accessed January 27, 2013, http://www.house.leg.state.mn.us/sessionweekly/art.asp?ls_year=86&issueid_=50&storyid=1531&year_=2010.

Damore, David F., Ted G. Jelen, and Michael W. Bowers. 2007. "Sweet Land of Liberty: The Gay Marriage Amendment in Nevada." In *Religious Interests in Community Conflict: Beyond the Culture Wars,* edited by Paul A. Djupe and Laura R. Olson, 51–71. Waco, TX: University of Baylor Press.

Demko, Paul. 2012a. "Amendments: from Anxiety to Elation at 'Vote No' Parties in Minnesota." *The Legal Ledger* (St. Paul, Minnesota). November 7. Accessed January 21, 2013, LexisNexis Academic.

Demko, Paul. 2012b. "Marriage Polls Have Infidelity Problem." *Politics In Minnesota.* October 12. Accessed October 12, 2012, http://politicsinminnesota.com/2012/10/marriage-polls-have-infidelity-problem/.

Demko, Paul. 2012c. "Minnesota Wins Add to Ad Shop's Cachet." *The Legal Ledger* (St. Paul, Minnesota). November 30. Accessed January 21, 2013, LexisNexis Academic.

Demko, Paul. 2013. "Minnesota Politician of the Year: 'Vote No' Campaigns Defied the Odds in Constitutional Referendums." *The Legal Ledger* (St. Paul, Minnesota). January 4. LexisNexis Academic (accessed January 21, 2013).

Diaz, Kevin. 1991. "Sodomy Law Still on Books, and No Challenge Is in Sight." *Star Tribune* (Minneapolis, Minnesota). August 31. Accessed February 2, 2013, ProQuest.

Dibblee, Michelle, and Bee Rongitsch. 2012. "Why Marriage and Why Now?" Notes from workshop "Making Marriage Equality a Reality in Minnesota" at Equality and Justice Summit, Minneapolis, MN, December 1. Accessed February 9, 2013, http://www.outfront.org/summit.

Elazar, Daniel, Virginia Gray, and Wyman Spano. 1999. *Minnesota Politics and Government.* Lincoln, NE: University of Nebraska Press.

Friedman, Marc. 2012. "2012 Guide to the Twin Cities Pride Festival." WCCO. June 16. Accessed December 16, 2012, http://minnesota.cbslocal.com/top-lists/guide-to-the-twin-cities-pride-festival/.

Gates, Gary J., and Abigail M. Cooke. ca 2011. "Minnesota Census Snapshot: 2010." The Williams Institute, UCLA School of Law. Accessed December 16, 2012, http://williaminstitute.law.ucla.edu/wpcontent/uploads/Census2010Snapshot_Minnesota_v2.pdf.

Gervino, Tony. 2012. "The Punter Makes His Point." *The New York Times.* October 19. Accessed October 20, 2012, http://www.nytimes.com/2012/10/20/sports/football/punter-chris-kluwes-voice-is-heard-in-same-sex-marriage-debate.html.

Gilman, Rhoda. 2000. "The History and Peopling of Minnesota: Its Culture." *Daedalus, 129*(3): 1–29.

Goins v. West Group. 635 N.W.2d 717 (Minn. 2001).

Goldberg, Michelle. 2011. "Bachmann's Unrivaled Extremism." *Daily Beast.* June 14. Accessed February 2, 2013, http://www.thedailybeast.com/articles/2011/06/14/michele-bachmanns-unrivaled-extremism-gay-rights-to-religion.html.

Grow, Doug. 2008. "Minnesota's Gay Community Purposely Moving Slowly on Gay Marriage Efforts." *MinnPost.* November 28. Accessed February 5, 2013, http://www.minnpost.com/politics-policy/2008/11/minnesotas-gay-community-purposely-moving-slowly-gay-marriage-efforts.

Hanson, Dan. 2009. *History of the Minnesota Gay and Lesbian Legal Assistance (MnGALLA).* Golden Valley, MN: Friends of the Bill of Rights Foundation.

Hauser, Tom. 2012. "'Vote No' Side Gains Ground on Marriage Amendment." *KSTP.* October 18. Accessed October 18, 2012, http://kstp.com/news/stories/S2802855.shtml?cat=1.

Hawkins, Beth. 2012a. "Archbishop Nienstedt's Latest Marriage Amendment Letter Adds to Catholic Turmoil." *MinnPost.* August 31. Accessed August 31, 2012, http://www.minnpost.com/politics-policy/2012/08/archbishop-nienstedts-latest-marriage-amendment-letter-adds-catholic-turmoil.

Hawkins, Beth. 2012b. "Engaging Congregations: A Q&A with Minnesotans United's Grant Stevensen." *MinnPost.* March 12. Accessed January 26, 2013, http://www.minnpost.com/minnpost-asks/2012/03/engaging-congregations-qa-minnesotans-uniteds-grant-stevensen.

Hawkins, Beth. 2012c. "Former Priests against Marriage Amendment Near 100 Signatory Mark." *MinnPost.* July 11. Accessed July 7, 2012, http://www.minnpost.com/politics-policy/2012/07/former-priests-against-marriage-amendment-near-100-signatory-mark.

Hawkins, Beth. 2012d. "In Targeted Calls, Volunteers Discuss Marriage Amendment with Latinos." *MinnPost*. August 17. Accessed August 17, 2012, http://www.minnpost.com/politics-policy/2012/08/targeted-calls-volunteers-discuss-marriage-amendment-latinos.

Hawkins, Beth. 2012e. "New Marriage-Poll Results: A Dramatic Change in Voters' Views—Or a Fluke?" *MinnPost*. July 24. Accessed July 24, 2012, http://www.minnpost.com/politics-policy/2012/07/new-marriage-poll-results-dramatic-change-voters-views-%E2%80%94-or-fluke.

Helgeson, Baird. 2012. "Winning Streak on the Line for Marriage Crusader." *Star Tribune* (Minneapolis, Minnesota). August 4. Accessed August 5, 2012, http://www.startribune.com/politics/statelocal/165028496.html?refer=y.

Helgeson, Baird. 2013a. "Minnesota Gay Marriage Opponents to Target State House Races." *Star Tribune* (Minneapolis, Minnesota). August 1. Accessed November 11, 2013, http://www.startribune.com/politics/statelocal/217953651.html.

Helgeson, Baird. 2013b. "PAC Backs Minnesota's Gay Marriage Coalition" *Star Tribune* (Minneapolis, Minnesota). May 15, 2013. Accessed November 11, 2013 http://www.startribune.com/politics/statelocal/207647641.html.

Helgeson, Baird, Mike Kaszuba, Eric Roper, and Rachel Stassen-Berger. 2011. "Shut Down: Both Sides Traded Bitter Words as Talks Toward a Deal Fell Apart; Dayton Renewed His Call to Tax the Rich; GOP Pointed to Harm of Long-term Debt." *Star Tribune* (Minneapolis, Minnesota). July 1. Accessed February 2, 2013, ProQuest.

Hicks, Dylan. 2004. "How the Twin Cities Pride Fest Helped Turn Minneapolis into the San Francisco of the Wheat Belt." *City Pages* (Minneapolis, Minnesota). June 23. Accessed December 26, 2012, http://www.citypages.com/2004-06-23/news/pride/.

"Hotdish Politics: Marriage Amendment Defeat Is Cause for Reflection." 2013. *Star Tribune* (Minneapolis, Minnesota). January 3. Accessed January 21, 2013, http://www.startribune.com/politics/statelocal/185759142.html?refer=y.

Human Rights Campaign. 2012. "Maps of State Laws & Policies." Accessed February 2, 2013, http://www.hrc.org/resources/entry/maps-of-state-laws-policies.

Jossi, Frank. 2012. "Kevin Lindsey Brings a New Energy to the Minnesota's Human Rights Efforts." *The Legal Ledger* (St. Paul, Minnesota). December 12. Accessed January 21, 2013, LexisNexis Academic.

Kimball, Joe. 2011. "Archbishop Nienstedt Wants Pro-Amendment 'Prayer for Marriage' Used in Mass." *MinnPost*. December 19. Accessed February 10, 2013, http://www.minnpost.com/political-agenda/2011/12/archbishop-nienstedt-wants-pro-amendment-prayer-marriage-used-mass.

Kimball, Joe. 2012a. "Brad Pitt Gives $100,000 For Gay Marriage Ballot Efforts in Minnesota and Other States." *MinnPost*. October 31. Accessed October 31, 2012, http://www.minnpost.com/political-agenda/2012/10/brad-pitt-gives-100000-gay-marriage-ballot-efforts-minnesota-and-other-stat.

Kimball, Joe. 2012b. "GOP Lawmakers and Supporters of Minnesota Marriage Amendment Sue over Title Change." *MinnPost*. July 9. Accessed July 9, 2012, http://www.minnpost.com/political-agenda/2012/07/gop-lawmakers-and-supporters-minnesota-marriage-amendment-sue-over-title-ch.

Lilly v. City of Minneapolis. 527 n.w. 2D 107. (Minn. Ct. App. 1995).

Linkins, Jason. 2012. "Chris Kluwe Quits St. Paul Pioneer Press over Marriage Equality Amendment Editorial." Huffington Post. November 3. Accessed November 3, 2012, http://www.huffingtonpost.com/2012/11/03/chris-kluwe-st-paul-pioneer-press_n_2069240.html.

Louwagie, Pam. 2001a. "State Sodomy Law Violates Constitution, Judge Rules/The Decision Affects Only the Eight Plaintiffs, but Their Lawyers Hope to Make It Apply Statewide." *Star Tribune* (Minneapolis, Minnesota). May 22. Accessed February 2, 2013, ProQuest.

Louwagie, Pam. 2001b. "State Won't Appeal Class-Action Sodomy Ruling/Critics Said a Decision to End a Ban on Certain Sex Acts Might Not Be Far-Reaching." *Star Tribune* (Minneapolis, Minnesota). September 1. Accessed February 2, 2013, ProQuest.

McIntee, Michael. 2012. "MN Sec. of State Asks Newspapers to Print Full Proposed Constitutional Amendments." *The Uptake*. October 22. Accessed October 23, 2012, http://www.theuptake.org/2012/10/22/mn-sec-of-state-asks-papers-to-print-full-proposed-constitutional-amendments/.

Milton, John. 2010. "20 Years After Senate First Tried, Minnesota Legislature Finally Gives Gays Civil Rights Protection." (Excerpt from Afterword to *Crossing the Barriers: The Autobiography of Allan H. Spear.*) *MinnPost.* October 22. Accessed January 19, 2013, http://www.minnpost.com/politics-policy/2010/10/20-years-after-senate-first-tried-minnesota-legislature-finally-gives-gays-c.

Minnesota Campaign Finance and Public Disclosure Board. 2013. "Ballot Question Political Committees and Ballot Question Political Funds." Reports submitted by campaigns. Accessed February 3, 2013, http://www.cfbreport.state.mn.us/rptViewer/viewRptsPCF.php#searchType=PCF&year=12&regnum=50053&letter=&name=.

Minnesota Family Council. 1999. "Minneapolis Officials Yet to Enforce Bathroom Ban." *Pro-Family News,* 5(6). Copy of newsletter stored in Internet archives: Accessed December 30, 2012, http://web.archive.org/web/19981206145041/http://www.mfc.org/.

Minnesota for Marriage. 2012. "Minnesota for Marriage Releases Finance Report" (news release). June 19. Accessed October 16, 2012, www.minnesotaformarriage.com/2012/06/minnesota-for-marriage-releases-finance-report/.

Minnesota Human Rights Act. 2012. Minnesota Statutes §363a.

Minnesota Legislative Reference Library (MLRL). 2012. "Resources on Minnesota Issues: Same-Sex Marriage in Minnesota." Accessed January 27, 2013, http://www.leg.state.mn.us/lrl/issues/issues.aspx?issue=gay.

Minnesota Legislature. 2003. A Bill for an Act Relating to Human Rights; Removing Sexual Orientation as a Protected Class Under the Human Rights Act and in Other Statutory Provisions; Amending Minnesota Statutes ... House File 341/Senate File 545.

Minnesota Rules. 2012. Chapter 8250–Ballot preparation.

Minnesota Secretary of State. 2012a. "Minnesota Estimated Voter Turnout." Accessed December 8, 2012, http://electionresults.sos.state.mn.us/ENR/Results/CountyStatistics/1.

Minnesota Secretary of State. 2012b. "Results for Constitutional Amendments." Accessed December 8, 2012, http://electionresults.sos.state.mn.us/ENR/Results/AmendmentResultsStatewide/1.

Minnesotans United for All Families. 2012a. "Cities." Accessed February 9, 2013, http://mnunited.org/cities/.

Minnesotans United for All Families. 2012b. "Full Coalition Partner List": Last updated: October 27, 2012. Accessed November 7, 2012, http://mnunited.org/wp-content/uploads/2012/10/CoalitionPartnerList_MASTER1.pdf.

Murphy, Kevin. 2010. "Gay Was Good: Progress, Homonormativity, and Oral History." In *Queer Twin Cities,* by Twin Cities GLBT Oral History Project, 305-318. Minneapolis, MN: University of Minnesota Press.

Murphy, Ryan Patrick, and Alex T. Urquhart. 2010. "Sexuality in the Headlines: Intimate Upheavals as Histories of the Twin Cities." In *Queer Twin Cities,* by Twin Cities GLBT Oral History Project, 40-89. Minneapolis, MN: University of Minnesota Press.

National Organization for Marriage (NOM). 2010a. "Marriage an Historic Winner at Polls" (news release). November 3. Accessed October 16, 2012, www.nationformarriage.org/site/c.omL2KeN0LzH/b.5075687/apps/s/content.asp?ct=8716865.

National Organization for Marriage (NOM). 2010b. "National Organization for Marriage Demands That Minnesotans Be Allowed to Vote on Marriage" (news release). May 18. Accessed October 16, 2012, www.nationformarriage.org/site/c.omL2KeN0LzH/b.5075687/apps/s/content.asp?ct=8400289.

National Organization for Marriage (NOM). 2010c. "National Organization for Marriage Launches Radio Ad Campaign in Minnesota," (news release). October 14. Accessed October 16, 2012, http://www.nationformarriage.org/site/c.omL2KeN0LzH/b.5075687/apps/s/content.asp?ct=8400289.

Noble, Scott. 2012. "Diverse Group Unites behind the Marriage Amendment." *Minnesota Christian Examiner*. October. Accessed December 29, 2012, http://www.minnesota.christianexaminer.com/Articles/Oct12/Art_Oct12_04.html.

OutFront Minnesota. ca 2007. "OutFront Minnesota: 20 Years of History." *OutFront.* Accessed January 9, 2013, http://www.outfront.org/docs/20years.pdf.

OutFront Minnesota. ca 2012. "Domestic Partnerships." Accessed February 9, 2013, http://www.outfront.org/library/marriage/dpregistry.

OutFront Minnesota. 2013. "Minnesota Safe Schools for All Coalition." Accessed February 9, 2013, http://www.outfront.org/resources/safeschools.

Pew Research Center for the People and the Press. 2012. "Behind Gay Marriage Momentum, Regional Gaps Persist." November 9. Accessed December 4, 2012, http://www.people-press.org/2012/11/09/behind-gay-marriage-momentum-regional-gaps-persist/.

Pew Research Center, Pew Forum on Religion and Public Life. 2012. "Changing Attitudes on Gay Marriage." Line graph showing annual survey data from 2001–2012. November. Accessed December 4, 2012, http://features.pewforum.org/same-sex-marriage-attitudes/index.php.

Phelps, David. 2003. "Same-sex Benefits Doomed; Supporters of Provision in State Worker Contracts Concede the Battle," *Star Tribune* (Minneapolis, Minnesota). February 12. Accessed November 12, 2012, ProQuest.

Post, Tim. 2013. "Anti-Bullying Bill Will Return Next Year, Supporters Say." *Minnesota Public Radio*. May 21. Accessed November 11, 2013, http://minnesota.publicradio.org/display/web/2013/05/21/politics/anti-bullying-bill-legislature.

Pretangelo, Tony. 2012. "The Rural-suburban Divide on the Minnesota Amendments." *Left.MN.* November 7. Accessed November 8, 2012, http://left.mn/2012/11/the-rural-suburban-divide-on-the-minnesota-amendments/.

Project 515. 2010. "Still Unequal under the Law." Accessed February 9, 2013, http://project515.org/files/2011/05/Still_Unequal_Under_the_Law.pdf.

Public Policy Polling. 2012. "Minnesota Miscellany." September 12. Accessed February 9, 2013, http://www.publicpolicypolling.com/main/2012/09/minnesota-miscellany.html.

Pugmire, Tim. 2012. "State Human Rights Commissioner Is Vocal Opponent of Proposed Amendments." Minnesota Public Radio. October 26. Accessed January 19, 2013, http://minnesota.publicradio.org/display/web/2012/10/26/politics/keving-lindsay-state-human-rights-commissioner-vocal-opponent-amendments.

Pugmire, Tim. 2013. "Auditor Issues a 'No Decision' against Ritchie and Lindsey." *Minnesota Public Radio*. Accessed February 5, 2013, http://minnesota.publicradio.org/collections/special/columns/polinaut/archive/2013/02/auditor_cant_as.shtml.

Ringham, Eric, and Sasha Aslanian. 2012. "Eighteen Months to History: How the Minnesota Marriage Amendment Was Defeated—Money, Passion, Allies." *Minnesota Public Radio*. November 9. Accessed November 9, 2012, http://minnesota.publicradio.org/display/web/2012/11/09/marriage-how/.

Romero, Adam P., Clifford J. Rosky, M. V. Lee Badgett, and Gary J. Gates. 2008. "Census Snapshot: Minnesota." The Williams Institute, UCLA School of Law. Accessed December 16, 2012, http://williamsinstitute.law.ucla.edu/wp-content/uploads/MinnesotaCensus2000Snapshot.pdf.

Rossman, Lyle. 1997. "Sexual Orientation Issues Impact K-12 Education." In *Gay/Lesbian/Bisexual/Transgender Public Policy Issues: An Administrator's Guide to the New Cultural Struggle*, edited by Wallace K. Swan, 63–74. Binghamton, NY: Harrington Park Press.

Scheck, Tom. 2012. "Capitol View Category Archive: Campaign 2012: Presidential Race." Collected news updates and blog posts. *Minnesota Public Radio*. Accessed January 29, 2013, http://minnesota.publicradio.org/collections/special/columns/polinaut/archive/2012/campaign-2012-p/.

Shaiko, Ronald. 2007. "Same-Sex Marriage, GLBT Organizations, and the Lack of Spirited Political Engagement." In *The Politics of Same Sex Marriage*, edited by Craig A. Rimmerman and Clyde Wilcox, 85 -103. London: University of Chicago Press.

Shenoy, Rupa. 2012. "Twin Cities Pride Festival Marks 40th Year." *Minnesota Public Radio*. June 23. Accessed December 16, 2012, http://minnesota.publicradio.org/display/web/2012/06/23/regional/gay-pride/.

Shenoy, Rupa, and Tom Scheck. 2012. "Minnesota Same-sex Marriage Activists Gather to Plan Strategy." Minnesota Public Radio. December 3. Accessed February 9, 2013, http://minnesota.publicradio.org/display/web/2012/12/02/politics/same-sex-marriage-summit.

Smith, Dane. 2006a. "A Kinship in Promoting the Marriage Amendment; Deep Faith and Fierce Commitment United Chuck Darrell and Jeff Davis. Their Two Groups Have Emerged as Combative Advocates of a Constitutional Ban on Same-sex Marriage and Its Equivalent." *Star Tribune* (Minneapolis, Minnesota). April 17. Accessed February 2, 2013, ProQuest.

Smith, Dane. 2006b. "Election 2006; The Record of Tim Pawlenty: A Conservative Tenure, with Shifts to Center; The GOP Governor Has Made His Mark on the State, but He Also is No Small-Government Purist." *Star Tribune* (Minneapolis, Minnesota). Oct 30. Accessed February 12, 2013, ProQuest.

Stassen-Berger, Rachel E. 2013. "Huge Sums Tossed at Ballot Questions in '12." *Star Tribune* (Minneapolis, Minnesota). February 1. Accessed February 2, 2013, http://www.startribune.com/politics/statelocal/189471121.html?refer=y.

Stone, Amy L. 2010. *Gay Rights at the Ballot Box*. Minneapolis, MN: University of Minnesota Press.

Stone, Amy L. 2012. "How Did Same-Sex Marriage Gain Historic Wins at the Ballot Box Yesterday? Three Ideas." *University of Minnesota Press* (blog). November 7. Accessed December 4, 2012, http://www.uminnpressblog.com/2012/11/how-did-same-sex-marriage-gain-historic.html.

Swan, Wallace. 1998. "The 'Wally Swan for Minnesota State Treasurer Campaign.'" Paper presented at the Human Rights Campaign "Out/Vote Conference," Washington DC, September 18–19.

Tyson, Amy M. 2010. "Skirting the Boundaries: Queer Bar Cultures in the Postwar Twin Cities." In *Queer Twin Cities,* by Twin Cities GLBT Oral History Project, 171–202. Minneapolis, MN: University of Minnesota Press.

Van Cleve, Stewart. 2012. *Land of 10,000 Loves: A History of Queer Minnesota*. Minneapolis, MN: University of Minnesota Press.

Whereatt, Robert. 2001. "Partners of State Workers Get Benefits; Insurance For Same-sex Domestic Partners Was OK'd Before Strike." *Star Tribune* (Minneapolis, Minnesota). October 17. Accessed November 12, 2012, ProQuest.

Chapter 7

North Carolina: A Disempowered State

Wallace Swan with Elizabeth Swanzy-Parker

Contents

Introduction

"North Carolina borders South Carolina and Georgia to the south as well as Tennessee to the west and Virginia to the north ... [It] ... is known as the Tar Heel State and the Old North State ... [It] ... is comprised of 100 counties" (Swanzy-Parker 2013, 1). Its capital is Raleigh, and its largest city is Charlotte.

The state is comprised of 72.1% white persons, 22% black persons, 1.5% American Indian and Alaska Native persons, 2.3% Asian persons, 0.1% Native Hawaiian and Other Pacific Islanders, and 1.9% persons reporting two or more races (U.S. Census Bureau 2011).

The First Marriage Statute

In 1996, North Carolina carefully defined marriage under its statutes in Chapter 51, Article 1.

> The precise language of the law reads "A valid and sufficient marriage is created by the consent of a male and female person who may lawfully marry, presently to take each other as husband and wife, freely, seriously and plainly expressed by each in the presence of the other, either (1) a. In the presence of an ordained minister of any religious denomination, a minister authorized by a church, or a magistrate; and b. With the consequent declaration by the minister or magistrate that the persons are husband and wife; or (2) In accordance with any mode of solemnization recognized by any religious denomination, or federally or State recognized Indian Nation or Tribe."*

The Proposed Constitutional Amendment (Consideration Deferred in the Legislature)

On Tuesday February 22, 2011, Republican Senator James Forrester of Gaston County filed a proposed Constitutional Amendment on marriage, with sponsors Tillman and Soucek, and 20 Republican cosponsors (Comer 2011). Forrester had served 11 terms in District 41, representing Gaston, Iredell, and Lincoln counties; and was a physician in family practice." This amendment stated that it was a "Bill to be Entitled An Act to Amend the Constitution to Provide Marriage Between a Man and a Woman is the Only Domestic Legal Union that shall be Valid or Recognized in this State."

Section 1, Article 14 of the Constitution was to be changed by adding "Section 6. Marriage between a man and a woman is the only domestic legal union that shall be valid or recognized in this State."

Section 2 would state: "The amendment set out in Section 1 of this act shall be submitted to the qualified voters of the State at the statewide general election on November 6, 2012, which election shall be conducted under the laws then governing

* North Carolina General Statues. 2013. Chapter 51 Marriage, http://law.onecle.com/north-carolina/51-marriage/index.html.

elections in the State. Ballots, voting systems, or both may be used in accordance with Chapter 163 of the General Statutes. The question to be used in the voting systems and ballots shall be: [] FOR [] AGAINST Constitutional amendment to provide that marriage between a man and a woman is the only domestic legal union that shall be valid or recognized in this State."* If there were to be a voting majority in favor, the amendment would become effective January 1, 2013.

The proposal was then introduced in the Senate and titled "S1, Senate Bill 106 ... February 23, 2011," again stating "Sec. 6 Marriage. Marriage between a man and a woman is the only domestic legal union that shall be valid or recognized in this State." The amendment would be voted on in the November election; then the State Board of Elections would certify the result to the Secretary of State, with the effective date of January 1, 2013.†

Attempted Passage in the Legislature

The measure was debated during the fall session that began September 12, 2011, in House Bill (HB) 777, after not getting enough votes in the spring.

> On September 12, 2011, 75 North Carolina CEO's signed an open letter to state officials asking them to halt efforts to approve the proposed amendment. [They included the following:]
>
> - Martin Eakes, CEO of Self Help and the Center for Responsible Lending;
> - Kel Landis, a partner in Pelux Capital;
> - Ping Fu, CEO of Geomagic;
> - Marc Noel, chairman of the Noel Group;
> - Ryan Allis, CEO of iContact;
> - Barbara Goodmon, president of the A.J. Fletcher Foundation;
> - Andy and Barbara Rotchschild, principals of Scientific Properties;
> - Gordon Grubb, CEO of Grubb Ventures;
> - Chuck Wilson, owner and president of CT Wilson Construction;
> - Scott Custer, CEO of Piedmont Community Bank;
> - Joseh DeSimone, founder of Liquidia Technologies. (Cornatzer 2011, 1)

The North Carolina House voted 75–42 to refer the proposed amendment to a state ballot on September 13, 2011 (Bonner 2011). Section 1. "Article 14 of the

---

* http://www.ncga.state.nc.u.s/Sessions/2011/Bills/Senate/HTML/S106v0.html.

† North Carolina General Assembly, http://www.ncleg.net/gascripts/BillLookUp/BillLookUp.pl?Session=2011&BillID=SB+106.

Constitution was amended by creating a new Section 6: 'Marriage is the union of one man and one woman at one time. No other relationship shall be recognized as a valid marriage by the State.' The 'Sponsors of the House version included Republican Representative David Lewis, Rayne Brown Sr., James Crawford Jr., and Dewey Hill'"(Swanzy-Parker 2013, 8–9).

Following discussion in the Senate, the vote would be on the Constitutional amendment that would be placed on the ballot saying "[] FOR [] AGAINST Constitutional amendment to provide that marriage between one man and one woman is the only domestic legal union that shall be valid or recognized in this State" (General Assembly 2011, 1).

Shortly thereafter, the State Senate (HB) 514 was approved as well by 30–16. The sponsor was Republican Senator Peter Brustetter, a three-term Senator who is an attorney (General Assembly of North Carolina 2013).

After Legislative Passage

"On March 1, 2012, the North Carolina Constitutional Amendments Public Commission prepare(d) explanation of the measure for media and election boards" (Swanzy-Parker 2013, 14).

Then "on March 17, 2012, the Durham County Republican party passed a resolution at their annual convention, expressing support for the amendment and arguing that the amendment gives citizens a vote on the issue before it can be decided in court or state without the people's consent. The resolution further argued that the amendment does not change existing law and can be revoked by voters in the future" (*Ballotpedia* 2012). After restating the provisions of the proposed Constitutional amendment, the "whereas" clauses give a rare insight into why supporters of the Constitutional Amendment wanted it passed:

> 2. Whereas, the Supreme Judicial Court of Massachusetts legalized marriage beyond that between a man and woman in 2003 by a narrow 4-3 decision based on its interpretation of the Massachusetts State Constitution;
> 3. Whereas, the voters of Massachusetts have been denied by their legislature the opportunity ever to vote on this issue;
> 4. Whereas, 29 states have responded to the Massachusetts decision by adopting marriage amendments to their constitutions in order to prevent courts altering the definition of marriage in opposition to the will of the people;
> 5. Whereas our legislature is providing the opportunity for North Carolina citizens to vote on this important issue;
> 6. Whereas the proposed amendment does not change the existing law in North Carolina;

7. Whereas courts and legislatures have used the power of the state to coerce religious institutions to accept government dictated definitions of marriage, thereby limiting our religious freedom;
8. Whereas the amendment does not limit the rights of private parties to contract;
9. Whereas the traditional institution of marriage is a bulwark for liberty and the common good;
10. Whereas this amendment in no way diminishes the existing rights and liberties of all North Carolinians;
11. Whereas the citizens of North Carolina have the right, duty and obligation to amend their constitution to protect our liberties;
12. Whereas, this amendment protects us from a fundamental change in our law by the judiciary or legislature without the vote of the people;
13. Whereas, the citizens of North Carolina can revoke this amendment in the future should they so wish;
14. Whereas this amendment enhances and protects the popular sovereignty of all North Carolinians;

BE IT RESOLVED THAT THE DURHAM COUNTY REPUBLICAN PARTY:
Expresses its appreciation to the North Carolina Legislature for providing for a popular vote on this amendment, insuring that the voice of the people is heard; and Supports the adoption of this Amendment to the North Carolina State Constitution; and Recommends that all voters vote YES on this question; and directs that this resolution be communicated to our Senators and Members of Congress, and all other parties, elected officials and the citizens of North Carolina as appropriate." (Durham County Republican Party 2012, 1–2)

Then on Friday, April 20, 2012, a rally was held in Raleigh, the state capital. "The widow of a lawmaker who was the driving force behind a gay marriage referendum on next month's ballot in North Carolina told thousands of conservative Christians it's now up to them to get people to the polls to change the state constitution" (Associated Press 2012, 1). One of the opponents of the amendment (from the Coalition to Protect North Carolina Families) indicated that the approach would eliminate health care benefits for married and unmarried couples, limit domestic violence provisions, and cause the state to be seen as a less progressive state in which to do business.

In order to analyze the forces in opposition to and in favor of the passage of the Constitutional amendment, we need to look at those who declared their support and the amounts of money raised by each side.

Organizations and People Opposed to the Constitutional Amendment

1. "Over 100 *CEOs and other business leaders* from all parts of the state spoke out as individuals against the 2012 North Carolina Constitutional amendment" (Swanzy-Parker 2013, 21).
2. A number of *professional leaders and associations* opposed the amendment, including: law experts at every school of law in North Carolina, North Carolina Association of Women Attorneys, National Association of Social Workers NC, North Carolina Psychological Association, North Carolina Pediatric Society, North Carolina Psychological Association, North Carolina Psychiatric Association, National Association of Social Workers, North Carolina Chapter and the Carolinas Chapter of the American Association of Clinical Endocrinologists, and Council for Entrepreneurial Development (CED) (Swanzy-Parker 2013, 21).
3. *Religious organizations* were opposed, including the "Association of Welcoming and Affirming Baptists" and over 500 individual religious leaders (Swanzy-Parker 2013, 21). A list of supportive religious organizations includes the following: The North Carolina Council of Churches, The North Carolina NAACP, Religious Affairs, The North Carolina Episcopal Diocese, Standing on the Side of Love, North Carolina Unitarian Universalists Organizing to Protect ALL Families, Methodist Federation for Social Action, The Baptist Peace Fellowship, People of Faith for Just Relationships (Asheville), Interfaith Voice (Winston Salem), Clergy for Equality (Charlotte), The Religious Coalition of Orange and Durham Against Amendment 1 (R-CODA-A1), and People of Faith Against Amendment One (Raleigh) (Protect All North Carolina Families 2013).
4. *Civic and community groups* opposed the constitutional amendment, including (Swanzy-Parker 2013, 21–22): NC NAACP, ACLU-NC, Advocates for Justice, Self-Help, Action NC, ARC of NC Covenant with North Carolina's Children, Democracy North Carolina, Disability Rights North Carolina, El Pueblo Institute for Southern Studies, Latin American Coalition, Lillian's List of NC, NARAL Pro-Choice NC, North Carolina National Organization for Women, Philip Randolph Institute, North Carolina Coalition Against Domestic Violence, North Carolina Coalition Against Sexual Assault, North Carolina Justice Center, North Carolina Policy Watch, Planned Parenthood Health Systems, Planned Parenthood of Central NC, Southern Coalition for Social Justice, and TrustWomenNC.
5. A number of *individuals and groups* positioned themselves against the amendment including President Barack Obama (Democrat), Senator Kay

Hagan (Democrat), Congresswoman Renee Ellmers (Republican), North Carolina Governor Bev Purdue (Democrat), John Hood (president and chairman of the conservative John Locke Foundation), Bob Orr (former justice of the N.C. Supreme Court), Harvey Gantt (former Democratic mayor of Charlotte), Richard Vinroot (former Republican mayor of Charlotte), Raleigh City Council, Durham City Council, City of Greenville, NC Asheville City Council, Greensboro City Council, Chapel Hill Town Council, Orange County Board of Commissioners, North Carolina Democratic Party, Libertarian Party of NC, Log Cabin Republicans, College Democrats of NC, Young Democrats of NC, Progressive Democrats of NC, Not Right NC (Republicans Against Amendment One), and North Carolina Alliance of Black Elected Officials among others (Swanzy-Parker 2013, 22–23).

Organizations and People in Favor of the Constitutional Amendment*

1. Legal professionals and law enforcement
   - Locke Bell, District Attorney, Gaston County, Dis. #27A
   - Phil Berger, Jr., District Attorney, Rockingham County, and Vice President of the North Carolina Conference of District Attorneys
   - Senator Phil Berger, Senate Leader, Dis. #26
   - Wallace Bradsher, District Attorney, Caswell and Person Counties, Dis. #09A
   - Raven Byrne, Family Law Attorney in Wake County
   - Garry Frank, District Attorney, Davidson and Davie Counties, Dis. #22B
   - Jay Gaither, District Attorney, Burke, Caldwell, and Catawba Counties, Dis. #25
   - Jeff Hunt, District Attorney, Henderson, Polk, and Transylvania Counties, Dis. #29B
   - Terry Johnson, Sheriff, Alamance County
   - Tom Keith, Former District Attorney, Forsyth County, Dis. #21
   - John Snyder, Former District Attorney, Union County, Dis. #20B
   - Jerry Wilson, District Attorney, Avery, Madison, Mitchell, Watauga, and Yancey Counties, Dis. #24
   - Carey Winders, Sheriff, Wayne County
   - Judge Paul Wright, Former District and Superior Court Judge
2. County endorsements
   - Ashe County Board of Commissioners
   - Avery County Board of Commissioners

* Swanzy-Parker, 2013, 22–29.

- Beaufort County Board of Commissioners
- Bladen County Board of Commissioners
- Brunswick County Board of Commissioners
- Caldwell County Board of Commissioners
- Catawba County Board of Commissioners
- Columbus County Board of Commissioners
- Craven County Board of Commissioners
- Davie County Board of Commissioners
- Gaston County Board of Commissioners
- Gates County Board of Commissioners
- Lincoln County Board of Commissioners
- McDowell County Board of Commissioners
- Robeson County Board of Commissioners
- Rockingham County Board of Commissioners
- Stanly County Board of Commissioners
- Stokes County Board of Commissioners
- Surry County Board of Commissioners
- Union County Board of Commissioners
- Wake County Board of Commissioners
- Watauga County Board of Commissioners
- Wilkes County Board of Commissioners
- Yancey County Board of Commissioners

3. Organizations
   - 6th Congressional District Republican Convention
   - Appalachian Republican Women
   - Billy Graham Evangelistic Association
   - Brunswick Baptist Association
   - Burke County Republican Party
   - Catholic Diocese of Charlotte
   - Catholic Diocese of Raleigh
   - Christian Action League
   - Craven–Pamlico Christian Coalition
   - Dan Forest For Lieutenant Governor
   - Dan Valley Baptist Association
   - Durham County Republican Party
   - Fellowship Baptist Church & Christian Academy
   - Mitchell Baptist Association
   - NathanTabor.com
   - National Organization for Marriage
   - NC4Marriage
   - NCFPC, North Carolina Family Policy Council
   - New Freedom Christian Fellowship
   - New River Baptist Association

- North Carolina Values Coalition
- Open Arms
- TheMarriageChannel.org
- Three Forks Baptist Association
- Town of Lilesville, Board of Commissioners
- Town of Spruce Pine Town, Council
- The Henderson Co. 9-12 Project

4. Churches
   - Central Baptist Church
   - Christian Community Church
   - Christian Fellowship Church
   - Cornerstone Community Church
   - Crystal River Church of God
   - East Lumberton Baptist Church
   - Emmaus Baptist Church
   - Fellowship of Praise Church of God
   - Flat Rock Baptist Church
   - Fletcher First Baptist
   - Gorman Baptist Church
   - Jacksonville Christian Church
   - King's Crossroads Original Free Will Baptist Church
   - Kingdom Life Fellowship
   - LaGrange Park Baptist Church
   - Lake Gaston Baptist Church
   - Midway Baptist Church
   - Mount Olive Baptist Church
   - Mt. Vernon Baptist Church
   - North Canton Baptist Church
   - North Carolina Baptists
   - Oak Level Baptist Church
   - Piney Grove Chapel Baptist Church
   - Plymouth Church of God
   - Powerhouse Church of Jesus Christ
   - Raleigh First Assembly of God
   - Sharon Baptist Church
   - Smith Grove Baptist Church
   - South Charlotte Baptist Church
   - South Raleigh Church of God
   - Southside Church
   - West Asheville Baptist Church
   - West Clayton Church of God
   - White Oak Church of God
   - Zina Christian Center

5. Church leaders
   - Anne Graham Lotz, AnGeL Ministries
   - Bishop Michael Burbidge
   - Bishop Peter Jugis
   - Dinesh D'Souza, *New York Times* Bestselling Author, President of King's College
   - Dr. Norman L. Geisler, Author, Apologist
   - Lady Goodman, Mt. Zion Baptist Church
   - Lay Leader Grissom, White Memorial Methodist
   - Pastor Arnold, CrossRoad Baptist
   - Pastor Bailey, Grace Baptist Church (Nashville)
   - Pastor Banks-Lee, New Freedom Christian Fellowship
   - Pastor Barbee, New Covenant Ministries P.H. Church
   - Pastor Barnes, Bible Missionary Baptist Church
   - Pastor Bearrer, Victory Baptist Church
   - Pastor Beck, Central Baptist
   - Pastor Bennett, Gospel Center Baptist Church
   - Pastor Blocker, Galillee Missionary Baptist Church
   - Pastor Breedlove, Harriett Baptist
   - Pastor Breland, Liberty Christian Church
   - Pastor Buchanan, Tabernacle Baptist
   - Pastor Bud Russell, Mt. Vernon
   - Pastor Carter, First Baptist Church of Oak Island
   - Pastor Clemmons, Mt. Olive Grove Baptist Church
   - Pastor Collins, North Topsail Shores Baptist Church
   - Pastor Cottrell, Pearce Baptist Church
   - Pastor David, Lake Gaston Baptist Church
   - Pastor Davis, Christian Community Church
   - Pastor Davis, Triad Cowboy Church
   - Pastor Dennis, Pole Creek Baptist Church
   - Pastor Dohan, Sovereign Redeemer Community Church
   - Pastor Frank, South Henderson Pentecostal Holiness Church
   - Pastor Fox, Popler Springs Baptist
   - Pastor Galyean, Dublin First Baptist Church
   - Pastor Garbett, New Hope Baptist Church
   - Pastor Gilbert, Good Shepherd Community Church
   - Pastor Golden, Piney Grove Baptist
   - Pastor Grainger, Cedar Grove Baptist
   - Pastor Haley, Harris Chapel Baptist Church
   - Pastor Harris, Joy in the Lord
   - Pastor James, Shallowford Baptist Church
   - Pastor Jefferys, Open Road Community Church
   - Pastor Jesse, Church of the Crossroads

- Pastor Jestory, Sandy Creek Baptist
- Pastor Johnson, Brunswick Baptist
- Pastor Jones, Highest Praise Ministries
- Pastor Key, Mt. Zion Baptist Church
- Pastor Lewis, First Baptist Church of Maysville
- Pastor Lewis, White Oak Baptist Church
- Pastor Mark Harris, First Baptist Church of Charlotte
- Pastor McNeill, Maple Springs Baptist Church
- Pastor Pendergrass, Freed Life
- Pastor Phillips, Cherry Grove Baptist Church
- Pastor Prewer, Freedom Life Church of God
- Pastor Randolph, New Born Church of Jesus Christ
- Pastor Ross, South Henderson Pentecostal Holiness Church
- Pastor Sledge, Oasis of Hope Ministries Inc.
- Pastor Smith, Soldier Bay Baptist Church
- Pastor Speight, Trinity Baptist
- Pastor Steve, High Cross Cowboy Church
- Pastor Sutherland, Fellowship Baptist Church & Christian Academy
- Pastor Upchurch, Anchor Baptist Church
- Pastor Wallenm, Oak Level Baptist Church
- Pastor Williams, Bethel Baptist Church
- Pastor Wood, Calvary Baptist Church
- Pastor Wood, Potters Hill Baptist Church
- Pastor Yopp, Salem Baptist Church, Inc
- Rev. Currin, Pine Ridge Baptist Church
- Rev. Clemmons, Mount Olive Baptist Church
- Rev. Harvey, United Church of Christ
- Rev. Hunter, Central Baptist Church
- Rev. Easter, Victory Baptist Church
- Rev. Hester, Riegelwood Baptist Church
- Rev. Kasey, North Henderson Baptist Church
- Rev. Larry Phillips, Midway Baptist Church
- Rev. Pegram, Westwood P. H. Church
- Rev. Winstead, Grace Baptist Church

Funding Reports from Organizations in Favor of Amendment

"The North Carolina reports for the ... biggest spenders in the May 8, 2012, constitutional amendment fight indicated the following state board's summary reports on WRAL" (Swanzy-Parker 2013, 30–31).

1. Vote for Marriage (Pro Amendment): $4,725,971.22. Major organizational contributors included: Christian Action League, National Organization for Marriage, North Carolina Values Coalition, Roman Catholic Dioceses of Charlotte, American Family Association, Bayleaf Baptist Church, First Baptist Church (Charlotte), and AMDG Medical, LLC.
2. Coalition to Protect All North Carolina Families (Anti-Amendment): $8,191,371.27. Major organizational contributors included: Human Rights Campaign, Replacements LTD, Bluepint NMC, HRC ZNZC Families PAC, Center for Community Self Help.

Primary Election Results

The primary election was held on May 8, 2012. The vote for the constitutional amendment was 1,317,178 (61.04%) and against was 840,802 (38.96%) (NC Board of Elections 2012). Out of 100 counties, 7 counties voted against the constitutional amendment (4 of which were located in the Triangle, which is typically a progressive area), while 93 counties voted in favor of the Constitutional amendment (Leslie 2012).

Minnesota and North Carolina Compared

What were some of the factors that made it possible for the people in Minnesota to defeat the "One Man, One Woman" constitutional amendment as opposed to factors that made it possible for North Carolina to pass its "One Man, One Woman Amendment":

1. Although North Carolina's anticonstitutional amendment forces raised approximately twice as much money as the proconstitutional amendment forces, in Minnesota the amount raised by the anticonstitutional amendment forces was dramatically larger than that raised by the proconstitutional Amendment forces.
2. Minnesota had a human rights law protecting the rights of lesbian, gay, bisexual, and transgender (LGBT) people since 1993, whereas North Carolina had such a provision in force only in a few large cities. This provided a base for organizing in Minnesota that was not possible in North Carolina.
3. Minnesota had almost 700 organizations signing on against the constitutional amendment. Minnesota organizers were careful to involve very large numbers of clergy and to make them obvious in media presentations. North Carolina ministers generally favored the amendment.
4. There is a significant difference in the basic demographics of the two states, in regard to those key socioeconomic issues that we have discussed elsewhere in the book (see Chapter 3).
5. Minnesota developed a coalition, Minnesotans United for All Families, which was exceptionally well organized.

Minnesota went on the next year to pass legislation allowing for same-sex marriage; again based upon the history of human rights legislation empowering LGBT people. North Carolina was left with a law implementing the "One Man, One Woman" principle for marriage.

References

Associated Press. 2012. "Thousands Rally to Back NC Marriage Amendment." *WRAL.com*. April 20. http://www.wral.com/news/state/nccapitol/story/11007080/.

Ballotpedia. 2012. http://ballotpedia.org/wiki/index.php/North_Carolina_Same-Sex_Marriage,_Amendment_1_May_2012.

Bonner, Lynn. 2011. "N.C. House OKs Amendment Banning Gay Marriage." *Newsobserver.com*. September 13. http://www.newsobserver.com/2011/09/13/1483783/house-oks-amendment-banning-gay.html.

Comer, Matt. 2011. "Anti-Gay Marriage Amendment Filed in N.C. Senate." February 22. http://goqnotes.com/10093/anti-gay-marriage-amendment-filed-in-n-c-senate/.

Cornatzer, Mary. 2011. "Business Leaders Ask Lawmakers to Think About Jobs, Not Marriage." Newsobserver.com. http://projects.newsobserver.com/under_the_dome/business_leaders_ask_lawmakers_to_think_about_jobs_not_marriage.

Durham County Republican Party. 2012. "Marriage Amendment." County Convention. http://durhamgop.com/wp-content/uploads/2012/03/Marriage_Amendment_Resolution.pdf.

General Assembly of North Carolina. 2011. Session Law 2011-409, Senate Bill 514. http://www.ncleg.net/Sessions/2011/Bills/Senate/PDF/S514v5.pdf.

General Assembly of North Carolina. 2013. Senator Peter S. Brunstetter (Rep). http://www.ncleg.net/gascripts/members/viewMember.pl?sChamber=S&nUserID=223

Leslie, Laura. 2012. "Breaking Down the Amendment Vote." WRAL. May 9. http://www wral.com/news/state/nccapitol/blogpost/11079387.

NC Board of Elections. 2012. Primary Election—Official Results. North Carolina, State Board of Elections. http://results.enr.clarityelections.com/NC/36596/85942/en/summary.html.

Protect All North Carolina Families.org. 2013. "Toolkit." http://www.protectncfamilies.org/content/faith-toolkit.

Swanzy-Parker, Elizabeth. 2013. "The Great Divide: Minnesota and North Carolina—The Battleground States," unpublished manuscript, April 28.

U.S. Census Bureau. 2011. "U.S. Census Bureau, State and County QuickFacts" (2011 estimate). http://quickfacts.census.gov/qfd/states/37000.html.

Chapter 8

Life in the Disempowered States

Wallace Swan

A while back, I had a conversation with a gay man who lives in a small town in South Dakota. He told me that he is in his 30s and he has his own business. I asked him how it was to live in a state that does not have human rights for lesbian, gay, bisexual, and transgender (LGBT) persons. He gave me something of a blank stare. I asked him if his state offered human rights protection for LGBT persons, and he talked with his friends and relatives, and they also had no idea of whether their state had human rights protections. Then I asked him if he was aware of any problems that he had experienced in his hometown as a result of being gay. He said no because he had had no negative experiences that he could recollect.

Contrast this with my experience in talking with a person who lives in a large city in a Central Plains state. I asked him about his experiences in living in a state that does not offer human rights protections for LGBT persons. He is in a partnership with another gay man. He told me that both he as well as other professional people he knows feel very much discriminated against. They do not feel comfortable in discussing their sexual orientation with other people, because of the fact that they might be discriminated against in their professional lives. Especially relevant is the fact that he is well-educated and looking for a position. Like many gay people in that situation, he does not want to move to another location because he loves his home. But he feels that if the information about his sexual orientation were to come out, then he might well lose a chance at any jobs he would be interested in having, especially in today's tight job market.

So what accounts for the difference between experience of the gay businessman in South Dakota and the professional in the Central Plains state? One factor might be that the gay man in South Dakota is not in a relationship and has thus not experienced the way in which heterosexual couples in a workplace have rights that single people do not have (especially since his workplace is his own). As we know, there are 1,138 federal rights that accrue to a heterosexual couple that are not available to a gay couple. Each state also has hundreds of additional rights that are provided to heterosexual couples as opposed to same-sex couples. A second factor might be that he has not tried to gain a position (e.g., an elective or appointed position) where people in his community might begin to analyze his qualifications based upon his identity as a gay person. A third factor might be that the quality of life for LGBT people has, at least in some ways, gotten better in the period since the Stonewall Rebellion in 1969: There are role models on television, people can connect with other gay people on the Internet, and there is essentially a socialization structure that has developed because of recognition of a gay identity. This cultural change is one that the person in South Dakota would certainly be aware of. And certainly this is true of the Central Plains, where many of the people we talked with are "out" despite the effect that this status may have upon their housing, education, and employability. Fourth, there has been a revolution in the belief system of many gays and lesbians. Having written for a number of years in the field, I can remember when, in the 1980s, it was a major accomplishment to persuade governmental agencies to provide basic human rights. Later, around 1994, it was a major issue to argue the Minneapolis School Board into providing domestic partners benefits for employees: It took years. The LGBT movement has now, in 2014, progressed in 18 states to provide marital benefits. Interestingly enough, the cultural expectation of people in today's LGBT community is simply that one should be able to have a partner who is the equivalent of a heterosexual marital partner. In a number of states (for example, the author's state of Minnesota) it is also a cultural expectation that rights of people with differing gender identity and orientation ought to be strongly affirmed. However, I think it is fair to say that this same level of affirmation is not present for bisexual people. In fact, there is sometimes a gay and lesbian presumption (which is clearly not the case) that people are either "gay" or "straight"; and that there is no intermediate position of "bisexual." The author has seen people shunned in the LGBT community if they move from gay or lesbian to "bisexual." And it is one of the purposes of this book to ensure that there continues to be recognition of the legitimacy of all points on the Kinsey continuum, as well as support for persons with differing gender orientation and identity.

My conversation about life in the disempowered states started with a presentation at the national conference of the American Society for Public Administration in Las Vegas. I had been asked to present a paper on a chapter I had coauthored in the book *Cultural Competence for Public Administrators*. The chapter, "Cultural Competency around Sexual and Gender Orientation and Identity," was the result of several years of intensive work with Kristen Norman-Major and Mark French. I decided to provide some of the highlights of this chapter in some PowerPoints that I prepared. After the presentation was completed, I was asked by a member of the audience whether I would be willing to meet with him back in my hometown of Minneapolis when he and his partner came there a few months hence. I said that I would be glad to, so that we could talk more at length about the issues raised in the chapter. I found that he and his partner were living in a Central Plains state that not only did not have partnership rights for LGBT people but also had no human rights. So, when they came to the Twin Cities (ironically for a heterosexual wedding) a few months later, I invited them to lunch at my downtown condo and they came over.

I found that this person, who had a master's degree and who was prominent in his professional association, did not currently have a job. After knowing so many of my LGBT friends having their homes foreclosed and rendered bankrupt by the Great Recession, this was not a surprise to me. But what I found especially problematic was that my new friend had to worry about divulging his identity to potential employers, who might rule him out of the workplace based upon who he was. Having lived in Minnesota prior to the passage of the Human Rights Amendment in 1993, I instantly remembered how it had been when I came out and was constantly badgered in my workplace. One prominent social service manager at the time asked me, "What should I tell people when they find out you were discussed in a gay newspaper?" I said, "Tell them that I am gay." And another leading social service manager told his staff that "we should place his desk as close to the north wall of the Hennepin County government center as possible, so that he will know that he could be pushed off the edge." I always learned about the bigotry of these managers, because their supervisees would warn me about what they had said. The conversation brought me back to the days when my very career and identity were at risk whenever I was honest. And I thought what a terrible thing it is that the majority of the states in this country still require LGBT people to live in fear like this.

Let us talk about some of the economic and social characteristics of the "disempowered states." These states may generally be divided into four categories:

1. Mountain/Western states, including Idaho, Utah, Montana, Wyoming, Arizona, and Alaska
2. Midwest states, including Indiana, Pennsylvania, Michigan, Ohio, and Missouri
3. Plains states, including Kansas, Nebraska, North Dakota, South Dakota, and Oklahoma
4. Southern ("Sunbelt") states, including Alabama, Arkansas, Florida, Georgia, Kentucky, Louisiana, Mississippi, North Carolina, South Carolina, Tennessee, Texas, Virginia, and West Virginia

The Mountain/Western states have always incorporated highly individualistic and conservative social values, which have moved steadily to the right over the years. Midwest states are ones that have been undergoing a technological shift from an industrial-based society, and have suffered major job losses. One may note that a number of these states (categorized variously by the author) may also be seen as falling within the Plains states or "Great Plains" (Montana, Wyoming, Kansas, Nebraska, North and South Dakota, Oklahoma, and Texas) which is, and has been for many years, undergoing a large degree of social, economic, and technological change. Small, individually owned farms have been replaced by much larger farms, crop supports have been almost eliminated, the area is dealing with major droughts, the use of irrigation (which made possible the use of enormous amounts of water from the Ogallala Aquifer) is threatened by the fact that this reserve may be almost eliminated by 2030, and farming income is being supplemented by wind power (Hylton 2012). And finally, the Southern states continue to be a world of their own, characterized by strong religious values, conservative social values, and low wages.

Richard Florida has documented the way in which the "creative class" has been migrating to regions that have certain characteristics present, and these areas typically do not include the Mountain, Midwestern, Plains, and Southern states. The result of his calculations has been the creation of a "creativity index," which evaluates how an area does in terms of its potential economic capabilities: "The three T's [talent, technology, and tolerance] are made upon indexes such as: visible minority, foreign born and gay/lesbian population share for Tolerance, a Tech-Pole index and patents per capita for Technology and Creative Class occupational share and educational attainment for Talent, amongst others" (Martin Prosperity Institute 2012). Taking a look at his chart in this article titled "Exhibit I: The Creativity Index for Top 20 Metros, 2010," one will find that out of the 20 top metros, there are creativity indexes for only five metropolitan areas that are located partially or totally in disempowered states: Tucson, Arizona; Atlanta–Sandy Springs–Marietta, Georgia; Austin–Round Rock Texas; Washington D.C.–Arlington, Virginia–Alexandria, Virginia/West Virginia; and Durham, North Carolina. The Minneapolis–St. Paul–Bloomington, Minnesota/Wisconsin area is partially in Minnesota, which allows same-sex marriage (Martin Prosperity Institute 2012). In some cases, the "Tolerance Index Rating" is already low and will likely move even lower.

We know that when federal dollars are distributed to states, most of the empowered states receive less than $1 worth of federal tax monies generated, while most of the disempowered states receive more than $1 worth of federal tax monies generated. What does this compilation of figures tell us? It provides us with some of the connection between the level of federal revenue collected and the level of federal expenditures for a number of states; and it suggests some interesting characteristics about the type of states that have discrimination bans and those states that prohibit discrimination. The former states are typically, but not always, states with fewer resources, which help to make them disempowered.

Another map of the United States also poses interesting questions about the disempowered states and the empowered states. The "Hate Map," which documents the existence of many hate groups in the United States, shows that of the 20 top states having the most hate groups, 16 of those states are disempowered states (Georgia, Florida, Texas, Mississippi, Tennessee, North Carolina, Pennsylvania, Virginia, Alabama, Ohio, Louisiana, South Carolina, Arkansas, Michigan, Missouri, and Indiana), while only 4 are empowered states (California, New Jersey, New York, and Illinois). By contrast, of the 20 states with the least hate groups, 12 states (Nevada, Massachusetts, Wisconsin, Maine, Connecticut, Delaware, Iowa, New Hampshire, New Mexico, Rhode Island, Vermont, and Hawaii) are empowered states (Southern Poverty Law Center 2012). Of course, the characterization of some states as hate states has been extremely controversial, but we present the information for the reader to make up their own mind.

Similarly the states that opted to not create their own health insurance exchanges generally are disempowered states. These include Alabama, Alaska, Arizona, Florida, Georgia, Indiana, Kansas, Louisiana, Maine, Mississippi, Missouri, Montana, Nebraska, New Jersey, North Carolina, North Dakota, Ohio, Oklahoma, Pennsylvania, South Carolina, South Dakota, Tennessee, Texas, Utah, Virginia, Wisconsin, and Wyoming (The Henry J. Kaiser Foundation 2013). Those states that opted out of Medicaid expansion generally are disempowered states: Alabama, Alaska, Florida, Georgia, Idaho, Indiana, Kansas, Louisiana, Maine, Mississippi, Montana, Nebraska, North Carolina, Oklahoma, South Carolina, South Dakota, Tennessee, Texas, Virginia, Wisconsin, and Wyoming (The Advisory Board Company 2013).

From a political point of view, the Congressional elections of 2010 consolidated many of the trends in these states. This election resulted in election of Scott Walker in Wisconsin as well as a number of "governors, including Rick Snyder of Michigan, John Kasich of Ohio, Rick Scott of Florida, Paul LePage of Maine, Tom Corbett of Pennsylvania, and … Chris Christie of New Jersey. The Republican-controlled state legislatures (have) proceeded to pass laws on social issues, including gay rights" (The Progressive Professor 2012). Scott Walker led the effort to limit collective bargaining rights for public employees in Wisconsin (as well as dealing with benefits of public employees). Rick Snyder of Ohio worked with the Michigan legislature to pass a right-to-work law. This group of governors also initiated a number of other initiatives (e.g., dealing with evolution, abortion, among others). The 2012 elections had a somewhat different effect in that some members of Congress were not reelected because of their positions on a variety of controversial issues.

Probably the most telling data that compares empowered and disempowered states is information collected by two comparative reports, both concerning same-sex marriage. A study involving 34,000 LGBT people looked at the psychological health of this group first in 2001–2002 and then in 2004–2005 (after marriage amendments were passed in 14 of the states). The same survey was used in both, and the second survey indicated that "participants reported …

increases of 36% for any mood disorder, 248% for generalized anxiety disorder, 42% for alcohol use disorder, and 36% for psychiatric comorbidity. In the comparable control group from states without such amendments during the same time period, there were no significant increases in these psychiatric disorders" (Buffie 2011, 987). The second study (titled "Effect of Same-Sex Marriage Laws on Health Care Use and Expenditures in Sexual Minority Men: A Quasi-Natural Experiment") is summarized as follows: "In the twelve months following the 2003 legalization of same-sex marriage in Massachusetts, gay and bisexual men had a significant decrease in medical care visits [13%], mental health care visits, and mental health care costs [14%], compared with the 12 months before the law change" (McQueen 2012, 1).

Conclusion

Perhaps it is because I was born in Nebraska and raised in eastern Washington and Northern Idaho (where I graduated from college) that I see this issue so clearly. The "creative class" has migrated to empowered states, the level of suicides is higher in the disempowered states, for every federal dollar raised an amount higher than that $1 goes to disempowered states, there are proportionately more hate groups in the disempowered states than the empowered states (e.g., one of my relatives in Idaho lives within 37 minutes of the new headquarters for a neo-Nazi group), and efforts to prevent affordable health care and Medicaid expansion are centered in the disempowered states.

Finally, we see that the states that have gone through the process of amending their constitutions (and, one might also surmise, passing legislation) to ensure that only heterosexual marriages are legal in the eyes of the state have also strongly contributed to significantly reducing the health outcomes for gay, lesbian, and bisexual people. Conversely, we have seen that where same-sex marriage has been legalized (the state of Massachusetts), this has had a positive impact upon the health outcomes for partnered as well as single gay men.

References

Buffie, William. 2011. "Public Health Implications of Same-Sex Marriage." *American Journal of Public Health, 101*(6), 987–990.

Hylton, Will. 2012. "Broken Heartland: The Looming Collapse of Agriculture on the Great Plains." *Harper's Magazine*, 23–35.

Martin Prosperity Institute. 2012. "Insight—Rise Revisited: Creativity Index." June 27, http://martinprosperity.org/2012/06/27/insight-rise-revisited-creativity-index/.

McQueen, Derrick. 2012. "Same-Sex Marriage Laws Reduce Doctor Visits and Health Care Costs for Gay Men." Union in Dialogue.org, January 4.

Southern Poverty Law Center. 2012. "Hate Map." http://www.splcenter.org/get-informed/hate-map.
The Advisory Board Company. 2013. "Where the States Stand on Medicaid Expansion." http://www.advisory.com/Daily-Briefing/Resources/Primers/MedicaidMap.
The Henry J. Kaiser Foundation. 2013. "State Decisions for Creating Health Insurance Marketplaces." http://kff.org/health-reform/state-indicator/health-insurance-exchanges/.
The Progressive Professor. 2012. "Republican Run State Government, Their Social Agenda, and the Effect on 2012 Elections." http://www.theprogressiveprofessor.com/?p=18237.

Chapter 9

Another Divide: Bisexuality in U.S. Politics

Victor J. Raymond

Contents

In order to understand the place of bisexuality within the larger discussion of lesbian, gay, bisexual, transgender, queer, or questioning (LGBTQ) issues and politics in the United States, one must first recognize the contested nature of bisexual identity. Bisexuality remains largely misunderstood, with different groups advancing their own conceptions of what bisexuality actually is and what it means within the constellation of LGBTQ identities. Within the context of the discussion of the "empowered" and "disempowered" states, bisexuality has been something of a strategic football, conceptually deployed, avoided, or erased as part of larger political efforts and struggles. This essay begins with the task of defining bisexuality, then moves to a consideration of bisexuality in recent political history, the role of bisexual erasure and its effect on the empowered and disempowered states, and finishes with five brief case studies.

Defining Bisexuality

In order to explore the dynamics of bisexuality and its place in the larger LGBTQ movement, we should first define what bisexuality is. This is—and has almost always been—more complicated than might be first expected. Some of these tensions are reflected in the range of definitions of bisexuality actually used by self-identified bisexuals (see later). The range of definitions is itself something of a conundrum, since ambiguity in relation to sexual orientation creates social tensions, from interpersonal interaction to relations at much higher levels between organizations. For the purposes of this essay, "bisexuality" should be understood as having attraction to more than one gender. This includes people attracted to both men and women, including when there may be attraction more to one gender than another. It also includes people whose sexual identity is fluid and may change over time. It also includes people who see their attraction as unrelated to gender, as well as people who dispute the idea that there are only two genders (Barker et al. 2012). Additionally, this definition does not immediately take into account differences between how people feel, how they act, and how they identify. The range of definitions originating *within* the bisexual community may also reflect a greater level of comfort among bisexual-identified people for different definitions but also poses problems for establishing a definition recognized by those on the *outside* of the bisexual community as legitimate and valid. To this extent, this also provides an opening for others—heterosexuals, lesbians, gays, and transgender people—to impose their own definitions. This tug-of-war also reflects the fact that those *outside* of the bisexual community do not agree on what bisexuality is. On first blush, bisexuality is often understood as having attractions to men and to women, but even this seemingly innocuous definition is seen by some as reifying and reinforcing a dualistic construction of gender. This has led some people to adopt terms such as "omnisexual" or "pansexual" in order to work around this somewhat limited view of sexuality and gender identity. Within the gay male community, bisexual is often not seen as a legitimate sexual orientation, but merely a phase or transitional state preceding acceptance of a more legitimate gay or lesbian identity (Fox 1996). For some lesbians, bisexuals and particular bisexual women are seen as being inherently problematic, with divided loyalties and compromised by potential attraction to men. Within some parts of the transgender community, bisexuality is defined as involving only cisgender attraction (i.e., attraction to people whose gender matches the sex assigned at birth)—a definition that recognizes only a small portion of people who would identify themselves as bisexual (see earlier) (Eisner 2013). When bisexuality is recognized as being potentially legitimate, it is defined in such a way as to render it rare, if not completely mythical; for example bisexuals are *only* those people who are *exactly* divided in their attractions, 50–50 men versus women, or bisexuals *might* exist, but they are rarely encountered, not unlike unicorns.

All of these attempts to define bisexuality from the outside of the bisexual community are inextricably tied up with questions of boundary maintenance, definitional simplicity, as well as attempts to legitimate other groups' self-definition at the expense of bisexuals and bisexuality (Eisner 2013). What must also be recognized is the centrality of white, middle-class, heteronormative cultural construction of gender and sexuality in these debates; little if any recognition is given to differing understanding of sexuality and gender originating in communities of color (Rust 1996).

A different and perhaps more easily understood parallel may be found with biracial and multiracial identity. Since the U.S. Supreme Court decision in *Virginia v. Loving* in 1967, the number of people with multiple racial and ethnic identities has grown significantly. Given the range of different racial and ethnic groups in U.S. society, it is perhaps conceptually easier to recognize the range of different definitions and kinds of biracial and multiracial people, along with the different kinds of discrimination targeted at biracial and multiracial people (Collins 2000).

Discrimination against bisexuality has taken on many forms. Among heterosexuals the acceptance of bisexuality is distinctly mixed, as well as distinctly gendered. Bisexuality among women is seen as acceptable only so long as it does not challenge the central and controlling position of heterosexual relationships. Bisexuality among men is not nearly so acceptable, and is often mistaken for and lumped together with homosexuality. Within the gay and lesbian communities, bisexuality is not considered as a legitimate sexual orientation, and bisexuals are often treated as sojourners, fair-weather allies, liable to pass for straight, and ready to take advantage of heterosexual privilege (Hutchins 1996, 240–259). As will be discussed later, the combination of discrimination and lack of acceptance by both heterosexuals and homosexuals leads to "bisexual erasure"—a social dynamic in which bisexuality as an intermediate category is rendered invisible or unacceptable due to tensions between groups at either end, namely, heterosexuals and homosexuals. If this were merely an abstracted phenomenon, with little in the way of larger social consequence or institutionalized discrimination, such erasure might seem irritating, at best. But when combined with political dynamics that have left bisexuals both atomized and yet unappreciated within the LGBTQ communities, the resulting dynamic leaves bisexuals at best as second-class citizens within a supposedly larger struggle for equality and liberty regardless of sexual orientation.

Background

The history of bisexual activism cannot be separated from the larger history and context of the struggle for lesbian, gay, bisexual, and transgender rights. Pre-Stonewall discrimination was sufficiently negative that there was little perceived need to distinguish between gay men, lesbians, bisexuals, and transgender people—all were seen as "deviant" and "queer." Organizations such as the Mattachine Society and Daughters of Bilitis had bisexual members without necessarily recognizing bisexual (or transgender) identity. Yet these organizations were relatively small, in terms of numbers, funding, and political efficacy. By the 1970s, this uniformity of discrimination and lack of differentiation meant that the emergent "gay rights" movement included bisexuals, lesbians, transgender, and gender-queer people, as well as gay men—yet that diversity is not always acknowledged in retrospect. This has led to the erroneous assumption on the part of some that gay men—and by implication, white middle-class gay men—were somehow at the forefront of the struggle for sexual liberation, when that was not necessarily the case at all.

Bisexuality in the Post-Stonewall Era

Bisexuals were active in many organizations labeled retrospectively as "gay" or "gay and lesbian." One notable example was Brenda Howard, an activist in the bisexual as well as BDSM communities in and around New York City. Howard was a key figure in the founding of the first Gay Pride parades. David Lourea was another early bisexual activist in the Bay Area and an early activist in the AIDS crisis of the 1980s and 1990s. It should not be surprising that bisexual activists were involved in various lesbian and gay organizations, given the common interest in same-gender attraction and related political and social issues, including civil rights, sexual freedom, and HIV/AIDS. But the very labeling of organizations as "gay" or "gay and lesbian" in the 1980s and 1990s leaves the erroneous retrospective impression that bisexuals—as well as transgender people (who themselves could be lesbian, gay, bisexual, or heterosexual)—were less involved or not members of such organizations. This was simply not the case, as various LGBTQ local, state, and national level organizations were often the *only* organizations dealing with issues of concern to bisexual individuals. The centrality of gay and lesbian identity in the naming and character of these organizations also illustrates the reality that bisexuals were not always welcome in those organizations, due to a variety of factors: assumptions of homosexual identity; prejudice toward bisexuals and a consequent discouragement of coming out as bisexual; and a lack of belief in bisexuality as a valid identity. In particular, the naming of organizations as "gay and lesbian" indicates the primacy of gay and lesbian identity in such groups—but not exclusivity, as many bisexual activists persisted in their involvement in these organizations, despite often being made to feel unwelcome or not full members (Hutchins and Kaahumanu 1991; Serano 2010).

Second, despite their small size and sometimes ephemeral character, there were organizations that specifically served the bisexual community and represented the interests of bisexuals from the 1970s onward. The San Francisco Bisexual Center was founded in 1976 and remained in existence until 1984, BiPOL in 1983, and followed by the Bay Area Bisexual Network in 1987. Various other organizations and groups emerged around the United States. during the 1970s and early 1980s, in places such as Boston, Chicago, Detroit, Minneapolis/St. Paul, and Miami (Hutchins and Kaahumanu 1991). While many of these organizations have closed their doors, a few have remained, notably the Boston Bisexual Women's Network, founded in 1983, and some organizations such as the Bisexual Organizing Project in the Twin Cities, are successors to now-defunct older groups (Burleson 2005). These early groups were supported by an increasing awareness of bisexuality in literature and media. Books such as *Bi Any Other Name*, coedited by Lani Ka'ahumanu and Loraine Hutchins; and Marjorie Garber's *Vice Versa: Bisexuality and the Eroticism of Everyday Life* raised awareness of bisexuality in U.S. society, and in so doing, provided support for various bisexual groups and organizations around the country. There was a bisexual contingent organized as part of the 1987 March On Washington for Gay and Lesbian Rights, which in turn led to the first National Conference on Bisexuality in 1990, which then led to the formation of the organization now known as BiNet USA (Hutchins and Kaahumanu 1991). All of this contributed to the slowly emergent formation of a national bisexual political movement by the end of the decade. This movement was marked by its grassroots character and the relative impermanence of formal bisexual organizations, echoing the initial waves of organizing in the aftermath of the Stonewall riots in 1969.

In some ways, the bisexual movement's early efforts to gain greater recognition for the "B" in LGBTQ has some parallel with efforts on the part of lesbian activists since the 1970s to encourage organizations to switch from "gay" to "gay and lesbian." The political position of lesbians as a distinct interest group began to diverge from that of gay men, due to a variety of factors: the growing realization of different earning potential between female–female couples and male–male couples, sexism on the part of gay white men, many lesbians having children with resulting variation in family formation and structure, and the different experiences of sexism between women and men. All of this was taking place in the mid-1970s and persisted into the 1980s and the early 1990s, roughly concurrent with the debate within the feminist movement about the place of lesbians within it (Vaid 1995).

Bisexuality in the 1990s

By the early 1990s, a national bisexual political movement began to emerge. Two national organizations, BiNet USA and the Bisexual Resource Center, provided a voice for bisexual activism and were assisted later by the American Institute on Bisexuality. Both BiNet USA and the Bisexual Resource Center were and are very small in comparison to more established national advocacy organizations such as the National Gay and Lesbian Task Force (NGLTF; originally the National Gay Task Force) or the Human Rights Campaign (HRC; originally Human Rights Campaign Fund). Bisexual conferences and the presence of a visible bisexual contingent at the 1993 National March on Washington for Lesbian, Gay and Bi Equal Rights and Liberation—including a bisexual speaker, Lani Kaahumanu, as part of the speaker lineup—and other events all served as reminders of bisexuality as a part of a larger movement for sexual orientation equality and liberation (Hutchins and Kaahumanu 1991). Even so, by the 1990s, national organizations advocating for bisexuals were (and still are) miniscule in size compared to a much larger and better-funded set of organizations that purported to serve the LGBTQ communities, but mainly represented the gay and lesbian communities (Vaid 1995).

The efforts of bisexual activists for greater recognition of bisexuality within the LGBTQ movement in the 1990s were also parallel with efforts on the part of transgender activists to seek full inclusion of transgender identity in the LGBTQ political movement. Early efforts at coalition building between bisexuals and transgender activists were initially quite successful, due in part to a recognition of shared interests and a mutual wariness of some gay and lesbian leaders who were sometimes actively hostile to bisexual and transgender involvement and gay and lesbian organizations, which were often not inclusive of bisexuals. It did not stop there; sometimes bisexuality and transgender identity were used by opportunistic conservative politicians to signal their distance from the gay and lesbian communities without appearing to be homophobic. For example, in the late 1990s, then-Mayor Norm Coleman of St. Paul, Minnesota declined to sign the LGBTQ Pride Proclamation because (as he put it) he had no difficulty with gays and lesbians, but bisexuality and transgender identity were "lifestyle choices"—coded language for his more conservative supporters (Lonetree 1994). In a meeting with LGBTQ leaders from around Minnesota (including the author of this essay), Coleman listened attentively to the objections raised by activists but did not back down from his earlier decision.

Despite these setbacks, bisexual and transgender activists continued to work together and with gay and lesbian leaders who were interested in truly diverse coalitions for social change. But the road to unity is not always clear or well-marked; recently, tensions have emerged between bisexuals and transgender people as some transgender activists have inaccurately defined bisexuality as only cisgender in nature (Serano 2010).

Bisexuality and the Marches on Washington

Taking place in 1979, 1987, 1993, 2000, and 2009, the various Marches on Washington served as catalysts for LGBTQ activism. The Marches are perhaps best thought of as exemplars of the evolution of the LGBTQ political movement from an organic and grassroots nature to a more institutionalized kind of activism, controlled by a set of established (some would say "entrenched") political advocacy organizations. The Marches on Washington also serve as snapshots of bisexual and transgender acceptance, going from no recognition to a grudging acceptance to finally a kind of erasure. Beginning in the 1980s, activists from BiNet USA and other bisexual organizations working with NGLTF exercised real leadership to raise the visibility of bisexuals, encountering tension with various gay and lesbian organizations and leadership, most notably HRC. Later Marches did not see the same kind of direct bisexual involvement; indeed, the 2000 March was actively boycotted by BiNet USA.

Bisexuality in the Current Era

From an institutional perspective, the emergence of distinct bisexual advocacy organizations on the national level happened just as national organizations primarily serving gay men and lesbians became larger political players on the national scene. Thus, national organizations dealing with sexual orientation were *originally* established with bisexual and transgender participation, but their later organizational cultures and programmatic activities were primarily focused on the gay and lesbian communities. This left those newly formed bisexual advocacy organizations as Davids among Goliaths in terms of their ability to exert political influence, both within the LGBTQ communities and the larger society as a whole.

The internal tensions between these different communities are illustrated by the slow evolution over time in the labels used to describe what we now think of as the LGBTQ political movement. Beginning with "gay" as in the Gay Liberation Front or the Gay Activists Alliance, then evolving into "gay and lesbian" as in the National Gay and Lesbian Task Force, still later into "gay, lesbian, and bisexual" and then "gay, lesbian, bisexual, and transgender." Since the 1990s, "queer" has been used in a reclaiming way as an umbrella term with political and activist connotations but is rejected by some elements of the LGBTQ communities. Sociolinguistic changes over time have thus led to bisexuals being left invisible within the larger context of LGBTQ, as "gay" and (to a lesser extent) "queer" have been used as umbrella terms but also as specific identifiers of sexual orientation identity—often without any attempt to distinguish one usage from the other, thus muddying the waters when attempting fully recognize a complex and diverse range of identities and communities. This has sometimes led to organizations adopting new names that reflect a common commitment to freedom and equality. In so doing, however, these organizations may inadvertently obscure the contributions of bisexual, transgender, and queer activists and members, if they have not fully integrated bisexuality and transgender identity and a deeper understanding of bisexual and transgender issues into their core values and mission (Burleson 2000; Serano 2007).

From the perspective of the larger heterosexual and heteronormative society, it is conceptually easier to lump all gender-variant and varieties of nonheterosexual attraction together, making discrimination easier. However, in an odd way, this overgeneralization contains one of the possible ways to ameliorate the lack of acceptance of bisexuality; an increasing number of polls indicate that younger Americans are far less concerned about sexual orientation as a form of normative deviance, instead taking a much more accepting view of same-sex attraction and other sexual minorities (James 2007; Malernee 2003; Morris 2006). It is possible that, over time, bisexuality will simply emerge (along with a number of others) as one of a variety of socially accepted sexual orientations. What augurs against this is the conceptual dominance of "gay" as an inclusive label, when it is manifestly not inclusive in how it is used within the lesbian and gay communities. Thus, the combined social, political, and linguistic tensions are reflective of what is now understood as *bisexual erasure.*

The Problem of Bisexual Erasure

In a landmark article in the *Stanford Law Review*, Kenji Yoshino (2000) advanced the concept of "bisexual erasure" arguing that not only were bisexuals invisible in U.S. society, but that bisexuality was *made* invisible as part of a mutually convenient social arrangement between heterosexuals and homosexuals. Yoshino labeled this arrangement an "epistemic contract of bisexual erasure" as it emerged from the interests of specific groups in society rather than from society as a whole.

Yoshino went on to discuss various strategies of bisexual erasure. Among heterosexuals, Yoshino argued that bisexuals were erased as an entire class (bisexuality is "just a fad"), and as individuals, and ultimately stigmatized and viewed only negatively. Gays also practice these three kinds of bisexual erasure but with significant differences from heterosexuals. Bisexuals and bisexuality as a category are misidentified as gay, lesbian, or queer, and identifying as bisexual is seen as a "phase." Yoshino notes that both heterosexuals and homosexuals as groups are invested in maintaining this erasure.

The implications of bisexual erasure are quite clear: bisexuality is not recognized as a legitimate part of the spectrum of sexual orientations and identities, neither by straight people nor by gay men, lesbians, and not by some transgender activists. The consequences of bisexual erasure are many and varied. In almost all cases, the existence of bisexual identity is never fully acknowledged, but instead is taken as a kind of "conditional" or "provisional" state.

A number of bisexual activists have highlighted the influence of the Cass model of sexual orientation identity development in which bisexuality is treated as a transitional state between heterosexual identity and homosexual identity. It is assumed that heterosexuality is the original or starting status, and the development or realization of homosexual orientation is the end state. Not surprisingly, the Cass model thus has an implicit dualistic model of sexual orientation and has been increasingly questioned as a result (Collins 2000; Diamond 2009). This assumption of duality between opposite-sex attraction and same-sex attraction matches the assumptions made in the larger society about sexual orientation, thus underscoring the power of bisexual erasure: It is not just that bisexuals are not fully included in the larger matrix of LGBTQ politics and social construction but that there is *no conceptual room* for them to occupy. The result of this "negative space" can be seen in the following ways.

Social Norm Enforcement of Binary Identity

On balance, bisexuality is not acknowledged as a legitimate or stable sexual orientation identity. On a simply conceptual level, this is what Yoshino has already laid out clearly. How this plays out in social terms is a kind of normative pressure on bisexual individuals to live up to a monosexual norm: either heterosexuality or homosexuality. The fact that this in turn also reinforces a dualistic construction of gender is generally not fully recognized or thought to be worth further attention. This lack of consideration is at times contradictory to the tentative and conditional acceptance of transgender identity within the LGBTQ communities, insofar as there is any acknowledgment of greater gender variation beyond male and female. Indeed, the very division between "gay" and "lesbian" also serves to reinforce a gender dichotomy; bisexuality seems to attract its own share of negative attention for supposedly reinforcing a gender binary. A number of transgender activists have pointed out that there are also social pressures to conform to certain acceptable kinds of gender presentation, particularly as it relates to sexual orientation, which in turn could reinforce gender binaries in not just the straight community, but also the lesbian, gay, and bisexual communities as well (Serano 2010).

Lack of Acknowledgment of Individual Bisexuals and Bisexuality

Besides the social norms already mentioned, there is also a kind of nonacknowledgment of bisexual individuals who publicly assert their bisexual identity. Within the LGBTQ communities, because of the conceptual erasure of bisexuality, the only value awarded to claiming the label of bisexual for oneself is a generalized reinforcement of same-sex attraction. Put another way, when someone publicly states they are bisexual in the company of lesbians and gay men, the specific assertion of "bisexuality" itself is not validated, except insofar as it is taken to mean "lesbian" or "gay"—and thus the bisexual person is assumed to be gay or lesbian, despite efforts to identify otherwise. A further form of this can be found in the boundary-keeping behavior often found within the lesbian and gay communities when bisexual individuals form what are thought of as "heterosexual" relationships. In such cases, the validity of any same-sex attraction on the part of the bisexual individual is called into question because of their present behavior, for example, "Oh, she was never really into women. She's with a man, now, so it's *obvious*" (Ochs 1996, 217–239). It is almost impossible to tease out the logical inconsistencies in attempting to use "heterosexual" and "homosexual"—likewise "gay" and "straight"—to describe relationships when the terms themselves relate more properly to individual orientation. Within the heterosexual community, the lack of acknowledgment is directly related to the oversimplification of sexual minorities into a single, homogenous group—the "gay community" as it is often described in the media. This lumping together of different groups is sometimes taken advantage of by gay and lesbian leaders and organizations, finding it advantageous when advocating for certain issues. On a more personal level, a bisexual within the heterosexual community is not validated for any different-gender attraction. Instead bisexual individuals are viewed as being merely "gay"—with the social stigma and halting social acceptance that that label now connotes. Acceptance of bisexuality within the larger community has been distinctly gendered. Bisexual behavior in women is increasingly deemed acceptable by the larger heterosexual society, so long as it does not actually challenge the centrality of heterosexuality. It is considered daring for two girls to kiss one another—so long as they appear relatively femme or conventionally attractive to men, and return to their boyfriends afterwards. Butch women, women who fit stereotypic notions of what a lesbian is supposed to look like, do not encounter such acceptance. When women attempt to assert a bisexual identity, they are often portrayed as femme and more attractive in the larger culture. Further, they are often hypersexualized and available for the male gaze and sexual satisfaction (Herek 2002). All of this reflects how homophobia is inherently tied up with sexism as a system of inequality (Pharr 1997). However, bisexuality in men remains stigmatized, partly due to fears of sexually transmitted diseases and partly due to stigma attached to homosexual sexual behavior between men. Within the gay and lesbian communities, bisexuality remains only conditionally accepted.

Lack of Institutional Support for Bisexuality

Organizations and efforts post-Stonewall have built on a tacit coalition across sexual orientation and gender identity lines, but have never fully recognized bisexuality or transgender identity. Current political organizations that supposedly represent LGBTQ people are now largely "gay and lesbian" oriented, with bisexual and transgender people treated as de facto second-class citizens within the larger political movement. Given the history of LGBTQ political and social organizations, it is not surprising to discover that many bisexual people became involved in the lesbian and gay communities as a means of validating themselves and finding a sense of community. Indeed, many bisexual people within the lesbian and gay communities had already come out as lesbians or gay men, and were active in the community, who realized they were bisexual and remained in the lesbian and gay communities and political movement. Not too surprisingly, bisexual activists were involved with LGBTQ political organizations because of common issues and also because such organizations provided employment opportunities. Many of these bisexual activists helped organize bisexual communities, organizations, and the bisexual political movement. However, the vast majority of lesbian and gay political and social organizations assume that the programs they offer to their gay and lesbian members or adherents are also automatically going to appeal to and be appropriate for their bisexual members and supporters. Combined with bisexual erasure, the implication of this is that bisexuality is only included insofar as it matches with social expectations to conform to lesbian and gay norms. The amount of programming and activities provided by lesbian and gay organizations that is specifically targeted to bisexuals is miniscule (Bowen 2012), yet these very same organizations claim to be "LGBT" in their literature and public representation. Whether by accident or by design, this serves as a kind of institutional reinforcement for conformity to lesbian and gay norms. When efforts have been made to be more inclusive of bisexuality, these have often faced the gauntlet of objections based on the belief that the existing allocation of resources is (1) just and (2) appropriate. Thus bisexuals are told that they ought not to expect very much, given the centrality of a monosexually defined and understood approach to same-sex attraction. Within the greater community, there is simply little if any institutional or organizational attention paid to bisexuality, much less programmatic support. An argument could be made that there is considerable support for bisexuals who are in different-sex relationships, particularly marriage (i.e., "taking advantage of heterosexual privilege"). Such a viewpoint misses the *hetero*normative character of this support. Efforts to press the issue within the LGBTQ community are often characterized as divisive and unnecessary: "If you bisexuals want to be recognized, why don't you go start your own organizations?" Such statements largely ignore the issue of who gets to "own" the organizations supposedly representing all nonheterosexual orientations. Thus, bisexuals and bisexuality are not fully welcomed within organizations that supposedly purport to serve their interests, and not acknowledged in a meaningful way by other institutions or organizations in society.

The picture is not universally bleak; some organizations within the LGBTQ communities have been active allies in recognizing bisexuality as a valid identity. In 2005, NGLTF coordinated a response to a highly biphobic article that had appeared in the *New York Times* titled "Straight, Gay—or Lying" (Carey 2005). Working in coordination with a number of bisexual activists and national organizations, NGLTF produced a fact sheet that raised significant questions about the article and the research referenced (NGLTF 2005). Later, in April 2010, the National Center for Lesbian Rights and the law firm K&L Gates filed a complaint in federal court in Seattle on behalf of three bisexual men of color whose team had been disqualified from a second place finish in the Gay Softball World Series organized by the North American Gay Amateur Athletic Alliance (NAGAAA) because they were believed to be "heterosexual." In November 2011, the lawsuit was settled out of court in favor of the plaintiffs, and NAGAAA agreed to further actions to recognize bisexuality and be more inclusive of bisexuals in their athletic activities (NCLR 2013). It is uncertain if these instances reflect a deeper change in national LGBTQ organizations or if they are data outliers.

Co-optation of Bisexual Activism

The lack of a distinct bisexual political network or infrastructure makes it more difficult for bisexuals to be recognized as full players in the LGBTQ political movement. Worse yet, bisexuals get co-opted into working locally, regionally, and nationally for supposedly bisexual-inclusive organizations and efforts that are actually not inclusive (see earlier). Throughout the history of the LGBTQ political and social movement, bisexuals have been involved in the organizations and activities that have formed the core of what is considered that movement, as was discussed earlier. But this has not resulted in a valuation of that involvement, rather the opposite. Bisexuals who have been motivated to become activists for LGBTQ rights often end up becoming involved in organizations dominated by lesbian and gay leadership, and lesbian- and gay-defined agendas. Similar processes have happened in the past, for example, lesbians seeking to overcome latent and many times blatant sexism within organizations dominated by gay men, or by LGBTQ people of color confronting a lack of diversity within organizations and activities dominated by whites. However, in these two cases—as well as with the transgender community—there has been as least some acknowledgment that lesbians, people of color, and transgender people actually exist. The same is more difficult to claim in the case of bisexuals, who are constantly bombarded with claims of their nonexistence. Thus, bisexual activists end up facing a higher standard of scrutiny when considering where they could commit their time and resources as activists—the only validated kind of activism is that which provides support to LGBTQ organizations and efforts. However, these are often exactly the same organizations that do not provide meaningful support for bisexuals in their programs and activities. Thus, bisexuals are asked to contribute time, energy, and effort to causes that are designed and constructed in ways that increasingly treat them as invisible, or more specifically as visible only when they are acting and presenting in ways compatible with gay and lesbian identity.

Bisexuality and the Great Divide

In political terms, bisexuality has sometimes been recognized as an element in the political battles between the LGBTQ and allied communities and anti-LGBTQ conservatives. This, in turn, has shaped the larger divide in U.S. politics between states with relatively progressive laws and social acceptance, and those states without legal protections and where social norms are less inclusive. Some examples help illustrate this point. In terms of the Great Divide, the effect of bisexual erasure has a marked effect:

1. In the "disempowered states" and the "battleground states," bisexuals and bisexual identity are most often conflated with gay and lesbian identity. Unlikely to be acknowledged as a distinct identity, the general public view of bisexuality is as an unstable phase in sexuality, more stereotype than an actual sexual orientation. To the relatively powerful anti-LGBTQ organizations and interest groups, "bisexuality" is simply a variation of "gay" or "lesbian" and therefore to be treated as essentially the same. The only reason to specifically acknowledge bisexuality is to be complete insofar as discrimination is concerned. Within the LGBTQ communities and for LGBTQ organizations and interest groups, however, there is not necessarily any recognition of bisexuality as a distinct identity or constituent population, but bisexual *individuals* are welcome as part of coalition efforts for political and social change. To the extent they conform to expectations of gay or lesbian self-presentation, they are accepted as legitimate members of the lesbian and gay community; otherwise they are lumped in with heterosexuals as "allies." In all of this, gay, lesbian, bisexual, and transgender people may find it strategically important to form alliances, since the general mentality is one of being under siege. Extending this one step further, LGBTQ organizations in the disempowered states are more likely to emphasize the similar goals and objectives between different sexual orientations and gender identities simply as a necessary aspect of community building and coalition formation, but this may not overcome the problem of bisexual erasure and lack of acceptance.
2. In the "empowered states," bisexuality may be questioned by some, but there is greater recognition of diversity of sexual orientation by the larger society. While there are still heteronormative social forces at work, bisexuality is more accepted simply because it is less likely for same-sex attraction to be considered as deviancy or to be otherwise stigmatized. The outcome of this is relatively straightforward: in urban and some suburban environments, bisexuality is unremarkable—but also therefore unremarked upon.

The divide between the empowered states and the disempowered states may be illustrated by five case studies, each focusing on a specific place and set of issues related to bisexuality.

Case Study 1: AIDS/HIV Crisis

The emergence of AIDS as a national health crisis in the early 1980s involved bisexuality from the very beginning, yet recognition of bisexuality was itself largely negative (Burleson 2005). The three populations initially identified by the Centers for Disease Control (CDC) as being at-risk for AIDS were gay men, IV drug users, and Haitians. LGBTQ activists quickly fought back against the stigmatization of gay men, but in the early years of the AIDS crisis, the U.S. populace was frightened by the prospect of a deadly disease with an as-yet-not-fully-understood cause and means of transmission. Bisexual men were immediately stigmatized, since they were characterized as "Typhoid Marys" who would spread the disease to an unsuspecting heterosexual population, having gotten it from their same-sex partners. Thus, the tacit contract of bisexual erasure broke down over concerns in the largely heterosexual segment of society about the transmission of the disease.

Several bisexual activists were at the forefront of responding to the AIDS epidemic, notably (but by no means limited to) Luigi Ferrer, Alexei Guren, Carol Leigh, David Lourea, Veneita Porter, and Alan Rockway. Their common argument was that the CDC, and state and local health authorities were making a critical public health error by assuming that only gay men were at risk of seroconversion. By including bisexuals, women, sex workers, and IV drug users, it would be possible to develop a much clearer picture of the spread of the disease. This perspective was part of what eventually led to a shift away from defining at-risk populations on the basis of *identity*, basing it more on actual sexual *behavior.*

Today, in the empowered states, relatively enlightened attitudes toward LGBTQ civil rights and fewer stigmas associated with diversity in sexuality have emerged concurrently with more effective public health programs to reduce HIV transmission, including a shift in focus on sexual behavior in sexuality and public health education, as well as needle-exchange programs in some places. By contrast, in the disempowered states, conservative forces have lumped bisexuals in with gay men in continued efforts to stigmatize same-sex sexual expression.

Case Study 2: Colorado and Oregon as Early Battleground States

In 1992, the *Colorado No Protected Status for Sexual Orientation* Amendment, better known as Amendment 2, sought to remove legal protections for homosexuality and bisexuality. The inclusion of bisexuality was not an accident. In a memo from Brian McCormick, the legal counsel for the anti-LGBTQ lobbying group Colorado Coalition for Family Values (1991), the inclusion of bisexuality along with homosexuality and lesbian orientation was considered necessary since bisexuality involved same-sex attraction and was therefore just as morally objectionable as being gay or lesbian, and if bisexuality were not included, gays and lesbians would evade restrictions on enacting special rights by claiming they were bisexual (!). The conception of "gay identity" revealed in this memo is completely disconnected with notions within the LGBTQ community about identity politics and stereotypes of bisexuality as an "intermediate stage" and "just a phase." The opposition to Amendment 2 was relatively disjointed and efforts to build a genuinely inclusive coalition failed, leading to the passage of Amendment 2 in November 1992. The law was later overturned in the historic *Romer v. Evans* U.S. Supreme Court decision in 1996 (Goldberg 1996). However, one outcome of the failure to stop

Amendment 2 was a realization on the part of LGBTQ activists and organizations in Colorado that they had fallen prey to a divide-and-conquer strategy. Observing the more successful effort in Oregon to defeat Proposition 9, Colorado activists began to understand the need to build a more inclusive political strategy, one that recognized bisexuality and transgender identity. It is somewhat ironic, then, to note that the Human Rights Campaign blog entry commemorating *Romer* v. *Evans* in 2011 (Yost 2011) did not have a single mention of bisexuality and, in fact, glossed over the inclusion of bisexuality in its summary of the proposed amendment, leaving the impression that the amendment was focused only on homosexuality.

In contrast to the passage of Amendment 2 in Colorado, the much more successful "No on 9" campaign in Oregon was in opposition to the Oregon Citizens Alliance effort to enact a similar referendum on LGBTQ rights. The "No on 9" campaign was based on the idea of inclusion and equality across sexual orientations and gender identity. Such an inclusive effort made it easier to build a statewide coalition, a coalition united by common belief in shared values, rather than in specific sexual or gender identities. Because of these experiences, both Colorado and Oregon have moved away from the politics of division and have increasingly recognized the rights of LGBTQ people and their position as equal members of society. Within the framework of the Great Divide, it is clear that both Colorado and Oregon were early battleground states. As such, it would be fair to say that the LGBTQ political movements in each state benefitted from more inclusive strategies—Oregon from the start and Colorado after having suffered a bruising defeat. With that in mind, the absence of any durable organization at the state level to advocate specifically for bisexuals minimized the degree to which bisexuals were recognized as a distinct group in LGBTQ advocacy efforts.

Case Study 3: Minnesota as an Ongoing Battleground State

In 1993, Minnesota became the eighth state to pass a law providing for protection from discrimination on the basis of sexual orientation and the first state to provide protection from discrimination on the basis of gender identity. Coming on the heels of the successful effort to provide such protections in the city of St. Paul, the coalition effort named "It's Time, Minnesota" sought to build an inclusive alliance across a wide political spectrum. It's Time, Minnesota was notable for having not only lesbian and gay activists, but also transgender and bisexual activists in positions of leadership. Susan Kimberly, a former St. Paul City Council President and (later) transgender activist, was instrumental in shaping the draft bill so it included gender identity as well as sexual orientation. I was the cochair of the People of Color Caucus, which provided significant support from the Native American, African-American, Latino and Asian communities for the legislative campaign. By actively building an effort that reached across political party lines, urban/rural divides, as well as working for racial and class diversity, it was relatively easy to recognize the value in bisexual and transgender inclusion.

Case Study 4: Bisexuality and the "Ex-Gay" Debacle

Starting in the mid-1990s, BiNet USA undertook a campaign to address the role of bisexuality in the (so-called) ex-gay movement. Much of the public debate regarding "reparative therapy" was centered on the question of whether gay people could change their orientation to becoming heterosexual. The ex-gay movement argued that it was possible, and provided a relatively small sample of ex-gays, once gay but now married and happily heterosexual, as proof of their position. The response on the part of the LGBTQ community had largely been (and continues to be) based on the idea that being homosexual is an in-born trait and no amount of reparative therapy would actually work. Similarly, various "ex-ex-gays" were seen as proof of this position. While oversimplified, this summary reveals a basic problem in the debate, namely, that the positions taken by each side do not really address the evidence provided by the other. Put another way, how could gay and lesbian activists explain the seeming evidence that there *were* ex-gays in heterosexual relationships? The general counterargument was that these ex-gays had merely gone back into the closet, and it was only a matter of time before they came out again as gay. But it is impossible to prove a negative, and partly due to that the debate has continued to rage on to greater or lesser degrees in the national spotlight. Bisexual activists working through BiNet USA saw this as an opening to provoke greater awareness of bisexuality, using this logic: What if some of those "ex-gays" were really not "gay" at all? What if instead, these ex-gays were actually bisexual? Given enough social conditioning and really big doses of stigmatization, some of the ex-gay success stories could be more easily explained as actually being bisexuals who were now repressing their attractions to their own gender. While the effort on the part of bisexual activists was only one response among many others, it did make a valuable contribution to the political debate around this issue (Political Research Associates 1998). What is notable is the fact that the anti-ex-gay movement would be in a significantly stronger political and social position, by simply accepting bisexuality as a valid sexual orientation, and using that as part of the political dialogue to show how the ex-gay movement is mistaken in its rationale. Such a rationale persists not only in the direct discussion of this issue but also in debates about marriage equality.

Case Study 5: Bisexuality and Marriage Equality

Long considered an unattainable goal, marriage equality has emerged as an important issue for bisexual and LGBTQ activists. A distinctly state-level issue, marriage equality has gathered momentum in the past several years, aided by a distinct shift in public opinion over the past generation. But the language initially used to describe marriage equality, "gay marriage," acted to erase the presence of bisexuals who were themselves in relationships with people of the same gender. The shift over time toward "same-sex marriage" placed the emphasis on gender instead of sexual orientation, and the term "marriage equality" was a strategic move to emphasize the unequal position same-sex couples were in, especially in states with state constitutional amendments banning same-sex marriage (so-called Defense of Marriage Acts or DOMAs, or in such cases Super DOMAs). These linguistic markers may seem to be splitting hairs, but they denote how bisexuality gets erased in the political discourse. In addition to the debate over terminology and labeling, there is a lingering suspicion within the gay and lesbian communities that bisexuals—particularly those with different-gender partners—will succumb to "heterosexual privilege." By being married and appearing as a heterosexual couple, these bisexuals have reentered the closet and are thus less dependable as allies in the fight for marriage equality (Boucai 2012). But such a position is fallacious; it would be as if light-skinned African-Americans *by their very nature* would be less committed to the cause of civil rights, and this is demonstrably not so. Appearances cannot predict beliefs, commitments, or personal identity.

So despite the active involvement of bisexuals in the fight for marriage equality, there has been a distinct lack of recognition of their presence and contribution to these efforts. Two cases are worthy of being mentioned: longtime bisexual activist Robyn Ochs and her partner, Peg Preble, were misidentified in the *Washington Post* as a "lesbian couple" when married in Massachusetts (Jones 2004). Another couple, Lindasusan Ulrich and her wife, Emily Drennen, were also misidentified as a lesbian couple after getting married. Beyond these individual examples, the recently successful effort in the battleground state of Minnesota for marriage equality saw friction emerge between the leadership of the bisexual community and the advocacy coalition Minnesotans United for All Families. Allegations were made that the leadership of Minnesotans United declined to specifically name bisexuals in public relations efforts, ostensibly because "bisexuality" as a concept was poorly received in market research (which may, in fact, have been true). Additionally, during the legislative session when the bill for marriage equality was being debated, opponents of same-sex marriage sought to use the example of an ex-gay activist to show that it was possible to "exit the homosexual lifestyle" (Ferguson 2013).

In all of these case studies, the tension between identity politics and the politics of inclusion cannot be stressed too highly. Because the institutions and social character of the LGBTQ communities have focused so strongly on identity politics and the legitimation of gay and lesbian identity, the possibilities of building stronger coalitions with bisexuals, transgender people, and other sexual minorities have often been missed or deemed lacking in value, or worst of all, undermining the legitimacy of lesbian and gay identity. The combination of a lack of institutional support and a conceptual erasure of bisexuality has left bisexuals inadequately represented in political discourse. "Gay identity" and "straight identity" act as centers of gravity that tend to leave the intervening space empty—there is considerable gravitational pull for anyone wanting to remain in-between the two, conceptually speaking. Until such a time as there are more institutional organizations representing bisexual interests politically and socially, forming a strong and cohesive national and state-level infrastructure, it is unlikely that bisexuals will be recognized as fully part of the struggle for sexual orientation equality and sexual liberation. It may seem ironic, therefore, to argue for the recognition of another sexual orientation as legitimate, but it is a necessary step in building an ultimately much stronger social and political movement based on shared values and beliefs.

References

Barker, Meg, Christina Richards, Rebecca Jones, Helen Bowes-Catton, Tracey Plowman, Jen Yockney, and Marcus Morgan. 2012. "The Bisexuality Report: Bisexual Inclusion in LGBT Equality and Diversity." Open University, Centre for Citizenship, Identities and Governance and Faculty of Health and Social Care.

Boucai, Michael. 2012. "Sexual Liberty and Same-Sex Marriage: An Argument from Bisexuality" *San Diego Law Review, 49*, 415–486. http://williamsinstitute.law.ucla.edu/wp-content/uploads/Boucai-SL-SSM-Aug-2012.pdf.

Bowen, Anthony. 2012. *40 Years of LGBT Philanthropy*. New York: Funders for LGBTQ Issues. http://www.lgbtfunders.org/files/40years_lgbtqphilanthrophy.pdf.

Burleson, William E. 2005. *Bi America: Myths, Truths and Struggles of an Invisible Community.* New York: Harrington Park Press.

Carey, Benedict. 2005. "Straight, Gay or Lying? Bisexuality Revisited." *New York Times*, July 5.

Collins, J. Fuji. 2000. "Biracial-Bisexual Individuals: Identity Coming of Age." *International Journal of Sexuality and Gender Studies, 5*(3), 221–253.

Diamond, Lisa M. 2009. *Sexual Fluidity Understanding Women's Love and Desire.* Cambridge: Harvard University Press.

Eisner, Shiri. 2013. *Bi Notes for a Bisexual Revolution.* Berkley, CA: Seal Press.

Ferguson, David. 2013. "Minnesota Legislator Introduces 'Ex-Gay' Friend during Marriage Equality Debate" *The Raw Story*, March 12. http://www.rawstory.com/rs/2013/03/12/minnesota-legislator-introduces-ex-gay-friend-during-marriage-equality-debate/.

Fox, Ron. 1996. "Bisexuality in Perspective—A Review of Theory and Research." In *Bisexuality: The Psychology and Politics of an Invisible Minority,* edited by Beth A. Firestein, 3–50. Thousand Oaks, CA: Sage Publications.

Garber, Marjorie. 1996. *Vice Versa: Bisexuality and the Eroticism of Everyday Life.* New York: Touchstone.

Goldberg, Suzanne B. 1996. "No Special Rights—Supreme Court's Amendment 2 Decision." *HRC Quarterly* (Human Rights Campaign), Summer 1996.

Herek, Gregory. 2002. "Heterosexuals' Attitudes toward Bisexual Men and Women in the United States" *The Journal of Sex Research, 39*(4), 264–274.

Hutchins, Loraine. 1996. "Bisexuality Politics and Community." In *Bisexuality: The Psychology and Politics of an Invisible Minority,* edited by Beth A. Firestein, 240–259. Thousand Oaks, CA: Sage Publications.

Hutchins, Loraine, and Lani Kaahumanu. 1991. *Bi Any Other Name: Bisexual People Speak Out.* Boston, MA: Alyson Publications.

James, Susan Donaldson. 2007. "Young Women Defy Labels in Intimacy with Both Sexes." *ABC News,* August 16. http://abcnews.go.com/US/LifeStages/story?id=3484082.

Jones, Tamara. 2004. "A Carefully Considered Rush to the Altar, Lesbian Pair Wed after 7 Years Together." *Washington Post,* May 18. http://www.washingtonpost.com/wp-dyn/articles/A34665-2004May17.html.

Lonetree, Anthony. 1994. "Coleman Won't Sign Gay Month Proclamation." *Star-Tribune* (Minneapolis), May 4.

Malernee, Jamie. 2003. "S. Florida Teen Girls Discovering 'Bisexual Chic' Trend." *Sun-Sentinel* (Broward/Palm Beach), December 30. http://articles.sun-sentinel.com/2003-12-30/news/0312300142_1_teen-girls-kiss-high-school-students.

McCormick, Brian M. 1991. "Re: Analysis of Language in Amendment Initiative. Memorandum." National Legal Foundation, June 13. (Memorandum held as ephemera in author's files.)

Morris, Alex. 2006. "The Cuddle Puddle of Stuyvesant High School." *New York*, February 6. http://nymag.com/news/features/15589/.

National Center for Lesbian Rights (NCLR). 2013. "Case: Steven Apilado, et al. v. North American Gay Amateur Athletic Association." http://www.nclrights.org/cases-and-policy/cases-and-advocacy/steven-apilado-et-al-v-north-american-gay-amateur-athletic-association/.

National Gay and Lesbian Task Force (NGLTF). 2005. "The Problems with 'Straight, Gay or Lying?'" NGLTF Factsheet. (Held as ephemera in author's files.)

Ochs, Robyn. 1996. "Biphobia: It Goes More than Two Ways." In *Bisexuality: The Psychology and Politics of an Invisible Minority*, edited by Beth A. Firestein, 217–239. Thousand Oaks, CA: Sage Publications.

Pharr, Suzanne. 1997. *Homophobia: A Weapon of Sexism*. Berkeley, CA: Chardon Press.

Political Research Associates, Equal Partners in Faith, and The Policy Institute of the National Gay and Lesbian Task Force. 1998. "Challenging the Ex-Gay Movement: An Information Packet." December.

Rust, Paula. 1996. "Managing Multiple Identities – Diversity Among Bisexual Women and Men." In *Bisexuality: The Psychology and Politics of an Invisible Minority*, edited by Beth A. Firestein, 53–83. Thousand Oaks, CA: Sage Publications.

Serano, Julia. 2010. "Bisexuality Does Not Reinforce the Gender Binary." *The Scavenger*, October 10. http://www.thescavenger.net/glb/bisexuality-does-not-reinforce-the-gender-binary-39675.html.

Vaid, Urvashi. 1995. *Virtual Equality*. New York: Anchor Books.

Yoshino, Kenji. 2000. "The Epistemic Contract of Bisexual Erasure." *Stanford Law Review*, 353–461. http://www.kenjiyoshino.com/articles/epistemiccontract.pdf.

Yost, Mike. 2011. "Know Your Colorado LGBT History: *Romer v. Evans*." Human Rights Campaign, December 18. http://www.hrc.org/blog/entry/know-your-colorado-lgbt-history-romer-v.-evans.

Chapter 10

An Eye to the Future: Perspectives on the National Transgender Discrimination Survey

Denise Burke

Contents

Introduction

A young trans woman glances about, afraid somebody might overhear what she is about to reveal. She whispers that she is afraid of being back in the community with no job and no place to live. She is afraid that with no income, she will return to prostitution and inevitably back to addiction.

Her fears are not irrational. Constrained by lack of education, lack of safe housing (which also has resources for treatment of addiction) for trans women who have not legally transitioned, a poor economy, and the specter of an addiction always watching from the sidelines, her odds look progressively worse.

Where will she find hope and possibility? Is there a way out of the maze? When and where will it all end?

This chapter proposes possible solutions and at least a glimmer of hope in facing those questions for trans women and men. I will utilize the structure provided by the National Transgender Discrimination Survey, a joint effort of the National Gay and Lesbian Task Force and the National Center for Transgender Equality (Grant, Mottet, Tanis, Harrison, Herman, and Keisling 2011).

As crucial as this survey has been for the transgender community, it does indicate some methodological challenges, not the least of which is the transgender community itself. Transgender people are not of one mind about how to define themselves or even if self-definition is a good idea. Although this writer follows the convention of describing "transgender" as an umbrella term that includes transsexual women and men, cross-dressers, drag performers, and gender queer people (people for whom the gender binary male–female makes no personal sense), that assertion is in continual debate.

Although I have not included intersexed people in this group, it is entirely possible that some intersexed people did respond to the survey.* This writer knows intersexed people personally who do self-identify as transgender and do in fact experience much the same degree and kind of violence and discrimination, as well as the issue of surgical intervention as early as postpartum before the person could possibly have input into such a momentous life decision as correcting genital anatomy.

* "Intersex" is a general term used for a variety of conditions in which a person is born with a reproductive or sexual anatomy that does not seem to fit the typical definitions of female or male. For example, a person might be born appearing to be female on the outside, but having mostly male-typical anatomy on the inside. Or a person may be born with genitals that seem to be in-between the usual male and female types. Or a person may be born with mosaic genetics, so that some of her cells have XX chromosomes and some of them have XY (Intersex Society of North America 2013).

This situation is complicated by an evolving nomenclature including the terms "gender variant" and "gender fluid," the latter term referring to people who move at times from one pole of the gender spectrum to the other pole, maybe in the same day.

The survey itself is subject to the vagaries of any self-reporting instrument (Hoskin 2013). The survey is an initial snapshot; these questions have not been applied to the same population over time. Can a person the subject of continuous discrimination and victim of systemic and episodic violence gain the introspective ability to accurately describe their life? Perhaps this is the case but not always. It is conceivable that a person in desperate straits may be inclined to always respond in certain ways.

The issue of honesty and image manipulation is affected by the prevalence of the "stealth phenomenon." Trans people all seem to know at least one other transsexual person (that is, a person who has transitioned full time into the gender opposite from birth identification) who has turned away from the larger trans community and insists that transition is complete. Such a person refuses to divulge that birth-identified gender and any previous transitioning status to anybody, sometimes including life partners. Those voices may not be expressed; there is no way to know presently how dependent that phenomenon is on fear of discrimination or violence.

Despite the necessary shortcomings of a self-reporting instrument, the survey does focus the anecdotal experiences of transgender people into a single compelling story of transgender life in the United States. The survey is the best, if not the only, existing tool to understand and to feel both the despair of people so firmly on cultural margins and the strength of their human determination and spiritual resilience. Both understanding and empathy are necessary ingredients in moving toward an end to violence and full inclusion of transgender people in American society.

Just How Bad Is It?

On the seasonably cold evening of November 20, 2013, people crowded into Living Table United Church of Christ in Minneapolis, Minnesota, for what has become the defining response to violence perpetrated on transgender people from Minneapolis and the rest of the United States and out into the world as far away as France, Russia, and Brazil. This international vigil started in memorial of Rita Hester, murdered on November 28, 1998, a murder like so many other trans murders not yet solved (Transgender Day of Remembrance 2013).

Names are read, candles lit, and pictures shown if they exist. The community of trans people and their allies—clergy, family, and friends—mourn those deaths, vowing that each person murdered held an intrinsic life value and even when unknown to us is known by the greater good of this universe and will not be forgotten.

Two themes emerge repeatedly in the annual vigil: (1) the outsized statistical representation of people of color and (2) the atrocious nature of these crimes. These murders frequently are far more than just one person shooting another. They often include dismemberment and other continued violence on the body, disposing of the body in a landfill, and burning (CBS Detroit 2011).

Transgender Day of Remembrance is a heart-wrenching reminder of just how bad it is for transgender people within and beyond the United States. Yet the National Transgender Discrimination Survey provides an intimate snapshot into just how bad it really is every day.

Discrimination in the Workplace

We start with discrimination in the workplace because a strong correlation exists between the extent of workplace discrimination and the overwhelming escalation of personal and social distress.

> Respondents who had lost a job due to bias also experienced ruinous consequences such as four times the rate of homelessness, 70% more current drinking or misuse of drugs to cope with mistreatment, 85% more incarceration, more than double the rate of working in the underground economy (illegal drug trafficking or sex work), and more than double the HIV infection rate, compared to those who did not lose a job due to bias. (Grant et al. 2011, 3)

The Human Rights Act of 1993 propelled Minnesota into the initial leadership position of providing workplace protection for both sexual orientation and gender identity. But how well does this work for the intended protected class of people?

Anecdotally, trans people still report not being hired based on gender identity. If prospective employers choose their words carefully and largely keep their opinions of trans people to themselves, discrimination can still happen with little legal recourse because the trail is obscured.

Some legal protection is of course better than none, but trans people are still reporting up to twice the rate of unemployment nationally. Here is our first indication of the added weight of racial bias as these rates for trans people of color increase to up to four times the national average (Grant et al. 2011, 3).

When 90% of trans people report harassment and discrimination at work, what does that look like? The spectrum of harassment can range from (a) the more egregious examples of attempted religious conversion/questioning the morality of transitioning, (b) limiting access to the appropriate identified public facilities (the bathroom/locker room question) to consistently (c) misgendering pronouns to (d) humiliating tactics often associated with general sexual harassment, such as unwanted sexual overtures and physical contact or demeaning jokes.

Legal protection does not prevent a person from *thinking* in biased patterns and perhaps acting on those thoughts in far more subtle fashion than regulation can address.

Discrimination When Seeking Shelter

Although direct homeless housing discrimination is extraordinarily high, perhaps the most distressing aspect of shelter discrimination are the 55% of respondents who report being harassed by staff or other residents and the 22% who report being sexually assaulted (Grant et al. 2011, 4). An astounding 12% report exchanging sex for housing, perhaps as workers in the underground economy (Grant et al. 2011, 115). These figures are out of all expected proportion compared to the U.S. general population (United States Conference of Mayors 2008,19).

The Salvation Army often appears in the middle of controversy regarding providing services such as emergency shelter to LGBT people and has been the subject of attempted boycotts stemming from a refusal to provide benefits for same-sex domestic partners.

The Human Rights Campaign acknowledges the Salvation Army official response, promoted on the website of the Salvation Army Northern Division (Salvation Army 2013). The response denies any discrimination and holds up the example of a 55-year-old trans woman on this webpage. She maintains that she was never disrespected or shamed and that the experience sparked a new sense of community service for her.

Questions still remain. The webpage includes a link to an op-ed article from *The Washington Times*, a noted conservative news outlet. Does staff actually support an official stance of nondiscrimination or do workers sometimes look the other way? If an employee should choose to ignore LGBT discrimination or qualify such discrimination (gay and lesbian clients are acceptable but trans women in particular are not because they are unable to sufficiently "pass" in their life gender to suit another's criteria*), is there an adequate investigation? Will the Salvation Army initiate contact with the trans community to identify needs and concerns/fears? Is there any discrepancy between enactment of this official position depending on which region of the United States is impacted? These questions yet remain unanswered.

Word travels fast on the street among the homeless. Fair or not, when fear and distrust overwhelm trans people, they will avoid necessary services. When trust is gained, trans people can be grateful and resilient people.

Discrimination in Public Accommodations

In the company of a gay friend, I step to the register of a chain restaurant in St. Paul, Minnesota. I reach in my purse and the restaurant manager asks, "How was your meal today, *sir* [emphasis added]?" While I dig for my credit card, I reply, "The meal was fine, but I do appreciate being called ma'am, not sir."

* "Among respondents who accessed a shelter, 42% reported that they were forced to live as the wrong gender to be allowed to stay. Being forced to live as the wrong gender can range from being required to alter a hairstyle or makeup to radically altering gender presentation from head to toe" (Grant et al. 2011, 118).

I look up, card in hand, to find that the manager is replaced behind the register with a younger associate.

Discrimination in public accommodations can be that subtle, a misgendering of pronouns that crosses a boundary between the casual mistake and intentional disrespect. Public accommodations can be much more overt, in particular, over the use of gender-specific bathrooms.

An example in point was Arizona Senate Bill 1432, an attempt by Sen. John Kavanaugh to make use of a public restroom facility a criminal offense by any person who could not produce a legal ID with gender marker and picture that matched that person's appearance (Think Progress 2013). Matched by similar attempts in such places as Massachusetts, proponents have traded on fears of sexual assaults perpetrated by trans people in public restrooms, which are fears without foundation. Political forces attempting to overthrow AB 1266, the California law protecting transgender students, have expanded this tactic now to include children. Although it looks like at this writing the repeal efforts to put the measure on an upcoming ballot will fail for lack of valid signatures, at this time the California Secretary of State has not officially made that determination.

Fear itself in such a marginalized population erects barriers against visibility and self-assertion, which perpetuate the cycles of discrimination. A trans person reschedules flights to avoid Phoenix International since her ID does not physically match her description. Another trans person avoids calling 911 or other services related to domestic violence from fear of harassment and so the danger persists.

The table "Experiences of Discrimination and Violence in Public Accommodations" clearly shows that no segment of public life is immune to this experience, ranging from emergency room services to public transportation to social support programs (Grant et al. 2011, 5).

Discrimination in Health Care

When I first revealed to my general practitioner that I am a trans woman, he shared that he was familiar with the health needs of trans people since he had served his residency in the emergency room of a Philadelphia hospital with a number of trans patients. According to the National Transgender Discrimination Survey, half of the rest of trans people cannot make a similar statement.

Some reports are particularly egregious. One percent of the respondents report being physically attacked while in a physician's office. That means that approximately 65 individuals responding to this survey were not safe to seek out medical care even within a highly structured setting.

Addiction issues are significantly greater for trans people using substances as coping mechanisms in the face of discrimination. HIV rates are far above the national U.S. average. Transgender people are specifically avoiding medical treatment, even setting aside the question of gender reassignment surgery (defined as genital confirmation surgery for trans women and mastectomies for trans men).

They avoid health care because they are caught in a complex web of potential violence and ridicule, lack of professional education, and a perceived willingness to discount people marginalized on several levels. Stories are shared within the community of such preventable deaths as a ruptured appendix.

Consequences

Attempting to gauge the depth of gender identity discrimination can be overwhelming. The National Transgender Discrimination Survey is replete with statistical evidence of just how pervasive this discrimination is. The correlation between discrimination and detrimental, even life-threatening, consequences cannot be overlooked.

I attend a class of pastoral students at the invitation of a former ethics professor to share some of my life as a trans woman. I ask the class if they know the percentage of the average U.S. population that reports attempting suicide. They do not. I say that the percentage is 1.6%. People shake their heads. That is a lot of people, they agree.

So I ask them if they know what the rate is for transgender people. They do not. I quote the statistic from the survey: 41%. Dead silence. The professor sitting next to me whispers, "I don't think we heard that quite right. Would you repeat that?"

I reply, again quoting the survey, "As a matter of fact, although people of color generally report smaller numbers in the general U.S. population, in the transgender community, that phenomenon is reversed. Native American and Alaskan trans people report a rate of 56%."

Persistent endemic discrimination of trans and gender-nonconforming people results in extremely high incidences of self-harmful behavior, including high-risk sexual behavior, substance abuse, and avoidance of medical treatment. Economically forcing trans people, in particular trans women, into sex work has a high correlation to the prevalence of HIV among this population.

Although studies demonstrating the economic and social costs of discrimination of this marginalized group are at best in their infancy, do policy creators and transgender activists and allies really need to wait until those details are complete before taking any action at all?

In the next section "Just How Good It Can Get," I intend to describe certain strategies that can be presently implemented, primarily through increasing visibility of transgender and gender-nonconforming people in physically and socially safe environments. Solutions do not have to wait.

Just How Good It Can Get

Inspired by the prophetic vision of *shalom* elucidated by Isaiah, chapter 65, in the Jewish scriptures, is a possibility and promise of hope which appears before the people. Whether or not we accept that vision as an article of spiritual faith, it does articulate from an ancient time a positive glimpse of the future. The vision looks to a future as yet unrealized in which distress passes away and people do not die before living a long and fulfilled life. The fruits of people's work belong to them. They live in houses and eat from the gardens of their own labor. Violence assumed to be the natural order of life is turned on its head as natural enemies become intimate.

The reality of Transgender Day of Remembrance is bleak. The physical violence extends beyond what people can barely describe. When the weight of institutional violence and systemic discrimination is added to the scale, possibility seems more like impossibility. Prophetic vision of the order of Martin Luther King evaporates and the young woman whose story starts this chapter ("A young trans woman glances about, afraid somebody might overhear what she is about to reveal") will not find an answer.

To find a way through the maze of gender identity discrimination to that vision of *shalom* requires in part a willingness on the part of trans people themselves to take the volatile risk of visibility.

Transgender Visibility

What propels a transgender worker through or around discriminatory employment roadblocks? How does that worker display the kind of resilience that enables successful transition?

The success starts with improved self-image. When people become "comfortable in their own skin," they start to outshine past work performance if given an opportunity.

> Of respondents who are living full-time in accordance with their gender identity, 78% said they felt more comfortable and their performance improved at work. Respondents in the higher income categories more often reported an increase in feeling comfortable and performing better after transitioning. Transgender men (78%) and transgender women (79%) who have transitioned reported nearly identical rates of improved job situation. (Grant et al. 2011, 64)

Without the fear of being outed or the pressure to conform to social expectations so utterly foreign to self-image, transgender people anecdotally report a favorable work experience.

One key seems to be if an employer or coworkers actually know a trans person, either from previous work experience or in their own family or circle of acquaintances. Familiarity breeds an easier relationship; a trans woman becomes one more woman in the workplace and from there to one more employee in the workplace.

Experience has taught some trans people that larger corporations with internal human resource departments tend to value diversity more in the workforce, not necessarily because employment regulation requires it (as valuable as legislation can be), but because trans employees can be as superior employees as is the case with the rest of the gay and lesbian community.

The year 2013 has seen a rise in requests from the business community for "transgender 101" workshops. Ellen Krug, a Twin Cities activist and author, and I have jointly held such a workshop for Metropolitan Health Plan (MHP), Hennepin County, Minneapolis. She recently provided a workshop for the Twin Cities United Way. Another trans activist and I have been requested to provide input to a gender-identity training course for Hennepin County Sheriff's Department in Minneapolis. In Minnesota the visibility tide is turning.

The tide seems to follow the outline of states also enacting marriage equality laws. I am a speaker at a conference for the Religious Coalition against Discrimination in Maine, one of four states that also enacted marriage equality in 2012.

The challenge is to translate that experience from an empowered state like Minnesota to a disempowered state like Tennessee or Texas. How will a trans woman in Memphis find the courage to seek out that foothold when she reports constant harassment from Memphis police because her proof of identity does not match her physical appearance? The trans man needs that courage as well every time he steps into a gender-appropriate restroom or locker room at work in Dallas.

Visibility implies risk. As the National Transgender Discrimination Survey demonstrates, sometimes this risk can be extreme. Mara Kiesling, the executive director of the National Center for Transgender Equality, recently said in a Minneapolis meeting of activists that the time has arrived to stop telling the world we are basically ordinary people. Although trans people want our culture to understand that we need to work, pay taxes, go grocery shopping, and attend school, trans people are really quite extraordinary. No other group of people in American society so carefully weighs the consequences of living authentically and then step ahead into the decision. Resilient trans people have discovered some way to live authentically every day and so become truly extraordinary.

Growth of Transgender Allies

The Oberlin College Multicultural Resource Center (Oberlin College 2013) is just one of many resources for information about how to become a stronger and more knowledgeable trans ally without feeling the pressure to be a gender-identity expert. The tools and skills in these resources are effective in any setting, be it workplace, government, or education.

Some skills useful when interviewing trans people requesting services or who have mustered the courage to appear at public hearings include the following:

- Do not assume that you know what services trans people need. Treat them as you would any other citizens with respect. Let them tell you.
- Realize that you may have to show some courage as well if you represent a state or community in which trans people are especially marginalized. You may come under pressure from constituents or coworkers. Formulate

and establish public policy based on what is right and lawful rather than expedient.

- Ask trans people which pronouns they prefer. The answer may not be what you expect. Considerable diversity happens in the trans community. Except when dealing with matters of strict legality, use the name preferred.

Areas of Public Policy Potential

Transgender voices themselves have identified the most immediate public policy needs. Within the short range of this chapter, I have included the top five (Grant et al. 2011, 178) (bringing together the concerns of insurance coverage of health care and improving sensitivity to health care needs under a single heading). In these voices is the framework for identifying where to start improving transgender life.

Passage of Workplace Protections That Include Gender Identity

Some measure of fear exists in the trans community that protection against discrimination for gender identity has been or will be a political bargaining chip for passage of antidiscrimination legislation, such as the Employment Non-Discrimination Act. Those fears have sometimes rightly dampened trans support for such landmark political successes as marriage equality.

This fear can be bridged by resisting the assumption that gay, lesbian, and bisexual people understand the *T* at the end of LGBT. The increasing visibility of trans people courageously sharing their stories and educating all in the LGBT as well as the larger community combined with an increasing willingness of natural allies to desire just policies contributes to a more cohesive, politically unified presence.

Legal sanctions against discrimination in any form do help create an environment of expectations. If a worker cannot lose his job because he (using the preferred pronoun) transitions on the job from female to male, human resource professionals do take that seriously. An increasing number of new internal corporate policies (such as the policy of the National Association of Realtors [2013]) that include gender identity may be influenced by increasing legal pressure for protection.

Insurance Coverage of Trans-Sensitive Health Care

The focus on trans health care often is limited to attempts to gain insurance coverage for mastectomies for trans men or gender reassignment surgery for trans women. Related surgeries such as breast enhancement (hormone replacement therapy can have individualized limitations) have been historically lumped together as "cosmetic" and by definition are usually not covered even when a high correlation exists between these surgeries and transitioning success.

General transition therapy (including hormone replacement therapy) coverage has improved and some improved anecdotal signs of surgical correction have started to appear in such states as Colorado (One Colorado 2013). Yet according to the National Transgender Discrimination Survey results, trans-specific health concerns are not the whole story.

The Center for Human Sexuality of the University of Minnesota routinely invites medical students to trans group-therapy sessions. Those students get an early exposure to the peculiar challenges of daily trans life. The goal is not to create surgeons trained in gender reassignment surgery but to at least increase a sensitivity to the patient as that person appears. Every student should be aware that trans people bridge the health concerns of all genders. For instance, a trans woman may well have completed gender reassignment surgery and yet contract prostate cancer. Even without gender reassignment surgery, a trans woman will need to start scheduling periodic mammograms. The insurance industry often shows no sign of openness to modifying procedures to accommodate the realities.

Refusal to offer emergency services to trans people on religious or ethical grounds or elevating a patient's gender to the status of a preexisting condition calls for corrective public policy responses. How the Affordable Care Act (and the pending case before the United States Supreme Court that would allow employers to opt out of providing as part of their health plan offerings) will impact these concerns is yet open to speculation.

Improvements to Hate Crime Law and Enforcement

Forty-seven percent of National Transgender Discrimination Survey respondents prioritize enactment and enforcement of hate crime law as being essential. They do not feel safe, not only on the street but in any environment.

A trans woman recounts on Facebook an evening in a Minneapolis club with a friend. An acquaintance of the friend introduces herself and immediately asks the trans woman when she decided to have gender reassignment surgery and escalates the conversation to a debate about whether any person should have the right to do that.

This sort of event is referred to as "being outed in public." Fueled by alcohol and lowered social inhibitions, the event becomes more than a nuisance. On at least one similar occasion, a patron overheard a similar conversation, retrieved a gun from a vehicle and shot a trans woman sitting in her car in the parking lot (*Huffington Post* 2012).

Fear of being targeted simply because a person is transgender is endemic to the United States, not to mention certain other countries with high rates of incited homicide.

A firm clear response to transgender violence is an obligation for democratic society. Calls for violence directed against transgender people by elected officials such as Tennessee Rep. Richard Floyd (R) (Transgender Law Center 2013) and extreme strategies involving forced encampment such as Todd Kincannon, former executive director of the South Carolina GOP (Parker 2013), should be categorically rejected by thoughtful and responsible citizens. Democracy itself stands on the effectiveness and universality of justice.

Improvements to Legal Documents and Records

Forty percent of respondents to the National Transgender Discrimination Survey identified legal documents as a public policy priority. State laws vary dramatically even in the same region, especially regarding the process of legal name and gender marker change, and the effect on those documents.

Minnesota allows any state resident to change a legal name upon application to district court and payment of a fee of $320 (a fee in itself often outside the reach of persons with limited incomes). The person applying will need to affirm that the request is not for any fraudulent purpose and will need to provide two character witnesses who will be asked in court to affirm who you are and how long they have known you. These forms are available through the website of OutFront Minnesota (2013) among other places.

The first catch comes with changing gender markers; that is, changing a driver's license or other state identification from male to female or vice versa. Many states require documentation of gender reassignment surgery (emphasis on *not reversible*) before granting gender marker change on any legal document including birth certificates. Any decree of a Minnesota district court is necessarily limited to the jurisdiction of Minnesota itself. A Minnesota district court decree allowing a gender marker change has no validity in Texas, as an example.

Even in such a progressive state as Minnesota, state statute seems particularly murky on this subject. Depending on the county of residence and the individual judge, the decree may or may not be granted in identical circumstances. If the request for gender marker change is made on the same form as the request for name change, the judge has the discretion to grant it. A petitioner may be asked if anything physically irreversible has been done: Hormone replacement therapy may qualify.

Moving on from state agencies and courts to the federal level brings another set of experiences. The Social Security Administration no longer shares gender information with employers and recently has revised its policy of gender marker change. An agent has told me that the Internal Revenue Service takes its cue from Social Security. And tacked on to this patchwork is a possible avenue for changing both name and gender marker on the DD214 discharge papers for transgender veterans, whose numbers have been estimated at least 300,000.

Attempting to thread a way through this maze requires an individual to be persistent, knowledgeable, and assertive. Assistance will be needed for a significantly larger group of people already marginalized.

Summary

The gulf between states like Minnesota that have enacted marriage equality as well as other forms of LGBT equality in contrast to states like Texas that have not is more profound than a single issue for what may be the most marginalized community of all: transgender people. The gross disparity of every factor of life from workplace to health care to public accommodations and safety on the surface is overwhelming and laden with heartbreaking stories. So much of the evidence for discrimination at present is caught up in anecdotes and much more research is needed.

The work of the National Transgender Discrimination Survey* is pivotal to moving the discussion past powerful anecdotes to the additional power of quantifying the despair. Empirical evidence will help policy creators and implementers to focus on areas of greatest need without effectiveness diluted.

Throughout all these stories and numbers, one fact remains in the center: the resilience of trans people. Gender variance is a human phenomenon that refuses to disappear. The trans men and women I have known from Vermont to Mississippi to Texas to Arizona to Montana still remain. Some thrive more than others, but being still alive is itself a triumph.

References

CBS Detroit. 2011. "Burned Body Found in Detroit Identified as Transgender Teen." CBS News. Accessed December 11, 2013, http://detroit.cbslocal.com/2011/11/11/body-found-in-detroit-identified-as-transgender-teen/.

Grant, Jaime M., Lisa A. Mottet, Justin Tanis, Jack Harrison, Jody L. Herman, and Mara Keisling. 2011. "Injustice at Every Turn: A Report of the National Transgender Discrimination Survey." Washington, DC: National Center for Transgender Equality and National Gay and Lesbian Task Force.

Hoskin, Rob. "The Dangers of Self-Report." Sciencebrainwaves.com. Accessed December 2, 2013, http://www.sciencebrainwaves.com/uncategorized/the-dangers-of-self-report/.

Huffington Post. 2012. "Brandy Martell, California Transgender Woman, Shot Down in Possible Hate Crime: Reports." Accessed December 11, 2013, http://www.huffingtonpost.com/2012/05/02/brandy-martell-california-transgender-woman-shooting_n_1471209.html.

Intersex Society of North America. 2013. "What Is Intersex?" Accessed December 11, 2013, http://www.isna.org/faq/what_is_intersex.

* The National Transgender Discrimination Survey, 2013, survey records instances of discrimination against transgender people across the United States, including Guam, Puerto Rico, and the Virgin Islands. Six months of data collection included interviewing nearly 6,500 people using an extensive questionnaire that covered critical topics such as employment, education, health care, housing, public accommodation, criminal justice, family life, and access to government documents. Accessed December 17, 2013, from http://transequality.org/Resources/.

National Association of Realtors. 2013. "Realtors Add Gender Identity." Accessed December 11, 2013, http://www.realtor.org/news-releases/2013/11/realtors-add-gender-identity-to-code-of-ethics.

National Center for Transgender Equality. 2013. "Resources." Accessed December 17, 2013, http://transequality.org/Resources/.

Oberlin College. 2013."Trans Ally 101 Workshop." Accessed December 11, 2013, http://new.oberlin.edu/office/multicultural-resource-center/workshops/trans-101.dot.

One Colorado. 2013. "What Coloradans Need to Know." Accessed December 11, 2013, http://www.one-colorado.org/what-coloradans-need-to-know-about-the-division-of-insurance-recent-bulletin-on-health-insurance/.

OutFront Minnesota. 2013. "Transgender Legal Issues." Accessed December 11, 2013, http://www.outfront.org/library/legal/trans.

Parker, Malloy. 2013. "Todd Kincannon, Former Executive Director of South Carolina GOP, Believes Transgender People Should Be 'Put in a Camp.'" *Huffington Post*. Accessed December 11, 2013, http://www.huffingtonpost.com/parker-marie-molloy/todd-kincannon-transgender-camps_b_4100777.html.

Salvation Army. 2013. "LGBT Discrimination: Debunking the Myth." Accessed December 4, 2013. http://salvationarmynorth.org/about-us/what-we-believe/debunking-the-lgbt-discrimintation-myth/.

Think Progress. 2013. "Arizona Lawmaker." ThinkProgress.org. Accessed December 11, 2013, http://thinkprogress.org/lgbt/2013/03/20/1748851/arizona-lawmaker-introduces-bill-to-prosecute-transgender-people-who-use-the-wrong-bathroom/.

Transgender Day of Remembrance. 2013. "About TDOR." Accessed December 2, 2013, http://www.transgenderdor.org/about-2.

Transgender Law Center. 2013. "Transgender Law Center Condemns Threat of Violence." Accessed December 11, 2013, http://transgenderlawcenter.org/archives/422.

United States Conference of Mayors. 2008. "Hunger and Homelessness Survey," p. 19. http://usmayors.org/pressreleases/documents/hungerhomelessnessreport_121208.pdf.

Chapter 11

Transgender Americans and Public Policy

Andrea Jenkins

Contents

Introduction

What does the *T* in LGBT stand for? This is a question that many policymakers ask themselves. According the UC Berkeley Gender Equity Resource Center (2013): "Transgender is an umbrella term for transsexuals, cross-dressers (transvestites), transgenderists, gender queers, and people who identify as neither female nor male and/or as neither a man or as a woman. Transgender is not a sexual orientation; transgender people may have any sexual orientation."

According to a 2011, UCLA (Williams Institute) study "about 9 million people in the United States identify themselves as lesbian, gay, bisexual or transgender. The estimate, which translates to about 3.5% of adults as LGBT and 0.3% of adults as transgender ...

argues that any estimate of the population is difficult because there are insufficient and inconsistent national surveys" ("Estimated 9 Million Americans" 2011).

The National Gay and Lesbian Task Force (2014) reports that 17 states (and the District of Columbia) have laws specifically protecting transgender people in the United States, which equals more than 45% of transgender Americans having housing, employment, and discrimination protections. Those states are

California
Colorado
Connecticut
Delaware
District of Columbia
Hawaii
Illinois
Iowa
Maine
Massachusetts
Minnesota
New Jersey
New Mexico
Nevada
Oregon
Rhode Island
Vermont
Washington
Wisconsin

There are a number of transgender-specific organizations and activists working to improve these numbers, but change requires persistent action. These organizations include the Transgender, Gender Variant and Intersex Justice Project; The Transgender Law Center; and the National Center for Transgender Equality.

What Are the Issues That Face Transgender Americans?

Harassment and Physical Violence

According to a recent report by the National Black Justice Coalition, National Center for Transgender Equality, and National Gay and Lesbian Task Force (2013), "Injustice at Every Turn: A Look at Black Respondents in the National Transgender Discrimination Survey":

> Black transgender people live in extreme poverty with 34% reporting a household income of less than $10,000/year … Black transgender people are affected by HIV in devastating numbers. Over one-fifth of

> Black respondents were HIV-positive (20.23%) and an additional 10% reported that they did not know their status ... Thirty-eight percent (38%) of Black transgender people who had interacted with the police reported harassment. Fourteen percent reported physical assault. Six percent reported sexual assault.

An Example of the Discrimination That Transgender People Face

To fully understand the need for more equitable public policies, let us look at the case of CeCe McDonald that sparked concern around the country and the world. On June 5, 2011, Chrishaun McDonald (an African-American transgender woman) became a statistic.

> Early in the morning ... outside the Schooner Tavern on Lake Street in Minneapolis, Chrishaun McDonald was verbally assaulted with racial slurs, sexual harassment, and transphobic and sexist attacks. When a larger brawl ensued, Ms. McDonald was hit in the face with a bottle. Her attacker ended up dead, and Ms. McDonald was taken to jail where she remains in solitary confinement. She has been charged with second degree murder. Ms. McDonald maintains her innocence, citing self-defense. "They were the ones who attacked us. It was evil what they called us." (Pizzuti 2011)

In spite of her gender, McDonald was transferred to St. Cloud, which is an all-male prison. The issue of her being imprisoned as a male was not even considered by the court. [*Editor's note:* CeCe McDonald was released from St. Cloud State Prison in January 2014.]

Some Signs of Progress

> The Matthew Shepard and James Byrd, Jr., Hate Crimes Prevention Act of 2009, 18 U.S.C. § 249, was enacted as Division E of the National Defense Authorization Act for Fiscal Year 2010. Section 249 of Title 18 and provides funding and technical assistance to state, local, and tribal jurisdictions to help them to more effectively investigate and prosecute hate crimes. It also creates a new federal criminal law which criminalizes willfully causing bodily injury (or attempting to do so with fire, firearm, or other dangerous weapon) when: (1) the crime was committed because of the actual or perceived race, color, religion, national origin of any person or (2) the crime was committed because of the actual or perceived religion, national origin, gender, sexual orientation, gender

> identity, or disability of any person and the crime affected interstate or foreign commerce or occurred within federal special maritime and territorial jurisdiction … Subsection (a)(2) of § 249 protects a wider class of victims. Subsection (a)(2) criminalizes acts of violence (and attempts to commit violent acts undertaken with a dangerous weapon) when motivated by the actual or perceived gender, disability, sexual orientation, or gender identity of any person. (U.S. Department of Justice 2014)

This is the first time that gender identity was included in national legislation.

Melissa Harris Perry, MSNBC Talk Show Host, April 13, 2012

Mara Keisling (2012), director of the National Center for Transgender Equality, wrote in an article for *Huffington Post*: "If you watch Sunday morning news shows, you may have noticed another unprecedented event for transgender people. Last Sunday MSNBC's Melissa Harris-Perry dedicated the second hour of her two-hour show solely to trans social and political issues, in a segment called, 'Being Transgender in America.'"

And while Melissa Harris Perry provided a national platform for transgender activists to discuss the issues facing this population, another media milestone was happening in Washington D.C. "The groundbreaking Transgender and Gender Identity Respect Campaign has been called by advocates the first government-funded campaign focused exclusively on the betterment of transgender and gender non-conforming people … the campaign aims to increase understanding and respect for the transgender and gender non-conforming communities" (Office of Human Rights 2012). There were five campaign ads appearing in bus shelters during 2012 in the fall and winter.

And More Progress

In April 2012, the Transgender Law Center publicized an Equal Employment Opportunity Commission ruling "that Title VII, the federal sex discrimination law, protects employees who are discriminated against because they are transgender" (Transgender Law Center 2012). This, however, can be easily overturned with a change of administrations because it is a federal regulation, not a statute. Despite the significant gains in the movement for transgender equality, there still remain strict barriers for transgender people when it comes to accessing health care, housing, education and economic advancement. "Even Vice President Joe Biden has expressed his belief that the severity of discrimination against transgender people is the 'civil rights issues of our time'" (Zeigler 2012).

Similarly the Employment Non-Discrimination Act has also been written in such a way as to ensure protection not only for lesbian, gay, and bisexual persons, but also for transgender people. The act has now been passed by the United States Senate but has not been enacted by the House of Representatives.

Why Rights Are Not Enough

In the book *Normal Life: Administrative Violence, Critical Trans Politics and the Limits of Law*, Dean Spade, author and associate law professor at the Seattle University School of Law, suggests that the transgender community has worked hard to gain antidiscrimination goals, equal accessibility and protection of rights; in the same way as mainstream lesbian and gay organizations. However, Spade (2011) indicates that because of the way in which transgender people are marginalized, they require additional protection because of the risk of violence and poverty and even early death.

References

"Estimated 9 Million Americans Identify as Lesbian, Gay, Bisexual or Transgender, Study Finds." 2011. *Los Angeles Times*, April 7. Accessed January 13, 2014, http://latimesblogs.latimes.com/lanow/2011/04/9-million-americans-identify-as-lesbian-gay-bisexual-or-transgender-study-finds.html?cid=6a00d8341c630a53ef0147e3ce823c970b.

Gender Equity Resource Center. 2013. "Definition of Terms." http://geneq.berkeley.edu/lgbt_resources_definiton_of_terms.

Keisling, Mara. 2014. "Reflections on a National Media Moment for Trans People." *Huffington Post*, April 20. Accessed January 13, 2014, http://www.huffingtonpost.com/mara-keisling/reflections-on-a-national_b_1437692.html.

National Black Justice Coalition, National Center for Transgender Equality, and National Gay and Lesbian Task Force. 2013. "Injustice At Every Turn: A Look at Black Respondents in the National Transgender Discrimination Survey." Accessed January 13, 2014, http://nbjc.org/sites/default/files/trans-adjustment-web.pdf.

National Gay and Lesbian Task Force. 2014. "State Nondiscrimination Laws in the U.S." Accessed May 21, 2014, http://www.thetaskforce.org/downloads/reports/issue_maps/non-discrimination_5_14color.pdf.

Office of Human Rights: District of Columbia. 2012. "Transgender and Gender Identity Respect Campaign." Accessed January 13, 2014, http://ohr.dc.gov/transrespect.

Pizzuti, Matthew. 2011. "Minneapolis Transgendered Woman Charged with Murder after Killing Verbal Attacker During Gay Bashing." *OutFront*, June 28. Accessed January 13, 2014, http://outfrontonline.com/ofcnow/minneappolos-transgendered-woman-charged-with-murder-after-killing-a-possible-attacker-during-gay-bashing/.

Spade, Dean. 2011. *Normal Life: Administrative Violence, Critical Trans Politics, and the Limits of the Law*. Brooklyn, NY: South End Press.

Transgender Law Center. 2012. "Groundbreaking! Federal Agency Rules Transgender Employees Protected by Sex Discrimination Law." Accessed January 13, 2014, http://transgenderlawcenter.org/archives/tag/eeoc.

U.S. Department of Justice. 2014. "Matthew Shepard & James Byrd Jr. Hates Crimes Prevention Act of 2009." Accessed January 13, 2014, http://www.justice.gov/crt/about/crm/matthewshepard.php.

Ziegler, Kortney Ryan. 2012. "Continuing the Fight for Transgender Rights." *HuffPost: Gay Voices*, November 8. Accessed January 13, 2014, http://www.huffingtonpost.com/kortney-ryan-ziegler-phd/continuing-the-fight-for-transgender-rights_b_2096629.html.

Chapter 12

Lesbian, Gay, Bisexual, and Transgender Inclusion: Business Imperative

Sam McClure

In the economy of 2014, diversity and inclusion (D&I) is an established market-driven industry and a cornerstone of sustainable business strategy in the United States. Work in this focus area began as a reaction to the early civil rights movements and progress has often been driven by changes in public policy relating to the treatment of women and ethnic minorities. The earliest work on diversity in the workplace was focused on enumeration. Put simply this involved work aimed at increasing the numbers of diverse people in total employee numbers. Today, however, the focus is on inclusion and engagement. Our multicultural society delivers a diverse workforce. The challenge for employers is to create workplace cultures that are fully inclusive and welcoming to every diverse identity and perspective. Creating and maintaining a fully inclusive workplace where employees bring their whole self to work every day without fear is solid management practice. Discrimination is not only morally unacceptable: It is inefficient. Chief executives and top managers understand that productivity is directly linked to employee trust and loyalty. A fully engaged workforce is the key to productivity and innovation. The strength and sustainability of the D&I industry is being driven from the top down. The Society for Human Resource Management's (SHRM) "Global Diversity and Inclusion Report" (2008) asks the question: Who are the main advocates of workplace Diversity and Inclusion policies in your organization? The answers were as follows: CEO and top management, 60%; head of human resources, 42%; employees, 21%; board of directors, 18%. "On August 18, 2011 The President of the United States, Barack Obama issued Executive Order #13583—*Establishing a Coordinated Government-wide Initiative to Promote Diversity and Inclusion In The Federal Workforce*" (White House 2011). While sexual orientation and gender identity/expression are not explicitly mentioned in the order, both are included in the "Guidance for Agency-Specific Diversity and Inclusion Strategic Plan" (Office of Personnel Management 2011a) and also in the "Government Wide Diversity and Inclusion Strategic Plan" (2011b), which was developed as a specific requirement of the Executive Order. Inclusion of lesbian, gay, bisexual, and transgender (LGBT) people in D&I efforts is standard business practice among the Fortune 500. This business trend is being driven more by market trends than public policy. President Obama's thoughtful and strategic use of Executive Order demonstrates a recognition that lawmakers are lagging far behind market-driven trends that demand a fully inclusive workplace.

There are no federal nondiscrimination laws for LGBT people. An LGBT person's vulnerability to discrimination depends largely on where they live. The year 2012 marks the first "Municipal Equality Index," published by the Human Rights Campaign (HRC), which measures: nondiscrimination laws, relationship recognition, municipality as employer, municipal programs and services, law enforcement and relationship with LGBT community. Currently only 4 states have nondiscrimination laws that include sexual orientation and only 17 that also include gender identity or expression (NGLTF 2014). Even with this inconsistent and disparate climate for protections within law it is standard business practice among large employers to include sexual orientation and gender identity and/or expression in nondiscrimination policy. According to the 2012 HRC Corporate Equality Index (CEI), 88% of the Fortune 500 include "sexual orientation" in their nondiscrimination policy, and 57% include "gender identity" NGLTF 2014. There are no federal laws that affirmatively allow same-sex relationship recognition; not marriage, civil union, or even simple domestic partnership, although a proposed piece of federal legislation would move the country in that direction. Workplaces began offering basic benefits to recognize domestic partnerships as early as 1982 when the *Village Voice* newspaper became the first private business to offer domestic partner benefits to their employees (Guillen 2013). According to the CEI 2012, the majority of the total Fortune 500 (62%) offer equivalent medical benefits between spouses and partners and 25% offer transgender inclusive benefits, including surgical procedures (Human Rights Campaign 2012). Today the trend is toward taking these benefits to the level of spousal equivalency, well beyond simple health insurance benefits to retiree benefits, family medical leave, and so on. Businesses recognize that inequality in relationship recognition creates inequities in compensation and they are actively seeking solutions and policies to correct this as a part of their broader efforts to create a fully inclusive and engaged workplace. For example: Two employees are performing the same work. One has benefits that recognize and extend to their family members and one does not. The monetary value of these benefits is considered compensation and the disparity between these two employees creates a risk for the employer to be perceived as unfair even though they are in compliance with the law. Once again the trends toward achieving a fully engaged workforce to achieve the highest levels of loyalty and productivity are driving employers to create workplaces where all people feel welcome and valued.

The standards, metrics, and accountability for this progress toward full inclusion of LGBT people in the workplace have been not only measured but also driven by the Human Rights Campaign's Corporate Equality Index. First published in 2002, it has created a roadmap for companies to follow. It was designed strategically as an incentivizing tool. Each new iteration of the survey adds new criteria and effectively raises the bar on the standards for LGBT inclusion policy. Among the criteria for 2013 is demonstrating an effort to include LGBT-owned businesses in corporate supplier diversity programs.

Business's attraction to the CEI was initially rooted in market research. As information became available concerning the purchasing power of LGBT people as a market segment, it became clear that this was a new frontier in the already established outreach to diverse markets. Just as businesses were working to make sure their products and services were reaching women, ethnic minorities, and all age groups, LGBT people were on this radar as well. This information, published by Deloitte in its online report "Diversity and Inclusion: Driving Business Performance," gives a powerful snapshot of diverse markets and their respective buying power.

The 2014 projection for African American buying power is $1.1 trillion, Hispanic $1.3 trillion, Asian American $696.5 billion, Native American $82.7 billion, and White $13.1 trillion (Humphreys 2009). LGBT projected buying power in 2014 is $835 billion (Witeck-Combs Communications). Credibility as a company that is committed to D&I is a critical competitive advantage in the marketplace. Our constantly shifting multicultural society means that these "minority" segments, when combined, are tipping the scales in terms of buying power and economic impact more broadly. I placed the word "minority" in quotes because when all of these identities are combined the word loses its meaning. It is important to note that the only demographic in the projections listed earlier that is not a minority has the largest buying power but the slowest rate of increase in that percentage.

It was and continues to be widely recognized that excluding or marginalizing the LGBT community as a diverse market would effectively be bad for business in a number of ways. Initially the business wants access to this attractive customer and published research indicates an extremely high level of loyalty to brands that demonstrate support for LGBT people. According to Harris Interactive (2011), "LGBT adults strongly prefer brands that support causes important to them and that also offer equal workplace benefits." Nearly 9 out of 10 or 87% of LGBT adults are likely to consider a brand that is known to offer equal employment policies to *all* of their employees including LGBT people. Combine this knowledge of market size and loyalty with the reality that HRC's CEI scores give a metric that is easy for the public to access quickly through publications like the HRC buyers guide, which is widely available in print and online. An additional consideration for business is access to high-quality talent. Recruiting and retaining talent is a business imperative and the CEI also includes an easy-to-use employer database that allows prospective employees to evaluate their potential employer's LGBT inclusion policies easily and quickly. Even more compelling than the ability to attract new talent is mitigating the risk of a potential LGBT talent drain. A highly placed executive within a company that is not addressing LGBT disparities with its employee policies becomes quite vulnerable to poaching by competitors who are more forward thinking. Ultimately providing fully inclusive employee benefits is a critical component in the race to be a competitive employer and attract and retain high-quality talent.

As D&I policies continued to improve and workplace cultures began to change, D&I thought leaders started to question the depth of these efforts and began pushing deeper more meaningful changes. If large employers are inclusive of LGBT people in workplace policies, language, antidiscrimination, cultural and historical respect, recognition and celebration, why does this culture of inclusion stop at the supply chain? "Supplier diversity" is intentional inclusion of marginalized and underrepresented businesses. These inclusion efforts methodically buy back from businesses owned by women and ethnic minorities. Why not LGBT people? The answer was at least in part a structural problem. In order for supplier diversity to include LGBT businesses in their diverse supply chain opportunities a third-party certification similar to that of women- and minority-owned businesses was needed, and also a way of accessing and working directly with those certified enterprises. The National Gay & Lesbian Chamber of Commerce (NGLCC) was formed in 2002 to become the economic voice for LGBT people. IBM was the first company to reach out to the NGLCC seeking a way to identify businesses as LGBT-owned and ultimately became the founding corporate partner in the formation of the NGLCC's LGBT Supplier Diversity Initiative, which created the exclusive third-party LGBT business certification. The LGBT business certification was modeled after existing, credible and rigorous certifications that identified women- and minority-owned businesses. In 2004 the LGBT business certification became the newest diverse business certification and made is possible for the supplier diversity industry to include LGBT business enterprises. With the leadership of IBM, many other corporations joined the list of founding partners and many other corporate partners followed in the next few years. Supplier diversity teams within these corporations began to seek out LGBT business enterprises (LGBTBEs) in addition to women- and minority-owned business enterprises (WBEs and MBEs). LGBT inclusion in diverse supply chains was acknowledged as a standard LGBT inclusion policy by being added to the CEI in 2009. It is now an established part of the lexicon of inclusion policies that define business cultures as "fully inclusive."

NGLCC is the largest LGBT business advocacy organization in the world, with 61 state, local, and international affiliate organizations. For LGBT business advocacy organizations there was a shift in focus as the NGLCC's Supplier Diversity Initiative and message of LGBT economic empowerment gained momentum. The earliest community organizing to support LGBT businesses resulted in the formation of local organizations such as the Golden Gate Business Association in 1974. The early organizational model focused on identifying gay-owned, -oriented, and -serving businesses, and driving consumers to them as well as creating safe spaces for LGBT business owners and professionals to gather, network and work together. This model was driven by disenfranchisement and a need for safety. The core products of the early organizational models were often aimed at small businesses that were largely doing business direct to consumer. The value and deep impact of this model was pivotal to early LGBT community development and organizing. Providing opportunities for LGBT business leaders to gather, network, and work together has always been a component of business organizations. When LGBT people began working together and sharing information about their business and professional experiences, they began to identify specific areas of marginalization and organizing to address these disparities. Out of these networking models, multiple organizational focuses evolved. Like-minded business leaders tend to group together: those LGBT people within large corporations became focused on workplace policy disparities and solid strategies to address these. Out & Equal founded in 1996 with a sole focus on developing training programs designed to address disparities within the workplace and the HRC formed its business council in 1997 and identified workplace among the many issues within their mission. The evolution and growth of these organizations was and continues to be a driving force today for the D&I industry trends toward full inclusion of LGBT people in the workplace.

The current local LGBT chambers of commerce models are shifting toward capitalizing on the LGBT community's own economic power and acknowledging the fundamental value of wealth in the pursuit of full equality in U.S. society. Economic empowerment has been a cornerstone in every pursuit of civil rights. For LGBT people these efforts are currently being driven by community organizing, the D&I and supplier diversity industry trends in the market economy more so than public policy. NGLCC's LGBT Supplier Diversity Initiative evolved as these powerful trends for LGBT inclusion started to reach the supplier diversity industry. Working within business trends has proven to be effective strategy and has brought change and progress at the pace of business imperatives versus the pace of public policy.

The NGLCC and local business advocacy organizations are leading LGBT business owners to think beyond the next single consumer transaction and shift their goals and focus toward long-term sustainable growth strategies. Many LGBT business owners are beginning to shift their business models from a focus on simple self-employment models (often started because of unwelcoming workplaces or unwillingness to hide one's full identity) to building legacy businesses and generational wealth, providing jobs, and taking a seat at the table of this powerful economy. This change in focus brings strength not only to the LGBT community but also to geographic communities. Businesses do not succeed or grow in a vacuum. They thrive in complex organic interdependent systems. When one business accesses a significant growth opportunity other businesses will grow. This is why supplier diversity and procurement opportunities are so critical for LGBTBEs (LGBT business enterprises). When one supplier wins a supply chain contract, the growth trajectory is not exclusive to that single enterprise: It also carries forward its own set of vendors and suppliers. As one business grows, so do its interdependent relationships. Each is adding strength to the economy in the area where they operate—more employment, more tax revenue, and more vendor and supply chain opportunities for others. When any businesses are locked out of opportunities to engage in this organic interdependent system, all economic growth is slower. Again, discrimination is not only morally wrong it is inefficient. In order to have real progress on the economic front, meaningful opportunities are essential.

The corporate supplier diversity industry is focused on opening opportunities to a wider and more diverse pool of possible vendors. This means more opportunities for diverse suppliers and also increased competition. Put simply, more vendors are looking at opportunities and offering a wider array of innovative value-driven solutions. The business case for LGBT supplier diversity inclusion within large corporations also includes: a demonstrated commitment to social responsibility, a reflection of customer base, and a requirement by other companies. For other minorities it may be a government requirement. Regardless of the initial motivation it becomes a question of staying competitive and relevant as a brand. This reality is driving economic trends and shifting power in our culture. For a company today not having and demonstrating a fully inclusive culture in workforce, vendors and customer base is a distinct disadvantage when it comes to recruiting and retaining high-quality talent, accessing innovative and cost-effective business solutions, and building market share.

Federal and municipal procurement (government spending) is a very large percentage of gross domestic product, 38.9% according to the Heritage Foundation, and these large supply chains are also making historic efforts to become fully inclusive. The White House Office of Public Engagement published an LGBT Fact Sheet to sum up the significant progress made in the first term of the Obama administration and reiterate commitments for the second term which includes supporting job creation among LGBT-owned business. It cites the Department of Commerce signing a memorandum of understanding (MOU) with the NGLCC to support federal contracting and exporting (White House n.d.).

On November 15, 2012, the NGLCC hosted the first federal procurement fair for LGBT business enterprises. It was held at the U.S. Department of Commerce and attendees were welcomed by acting Secretary Dr. Rebecca Blank; Deputy Assistant Administrator of the Small Business Administration Eugene Cornelius;

and the White House Associate Director of Public Engagement and LGBT Liaison Gautam Rhagavan. LGBT business owners continue to gain access to opportunities within federal procurement through a series of historic memorandums of understanding between the NGLCC and an increasing number of U.S. federal agencies such as the Department of Interior, Department of Commerce, Department of Labor, and the Small Business Administration. These MOUs open opportunities for LGBTBE's to bid on federal contracting opportunities and gain access to educational and business development programs. The NGLCC has worked closely with the Department of Commerce and the White House to demonstrate the economic impact of LGBT businesses on every aspect of the U.S. economy including international trade and export. President Obama's Executive Order #13534, which launched the National Export Initiative, laid out an aggressive plan to double U.S. exports. The NGLCC made history by taking the first fully sanctioned trade mission specifically for LGBT businesses to Colombia in 2012. This mission opened opportunities for LGBT business owners to explore the strategic growth opportunities connected to export and demonstrates the Obama administration's deep commitment and consistent track record of working for full inclusion. The Obama administration demonstrated an early commitment and fundamental understanding of the importance of LGBT business owners by inviting and including the NGLCC in meetings and briefings not only concerning LGBT issues but also all business and economic issues during the earliest days of the administration taking office, including an invitation to address the transition team.

The NGLCC's mission to advocate for LGBTBEs goes beyond providing access to supply chain and procurement opportunities. In collaboration with corporate partners and federal agencies they are giving access to education and mentoring programs that provide resources and information that guide LGBTBEs as they bring their businesses to scale, develop strategic growth plans, and shift from survival mode to legacy mode.

On June 25, 2005, the NGLCC made history by being the first LGBT organization to ring the closing bell at the New York Stock Exchange.

> Washington, DC—On Monday, June 20, 2005 the National Gay & Lesbian Chamber of Commerce became the first LGBT organization ever to ring the bell at the New York Stock Exchange (NYSE). NGLCC co-founders Justin Nelson and Chance Mitchell joined NGLCC board member and gfn.com founder, Walter Schubert, in ringing the NYSE Closing Bell™ at 4 p.m. EST. Nelson, Mitchell and Schubert were joined by NYSE CEO John Thain, NGLCC Board Chair, Patricia Vivado, Vice President of Lehman Brothers, as well as Howard Buford of Prime Access and Zoa Martinez of Zona Design, both member businesses of the NGLCC.
>
> "In a time when our community is under constant and vicious attacks from the far right, having the very public recognition of our work from

> the NYSE, the nerve center of the U.S. business community, speaks volumes about our mission" said Nelson. "The world's largest marketplace has stated loud and clear that LGBT businesses and investors matter, and our message of economic empowerment is resonating." The NYSE invited the NGLCC to ring the bell as a result of the organization's work within the business sector and in honor of Gay Pride Month, a first for the Exchange. Recognition by the NYSE that the gay community is "an important part of the American economy, should send a signal to everyone, that discrimination in any form only weakens our country," Schubert said.
>
> "LGBT America is open for business," cheered Mitchell after the bell ringing ceremony concluded. "The symbolism of this historic bell ringing should make all members of the LGBT community feel proud." The Closing Bell™ is seen by roughly 120 million viewers around the world according to the NYSE. Several gay and lesbian members of the NYSE staff also appeared with the NGLCC on the podium. John Thain, Chief Executive Officer of the NYSE, presented each participant with a commemorative coin in recognition of Gay Pride Month. (National Gay & Lesbian Chamber of Commerce, 2013, http://www.nglcc.org/news/pressreleases/20050623)

All of the economic progress for LGBT people addressed in this chapter has happened prior to any federal protection or recognition. This is dramatically different than the path of inclusion for women- and minority-owned business, which was driven by public policy. The early history of diversity efforts was driven by President John F. Kennedy's 1961 Executive Order #10925 (White House 1961), which established the President's Equal Employment Opportunity Committee and ultimately the Equal Employment Opportunity Commission (EEOC) (2013). Table. 12.1 demonstrates

Table 12.1 Evolution of Workplace Diversity

	Focus	*Driver*	*Benefits*	*Foundation*
Affirmative action (remedial)	Equal opportunity	Laws	Targeted groups	Assimilation model
Valuing diversity (idealistic)	Appreciation of differences	Ethics	All employees	Diversity model
Managing diversity (practical)	Building skills and changing policies	Corporate Strategy	Organization and all employees	Synergy model

Source: American Society of Mechanical Engineers, 2013, http://www.professional-practice.asme.org/MgmtLeadership/Diversity/History.cfm.

the course of history for the D&I industries, evolving from that starting point to the current era of inclusion work that is dramatically more market driven.

Although these eras may look like three vastly different models for advocating for economic opportunities, this view may be overly simplistic. It is more accurate to acknowledge that one era was built on the traction gained by the former. Historians will have to sort that out, but for today, the attitude of thought leaders on the front line of the current market-driven D&I trends is liberty. Liberty means more than simply not being held captive or suppressed. It means having the freedom to access opportunities for meaningful work and full engagement in the economy. For many this will mean access to opportunities for higher levels of education and employment, and for others it means access to capital to start ventures and build sustainable business models that create innovative solutions to societal challenges. There is a realization that suppressing anyone's full engagement in our economic system ultimately slows our economy and stifles creativity and innovation. Our nation is a stronger, more vibrant, and sustainable economic force when all people are at the table.

Equally suppressive to the growth of our economy is any legislation or absence of legislation that inhibits one's ability to organize and protect one's family. This dynamic is ultimately antiwealth and therefore anticonsumer. When public policy creates barriers to solid financial planning and people's ability to build wealth, it is not only oppressive to people it is ultimately suppressing consumer activity and stifling economic growth. It is very clear by the power, impact, and pace of the D&I industry's LGBT inclusion that this basic principle is recognized and understood by corporate America. In the most recent state marriage equality battles, corporate leaders are weighing in. During Minnesota's recent ballot initiative battle and ultimate victory (the first state ever to defeat a constitutional amendment ballot initiative banning same-sex marriage) the *Minneapolis/St. Paul Business Journal* ran an article on June 25, 2012, titled "General Mills: Gay Marriage Ban Bad for Business" (Hammerand 2012). General Mills Vice President of Global Diversity Ken Charles is quoted: "While General Mills doesn't normally take positions on ballot measures, this is a business issue that impacts our employees," Charles wrote, later saying, "We believe a diverse, inclusive culture produces a stronger, more engaged workforce—and strengthens innovation. Inclusive communities are more successful economically as well."

In this powerful blog post Charles writes of his experience testifying before the U.S. Senate in strong support of the Employment Non-Discrimination Act (ENDA) in the same week that CEO Ken Powell publicly announced that General Mills opposes the constitutional amendment. These two strong and very public positions on legislative issues favorable to LGBT equality were born out of and nurtured by the clear business case for full inclusion.

While there is significant progress because of the strong market-driven push for full inclusion of LGBT people in the workforce, there are still big challenges ahead and the journey to true equality for LGBT people will be a long one. In most corporate structures there is a huge chasm gaping between the ivory tower of human resources departments where policies are changing and the day-to-day experience of an employee working at the cash register or on the loading dock. Policies change much faster than actual cultures. These culture changes will be positively influenced by higher levels of visibility, as increasing numbers of LGBT people are living "out" and the idea that people should hide their sexual orientation or gender identity is no longer a cultural norm. There are many examples of this tipping point in public opinion; however the most powerful was the second inaugural speech of President Barak Obama. With a few simple words this speech addressed a nation with an acknowledgement and a call to action.

> We, the people, declare today that the most evident of truths—that all of us are created equal—is the star that guides us still; just as it guided our forebears through Seneca Falls, and Selma, and Stonewall; just as it guided all those men and women, sung and unsung, who left footprints along this great Mall, to hear a preacher say that we cannot walk alone; to hear a King proclaim that our individual freedom is inextricably bound to the freedom of every soul on Earth.
>
> It is now our generation's task to carry on what those pioneers began. For our journey is not complete until our wives, our mothers and daughters can earn a living equal to their efforts. Our journey is not complete until our gay brothers and sisters are treated like anyone else under the law, for if we are truly created equal, then surely the love we commit to one another must be equal as well. (White House 2013)

While these remarks seem laser focused on marriage equality, if LGBT people are to be "treated like everyone else under the law" this call to action will be the harbinger for much more including public policy changes addressing inequities in opportunities to fully participate in the U.S. economy.

References

Charles, Ken. 2012. "There Is Something We Need to Discuss." http://blog.generalmills.com/2012/06/there-is-something-we-need-to-discuss-%E2%80%A6/.

Guillen, Lina. 2013. "Brief History of Domestic Partner Benefits." Nolo.com. http://www.nolo.com/legal-encyclopedia/domestic-partnership-benefits-29916.html.

Hammerand, Jim. 2012. "General Mills: Gay Marriage Ban Bad for Business." *Minneapolis/St. Paul Business Journal.* June 25, morning edition. http://www.bizjournals.com/twincities/morning_roundup/2012/06/general-mills-gay-marriage-ban-bad.html.

Harris Interactive. 2011. "LGBT Adults Strongly Prefer Brands That Support Causes Important to Them and That Also Offer Equal Workplace Benefits." http://www.harrisinteractive.com/NewsRoom/PressReleases/tabid/446/mid/1506/articleId/835/ctl/ReadCustom%20Default/Default.aspx.

Human Rights Campaign. 2012. "Municipal Equality Index 2012 Report." Corporate Equality Index 2013 Report. http://www.hrc.org/files/assets/resources/CEI_2013_Final_low.pdf.pdf.
Human Rights Campaign. 2013. "Municipal Equality Index 2012 Report." http://www.hrc.org/files/assets/resources/MEI_2012_Report.pdf.
Humphreys, Jeffrey M. 2009. "The Multicultural Economy 2009." Selig Center for Economic Growth.
National Gay & Lesbian Chamber of Commerce. 2013. http://www.nglcc.org/news/pressreleases/20050623.
National Gay and Lesbian Task Force. 2014, May 21. "State Nondiscrimination Law in the U.S." http://www.thetaskforce.org/downloads/reports/issue_maps/non-discrimination_5_14color.pdf.
Office of Personnel Management. 2011a. "Guidance for Agency—Specific Diversity and Inclusion Strategic Plan." United States Office of Personnel Management, November. http://www.opm.gov/diversityandinclusion/reports/DIAgencySpecificStrategicPlanGuidance.pdf.
Office of Personnel Management. 2011b. "Government-Wide Diversity and Inclusion Strategic Plan."
Society for Human Resource Management (SHRM). 2008. "Global Diversity and Inclusion Report." Economist Intelligence Unit, *The Economist*.
White House. 1961. "Establishing the President's Committee On Equal Employment Opportunity." Executive Order #10925. http://www.eeoc.gov/eeoc/history/35th/thelaw/eo-10925.html.
White House. 2011. "Establishing a Coordinated Government-wide Initiative to Promote Diversity and Inclusion in the Federal Workforce." Executive Order #13583. http://www.whitehouse.gov/the-press-office/2011/08/18/executive-order-establishing-coordinated-government-wide-initiative-prom.
White House. 2013. "Inaugural Address President Barack Obama." http://www.whitehouse.gov/the-press-office/2013/01/21/inaugural-address-president-barack-obama.
White House. n.d. "The Obama Administration's Commitment to Winning the Future for the LGBT Community." http://www.whitehouse.gov/sites/default/files/rss_viewer/lgbtfactsheet.pdf.
Witeck-Combs Communications. "The Buying Power of Gay Men and Lesbians in 2008."

Chapter 13

Data-Driven Health Care and Senior Care Analysis

Wallace Swan

Contents

Introduction

Is it fair that lesbian, gay, bisexual, and transgender (LGBT) people have lower incomes (Albelda, Badgett, Schneebaum, and Gates 2009) even though they are better educated than the rest of the population? Was it fair that heterosexual people were able to marry when gay and lesbian couples in a number of states did not have the same opportunity? Is it fair that lesbian and gay couples in some states cannot adopt children or provide foster care when heterosexual couples are able to do so (Ryan, Bedard, and Gertz 2003)? Is it fair that heterosexual couples are able to get financial and legal benefits at work in their corporation, government agency, or nonprofit when gay and lesbian couples are not able to? An approach emphasizing equality and morality has been effective up to a point in the effort to ensure civil rights for LGBT people, but there needs to be proof that this inequality really does make a difference in the life of LGBT singles and couples. In our culture, the use of empirically driven analysis is essential for every group that wishes to achieve their own rights.

Since the 1990s, the U.S. Census has collected data about gay and lesbian couples. As a result, it is now possible to document the numbers of gay and lesbian couples who have been deprived of the benefits routinely given to heterosexual couples. However, the numbers of single gay and lesbian people are not included within the U.S. Census data. And the same is true for transgender and bisexual people: There are not even any questions included in the U.S. Census to collect data about single gay and lesbian, transgender, and bisexual people; and consequently there is no information available upon which to make decisions about policy. In this chapter, we will see what a difference having some of this data actually makes for nonprofit and public administration and policy.

Hennepin County, Minnesota, SHAPE 2010 Data

For a number of years, Hennepin County, Minnesota, staff researchers have been collecting randomly sampled data about the health status of residents of their county (which includes Minneapolis and suburbs). In 2010, the study (which included 7001 residents who responded) was repeated. The simple inclusion of LGBT questions is unusual in the United States. The data was collected in such a way as to allow comparisons between LGBT populations and the general population of the county. Some of the indicators of overall health and mental health are the same for both populations, while some are better (or, more accurately, higher) and some are worse. Table 13.1 shows some of the more striking data in cases in which there is a major variation between LGBT and general population responses (Hennepin County Public Health Department 2010, 1–11).

Rainbow Health Initiative—Voices of Health: A Survey of LGBTQ Health in Minnesota (2012)

Rainbow Health Initiative, a non-profit based in Minneapolis, does an annual LGBTQ community health survey. The data is not collected by random sampling, which makes it less methodologically rigorous than the previous SHAPE 2010 study.

Table 13.1 Data Derived from Hennepin County Shape Study (2010)

Hennepin Shape 2010 Indicator	*Rate for LGBT Adults*	*Compare to Adults Not LGBT*
Overall Health, Chronic Diseases, and Conditions		
Currently having asthma	10.8%	6.5%
Mental Health (MH)		
Frequent mental distress: Mental health was not good for 14 days or more during the past 30 days	16.3%	8.4%
Depression: Ever been diagnosed	43.3%	23.2%
Anxiety or panic attack: Ever been diagnosed	26.6%	16.0%
Serious psychological distress (SPD), SPD measures serious mental health (SMI) in population	7.4%	2.5%
Any psychological distress, based on scale for SPD	27.1%	14.8%
Activity Limitation or Disability		
Activity limitation: Respondent is limited in any activities because of physical, mental, emotional problems	28.5%	19.6%
Work limitation: Respondent has difficulty in getting, keeping, or working at a job or business because of any impairment or health problem	14.0%	7.7%
Health Access and Utilization		
Currently uninsured	10.6%	6.4%
Uninsured at least sometime during the past 12 months	20.0%	10.0%
Having no regular source of care (personal doctor or health care provider)	33.9%	28.3%
Felt being discrimination against when seeking health care during the past 12 months	5.7%	2.2%
Experienced unmet medical care needs	26.4%	15.5%
Experienced unmet mental health care needs	33.3%	13.7%

Continued

Table 13.1 (*Continued*) Data Derived from Hennepin County Shape Study (2010)

Hennepin Shape 2010 Indicator	*Rate for LGBT Adults*	*Compare to Adults Not LGBT*
Preventive Care Indicators		
Complete physical exam within the past year	43.0%	55.2%
Mammogram within the past year (among women aged 40 and older)	49.7%	65.2%
At Last Clinic Visit, Health Care Provider Asked About ...		
Smoking or other tobacco use	54.2%	45.0%
Stress	50.1%	39.9%
Alcohol use	48.5%	42.0%
Lifestyle and Risk Behavior Indicators		
Currently smoking	18.8%	11.7%
Heavy drinking (more than 2 drinks per day for males and 1 drink per day for females)	18.3%	11.7%
Binge drinking (having more than 5 drinks for males and 4 drinks for females in one occasion, at least once during the past 30 days)	39.9%	28.7%
Community and Neighborhood Indicators		
This is a good community to raise children	82.1%	88.1%
Involved in school, community, and neighborhood activity often	17.6%	28.9%
Connect with friends or neighbors often, at least weekly	89.9%	84.4%
Go to a church, temple, mosque, or other places of worship or other activities often (at least weekly)	12.8%	33.8%
Strongly Agree or Agree with Statement about Where You Live		
People in this neighborhood know each other	63.7%	70.3%
People in this neighborhood can be trusted	77.7%	83.4%

Table 13.1 (*Continued*) Data Derived from Hennepin County Shape Study (2010)

Hennepin Shape 2010 Indicator	*Rate for LGBT Adults*	*Compare to Adults Not LGBT*
People in this neighborhood are afraid to go out at night due to violence	30.0%	19.3%
Gangs are a serious issue in this neighborhood	20.6%	11.0%
Children are safe in this neighborhood	83.6%	89.3%
Economic Distress and Residential Stability		
Experienced food insecurity	19.4%	13.3%
Experienced housing insecurity	11.4%	8.4%
Difficulty in paying for prescription medication each month	17.7%	11.6%
Residential instability (moved more than 2 times during the past 2 years)	15.5%	9.3%

Note: Percentages are not additive.

In 2012, 1,144 people who identified as LGBTQ completed the survey, which was distributed at LGBTQ venues throughout the state (Pride Festivals, Rainbow Health Initiative events, etc.). See Table 13.2.

University of Washington Aging and Health Report

The concerns of LGBT seniors throughout the nation have not been expressed well in the past because of lack of available data on the subject. In a chapter I recently coauthored with Kristen Norman-Major and Mark French titled "Cultural Competency Around Sexual and Gender Orientation and Identity," I was struck by how little available data there was available on LGBT seniors (Norman-Major and Gooden 2012). However, this has begun to change because of the study titled "The Aging and Health Report: Resilience and Disparities among Lesbian, Gay, Bisexual, and Transgender Older Adults" (Fredrikson-Goldsen et al. 2011). This study was initially done using data from the "Behavioral Risk Factor Surveillance System" in Washington State (BRFSS 2013); but then was augmented by data collected by a group of community partners, including agencies in New York, Los Angeles, San Francisco, Boston, Chicago, Seattle,

Table 13.2 Data Derived from Rainbow Health Initiative "Voices of Health" Survey (2012)

RHI Category	
Individual Health	
Smoked every day or some days per week	30.8%
Diagnosed with depression	41.8%
Diagnosed with anxiety	37.0%
Health Attitudes	
Did not know there are higher rates of tobacco use among LGBTQ people	59.7%
Saw expense as a major barrier to eating more fruits and vegetables	56.5%
Saw a lack of safe and convenient places to exercise	13.6%
Experiences with Health Care	
Have health insurance	81.2%
Were out to their doctor about their sexual identity and gender identity	61.7%
Bisexual people were the least likely to be out	48.6%
Gay and out	72.0%
Lesbian and out	74.4%
Thought their doctor was very competent about LGBTQ health issues	33.0%
Quality of Care	
Reported receiving poor quality care because of their sexual orientation or gender identity	26.2%
Queer people reported the highest rates of poor quality care	43.2%
Trans people experienced poor quality care at a higher rate	44.0%

Source: Rainbow Health Initiative, "Voices of Health: A Survey of LGBTQ Health in Minnesota," 2012, p. 4.

Milwaukee, Minnesota, and St. Louis. Some of the findings about LGBT aging and health include the following:

- Nearly one-half have a disability; nearly one-third report depression.
- Ninety-one percent engage in wellness activities.
- Almost two-thirds have been victimized three or more times.

- Thirteen percent have been denied health care or received inferior care.
- More than 20% do not disclose their sexual or gender identity to their physician.

According to the survey, these LGBT seniors need services like housing, social events, legal, and transportation (Fredrickson-Goldsen et al. 2011).

PFund Foundation Surveys

PFund (2013) is a foundation in Twin Cities, Minnesota, which provides grants and scholarships, develops leaders and deals with LGBT regional organizations in building their infrastructure. It has been working for the past few years in ensuring that health and social service capabilities are developed by LGBT senior organizations.

Ready to Serve? PFund Foundation Report of the Aging Network and Lesbian, Gay, Bisexual, and Transgender Older Adults

Ready to Serve? was compiled by PFund coauthors as an online survey. It was designed to assess the readiness of 24 organizations in the PFund region to provide services to LGBT seniors (Upper Midwest), all of which are member agencies in the Aging Network (Area Agencies on Aging, State Units on Aging, and related agencies).

The major findings were as follows: "More than half of the agencies have offered or funded staff training about LGB and T aging, yet only one agency is providing services and outreach targeted to the LGB and T community and only two agencies had received a request to assist an LGB and T old person in the previous year. … [F]ull staff training … is likelier to result in welcoming, appropriate services that LGB and T older adults trust" (Knochel, Abel, Moone, and Quam 2010, 4).

The policy result of this study was to move a community agency, Training to Serve, into the business of providing LGBT cultural competency training to agencies serving seniors in the Twin Cities region.

2012 Twin Cities LGBT Aging Needs Assessment Survey

The 2012 Twin Cities LGBT Aging Needs Assessment Survey was compiled as a follow-up to a similar study (a needs assessment) that was done in 2002. Twenty-one LGBT partner agencies and organizations participated, resulting in 792 people responding to the questionnaire, of which 495 met the requirements of the study. The key results are summarized as follows: "The LGBT older adults who participated in the study were nearly twice as likely to be a caregiver. However, they were more likely to live alone, less likely to have a caregiver, and less likely to have children" (Croghan, Moone, and Olson 2012).

One of the policy outcomes of this particular study has been to allocate money from a special PFund grants program. "PFund, in partnership with Greater Twin Cities United Way, (as part of the LGBT Aging Initiative) awarded $25,000 to innovative and collaborative projects that address ageism and create widespread community impact to ensure LGBT older adults can thrive and age with dignity, safety and equitable care" (PFund 2013).

Conclusion

These studies have begun to provide a base for decision making on LGBT people, a subfield of knowledge that previously had little or no data available to decision makers. Given this information, government agencies, foundations, and nonprofits are beginning to focus their attention upon the needs of a dramatically underserved population.

References

Albelda, Randy, M. V. Lee Badgett, Alyssa Schneebaum, and Gary Gates. 2009. "Poverty in the Lesbian, Gay, and Bisexual Community." Los Angeles, CA: Williams Institute.

Croghan, Catherine, Rajean Moone, and Andrea Olson. 2012. "2012 Twin Cities LGBT Aging Needs Assessment Survey." Minneapolis, MN: PFund Foundation.

Fredrikson-Goldsen, Karen, Hyun-Jun Kim, Charles Emlet, Anna Muraco, Elena Hoy-Ellis Charles Erosheva, Jayn Goldsen, and Heidi Petry. 2011. "Executive Summary: The Aging and Health Report: Resilience and Disparities among Lesbian, Gay, Bisexual, and Transgender Older Adults." Seattle, WA: Institute for Multigenerational Health, University of Washington.

Hennepin County Public Health Department. 2010. "Overall Health and Mental Health Indicators at a Glance: Hennepin County LGBT Adults 2010," pp. 1–11. Minneapolis, Minnesota.

Knochel, Leyy Abel, Catherine Croghan, Rajean Moone, and Jean Quam. 2010. "Ready to Serve? PFund Foundation Report of the Aging Network and Lesbian, Gay, Bisexual, and Transgender Older Adults." Minneapolis, MN: PFund Foundation, p. 4.

Norman-Major, Kristen, and Susan Gooden. 2012. "Cultural Competency for Public Administrators." In *Cultural Competency Around Sexual and Gender Orientation and Identity*, edited by Wallace Swan, Mark French, and Kristen Norman-Major, 141–169. Armunk, NY: M. E. Sharpe.

PFund. 2013. "The LGBT Aging Initiative: LGBT Aging Initiative Fund Update." http://www.pfundonline.org/aging.html.

Rainbow Health Initiative. 2012. "Voices of Health: A Survey of LGBTQ Health in Minnesota," p. 4.

Ryan, S. D., L. Bedard, and M. Gertz. 2003. "Florida's Gay Adoption Ban: What Do Floridians Think?" *University of Florida Jacksonville & Public Policy, 15*, 261.

Washington State Department of Health. 2013. Behavioral Risk Factor Surveillance System (BRFSS). http://www.doh.wa.gov/DataandStatisticalReports/HealthBehaviors/BehavioralRiskFactorSurveillanceSystemBRFSS.aspx.

Chapter 14

Lesbian, Gay, Bisexual, and Transgender Health Issues

Sid Guthrie

Contents

Introduction

Since the *Handbook of Gay, Lesbian, Bisexual, and Transgender Administration and Policy,* edited by Wallace Swan, was published in 2004, significant changes within the lesbian, gay, bisexual, and transgender (LGBT) community have occurred. The state and national quests for legitimization of marriage between same-sex couples have advanced significantly and the ability of LGBT service members to serve openly in the armed forces has substantially increased the visibility of the LGBT community. Great strides have been made in the care of AIDS and although the numbers of men becoming infected in the United States have decreased, it still remains a priority health care issue for the LGBT community. LBGT politics over that last eight years has shifted from increasing awareness and funding for HIV-related issues to marriage equality and allowing gays and lesbians to serve openly in the military. In tandem with marriage equality is the increased number of LGBT people who are choosing to have children biologically or through adoption.

Thanks to the data collection methodology used during the 2010 Census collection and work done by the Williams Institute,* a better idea of the composition and demographics of the LGBT community and the ability to identify potential needs (including the area of health) is now obtainable. Concurrently the work done by national and some state organizations on cultural competence and access to care has broadened the discussion and interest among top federal and private health care organizations to begin exploring LGBT health care issues beyond HIV diseases. In 2011 after spending several years with hundreds of experts, the Institute of Medicine released its landmark report on health care needs of the LGBT community.† In its summation, the Institute of Medicine advocated that more research dollars need to be committed to better understanding the health care needs of the LGBT community and providing better models of care.

The purpose of this chapter will be to briefly cover some of the most pressing health care issues affecting the LGBT community. These are areas that influence the overall physical, mental, and economic stability for the community at large. There will be discussion and comparison between empowered and disempowered states on how health care is legislated, offered, and accounted for. In contrast to

* Williams Institute. Accessed January 7, 2013, http://williamsinstitute.law.ucla.edu/category/research/census-lgbt-demographics-studies/.

† Institute of Medicine. 2011. "The Health of Lesbian, Gay, Bisexual, and Transgender People Building a Foundation for Better Understanding." Washington, D.C.: National Institutes of Health. http://www.iom.edu/~/media/Files/Report%20Files/2011/The-Health-of-Lesbian-Gay-Bisexual-and-Transgender-People/LGBT%20Health%202011%20Report%20Brief.pdf.

the African-American, Asian, and Hispanic populations in the United States, the LGBT community is relatively new to the stage of health care disparities research. Fortunately the interest and building blocks are in place to offer the LGBT population the outstanding health care it wants and needs in order to further their personal, political, and economic objectives.

Priority Health Care Issues for the LGBT Community

Gay Men

Cardiovascular disease. According to the Substance Abuse and Mental Health Services Administration (SAMHSA), cardiovascular disease is a major issue for the LGBT community. Heart disease remains the top risk for adults in general. Studies indicate that gay men have a higher prevalence of heart disease. Two significant leading risk factors for heart disease in gay men are the incidence of smoking and alcohol use (American Lung Association 2010).

Cancer. Prostate, testicular, and colon cancer among gay and bisexual men may be increased due to lack of education and awareness that can happen when there is no regular provider seen and a family history is not picked up and documented in the medical record (Asencio, Blank, Descartes, and Crawford 2009). Not having insurance or lack of a primary care provider who does not have enough information on the patient to suggest various cancer screening techniques may have been contributors to the higher rates. Difficulty revealing types of sexual activities to a provider one may not know well or trust may be a factor in care. For example, a patient may not wish to discuss exposure to human papillomavirus (HPV) that can cause genital and anal warts and possibly contribute to the development of anal cancer (Heslin, Gore, King, and Fox 2008).

Mental health and substance abuse. In the area of mental health and substance use, gay men have been found to experience higher levels of depression and anxiety than heterosexual men. Higher rates of suicide have been found among gay men in comparison to the public at large (Berg, Mimiaga, and Safren 2008). Some of this could be the result of increased substance abuse, but some has been attributed to issues related to coming out and the feeling of isolation. Some studies suggest that bisexual men have a higher rate of suicide attempts than gay men (Dobinson 2007).

Sexually transmitted disease. HIV prevalence within the gay and bisexual community remains a significant issue. According to data from the Centers for Disease Control and Prevention (CDC), gay and bisexual men still account for about 48% of the population living with HIV infection: Regarding the rate of newly acquired HIV infection, African-American gay and bisexual men have a rate of infection that is 44 times higher than Caucasian and Hispanic men.

Injury and violence. Injury and domestic violence are also priority issues that plague gay men. Gay men have a higher incidence of being victimized in society at large because of their sexual orientation. Also they have been found to be at increased risk of violence from a domestic partner (Houston and McKirnan 2007).

Lesbians

Cancer. Lesbians have been found to be at higher risk of developing breast cancer through their lifetime in comparison to heterosexual women (Dibble, Roberts, and Nussey 2004). The reason given for this is that a lower percentage of lesbians give birth to children than heterosexual women. During pregnancy and breastfeeding, hormones that protect women against breast cancer are developed. Since this is less likely for lesbians, breast cancer will be more of a risk. There is also a higher incidence of endometrial and ovarian cancer found in the lesbian community, which is also attributed to the lack of protective hormones in conjunction with a higher rate of obesity. Studies have also shown that fewer lesbians visit providers for regular screenings that include Pap screenings than do heterosexual women (U.S. Office on Women's Health 2005).

Cardiovascular disease. Prevalence is higher for heart disease for lesbians in comparison to heterosexual women. Once again this is attributed to a higher rate of obesity and smoking in addition to minority stress.

Injury and violence. Lesbians report almost a 30% rate of domestic violence (Lockhart, White, Causby, and Isaac 1994). They also report a higher percent of violence from family members than do heterosexuals.

Bisexual Men and Women

Cardiovascular disease. Both bisexual men and women reported being at higher risk for heart disease. Bisexual women reported a higher level of heart disease than heterosexual women but a lower level than lesbians (VanKim and Padilla 2010).

Cancer. Bisexual men who have anal sex are at a higher risk of developing anal cancer, second only to increased risk to exposure to HPV.*

Injury and violence. Both bisexual men and women have been found to have a higher rate of domestic violence that heterosexual men and women (VanKim and Padilla 2010).

Mental health and substance abuse. Bisexual women reported that they had more anxiety than heterosexual women during their teenage years. Bisexual women were found to have more issues surrounding eating disorders than lesbians (Koh and Ross 2006). Studies suggest that bisexual men and women were twice as likely to report depression and three times more likely having had suicidal ideations than their heterosexual counterparts (VanKim and Padilla 2010). Bisexual men and

---

* Dobinson, Cheryl. 2007. "Top Ten Bisexual Health Issues." As cited in *Bisexual Health: An Introduction and Model Practices for HIV/STI Prevention Programming*, by Marshall Miller, Amy André, Julie Ebin, and L. Bessonova. New York: National Gay and Lesbian Task Force Policy Institute. See Appendix A.

women have been found to have higher rates of binge drinking. Both bisexual men and women have higher rates of smoking.

Transgender

Injury, violence, and mental health. Due to the significant gap in data collection on health indicators, identifying priority issues for transgender people in regard to health has been difficult to accomplish. Difficulties involved in getting and maintaining health care remain problematic, although this will change with the passage of the Affordable Care Act (ACA). What is known is that some studies have shown that over 60% of transgendered people have been victims of violence resulting in injury. With rates of injury that high, it is not surprise that depression and anxiety are key mental health issues for this community.

Substance abuse. Tobacco, alcohol, marijuana, and crack cocaine are found to be used more among the transgendered population. Alarmingly, there also has been an increase in the use of methamphetamines. There has been growing concern about the increasing use of injecting methamphetamines (Risser et al. 2005).

Sexually transmitted diseases. Studies on the prevalence of HIV infections have been difficult to calculate although it is suggested that male-to-female transgender women of color have higher rates of infection than other transgendered groups (Tooru 2001).

Summary

For the LGBT community, priority health care issues focus on access and continuity of care, although this will hopefully diminish in importance with the full implementation of the Affordable Care Act starting in 2014. Cardiovascular disease and cancer remain problems, but both of these issues are exacerbated by lifestyle issues such as the increased rate of smoking and substance abuse found in the LGBT community. With new tools and data systems that will be part of the ACA, prevention and intervention goals will need programs to decrease the prevalence of these diseases and outcome measures set. Stress and substance abuse among minorities can probably be linked to the increased anxiety, depression, and suicide found in the LGBT community. Interestingly enough, Blackwell (2012) points out a potential link between internalized homophobia and substance abuse. There has not been much research done on internalized homophobia, but the ramifications might not be detrimental only to the individual but to the LGBT community as a whole.

HIV remains and will continue to be a significant health care issue for gay/bisexual men and transgendered persons. New drugs are helping those who are HIV positive avoid infections and complications that increased mortality rates in the past. There is concern about the recent increased rates of HIV infection among younger gay and bisexual (especially African-American) men.

Specialty Populations

LGBT Aging

As with the population at large, the aging LGBT population has more chronic health problems that can accompany the aging process. In addition, those men who have been treated for HIV-related diseases are living longer with chronic health problems.

About three quarters of LGBT seniors live alone and up to 80% live alone without a partner. Many LGBT seniors do not have children and lack traditional support networks that can assist them in time of need.

An area that needs to be identified and fully explored is when those LGBT persons who have been on Medicaid or private insurance transfer to Medicare. Smooth transition of treatment for needs and caregivers should be considered when moving to Medicare coverage. Legislative changes will need to be considered as the ACA rolls out so that there is not significant disruption of care coverage when moving into retirement. Also relationships, advanced directives, and power of attorney need to be honored across the lifespan.

About 65% to 70% percent of the aging LGBT population will have long-term care needs.* Depending on the area of the country in which the person is living, education on cultural sensitivity may be lacking or inconsistent among providers. Those who rely exclusively on Medicare for their insurance coverage may find themselves unable to have much choice of providers if they are unable to supplement their insurance plan with alternative financial resources. Placement in transitional care units or nursing homes may be dependent entirely on financial coverage and not on cultural competence or choice.

Family Health and Active Duty Military

With the increasing number of LGBT persons who have children, health insurance not only for the partners but also for the children in our legal system becomes problematic. Employer-based health insurance is a staple for most employed Americans. Even in states that offer marriage or domestic partnership benefits, unless both parents adopt the child, coverage can become an issue if the parent with the primary insurance does not have custody of the child. Even if the child is in the custody of the parent who has employer-based health insurance, then the other parent must seek private insurance that may add considerable expense.

For active-duty military, benefits will be provided to legally married couples regardless of their state of residency (see p. 358).

* LGBT Aging Center. 2010. "LGBT Older Adults: Facts at a Glance." Accessed January 7, 2013, www.lgbtagingcenter.org/resources/pdfs/LGBTOlderAdultsFactsataGlance.pdf.

All couples with children need to understand the state laws in regard to parent recognition, which can be found in a table titled "State Same Sex Parenting Laws" (Movement Advancement Project 2012).

What makes matters worse is that in some states it depends on the jurisdiction as to where the custody was issued and may not apply throughout the state. These considerations need to be thought through when making decisions on moving due to employment or other reasons.

Custody plays an important part in visitation rights and making decisions on medical treatment for children in an emergency. Same-sex parents without dual custody may have problems obtaining any information on their hospitalized child until the custody status is determined or designated in the health care records. These are stressors that heterosexual married couples do not need to consider but are going to necessitate major legal changes in regard to same-sex parenting.

Health Care Systems and Access

Access

Access to care has remained a problem for transgender persons, lesbians, and bisexual women. Lesbian and bisexual women have a higher rate of being uninsured or underinsured (Diamont, Wold, Spritzer, and Gelberg 2000). Also, findings show that many of these women are reluctant to share their sexual orientation with physicians especially if they do not see a regular provider.

Due to increased unemployment rates, transgendered persons also run into difficulties maintaining consistent medical care due to lack of insurance (Kenagy 2005). Additionally, they have difficulty finding a provider that has the knowledge and comfort level to treat them. Adequate transgender care involves being familiar with the stages and transitions transgender clients go through. This takes an expertise that is usually not part of the educational experience for most providers. Often what might appear to be refusal of care to a client may in actuality be a concern that the provider is not feeling fully confident in determining the care of this person.

Cultural Competency

Many medical schools have started taking steps to teach medical students and residents how to care for LGBT clients. Several organizations, including the Gay and Lesbian Medical Association and Human Rights Foundation, have worked with health care organizations on cultural competency education for LGBT clients. With the introduction of the Affordable Care Act, collaboration with these and similar groups is needed to provide the curriculum for this type of much needed education for all health care personnel.

Health Care Quality

Health Care Quality Index

Since the early 2000s, LGBT organizations have been increasing their attention to health care given to the LGBT population. The Human Rights Foundation (HRF) has done excellent work in putting together foundational criteria for evaluation of health care organizations. The foundation developed four core elements that it thought health care organizations should foster in order to be considered LGBT friendly. These core four criteria are patient nondiscrimination, equal visitation, employment nondiscrimination, and training in LGBT patient care. A table titled "Hospital Visitation Rights" summarizes these visitation rights: Health care organizations who responded have their results posted on the website* and these can be used by consumers (HRC 2013). They also provide information on LGBT friendly providers and facilities on its website. The HRC website also has a Corporate Equality Index that gives information about companies surveyed that offer LGBT friendly benefits and employment policies. For 2013, after surveying 688 U.S. businesses, it found that 55% offer domestic partner benefits. In 2010, President Obama mandated that all health care facilities that received Medicare and Medicaid funding give equal visitation rights to same-sex partners. Health care organizations have been in the process of revising their policies to reflect the change.

Other national organizations (such as the National Coalition for LGBT Health, Movement Advancement Project, National Gay and Lesbian Task Force, the Gay and Lesbian Medical Association) collect data, institute educational programs, and sponsor research. It will be important as the ACA rolls out that these organizations not only participate in building of legislation for these programs, but also use their websites and chapter affiliates to get the word out to the larger LGBT community.

Healthy People 2020

The Department of Health and Human Services in 2010 began to work with the LGBT community on how to decrease health care disparities in the LGBT community. Health disparity issues were identified. They were then incorporated into the Healthy People 2020 project in efforts to expand the work on health care disparities in the LGBT community. Evidence-based data on priority health care issues and recommendations on how to address them will be one of many outcome measures.

* See http://www.hrc.org/hei.

Affordable Care Act

In 2010 President Obama signed into law the Affordable Care Act (ACA). This bill was not only a landmark for the United States population as a whole but served as a cornerstone for important changes that now can occur for the LGBT community. For the first time, comprehensive health coverage would become available to more Americans who previously were unable to afford it because of expense or because it was not provided through their place of employment. The development of coverage will be based on essential health benefits taking into account the diverse populations that will be served through this act. Although not directly stated, foundational to the building of the ACA was to decrease health care disparities while still providing affordable care. The hope was the desire to create insurance products that embedded these principles.*

Most promising is that the Center for Medicare and Medicaid (CMS) will be providing oversight for the previously uninsured, who become Medicaid eligible. CMS is an agency that oversees federal health care programs and determines quality indicators that are publicly reportable. CMS and the Joint Commission on Accreditation of Hospitals and Health Care Organizations have been the main drivers behind the movement to improve quality, decrease costs, improve coordination, and increase patient satisfaction. Their recommendations and outcome criteria are based on current research. Both of these organizations advocate for decreasing health care disparities and include public input in any changes made. Both Medicare and Medicaid have been leaders in advocating and have initiated demonstration projects for partial reimbursement based on outcome performance and patient satisfaction from practitioners and systems.

The transgender community will benefit the most from the ACA since historically up to 50% of them have been denied service by providers. Additionally, due to underemployment and unemployment up to 60% of transgender persons in some studies reported being unable to get insurance. Despite the research that has been done with the transgender community in regard to health needs, coverage for transgender-specific health care is severely lacking (Transgender Law Center 2009).

On the down side, at this time 21 states have opted out of the Medicaid expansion and will continue to use the "current" criteria for eligibility for enrollment and continue the same benefits. Twenty-five states have decided to accept federal funding for Medicaid expansion. Four other states—Missouri, New Hampshire, Pennsylvania, and Utah—are still considering expansion. [*Editor's note*: New Hampshire approved expansion.] Although most of these are disempowered states, ironically one of the states, Maine, has legalized same-sex marriage (The Advisory Board Company 2013).

It is estimated that there will be a significant influx of Medicaid patients added to the federal government program. People with cancer will be able to get the ongoing care they need. Also will be no lifetime caps on health care costs that have often

* Healthcare.gov. Accessed January 7, 2013, www.healthcare.gov/law/full/index.html.

resulted in significant increases in medical bankruptcies over the last several years. Yearly out-of-pocket deductibles will be redefined on an annual basis and determined by community standards.

Identification and prevention of illness have been identified as a high priority for the ACA. With the ability to have access to quality primary care, early identification of health care deficits can be identified and health promotion incorporated into visits in order to maintain optimum health.

The ACA is fully implemented in 2014. It is imperative that LGBT organizations become involved in defining what and how LGBT health care needs will be addressed and what outcome measures will be used. Information on sexual orientation or identification as well as the family structure will need to be part of the data-gathering process. The intake and ongoing data collection regarding the LGBT health issues will need to be standardized and agreed upon by all states. LGBT community health care facilities, providers, and consumers should be included in determining what data is obtained and how it is used.

Health Insurance Exchanges

In 2014, adults who are not eligible for private health care coverage through work and do not meet the requirements for subsidized or full Medicaid benefits will need to purchase insurance under the individual mandate section of the law. There is a penalty applied if coverage is not purchased. The government will subsidize the premium rates for those who fall below the federal poverty level. The law also requires businesses with over 50 employees to provide insurance to their employees. The ACA employer mandate was to start in 2014 but has been extended to 2015. Large businesses with over 50 employees may not use the health insurance exchanges initially for the first three years. Tentatively, in 2017, these businesses can opt to join the state insurance exchanges, although this date is subject to change.

All of the insurance plans will be required to provide a defined basic package of health care benefits determined by the Secretary of the Department of Health and Human Services. At this point the states may create them or if they opt not to do that, then the federal government will offer a plan. All states must offer at least one plan. All plans will have the same basic benefits and will be affordable. Choices made will be by the consumer who can pick the plan that fits their income and needs. Small businesses that have less than 100 employees can participate to keep their benefit costs down. Businesses can either cover the full premium or give the employees vouchers so that they can pick their own plans. All people must be insured and if they decide not to, there will be a federal penalty for not having insurance. Competition between insurance offerings will be based on pricing and additional benefits that may be added to the individual plans. Denials of care based on previous health history will no longer be allowed for those with preexisting diseases, such as HIV or other health care problems. There will no longer be a lifetime cap on insurance and the yearly premiums and out-of-pocket maximum deducible will be developed by a community standard formula.

During the development process, the states chose how they wanted to go about creating and managing state exchanges. The federal government worked hard with the states to make sure they had the information they need to get started and timelines set to let the federal government know how far they have progressed. One of the major benefits of this program is that the federal government, from the beginning, worked with the Department of Health in using cloud computer technology whereby states can share information with each other. It makes it easier for individual states to keep up with new information and to have a forum to ask questions as the exchanges develop. This will probably be the precursor to a large database that will retain all health care–related information so that states can use the data for performance improvement and research. This has huge potential for the LGBT community, but it also has risks.

Here is an example of what could occur over the next several years when empowered states come together to develop their health insurance exchanges under the Affordable Care Act (RFR 2012). Because Massachusetts was an early adopter, it received grant funding early under an innovations project to develop information technology to create health insurance exchanges. Massachusetts created the Massachusetts Connector that began to put a plan together to build the framework for the state exchanges: This involved an eleven-member board that included governmental leaders, academics, and leaders within the health care community (Yang, Flint, and Apicella 2012). The Massachusetts Connector began to gather information from current state health plans and at the same time develop an educational curriculum that will eventually accompany the rollout of the health insurance exchanges. Additionally they started exploring insurance options that could be developed for small business with less than 100 employees, so that they could offer coverage to their employees at a reasonable cost. Since Massachusetts received innovation money to develop the information technology (IT) infrastructure, this gives it leeway to begin setting up the informational databases that will be used in 2013 when the first wave of eligible Medicaid recipients will be applying for benefits.

Massachusetts is also a member of the newly created New England States Collaborative Insurance Exchange. Other states included in this collaborative are Connecticut, Maine, New Hampshire, Rhode Island, and Vermont. Massachusetts, New Hampshire, Vermont, and Maine all recognize same-sex marriages. One would assume that within this collaborative where the majority of states involved have same-sex marriage provisions for married same-sex couples, the health care needs for the entire LGBT community will be strongly considered when building essential elements into health insurance plans. These plans will be piloted and will probably be the benchmark for other states that have same sex marriage laws or domestic partnerships that include health care benefits.

Massachusetts got a head start on data collection in 2009 when the Massachusetts Department of Health did a study on the health of the LGBT community. Demographics it collected went beyond health-related issues and covered areas such as whether, if coupled, the people had access to partnership coverage. The health department asked questions about how people felt about their overall physical health, mental health, and exposure to violence. Their study showed that the overall health indicators regarding wellness were lower than for heterosexuals: This correlates with other studies done on the LGBT population. They did however find a higher rate of health insurance coverage for those who were married to same-sex partners compared to those who were in domestic partnership arrangements.

Other states too have begun to study their LGBT population as well. The largest urban county in Minnesota has begun to share LGBT-related data in a study titled "SHAPE 2010." SHAPE is an annual survey that looks at the overall health of Hennepin County. The county collected data on overall health, health care access, lifestyle, and behaviors related to a healthy lifestyle and social–environmental factors. This is one of the few instances that a county specifically took a look at the LGBT community from a health care point of view and compared it with the broader population of the county. Both Massachusetts and Minnesota used state dollars to finance their research. Both also are considered empowered states.

Another state that has a ban on same-sex marriage and would not be considered "empowered" also recently completed a demographic study on its LGBT populations. The "Missouri Foundation Series: Responding to LGBT Health Disparities," has released its study in 2012. It collected much of the same demographic information that the other states did. What was interesting was that Blue Cross and Blue Shield Insurance financed the study. Despite a ban on marriage at that time, one of the first recommendations made on changes that needed to come about as a result of the studies was that same-sex marriage should be legalized.

Opportunities

One of the other recommendations that the Affordable Care Act requires is the development of community-based health centers that can provide preventative health screening, primary care, and continuity of care. There are scattered LGBT community health centers in a variety of locations throughout the United States. Many started during the AIDS epidemic due to the lack of culturally sensitive care and the increased social needs that infected patients required in tandem with their drug therapies.

One of the most well-known is the Fenway Institute in Boston. Its leadership has been instrumental in creating an institution that has changed and expanded their health care to meet the changing needs and demographics of a changing LGBT community. The Fenway Institute not only focuses on medical care but also takes a more holistic approach to the patients they serve. Family-centered care including maternity care and pediatrics as well as the full spectrum of transgender care needs are met within the facility. The institute has ongoing research and developed an education program of culturally competent care covering the full range of needs for the LGBT community. This information is available to professionals nationally.

In closing, the health and wellness of the LGBT community stands to benefit greatly from the changes in health care brought about by the Affordable Care Act as well as other initiatives undertaken by the federal government, some states, and foundations. This will require significant leadership and support from the gay community at large and most important its leading institutions. There will certainly be legal battles ahead as well and tough choices to make in regard to costs and coverage. In times when money is tight, the LGBT community will need to work closely and develop strong relationships with state and federal health departments, private insurance companies, and government officials. Also, more time and energy will need to be devoted to areas of the country that have outstanding relationships with their LGBT communities, since they are going to have to develop the benchmarks that will drive improvement in other areas of the country. At least in health care we can minimize if not eliminate any perceived "great divide."

References

American Lung Association. 2010. "Smoking Out a Deadly Threat: Tobacco Use in the LGBT Community." Accessed September 3, 2012, http://www.lungusa.org/about-us/our-impact/top-stories/smoking-out.html.

Asencio, Marysol, Thomas Blank, Lara Descartes, and Ashley Crawford. 2009. "The Prospect of Prostate Cancer: A Challenge for Gay Men's Sexualities as They Age." *Sexuality Research & Social Policy, 6*(4):38–51.

Berg, Michael B., Matthew J. Mimiaga, and Steven A. Safren. 2008. "Mental Health Concerns of Gay and Bisexual Men Seeking Mental Health Services." *Journal of Homosexuality* 54(3):293–306.

Blackwell, Christopher W. 2012. "Addressing Alcohol Abuse in Gay Men." *American Journal of Lifestyle Medicine*, 6(1): 90–91. doi:10.1177./1559827611402595.

CDC Fact Sheet. 2010. "HIV AIDS among Gay and Bisexual Men." Centers for Disease Control, June. http://www.cdc.gov/nchhstp/newsroom/docs/FastFacts-MSM-FINAL508COMP.pdf.

Diamant, Allison L., Cheryl Wold, Karen Spritzer, and Lillian Gelberg. 2000. "Health Behaviors, Health Status, and Access to and Use of Health Care: A Population-Based Study of Lesbian, Bisexual and Heterosexual Women." *Archives of Family Medicine, 9*(10):1043–1051.

Dibble, Suzanne L., Stephanie A. Roberts, and Brenda Nussey. 2004. "Comparing Breast Cancer Risk between Lesbians and Their Heterosexual Sisters." *Women's Health Issues, 14*(2):60–68.

Dobinson, Cheryl. 2007. "Top Ten Bisexual Health Issues." In *Bisexual Health: An Introduction and Model Practices for HIV/STI Prevention Programming,* by Marshall Miller, Amy André, Julie Ebin, and L. Bessonova. New York: National Gay and Lesbian Task Force Policy Institute, the Fenway Institute at Fenway Community Health, and BiNet USA.

Heslin, K. C., J. L. Gore, W. D. King, and S. Fox. 2008. "Sexual Orientation and Testing for Prostate and Colorectal Cancers among Men in California." *Medical Care, 46*(12):1240–1248.

Houston, Eric, and David J. McKirnan. 2007. "Intimate Partner Abuse among Gay and Bisexual Men: Risk Correlates and Health Outcomes." *Journal of Urban Health, 84*(5):681–690. http://www.ncbi.nlm.nih.gov/pubmed/17610158.

Human Rights Campaign (HRC). 2013. "Resources: Health & Aging." Accessed January 7, 2013, www.hrc.org/resources/category/health-and-aging.

Kenagy, Gretchen P. 2005. "The Health and Social Service Needs of Transgender People in Philadelphia." *International Journal of Transgenderism, 8*(2/3):49–56. http://www.iom.edu/~/media/Files/Report%20Files/2011/The-Health-of-Lesbian-Gay-Bisexual-and-Transgender-People/LGBT%20Health%202011%20Report%20Brief.pdf.

Koh, A. S., and L. K. Ross. 2006. "Mental Health Issues: A Comparison of Lesbian, Bisexual and Heterosexual Women." *Journal of Homosexuality, 51*(1):33–57. http://www.ncbi.nlm.nih.gov/pubmed/16893825.

Lockhart, Lettie L., Barbara W. White, Vicki Causby, and Alicia Isaac. 1994. "Letting out the Secret: Violence in Lesbian Relationships." *Journal of Interpersonal Violence, 9*(4):469–492.

Movement Advancement Project (MAP). "Equality Maps." 2012. Accessed December 10, 2012, http://www.lgbtmap.org.

RFR. 2012. "Request for Response for Massachusetts Health Insurance Exchange and Integrated Eligibility System." Independent Verification and Validation Services, University of Massachusetts Medical School. (CW12-JD-0038-0001 RFR).

Risser, Jan MH, Andrea Shelton, Sheryl McCurdy, John Atkinson, Paige Padgett, Bernardo Useche, Brenda Thomas, and Mark Williams. 2005. "Sex, Drugs, Violence, and HIV Status among Male-to-Female Transgender Persons in Houston, Texas." *International Journal of Transgenderism, 8*(2/3):67–74.

The Advisory Board Company. 2013. "Where the States Stand on Medicaid Expansion." Accessed December 12, 2013, http://www.advisory.com/Daily-Briefing/Resources/Primers/MedicaidMap.

Tooru, Nemoto. 2001. "Critical Health Needs for MTF Transgenders of Color—Preliminary Findings." San Francisco, CA: University of California at San Francisco, Center for AIDS Prevention Studies. http://caps.ucsf.edu/uploads/projects/TRANS/pdf/TRANScriticalneeds.pdf.

Transgender Law Center. 2009. "The State of Transgender California Report—Results from the 2008 California Transgender Economic Health Survey." San Francisco, CA: Transgender Law Center. Accessed June 15, 2012, http://www.transgenderlawcenter.org/pdf/StateTransCA_report_2009Print.pdf.

U.S. Office on Women's Health. 2005. "Lesbian Health: Frequently Asked Questions." Accessed January 1, 2005. http://womenshealth.gov/faq/lesbian-health.cfm.

VanKim, Nicole A., and James L. Padilla. 2010. "New Mexico's Progress in Collecting Lesbian, Gay, Bisexual, and Transgender Health Data and Its Implications for Addressing Health Disparities." Albuquerque, NM: New Mexico Department of Health.

Swan, Wallace, ed. 2004. *Handbook of Gay, Lesbian, Bisexual, and Transgender Administration and Policy*. New York: Marcel Dekker.

Yang, Jean, John Flint, and Daniel Apicella. 2012. "Commonwealth Care FY2013 Procurement." Massachusetts Health Connector, Board of Directors meeting, February 9. http://archives.lib.state.ma.us/bitstream/handle/2452/119156/ocn793126391.pdf?sequence = 1.

Chapter 15

Lesbian, Gay, Bisexual, and Transgender Aging in These Divided States

K. Abel Knochel and Jean K. Quam

Contents

A significant divide exists in this country between the young and the old and the divide is getting greater. Increasingly, concerns are expressed that a shrinking population of middle-aged and young adults will support a rapidly expanding population of old adults. Despite the fact that the retirement age is moving upward and many older people are working part time or full time, old adults are living longer and will require more social and health-related services. Over 2,000 adults in the United States were surveyed in a recent Gallup survey. Older adults are planning for retirement beyond age 65 because they are concerned that their savings will not support them; costs for housing, food, and health care are going up; and they may earn more if they wait longer to retire (Brandon 2010).

How does the "Great Divide" apply to a population of old lesbian, gay, bisexual, and/or transgender (LGB and T) adults? As with any cohort, there may be significant, within-group differences based on race/ethnicity, gender, age, geography, socioeconomic status, or religious affiliation. LGB and T older adults may also differ based on physical and mental health, age cohort ("Baby Boomer" or "oldest old"), and geography (rural, suburban, or urban locales with policies that either protect or discriminate against LGB and T people).

Even the term "LGBT," an acronym for lesbian, gay, bisexual, and transgender, is something of a divide. Gender identity and sexual orientation are separate identities. A person's gender identity is their sense of themselves as a man, a woman, or a gender that combines or is outside of these genders. A person's attraction toward certain types of people and their expression of that attraction indicate their sexual orientation. These two identities are often conflated in the mainstream in a way that subsumes transgender identity as a category within sexual orientation. Further, organizations that use the acronym LGBT in their name and mission statement may claim to represent all of these identities while primarily dedicating their resources and work to issues of sexual orientation. We use the term LGB and T to draw attention to the distinctions between these identities. For purposes of this paper, we consider "old" as over the age of 65 years, which is a generally accepted definition.

Many studies acknowledge that LGB and T old adults are a group that may not want to or is not yet able to be counted (Meezan and Martin 2011). For the oldest members of this group, early life experiences have led to fear and mistrust of "coming out" to anyone. A number of different models exist of stages of the coming out process (Hunter 2007). However, it is clear that self-identification as a gay, lesbian, bisexual and/or transgender person is unique at different stages of the life cycle. Coming out involves disclosure to self and others (e.g., family, friends, work colleagues, neighbors) and living actively in a nondominant gender identity, gender expression, or sexual orientation. One may have more emotional and psychological resources when the coming out process occurs later in life or one might be so entrenched in a heterosexual or cisgender identity of many years that coming out is far more difficult than it might have been when one was younger.

In addition, there is not yet an accurate census of LGB and T people. Thus, estimates of the size of this group have been just that—estimates. As such, these numbers for the LGB and T population vary widely. Because very few aging studies or general questionnaires ask about gender identity and/or sexual orientation, *Outing Age* surveyed leading LGBT researchers in 2009 and they "reviewed the limited existing data and literature to determine a demographic estimate of the LGBT community in the United States as ranging between five percent and 10% of the population at large ... or approximately nearly two million to as many as seven million LGBT elders in the United States" (Grant 2011, p. 26). This number is supported by Fredriksen-Goldsen et al. (2011), who used a narrative approach to review articles that studied LGB adults aged 50 and above and that were published between 1984 and 2008.

One "divide" that has been somewhat overlooked is sex and gender. Averett and Jenkins (2012) reviewed twenty-eight research articles about older lesbians published from 1997 until 2010. They concluded that articles focused on studies with gay men and studies with lesbians discussed these separate populations as "one and the same" (p. 539). In some studies with a predominance of gay males, the researchers assumed that findings that applied to gay males would also be valid for lesbians. Despite the fact that some of the earliest research focused on both old gay men and lesbians as a group with common concerns, studies have shown that concerns of old lesbians may be more similar to those of old women in general than issues of concern to old gay men (e.g., Quam and Whitford 1991). In addition, studies of older lesbians and gay men generally assume the participants are cisgender, neglecting to identify distinctions between sex (i.e., a person's biological makeup) and gender identity (i.e., the gender a person understands themselves to be, irrespective of their sex or the gender they were assigned at birth). *Cisgender* is a term used to classify people whose sex (e.g., male, female), gender identity (e.g., man, woman), and expression of their gender (e.g., masculine, feminine) are congruent, in contrast to the term *transgender*. Another term, *trans**, is sometimes used to include both people who self-identify as transgender and those who self-identify as transsexual. The terms *transgender* and *trans** will be used interchangeably in this paper.

Division by Age Cohort

Who are LGB and T old adults? As early as the 1950s, Bernice Neugarten recognized divisions within the population of old adults or those who are over the age of 65. She referred to the "young-old" and the "old-old" (Neugarten 1974). The younger group was healthier, more recently retired, with higher incomes and more likely to have larger social networks and to be engaged in many different activities (e.g., social, religious, recreational, educational, and physical). The old-old, who are sometimes defined by age (e.g., over 80 or 85 years of age), are more likely to be referred to today as the "frail elderly." These individuals have often experienced a significant change in their physical abilities, an increase in the number of chronic conditions (e.g., high blood pressure, diabetes, asthma, hearing or vision loss), and possibly a change in their living situation to a more structured setting with services available as needed. As individuals live longer, some writers have suggested that this oldest age group may have multiple age groupings within it and greater variation within groups. For example, a healthy 95-year-old female may live on her own and have financial independence, whereas a 68-year-old female may require full-time nursing care received through Medicaid support.

In addition to distinctions based on aging, the young-old (Baby Boomers) and old-old LGB and T adults are divided by the influences of the time in which they came into their LGB and T identity. Society in the 1950s was harsher toward gay and lesbian people, for example, and gay and lesbian people who emerged into 1950s society may continue to practice a way of being they learned at the time: living as who they are without calling the name of it, for example, and socializing in hidden networks. By contrast, the young-old who came out as gay or lesbian in the 1970s may have found a culture that acknowledged them and stories of the community actively embracing an out and collective identity. As older adults, they may call the name of who they are more publicly and socialize more publicly. These two different ways of surviving and being may clash as these different age cohorts mix in public as well as in long-term care and other senior living environments.

Division by Geography

Rural and Urban

The earliest accounts of LGB and T aging were stories or qualitative analyses of small groups of gay or lesbian adults or anecdotal stories of exceptional LGB or T individuals. Frequently, individuals who were studied were friends or acquaintances of the researcher. From the earliest accounts, a reader would assume that anyone who was gay or lesbian lived in New York, San Francisco, or another large urban area, but rarely anywhere else. The assumption was that if you were gay or lesbian, you wanted to live in a big city where you could be anonymous and yet feel safe and find friends among people who shared your sexual orientation.

Definitions of "rural" are complex ones. Rurality can be seen as a continuum with variations such as small towns, sparsely populated communities, and even suburban areas. According to the U.S. Census Bureau website (www.census.gov), rural areas are defined as fewer than 2,500 people in a given area. Older adults are about 12.8% of everyone who is living in rural areas, although there are great variations in even what individuals consider to be a rural area for their home. Older adults in rural areas are more likely to be homeowners, but their homes tend to be older and in more need of repair. Although rural areas generally lack sufficient formal services for individuals as they age, including an absence of public transportation, mobile meals, and a variety of social services, informal services such as neighbors, friends, and congregational support may be more available (Kaye and Butler 2003).

Quantitative studies that include geographic differences tend to have difficulty finding rural subjects. Rural studies underrepresent lesbian, gay, bisexual and trans* older adults (Lee and Quam 2013, 112). Using a national sample of LGB and T baby boomers (ages 45 through 64), Lee and Quam (2013) found that LGB and T adults living in rural communities are not likely to "come out" and they tend to find friends who will serve as supporters as they age. Some small groups of rural LGB and T adults have designed and provided their own services once they are identified to each other, consonant with the informal support for older adults that Kaye and Butler (2003) found to be prevalent in rural communities.

Next to Alaska, Wyoming is the least populated state in the country, with fewer than 5.1 people per square mile. Leedy and Connolly (2008) took a look at over 80 middle-aged LGB and T adults who lived in Wyoming. While very little is known historically about LGB and T adults in rural areas such as Wyoming, Leedy and Connolly concluded that "the characterization of rural life as being hostile to LGB persons has remained fairly constant over time" (p. 18). The beating death of Matthew Shepard, a young college student, brought attention to Wyoming, a state that LGB and T individuals identified as lacking services or even safe places to be "out." No gay bars or bookstores existed in individual communities in Wyoming, and many gay and lesbian adults created their own communities of friends as they aged.

Division by States' LGBT-Related Legal Rights

The federal government has instituted a few policies and laws that benefit all LGB and T older adults, including the right to designate hospital visitors and nursing home visitors (Centers for Medicare and Medicaid Services 2013; U.S. Department of Health and Human Services 2010). These rights were expanded in 2013 for couples of the same legal sex who are in a federally recognized marriage, regardless of state of residence. However, the quality of life and level of equality vary between states based on state laws, enforcement of policies, and education of frontline workers and others responsible for implementing these policies. Some states have enacted laws to protect LGB people and transgender people from discrimination, while many other states permit such discrimination. Some states recognize relationships outside of heterosexual marriages, while other states have enshrined rejection of such relationships into their constitutions and laws. These policies and their impact on older adults are considered next.

Housing and Public Accommodations Nondiscrimination Policy

The federal Fair Housing Act provides protection from housing discrimination based on gender identity, per a 2011 Housing and Urban Development (HUD) guideline that expanded the definition of gender nondiscrimination (Chin 2012). This provides recourse for trans* older adults. Other recent HUD guidelines provide more limited protection for LGB people, including protection from discrimination in Section 8 and other HUD rental and home ownership programs and a willingness to jointly investigate public housing discrimination (Chin 2012). These administrative policies provide some protections in the absence of a federal law prohibiting LGB and T discrimination in housing. LGB and T older adults have more recourse in states that have LGB and T-inclusive nondiscrimination policies.

The Federal Nursing Home Reform Act, passed in 1987, provides protection from discrimination and the right to "reasonable accommodation of individual needs and preferences" for residents of facilities that are funded through Medicare and Medicaid (Chin 2012). An LGB or T older adult can use the provisions of this act to address, for example, a nursing home's refusal to recognize a trans* person's preferred pronouns and name, its denial of visits by a gay resident's partner, or its isolation of a lesbian due to complaints from other residents. The level of reported discrimination and LGB and T elders' fear of discrimination in long-term care (NSCLC, NGLTF, SAGE, Lambda Legal, NCLR, and NCTE 2010) indicate that the language of this law, absent active monitoring and enforcement, is insufficient to protect older LGB and T adults from discrimination. Although the law exists to protect people across the nation, LGB and T older adults can be expected to fare better in states with nursing home licensing and certification agencies, long-term care ombudsmen, and adult protective services that are well-resourced and that have trained their workers to be sensitive and appropriate around issues of sexual orientation and gender identity.

Twenty-one states and the District of Columbia have passed laws to protect people from discrimination in housing and public accommodations based on sexual orientation (Movement Advancement Project [MAP] 2013). Seventeen of these states extend housing protection to people based on their gender identity or expression, and 16 states extend such protection in public accommodations (NGLTF 2014). These laws make it illegal to deny housing or otherwise discriminate against an LGB person or a trans* person in a nursing home, assisted-living facility, or senior housing based on their sexual orientation or their gender identity, thus bolstering and expanding the federal protections. These laws also protect LGB and T people from discrimination in senior centers or other public accommodations utilized by older adults. As a result, LGB and T adults face different levels of protection based on state of residence. A gay man who is transferred to the dementia ward due to discomfort of other residents with his sexual orientation is likely to have an easier time getting the situation remedied if he lives in New York, for example, than if he lives in Pennsylvania.

Employment Nondiscrimination

Title VII of the Civil Rights Act prohibits trans* discrimination per a 2012 Equal Employment Opportunity Commission (EEOC) ruling that sex discrimination includes bias due to gender identity and expression (EEOC 2013). This provides a basis for employment protection in the absence of a federal law prohibiting such discrimination, yet 90% of trans* people report employment harassment and discrimination (Grant et al. 2011) and a parallel EEOC ruling does not exist based on sexual orientation.

Seventeen states and the District of Columbia protect LGB and T people from discrimination in employment (MAP 2013). An additional 4 states provide such protection for sexual orientation, but not for gender identity or expression (MAP 2013). Most of these laws came into existence in the first decade of the 21st century (National Gay and Lesbian Task Force [NGLTF] 2013a). An older LGB or T person would have been a working-age adult for 35 or more years without protections in these states, and may have spent all of their working years without job protection.

Many older adults continue to work part time or full time based on economic necessity. This may be especially true for LGB and T older adults who have fewer savings due to the cumulative effects of employment discrimination (Grant et al. 2011; MAP, CAP, and HRC 2013). Nondiscrimination statutes may help older LGB and T workers find and maintain needed employment. Their employment status may be more precarious in states that do not provide such protection.

Employment nondiscrimination statutes and the EEOC ruling may be particularly important for trans* older adults, who often transition in midlife or later. Employment protection can help them retain employment while undergoing transition and once they have completed transition. Given the high rates of employment discrimination reported by trans* people (Grant et al. 2011) and the costs associated with transition, job protections are vital.

In states that lack employment protection based on gender identity and expression, trans* people may simply decide not to transition or may wait until they are retired or no longer able to work. However, the EEOC's 2012 ruling may impact this somewhat. In states that lack protection based on sexual orientation, older LGB adults may remain hidden (i.e., in the closet) while working in order to maintain their job. While remaining hidden may provide a level of income security, it exacts a mental and emotional cost.

People who have experienced employment discrimination over the life course, as is true for many LGB and T people, are more likely to enter old age with fewer savings and to have greater reliance on Social Security benefits. Social Security benefits, in turn, may be negatively impacted by past job discrimination (i.e., lower wages resulting in lower benefits or too few quarters of recorded work to qualify for full benefits). Social Security retirement and survivor benefits began to be extended to couples in legal same-sex marriages in

August 2013, although it is unclear whether these benefits will extend to such married couples in states that do not recognize their marriages (U.S. Social Security Administration 2013). Policies regarding relationship recognition are considered in the next section.

Relationship Recognition

The Defense of Marriage Act (DOMA), which declared marriage and the accompanying federal benefits as the domain of a man and a woman in a legally sanctioned marriage, was in place at the federal level from 1996 until June 2013. DOMA and the maintenance of more than 1,000 federal benefits exclusively for opposite-sex couples have negatively impacted older LGB and T adults in many ways, including the inability to access Social Security survivor benefits and the taxation of joint assets at the death of a partner. In addition, some states have extended the right of same-sex couples to maintain their dwelling and still qualify for Medicaid if one member of the couple needs a nursing home, while most states have thus far refused to extend this benefit (Pizer, Konnoth, Mallory, and Sears 2012).

Courts in some states have upheld the legality of marriages that include a transgender partner, while such marriages have been invalidated in other states. Many of these court cases have revolved around the right to inherit or the right to a deceased spouse's pension. The legality of marriages involving one or more trans* people remains in question even with the repeal of DOMA, injecting uncertainty into the lives of older trans* adults and their spouses, and potentially denying them access to Social Security and other needed financial benefits.

Between 2004 and June 2014, 18 states and the District of Columbia made marriage legal for same-sex couples, and same-sex marriages in utah were halted pending a legal appeal (NGLTF 2014). Three additional states have passed other forms of relationship recognition, including civil unions, reciprocal beneficiary agreements, and domestic partnerships (NGLTF 2014). Vermont and the District of Columbia offer both marriage and another form of relationship recognition (NGLTF 2014). Relationship recognition at the state level has provided access for same-sex couples to some or all of their state's marriage-related benefits. Such benefits include inheritance and pension rights.

There are 28 states with statutory prohibition against same-sex marriage, 10 constitutional amendments banning same-sex marriage, 7 statutes with broader prohibitions against same-sex marriage, and 19 constitutional amendments with broader prohibitions against same-sex marriage (NGLTF 2014).

The June 2013 Supreme Court ruling on DOMA adds another layer of difference in the treatment of LGB and T people based on state of residency. These differences may be particularly acute for older adults. The court ruling requires federal recognition of the marriage of a same-sex couple that has had its marriage sanctioned at the state level. At this writing, the executive branch of the U.S. government has declared that legally married same-sex couples have the same federal tax rights and responsibilities as other legally married couples regardless of state residence, but it is unclear whether Social Security benefits and other federal marriage-related rights and responsibilities will apply to legally married same-sex couples who live in states that do not recognize their marriages. The U.S. Congress has jurisdiction over making a change to extend benefits provided by Social Security and by Veterans Affairs to same-sex married couples regardless of state of residency, but thus far has not pursued these changes. Although the Obama administration is taking steps to extend such rights within its authority, these changes can be challenged and they can be reversed by subsequent administrations unless the U.S. Congress changes the laws.

Absent these changes, older adults in same-sex relationships who married in Washington, D.C. or in one of the states that sanction these marriages *and* who reside in those states will enjoy both federal and state marriage benefits, whereas those who were married in one of these states but reside in a state without such protections are denied these benefits. In addition, LGB and T older adults who have recognition of these relationships only through a civil union, reciprocal beneficiary agreement, or domestic partnership, and those with relationship configurations not recognized in any state, will continue to age without full legal protections for their families. Some of these legal protections, such as power of attorney and a living trust, can be obtained by drawing up documents through legal counsel, but this protection is piecemeal and comes with a significant cost.

States' Distinctions in Aging Services

The Older Americans Act (OAA), the major federal legislation providing funding and guidelines for services to older adults, does not include LGB and T people among populations designated as receiving priority due to having the "greatest social need." The individual Area Agencies on Aging (AAAs), Tribal Aging Units (TAUs), and State Units on Aging (SUAs), funded under the OAA, can define additional vulnerable populations for special programming and for protection, however. LGB and T older adults who live in the jurisdiction of a AAA, SUA, or tribal unit that has planned for them may enjoy home visits or meal delivery from an LGB or T volunteer, LGB and T-friendly congregate dining, and other services and programming (Knochel 2010). Few AAAs offer such services, however. Knochel, Croghan, Moone, and Quam found that, in 2010, only 8% of AAAs offered services targeted to LGB and T populations, while 12% offered targeted outreach (2012, 432).

Private housing has been developed and marketed to gay and lesbian older adults and, in some instances, LGB and T older adults. This provides a choice for LGB and T older adults, who often fear discrimination based on sexual orientation or gender identity (Knochel 2011; MetLife Mature Market Institute 2009).

However, the price of this housing places it out of the reach of most LGB and T older adults. Several affordable housing developments, including one each in Minneapolis, Minnesota, and Hollywood, California, and ones planned for Chicago, Philadelphia, and San Francisco, are targeted for LGB and T older adults. Together, these will provide several hundred affordable housing units, serving a small fraction of the population.

The need and demand for LGB and T-specific aging services, housing, and programming will exist until discrimination based on sexual orientation, gender identity, and gender expression ceases to be a part of the experience of aging and old LGB and T people. Limited resources preempt separate housing, services, and programming sufficient to meet the need and demand. Thus, there is a need to develop a range of mainstream aging services that offer welcoming, nondiscriminatory, and appropriate care to LGB and T older adults. State-level and national studies of agencies that serve older adults have found that the agencies say that they welcome LGB and transgender adults into their programs and that they would like to see more training for their staff (Hughes, Harold, and Boyer 2011; Knochel, Quam, and Croghan 2011; Knochel et al. 2012). Knochel et al. (2012) found that this willingness to receive training on LGB and T aging issues held true across all regions of the nation. However, agencies also reported that LGB and transgender clients are underrepresented at their agencies, that their agencies do not ask an individual's sexual orientation or gender identity, and that they are unclear why their agencies do not attract LGB and trans* clients (Hughes et al. 2011; Knochel et al. 2011, 2012). The silence of the individual staff members leads to poor if not inappropriate service and the likelihood that a client will not return for care if given a choice.

Promisingly, several studies have examined training in cultural competence, diversity, and prejudice reduction among providers of aging services and found evidence of their effectiveness (Knochel et al. 2011, 2012; Leyva, Breshears, and Ringstad 2013; National Resource Center on LGBT Aging, 2012). Training offered to providers of aging and LGB and T services across the nation positively impacted providers' understanding of LGB and T older adults' needs; their compassion toward LGB and T older adults; their knowledge of how to develop a welcoming, supportive atmosphere; and, in more intensive training, their ability to recognize bias in their organization, program, or service (National Resource Center on LGBT Aging, 2012). These results are mirrored in a study of providers of aging services in central California (Leyva, Breshears, and Ringstad 2013). Knochel et al. (2012), too, in their national survey of AAAs, found that those agencies that had provided LGB and T-related training for their staff were more likely to believe in addressing the issues faced by LGB and T older adults. In addition, Knochel et al. found that programs that had provided such training were more likely to be approached for services by someone who is LGB or transgender, and more likely to offer services targeted to LGB and T people (2012).

Division by Social Identity

Dynamics of privilege and oppression factor into LGB and trans communities. Other social identities, such as race, gender, and class, provide additional challenges that factor into the state in which LGB and trans* people enter and move through older age.

Race and Ethnicity

The pervasiveness of discrimination based on race and ethnicity is as true for LGB and trans* communities as for the population at large. The vast majority of research that has been completed has included few non-white LGB and T adults and has not examined differences based on race. The accumulated effects of discrimination over one's lifetime contribute to high levels of stress and reduced incomes. Significant health and economic disparities exist between non-white LGB and T adults and their white counterparts as well as between specific racial and ethnic groups within the LGB and T population. In one of the larger national studies of LGB and trans* aging and older adults, which paid particular attention to race, Fredriksen-Goldsen et al. (2011) found that Latino participants had fewer social supports; Latino and Native Americans reported more depression and more stress; Latino and Black older adults were more likely to be neglected; and Native Americans were more likely to describe themselves as lonely. However, it was not clear how extensively the significant health and economic disparities contributed to these conclusions.

Gender

As stated earlier, it is important to note that early gerontological research assumed that an understanding of how males aged could easily be applied to female aging. Thus it was not difficult to see the logic in assuming that early research on gay male aging also applied to aging lesbians. As research has advanced, critical empirical differences have emerged within gender groups. For aging gay men, for example, one of the more surprising findings in the MetLife Mature Market Institute 2010 study was that gay men were equally as likely to be functioning as a caregiver, usually for a parent or a partner, as older women. Caregiver fatigue and stress is a significant risk factor for poor physical health as one ages. This is an important finding to fully understand the roles and responsibilities of aging in gay men.

Although gay men and lesbians both are less likely to seek health care than heterosexuals, lesbians with childbearing histories of fewer or no pregnancies and breastfeeding are at a higher risk for breast or ovarian cancer than women in the general population. For lesbians at all ages, there is a tendency to be less likely to use cancer screenings or mammograms. Information about lesbians at older ages is not available, but given reduced incomes into old age, there is no reason to believe that there is a positive change in this behavior (Kerker, Mostashari, and Thorpe 2006;

Zaritsky and Dibble 2010). This too becomes an important finding to understand the health care needs of aging lesbians.

Religion and Spirituality

Affiliation with an organized religion, past experiences with religion and religious figures, and spirituality all may be additional dividing issues in the LGB and T community. For many old adults, being gay, lesbian, bisexual, and/or trans* was seen as sinful or wrong in addition to being unlawful. Stories abound of adolescents and young adults who were told that they would "go to hell" or be "eternally damned" for thinking about, much less engaging in, same-sex attraction or questioning their gender identity.

In surveys, adults are frequently asked to identify their affiliation with a religion or a religious preference. However, that information does not provide us with an understanding of what role religion or spirituality plays in one's life. For every example of someone being rejected by a church or synagogue, there is another example of support that is provided for the full expression of one's identity. Certainly, no area has been more controversial or experienced more change than the role of religion in the lives of LGB and T adults.

Division by Health

Mental Health

Over half of all older adults will have experienced at least one mental health disorder or substance abuse or misuse by age 75 (Kessler et al. 2005). As many as one-third of older adults who misuse alcohol will also experience a primary mood disorder. Depression, which is common as one ages, results from significant and frequent losses. It is not uncommon for adults to experience situational depression as they age due to the deaths of friends and family, a move to a new location, and the loss of employment to name a few examples. However, chronic depression frequently leads to drug and alcohol abuse.

Physical Health

LGB and T adults consistently rate their health more poorly at all ages than do heterosexual and cisgender people. This may be due to a lifetime of stigma and its consequences that build over time. The first national project that was funded by the National Institutes of Health and the National Institute on Aging surveyed over 2,500 LGB and T adults ages 50 to 95. This study, called "Caring and Aging with Pride," found that almost half (47%) of the subjects reported a disability defined by a limitation in any activity due to physical, mental, or emotional problems, or use of special equipment (Fredriksen-Goldsen et al. 2011, 22). A positive sign was that almost all of the respondents were involved in some type of wellness activity, such as exercise, running, or aerobics (Fredriksen-Goldsen et al. 2011).

In the 2006 MetLife study, LGB individuals (1,000 adults ages 40 to 61) anticipated long and healthy lives. Sixty percent expected to live to age 80 or older and 20% anticipated survival to age 90 or longer (MetLife Mature Market Institute 2006, 15). Those who were in a relationship were more likely than those without a partner to say that they expected to live longer. These findings are consistent with other research that finds that heterosexual adults with spouses have better mental and physical health and expect to live longer. What was concerning in this report was the finding that many LGB adults have not prepared advanced care directives or talked with friends or relatives about their wishes concerning how they prefer to be cared for when they are dying. They expect to receive end-of-life care in their own homes. To try to ensure this, they are more likely to have completed living wills, health care proxies, rights of visitation, or partnership agreements than their heterosexual counterparts.

In a similar MetLife study three years later, over 1,200 LGB and T 45 to 64 year olds were sampled. The study revealed that concerns as one ages were similar in populations LGB, heterosexual, transgender, and cisgender (MetLife Mature Market Institute 2009). Issues such as becoming unable to care for one's self, becoming dependent on others, becoming sick or disabled, becoming confused or demented, and outliving one's income were common responses for both groups.

A large, national study asked open-ended questions of old adults about whether being LGB and T had helped to prepare them for aging or had made preparation for aging more difficult (MetLife Mature Market Institute 2009). For those who saw being LGB or T as a handicap or a disadvantage, there were concerns about the difficulty of finding a new relationship as one aged, fear of discrimination, feeling vulnerable with health care providers, and being socially isolated. However, many subjects also saw the benefits of being gay, lesbian, bisexual, or trans* as they aged. These benefits included being more accepting of others, being more resilient to change and challenges, being more cautious in financial matters, and having chosen family and friends who can support them. For the most part, the fears and concerns about aging are not much different for any person who is growing older, with the exception of the fear of discrimination. Thus, one's fear of vulnerability with health care providers may be universal, but there is an additional layer of fear for the LGB or T adult that the health care provider may be homophobic or transphobic. Fears are exacerbated if one has not been "out" or felt safe with one's identity.

Conclusion

Years of fear of (or actual) discrimination as an LGB and T individual can take a toll financially, mentally, and physically. It is extremely difficult for an older person to trust that the world is changing around them in a positive way—that there is more acceptance of differences and less overt discrimination. One of the most historic decisions regarding the rights of LGB and trans* older adults was the U.S. Supreme Court's decision in 2013 to strike down the discriminatory Defense of Marriage Act (DOMA). Federal rules and regulations in such areas as Social Security, military benefits, housing, income support, and taxes are affected by one's legal marital status. Although there are an increasing number of states that are permitting same-sex marriages, less than half of states have done so. One of the biggest legal divides between same-sex couples and heterosexual couples is in the process of disappearing, although the fate of married couples that include a trans* individual remains unclear. The effects of these legal changes have yet to be fully realized and studied.

The population of old lesbian, gay, bisexual, and trans* adults who are aging is a diverse group with many "divides" within it. As we learn more about the uniqueness of the many different segments of this population, we can advocate for creation and enforcement of better laws and policies, and provide improved services to facilitate the process of aging well for LGB and T older adults.

References

Averett, P., and C. Jenkins. 2012. "Review of the Literature on Older Lesbians: Implications for Education, Practice and Research." *Journal of Applied Gerontology 31*, 537–561.

Brandon, E. 2010. "The 10 Biggest Sources of Retirement Income-US News and World Report." *Business News and Financial News-US News Business.*

Centers for Medicare and Medicaid Services (CMS). 2013. "Reminder: Access and Visitation Rights in Long Term Care Facilities." Accessed June, 2013, http://www.cms.gov/Medicare/Provider-Enrollment-and-Certification/SurveyCertificationGenInfo/Downloads/Survey-and-Cert-Letter-13-42.pdf.

Chin, N. 2012. "Fair Housing Federal Law: A Fact Sheet for LGBT Older Adults, 2012." Accessed June 2013, http://www.lgbtagingcenter.org/resources/resource.cfm?r=400.

Chokshi, N. 2013. "Utah Plans to Take Its Gay-marriage Fight to Supreme Court … Soon." *Washington Post,* December 27. Accessed December, 2013, http://www.washingtonpost.com/blogs/govbeat/wp/2013/12/27/utah-plans-to-take-its-gay-marriage-fight-to-the-supreme-court-soon/.

Equal Employment Opportunity Commission (EEOC). 2013. "Sex-based Discrimination." Accessed June, 2013, http://www.eeoc.gov/laws/types/sex.cfm.

Fredriksen-Goldsen, K. I., H. Kim, C. A. Emlet, A. Muraco, E. A. Erosheva, C. P. Hoy-Elis, J. Goldsen, and H. Petry. 2011. "The Aging and Health Report: Disparities and Resilience among Lesbian, Gay, Bisexual, and Transgender Older Adults." Institute for Multigenerational Health.

Grant, J. M. 2011. *Outing Age 2010: Public Policy Issues Affecting Lesbian, Gay, Bisexual and Transgender Elders.* New York: National Gay and Lesbian Task Force Policy Institute.

Grant, J. M., L. A. Mottet, J. Tanis, J. Harrison, J. L. Herman, and M. Keisling. 2011. "Injustice at Every Turn: A Report of the National Transgender Discrimination Survey." Washington, D.C.: National Center for Transgender Equality and National Gay and Lesbian Task Force.

Hughes, A. K., R. D. Harold, and J. M. Boyer. 2010. "Awareness of LGBT Aging Issues Among Aging Services Network Providers." *Journal of Gerontological Social Work, 54*(7), 659–677.

Hunter, S. 2007. *Coming Out and Disclosures: LGBT Persons Across the Life Span*. New York: Haworth Press.

Kaye, L. W., and S. Butler. 2003. *Gerontological Social Work in Small Towns and Rural Communities*. New York: Haworth Press.

Kerker, B., F. Mostashari, and L. Thorpe. 2006. "Health Care Access and Utilization Among Women Who Have Sex with Women: Sexual Behavior and Identity." *Journal of Urban Health, 835*, 970–979.

Kessler, R. C., P. Berglund, O. Demler, R. Jin, K. R. Merikangas, and E. E. Walters. 2005. "Lifetime Prevalence and Age of Onset Distributions of DSM-IV Disorders in the National Comorbidity Survey Replication." *Archives of General Psychiatry, 62*, 593–602.

Knochel, K. A. 2010. "How To Advocate For AAA Involvement in LGBT Communities." *Aging Today Online, 1*(4).

Knochel, K. A. 2011. "Are They Prepared? A Look at Midlife Transgender People and Their Anticipated Adaptation to Aging." Ph.D. dissertation, University of Minnesota, ProQuest 3466964.

Knochel, K. A., C. F. Croghan, R. P. Moone, and J. K. Quam. 2012. "Training, Geography and Provision of Aging Services to Lesbian, Gay, Bisexual, and Transgender Older Adults." *Journal of Gerontological Social Work, 55*, 426–443.

Knochel, K. A., J. K. Quam, and C. Croghan. 2011. "Are Old Lesbians and Gay People Well Served? Understanding the Perceptions, Preparation and Experience of Aging Service Providers." *Journal of Applied Gerontology, 30*, 370–389.

Lee, M. G., and J. K. Quam. 2013. "Comparing Supports for LGBT Aging in Rural Versus Urban Areas." *Journal of Gerontological Social Work, 56*, 112–126.

Leedy, G., and C. Connolly. 2008. "Out in the Cowboy State: A Look at Lesbian and Gay Lives in Wyoming." *Journal of Lesbian and Gay Social Services, 19*, 17–34.

Leyva, V. L., E. M. Breshears, and R. Ringstad. 2013. "Training for Aging Services Providers in California's Central Valley." *Journal of Gerontological Social Work*. Published online. Accessed December, 2013, http://www.tandfonline.com/action/showAxaArticles?journalCode = wger20#.Ur8jkrTAGbg.

Meezan, W., and J. I. Martin. 2011. *Research Methods with Gay Lesbian Bisexual and Transgender Populations*. New York: Haworth Press.

MetLife Mature Market Institute. 2006. *Out and Aging: The Midlife Study of Lesbian and Gay Baby Boomers*. Westport, CT: MetLife Mature Market Institute.

MetLife Mature Market Institute. 2009. *Still Out, Still Aging*. Westport, CT: MetLife Mature Market Institute.

Movement Advancement Project (MAP). 2013. "Non-Discrimination Laws." Accessed December 2013, http://www.lgbtmap.org/equality-maps/non_discrimination_laws.

Movement Advancement Project and Services and Advocacy for GLBT Elders. 2010. *Improving the Lives of LGBT Older Adults*. Denver and New York: MAP and Sage.

Movement Advancement Project (MAP), Center for American Progress (CAP), and Human Rights Campaign (HRC). 2013. "A Broken Bargain: Discrimination, Fewer Benefits, and More Taxes for LGBT Workers." Accessed December 2013, http://www.lgbtmap.org/file/a-broken-bargain-full-report.pdf.

National Gay and Lesbian Task Force (NGLTF). 2014. "Relationship Recognition for Same-Sex Couples in the U.S." Accessed May 2014, http://www.thetaskforce.org/downloads/reports/issue_maps/rel_recog_5_20_14_color.pdf.

National Gay and Lesbian Task Force (NGLTF). 2013b. "Relationship Recognition for Same-Sex Couples in the U.S." Accessed December 2013, http://www.thetaskforce.org/downloads/reports/issue_maps/rel_recog_12_20_13_color.pdf.

National Gay and Lesbian Task Force (NGLTF). 2013c. "State Laws Prohibiting Recognition of Same-Sex Relationships." Accessed December 2013, http://www.thetaskforce.org/downloads/reports/issue_maps/samesex_relationships_5_15_13.pdf.

National Resource Center on LGBT Aging. 2013. "Cultural Competency Training Results: July 2011–July 2012." Accessed December, 2013, http://www.lgbtagingcenter.org/resources/resource.cfm?r = 532.

National Senior Citizens Law Center (NSCLC), National Gay and Lesbian Task Force (NGLTF), Services and Advocacy for GLBT Elders (SAGE), Lambda Legal, National Center for Lesbian Rights (NCLR), and National Center for Transgender Equality (NCTE). 2011. "LGBT Older Adults in Long Term Care Facilities." Accessed December 2013, http://www.nsclc.org/wp-content/uploads/2011/07/LGBT-Stories-from-the-Field.pdf.

Neugarten, Bernice. 1974. "Age Groups in American Society and the Rise of the Young-Old." *The Annals of the American Academy of Political and Social Science*, 4, 187–198.

Pizer, J. C., C. J. Konnoth, C. Mallory, C., and B. Sears. 2013. "Extending Long-Term Care Impoverishment Protections to Same Sex Couples." Williams Institute. Accessed December 2013, http://williamsinstitute.law.ucla.edu/wp-content/uploads/Medicaid-Overview.pdf.

Quam, J. K., and G. S. Whitford. 1991. "Adaptation and Age-Related Expectations of Older Gay and Lesbian Adults." *The Gerontologist, 32*, 367–374.

U.S. Department of Health and Human Services. 2010. "Medicare Finalizes New Rules to Require Equal Visitation Rights for All Hospital Patients." Accessed December 2013, http://www.hhs.gov/news/press/2010pres/11/20101117a.html.

U.S. Social Security Administration. 2013. "Benefit Eligibility for Couples in States that Prohibit or Do Not Recognize Same-Sex Marriages or Other Legal Same-Sex Relationships." Accessed September 2013, http://ssa-custhelp.ssa.gov/app/answers/detail/a_id/2503.

West, C., and D. H. Zimmerman. 1987. "Doing Gender." *Gender & Society, 1*, 125–151.

Zaritsky, E., and S. E. Dibble. 2010. "Risk Factors for Reproductive and Breast Cancers among Older Lesbians." *Journal of Women's Health, 19*, 125–131.

Chapter 16

Lesbian, Gay, Bisexual, and Transgender Youth (and Adult) Homelessness

Stephanie Kimble

Contents

Defining a Lesbian, Gay, Bisexual, and Transgender (LGBT) Youth Homeless Population in the United States

Homelessness in the United States is a phenomenon that concerns not only those considered homeless but the general population as well. The number of individuals who are homeless rises as at-risk persons are faced without the resources to maintain stable and permanent housing. The U.S. Department of Health and Human Services (HHS) notes that "some 2–3 million individuals, experience a night of homelessness that puts them in contact with a homeless assistance provider, and at least 800,000 people are homeless in the United States on any given night" (Leavitt 2007, 1). Throughout the literature the word "estimate(s)" qualifies the number of homeless individuals accounted for within a given study. There are several possible reasons for such large discrepancies within the total number reported. In addition to recognizing that not all individuals are willing participants or may lie to their surveyors regarding to what degree they suffer from homelessness, another reason for the discrepancies is that of the accessibility of outreach to "qualified" homeless individuals. The degree to which homeless individuals qualify for survey participation varies largely by study. Therefore there is a need to first define the word "homeless" as it relates to this chapter.

Studies have tended toward a narrower focus to include only those individuals considered traditionally homeless defined as follows: "people who have spent at least some time in homeless shelters or living on the streets or in other unconventional settings" (Haber and Toro 2004, 124). This definition, while a necessary piece to consider, is arguably not the only representation of this vulnerable population to be counted. More specifically, as this chapter intends to report on issues faced by the sexual minority (i.e., gay, lesbian, bisexual, transgender, and questioning [LGBTQ], homeless youth population), a broader definition must be adopted. Haber and Toro pose several questions when defining the term homeless in order to create an understanding of both the reasons for the lack of broad definitions across studies as well as to explain the reason these additional subgroups should not be overlooked.

For instance, Ray (2006, 1) reports that the HHS "estimates that the number of homeless and runaway youth ranges from 575,000 to 1.6 million per year." Further according to the HHS 2007 strategic plan, "homeless youth are defined as persons between the ages of 16–24" (Leavitt 2007, 1), classified as unaccompanied because they live in shelters or on the street. Unfortunately "unaccompanied" can mean so much more. As Haber and Toro (2004) indicate, these individuals may also be youth who are no longer welcomed or perceived to be welcomed in their primary caregivers' or guardians' home, if one exists, and therefore may be "doubled up with family or friends" (p. 124).

According the Minnesota-based Amherst Wilder Foundation's website, during fall 2009, "Wilder's statewide study counted 9,654 homeless adults, youth and children—a 25 percent increase" (Wilder Research 2009, 1), from the number counted in the previous survey. The study, which is conducted triennially, surveys individuals living in nontraditional housing, such as in emergency shelters, transitional housing, and "in a place not meant for human habitation" (National Alliance to End Homelessness), that is, street homeless. While this "one-night" (Wilder Research 2009, 2) count of Minnesota homeless individuals is high, this number is likely only a fraction of the true number of homeless persons within the state. This is demonstrated through Wilder's estimate that beyond this total number there are many homeless people who perhaps go uncounted, even in its own study. In its 2009 report of homelessness in Minnesota, the Amherst Wilder Foundation indicated that in addition to the number of homeless individuals, families, and unaccompanied youth counted on October 22, 2009, an estimated several thousand "youth were 'doubling up'" (p. 3).

The HHS definition as noted earlier does not necessarily account for those youth living with other family members. Therefore researchers have not tended to include these individuals since they are difficult to identify. It may be somewhat easier to consider those individuals living in transitional housing or who have had dealings with the juvenile justice system as these youth are likely already being accounted for. However this number is often only partially representative as "many homeless youths avoid contact with shelters, medical services, and the police, service providers who might otherwise estimate their numbers" (Ringwalt, Greene, Robertson, and McPheeters 1998, 1325). These youth may favor a status of doubling up and in extreme cases in which a known friend or family is unable to help house the youth, may even resort to riskier "survival strategies" (Hein 2011, 274) such as staying with strangers in return for providing a sexual service.

Additionally, although the HHS definition does take into account those individuals over age 18 who are unaccompanied and still in a vulnerable state, it also considers a minimum age of only 16 years old. As reported, the vast majority of adolescents who are homeless and on their own appear to be aged 13 or older (Haber and Toro 2007). Although "young adults ages 18 to 24 years old are especially vulnerable to homelessness in the United States: Estimates of those experiencing an episode of homelessness each year have ranged from 750,000 to 2 million" (Zerger, Strehlow, and Gundlapalli 2008, 824), there is still a need to report on the services available to and the experiences of unaccompanied youth in the three years before the age of 16 years.

One reason for this, with regard to sexual minority youth, is that, as cited by Robinson and Espelage (2011), same-sex attraction was often made aware within a youth early in life: "by age 10 or 11 years, whereas the mean age of non-heterosexual self-labeling ranges between 14 and 16 years … for 24 self-identified transgender individuals, the mean age of awareness was 10.4 years (ranging from ages 6–15)" (p. 316). When the transgender people labeled themselves, the mean age was 14.3 (Robinson and Espelage 2011, 316).

The report, as it studies middle-school- and high-school-aged students, therefore suggests that sexual minorities as young as 13 should certainly be considered in terms of need for services. Unfortunately, as Ray (2006) found, although in large urban areas such as New York City there are medical service providers whose treatment such as "the Callen-Lorde Community Health Center offers comprehensive health-care to trans-identifying clients regardless of their health insurance status" (Ray 2006, 63), transsexual individuals not yet having reached age 18 are exempt from service as a liability against the center is a major concern. These and other sexual minority youths face serious concerns with regard to mental health issues, according to Mustanski, Garofalo, and Emerson (2010) in an analysis that uses the "*Diagnostic and Statistical Manual of Mental Disorders, Fourth Edition (DSM-IV)* ... Overall, one third of participants met diagnostic criteria for at least 1 diagnosis" (p. 2427–2429), which include posttraumatic stress disorder, major depression, conduct disorder, suicidal ideation, suicide plan, and suicide attempt (in table 3 of the study).

Robinson and Espelage (2011) found that most sexual minority youth do not face heightened risk of reported suicidal ideation: They also found that these youth are in fact able to grow into healthy young adults: There does still exist a correlation between the increased risk when comparing sexual minority youth to heterosexual youths, in both suicidal thoughts and, more concerning, actions (Robinson and Espelage 2011). Other research concludes that LGBTQ youth may be at an increased risk for suicide, but that the heightened risk may not be initiated based on sexual orientation but rather sexual orientation coupled with other risk factors (Savin-Williams, and Ream 2003).

Homelessness is a risk factor for increased depression and suicide and other destructive behaviors, leading to a seemingly reasonable conclusion that behaviors such as substance abuse and risky sexual encounters might occur in the LGBTQ youth population. Thus, this chapter accepts the broadest definition of LGBTQ youth homelessness available. It notes that youth as young as 10 may be in danger of increased stress related to their status as LGBTQ-identified and that typically the earliest age of reported unaccompanied homeless youth is 13 years of age; and that the most commonly accepted age limit for the term youth is 24 years of age. In addition, the chapter recognizes that LGBTQ homeless youth may include those youth traditionally considered homeless as well as to those staying with friends or family and those using survival strategies and staying with strangers, that is, any youth living in a place other than with a primary caregiver or guardian. Unfortunately only some research supports this definition and studies need to continue to more accurately represent the age and status within these homeless demographics.

What the Numbers Show

There continue to be large discrepancies in the number of reported homeless LGBTQ-identifying youth. Ray (2006, 1) indicates that LGBT homeless youth are somewhere between 20% and 40% of the homeless youth population. Ryan, Huebner, Diaz, and Sanchez (2009, 350) suggest that "LGB youth are overrepresented in foster care, juvenile detention, and among homeless youth." Additionally some researchers have found significantly smaller numbers being reported. The LGBTQ homeless youth count varies so greatly in part due the locations at which youth are counted.

For instance, studies of youth homelessness tend to focus upon individuals living in large urban areas such as Los Angeles, San Francisco, and New York. Haber and Toro (2004) acknowledge that rural community homelessness is a phenomenon that is largely underreviewed among academics noting that the low number of studies "that have documented recruitment of rural adolescents who are on their own have tended to recruit them in fairly small numbers" (p. 129). Questions remain whether larger studies reporting an overrepresentation of LGBTQ homeless youth are entirely representative or if a broader search in smaller more rural areas would lead to a more accurate count. However, this chapter will proceed using the 20% to 40% figures as noted earlier, as they are the most widely accepted numbers available to date.

Regardless of any possible disconnect within the findings as they relate to the total number of LGBTQ homeless youth, there exists real concern that there are any youth who find themselves without access to suitable housing. LGBTQ youth like heterosexual youth identify a myriad of reasons for their personal homeless outcome. But, the National Gay and Lesbian Task Force, while recognizing that as individuals each circumstance behind homelessness is different, the underlying commonality is that conflicts within the home is the primary cause. Ray (2006) goes on to report that a Canadian (specifically Alberta) study noted that survey-takers identified that direct parental conflicts are not the only contributing factor to their status of living away from their primary residence. Some of these other factors include: loss of a stable environment due to divorce, a youth's view that the primary caregiver does not provide nurturing, physical violence between any parties in the house, caregiver substance abuse, and caregiver dealings with the criminal justice system (Ray 2006).

In her study, Ferguson (2009) also cited home instability as playing a significant role in youth homelessness. The study said that "youth experienced a great deal of instability, insecurity, and uncertainty in their home environment" (p. 1881) and then further discussed youth abandonment, substance abuse, and abuse between caregivers and other family members. Any number of these factors may influence the circumstances that lead to youth becoming homeless, as defined by Ray (2006, 15), including those characterized as runaways, throwaways, street youth, and systems youth.

Factors leading to youth homelessness are broadly studied. Unfortunately, however, the literature as it relates specifically to homeless LGBTQ youth spends far more time discussing the issues LGBTQ youth face once they have become homeless. While so much more needs to be researched with regard to the discussion of how LGBTQ youth find themselves homeless, those studies that do provide reasons for LGBTQ youth homelessness seem to focus significantly on what can be presumed as only half of the story.

In addition to the reasons previously stated for homelessness among the youth population, Kempf-Leonard and Johansson (2007) reported that one reason for leaving or being thrown from the home was due to the youth "being forsaken because their families can no longer support them" (p. 310). This statement seems to view the lack of support as a financial burden on the family. And while severe poverty is widely known as directly resulting in homelessness, the research, possibly in order to strongly portray the devastating accounts of LGBTQ disapproval, more frequently reveals that disapproval is the contributing factor of sexual minority youth homelessness.

One example of this is the study that Ray (2006, 2) references, noting that when gay males told their parents they were gay, 50% of them received a negative response and 26% of them were told to leave the home. Reasons such as family breakdown, family substance abuse, or family incarceration are also strong predictors of a youth's potential to become homeless, but we are excluding them from our analysis. Therefore, as the research seems to focus more directly on the population that is unwelcomed at home for reasons of parental discontent with the youth's LGBTQ status, so too will this literature review.

Factors Resulting in LGBTQ Youth Homelessness

Involvement in parental child abuse is widely considered one of the most inhumane environments to raise a child. Those parents that ultimately turn out to be an abuser may even have, at one time or another, found it an inconceivable thought to raise a hand or disparaging word to their child. Unfortunately even though "the intimate life of the Western developed world is going through a process of transformation and transition that is creating the possibility for sexual/gender diversity to flourish" (McDermott, Roen, and Scourfield 2008, 816), all too often LGBTQ children find themselves as victims of physical, emotional, or sexual abuse as related to their sexual minority status (Friedman et al. 2011; McDermott et al. 2008; Ray 2006; Roberts, Rosario, Corliss, Koenen, and Austin 2012).

Abuse is one of the most common reasons reported as leaving home without parental consent. Whitbeck, Hoyt, and Bao (2000) state in their findings of the relationship between depressive symptoms, runaway youth, and abuse within the home that "[b]y the time young people are pushed out, drift out, or actively make the decision to leave home, they are likely already to have been physically or sexually abused" (p. 723). According to the Amherst Wilder Foundation's 2003 study of homelessness approximately half of respondents had been physically harmed or taken advantage of in a sexual manner and even more individuals found themselves victims of full sexual abuse (Wilder Research 2009).

It is important to note that the figures reported by the Amherst Wilder Foundation reflect instances of abuse without consideration of sexual orientation status. However, it is also important to remember that "families can be influenced by the stigmatizing attitudes in their social and cultural environments, and when a son or daughter discloses a gay, lesbian, or bisexual orientation, some families respond with hostility and distress" (Saewyc et al. 2006, 197). This hostility and distress may in turn result in violence in homes where previously there was not a problem (until sexual orientation or gender nonconformity manifested itself).

Studies indicate that LGBTQ status may be the sole reason that abuse occurs within the family unit. In their research Friedman et al. (2011) state, "One risk factor for experiencing these types of abuse may be sexual orientation" (p. 1481). Research completed by House, Van Horn, Coppeans, and Stepleman (2011) supports this hypothesis citing a study comparing

> a large sample of GLB individuals with their heterosexual siblings and found that sexual minority status was associated with an increased risk of child physical abuse, child psychological abuse, child sexual abuse, psychological abuse by an intimate partner, physical assault by an intimate partner, and rape. (pp. 76–77)

Additionally studies have found that physical or sexual assault is, at times, a direct response to news that a child is LGBTQ-identified; this can be true of both a primary caregiver as the offense-committing adult (Ray 2006), or in the case of bisexual male and female youth, the perpetrator is a heterosexual peer (Saewyc et al. 2006). Finally, Roberts et al. (2012) state that "if parents are uncomfortable with homosexuality, nonconformity may lead to the child being targeted for abuse. Some parents also believe their own parenting can shape their child's gender nonconformity … thus, their parenting may become more physically or psychologically abusive" (p. 414). Roberts et al. 2012 determined that this additional abuse is meant to redirect the youth's gender nonconformity back toward acceptance of their birth gender.

Parental abuse as a reason for leaving home is a significant predictor, but violence or abuse of any kind may be derived from other familial, peer, or societal interactions as well, for example, in restrictive neighborhoods in which at risk youth reside, studies have shown that loving parents may not have the capability of protecting their LGBTQ children (Ferguson 2009). Youth may view these other abusive situations as hopeless, further resulting in increased instances of homelessness. Students, who fear parental reprisal if academic standards not met, may further be at risk of becoming homeless (Ray 2006). And the stress related to systemic bullying found in institutions such as schools is widely accepted as one reason for low performance (Kim, Sheridan, and Holcomb 2009; Larrabee and Moorhead 2010; Murdock and Bolch 2005; Ray 2006).

University of Illinois at Chicago Professor Stacey Horn is credited in the National Education Association's *A Report on the Status of Gay, Lesbian, Bisexual and Transgender People in Education: Stepping Out of the Closet, Into the Light* with stating that "homophobic bullying is fueled by 'sexual prejudice' or attitudes and beliefs reflecting negative assumptions and stereotypes about sexual orientation and gender identity" (Kim et al. 2009, 19). School victimization occurs in the same overt ways as in the forms of physical violence and verbal abuse such as taunting and harassment, but studies indicate that just as harmful to the student is the act of "exclusion from mainstream school life" (Murdock and Bolch 2005, 160).

Pilkington and D'Augelli (1995, 44) found, indicating exclusion, that "when asked about friends, 43% of the males and 54% of the females said they had lost at least one friend as a result of the disclosure of their sexual orientation." Exclusion can also occur in correlation with other forms of bullying, in particular verbal harassment. "It is clear that students across the life span attend classes in which being anything but heterosexual places them at risk for victimization and humiliation. In fact it appears that being anything but heterosexual equals something bad as early as elementary school" (Espelage and Swearer 2008, 158).

Words used to describe sexual minority youth are used synonymously with words describing stupidity or disgust, and can be considered commonplace among school-aged youth (Bishop and Casida 2011, 84). Phrases such as "That's so gay" are intended to ostracize and have the added effect, whether intended or not, of creating a hostile space in which students are expected to learn. Although these negative epithets are thrown around in a teasing manner, they are also often used to intimidate LGBTQ students. This means that the words originally designed only to describe an individual's sexual or gender nonconforming status are turned around and "are inappropriately used as putdowns and are directed toward sexual minority students or perceived sexual minority students" (Bishop and Casida 2011, p. 134).

This form of victimization can lead to outcomes of diminished academic success. Students who do not attend school cannot learn and when comparing LGBTQ-identified youth with their heterosexual colleagues, the former "were 100% more likely to skip school" (Robinson and Espelage 2012, 313). "Sexual minority youths also face more difficulties in getting along with peers, teachers, parents, and they are emotionally less attached to each other" (Ueno 2005, 269). Therefore, within the confines of a school institutional setting, students may find themselves the direct or indirect victims of antihomosexual retorts and sentiments. It should be noted that states that do not protect against bullying (by enumeration) tend to be those that are also the "disempowered states."

And as technology advances so to do the media in which youth may be taunted. "Cyberbullying" is a term coined to represent the distress caused by posting defamatory comments, photos, and videos on the Internet. Social media sites offer a sounding board for individuals to promote their thoughts and beliefs, and in some instances individuals post to these sites with the intent of publically humiliating and harming others. Bullying through these online public forums is more difficult to police than are more traditional bullying interactions. But what are the ramifications when bullying interventions are possible to put in place and authority figures choose to look the other way and pay little to no attention to stopping LGBTQ bullying in places where societal stigmatization still exists?

Espelage and Swearer (2008) surmise that their research implies that the lack of an immediate hard stop to antigay actions and remarks will continue to promote, whether or not the promotion is intentional, an environment of hostility against LGBTQ youth. Bishop and Casida (2011) suggest that this stigma may in fact diminish a teacher or administrator's instinct to protect and lead to "the harassment of sexual minority students (gay, lesbian, or bisexual) and students who are perceived by others as being sexual minorities" (p. 134). On the other hand educators may be inclined to present ideas regarding the acceptance of individuals within the LGBTQ community.

In fact school climates vary across the country, and administrators, educators, and students are not the sole predictor of whether LGBTQ persons find it difficult to remain in the educational setting and the home (Ueno 2005). Therefore, in situations in which institutional prejudices exist, educators are unable to find the support needed to present positive examples of LGBT history and role models. Additionally, some of these educators may choose not to portray these successes in the LGBTQ community because of feelings of being unequipped in accurately presenting appropriate information (Dessel 2010). Some disempowered states require "neutrality" regarding discussions of LGBT people; for example, South Carolina.

For instance, Sherwin and Jennings (2006) set out to study what if anything was being taught in university and college's teacher preparatory programs. The researchers surveyed institutions across seven states and targeted collegiate-level teacher preparation curriculum across the varying regions of the United States. The study asked program coordinators whether these curriculum included diversity training; the study broke diversity training into several categories, which included a designation of sexual orientation, "using a six-point Likert-type scale and ranged from 'most emphasized (6) to 'least emphasized' (1) and also included the option 'don't cover at all' (0)" (Sherwin and Jennings 2006, 211). Their findings showed that "no programs ranked 'gender diversity' or 'sexual orientation diversity' as most emphasized" (p. 212). The largest number of respondents to the Sherwin and Jennings study found that sexual orientation as a curriculum topic had the least emphasis placed upon it and more than a significant number of programs gave the topic no attention at all. "The school community as a whole is negatively influenced by sexual orientation harassment" (Dessel 2010, 558) through the systemic lack of consideration for the overall development of sexual orientation pedagogy.

School's administrations and teaching preparatory programs are not the only entities to examine the lack of school support of LGBTQ students. Some county and state governments demonstrate community lack of support for sexual minorities and gender nonconforming individuals. For instance, according to Robinson and Espelage (2011), legislation in Tennessee and Missouri will expressly forbid healthy discussions of sexual orientation and its role in history, while the state of Missouri goes further disallowing the formation of Gay Straight Alliance (GSA) student organizations. In another case, Robinson and Espelage (2012) reported, "Anoka-Hennepin School District, which implemented a policy aimed at reducing bullying in general but that explicitly prohibited both positive and negative discussions regarding sexual identity" (p. 309). These and other LGBTQ stigma may in many cases perpetuate youth's fear of disclosure of their sexual minority or gender nonconformity status to the community at large.

In one study, nearly 30% of youth went so far as to express a fear of identifying as LGBTQ openly within their general community (Pilkington and D'Augelli 1995). Fear of the community is a precursor to fear of authority and fear of those whose jobs are to protect victims of harassment or abuse. Pilkington and D'Augelli (1995) reported that respondents vocalized hopeless feelings: "Nothing would be done," "Authorities don't recognize bias crimes against gays," "It seems useless in today's system" (p. 45). These feelings of hopelessness may be an additional factor leading to homelessness. Youth may find it necessary to take matters into their own hands rather than reach out for help from caretakers, teachers, and school administrators, and potentially social service agencies or the police after homelessness occurred.

Why Abuse in the Home, School Setting, and Community Matters

Findings indicate that sexual minority youth is one group that is most susceptible to being physically and sexually victimized after becoming homeless (Cochran, Stewart, Ginzler, and Cauce 2002; Whitbeck, Chen, Hoyt, Tyler, and Johnson 2004). The reasons for this continued victimization beyond the youth's given circumstances (e.g., primary caretaker's home, school, and community) have not been significantly studied. Most studies discussing LGBTQ youth focus on the experiences of the youth being victimized, some ask questions about whether experiences of verbal, physical, or sexual abuse were as a result of the youth's perceived sexual orientation, but none were found to have surveyed youth perpetrating such events. Therefore, other factors may play a role, be it significant or minor, in the youth's experience and subsequently there is a need for additional studies to determine the reason for continued victimization of this homeless subpopulation.

Assuming, for the time being however, that these events of violence were perpetrated in part or solely due to the youth's perceived or actual sexual orientation, it can be determined that LGBTQ homeless youth are in a position of heightened need for services. As victims of violence, however, sexual minority homeless youth are reported to feel resistant to report crimes against them. Ray (2006) reports that violent crimes against LGBTQ homeless youth go unreported nearly two-thirds of the time. One prominent reason for this is that these youth may be participating in criminal activity at the time during which the violent offense is committed.

Implications of Survival as the Sole Consideration

Hein (2011) in her research found that homeless sexual minority youths were far less likely than homeless heterosexual youths to employ the services of shelters in order to survive. As LGBTQ youth shy away from social service providers, their dependence on creating a pattern of survival increases. It is widely accepted that homeless individuals in general face a great deal of discrimination due to the many vulnerabilities that come from the challenges of living on the street, but reports demonstrate that additional discrimination is felt by LGBTQ homeless youth due to their sexual minority status (Ray 2006).

"Psychosocial problems associated with homelessness (i.e., causes or correlates) include negative peer and family relationship, mental health issues, sexually transmitted diseases (STDs) and sexual risk, and substance use" (Gattis 2009, 1066–1067). Many of the psychosocial problems listed here are a direct result of the survival strategies that befall homeless youth and, in large proportion, homeless sexual minority youth. Studies indicate that homeless youth are often likely to employ survival strategies after having spent time directly on the streets. Unfortunately survival itself can lead to outcomes creating further disturbances in the lives of LGBTQ homeless youth.

One of these strategies is that of "survival sex," meaning that homeless youth will trade acts of sex for shelter, drugs, food, and money (Ray 2006; Whitbeck et al. 2004). Sexual minority homeless youth are the most common participants in survival sex. Whitbeck et al. (2004) found that "gay males (27.8%) were more likely than heterosexual males (9.0%) to report that they engaged in survival sex" (p. 334). Walls and Bell (2011) note, "Consistent with previous findings, we found that gay, lesbian, and bisexually identified homeless youth and young adults were significantly more likely than heterosexually identified youth to have engaged in survival sex" (p. 432).

Additionally, studies show that transgender homeless youth are further likely to participate in survival sex strategies (Hein 2011). It is important to note that the extremely high rates of transgender participation, for example, "100% of transgender youth," (p. 279) in Hein's (2011) study, are likely, to one degree, exaggerated due to a very small transgender study group. However, regardless of the small sample size, the number of sexual minority and gender nonconforming homeless youth entering into survival sex is overwhelming.

After discussing the health pitfalls of survival sex, Ray (2006) goes on to identify this severely vulnerable population to include those homeless sexual minority individuals who were abused as youth. Additionally, when tying instances of survival sex to previous instances of sexual abuse committed by a caretaker Whitbeck et al. (2004) found that the propensity toward a survival sex strategy doubled. As discussed earlier homeless sexual minority youth often refer to caretaker abuse as the reason for their homeless status, continuing a cycle of revictimization of these youth.

As these youth continue to participate in risky sexual behaviors such as survival sex they become further at risk of the dangerous effects of revictimization and other health impacts including sexually transmitted infections (STIs) and HIV/AIDS. Regardless of whether the sexual act is performed with expectations of a trade scenario or for other reasons, studies indicate that LGBTQ homeless youth are at a heightened risk of developing HIV/AIDS and other STIs. For instance, in their study, Cochran et al. (2002) found that "LGBT youths reported a higher number of lifetime sexual partners than did heterosexual youths ... LGBT youths were significantly younger than heterosexuals in regard to age at first voluntary intercourse" (p. 775). The study also found that "LGBT youths reported higher rates of unprotected intercourse" (p. 775).

In a study conducted 10 years after the Cochran et al. (2002) study, researchers determined that homeless LGBTQ youth are all too aware of the consequences that unprotected intercourse has on their health and potentially their lives. Unfortunately this knowledge is often ignored as homeless LGBTQ youth listed reasons related to pleasure, partner trust, and fear of accusations of being unfaithful among other reasons (Ream, Barnhart, and Lotz 2012). "These participants also employed situational ethics. They were very aware of the risks associated with survival sex, sex work, casual encounters, and substance use. Some acknowledged various degrees of risk behaviors, but most reported being strictly safe in those situations" (p. 7).

This information would seem to point to the fact that homeless LGBTQ youth are typically likely to use safe-sex practices during situations in which they are entering into risky sexual behaviors. However, evidence exists showing that these youth may be more likely to choose to employ safe practices in theory and not necessarily in life experience. For instance, studies show that youth who feel low self-worth are less likely to engage in safe-sex practices as a result of their emotional distress. Ream, Barnhart, and Lotz (2012) interviewed homeless LGBTQ youth regarding their decision-making process when related to condom use and homelessness, and found that youth who have dealt with severely detrimental life experiences as a result of their sexual minority status were, per their own accounts, less likely to use condoms during high-stress times.

Reisner, Mimiaga, Safren, and Mayer (2009) "surveyed men in Massachusetts who reported having sex with other men and of whom 73% self-identified as homosexual" (p. 1484). The study intended to determine whether there is a causal effect of "men who have sex with men (MSM)"(p. 1481), on their potential risk of contracting HIV and other STIs when considering posttraumatic stress disorder (PTSD) as a predictive factor. The researchers concluded that MSMs who suffered from PTSD were in fact more likely to engage in unprotected sexual behaviors.

One of the measures of PTSD according to the American Psychiatric Association (APA) *Diagnostic and Statistical Manual of Mental Disorders*, 5th edition (*DSM-5*) is "Criterion A: stressor. The person was exposed to death, threatened death, actual or threatened serious injury, or actual or threatened sexual violence" (p. 1). As discussed throughout this chapter, LGBTQ status is sometimes a predictor of physical, emotional, or sexual violence against youth in the home, school, and in the community due to a pattern of heterosexism exhibited throughout these populations.

Additionally, "findings suggest that GLB individuals may be at increased risk for sexual violence victimization as compared to their heterosexual counterparts"

(Rothman, Exner, and Baughman 2012, 57), even when extended to include lifetime instances of violence.

PTSD and "the consequences of homelessness are dire and often include unemployment, poverty, morbidity, and mortality" (Gattis 2009, 1067) falling under another criteria, "Criterion G: functional significance. Significant symptom-related distress or functional impairment (e.g., social, occupational)" (*DSM*-5). In a study completed by Ueno (2005), the researcher "confirmed ... sexual minority adolescents experience higher levels of psychological distress than majority adolescents" (p. 269). The distress if derived from "victimization perceived as homophobic may have added effects beyond general victimization for LGBTQ youth because it further denigrates their identity and emphasizes their marginalized position" (Poteat, Mereish, DiGiovanni, and Koenig 2011, 597).

Homeless youth suffering from PTSD due to a single or long-term exposure to traumatic life event(s) may find it difficult to overcome the stigma that the trauma, such as physical, emotional, or sexual abuse, may have caused. For example, one study that surveyed both homeless and nonhomeless sexual minority youth found that "hopelessness was reported by 57.53 percent of the respondents" and that "slightly less than one-half reported verbal and/or physical abuse by their family of origin" (Walls, Hancock, and Wisneski 2007, 190). The same report demonstrated that homeless sexual minority youth were significantly more likely than their sexual minority nonhomeless counterparts to report both familial abuse and feelings of hopelessness.

This leads to the idea that in addition to the challenges faced as the marginalized group based on sexual orientation, sexual minority youth who are homeless doubly suffer from the stresses of their circumstance. This suggests that "the challenge for transient homeless youth who must constantly reestablish support networks in new locations may slowly recover from victimization, elevating the risk of PTSD" (Bender, Ferguson, Thompson, Komlo, Pollio 2010, 166). While the study does not distinguish LGBTQ youth from their heterosexual counterparts, it does help to develop a background demonstrating that highly transient homeless youth suffering from PTSD may also find it more difficult to mainstream back into the general population after having become homeless. Additionally if, as the studies identified in this chapter indicate, sexual minority youth suffer from heightened rates of PTSD, depression, and other mental health concerns as well as homelessness, these youth are at an increased need for preventative services.

Further, the research indicates that there are some discrepancies among the outcomes that befall homeless LGBTQ youth as a result of the reported level at which they suffer from PTSD, depression, and other mental health concerns. For instance, research indicates that findings across studies confirm the hypothesis that sexual minority youth are more likely than their heterosexual counterparts to have suicide ideation and for some suicide attempt follow through. However, there is debate regarding the efficacy of these studies due in part to their small population sizes, limited methods of data collection, and the broad considerations taken in reports of suicide attempts (Savin-Williams 2001).

Although researchers' concerns may be valid, there seems to be little research done to dispute the claim that mental health concerns are manifested higher in sexual minority youths than in sexual majority youths. Gattis (2009) found that among male adolescents gay individuals were significantly more likely to meet the diagnostic criteria of severe depression. Additionally, Walls and Bell (2011, 430) studied homeless youth and young adults, comparing two groups: those who had engaged in survival sex and those who had not. Homeless individuals who had participated in survival sex were 30% more likely to have at least one report of attempted suicide.

Additionally, as reported previously in the chapter, the literature shows that sexual minority youths are far more likely to enter into survival sex scenarios. Further, one study, when surveying homeless youth regarding the implications that having used social services and survival sex have on suicide attempts, found that gender differences in suicide attempt were less significant when also considering LGBTQ status or survival sex history (Walls, Potter, and Van Leeuwen 2009). The researchers noted the presence of limitations with regard to the targeted sample survey and so cautioned against generalizing their findings.

However, Walls et al. (2009) through their literature review determined that homeless sexual minority youth as a double marginalized population were shown to suffer from higher rates of suicidal ideation and attempts than were homeless heterosexual youth. Therefore, separating attempts that resulted in little to no bodily harm from those that resulted in serious injury do not seem necessary until the mental health status of heterosexual individuals can be proved to match directly with LGBTQ mental health concerns when determining for rates of higher instances of suicide alone.

Suicide ideation and attempts by LGBTQ youth, as a health concern, must be addressed and eradicated. However, suicide is not the only factor in mental health that may be a result of, or result in, homelessness. For instance, whether "youths aged 14–17, in comparison to older youths, ever attempting suicide was related to greater lifetime and recent substance use" (Salomonsen-Sautel, Van Leeuwen, Gilroy, Boyle, Malberg, and Hopfer 2008, 230–231). Additionally, depending on the severity of the drug as well as the frequency of use, this and other studies have found links between suicide and drug use noting, "Respondents who had used intravenous drugs were 2.5 times as likely to report attempting suicide" (Walls, Potter, and Van Leeuwen 2009, 245).

Throughout the literature, drug and alcohol misuse have been identified as having a correlation to many of the stigmas from which homeless youth and further homeless sexual minority youths suffer, for example, victimization (Balsam, Lehavot, and Beadnell 2011), survival sex (Walls and Bell 2011), negative health outcomes (Ryan et al. 2009), and, as noted earlier, suicide (Walls et al. 2009). And while one study found that overall alcohol use among homeless LGBTQ youth did not differ significantly from their LGBTQ housed counterparts leading to the possible conclusion that sexual minority youths in general are at an increased risk of substance abuse, homeless LGBTQ youth were found to have engaged in drinking "on more of the previous 30 days than were non-homeless sexual minority youths" (Walls et al. 2009, 194).

Walls et al. (2007) specifically surveyed youth on their reported use of marijuana, cocaine, and methamphetamine; all were found to be used at a "significantly" (p. 194) higher rate in homeless sexual minority youth versus sexual minority youth considered not homeless. Additionally, "data indicate that about half of this sample of young LGB adults show considerable mental health and substance use problems" (Ryan et al. 2009, 349). Further, the study by Salomonsen-Sautel et al. (2008) found that the older homeless youth (i.e., ages 18–24) who reported being a member of the LGTBQ community also reported higher rates of lifetime drug use.

The discussions of this chapter have centered on the issues faced by homeless sexual minority youth. As noted, LGBTQ homeless individuals are victimized at home and school prior to homelessness, and on the streets, and while receiving social services after homelessness occurs. This victimization may lead to outcomes of recurrent victimization, substance misuse, mental health concerns, and suicide ideation or actualization (Ray 2006). Although not specific only to LGBTQ homeless youths, the most recent literature demonstrates that the issues faced by homeless youth more frequently restrict the quality of life of the LGBTQ homeless subpopulation. It is therefore imperative that the distinctive social service needs of sexual minorities and gender nonconforming persons be addressed in coordination with meeting the needs of their homeless status.

Reducing the Symptoms through Systemic Changes to the Care Approach

As the barriers to regaining a foothold in the general population continue to be issues of concern for homeless persons and more specifically LGBTQ persons suffering from or on the verge of homelessness, it is important that social service providers are given the tools needed to better serve the LGBTQ homeless population. Greene (2005) notes:

> Identity represents an interaction between the social and internal world ... when the external, social world distorts one's identity and imposes barriers to opportunities based on that identity, the groundwork has been laid for a distorted image of one's self, sense of self-worth, and a distorted perception of others. (p. 296)

In part, better serving this population begins by removing the heterosexism that may exist in institutions that have not yet adopted or enforced an inclusion policy that specifically cites the concerns of LGBTQ persons. As noted earlier, although the vast majority of Americans agree that bullying in the United States is an issue that must be immediately dealt with, some anti-bullying policies and procedures in many states make no mention of acts perpetrated against LGBTQ youths. "Continued advocacy is needed to change oppressive social norms … that support violence against GLB people, including homophobia and the use of violence to control others" (Rothman, Exner, and Baughman 2011, 63).

Ray (2006) interviewed representatives of organizations providing shelter to homeless youth during the time the book was being written and found that there existed social service agencies across the country in which LGBTQ homeless youth were inadequately cared for. Stories were reported of humiliation tactics, violence, and lack of protection for sexual minority and more extensively gender nonconforming youth. Additionally, in some cases known LGBTQ youth were simply turned away from receiving services or services were discontinued after sexual orientation identity was discovered. In the cases of faith-based organizations, inclusion is not always the norm so that individuals greatly in need of services may forego seeking out services during instances in which they feel that their life experiences are in direct contradiction to the service provider's expressed beliefs.

However, as previously noted, educational system employees often feel less than qualified to work with and teach issues important for the safety and inclusion of sexual minority and gender nonconforming youth. Therefore teacher education programs within colleges and universities must work to provide more in-depth curriculum to better prepare educators, administrators, and social workers to understand how best to meet youth at a level that instills trust and acceptance.

Social workers who are able to determine that an issue exists for LGBTQ youth may be, as a trusted adult, able to work with LGBTQ youth to evaluate the home life and find an alternative emergency living situation for the youth. Walls et al. (2007) cited another recommendation in their work noting that social workers and educators would better serve youth by noticing more frequent instances of absenteeism and through providing safety within school institutions.

These two steps will likely go a long way to help prevent homelessness, but homelessness prevention is not the only need. Beyond prevention exists the need to support individuals already facing homelessness or who may face homelessness regardless of instances of family support. As mentioned earlier nearly half of sexual minority youth identify family discontent as a cause for leaving or being forced out of their homes. This leads to a conclusion that some LGBTQ youth are homeless for other reasons and may therefore end up homeless regardless of positive family intervention tactics. Therefore it is necessary to also consider how well agencies serving homeless individuals care for sexual minority and gender nonconforming persons.

As has been noted in this chapter, homeless sexual minority youth are often uncomfortable seeking social services for fear of additional discriminatory practices among providers and other service recipients. LGBTQ youth have traditionally shied away from child welfare systems or group homes for this expressed purpose. These institutions have been categorized as not being accepting of sexual minority persons, according to Wall et al. (2007). Yu (2010) agrees stating that these individuals "who do seek shelter, foster care placement, or other services face discrimination and victimization in these settings" (p. 342). As these experiences are reported on the streets, it will likely only discourage newly homeless LGBTQ youth from accessing services and encourage them to stay on the streets. Social Service agencies then must ensure that staff is made aware and fully comply with policies that identify safety procedures and positive housing conditions for sexual minority and gender nonconforming youth.

One way to do so may be to hear directly from sexual minority and gender nonconforming youth. Spiro, Dekel, Peled (2009) discuss the benefits of client satisfaction surveys in determining whether providers are supporting individuals based on the aspects of care that are most important to them. Spiro et al. (2009) go on to state that "client satisfaction surveys empower clients by giving them a voice in the evaluation and, indirectly, in the management of services. This is of special significance in the case … among the most powerless clients of social services" (p. 262). Again this study does not specifically identify the individual experiences of LGBTQ homeless youth and therefore the results found within the confines of their research are likely not truly representative of this population, but the researchers' findings do point to the general idea that supportive staff–client relationships lead more often to a positive shelter/service experience.

Research done just prior to the Spiro et al. (2009) study states that actively listening to the anecdotal experiences of homeless youth would likely lead to a stronger understanding by service providers as to the needs of said individuals. Additionally these youth may be found to have valuable insights into the types of service delivery that would bring about a focus on survival and thriving within their environment. The study goes on to state that not only do youth have a first-hand perspective of what needs should be met in order to help them survive and potentially exit homelessness, but so too do those who already work with homeless youth (Zerger et al. 2008).

In the instances in which youth and these practitioners are heard, opportunity as well as necessity has allowed supportive, nurturing organizations to develop programs that are designed to more effectively provide for the needs of LGBTQ homeless individuals (Ray 2006). In these cases agencies need to take special care to seek sexual minority and gender nonconforming homeless youth where they gather in order to better succeed in gaining trust among this homeless subpopulation (Zerger et al. 2008). Doing so may bring hope to LGBTQ homeless individuals that otherwise would not exist.

Beyond solely considering the needs of homeless sexual minority and gender nonconforming youth versus their homeless heterosexual counterparts, Walls et al. (2007) discuss the need for social service agencies to consider the needs of these LGBTQ homeless youth as they differ from their LGBTQ housed counterparts as well. One study concludes that while there exists an understanding that the different homeless subpopulations needs, including that of sexual minorities, should be cared for, researchers are still not fully considering the implications that not categorizing the different experiences of these subpopulations within their studies creates. Ensuring more specificity within the results of these studies may lead to a better understanding of more appropriate service interventions.

Further, in addition to preventing homelessness when possible and providing LGBTQ homeless individuals with the services needed to survive during episodes of homelessness, assisting LGBTQ individuals to exit homelessness should also be a high priority of social service agencies. For instance, sexual minorities must be treated for the abuse and other victimization, substance misuse, and mental and physical health concerns suffered as a result of their sexual minority or gender nonconforming status in conjunction with being served as homeless in general.

Ending the Cycle of Homelessness

Without treating the whole person, a case could be made that these individuals will be far less successful in recovering from homelessness, as their complete needs will not have been met. There is some evidence that exiting homelessness is most successful when homeless individuals have a support system in place prior to regaining stable housing. As noted, disaffiliation, the "decreased contact with friends and family, under-utilization of needed services" (Zlotnick, Tam, and Robertson 2003, 592), is a strong contributing factor to homelessness and further unsuccessful reentry into the general housed population (Milburn et al. 2009; Zlotnick et al. 2003).

The Milburn et al. (2009) study centered its discussion on newly homeless youth and did not determine that using social services while homeless was a contributing factor to exiting homelessness for those newly homeless youth. It suggested that early intervention is important because strong maternal–child bonds and peer connectivity help to reduce the risks of chronic homeless behaviors.

Additionally, Milburn, Ayala, Rice, Batterham, and Rotheram-Borus (2006) further noted that LGBTQ youth and more specifically LGBTQ homeless youth are often discriminated against. Their report finds that LGBTQ youth are more frequent victims of discrimination at home and at school as well as, once homeless, by police. The study goes on to note that as a doubly marginalized population, it continues to be seemingly more acceptable to be outwardly discriminatory due to an individual's sexual orientation status more than any other marginalized homeless or nonhomeless population.

By providing additional and ongoing inclusion training LGBTQ homeless individuals will likely find more acceptance from institutions before, during, and after homelessness. This in turn may help to reduce the possibility of homelessness for those members of the LGBTQ homeless population who, without the added stigmatized affects of being a part of the sexual minority or gender-conforming population might not otherwise face homelessness. Although it is not within the scope of this chapter to identify specific practices for addressing institutional mistreatment and inadequacies in addressing the unique needs of the LGBTQ homeless population, the research does point to the need for additional education and advocacy to provide educators, civil service officials, and social service providers with best practice approaches in supporting the LGBTQ homeless population. [*Editor's Note:* As this chapter was being written, a December 2, 2013, article in the *New York Times* highlighted the fact that a recent San Francisco study found that 29% of LGBT adults and seniors in that jurisdiction are homeless. Thus, discrimination that begins for LGBT youth continues at roughly the same level for LGBT adults. This highlights the need for additional research to ensure that the effect of societal discrimination against all LGBT people (young or old) is minimized.]

References

Balsam, Kimberly F., Karen Lehavot, and Blair Beadnell. 2011. "Sexual Revictimization and Mental Health: A Comparison of Lesbians, Gay Men, and Heterosexual Women." *Journal of Interpersonal Violence, 26*, 1798–1814. doi: 10.1177/0886260510372946.

Bender, Kimberly, Kristin Ferguson, Sanna Thompson, Chelsea Komlo, and David Pollio. 2010. "Factors Associated with Trauma and Posttraumatic Stress Disorder among Homeless Youth in Three U.S. Cities: The Importance of Transience." *Journal of Traumatic Stress, 23*, 161–168. doi: 10.1002/jts.20501.

Bishop, Holly N., and Heather Casida. 2011. "Preventing Bullying and Harassment of Sexual Minority Students in Schools." *The Clearing House, 84*, 134–138. doi: 10.1080/00098655.2011.564975.

Cochran, Bryan N., Angela J. Stewart, Joshua A. Ginzler, and Ana Mari Cauce. 2002. "Challenges Faced by Homeless Sexual Minorities: Comparison of Gay, Lesbian, Bisexual, and Transgender Homeless Adolescents with Their Heterosexual Counterparts." *American Journal of Public Health, 92*, 773–777.

Dessel, Adrienne B. 2010. "Effects of Intergroup Dialogue: Public School Teachers and Sexual Orientation Prejudice." *Small Group Research, 41*, 556–592. doi: 10.1177/1046496410369560.

Espelage, Dorothy L., and Susan M. Swearer. 2008. "Addressing Research Gaps in the Intersection between Homophobia and Bullying." *School Psychology Review, 37*, 155–159.

Ferguson, Kristin M. 2009. "Exploring Family Environment Characteristics and Multiple Abuse Homeless Youth." *Journal of Interpersonal Violence, 24*, 1875–1891. doi: 10.1177/0886260508325490.

Friedman, Mark S., Michael P. Marshal, Thomas E. Guadamuz, Chongyi Wei, Carolyn F. Wong, Elizabeth M. Saewyc, and Ron Stall. 2011. "A Meta-Analysis of Disparities in Childhood Sexual Abuse, Parental Physical Abuse, and Peer Victimization Among Sexual Minority and Sexual Nonminority Individuals." *American Journal of Public Health, 101*, 1481–1494.

Gattis, Maurice N. 2009. "Psychosocial Problems Associated with Homelessness in Sexual Minority Youths." *Journal of Human Behavior in the Social Environment, 19*, 1066–1094. doi: 10.1080/10911350902990478.

Greene, Beverly. 2005. "Psychology, Diversity, and Social Justice: Beyond Heterosexism and Across the Cultural Divide." *Counseling Psychology Quarterly, 18*, 295–306. doi: 10.1080/09515070500385770.

Haber, Mason G., and Paul A. Toro. 2004. "Homelessness among Families, Children, and Adolescents: An Ecological-Development Perspective." *Clinical Child and Family Psychology Review*, 7, 123–164. doi: 1096-4037/04/0900/0123/0.

Hein, Laura C. 2011. "Survival Strategies of Male Homeless Adolescents." *Journal of the American Psychiatric Nurses Association, 17*, 274–282. doi: 10.1177/1078390311407913.

House, Amy S., Elizabeth Van Horn, Christopher Coppeans, and Lara M. Stepleman. 2011. "Interpersonal Trauma and Discriminatory Events as Predictors of Suicide and Nonsuicidal Self-Injury in Gay, Lesbian, Bisexual, and Transgender Persons." *Traumatology, 17*. doi: 10.1177/1534765610395621.

Johnson. 2004. "Mental Disorder, Subsistence Strategies, and Victimization among Gay, Lesbian, and Bisexual Homeless Runaway Adolescents." *The Journal of Sex Research*, 41, 329–342.

Kempf-Leonard, Kimberly, and Pernilla Johansson. 2007. "Gender and Runaways: RiskFactors, Delinquency, and Juvenile Justice Experiences." *Youth Violence and Juvenile Justice*, 5, 308–327. doi: 10.1177/1541204007301293.

Kim, Robert, David Sheridan, and Sabrina Holcomb. 2009. "A Report on the Status of Gay, Lesbian, Bisexual and Transgender People in Education: Stepping Out of the Closet, into the Light." iBook edition. National Education Association.

Larrabee, Timothy G., and Pamela Morehead. 2010. "Broadening Views of Social Justice and Teacher Leadership: Addressing LGB Issues in Teacher Education." *Issues in Teacher Education, 19*, 37–52.

Leavitt, Michael O. 2007. "U.S. Department of Health and Human Services: Strategic Action Plan on Homelessness." Strategic Action Plan on Homelessness. U.S. Department of Health and Human Services. March. Accessed May 2011, http://www.hhs.gov/homeless/research/endhomelessness.html.

McDermott, Elizabeth, Katrina Roen, and Jonathan Scourfield. 2008. "Avoiding Shame: Young LGBT People, Homophobia and Self-Destructive Behaviors." *Culture, Health & Sexuality, 10*, 815–829. doi: 10.1080/13691050802380974.

Milburn, Norweeta G., George Ayala, Eric Rice, Phillip Batterman, and Mary Jane Rotheram-Borus. 2006. "Discrimination and Exiting Homelessness among Homeless Adolescents." *Cultural Diversity and Ethnic Minority Psychology, 12*, 658–672. doi: 10.1037/1099-9809.12.4.658.

Milburn, Norweeta G., Eric Rice, Mary Jane Rotheram-Borus, Shelley Mallett, Doreen Rosenthal, Phillip Batterham, Susanne J. May, Andrea Witkin, Naihua Duan, et al. 2009. "Adolescents Exiting Homelessness Over Two Years: The Risk Amplification and Abatement Model." *Journal of Research on Adolescence, 19*, 762–785.

Murdock, Tamera B., and Megan B. Bolch. 2005. "Risk and Protective Factors for Poor School Adjustment in Lesbian, Gay, and Bisexual (LGB) High School Youth: Variable and Person-Center Analysis." *Psychology in Schools, 42*, 159–172. doi: 10.1002/pits.20054.

Mustanski, Brian S., Robert Garofalo, and Erin M. Emerson. 2010. "Mental Health Disorders, Psychological Distress, and Suicidality in a Diverse Sample of Lesbian, Gay, Bisexual, and Transgender Youths." *American Journal of Public Health, 100*, 2426–2432.

Pilkington, Neil W., and Anthony R. D'Augelli. 1995. "Victimization of Lesbian, Gay, and Bisexual Youth in Community Settings." *Journal of Community Psychology, 23*, 34–56.

Poteat, V. Paul, Ethan H. Mereish, Craig D. DiGiovanni, and Brian W. Koenig. 2011. "The Effects of General and Homophobic Victimization on Adolescents' Psychosocial and Educational Concerns: The Importance of Intersecting Identities and Parent Support." *Journal of Counseling Psychology, 58*, 597–609. doi: 10.1037/a0025095.

Ray, Nicholas. 2006. "Lesbian, Gay, Bisexual and Transgender Youth: An Epidemic of Homelessness." New York: National Gay and Lesbian Task Force Policy Institute and the National Coalition for the Homeless. iBook edition.

Ream, Geoffrey L., Kate F. Barnhart, and Kevin V. Lotz. 2012. "Decision Process About Condom Use Among Shelter-Homeless LGBT Youth in Manhattan." *AIDS Research and Treatment,* 1–9. doi: 10.1155/2012/659853.

Reisner, Sari L., Matthew J. Mimiaga, Steven A. Safren, and Kenneth H. Mayer. 2009. "Stressful or Traumatic Life Events, Post-traumatic Stress Disorder (PTSD) Symptoms, and HIV Sexual Risk Taking among Men Who Have Sex With Men." *AIDS Care: Psychological and Socio-Medical Aspects of AIDS/HIV, 21*, 1481–1489. doi: 10.1080/09540120902893258.

Ringwalt, Christopher L., Jody M. Greene, Marjorie Robertson, and Melissa McPheeters. 1998. "The Prevalence of Homelessness among Adolescents in the United States." *American Journal of Public Health, 88*, 1325–1329.

Roberts, Andrea L., Margaret Rosario, Heather L. Corliss, Karestan C. Koenen and S. Bryn Austin. 2012. "Childhood Gender Nonconformity: A Risk Indicator for Childhood Abuse and Posttraumatic Stress in Youth." *Pediatrics,* 410–417. doi: 10.1542/peds.2011-1804.

Robinson, Joseph P., and Dorothy L. Espelage. 2011. "Inequities in Educational and Psychological Outcomes Between LGBTQ and Straight Students in Middle and High School." *Educational Researcher, 40*, 315–330. doi: 10.3102/0013189X11422112.

Robinson, Joseph P., and Dorothy L. Espelage. 2012. "Bullying Explains Only Part of LGBTQ-Heterosexual Risk Disparities: Implications for Policy and Practice." *Educational Researcher, 41*, 309–319. doi: 10.3102/0013189X12457023.

Rothman, Emily F., Deinera Exner, and Allyson L. Baughman. 2011. "The Prevalence of Sexual Assault Against People Who Identify as Gay, Lesbian, or Bisexual in the United States A Systematic Review." *Trauma, Violence, and Abuse, 12*, 55–66. doi: 10.1177/1524838010390707.

Ryan, Caitlin, David Huebner, Rafael M. Diaz, and Jorge Sanchez. 2009. "Family Rejection as a Predictor of Negative Health Outcomes in White and Latino Lesbian, Gay, and Bisexual Young Adults." *Pediatrics, 123*, 346–352. http://pediatrics.aappublications.org/content/123/1/346.full.html.

Saewyc, Elizabeth M., Carol L. Skay, Sandra L. Pettingell, Elizabeth A. Reis, LindaBearinger, Michael Resnick, Aileen Murphy, and Leigh Combs. 2006. "Hazards of Stigma: The Sexual and Physical Abuse of Gay, Lesbian, and Bisexual Adolescents in the United States and Canada." *Child Welfare,* 195–213.

Salomonsen-Sautel, Stacy, James M. Van Leeuwen, Christine Gilroy, Susan Boyle, Danielle Malberg, and Christian Hopfer. 2008. "Correlates of Substance Use Among Homeless Youths in Eight Cities." *The American Journal on Addictions, 17*, 224–234. doi: 10.1080/10550490802019964.

Savin-Williams, Ritch C. 2001. "Suicide Attempts Among Sexual-Minority Youths: Population and Measurement Issues." *Journal of Consulting and Clinical Psychology, 69*, 983–991. doi: 10.1037//0022-006X.69.6.983.

Savin-Williams, Ritch C., and Geoffrey L. Ream. 2003. "Suicide Attempts among Sexual-Minority Male Youth." *Journal of Clinical Child and Adolescent Psychology, 32*, 509–522.

Sherwin, Gary, and Todd Jennings. 2006. "Feared, Forgotten, or Forbidden: Sexual Orientation Topics in Secondary Teacher Preparation Programs in the USA." *Teaching Education, 17*, 207–223. doi: 10.1080/10476210600849664.

Spiro, Shimon, Rachel Dekel, and Einat Peled. 2009. "Dimensions and Correlates of Client Satisfaction: An Evaluation of a Shelter for Runaway and Homeless Youth." *Research on Social Work Practice, 19*, 261–270. doi: 10.1177/1049731508329395.

Toro, Paul A., Amy Dworsky, and Patrick J. Fowler. 2007. "Homeless Youth in the United States: Recent Research Findings and Intervention Approaches." Toward Understanding Homelessness: The 2007 National Symposium on Homelessness Research. U.S. Health and Human Services. http://aspe.hhs.gov/hsp/homelessness/symposium07/toro/.

Ueno, Koji. 2005. "Sexual Orientation and Psychological Distress in Adolescence: Examining Interpersonal Stressors and Social Support Processes." *Social Psychology Quarterly, 68*, 258–277. doi: 138.192.25.68.

US Department of Veteran Affairs. 2013. "DSM-5 Criteria for PTSD." http://www.ptsd.va.gov/professional/pages/dsm5_criteria_ptsd.asp.

Walls, N. Eugene, Cathryn Potter, and James Van Leeuwen. 2009. "Where Risks and Protective Factors Operate Differently: Homeless Sexual Minority Youth and Suicide Attempts." *Child Adolescent Social Work Journal, 26*, 235–257. doi: 10.1007/s10560-009-0172-2.

Walls, N. Eugene, and Stephanie Bell. 2011. "Correlates of Engaging in Survival Sex among Homeless Youth and Young Adults." *The Journal of Sex Research, 48*, 423–436, doi: 10.1080/00224499.2010.501916.

Walls, N. Eugene, Pam Hancock, and Hope Wisneski. 2007. "Differentiating the Social Service Needs of Homeless Sexual Minority Youths from Those of Non-Homeless Sexual Minority Youths." *Journal of Children & Poverty, 13*, 177–205. doi: 10.1080/10796120701520309.

Whitbeck, Les B., Xiaojin Chen, Dan R. Hoyt, Kimberly A. Taylor, and Kurt D. Johnson. 2004. "Mental Disorders, Subsistence Strategies, and Victimization among Gay, Lesbian, and Bisexual Homeless and Runaway Adolescents." *The Journal of Sex Research*, 41(4), 329–342.

Whitbeck, Les B., Danny R. Hoyt, and Wa-Ning Bao. 2000. "Depressive Symptoms and Co-Occurring Depressive Symptoms, Substance Abuse, and Conduct Problems among Runaway and Homeless Adolescents." *Child Development, 71*(3), 721–732.

Wilder Research. 2009. "Minnesota Homeless Study Homeless Children and Their Families." Accessed May 2011. http://www.wilder.org/Wilder-Research/Publications/Studies/Homelessness%20in%20Minnesota,%202009%20Study/Homelessness%20in%20Minnesota%202009,%20Full%20Report.pdf.

Yu, Van. 2010. "Shelter and Transitional Housing for Transgender Youth." *Journal of Gay & Lesbian Mental Health*, 14, 340–344. doi: 10.1080/19359705.2010.504476.

Zerger, Suzanne, Aaron J. Strehlow, and Adi V. Gundlapalli. 2008. "Homeless Young Adults and Behavioral Health: An Overview." *American Behavioral Science, 51*, 824–841. doi: 10.1177/0002764207311990.

Zlotnick, Cheryl, Tammy Tam, and Marjorie J. Robertson. 2003. "Disaffiliation, Substance Use, and Exiting Homelessness." *Substance Use & Misuse, 38*, 577–599. doi: 0.1081/JA-120017386.

Chapter 17

A Primer on LGBT Immigration Issues

Wallace Swan

Contents

Demographics of Immigration

Based upon the work of Gary Gates elsewhere in this book (see Chapter 1):

> There are more than 900,000 LGBT [lesbian, gay, bisexual, and transgender] foreign-born adults living in the United States. Of that group, an estimated 267,000 are undocumented, immigrant population, representing approximately 2.7% of undocumented adults in the United States. Approximately 637,000 LGBT-identified individuals are among the adult documented immigrant population, representing approximately 2.4% of documented adult immigrants in the United States. Compared to their documented and undocumented counterparts, LGBT immigrants are more likely to be male and are younger … the data provide no information

> about the visa status of individuals that would allow for a determination of what portion of (same-sex couples) might be undocumented. There are an estimated 113,300 foreign-born individuals (naturalized citizens and noncitizens) who are part of a same-sex couple ... An estimated 54,600 of these individuals are not U.S. citizens. Approximately 32,300 same-sex couples are binational (one U.S. citizen and one noncitizen) and 11,700 same-sex couples are comprised of two noncitizens. Nearly 7,000 same-sex couples that include two noncitizens (58%) are raising an estimated 12,400 children under age 18. (Gates, this volume, 15)

Binational Couples

The History

The issue of immigration for lesbian, gay, bisexual, and transgender (LGBT) people has been a perplexing one for many years. Formal and informal immigration practices have led to systematic discrimination against LGBT people from countries other than the United States. The passage of the Defense of Marriage Act made this discrimination even worse: The result was the disruption of LGBT families in many ways that were cruel and heartless. For example, if a heterosexual man fell in love with a woman from another country, and they decided to get married, then if they decided to live in the United States, the woman would automatically become a citizen of the United States. By contrast, if a gay man met another gay man from another country and fell in love, then the gay man from outside the United States would need to go through extremely complex procedures that are designed for single people. A wide variety of procedural issues would then come up.

Current Reality

For many years, the issue of binational couples has been a central issue for LGBT people concerned about immigration. The sad stories of binational couples being torn apart were on the minds of many LGBT people. However, with the repeal of Section 3 of the Defense of Marriage Act (DOMA), occasioned by the decision of the United State Supreme Court in *United States Petitioner v. Edith Schlain Windsor, in her Capacity as Executor of the Estate of Thea Clara Spyer, et al.*, times have changed. As Maya Rupert notes, "The Federal government now recognizes marriage. Immigration law is now based upon 'Place of Celebration' (the place where they got married), as opposed to 'Place of Residence' (where the parties currently live)" (Rupert 2013). The Board of Immigration Appeals (BIA) affirmed this interpretation in *Matter of Zeleniak*, a decision issued less than a month after the *Windsor* decision. The BIA stated explicitly, "'The Supreme Court's ruling in

Windsor has removed section 3 of the DOMA as an impediment to the recognition of lawful same-sex marriages and spouses if the marriage is valid under the laws of the State where it was celebrated.' There is no longer any reason to deny to same-sex couples the protections our immigration laws extend to those who are lawfully married" (Gorenberg 2013, 1).

Unfortunately, even with these changes, LGBT immigrant issues of a major nature still remain. Even in regard to marriage, it is important that the regulations developed in response to the *Windsor* case be put into statutory form, so that they will not be repealed by a future Republican administration.

And, let us look at seven major categories of statuses that are impacted by DOMA:

1. Both partners live in the United States—If both partners were married in a marriage equality state and have domicile in a marriage equality state, then a partner may file for citizenship for their partner in the same way as a different-sex marriage. If the couple lives in a non-marriage-equality state but was married in a marriage-equality state, the citizenship application will be handled the same as a different-sex marriage since the decision is based upon the state of "celebration" not domicile. If the couple was granted a civil union or domestic partnership, the answer is not quite so clear, and the couple would presumably be better off getting married.
2. The immigrants are in lawful immigration status—If the person is in the United States on a nonimmigrant visa (e.g., H1B or L1 visa) and they are married, their partner may file a green card application for them. If the applicant came to the United States on a tourist or student visa that indicated that the person was not coming here with intent to immigrate, then the issue is a bit more foggy: If they were a student and fell in love over an extended period of time, that is one thing; but if they came here on a tourist visa for three weeks and this happened, that is another case.
3. For immigrants who are "out of status"—If a person entered the United States a couple of years ago, and they never left, they can "adjust status" (to green card) since they are a spouse of a United States citizen.
4. If a person entered the United States without a visa and without inspection from Mexico, one might ask whether their spouse can sponsor them for a green card—Generally, if a person entered the United States without inspection, they cannot file for a green card within the United States. They must return to their home country and then apply for the green card through consular processing. But when they leave the United States there will be a bar of from 3 to 10 years because of unlawful presence. One could apply for a provisional waiver from within the United States, but this is a complex process requiring a lawyer.
5. Within a marriage, one partner lives in the United States but the other partner lives in another country because they cannot get a green card—The two partners can file a marriage-based green card application. The U.S. consulate

will interview the person living outside the United States there. If approved and the partner enters the United States, the partner should be a "lawful permanent resident."

6. Both partners live outside the United States because of previous U.S. restrictions—The U.S. citizen must reside in the United States or file intent to reside in the United States. The person should actually intend to live in the United States, if they wish to file an application for lawful permanent residence.
7. Citizen lives in the United States in a marriage-equality state and partner has no green card or visa and cannot marry in their own country—In this case, a fiancé visa application for them should be filed: The couple must marry within 90 days for green card; or get married, then go back to home country, and go through the consular process. If there is no visa, a person could file a fiancé visa application or the persons could be married in a third country. (Human Rights Campaign 2013)

Essentially, a whole series of issues have been somewhat simplified by the U.S. Supreme Court decision, but numerous issues remain.

Remaining Issues

There are many difficult issues that may still be faced by the potential applicant: (1) the issue of marriage may be only one possibly difficult situation to cope with, depending upon the circumstances of the couple; (2) the person may identify as bisexual or transsexual; (3) the applicant does not "appear to be gay"; (4) the person may return to their own country, where they would also contend that it would be dangerous for them to live in their own country, thereby constituting a seeming contradiction; (5) the applicant may have a criminal record; (6) the person may be employed by their own government, while simultaneously contending that it is dangerous to live in their own country, thereby constituting a seeming contradiction; and (7) the person may have dual citizenship and could choose to live in another country that is comfortable with LGBT people; thereby constituting a seeming contradiction (Immigration Equality 2013).

Comprehensive Immigration Reform

Many have wanted comprehensive immigration reform, which would deal with the aforementioned and many other seeming inconsistencies. However, what they have gotten from Congress, as Matthew McClellan (2013) has noted, is a Senate Bill that passed on June 2013 with a 13-year path to citizenship: "(1) It includes border search provisions, (2) It includes a wall, (3) It does not include LGBT people, and (4) the one-year asylum bill causes all kinds of problems. By contrast, the House has twelve different routes to immigration reform. There are 198 people signed onto H.R. 15, but there is a need to have 217. John Boehner is interested in a piecemeal approach."

The issue of asylum is very much alive as well. "Refugees and (asylees) made up 13 percent of all immigrants who obtained legal permanent status in 2012. Whether a person is considered a refugee or an asylee depends on where the person seeking protection was living at the time of the application. Refugees are people who apply from outside the U.S." By contrast, those who seek asylum already are living in the U.S. (Hesson 2013). When a person comes to the United States and claims asylum, they have a one-year period during which they may claim asylum. Many people do not realize this, and as a result they may become at risk for being deported.

Another issue of great importance is that of detention. As McClellan (2013) has noted "what is needed is attention to the issue of *detention*—LGBT people get no legal counsel and as a result the average length of stay is 102 days. This is inhumane. Both HR 15 and the Senate bill deal with this." Sometimes detention is chosen as an option for LGBT people, simply to protect them from other detainees, but when heterosexual detainees are held for a few days in detention and LGBT people are held for a disproportionately long period of time, there is a problem. Maya Rupert (2013) notes, "Detention is one of the most important issues for LGBT people. It sounds legal so it scares people. Asylum resulting from torture leads to detention: There is a huge lack of oversight of ICE (Immigration and Customs Enforcement). LGBT people are put into solitary confinement: They are trying to keep LGBT people (especially 'Trans-women') into a protected situation." According to Congressman Takano (2013), "There is no legal access for detention cases, there is no trial system. Cases are going to an Immigration Judge, and it takes 3–4 years before the cases actually go to the courts."

Another issue of great importance is that of deportation, which has recently received considerable attention. Under President Barak Obama, "2 million people have been deported by President Obama. These people will be left out of the reform" (Takano 2013). [*Editor's note*: Other writers have questioned this number.]

Another issue of importance is that of access to benefits. As Rupert (2013) notes, "LGBT people have lower socio-economic status and higher levels of poverty, as well as health issues. Immigrants are prevented from access to the Affordable Care Act if they are on the (13 year) path to citizenship: We are shooting ourselves in the foot if we do this, because 11 million people will have to use Emergency Rooms as a result of this. They also are not able to work if they are on the path to citizenship."

On the state level, we also see a number of restrictive laws being put into place. In Wisconsin, we see "they (Republicans) have done terrible things to immigrants: (1) They have repealed Tuition Equity—now the applicants must prove graduation from a Wisconsin high school, and must live there for 3 years, (2) They have an Arizona copy-cat law—where people must show their ID card" (Zamarripa 2013).

Finally, we see the damage that is being caused to our Gross Domestic Product by not enacting Comprehensive Immigration Reform, which would deal with these problems. Since there are, according to Representative Zamarripa, "11 million undocumented people, almost 300,000 undocumented LGBT people, and 20–50,000 transgender immigrants—some of whom are kept in solitary for up to 8 months," we have the result that "the Congressional Budget Office estimates that Gross Domestic Product would increase from 3.6% to 4.2% with Immigration Reform. Republicans want this; High Tech and Agricultural industries want this; the U.S. Chamber of Commerce supports this. It will extend the solvency of the Social Security Trust Fund" (Takano 2013). And yet we persist in not solving these problems because of Congressional inaction.

References

Gorenberg, Hayley. 2013. "Carving LGBT Families Out of Immigration Protections: Wrong and Harmful." Lamda Legal, July 19. http://www.lambdalegal.org/blog/carving-lgbt-families-out-of-immigration-protections-is-wrong-and-harmful.

Hesson, Ted. 2013. "Should There Be a One-Year Limit on Asylum Claims?" October 9. http://fusion.net/justice/story/year-time-limit-asylum-claims-15294.

Human Rights Campaign. 2013. "After DOMA, What It Means for You: Immigration." http://www.hrc.org/files/assets/resources/Post-DOMA_FSS_Immigration_v2.pdf.

Immigration Equality. 2013. "Immigration Basics: Thorny Issues in LGBT/H Asylum Cases." http://immigrationequality.org/issues/law-library/lgbth-asylum-manual/thorny-issue

McClellan, Matthew. 2013. "LGBT Issues in U.S. Immigration." Presentation at LGBT Leaders Conference, Denver, Colorado.

Rupert, Maya. 2013. "LGBT Issues in U.S. Immigration." Presentation at LGBT Leaders Conference, Denver, Colorado.

Takano, Mark. 2013. "LGBT Issues in U.S. Immigration." Presentation at LGBT Leaders Conference, Denver, Colorado.

Zamarripa, JoCasta. 2013. "LGBT Issues in U.S. Immigration." Presentation at LGBT Leaders Conference, Denver, Colorado.

Chapter 18

The Need for a National Solution for Our Bipolar Educational System for Lesbian, Gay, Bisexual, and Transgender Students

Tracy Phariss

Contents

Introduction

When a high school teacher is completing a college recommendation for a student, the teacher is often asked what three words best describe this student. What three words sum up the response of the national educational system to gay, lesbian, bisexual, and transgender (LGBT) students? The first two words could be *repulsion* and *nurturance*, according to the Riddle Scale of Homophobia, a psychometric scale (Weintrob 2010). The third word could be *bipolar* (Brauser 2011). It is a diagnosis from the fifth edition of the *Diagnostic and Statistical Manual of Mental Disorders* (*DSM-5*) approved by the American Psychiatric Association (Grohol 2012). *Bipolar* describes the result of the discrepancy between the first two words—and all three words indicate the importance and seriousness of the treatment of LGBT issues in education, for healthy development of our youth and society, regardless of sexual orientation or gender identity and expression.

The United States educational system is influenced by many people including students, their families, their teachers, their local communities, and the society at large, each pulling and pushing their own beliefs and ideas. Each state is responding to the different voices they hear. In some states, LGBT students have extremely high energy levels and feel wonderful about themselves because of the way they are nurtured by their schools. In other states, LGBT students are often in a depressive state because of the way they are rejected by their schools. It is no wonder that the educational system in the United States is bipolar, with emotional highs and lows, when it comes to the treatment of LGBT issues in schools.

The Riddle Scale was created by Dorothy Riddle of Richmond College in 1974 for the American Psychological Association Task Force on Gays and Lesbians (Weintrob 2010). The range of the psychometric scale goes from the most homophobic/heterosexist level of attitude (repulsion) to the eighth term that is the most positive level of attitude (nurturance). Every state can be classified for its handling of LGBT issues in education along this scale: repulsion, pity, tolerance, acceptance, support, admiration, appreciation, and nurturance (Riddle 1974). The inequality of LGBT students' physical, social, and emotional development in United States public schools has resulted from a very distinctive system in which the states either empower or disempower their schools.

Empowerment of LGBT Students

When students are empowered by an educational system, the LGBT students are supported, admired, appreciated, or nurtured (Riddle 1974). Many organizations have tried to classify best practices for positive youth development. For example, the Federal Administration for Children and Families (2001) refers to significant components of positive youth development (Family and Youth Services Bureau, 2001).

Key elements of positive youth development are

- Physical and psychological safety.
- Continual development from childhood to adulthood with increased age-appropriate responsibility and involvement in decision-making.
- Emotional and moral support from adults.
- Personable relationships with peers that reinforce and support healthy attitudes and behaviors.
- Advancement to personhood with developed personal values and citizenship with developed social values and norms.
- Strong bonds with family members, fellow students, and other community members, thus providing an opportunity to contribute and a sense of mattering.
- Situations that provide for the development of new skill building and mastery, thus providing confidence in one's self.

The basis of these elements can be found in many educational settings where the public schools use their privilege and power in a positive way, thus increasing positive youth development. Empowered LGBT students who have experienced the aforementioned elements will enter into adulthood and society well prepared.

To enumerate school district policies and procedures protecting LBGT students, teachers and staff members are creating a variety of ways to support LGBT issues in education. These include the passing of comprehensive and enumerated anti-bullying and nondiscrimination laws at the state and federal level; adopting, implementing, and enforcing enumerated school district policies and procedures protecting LGBT students and teachers; encouraging the establishment of student clubs that support LGBT students (gay–straight alliances); implementing safe school programs; developing inclusive curriculum regarding LGBT people and history; and training school personnel to increase the number of staff members supportive of LGBT individuals and issues (Kosciw et al. 2012).

Enumeration in anti-bullying laws and school district policies generally refers to a list that identifies types of individuals or groups that need to be protected. It also often includes protection based on those characteristics that are actual or just perceived. The wording in enumerated lists protects students based on a student's actual or perceived race, color, national origin, sex, gender, disability, sexual orientation, gender identity or expression, religion, or any other distinguishing characteristics that may be defined by a state or local education agency (Gay, Lesbian, and Straight Education Network 2010, 1).

Even though this inclusive education system would support positive LGBT youth development, the adoption of these elements is often met with resistance and hostility from antigay organizations and community activists. Antigay organizations have falsely stated that an inclusive and safe education system is an attempt by "homosexuals [to] recruit public school children" (Sheldon 2001, 1). "Homosexual recruitment" is a popular cry to stop the "use of tax dollars to fund homosexual recruitment programs in the public schools" (Traditional Values Coalition 2005).

Disempowerment of LGBT Students

When LGBT students are disempowered by an educational system, they are repulsed, pitied, tolerated, or just barely accepted (Riddle 1974). When schools use their privilege and power negatively, they are decreasing youth development. When local communities and some educators use their privilege and power negatively, LGBT students feel the oppression of homophobia and heterosexism. LGBT students experience bullying, harassment, discrimination, intimidation, and violence within states' educational systems when this occurs. Often, LGBT students pull away from things they once enjoyed to a point where it affects them in a negative way. High school seniors are contemplating their future careers, and a young man may be discouraged from thinking about being a ballet dancer; the artist that may give up being an artist. The teenager who loves teaching games to toddlers on the playground may never become a kindergarten teacher.* These experiences disempower all students including LGBT students, and denigrate their mental and physical health (Hines and Krehely 2011).

Disempowered LGBT students are repulsed by the schools because they are seen as strange, sick, crazy, and aversive. Society may influence administrations to be negative, believing, "Anything which will change them to be more normal or a part of the mainstream is justifiable" (Riddle 1974, 1). There are a number of disempowered states that through laws and educational policies force school districts to not respectfully deal with the LGBT students in their care. Mention of homosexuality or LGBT individuals by teachers is prohibited in the classroom unless done in a negative light. Several state laws will not allow affirmation of same-sex relationships by school personnel, as confirmed in January 2014.†

* Author's personal conversations with middle and high school students during 27 years of teaching in a suburban school district.

† Confirmed by reviewing every state's laws and some state's department of education policies on websites.

The Arizona Revised Statues §15-716 (C) states, "No district shall include in its course of study instruction which: 1) Promotes a homosexual life-style. 2) Portrays homosexuality as a positive alternative life-style. 3) Suggests that some methods of sex are safe methods of homosexual sex." Utah Code Annotated 53A-13-101 prohibits the "advocacy of homosexuality." Similarly, South Carolina Code Annotated §59-32-30 (A) (5) "may not include a discussion of alternate sexual lifestyles from heterosexual relationships." Alabama Code § 16-40A-2 (c) 8 goes even further and requires teachers to teach "that homosexuality is not a lifestyle acceptable to the general public and that homosexual conduct is a criminal offense under the laws of the state." This is still on the books even though the United States Supreme Court struck down sodomy laws because they violate the Constitution (*Lawrence v. Texas* 2003). Even the Texas Health and Safety Code §85.007 (b) 2 still requires teachers to teach "that homosexual conduct is not an acceptable lifestyle and is a criminal offense." Eight states have laws that disempower LGBT students by not allowing professional educators to discuss LGBT issues, including sexual health and HIV/AIDS awareness, in a positive light. These eight states (Alabama, Arizona, Louisiana, Mississippi, Oklahoma, South Carolina, Texas, and Utah) disempower LGBT students by not providing accurate, positive information about LGBT people including famous LGBT people throughout history (Gay, Lesbian, and Straight Education Network 2012c).

Illinois is supportive of inclusive anti-bullying measures with laws that protect students based on sexual orientation and gender identity (Hunt 2011). However, even in an empowering state, local school districts with support from the religious community work to ensure that LGBT students remain disempowered. In April 2012, the Erie Community Unit School District in a small northwest Illinois town voted to ban the use of material created by the Gay, Lesbian, and Straight Education Network (GLSEN). The forbidden GLSEN programs include "No Name-Calling Week" and "Ready, Set, Respect!" (Gay, Lesbian, and Straight Education Network 2012a). This curriculum depicted same-sex parents and included anti-LGBT bullying information, which was challenged by a few local Christian church leaders and a small number of community parents. The school board voted 5–2 to ban GLSEN material throughout the school district even though the National Association for the Education of Young Children and the National Association of Elementary School Principals endorse these programs and resources (Gay, Lesbian, and Straight Education Network 2012a).

In an extreme case, the Michigan Senate originally discussed a bill that allowed bullying and harassment of LGBT students if the perpetrator claimed that their actions were rooted in a "sincerely held religious belief or moral conviction" (Hibbard 2011, 1). Their view is that students who are LGBT choose to be that way and being different is definitely immature, and they need to help these unfortunate individuals by *reinforcing normal* behavior (Riddle 1974). After a great outcry, dropping this bill, then creating an improved bill, Michigan's Public Act 451 does prohibit harassment and bullying at school without the exemption. Even with an improved bill, Michigan is still disempowering LGBT youth because the anti-bullying laws do not specifically state sexual orientation or gender identity as categories of protection.

Diversity of State Laws

State laws and school policies that address bullying, harassment, discrimination, intimidation, and violence are supportive tools for creating safe and equitable learning environments for all students. A comprehensive law explicitly enumerates protections, requires educator training, and includes procedures for reporting incidents to school authorities.

As of June 2014, 18 states and the District of Columbia have anti-bullying laws with enumerated categories, including sexual orientation and gender identity.* States that currently include protection based on sexual orientation and gender identity (i.e., with enumerated laws) are Arkansas, California, Colorado, Connecticut, Delaware, Illinois, Iowa, Maine, Maryland, Massachusetts, Minnesota, New Hampshire, New Jersey, New York, North Carolina, Oregon, Rhode Island, Vermont, and Washington (as well as the District of Columbia) (Kosciw et al. 2012; Movement Advancement Project 2012; Stopbullying.gov 2010). One state, Wisconsin, has anti-bullying laws that protect students based on sexual orientation but not gender identity (Stopbullying.gov 2010). Five states contain teacher codes or state department of education regulations that prohibit discrimination based on sexual orientation—Georgia, Hawaii, New Mexico, Pennsylvania, and Utah—which overlaps states with anti-LGBT school laws and states with or without enumeration (Movement Advancement Project 2014).

The Wisconsin Statue §118.46 requires local school boards to adopt an anti-bullying policy and the Wisconsin Department of Public Instruction to create a sample policy. The policy recommended includes sexual orientation and gender identity in its enumeration. Therefore, Wisconsin does not protect students based on sexual orientation and gender identity but does through the Department of Public Instruction. In a different approach, the Delaware Code Annotated Title 14, §4112D—School Bullying Prevention does not enumerate who is protected but does require the investigating of bullying based on "the target's race, age, marital status, creed religion, color, sex, disability, sexual orientation, gender identity or expressions, or national origin." Two states contain teacher codes or state department of education regulations that prohibit discrimination based on sexual orientation—Hawaii and Delaware and five states Georgia, New Mexico, Pennsylvania, Utah, and West Virginia prohibit discrimination based on sexual

* Confirmed by reviewing every state's laws and some state's department of education policies on websites.

orientation and gender identity—which overlaps states with anti-LGBT school laws and states with or without enumeration (Movement Advancement Project 2014).

States with anti-bullying laws that are without enumeration categories are Alabama, Alaska, Arizona, Florida, Georgia, Hawaii, Idaho, Indiana, Kansas, Kentucky, Louisiana, Michigan, Mississippi, Missouri, Nebraska, Nevada, New Mexico, North Dakota, Ohio, Oklahoma, Pennsylvania, South Carolina, South Dakota, Tennessee, Texas, Utah, Virginia, West Virginia, and Wyoming (Kosciw et al. 2012; Movement Advancement Project 2014; Stopbullying.gov 2010).

In states that do not have enumerated anti-bullying laws, the local school boards can still pass anti-bullying and harassment policies that are enumerated. However, local school districts are not required to approve enumerated policies to cover students, which means that many LGBT students in these states will go without protection. Missouri and South Dakota go further and prohibit individual school districts from having enumerated policies (Gay, Lesbian, and Straight Education Network 2012c).

Forty-nine states have anti-bullying laws in place; only one state does not: Montana. Montana's Office of Instruction recommends a nonenumerated anti-bullying policy based on a 2013 rule for Montana's Standards of Accreditation (Bully Free Montana 2014). The Department of Education acted, since the legislative branch was not able to pass a statewide law (Hunt 2011).

Since 2000, anti-bullying laws have greatly increased in the United States (Cianciotto and Cahill 2012). However, as 31 states do not have enumerated anti-bullying laws, GLSEN is working to safeguard and advance the number of states that do (Gay, Lesbian, and Straight Education Network 2010). GLSEN research has shown that all students with this protection experience less bullying, feel safer overall, and have decreased absenteeism from feeling unsafe; and educators are more likely to intervene in bullying incidents when enumerated laws are in place (Gay, Lesbian, and Straight Education Network 2010). Enumeration is important if the laws are designed to protect all students. Enumeration still protects all students but simply places emphasis on a particular group that research shows is most likely to be bullied or harassed. The enumerated groups are also less likely to be actually protected with the implementation of nonenumerated anti-bullying and harassment laws and policies (Gay, Lesbian, and Straight Education Network 2010). The Supreme Court ruling in 1996, *Romer v. Evans,* recognized that enumerating laws is necessary for equitable implementation. Justice Anthony Kennedy, in his majority opinion, declared that "enumeration is the essential device used to make the duty not to discriminate concrete and to provide guidance for those who must comply (*Romer v. Evans* 517 U.S. 620 (1996))" (Gay, Lesbian, and Straight Education Network 2010, 1).

When states were left to their own devices, they created a variety of statutes that protected LGBT youth through anti-bullying laws that enumerated or not, required educational employee training programs or not, devised a code of ethics for educators or not, gave permission for school districts to enumerate safe school policies or not, included cyberbullying or not, and adopted harassment and intimidation school district policies that enumerated or not.* The state laws and school district policies are complex and quite varied throughout the nation. The LGBT and non-LGBT students meant to be protected by these policies are often left wanting, with the students, parents, guardians, teachers, administrators, and legislators finding it difficult to interpret and enforce these laws and policies. LGBT students will continue to face hostile and inequitable school environments until national laws are passed, implemented, and uniformly enforced in every state.

National Laws to Protect LGBT Students

At the national level, there are three pieces of legislation aimed at eliminating the difference between the empowering and disempowering states. The Safe Schools Improvement Act (SSIA) was first introduced in 2009 and addresses bullying and harassment of LGBT students. The Student Non-Discrimination Act (SNDA) was first introduced in 2011 and addresses discrimination of LGBT students. Each bill would establish uniform treatment for all students throughout the nation (Hunt 2011). During the 112th United States Congress SSIA and SNDA were reintroduced and in 2012, President Obama endorsed the SSIA (Geidner 2012). In 2013, the SSIA and SNDA were incorporated into the bill commonly known as Leave No Child Behind Act; officially named the Strengthening America's Schools Act of 2013 and is the reauthorization of the Elementary and Secondary Education Act of 1965 (Shah 2013).

The SSIA would for the first time establish a federal definition of bullying and protect all students nationwide. Schools and districts that receive federal funding would adopt, implement, and enforce stricter and more uniform anti-bullying policies and codes of conduct that prohibit bullying or harassment on the basis of perceived or actual disability, race, color, religion, national origin, sex, sexual orientation and gender identity. The SSIA would also require states and thus local school districts to document, summarize, and then report data on bullying, harassment, and discrimination to the U.S. Department of Education (Hunt 2011, 6).

SNDA would add sexual orientation and gender identity to the federal education nondiscrimination law and would prohibit discrimination in all school districts that receive federal funds. SNDA also allows individuals to seek monetary damages and court costs if they are successful in a legal action based on discriminatory claims covered by SNDA (Hunt 2011, 6).

Neither bill made it out of committee for a floor vote in either the U.S. Senate or House before the 112th Congress was over in 2012. During the 113th United States Congress, SSIA was reintroduced by Senator Casey on February 28, 2013, and Congresswoman Sanchez on March 14, 2013; SNDA was introduced by Congressman Polis and Congresswoman Ros-Lehtinen on April 18, 2013,

* See Appendix.

and Senator Al Franken on June 4, 2013; and the Strengthening America's Schools Act of 2013 was introduced by Senator Harkin on June 4, 2013. When Congress finally has passed such bills, all schools will be empowering places for all students, regardless of sexual orientation or gender identity/expression.

Regional Difference in the Protection of LGBT Students

Even with the uncertainty of federal intervention, it is important that all public schools be a safe and supportive environment for all students, regardless of sexual orientation and gender identity. Federally funded public schools should be empowering all students for positive youth development even if this might differ from the attitudes of states, local communities, and families. According to the GLSEN 2011 National School Climate Survey, there are great differences in how LGBT students experience life and the school climates in which they are required to live each school day (Kosciw et al. 2012). GLSEN placed students into regions based on the state the respondents were from:

Northeast—*Connecticut*, *<u>Delaware</u>*, *Maine*, *Maryland*, *Massachusetts*, *New Hampshire*, *New Jersey*, *New York*, *<u>Pennsylvania</u>*, *Rhode Island*, *Vermont*, *Washington, DC*
South—Alabama, *Arkansas*, Florida, *<u>Georgia</u>*, Kentucky, Louisiana, Mississippi, *North Carolina*, South Carolina, Tennessee, Texas, Virginia, *<u>West Virginia</u>*
Midwest—*Illinois*, Indiana, *Iowa*, Kansas, Michigan, *Minnesota*, Missouri, Nebraska, North Dakota, Ohio, Oklahoma, South Dakota, Wisconsin, Wyoming
West—Alaska, Arizona, *California*, *Colorado*, *<u>Hawaii</u>*, Idaho, **Montana**, Nevada, *<u>New Mexico</u>*, *Oregon*, *<u>Utah</u>*, *Washington*[*]

There are 23 states in the West and Northeast and 27 states in the South and Midwest, according to GLSEN's regions. Eighteen states of West (7) and Northeast (11) states have inclusive anti-bullying laws, policies, or codes (18/23 = 78%), whereas only seven states in South (4) and Midwest (3) protect LGBT students (7/27 = 26%). In general, the GLSEN 2011 survey shows that students in the Northeast and the West have access to positive LGBT resources and support, and thus LGBT students in these regions have been shown to experience less frequent victimization by bullying, harassment, intimidation, discrimination, and violence. Students in the South and Midwest are less likely to have access to positive LGBT resources and thus have higher frequency of victimization and hearing antigay

* *Italics*, state anti-bullying laws for sexual orientation and gender identity; *<u>italics and underlined</u>*, statewide teacher codes or department of education regulations; normal typeface, anti-bullying laws without enumeration; **bold**, no anti-bullying laws.

bullying remarks (Kosciw et al. 2012). Previous research indicates that the South and Midwest are probably more conservative than the West and Northeast (Lindhorst 1997; Swank, Frost, and Fahs 2012). The victimization of LGBT youth in disempowered states is directly correlated with a negative impact on the LGBT youth development: lower educational aspirations, lower grades, and higher absenteeism rate because the schools lack LGBT resources and support (Kosciw et al. 2012).

The GLSEN 2011 National School Climate Survey showed that school settings in the South and Midwest may pose significant obstacles for positive LGBT youth development (Kosciw et al. 2012). At the end of 2012, GLSEN also released a report about the experiences of LGBT students in rural and small town schools. These students are generally the most physically isolated but also isolated in terms of positive LGBT resources and support (Palmer, Kosciw, and Bartkieqicz 2012). Opposition to education including LGBT issues has been the strongest in states with large rural populations and in the South. "A Tennessee high school senior, Morgan Yeager stated, 'As bad as bullying can be at all schools, it seems to be amplified in the South and magnified in rural communities'" (Gay, Lesbian, and Straight Education Network 2012d).

Ensuring All LGBT Students Are Empowered

Because of this difference in how the empowering and disempowering states deal with LGBT issues in education, it is best to target education and advocacy efforts in rural locations in the South and Midwest; or even better, pass the inclusive Strengthening America's Schools Act. The resources needed to change the school cultures and practices are student clubs like gay–straight alliances, inclusive curriculum, supportive teachers and staff members, comprehensive anti-bullying and harassment policies with enforcement, and community education. These resources change the school culture and improve LGBT youth development by leading to higher self-esteem, lower depression, higher grades, less victimization, greater attachment to school, higher educational aspirations, increased likelihood of enrollment in postsecondary education, more accepting peers, lower frequency of hearing antigay remarks and negative remarks about gender expression, and better psychological well-being (Kosciw et al. 2012). Educators, attorneys, the Office of Civil Rights and the Department of Education will need to continue their work to enforce the Equal Protection Clause, the First Amendment, Title IX, and the Equal Access Act.

Action at the Federal Level

The Equal Access Act ensures that students have the right to form student clubs like gay–straight alliances in support of LGBT issues in public schools. On June 14, 2011, Secretary of Education Arne Duncan sent a letter to colleagues throughout the United States to help stop the harassment and bullying of LGBT students (Duncan 2011). He cited the 1984 Equal Access Act as it applies to equal treatment of student-initiated groups that address issues relating to LGBT students and matters involving sexual orientation. Student-initiated noncurricular clubs that support LGBT issues in education (gay–straight alliances) have been shown to have the general effect in reducing all bullying and harassment of all students, not just LGBT students (Kosciw et al. 2012).

Title IX of the Educational Amendment of 1972 (20 U.S. Constitution §1681) does not specifically mention sexual orientation or gender identity/expression. It does, however, protect all students from sexual harassment. A student may have a Title IX claim if (1) a student can show that the harassment is based on their actual or perceived sexual orientation and (2) if there is same-sex sexual harassment or harassment because of student's gender nonconformity. As an example, a student who is harassed for not dressing or acting according to the stereotypical gender-based expectations of their classmates could seek a Title IX claim (U.S. Department of Education 2012).

The First Amendment to the United States Constitution protects LGBT youth by ensuring students can express their identity in words or clothing, wear clothing that matches their gender identity, and access age-appropriate LGBT websites using school district computers with filtering software. There are limits on items that substantially disrupt the education of others or contain language that is lewd, vulgar, obscene, or threatening (Fisher 2012).

The Equal Protection Clause of the Fourteenth Amendment to the U.S. Constitution (§ 1983) requires schools to protect *all* students from harassment and discrimination if they protect *any* students. The student's right to equal protection is often utilized in lawsuits when schools fail to protect LGBT students. Schools must also treat transgender students as they would treat students of the same gender identity as that expressed by the transgender student (Fisher and Kennedy 2012).

Organizations working to change disempowering states into empowering states need to focus on halting the negative effects (using lawsuits against school districts), and work to ensure that students in rural or the Southern states receive an equitable and safe education. A number of national organizations are currently working and they need to continue to work together to pass national laws:

American Civil Liberties Union, ACLU
Children of Lesbians and Gays Everywhere, COLAGE
Gay and Lesbian Advocates and Defenders, GLAD
Gay, Lesbian, and Straight Education Network, GLSEN
Gay–Straight Alliance Network, GSA Network
Human Rights Campaign, HRC
Lambda Legal
Matthew Shepard Foundation

National Center for Transgender Equality
National Center of Lesbian Rights
National Gay and Lesbian Task Force, NGLTF
National Youth Advocacy Coalition, NYAC
Parents, Families, and Friends of Lesbians and Gays
Safe Schools Coalition

A multiprong approach is best. Organizations need to work to ensure that the current laws and policies are implemented and enforced equitably throughout the state. While pursuing the passage of national laws, organizations need to continue their present missions of supporting LGBT issues in education, and for individual students and their families.

Action at the State Level

As of June 2014, in only seven states are students protected on the basis of their connection with a person in a enumerated group, like having a gay parent, being friends with an out LGBT student, or having a family with same-sex parents: California, Connecticut, Illinois, Iowa, Massachusetts, North Carolina, Vermont, and the District of Columbia (Movement Advancement Project 2014). In other states, LGBT parents and students with LGBT parents both report negative experiences with schools. LGBT parents often face hostility from students, parents, and even staff members of the school their child attends. In extreme cases, LGBT parents were questioned about their parenting skills based solely on their LGBT identities (Kosciw and Diaz 2008). Students with LGBT parents may face bullying and discrimination based on their own perceived sexual orientation as well as their parents' LGBT status. According to one study, about 25% of the students felt unsafe at school because of the LGBT status of their family and 15% of the students heard negative comments about their parents (Kosciw and Diaz 2008). This is one area of protection that should be expanded especially in states that already have inclusive anti-bully, harassment, or nondiscrimination laws.

California social science curriculum is required to present positive and factual information about the LGBT civil rights movement and includes the economic, political, and social contributions of LGBT people and persons with disabilities into existing lessons. Since 2011 California's Fair, Inclusive, and Respectful (FAIR) Education Act also prohibits the adoption of all textbooks and other instructional material that discriminates. California schools are further prohibited from sponsoring negative activities based on race, ethnicity, nationality, sexual orientation, religion, gender, and disability (Burdge 2012). Schools that have supportive LGBT issues in the curriculum are less likely to have LGBT students miss school, have a greater sense of personal relationship to the school and school personnel, and report less bullying and harassment based on sexual orientation and gender identity or expression (Kosciw et al. 2012).

For the first time since 2005, the GLSEN National School Climate Survey has shown an increase in positive youth development with downward trend in LGBT student bullying and harassment, which can be correlated to the number of states that have created safer and more affirming learning environments for all students (Kosciw 2012). It is important to continue an upward trend of positive youth development at the state level by passing comprehensive anti-bullying, harassment, and nondiscrimination laws.

Action at the School Level

Individuals and organizations working at the federal and state levels need to also work with local school districts and individual schools if the state and federal legislators do not act to protect all students in their care. An individual school (except in Missouri and South Dakota) can adopt, implement, and enforce inclusive anti-bullying, harassment, and nondiscrimination polices that enumerate sexual orientation, gender identity, and gender expression (Gay, Lesbian, and Straight Education Network 2012c).

School policies and practices need to promote positive youth development so that all students have the opportunity to learn and succeed in school. School policies and especially individual educators' practices should not discriminate against LGBT students as to dress codes, school dances, gay–straight alliances, sex education classes, inclusive curricula, library books and resources, and access to accurate and age-appropriate information on school computers.

Conclusion

For educators, personal beliefs or feelings about sexual orientation, gender identity, or gender expression must not override their moral obligation to support positive youth development of all students. Regardless of their personal beliefs or feelings, educators must work to ensure all students are treated equitably in a safe and supportive environment. If an educator becomes aware of a bullying, harassment, intimidation, or discrimination, they must take action since every LGBT student has a fundamental right to expression and equality in a safe and supportive school environment.

In the United States, moving beyond school safety to nurturing all, including LGBT students, is gradually becoming a societal norm. Nurturance assumes the "differences in people are indispensable in society" (Riddle 1974). People at this level of attitude view these differences with "genuine affection and delight, and are willing to be advocates of those differences" (Riddle 1974). Nurturers empower LGBT youth to ensure they have positive physical, social, and emotional development in the United States' schools, with the results of better academic achievement as well, and are sure that to accomplish this will improve society in the long run.

Appendix: Individual State Statutes and Codes

Web links checked: June 6, 2013
Keyword search: bullying, harassment, sexual orientation, gender identity, gender expression

Alabama: http://alisondb.legislature.state.al.us/acas/ACASLoginie.asp
Arizona: http://www.azleg.gov/ArizonaRevisedStatutes.asp
Arkansas: http://www.arkleg.state.ar.us/SearchCenter/Pages/historicalbil.aspx
California: http://www.legislature.ca.gov/research_and_publications/laws_and_constitution/laws_and_constitution.html
Colorado: http://www.lexisnexis.com/hottopics/colorado/
Connecticut: http://search.cga.state.ct.us/dtsearch_pub_statutes.html
Delaware: http://delcode.delaware.gov/
District of Columbia: http://www.lexisnexis.com/hottopics/dccode/
Florida: http://www.leg.state.fl.us/Statutes/index.cfm?Submenu=2&Tab=statutes&CFID=297707254&CFTOKEN=33430925
Georgia: http://www.lexisnexis.com/hottopics/gacode/Default.asp
Georgia: Code of Ethics for Educators: http://www.gapsc.com/Ethics/CodeOfEthics.aspx
Hawaii: http://www.capitol.hawaii.gov/
Hawaii: Teachers Standards Board http://www.htsb.org/
Idaho: http://legislature.idaho.gov/idstat/TOC/IDStatutesTOC.htm
Illinois: http://www.ilga.gov/legislation/ilcs/ilcs.asp
Indiana: http://www.in.gov/legislative/index.htm
Iowa: http://search.legis.state.ia.us/nxt/gateway.dll/ic?f=templates&fn=default.htm
Kansas: http://www.kslegislature.org/li/b2013_14/statute/
Kentucky: http://www.lrc.ky.gov/statrev/frontpg.htm
Louisiana: http://www.legis.la.gov/legis/lawsearch.aspx
Maine: http://www.mainelegislature.org/legis/statutes/search.htm
Maryland: http://www.lexisnexis.com/hottopics/mdcode/
Massachusetts: https://malegislature.gov/Laws/GeneralLaws/Search
Michigan: http://www.legislature.mi.gov/(S(r0oz0155otrvwi55snlzcdnj))/mileg.aspx?page=chapterindex
Minnesota: https://www.revisor.mn.gov/statutes/
Mississippi: http://www.lexisnexis.com/hottopics/mscode/
Missouri: http://www.moga.mo.gov/
Montana: http://data.opi.mt.gov/bills/mca_toc/index.htm
Nebraska: http://nebraskalegislature.gov/laws/laws.php
Nevada: http://search.leg.state.nv.us/NRS/NRS.html
New Hampshire: http://www.gencourt.state.nh.us/rsa/html/indexes/default.html
New Jersey: http://www.njleg.state.nj.us/
New Mexico: http://public.nmcompcomm.us/nmpublic/gateway.dll/?f=templates&fn=default.htm
New Mexico: Code of Ethical Responsibility: http://www.nmcpr.state.nm.us/nmac/parts/title06/06.060.0009.htm
New York: http://public.leginfo.state.ny.us/menugetf.cgi?COMMONQUERY=LAWS
North Carolina: http://www.ncleg.net/gascripts/statutes/Statutes.asp
North Dakota: http://www.legis.nd.gov/general-information/north-dakota-century-code

Ohio: http://codes.ohio.gov/orc/
Oklahoma: http://www.oklegislature.gov/
Oregon: http://www.leg.state.or.us/ors/
Pennsylvania: http://www.pacode.com/secure/search.asp
Pennsylvania: Code of Professional Practice/Conduct: http://www.pacode.com/secure/data/022/chapter235/chap235toc.html
Rhode Island: http://webserver.rilin.state.ri.us/Statutes/
South Carolina: http://www.scstatehouse.gov/query.php?search=FIRST&searchtext=&category=CODEOFREGS
South Dakota: http://legis.state.sd.us/statutes/StatutesTextSearch.aspx
Tennessee: http://www.lexisnexis.com/hottopics/tncode/
Texas: http://www.statutes.legis.state.tx.us/Search.aspx
Utah: http://le.utah.gov/UtahCode/title.jsp
Utah: Utah's Educator Standards: http://www.rules.utah.gov/publicat/code/r277/r277-515.htm
Vermont: http://www.leg.state.vt.us/statutes/statutetextsearch.cfm
Virginia: http://leg1.state.va.us/000/src.htm
Washington: http://apps.leg.wa.gov/rcw/
West Virginia: http://www.legis.state.wv.us/WVCODE/Code.cfm
Wisconsin: http://legis.wisconsin.gov/rsb/stats.html
Wyoming: http://legisweb.state.wy.us/statutes/statutes.aspx

References

Administration for Children and Families. 2001. "Positive Youth Development." Family and Youth Services Bureau. Accessed June 6, 2013, http://www.acf.hhs.gov/programs/fysb/positive-youth-development.

Brauser, Deborah. 2011. "Criteria Changes for Bipolar Disorder Proposed for *DSM-5*." 9th International Conference on Bipolar Disorder. University of Pittsburgh School of Medicine, Pennsylvania.

"Bully Free Montana." *Montana Office of Public Instruction.* May 13, 2014. Accessed June 7, 2014, http://opi.mt.gov/Programs/TitlePrgms/SafeSchools/bully.html.

Burdge, H., K. Sinclair, C. Laub, and S. T. Russell. 2012. "Lessons That Matter: LGBTQ Inclusivity and School Safety." Research Brief No. 14. San Francisco, CA: Gay Straight Alliance Network and California Safe Schools Coalition.

Cianciotto, Jason, and Sean Cahill. 2012. *LBGT Youth in America's Schools.* Ann Arbor, MI: University of Michigan Press.

Duncan, Arne. 2011. "Key Policy Letter from the Education Secretary and Deputy Secretary." U.S. Department of Education, June 14. Accessed Novermber 27, 2012, http://www2.ed.gov/policy/elsec/guid/secletter/110607.html.

Fisher, S. F., and Kelly S. Kennedy. 2012. *Responsive School Practices to Support Lesbian, Gay, Bisexual, Transgender, and Questioning Students and Families.* New York: Taylor & Francis.

Gay, Lesbian, and Straight Education Network. 2010. "Enumeration: A Tool for Advocates." GLSEN. Accessed June 6, 2013, http://www.glsen.org/binary-data/GLSEN_ATTACHMENTS/file/000/000/754-3.pdf.

Gay, Lesbian, and Straight Education Network. 2012a. "Erie, IL: Reverse the Ban." GLSEN. Accessed Novermber 27, 2012, http://www.glsen.org/binary-data/GLSEN_ATTACHMENTS/file/000/002/2072-1.pdf.

Gay, Lesbian, and Straight Education Network. 2012b. "Model State Anti-bullying & Harassment Legislation." GLSEN. Accessed June 9, 2014, http://glsen.org/download/file/MjK10Q==.

Gay, Lesbian, and Straight Education Network. 2012c. "States with Safe School Laws." GLSEN. Accessed June 9, 2014, http://glsen.org/article/state-maps.

Gay, Lesbian, and Straight Education Network. 2012d. "Strengths and Silences." GLSEN. Accessed June 9, 2014, http://glsen.org/ruralreport.

Geidner, Chris. 2012. "White House Endorses Safe Schools Bill and Student Non-Discrimination Act." *Metroweekly.com,* April 20. Accessed June 6, 2013, http://www.metroweekly.com/poliglot/2012/04/white-house-endorses-safe-schools-bill-and-student.html.

Grohol, John M. 2012. "Final DSM 5 Approved by American Psychiatric Association." *PsychCentral,* December 2. Accessed June 6, 2013, http://psychcentral.com/blog/archives/2012/12/02/final-dsm-5-approved-by-american-psychiatric-association/.

Hibbard, Laura. 2011. "Michigan's Matt's Safe School Law Allows Bullying with Religious, Moral Reasons." *The Huffington Post,* November 4. Accessed June 6, 2013, http://www.huffingtonpost.com/2011/11/04/michigans-matts-safe-schools-law-allows-bullying_n_1076494.html.

Hines, Mark, and Jeff Krehely. 2011. "Comprehensive Federal Approach Needed to Create Safe Schools for All Students." Center for American Progress. Accessed June 6, 2013, http://www.americanprogress.org/issues/lgbt/report/2011/09/08/10240/comprehensive-federal-approach-needed-to-create-safe-schools-for-all-students/.

Hunt, Jerome. 2011. "Bullying Should Not Be a Teenage Rite of Passage" (Issue brief). Center for American Progress.

Kosciw, J. G., and E. M. Diaz. 2008. "Involved, Invisible, Ignored: The Experience of Lesbian, Gay, Bisexual and Transgender Parents and Their Children in Our Nation's K-12 Schools." Gay, Lesbian, and Straight Education Network. Accessed June 6, 2013, http://www.glsen.org/binary-data/GLSEN_ATTACHMENTS/file/000/001/1104-1.pdf.

Kosciw, J. G., Greytak E. A., Bartkiewica, M. J., Boesen, M. J., and Palmer, N. A. 2012. "The 2011 National School Climate Survey: The Experiences of Lesbian, Gay, Bisexual and Transgender Youth in Our Nation's Schools." Gay, Lesbian, and Straight Education Network. Accessed June 6, 2013, http://www.glsen.org/binary-data/GLSEN_ATTACHMENTS/file/000/002/2105-1.pdf.

Lindhorst, Taryn. 1997. "Lesbians and Gay Men in the Country: Practice Implications for Rural Social Workers." In *Rural Gays and Lesbians: Building on the Strength of Communitites,* edited by James D. Smith and Ronald J. Mancoske, 1–11. New York: Harrington Park Press.

Movement Advancement Project. 2014. "Safe Schools Laws." June 6. Accessed June 7, 2014, http://www.lgbtmap.org/equality-maps/safe_school_laws.

Palmer, N. A., J. G Kosciw, and M. J. Bartkieqicz. 2012. "Strengths and Silences: The Experiences of Lesbian, Gay, Bisexual, and Transgender Students in Rural and Small Town Schools." Gay, Lesbian, and Straight Education Network. December 11. Accessed June 6, 2013, http://www.glsen.org/binary-data/GLSEN_ATTACHMENTS/file/000/002/2132-1.pdf.

Riddle, Dorothy. 1974. "Attitudes Towards Differences: The Riddle Scale." Colorado Safe Schools. Accessed June 6, 2013, http://www.coloradosafeschools.org/background/worldriddle.htm.

Shah, Nirvi. "Proposed No Child Left Behind Rewrite Would Protect LGBT Students." *Education Week*. June 5, 2013. Accessed June 11, 2013, http://blogs.edweek.org/edweek/rulesforengagement/2013/06/no_child_left_behind_revision_pushes_specific_protection_for_lgbt_students.html.
Sheldon, Louis P. 2001. "Homosexuals Recruit Public School Children." Special Report 18, Traditional Values Coalition.
Stopbullying.gov. 2010. "Policies & Laws." Accessed November 28, 2012, http://www.stopbullying.gov/laws/index.html.
Swank, Eric, David M. Frost, and Breanne Fahs. 2012. "Rural Location and Exposure to Minority Stress among Sexual Minorities in the United States." *Psychology & Sexuality* *3*(3): 226–243.
Traditional Values Coalition. 2005. "Archived: Let's End Taxpayer Supported Homosexual Recruitment Programs in Public Schools." Internet Archive Wayback Machine. Accessed January 1, 2013, http://www.traditionalvalues.org/modules.php?sid = 103.
U.S. Department of Education. 2012. "Helping to Ensure Equal Access to Education." Report to the President and Secretary of Education, Under Section 203(b)(1) of the Department of Education Organization Act, FY 2009-12, Office of Civil Rights.
U.S. Department of Health & Human Services. 2010. "Stop Bullying." Accessed June 6, 2013, http://www.stopbullying.gov/laws/index.html.
Weintrob, Lori R. 2010. "Staten Island Gay, Lesbian, Bisexual, & Transgender History." Staten Island LGBT Community Center. Accessed June 6, 2013, http:// www.silgbtcenter.org/lgbt-history-timeline.

Chapter 19

Lesbian, Gay, Bisexual, Transgender, Queer, Intersex, and Asexual Support Systems within Higher Education

Michael Grewe

Contents

Introduction

Lesbian, gay, bisexual, transgender, queer, intersex, asexual (LGBTQIA) and allied students, staff, faculty, and alumni learn, teach, live, and exist on college and university campuses across the United States. These individuals make enormous contributions to the academic curriculum, to campus leadership, and to the general culture of every institution of which they are a part. LGBTQIA students, staff, and faculty members deal with many unique challenges, including whether to "come out" and to whom they will choose to disclose their gender or sexual identity; dealing with biphobic, homophobic, and transphobic language and situations from classmates, professors, coworkers, and administrators; and attempting to foster a healthy self-image in a heteronormative and gender conformist world (Sanlo and Espinoza 2012, 477). And the lived realities of LGBTQIA individuals can vary from campus to campus, depending on the policies, the philosophies, the politics, and the culture of an institution. Though LGBTQIA people are part of the fabric of thousands of colleges and universities across the country, many of these institutions make both conscious and unconscious choices to restrict and to impede LGBTQIA individuals' ability to participate fully within classrooms, residence halls, athletics, cocurricular activities, departments, and other facets of campus life.

Over the past ten years, higher education has continued to adapt its response more fully to the needs of LGBTQIA students, resulting in a number of positive changes. A sign of this progress is seen in the way undergraduate admissions departments across the country have taken an interest in recruiting gender and sexual minority students. For example, colleges and universities have noted that students prioritize their decision on where to apply based on whether a campus has an LGBTQIA student organization or a queer-friendly atmosphere (Burleson 2003, 12). As a result, institutions have begun to market themselves specifically to incoming LGBTQIA students and their allies: Pictures of LGBTQIA students and members of LGBTQIA student organizations are featured in promotional materials, and some have attended college fairs that are geared exclusively for LGBTQIA students (Cegler 2012, 20–21). Other colleges and universities have begun to ask applicants to note their "preferred gender identity" on college applications in addition to the female–male binary question that currently exists on the Common Application (Cegler 2012, 20). And in 2012, Iowa State University announced that it would become the first public university in the country to include an optional question asking about prospective students' membership in the LGBT community.* These questions are aimed to identify LGBTQIA populations on specific campuses for programmatic and retention purposes.

Colleges and universities are also entering the public sphere to make political statements in support of the LGBTQIA community. For example, in November 2012, Minnesota voters were asked whether they wanted to approve an amendment that would prohibit same-sex marriage in the state constitution.† In response, the administrations of Augsburg College, Capella University, and Macalester College officially came out against this amendment and joined the coalition working to defeat this ballot initiative.‡ Moreover, student, staff, and faculty senates at other institutions came out against the proposed amendment.§ Thus, higher education is not only implementing strategies to recruit LGBTQIA students, but they are also taking very public stances on controversial political issues to show solidarity with those in their campus communities (and those who potentially could become part of those communities) who identify as LGBTQIA.

By December 2004, there were at least 110 institutions of higher education that had a graduate student or a professional staff person (working at least half time) whose job function included explicitly supporting LGBTQIA students on campus; by December 2012, there were at least an additional 70 campuses that had such a position.¶ Moreover, a number of institutions offer students the opportunity to minor or to concentrate in LGBT or queer studies during their undergraduate or graduate tenures.** These staffed positions and course offerings afford both programmatic support to and academic visibility for LGBTQIA communities at campuses where these are housed. Moreover, these opportunities allow for LGBTQIA and allied individuals to come together as a larger community on campus, both within and outside of the classroom.

* Foley, Ryan J. 2012. "U. Iowa Adds Optional LGBT Question to Application," *Associated Press*, December 12, 2012, accessed December 26, 2012, http://bigstory.ap.org/article/u-iowa-adds-optional-lgbt-questions-application.

† Baran, Madeleine, Sasha Aslanian, and Curtis Gilbert. 2012. "Minnesota Voters Reject Marriage Amendment," *Minnesota Public Radio*, November 7, accessed December 26, 2012, http://minnesota.publicradio.org/display/web/2012/11/06/politics/elex-night-marriage-amendment/.

‡ Rode, Caroline. 2012. "St. Thomas Stands Neutral on Marriage Amendment," *Tommie Media*, October 10, accessed December 26, 2012, http://www.tommiemedia.com/news/st-thomas-stands-neutral-on-marriage-amendment/.

§ Minnesotans United for All Families. "Faculty at St. Olaf College Vote to Oppose Amendment Limiting the Freedom to Marry," accessed December 26, 2012, http://mnunited.org/news/faculty-at-st-olaf-college-vote-to-oppose-amendment-limiting-the-freedom-to-marry.

¶ Consortium of Higher Education LGBT Resource Professionals. "Higher Education LGBT Support Services Map," accessed December 26, 2012, http://www.lgbtcampus.org/lgbt-support-services-map.

** College Equality Index. 2010. "List of Colleges with LGBT Minors," accessed December 26, 2012, http://www.collegeequalityindex.org/list-colleges-lgbt-minors.

The consequences of overt and convert discrimination are many and powerful, including but not limited to harassment, physical violence, sexually transmitted diseases, substance abuse, depression, anxiety, poor academics, and suicidal ideation (Sanlo and Espinoza 2012, 477; Wolff and Himes 2010, 446–454). In spite of these known challenges, the vast majority of institutions offer little to no formal support for or programming about LGBTQIA communities on their campuses. Moreover, LGBTQIA students continue to report feeling isolated and harassed on campus (Goldstein and Davis 2010, 478), with a study finding "20 percent … [fearing] for their physical safety because of their sexual orientation or gender identity" and "most faculty (73 percent), students (74 percent), administrators (81 percent), and staff (73 percent) [describe] their campus climates for LGBT people as homophobic" (Rankin 2005, 19). And a significant number of college administrators have been found to believe that their institutions do little to support LGBTQIA communities (Rankin 2005, 19).

Although *every* institution of higher education has challenges and substantial work to be done in regard to creating a more welcoming, inclusive, and safe campus climate for LGBTQIA students, staff, faculty, and visitors, a divide does exist among campuses that offer support and campuses that do not. Though institutions are sometimes limited in the extent of support or programming they can provide based on structural and financial realities (e.g., lack of on-campus housing, disparities in the number of staff providing student support services, etc.), many institutions intentionally choose not to provide this support in spite of having the resources to do so. And though public institutions are bound to the antidiscrimination laws within their respective jurisdictions, private institutions are allowed and have been given significant constitutional leeway in discriminating against and even expelling individuals who engage in actual or perceived same-sex sexual behaviors or simply identify as part of the LGBTQIA community (Bingham 2007, 273). Furthermore, the tendency to have LGBTQIA-specific staff or programming has been found to be correlated around a number of factors, including an institution's "number of total students," its designation as public or private, and whether the campus is considered to be a "liberal political environment" (Fine 2012, 289). For instance, nearly four out of every five institutions that have practitioners focused on working with LGBTQIA students are located within states* that voted for President Barack Obama in the 2012 United States presidential election.† Generally, many states in the Southern and Central United States have few if any colleges or universities that provide such support staff or services. Thus, a "Great Divide" exists among those institutions that support their LGBTQIA students and those that refuse to do so.

* Consortium of Higher Education LGBT Resource Professionals. 2012. "Higher Education LGBT Support Services Map," accessed December 26, 2012, http://www.lgbtcampus.org/lgbt-support-services-map.

† "Election 2012: Results." 2012. *CNN*, last modified December 10, 2012, accessed December 26, 2012, http://www.cnn.com/election/2012/results/main.

Nondiscrimination Policies

An institution's nondiscrimination statement is a start in determining if a college or university is committed to gender and sexual diversity on its campus. Specifically, the presence or absence of "gender expression," "gender identity," or "sexual orientation" can paint a broad picture of the challenges and opportunities facing the students, staff, and faculty members who identify as part of the LGBTQIA community. Hundreds of colleges and universities across the country incorporate "sexual orientation" as a protected class within their antidiscrimination and equal opportunity employment clauses, including those in states that mandate nondiscrimination within public education, such as Minnesota.* Moreover, in April 2014, 731 colleges and universities included "gender identity" or "gender expression" as protected classes within such policies, including nearly 50 institutions in Minnesota.†

These protections are critical for a number of reasons. First, an antidiscrimination policy that includes "gender expression," "gender identity," and "sexual orientation" enables students, staff, and faculty members to seek redress in cases of "ostracism, harassment, and violence" on account of one's actual or perceived gender or sexual identity (Getz and Kirkley 2006, 859). Individuals can reference such policies—often stated within an institution's student code of conduct, employment manual, or faculty handbook—and seek punitive consequences for any individuals who took part in actions or behaviors that were discriminatory. This ability empowers LGBTQIA individuals and enables them to take control of what may seem to be an uncontrollable situation, particularly if such prejudice is coming from a roommate, a tenured faculty member, or an administrator. Second, it provides much needed employment security for those who work at an institution of higher education (Getz and Kirkley 2006, 859). Finally, such policies hold colleges accountable for creating an atmosphere of inclusion for LGBTQIA people on campus. Instead of simply reacting to bias-related incidents, institutions are concurrently responsible for teaching a curriculum and providing programming that includes voices and experiences of LGBTQIA communities.

The consequences of having no institutional protections against discrimination are profound. In 2005, Rankin found that over half of LGBTQIA-identified college students "concealed their sexual orientation or gender identity to avoid intimidation" (p. 19). In addition, colleges do not necessarily have the legal or political incentive to implement organizational and policy changes that would benefit LGBTQIA individuals on campus. Concerns focusing on the general curriculum, housing, athletic participation, student safety, and much more may not be considered priorities of the college in the absence of a comprehensive antidiscrimination policy.

---

* Minnesota Department of Human Rights. 2012. "MDHR History," accessed December 26, 2012, http://www.humanrights.state.mn.us/about/history.html.

† Campus pride. 2014. "Colleges and Universities with Nondiscrimination Policies that Include Gender Identify/Expression," last modified April 21, 2014, accessed May 8, 2014, http://www.campuspride.org/tpc-nondiscrimination.

Though many public institutions are legally mandated to provide such antidiscrimination protections, many private—and even religious—institutions have also implemented such policies. Augsburg College, a private liberal arts college in Minneapolis affiliated with the Evangelical Lutheran Church in America (ELCA), includes "gender expression," "gender identity," and "sexual orientation" as protected classes within its nondiscrimination statement and additional policies.* These protections were part of a larger effort within the ELCA to create "acceptance and full participation of people of all sexual orientations and gender identities within the Lutheran communion."† In 2009, the Augsburg College Board of Regents officially voted to make Augsburg a "Reconciling in Christ" institution within the ELCA, meaning "[people] of all sexual orientations and gender identities are expected and encouraged to share in the common life of [the] college."‡ In doing so, Augsburg became the second institution of higher education in Minnesota to adopt "gender identity" and "gender expression" as protected classes in its nondiscrimination policy (after the University of Minnesota system).§ Moreover, Augsburg College has shown its commitment to empower students, staff, and faculty members to report bias-related incidents in an easy, streamlined manner: Individuals may report any discriminatory incident that is incurred by any fellow student, staff, faculty member, or on-campus visitor.¶ Individuals may choose to remain anonymous, and administrators—including the coordinator of LGBTQIA Services—will work with students to ensure that appropriate action is taken. Therefore, the existence of antidiscriminatory policies provides a clearer avenue for individuals to report and to seek redress for biphobic, homophobic, and transphobic incidents.

Institutional Support

Many campuses have provided official support by creating certain positions on campus to work specifically with LGBTQIA communities (Beemyn 2007, 42). The first such position was created in 1971 at the University of Michigan–Ann Arbor, followed by Minnesota State University, Mankato in 1977.** These positions can range

* Augsburg College. 2012. "Non-Discrimination Statement," accessed December 26, 2012, http://www.augsburg.edu/discrimination/non-discrimination-statement.

† Reconciling Works. 2012. "Vision, Mission and Values," accessed December 26, 2012, http://www.reconcilingworks.org/reconcilingoworks/about-reconcilingworks/vision-mission-and-values.

‡ Augsburg College. 2012. "Lesbian, Gay, Bisexual, Transgender, Questioning, Intersex, and Asexual Services," accessed December 26, 2012, http://www.augsburg.edu/lgbtqia-services.

§ Transgender Law and Policy Institute. 2012. "Colleges/Universities," last modified November 30, 2012, accessed December 26, 2012, http://www.transgenderlaw.org/college.

¶ Augsburg College. 2012. "Discrimination and Bias Incident Reporting," accessed December 26, 2012, http://www.augsburg.edu/discrimination.

** Consortium of Higher Education LGBT Resource Professionals. 2012. "Higher Education LGBT Support Services Map," accessed December 26, 2012, http://www.lgbtcampus.org/lgbt-support-services-map.

from a part-time graduate student to a full-time professional staff person working in an office designated specifically for LGBTQIA-specific programs and initiatives. These LGBTQIA-focused practitioners can be tasked with a number of varying assignments, including but not limited to alumni relations, campus climate assessment and change, counseling, education and training, human resources advocacy, leadership development and recognition, programming, recruitment, retention, policy and organizational change, and student advising.

Religiously Affiliated Institutions

Though a number of colleges and universities employ such practitioners to work with their LGBTQIA-identified students, the Great Divide results in many institutions lacking in funding, programming, or support for LGBTQIA populations altogether (McEntarfer 2011, 309–331). This deficit in support structures is sometimes very intentional, particularly from religiously affiliated institutions that have no obligation to provide protections for gender and sexual minorities on their campuses (Bingham 2007, 276). Indeed, some colleges and universities go as far as to expel students for engaging in same-sex sexual behaviors or for simply identifying as LGBTQIA: As of 2008, at least seven of these institutions were located in Minnesota (Minnesota GLBTA Campus Alliance 2008).

Moreover, many religiously affiliated campuses are associated with denominations that have been historically and currently known to denounce LGBTQIA individuals. Roman Catholic, Mormon, and Southern Baptist denominations, among many others, have been part of the backbone and grassroots support to fund antiequality campaigns preventing same-sex marriage and nondiscrimination laws.* Thus, many of the campuses that are affiliated with these religious groups can harbor hostile—if not toxic—attitudes toward LGBTQIA individuals from students, staff, faculty, alumni, and administrators. In fact, some college and university administrators have been found to condone anti-LGBTQIA behavior, as "[pursuing] action against such perpetrators" would contradict their beliefs that "homosexuality is immoral" (Wolff and Himes 2010, 448). Moreover, some of these institutions would provide some form of support if it were not for the potential "backlash from students, parents, donors, and alumni [that] could cause problems or (particularly during an economic downturn) financial loss" (McEntarfer 2011, 316). Nevertheless, LGBTQIA students, staff, and faculty members do exist in every facet on life at these campuses, and they face unique challenges in regard to the attitudes harbored by their peers, their professors, their colleagues, and their administrators.

Though many institutions refuse to fund direct programming for and about LGBTQIA communities, some do allow students to organize in the form of

---

* McKinley, Jesse and Kirk Johnson. 2008. "Mormons Tipped Scale in Ban on Gay Marriage," *The New York Times,* November 14, accessed December 26, 2012, http://www.nytimes.com/2008/11/15/us/politics/15marriage.html.

student organizations. Citing freedom of speech and freedom of association, some college administrators permit students to form LGBTQIA student groups, which in turn provide programming to the student body at large, though many "continue to face resistance" by students, staff, and faculty members at these institutions (McEntarfer 2011, 313). For example, before the LGBTQIA Services office was founded at Augsburg College, Queer and Straight in Unity (QSU)—the LGBTQIA student organization on campus—provided general community support for gender and sexual minority students through group meetings, as well as programming in the form of speakers, workshops, and other events. These activities were funded by student activity fee dollars that were directly allocated by the student body senate, rather than through tuition funds that were allocated by the administration.* Despite these programs being offered by student organizations on many campuses, students are left responsible not only for their academic responsibilities and cocurricular activities but also for planning activities and events that, on campuses that provide funding and support for LGBTQIA initiatives, are done by graduate students or paid practitioners. Thus, while student organizations are fundamentally important and needed on college campuses to foster activism and to mobilize the LGBTQIA student population, they cannot and should not be solely responsible for providing support to LGBTQIA students at any institution.

Nevertheless, there are religiously affiliated campuses that house offices or positions that specifically support LGBTQIA students. As of 2012, there are at least 15 such institutions in the United States,† as well as additional ones that offer some form of support, including staff that may dedicate part of their time to LGBTQIA student needs. These positions often are created after some sort of campus climate assessment (which resulted in the founding of the University of Minnesota's GLBTA Programs Office)‡ or even after a student-led demonstration. For example, in 2003, after a number of anti-LGBTQIA incidents occurred at Augsburg College, students there staged a protest by occupying several of the college administration's offices. After hearing student concerns about the hostile campus climate and general lack of support for students, the college decided to establish and to fund the GLBTQIA Student Services office, which opened in the fall of 2004. This office was staffed by one half-time professional and generally focused on advising the college's LGBTQIA student organization and on providing counseling and support to LGBTQIA individuals. In 2006, the office changed its structure and was now staffed by a full-time practitioner (though that staff person had additional responsibilities outside of the LGBTQIA Services office). The office began to offer

* Augsburg College Campus Activities and Orientation. 2013. "2012–2013 Student Groups Handbook." Minneapolis: Augsburg College.

† Consortium of Higher Education LGBT Resource Professionals. 2012. "Higher Education LGBT Support Services Map," accessed December 26, 2012, http://www.lgbtcampus.org/lgbt-support-services-map.

‡ University of Minnesota GLBTA Programs Office. 2012. "History," accessed December 26, 2012, https://diversity.umn.edu/glbta/history.

direct programming and services to students, to provide comprehensive educational workshops and trainings, and to coordinate and to lead committees in order to assess the campus climate for LGBTQIA students.

Thus, work is being done at religiously affiliated colleges across the country to develop LGBTQIA-inclusive policies, practices, and procedures to ensure that all students, staff, faculty, alumni, and visitors are welcomed and affirmed on their respective campuses. Nevertheless, there is much work to be done: Hundreds of campuses across the United States still actively employ discriminatory policies and proactively allow deep-seated biases and prejudices to be harbored against LGBTQIA people.

Creating Community and Identity Development

LGBTQIA students face the "task of trying to resolve the conflict between their sexual and/or gender feelings and societal messages" (Berzon 1992; Zubernis and Snyder 2007, 76). Many students have spent their teenage years wrestling with competing ideas: These individuals have both attempted to develop a "positive [LGBTQIA] identity" and concurrently deal with the stigma associated with those who are gender and sexual minorities in society (Zubernis and Snyder 2007, 76). Thus, entering college may be the first time a student enters a space where they are either free to explore their identity or to meet those who also identify as LGBTQIA. As a result, many college and university campuses now offer specific programs that are aimed at developing the identity of LGBTQIA students (Bilodeau and Renn 2005, 33). One of the ways this is being done is through increased visibility accomplished by creating an intentional community on campus. This community building is done to provide space for those with similar and varying identities to network, to build relationships, and to discover meaning in their shared experiences (Poynter and Washington 2005, 44–46). Research has shown that increased LGBTQIA community visibility is correlated with reduced feelings of loneliness; a dampening of internalized biphobic, homophobic, and transphobic attitudes; and increased self-esteem, particularly around one's gender and sexual identity (Zubernis and Snyder 2007, 76–77). Thus, programming that enables students to reflect on their social identities and bond with others are essential to healthy development.

Support and social groups are examples of such programs. Students are coming out at earlier ages before they enter college: "Recent studies state that the average age at which youth are 'coming out'... is somewhere between 13.5 years and 16 years" in comparison to the 1970s "when the average age of coming out was in the mid-20s, (Cegler 2012, 20; Ryan 2009). However, many students still enter college questioning or coming to terms with their gender identity or sexual orientation, particularly in colleges where LGBTQIA communities are invisible or unsupported (D'Augelli 2006, 209), or where individuals must hide their gender or sexual identity to avoid harassment or violence (Rankin 2005, 19). Thus, such groups can provide an intentional space to develop an LGBTQIA community and to build relationships. These support groups can come in many forms, including "coming out" support groups for students questioning their gender or sexual identities, student organizations that meet weekly and plan common activities, and student activist groups that work to foster change on campus.

Working Across the Great Divide

Despite the existence of the Great Divide, partnerships can and are created among institutions with differing levels of support for LGBTQIA students. For example, five colleges make up the Associated Colleges of the Twin Cities (ACTC): Augsburg College, Hamline University, Macalester College, St. Catherine's University, and the University of St. Thomas.* Four of these institutions are religiously affiliated, and each of these institutions has differing attitudes and varying levels of programming for LGBTQIA students and their allies. However, despite some institutions providing more support than others, all have a limited number of funding and staff support.

Because of these limitations, in 2011, students, staff, and faculty members from all five institutions came together to plan the first ACTC LGBTQIA Student Leadership Retreat. The program was modeled after a similar initiative from the University of Minnesota system.† Varying levels of funding and support were obtained from all five campuses. Goals and participant outcomes were collectively established. A weekend of workshops and activities were planned to help students self-reflect on their multiple identities, foster awareness around gender and sexual equity, and develop leadership and activism skills through a social justice framework. Because of this collaboration, many students were able to attend an event they otherwise could not have if this program had only been developed by a single institution. Furthermore, this partnership allowed for students from all five institutions—all which had unique challenges and opportunities—to develop their own set of skills in which they could then enact and model on their respective campuses. This enabled participants to teach what they learned to fellow students and classmates, as well as to help foster needed change within their institutions.

All-Gender Facilities and Programming

Over the past decade, colleges and universities have been contending with issues around how to include individuals of all gender identities and gender expressions within all campus systems, programming, and curriculum development. Specifically, many of the systems within higher education have been intentionally designed around the female–male gender binary: Athletic programs, restroom and shower facilities, fraternities and sororities, residential spaces, scholarship and

* Associated Colleges of the Twin Cities. 2012. "About ACTC," accessed December 26, 2012, https://sites.google.com/a/actc.mn.org/actc/home/about.

† University of Minnesota, Crookston. 2009. "Crookston Students Attend Leadership Retreat," *2009 Year in Review, 2*(1).

mentor programs, and even some colleges themselves require an individual to identify oneself legally as a woman or as a man. Consequently, for many transgender and gender nonconforming students, navigating these constrained gendered spaces and structures can be confusing, complex, and even hazardous to one's own physical or psychological health and safety. Additionally, research has shown that "[transgender] college students [experience] distress at rates that [are] overwhelmingly higher than those for students with a traditional gender identity (men and women)" (Effrig, Bieschke, and Locke 2011, 154). These realities create barriers and prevent gender nonconforming students from full participation in every level on campus. To meet the changing needs for these students, many institutions have begun to create intentional spaces and programming that are inclusive for individuals of all gender identities and gender expressions.

On-Campus Housing

Students who choose to live within available on-campus housing are greatly impacted by their experiences during their residency within those facilities: "The overall impact upon students living in residence halls is profound in several areas, including involvement and satisfaction; persistence and graduation; and strengthening of values, attitudes, and moral judgment" (Fanucce and Taub 2009, 25–26). Within these residential spaces, students undergo significant development in regard to their gender, sexual, racial, and other social identities, as well as create long-lasting friendships with peers. Moreover, students tend to surround themselves with those who are (1) accepting of them as a person and (2) "similar to oneself" in regard to their identities (Poynter and Washington 2005, 44). However, many students who are gender nonconforming find themselves living within restrictive gendered spaces with which they do not identify, with roommates that are ignorant or even hostile (Getz and Kirkley 2006, 857) toward trans-identified individuals, or residing on a floor that contains a shared gendered restroom in which they feel uncomfortable or unsafe to ever use (Fanucce and Taub 2009, 35). Furthermore, many students—regardless of gender identity or gender expression—are requesting living spaces in which they can room with friends or acquaintances of differing gender identities. Consequently, to meet the inherent safety and residential needs of trans-identified students, as well as the demands of a larger campus populace that wants more freedom around roommate choice, a number of institutions have now begun to offer gender-neutral housing options for their students.

As of April 2014, 149 institutions of higher education in the United States had implemented some form of gender-neutral housing on their campuses.* The types of these all-gender housing facilities vary, and they include but are

* Campus Pride. 2014. "Colleges and Universities that Provide Gender-Inclusive Housing," last modified April 21, 2014, accessed May 8, 2014, http://www.campuspride.org/tpc-gih.

not limited to a single floor that is specifically marketed and geared toward LGBTQIA- and ally-identified students, or entire buildings that are designated as all-gender regardless of the bedroom or bathroom configurations within each unit. Creating these gender-neutral housing options creates potential spaces on campus where students of all gender identities and all gender expressions can feel welcomed, affirmed, and safe, providing opportunities to grow within their own identities. They can develop friendships with other students, and excel at their academics and other cocurricular programs (Beemyn, Curtis, Davis, and Tubbs 2005, 52–54).

Augsburg College, for example, has been moving in the direction of providing more comprehensive gender-neutral housing facilities for its student population. Beginning in the mid-2000s, the college enacted a policy that began to allow trans-identified students to reside on the gendered (female- or male-identified) floor in which they identified. However, if a gendered space was not feasible for a student (particularly if a student felt unsafe or they identified outside the female–male binary, such as "genderqueer") the Department of Residence Life would work with a student to attempt to find other acceptable housing on campus, often within a single room that had its own bathroom space.

Nevertheless, this system, while attempting to be inclusive, was still reactionary and modeled around accommodating the female–male gender binary rather than being proactive and attempting to transform systems to be equitable for individuals of all genders. To address this issue, several students applied to create an LGBTQIA- and ally-specific community living space within the residence halls for the 2010–2011 academic year. The mission of this floor would be to create a space where individuals of all gender expressions, gender identities, and sexual orientations could live safely and in community with one another. The students affectionately named the space the "Everybody Loves Everybody," or "ELE," floor. Moreover, the Department of Residence Life also allowed for at least one bed to be on reserve for an incoming first-year or transfer student. In its first year, 16 students lived on the ELE floor. However, existing policies still mandated that students were required to live in an apartment with those of the same gender identity, with some exceptions made.

For its second year, LGBTQIA Services and the Department of Residence Life worked together to craft ELE into a gender-neutral living space. This meant that students could live with anyone they wished, regardless of the bedroom or bathroom configuration of the room. When students were given the opportunity to register for living spaces for the upcoming year, 70 individuals opted to live on the ELE floor. The space proved not only to be successful the following year but also demonstrated the demand by the broader student body for gender-neutral living facilities. As a result, in addition to the ELE floor, two entire residence hall buildings have now been officially designated as gender-neutral housing facilities, with more spaces potentially to follow in upcoming years.

Restrooms

Transgender and gender-nonconforming students, staff, faculty, and visitors often experience discrimination, harassment, and even violence within gendered public restrooms on campus: "Anecdotal and research evidence suggest that transgender people often face verbal and physical assault and risk being questioned or even arrested by the police when they use gender-specific facilities" (Beemyn, Curtis et al. 2005b, 55). Thus, many individuals do not have a safe place on campus simply to use the restroom. As a result, many colleges and universities are taking steps to create more gender-neutral (or unisex) restrooms in their buildings. In 2008, Augsburg College's Queer Issues Committee did a complete inventory of campus restrooms and noted if they were designated as women's, men's, or unisex; if they were single stall or multistall; and if the outside door was lockable. Using this information, the college was able to determine spaces that were easily convertible to gender-neutral facilities: Those that were single stall, gendered, and had lockable doors could simply be converted by changing the signage on the door. Moreover, work is being done within the Queer Issues Committee to identify restrooms in every building that can be converted in the long term, as well as to ensure that any future buildings are designed with these facilities in mind. These specific steps are in accordance with identified best practices around creating gender-neutral restroom facilities on college and university campuses (Beemyn, Domingue, Pettitt, and Smith 2005, 92).

Once such restrooms are created, a significant challenge involves ensuring that students, staff, and faculty members know about these facilities. Such spaces not only benefit transgender and gender nonconforming individuals, but also those with different-gendered children, people with disabilities, and many who prefer privacy when using such a facility. Consequently, many colleges and universities have begun to publish a listing of on-campus gender-neutral restrooms on their websites, including Augsburg College,[*] Hamline University,[†] and the University of Minnesota-Twin Cities.[‡] Moreover, at institutions such as Augsburg, this listing is made available to the larger student body during programs such as first-year and transfer student orientation. With every student, staff, faculty, and visitor having the inherent right to have a safe space to use the restroom, it is imperative that not only gender-neutral restrooms be available but also that these locations are advertised and visible across campus.

---

* Augsburg College. 2012. "All-Gender Restrooms," accessed December 26, 2012, http://www.augsburg.edfu/lgbtqia-services/all-gender-restrooms.

† Hamline University Safe Zone Network. 2012. "LGBTQIA Resources," accessed December 26, 2012, http://www.hamline.edu/offices/misa/safe-zone-resources.html.

‡ University of Minnesota GLBTA Programs Office. 2012. "Gender-Neutral Restrooms Map," accessed December 26, 2012, https://diversity.umn.edu/glbta/restrooms.

Athletics

College-level athletic programs have historically placed a number of barriers for full participation by transgender and gender nonconforming student-athletes. However, that has not stopped many trans-identified athletes from demanding the ability to play on the team of their choice. Kye Allums, a transman student-athlete from George Washington University, transitioned while playing for the college's women's varsity basketball team in 2010. Allums is believed to be the "first Division I college basketball player to compete publicly as a transgender person, although not the first to play as a college athlete."* Because of the need for full inclusion and equal opportunity in the realm of college athletics, and because many institutions of higher education now have nondiscrimination policies that include "gender expression" and "gender identity" as protected classes, many colleges have been calling for guidance on how to move forward.

In 2011, the National Collegiate Athletic Association's (NCAA) Office of Inclusion developed policy and best practice recommendations for colleges and universities in regard to including transgender student-athletes.† In particular, the NCAA recommends that institutions of higher education with athletic programs establish "inclusive non-discrimination and harassment [policies]" that "[include] gender identity and expression" and provide information about a campus' gender equity policies on "all official department documents and web sites."‡ It also calls for all coaches, athletic administrators, and student-athletes to be educated about trans issues, including "transgender [identities], preferred terminology" and "respectful language."§

Despite this move toward gender equity in its best practices guidelines, the NCAA does place official restrictions on who can and cannot play. Specifically, transmen who are undergoing hormonal treatment may play on men's teams but not women's teams (without them being designated as a "mixed team"); conversely, transwomen who are "being treated with testosterone suppression medication" may play on a men's team but cannot play on a women's team until after one full year of treatment (otherwise, the team will be designated as mixed).¶ These restrictions also cross over into playoffs. Because men's teams are never designated as "mixed teams" in this situation, they are always eligible for normal NCAA tournament play; however, women's teams with transmen undergoing testosterone treatment

---

* Thomas, Katie. 2012. "Transgender Man Is on Women's Team," *New York Times*, November 1, accessed December 26, 2012, http://www.nytimes.com/2010/11/02/sports/ncaabasketball/02gender.html.

† NCAA Office of Inclusion. 2011. "NCAA Inclusion of Transgender Student-Athletes." Indianapolis: NCAA, 10–21.

‡ Ibid., 16.

§ Ibid., 16–18.

¶ Ibid., 13.

are not fully eligible.* Thus, the risk remains that college teams may feel compelled to discriminate against trans-identified athletes due to the fear of not being able to participate in championship games or postseason play. Nevertheless, these policy recommendations represent a first step in a positive direction toward gender equity and full inclusion for college-level transgender and gender nonconforming student-athletes.

Transgender student-athlete inclusion not only refers to team participation but also the structure of athletic facilities. Locker rooms are established as gendered spaces, and shower areas may be constructed without private stalls. Consequently, this design creates a number of safety concerns, especially for those who are not out about their transgender identity to other classmates, athletes, or even coaches. Many colleges and universities have begun to look at creating private changing rooms and showering stalls, both makeshift and permanent (Beemyn, Domingue et al. 2005, 92).

Challenges

The Great Divide between campuses with LGBTQIA-specific staff and resources and those that lack them creates an extremely large disparity between gender nonconforming students at different institutions. More often, policy and structural changes toward gender equity in regard to housing facilities, restroom and shower access, and athletic participation come from having vocal advocates on campus. Though these individuals can be and often are students and faculty members, paid professional staff members who officially hold this advocacy role within their job descriptions can be very effective at ensuring that administrators follow through on such institutional changes (Beemyn 2007, 42). However, as previously stated, though these positions have significantly increased over the past two decades, the vast majority of colleges and universities have no such practitioner on campus. Consequently, many institutions of higher education may and do find such organizational and structural changes more difficult to implement, thus making themselves less responsive to the needs and lived experiences of their trans-identified and gender nonconforming students.

Education and Training Initiatives

Over the past two decades, colleges and universities have implemented programs that aim to educate and to empower both LGBTQIA and non-LGBTQIA students, staff, and faculty members to interrupt biphobia, homophobia, and transphobia within classrooms, residence halls, and other spaces on campus. These programs, believed to have started in the early 1990s, were initially coined using the word "safe": Such programs included but were not limited to "Safe Zone,"

* Ibid., 12.

"Safe Space," and "Safe Harbor" (Poynter and Tubbs 2007, 122). Such education and training initiatives have a number of desired outcomes, including but not limited to "improving campus climate, increasing awareness, enhancing conversations around LGBT issues, providing safe space, [and] educating and providing skills to members to confront homophobia, transphobia, biphobia, or heterosexism" (Poynter and Tubbs 2007, 122–123). After going through these trainings, frontline support staff, faculty, and student leaders are expected to have the cultural competency skills necessary to interact effectively with those identifying as gender and sexual minorities.

However, because the concept of "safety" is relative (that is, what is perceived as "safe" by one person may be perceived to be "unsafe" by another), many institutions have moved away from the "safe" model to an "ally" model. An "ally" can refer to "a person who is a member of the 'dominant' or 'majority' group who works to end oppression in [one's] personal and professional life through support of, and as an advocate for, the oppressed population" (Washington and Evans 1991, 195). This paradigm shift has placed responsibility on heterosexual and gender conforming individuals to take responsibility for the power and privileges they have around their identities, as well as leveraging those privileges to make individual and institutional changes on college and university campuses to eliminate systems of biphobia, homophobia, and transphobia.

Thus, in the context of LGBTQIA climate change work, an "ally" can refer to someone who is heterosexual and/or gender conforming who is an advocate for LGBTQIA communities and is working to end heterosexism (the ideology that heterosexuality is "better, more normal, and more natural or morally right than" other sexual orientations [Hodges and Parkes 2005, 10]) and "genderism" (the ideology that individuals must adhere "to traditional expectations based on gender" and "punishing or excluding those who [do not] conform to traditional gender expectations"*). Moreover, research has shown that allies undergo identity development similar to those of other social identities: Goldstein and Davis described the journey allies take to discover their identity, detailing how they saw "LGBT-affirmative attitudes and behaviors" being normalized and were exposed to the "direct or indirect … oppression of others, including LGBT peers and adults" (Goldstein and Davis 2010, 479). Consequently, any education and training initiatives must include a component of self-reflection to help allies see the connection between their identities, their privileges, and systems of gender and sexual oppression.

The "Safe Space" program at Augsburg College began in full earnest in the spring of 2006, which was renamed "Ally Training" in the fall of 2008. Sessions are typically three hours and are open to all students, staff, and faculty members, though some sessions are tailored for specific student groups or campus departments.

* University of California, Berkeley Gender Equity Resource Center. 2012. "Definition of Terms," accessed December 26, 2012, http://geneq.berkeley.edu/lgbt_resources_definition_of_terms.

Participants usually examine the importance of confronting myths and stereotypes against LGBTQIA communities; discuss definitions and terminology; deconstruct models and systems of sex, gender, and sexual orientation; brainstorm heterosexual and gender-conforming privileges; practice responding to various scenarios; and reflect on action items they could be accountable for as an individual, within their spheres of influence (i.e., classmates, friends, coworkers, etc.) and at Augsburg College as a whole. All participants receive a rainbow-colored placard that says "Augsburg College Ally" that they can display in or outside their office or residence hall room. As of 2014, approximately half of all employees and several hundred students at the college have undergone the training in some form.

However, the format and composition of an ally training curriculum can vary campus to campus. Poynter and Tubbs (2007, 126) give a general outline for such a program that includes many of the components stated in the above example as well as (a) suggesting resources for LGBTQIA individuals on campus and (b) leading an "LGBT and Ally Panel" with campus community members of varying identities. Though a lot of information is covered with these trainings, participants begin to gain the tools, knowledge, and resources needed to create positive change to eliminate heterosexist and genderist systems within a college or university.

Worthen found that on-campus education and training initiatives focusing on LGBTQIA communities "may have positive effects on undergraduate student attitudes toward LGBTQ individuals" (Worthen 2011, 369). Moreover, assessment of such programs across the country found that they "increased visibility, improved the environment, [and] improved conversations" for LGBTQIA communities on campus (Poynter and Tubbs 2007, 129). Consequently, to gauge any progression of changed attitudes or new knowledge learned by participants (Yorke 1998, 106), evaluation must be an essential component of any safe space or ally training program. This is important for accountability reasons (Yorke 1998, 105): It not only holds the training's facilitators accountable to the curriculum's outcomes but also holds the administration accountable for ensuring that quality training reaches new areas and departments on campus. Moreover, evaluation can demonstrate that the intended training outcomes (e.g., increased awareness, learned skills to confront oppressive situations, knowledge of definitions and terminology, etc.) are, in fact, occurring.

Campus Climate Change: An Example

The Minnesota GLBTA Campus Alliance, founded in 2006, "strives to build a statewide network of individuals and organizations working ... [to] create welcoming, affirming, and safe environments on college and university campuses throughout the state of Minnesota."* This network included students, staff, faculty, alumni, and community members who were unaffiliated with a campus from across the state.

* Minnesota GLBTA Campus Alliance. "About the Minnesota GLBTA Campus Alliance," accessed December 26, 2012, http://www.mncampusalliance.org/about.php.

Some of these members were coming from campuses that had offices, professional staff, student organizations, faculty allies, and student leaders that were resourced, funded, and supported by their respective institutions. Moreover, many of the members came from campuses that had little to no such resources or support. An institution's size, geographic location, and status often determined whether such resources existed at a particular college or university, exacerbating the Great Divide between various campuses (Fine 2012, 289). As a consequence, the Minnesota GLBTA Campus Alliance sought to pool various resources from participating offices, student organizations, and members to affect change at all institutions across the state in order to shrink and even eliminate this LGBTQIA support divide between various campuses.

One of the organization's major initiatives included a training and education program. Because the vast majority of colleges and universities in the region did not have self-sustaining LGBTQIA training programs, the Minnesota GLBTA Campus Alliance decided to offer its own curriculum to campuses across the region. To do this, it combined the existing curriculum from participating institutions with new material developed by members. Furthermore, it began a grassroots, volunteer train-the-trainer program: Those individuals who had previously led LGBTQIA-specific trainings in the past educated students, staff, faculty, alumni, and community members who had never facilitated such a program. These volunteers, in turn, became the educators, and they were asked to train individuals from every type of campus across the state: public and private; religious and secular; four-year, community, and technical.

Many of the institutions that took advantage of this training had never offered *any* LGBTQIA-specific workshops or educational programs to their students, staff, or faculty members. Had the Minnesota GLBTA Campus Alliance not pooled resources together to form such a program, these campuses may not have been given an opportunity to be educated on ways of supporting LGBTQIA communities. Moreover, many institutions invited facilitators back to do additional follow-up programs, including their own train-the-trainer programs, giving students, staff, and faculty members at those respective campuses the opportunity to develop the skills, knowledge, and resources needed to create and to sustain their own LGBTQIA-specific trainings.

Between 2006 and 2010, trainings were completed at 33 different college and university campuses across Minnesota, South Dakota, and Wisconsin, with at least five of these institutions eventually developing ally training programs of their own. Moreover, 30 individuals were trained as either community panelists or trainers of the curriculum, the vast majority of whom had never facilitated such trainings before joining the Minnesota GLBTA Campus Alliance. Thus, this partnership not only provided a medium through which to educate individuals around ways of interrupting biphobia, homophobia, and transphobia on campus, but it also intimately connected students, staff, faculty, alumni, and community members from across the state to develop mentor–mentee relationships that would develop a new generation of LGBTQIA community leaders. Moreover, it bridged the Great Divide between those institutions with and without LGBTQIA-specific resources: Campuses came together to share their resources and ensure that any student, staff, or faculty member could participate in ally training regardless of the institution of which they were a part. Since 2008, similar alliances have formed in other regions to connect different institutions and to pool together resources, including those in North and South Dakota* and Michigan.†

Conclusion

The past decade has seen significant change take place toward full access, participation, and inclusion of LGBTQIA students, staff, and faculty members within higher education. Support services for gender and sexual minority students have increased, training programs for students and employees are growing, and the number of institutions that protect individuals on the basis of gender expression, gender identity, and sexual orientation is increasing monthly. Nevertheless, despite this progress, the evidence of both the existence and the disproportionate size of the Great Divide demonstrates that much more work has to be done. Consequently, college and university administrators must be held accountable for identifying and dismantling barriers that currently prohibit LGBTQIA students, staff, and faculty members from full participation, inclusion, and equity on campus.

Policies, facilities, curricula, and support structures should be reconstructed to provide full access for LGBTQIA students, staff, and faculty members. Making campuses more welcoming, inclusive, and safe for LGBTQIA students must be an inherent priority of an institution's strategic plan. The structure and layout of residence halls, restroom facilities, locker rooms, intramural and varsity sports, and other gendered systems must be scrutinized and redesigned with an emphasis toward complete gender equity. The curriculum must reflect the lived experiences and realities of LGBTQIA individuals, as well as critically analyzing the ways that oppression against gender and sexual minorities hurt not only those communities but also society as a whole. Simply accommodating and reacting as LGBTQIA individuals request services and then demanding change does not eliminate the inherent heterosexism and "genderism" from a campus' policies and organizational systems.

Despite these challenges, the Great Divide between various campuses can be bridged. The Minnesota GLBTA Campus Alliance is an example demonstrating that despite differences in geography, institution size, funding, philosophy,

---

* North Dakota State University. 2012. "Dakota Campus Alliance," accessed December 26, 2012, http://www.ndsu.edu/lgbtq/groups_and_meetings/lgbtq_dakota_campus_alliance.

† Carreras, Jessica. 2008. "Michigan Campus Alliance Works to Connect LGBT Groups from Schools Across the State," *Pride Source*, August 21, accessed December 26, 2012, http://www.pridesource.com/article.html?article=31626.

and identity, students, staff, faculty, alumni, and community members can come together and make meaningful, positive, and sustainable change. Working together, those within higher education can ensure that all lesbian, gay, bisexual, transgender, queer, intersex, and asexual individuals are welcomed, affirmed, and supported on every college and university campus across the United States.

References

Beemyn, Brett. 2007. "Serving the Needs of Transgender College Students." *Journal of Gay and Lesbian Issues in Education, 1*(1), 33–50.

Beemyn, Brett, Billy Curtis, Masen Davis, and Nancy Jean Tubbs. 2005. "Transgender Issues on College Campuses." *New Directions for Student Services,* 111, 49–60.

Beemyn, Brett Genny, Andrea Domingue, Jessica Pettitt, and Todd Smith. 2005. "Suggested Steps to Make Campuses More Trans-Inclusive." *Journal of Gay and Lesbian Issues in Education, 3*(1), 89–94.

Berzon, Betty. 1992. *Positively Gay: New Approaches to Gay and Lesbian Life*. Berkeley, CA: Celestial Arts.

Bilodeau, Brent L., and Kristen A. Renn. 2005. "Analysis of LGBT Identity Development Models and Implications for Practice." *New Directions for Student Services, 111*, 25–39.

Bingham, Tacasha. 2007. "Discrimination in Education: Public Versus Private Universities." *Journal of Law and Education, 36*(2), 273–279.

Burleson, Douglas A. 2003. "Sexual Orientation and College Choice: Considering Campus Climate." *About Campus, 14*(6), 9–14.

Cegler, Tyler D. 2012. "Targeted Recruitment of GLBT Students by Colleges and Universities." *Journal of College Admission, 215*, 18–23.

D'Augelli, Anthony R. 2006. "Coming Out, Visibility, and Creating Change: Empowering Lesbian, Gay, and Bisexual People in a Rural University Community." *American Journal of Community Psychology, 37*(3/4), 203–210.

Effrig, Jessica C., Kathleen J. Bieschke, and Benjamin D. Locke. 2011. "Examining Victimization and Psychological Distress in Transgender College Students." *Journal of College Counseling, 14*(2), 143–157.

Fanucce, Michael L., and Deborah J. Taub. 2009. "The Relationship of Homonegativity to LGBT Students' and Non-LGBT Students' Perceptions of Residence Hall Climate." *The Journal of College and University Student Housing, 36*(2), 25–41.

Fine, Leigh E. 2012. "The Context of Creating Space: Assessing the Likelihood of College LGBT Center Presence." *Journal of College Student Development, 53*(2), 285–299.

Getz, Cheryl, and Evelyn Kirkley. 2006. "Shaking Up the Status Quo: Challenging Intolerance of the Lesbian, Gay and Bisexual Community at a Private Roman Catholic University." *College Student Journal, 40*(4), 857–859.

Goldstein, Susan B., and Denise S. Davis. 2010. "Heterosexual Allies: A Descriptive Profile." *Equity and Excellence in Education, 43*(4), 478–494.

Hodges, Nigel, and Neville Parkes. 2005. "Tackling Homophobia and Heterosexism." *Learning Disability Practice, 8*(3), 10–16.

McEntarfer, Heather Killelea. 2011. "'Not Going Away': Approaches Used by Students, Faculty, and Staff Members to Create Gay-Straight Alliances at Three Religiously Affiliated Universities." *Journal of LGBT Youth, 8*, 309–331.

Minnesota GLBTA Campus Alliance. 2008. *Campus Resource Guide*. Minneapolis, MN: Minnesota GLBTA Campus Alliance.

Poynter, Kerry John and Nancy Jean Tubbs. 2007. "Safe Zones: Creating LGBT Safe Space Ally Programs." *Journal of LGBT Youth, 5*(1), 121–132.

Poynter, Kerry John, and Jamie Washington. 2005. "Multiple Identities: Creating Community on Campus for LGBT Students." *New Directions for Student Services, 111*, 41–47.

Rankin, Susan R. 2005. "Campus Climates for Sexual Minorities." *New Directions for Student Services, 111*, 17–23.

Ryan, Caitlin. 2009. *Supporting Families, Healthy Children: Helping Families with Lesbian, Gay, Bisexual, and Transgender Children*. San Francisco, CA: Marian Wright Edelman Institute, San Francisco State University.

Sanlo, Ronni, and Lily Espinoza. 2012. "Risk and Retention: Are LGBTQ Students Staying in Your Community College?" *Community College Journal of Research and Practice, 36*(7), 475–481.

Washington, Jamie, and Nancy J. Evans. 1991. "Becoming an Ally." In *Beyond Tolerance: Gays, Lesbians, and Bisexuals on Campus*, edited by Nancy J. Evans and Vernon A. Wall, 195–204. Alexandra, VA: American College Personnel Association.

Wolff, Joshua R., and Heather L. Himes. 2010. "Purposeful Exclusion of Sexual Minority Youth in Christian Higher Education: The Implications of Discrimination." *Christian Higher Education, 9*(5), 439–460.

Worthen, Meredith G. F. 2011. "College Student Experiences with an LGBTQ Ally Training Program: A Mixed Methods Study at a University in the Southern United States." *Journal of LGBT Youth, 8*, 332–377.

Yorke, Mantz. 1998. "The Management of Assessment in Higher Education." *Assessment and Evaluation in Higher Education, 23*(2), 101–116.

Zubernis, Lynn, and Matthew Snyder. 2007. "Considerations of Additional Stressors and Developmental Issues for Gay, Lesbian, Bisexual, and Transgender College Students." *Journal of College student Psychotherapy, 22*(1), 75–79.

Chapter 20

Understanding Economic Power Dynamics as a Method to Combat Lesbian, Gay, Bisexual, and Transgender Homicides

Dallas S. Drake

Contents

Introduction

Empowered states help produce wealth through public policies that support diversity as well as a variety of other economic development initiatives. However, there is no evidence supporting an attendant decrease in lesbian, gay, bisexual, and transgender (LGBT) homicide. The impact of wealth and diversity on lethal violence in LGBT communities is unclear at this time. The ability of LGBT people to recover tax dollars through typical legitimate governmental funding streams is still quite limited. This effectively caps the amount of resources available to socially organize an effective response to the problem of violence against LGBT people. Collateral funding and collateral power gradually trickles in, but the change needed to stop the killing is more ideological and intrapsychic. Therefore, the effectiveness of current strategies to prevent or reduce LGBT homicide is limited. Economics are not only of a financial nature but also about relational power dynamics; these dynamics are impacted by the larger economic environment. The class status of LGBT people fosters a situation where violence more easily occurs, thus reinforcing a lower class status.

What Is Known about LGBT Homicide?

To better understand the problem of LGBT homicide and violence, it is first necessary to examine who produces knowledge on this subject and to question how they know what they know. The original experts on the topic should be law enforcement and yet very little of what is known about LGBT homicide comes from the police.

LGBT homicide was once exclusively the purview of the street activists.* They understood antigay killing as part of a larger violence issue, which at times has imbued our understanding with errant information that distorted the picture

* New York Anti-Violence Project. "AVP History," accessed December 28, 2012, http://www.avp.org/about-avp/history.

of LGBT homicide. Homicide is part of a larger constellation of violence and aggression, but what makes homicide unique is the unifying feature that this violence ended in a death. Lethal violence is quite different than nonlethal violence; it trends differently than assaults and the internal dynamics of the killing are often quite remote from other types of crimes (Harries 1997; Harris et al. 2002). Taking a political approach to addressing homicide often leads to observational or cognitive distortions.

Sources of Information

In a perfect world, the police or law enforcement investigators would have been holders of this knowledge. Policing involves the "maintenance of order [which] is an inherently conservative function" of government (Waddington 1999, 297). "The police represent the conservative elements in society. Homosexuality is not seen by them as representing conservative ideals" (Burke 1994, 193). Robert R. Surgenor (2012, 1), a retired detective, describes the police overwhelmingly as "extremely conservative." Due, however, to their position of defending and maintaining society's social norms, police have been predominantly disinterested at the least and openly hostile at the worst toward the LGBT community (Jay 1992; Shilts 1988; Harry 1992). Therefore, the governmental resource (police) most likely to be in a position to help address the issue of LGBT homicide has been predominantly unavailable depending on the jurisdiction. In recent years there are signs this is changing but seemingly at a crawling pace.

The second source of LGBT homicide information comes through academics. These are of the same groups that refused to publish gay information, empirical or otherwise, in journals. The first journal studying gay life was the *Journal of Homosexuality*. It was started in an effort to overcome the gate-keeping discrimination that prevented gay information from being published mainstream. Today, dozens of journals exist that provide outlets for such publication, but the long history of prejudice and discrimination against academics who might undertake gay research has created a chilling effect on this topic. This is especially true for such a conservative landscape of criminological thought—criminal justice.

Much of what is known about LGBT homicide has been learned in the last 10 years. Until this time, there was little empirical data (actual case data) that could be analyzed. Empirical data is currently being collected by the Center for Homicide Research in Minneapolis, Minnesota, where researchers have amassed over 3,000 cases of LGBT homicide. At the center, variables are collected that include a crude measure of the victim's economic status, revealing that the majority of LGBT homicide victims are of low economic status (National Database of LGBT Homicide, 1969–Present). The center has dramatically changed the way research on this community is carried out. Whereas activists routinely only monitor and track LGBT victims, center researchers have overhauled the entire process to capture homicides involving LGBT offenders as well as incidents with only a homosexual or transsexual motive. This purging of activism from the conceptual process has made it possible to perceive other impacts of LGBT homicide not previously known.

Early in the process, researchers at the center rediscovered the previously established knowledge—known since at least the late 1940s—that gay male homicides, of which are the vast majority of LGBT homicides, have a very distinctive character (Drake 2004a). This includes the presence of a nude (24%)* or partially nude (10.9%) male body, either found in a bedroom or sleeping area of the home, but did not appear to be sleeping at the time of the assault. When the homicide occurs in a residence (64.7%), usually an apartment, the body is typically found in the bedroom (57%). There are signs of overkill present (43.5%) with the dominant weapon being a knife (44%). The motor vehicle may be stolen (36%) along with keys and credit cards; however, there is no sign of forced entry (Drake 2004b).

Types of Homicide

The importance of recognizing the paradigm or profile of a gay male homicide or an LGBT homicide is that it frames the action of the homicide into an identifiable pattern (Drake 2004a), thereby pointing toward a narrowing range of possible offenders (Turvey 2003). Lesbian homicides differ, as do transgendered homicides. Transgender homicides are more likely to involve the use of a firearm. Little is known about the differentiation of bisexual homicides from the other types based on theoretical obstacles that have yet to be overcome. As with each of these subtypes, intimate-partner violence is common, though no more so than for their heterosexual counterparts (Drake 2004a).

When speaking of the varying types of homicide, criminologists refer to the clustering characteristics of the homicides as syndromes (Block and Block 1992). Of the many syndromes found in LGBT homicide, a few make up the majority of types. Using data from the National Database of LGBT Homicides† we find that sexual homicide comprises at least 28% of these killings. Shame attacks‡ involve approximately 23%, and intimate-partner homicides comprise 12.8% of

* National Database of LGBT Homicide 1969-Present. Accessed December 17, 2012, Minneapolis, MN: Center for Homicide Research. These percentages are drawn from the National Database unless otherwise marked and were not part of the original report.

† National Database of LGBT Homicide 1969-Present. Accessed December 17, 2012, Minneapolis, MN: Center for Homicide Research.

‡ A shame attack commonly occurs during or after two men have sex for the first, or first few times, and is caused by the breaking of a same-sex taboo. To some degree, it involves a disintegration of a previously composed identity but with the added realization that one possesses an innate and stigmatized homosexual orientation. Subjects become very angry in an effort to neutralize and externalize their own discomfort. The result can be homicidal.

gay male homicides. Of all types, hate crimes surprisingly only involve 15.8% of LGBT cases. The rest of LGBT homicide is made up of the usual types of violence such as altercations or arguments, gang killings, child homicides, and robbery homicides. It should be noted here that researchers at the Center for Homicide Research agree with other researchers that few true cases of robbery homicide exist. When items are taken from the scene of lethal violence, it is often to cover up a sexual motive (Drake 2004a; Douglas et al. 1992; Geberth 1996, Schleshinger 2004). In some cases, the wallet or other property is simply taken as an afterthought (Loftin 1986; Karmen 2013).

Economics

This brings us to the present issue concerning economics and homicide. What is the relevance of economic factors in LGBT killings? Economics involves the relationship between two or more people that subsequently structures the preceding power dynamic (Nanda and Warms 2004) and perhaps promotes the homicide. As a result, the relationship operates within the homicide to produce the end consequence—an intentional death. Several books have been written on LGBT economics and a dozen or so journal articles have been written on gay male homicide. However, no effort has yet been made to examine the impact of the economic structure on any of the subgroups of LGBT homicides, nor has there been interest in teasing apart the layers that help determine when, where, how, and why an LGBT homicide occurs. On the surface of LGBT homicide we can quickly detect a unique character. LGBT homicides do not look like non-LGBT homicides (Drake 2004a). Power relations between potential actors are highly determined by economic factors and likely contribute to this unique character.

Prevalence of LGBT Homicide

A requisite step to addressing any crime problem is to determine its extent. The frequency of the phenomenon serves to help establish relevance but also frames the topic in a way that is an aid to sense making.

Little has been done to determine prevalence of LGBT homicide. The National Coalition of Anti-Violence Programs (NCAVP) provides an incidence list each year. While this service is important and helps to make a political case for addressing the issue of ideologically motivated homicides, the NCAVP outlines several caveats to using their list for any statistical purpose. According to the NCAVP, "[its] report is not a complete characterization of the incidence of anti-gay violence in the United States. Such a report is perhaps not possible to obtain at this time." Although the NCAVP does address LGBT-on-LGBT violence, it relies on "direct reports of victims" (NCAVP 1999, 5). The NCAVP also "lacks sufficient member organizations and resources to collect data on a truly national scale. Further, even within the NCAVP, the capacity to collect and compile data for inclusion in this report is not uniform" (p. 5). For example, in some years, due to budget cuts, various cities are dropped from the report, while others might be added. The number of cities reporting has varied over the years, thus impacting the counts.

Another attempt at determining prevalence of LGBT homicide victimization began with the establishment of the Minnesota Gay Homicide Study (MGHS), which is now a program of the Center for Homicide Research. While the investigation of the incidents of homicides is still part of an ongoing study, the initial estimate is that 3% of all homicide victims are LGBT (MGHS Database 2000). This of course is dependent on the relationship LGBT homicide has with various other types of homicide at the time. The center has found that particular kinds of homicide drive the overall homicide trend at any particular moment. In this present case, drug and gang homicides were the prevailing types. This means that as drug and gang homicides continue to drop throughout the United States (Beeghley 2003, 131; Blumstein, Rivara, and Rosenfeld 2000), the proportions (as a percent) that are LGBT homicides will increase. It is probable that the U.S. rate of LGBT homicide may reach as high as 10% of all homicides as drug and gang homicides decline.

In the preceding discussion only homicide victimization was discussed. LGBT people are also offenders in homicide. Although focusing on LGBT offending might initially be viewed as antigay, there are good reasons to do so. The study of lethal violence has long held that homicide is the result of an interaction between two parties. The assignment of blame is highly problematic because the outcome of any altercation is often determined by chance. A victim fights back and sometimes becomes an offender. Offenders often base actions more on pressures of the social structure than on individual choice. One such pressure is to only interact with others socially similar to one's own self—other LGBT people. After all, these are the people with whom most conflict is likely to develop. This homogeneous mixture will vary by region of the country and may shift the incidence of homicide type from hate-crime predation to gay-on-gay homicides.

The criteria for including a homicide as LGBT are based on the sexual orientation of either the victim or the offender. Sexual orientation is often a difficult aspect to determine (Drake 2003; Leahy, Francis, and Miller 2004). The Center for Homicide Research uses three criteria in its research. First, sexual orientation can be measured as expressed as one's sexual identity. This requires outward sharing of an individual's self-concept, oftentimes referred to as *coming out*. Second, a person's social sexual history can be assessed. In this way, a person's sexual behavior can be conflated over time to show an overarching or generalized pattern of orientation of affection. Last, sexual behavior engaged in as part of the homicidal event should be considered. Any time evidence of victim nudity exists (along with a probable same-sex offender), explicit same-sex acts are apparent, or behaviors that are part of sexual homicide syndromes are evident (between same-sex participants), a homicide should be labeled LGBT. This relieves some of the burden of having to positively determine sexual orientation, but does little to confirm or exclude a hate-crime motivation.

Demographics

Victims of LGBT homicide are quite varied in their demographics, yet are somewhat similar to how victims of all homicide appear. For instance, the National Database of LGBT Homicide 1969–Present, reveals that of cases where the race is known, 34% of LGBT homicide victims are black or African-American. Nationwide, half of all homicide victims are African-American.* African-American LGBT victimization is likely higher than shown in the National Database because of poor news coverage of black victims in larger urban centers, especially during intense crime waves. In addition, throughout the 1970s, many media organizations changed the way they reported on race, to only include it if directly relevant to the story at hand (Christian, Jacobsen, and Minthorn 2012). As a result, race shows up in federal statistics, but is difficult to assess using open sources such as is available to a nonprofit research center. Only 13% of African-Americans were deemed of low-income status as coded by a trained researcher, compared to 4% assessed as wealthy.†

Prevalence rates in other countries are even more difficult to assess. Britain reports a 1.5% overall rate, but a rate of 2.5% when compared to homicides of adult males (Leahy et al. 2004, ii). Brazil, a "major emerging economy," lays claim to the worst LGBT homicide rate in the world (Jebsen 2012, 1). In 2011 alone, 272 people were murdered, 98 of whom were transgendered. Although no mutual verification has occurred, Brazil's database is substantial and contains "2,998 victims of such killings between 1980 and 2008" (Frayssinet 2012, 1). Possible criticisms of this database include that it is an activist form of research, open to observer bias, and only documents victimization, not offending.

Iraq is another international example where human rights watchers are monitoring LGBT homicide. Advocates say that 678 LGBT murders were documented from 2004 through July 2009 (Institute for War & Peace Reporting [IWPR] 2009). These killings, now referred to as "sexual cleansing" by rights

* Violence Policy Center. 2010. "Black Homicide Victimization in the United States: An Analysis of 2007 Homicide Data." Violence Policy Center, Washington, D.C. This analysis used data from the Federal Bureau of Investigation's Supplemental Homicide Reports, concluding that 49% of all homicides in the United States were of African-Americans.

† National Database of LGBT Homicide 1969–Present. Accessed December 17, 2012, Minneapolis, MN: Center for Homicide Research.

workers (Tatchell 2008), began after a fatwā* was issued by the Grand Ayatollah Ali al-Sistani, an Iraqi Shiite Muslim leader (Ireland 2009). They have also targeted "those who dress in a distinctive, Western-influenced style called 'emo,' which some Iraqis mistakenly associate with homosexuality" (Reuters 2012, 1).† Approximately 4,000 people a year are murdered in Iraq currently (Iraq Body Count 2012a,b), indicating an LGBT homicide rate of 3.4% of the overall homicide count.

In the United States, South Dakota, which falls into the rankings of being a disempowered state, has a very high rate of LGBT homicide (National Database of LGBT Homicide).‡ High homicide in empowered states might have resulted from that state having a large LGBT population center. There is a relatively small openly gay LGBT population in South Dakota, however (Gates and Ost 2004), with few LGBT-specific community organizations.§

South Dakota is termed a frontier rural state, meaning that not only is it rural but most of the population is isolated from core urban centers, which may explain a rural–urban divide (Ciarlo 1997; Crist 1997; Hirsch 2006). A comparison with North Dakota, which is similar in geography and demography, shows this northern neighbor with no elevated rate. For instance, the median income in 2004 was quite similar between the two states (North Dakota $39,594 compared to South Dakota $40,519) (U.S. Census Bureau 2012). Therefore, at least some of the difference in rate of LGBT homicide between states cannot be explained by frontier characteristics or by poverty. One might wonder if things were so bad in North Dakota that perhaps all the sexual minorities fled the region leading to a low or at least a normal rate of antigay killing. This myth however has been partly debunked by Schneider (1997) who maintains that the advent of the HIV/AIDS crisis led many gay men to remain in or return to their rural communities (Verghese 1994).

Gender Differences in LGBT Homicide

Taking a look at gender, women are disproportionately unlikely to be victims of homicide. Seventy-six percent of all victims of homicides are male.¶ Males tend to participate in behaviors that may predispose them to the risk of lethal violence, such as drinking, asserting dominance through masculinity, and by being more competitive and independent. Therefore, lesbian women are less likely to be victimized

---

* A *fatwā* is a religious order or decree based in Islamic law.

† "Emo" is a subculture of youths who can be visually identified due to hair-style, clothing, and mellow dramatic affect.

‡ National Database of LGBT Homicide 1969–Present. Accessed December 17, 2012, Minneapolis, MN: Center for Homicide Research. Data is collected through open-source data collection, which is augmented by official records where possible.

§ Equality South Dakota. Accessed December 18, 2012, http://www.eqsd.org/resources/24-sd.html.

¶ Uniform Crime Reports, Federal Bureau of Investigation, computed over 21 years, 1976–1997.

by homicide in large part due to what is termed a "gender ratio difference" (Drake 2004a; Ellis 2008). This is the difference between males and females in a population or sample. Found in every species on Earth, this disparity between the sexes varies, though in humans the disparity is slight.

Studies of population have consistently shown that the gender-ratio difference between gay men and lesbian women is 2 to 1; this is true of all known studies (Swan and Drake 2004). It should come as no surprise then that few lesbians are victims of homicide. Lesbians are a numerical minority in the population (Black, Gates, Sanders, and Taylor 2000; Ellis 2008), which should always be considered whenever interpreting crime statistics.

Poverty–Homicide Correlates

Poverty's Role in Developing Homicide Offending

Interactions of economics and homicide can be examined in two different ways. These interactions are located, first, at the macro level structural analysis of homicide and, second, by determining how structural features organize individual behavior to incubate and develop homicide offending.

Poverty is perhaps the most widely accepted link to homicide (Beeghley 2003; Reed 1991). Scientists however do not agree to its causal effects (Hannon 2005; O'Connor 2011; Wilson 2011) and empirical evidence remains somewhat inconsistent (Messner and Rosenfeld 1999). This is because poverty is an aggregated correlate that artfully merges a myriad of interacting subvariables such as income, unemployment, inequality, and concentrations of poverty (Hannon 2005).

One of the earliest conceptualizations laying out the link between poverty and crime is Merton's 1938 strain theory. It proposes that poverty leads to social "strain that can push or pressure people to commit acts of lethal violence" (Messner and Rosenfeld 1999, 29). Resource deprivation therefore is cited as an overall cause of this strain and "one of the most important explanatory factors" (Land, McCall, and Cohen 1990). Cohen and Felson (1979), however, think poverty may at times increase homicide and resource deprivation may be viewed differently in America where confusion exists between what is expected and what is actually needed. Poverty, for example, is a major determinant of homicide in some but not all groups. Criminologists Messner and Rosenfeld (1999) maintain that poverty is an explanation of "homicide offending for whites, but not for blacks" (p. 37).

Predation, when considered in the course of homicide, can have a couple of different meanings. First, "predatory murder is committed to gain some material or other advantage, in contrast with killing that appears to be stimulated by powerful emotion" (Rapaport 1991, 370). According to criminologist Donald Black, most crime is not predatory (1983). Cooney laments that although there are no good numbers, he estimates a predatory prevalence range from only 20% to 40% depending on the data source (1998). A different take on predation includes acts "motivated precisely by the desire to make the victim worse off, and [the perpetrator] is willing to expend resources and incur costs to do so" (Gale, Heath, and Ressler 2002, 204). These would include hate crimes but might also ensnare sexual killings where sexual activity or sexual sadism is the primary gain.

Linking poverty to hate crime contains its own problematic dimensions. While an argument could be made that many hate-crime offenders might come from the lower class, only 5% of all homicides are actually considered predatory, that is, not poverty related (Black 1983; Daly and Wilson 1988). Predatory homicide is considered an intentional and premeditated killing (Glaser 1971). Only 5% of homicides are considered to be premeditated (Wolfgang and Ferracutti 1967). Other descriptors, used by Declercq, Willemsen, Audenaert, and Verhaeghe (2012, 60), include: "'proactive', 'attack', 'instrumental', 'cold-blooded', and 'predatory'. These terms describe acts of violence that are more purposeful and controlled and that lack an emotional display."

Homicide happens to the poor in every culture. The value of understanding how poverty and homicide interact is that poverty can tell us where a homicide will occur. Homicides have been occurring in the same areas of our cities in successive years and often in successive decades as well. This geographic regularity can help police and community advocates identify the occurrence of LGBT homicides. An analysis conducted by the Center for Homicide Research of homicides in Minneapolis, Minnesota, over 35 years shows fairly conclusively that LGBT homicides tend to cluster in LGBT neighborhoods (where minority population is the highest) and the cluster of LGBT homicides occur in areas of a city separate from the non-LGBT homicide clusters.

Many neighborhoods in U.S. cities are relatively *homicide free*, whereas other neighborhoods experience much more prevalent homicide rates (Drake 2011; Drake, Proskin, and Crain 2010). These homicide rates are largely determined by poverty. Nearly all states have homicides, though California, Texas, Florida, and New York have the most (Federal Bureau of Investigation, Uniform Crime Reporting Statistics [FBI UCR] 2010). Louisiana, Mississippi, New Mexico, and Maryland were actually the most lethal in 1999 when adjusted by population (Beeghley 2003). Their accompanying economic position out of 50 states is Louisiana 42nd, Mississippi 50th, New Mexico 41st, and Maryland 1st (U.S. Census Bureau 2012). Maryland is skewed by the city of Baltimore, which has a homicide rate of 31.3 per 100,000 compared to statewide rate, which is 6.8 per 100,000 (Disaster Center 2012; Federal Bureau of Investigation [FBI] 2011).

Poverty may also hold important clues as to how homicide can be prevented. Understanding the causes and linkages of homicide facilitates better policy development. The more understandable homicide is, the more preventable it will be.

Much of homicide research focuses on building understanding. Spatial analysis of homicide, whether by state or by neighborhood, is therefore an important part of homicide prevention.

Facilitative Process of Poverty to Create Gay Homicide

One way to view gay homicide is to see it as part of a structural process of homicide promotion through the use of social injustice. As with racial injustice, this is not in most instances a conscious decision to oppress. Instead, it is the promotion of killing, perhaps based more on apathy and dependent on impoverished conditions, socially structured over time, which is highly resistant to change. At first glance, it would be easier to link homicide directly to poverty, but the problem is more complex. Criminologists step in to clarify that homicide and crime are caused more specifically by concentrations of poverty (Hannon 2005; Kubrin and Wietzer 2003), neatly sidestepping the composition of the marginalized class, which is predominantly comprised of racial minorities, immigrants, sexual minorities, and current and former criminals.

Linking homosexuals with poverty is a quick and easy way to devalue homosexuals. For example, rape victims are often devalued in a similar manner. "Blaming the victim of rape was associated with blaming the victim of poverty ... attitudes about the economically disadvantaged were less associated with endorsement of rape myths than were attitudes toward lesbians and gay men" (Stevenson and Medler 1995, 6). Associating homosexuality with dirt or filth in the minds of Americans has also served to link poverty to gayness. Sex has historically been viewed as dirty or polluted (Fischer 2006). John Wesley remarked that cleanliness is next to godliness (Morris and Morris 1988), therefore implying that dirtiness was a "mark of depravity" (Fine and Hallett 2003, 4).

One of the persistent myths of homosexuality has been that in addition to being few in number, they are dirty and poor. Perhaps when evangelicals went to Uganda in 2009 their comments to African tribes that they should cleanse themselves of homosexuality (Gettleman 2011) was an attempt at linking homosexuality to the impoverishment of poor black tribesmen. Ugandan religious leaders wasted no time in promoting legislation authorizing the murder of any homosexual that would not convert to Christianity and renounce their homosexuality and of any family member who would not report and surrender their relative (Alsop 2009). At the same time this characterization served stateside to cast homosexuality as being an uncivilized condition associated with minority blacks.

Interlinkages

Race, class, and gender issues are mutually reinforcing upon one another and therefore a discussion of any single element is not useful. The interlinkage between race and class prejudice (Collins 1990) is part of how class status is strengthened using homophobia. In his book on race and homosexuality, historian Allan Bérubé (2001, 255) outlines how "gay whitening practices" act as a wedge against black gays in America. Ugandans seek to keep Western (interpreted as white) values out of Africa. As a result, homosexuality becomes viewed as a white characteristic and therefore not easily embraced. Uganda is an example of an attempt by American conservatives to use this wedge all the while redirtying homosexuality to the American audience back home without being viewed as explicitly racist.

Some practitioners of religion have long used the poor in the social construction of evil. According to them, the poor and destitute of society results from godlessness, which they assert leads to poverty. Poverty is often characterized in a veiled way as poverty of the spirit (Friend of God 1954; Osteen 2004). In a *Time* magazine poll, "Sixty-one percent of Christians believed God wants us to be prosperous" (Van Biema and Chu 2006, 49). The poor, however, are a sign of failure to believe in God, and thus the solution to poverty and homelessness is intrinsically linked to religious practice. As a result, many homeless shelters, including The Salvation Army, require religious participation in exchange for food and shelter.[*,†]

Linking victimization to godlessness is a form of blaming victims for their own poverty. Throughout the 1800s people were sent to the poorhouse, which was considered very shameful. Once there, inmates[‡] were subjected to corporal punishment, including whipping (Wagner 2005) to "beat the devil out" of them (Nash 1963, 296) or reduce their godlessness (Straus, Gelles, and Steinmetz 1980). This type of treatment is founded on a principle grounded in the Gospel of Prosperity (Bromley and Shupe 1990) wherein prosperity is linked to moral acceptability. At the individual level, homicide is considered immoral, yet at a structural level homicide and crime clustering is found in impoverished areas of cities but not wealthy areas (Paulsen and Robinson 2004; Shaw and McKay 1942).

The impact of this line of thinking is that people do not care much about the poor, especially where they are linked with deviant behaviors such as sex or violence. This is a catch-22 in that LGBT homicide occurs at the intersection of sex, poverty, and violence.

Violence has been identified as a precipitating factor for poverty in at least two kinds of lethal violence: suicide (Hamermesh and Soss 1974) and intimate-partner

---

* See *Intermountain Fair Hous. Council* v. *Boise Rescue Mission Ministries*, 657 F.3d 988 (U.S. App. 2011).

† Salvation Army. 2012. "Program Participation," Accessed December 4, 2012, http://www.salvationarmyusa.org/usn/www_usn_2.nsf/vw-text-dynamic arrays/741C878FA44CC46F8525742C006934A9?openDocument.

‡ Wagner, David. 2005. The Poorhouse: America's Forgotten Institution. Lanham, MD: Rowman & Littlefield. See page 28, where poorhouse residents are rather uniformly referred to as inmates. Poorhouses were the early form of asylums and present day correctional workhouses. Correcting inmates is alleged to have been more popular in the developmental era of the poorhouses but the fact that their facilities evolved into correctional facilities somewhat belies that claim.

homicide (Johnson and Ferraro 2000). The impact of experiencing violent deaths is both emotional as well as financial. Depression following the loss of a loved one can make it difficult to maintain employment or engage in required domestic duties such as paying bills or caring for family members. The direct costs of an unexpected family death include the funeral, burial, and any grief counseling expenses. In neighborhoods where homicide is concentrated, high rates of housing foreclosures and joblessness exist. Poverty and homelessness have previously been identified as a deleterious impact of intimate-partner violence (Johnson and Ferraro 2000; Zorza 1991). LGBT intimate-partner homicides most likely link to poverty in a similar manner.

As has been discussed, poverty has several mutually supporting linkages, and includes the value of constructing a pathway to social exclusion and eventual expulsion. In American society, we have permission to expel and sometimes even kill what we hate or what society devalues (i.e., blacks or gays). This inducement of death is not always a direct pathway. It does not always provide a smoking gun. Nevertheless the result is the same; death can be caused by social injustice of varying kinds, including expulsion, rejection, or social isolation. The attenuation between cause and effect is reminiscent of the Food Wars* used to kill enemy combatants in time of war (Erdkamp 1998; Messer 1990). Once the crops are burned, the people starve to death as if they had been executed with a bullet. Homicide and its accompanying apathy is a consistent and persistent result of poverty and economic injustice.

Religion has a long history of using passive mechanisms to cause death with the exception perhaps of stoning and crucifixion, which are more direct. Excommunication, disowning, and ostracism or shunning have all been used by religionists to expel and isolate their unwanted members. People experiencing this kind of isolation may die by suicide as a result of it having created a "social death" (Jones 2010, 236; Patterson 1982). LGBT people are also victims of homicide, another type of lethal violence where aggression is externalized rather than internalized.

Expelling trash is part of a genocidal narrative that involves the concept of social cleansing (Walling 2000). To expel the *other* is part of a participatory membership ritual used to build solidarity within the empowered group while simultaneously eliminating members of the undesirable group. Economic disempowerment helps communicate a devaluing of the targeted group, while at the same time providing a classist excuse: "They were poor trash anyway." This neatly fits the empowered group's narrative of godless poverty citing "What did they expect?" Clearly society is sending a message that LGBT people—poor people—in our society are expendable and in a subtle way are promoting and excusing when they fall victim to homicide.

---

* *Food Wars* is a term that denotes the strategy of targeting food stores for destruction as a means of starving out the enemy during time of war. It is an efficient means of killing because the enemy need not be located, and it saves much needed ammunition.

Social Control

Police in the United States have routinely engaged in police *sweeps* to clean up homosexuality and the deviance associated with it.* Sometimes journalists substitute the term *raid* when reporting police actions at businesses such as gay bars or adult bathhouses. Sweeps are predominantly outdoor events, while raids take place indoors. Police sweeps are a common response to homicides and crime (Tirellas 1996), especially involving the poor or homeless (Baker 1990) "and are reminiscent of holocaust roundups in Nazi, Germany" (Stoner 1995, 161). A raid refers to an attack, usually engaged in during warfare that is temporary in nature and comes as a surprise to those involved.† The historic report of the attack on the Stonewall Inn, a New York City gay bar, was characterized as a raid although they were quick to sweep people into the paddy wagons. The sweeping action connotes movement of human bodies.

In 1974, the *San Francisco Chronicle* reported that there was "a sweep to clear the Castro Street sidewalks," to which Harvey Milk responded that the only reason for arresting these men was because of their gayness (Stewart-Winter 2009, 14). In 1981, police raided Polk Street in San Francisco in a sweep that apprehended over 400 people. This area was a well-known gay district during this time (Rubin 1999).

Sweeps are a *law & order* form of social control that is rooted in the rigorous enforcement of laws (Beckett 1999). Sweeps and raids send messages to offenders and potential homicide offenders that killing people who are LGBT is excusable because it simply serves to clean up homosexual poverty. Interestingly, this poverty often positions uneducated, heterosexual, working-class youths in the same environment as LGBT youths, where straight thugs can build social status by simply killing a fag. Bragging after the fact can facilitate this status-building component. "Bigotry that lingers in the hearts and minds of many officers, together with unfair laws and discriminatory enforcement of laws, continue to create bad blood between policemen and homosexuals" (Jay 1992, xxxvi). This attitude contributes to LGBT homicide in that it removes capable guardians (Cohen and Felson 1979) from the traditional formula that one might serve to prevent LGBT citizens from antigay and antitranssexual predation.

Structural Evidence

Geographic evidence of the LGBT homicide–poverty connection is the violence associated with gay ghettos across the country. Although a somewhat controversial topic, LGBT people often do live in ghettos (Gluckman and Reed 1997;

* Herdt, Gilbert, ed. 1992. *Gay Culture in America: Essays from the Field*. Boston, MA: Beacon Press. Interestingly, Herdt describes how the development of the gay ghetto internally served a cleansing function to purify LGBT people from the negativity of a heterosexual society and resocialize its residents in a positive way (p. 10).

† Lonsdale, M. V. 1992. *Raids: A Tactical Guide to High Risk Warrant Service*. Los Angeles, CA: Specialized Tactical Training Unit.

Harry 1974; Herdt 1992; Rosenblum 1995) or concentrated gay neighborhoods. In Minneapolis, Minnesota, Loring Neighborhood has been associated with a homosexual population since at least as early as the 1940s. It peaked in the 1970s and has since then been in apparent decline. Sexual minorities clustered in this neighborhood for a number of reasons, though due mostly to similarity of social interests as well as the presence of young, single adults; and sexual cruising in and around the park (Halfhill 1986, 156).

Loring Neighborhood reveals the development of a homicide cluster that is LGBT-centric and does not follow the citywide homicide pattern. Loring Neighborhood is a dangerous place with many beatings and muggings of LGBT people, including murders (Mosedale 2006; Murphy and Urquhart 2010). According to data from the Minnesota Gay Homicide Study, the main LGBT homicide cluster of the city hovers directly over Loring Neighborhood.

The racial and ethnic diversity of Loring Neighborhood is a microcosm of the city. Sexual minority status is somewhat of a unifying status, though racism is well known in the LGBT community (Winegar 1990). The Loring district provided a hub of commercial enterprise in the form of prostitution but was also close to downtown theaters and restaurants, crucial to any impoverished population seeking lower wage employment. African-Americans who are LGBT may have moved into the neighborhood to rub shoulders with a perceived white gayness (Bérubé 2001). Black urban communities have been particularly hard hit by poverty and its incumbent violence, although white poverty may be more rural and hidden. However, moving into the gay ghetto did not turn out to be a protective factor for everyone. Already impoverished African-Americans traded one form of poverty for another.

Another example of a gay ghetto is Dupont Circle in Washington, DC (McChesney 2005). Mapping of homicides by the Center for Homicide Research in 2012 revealed an LGBT homicide cluster including this area. Homicides occurred over the course of 30 years from 1974 to 2004 and occur in nearby neighborhoods of Logan Circle and Shaw as well. Myslik (1996) observed that people who were LGBT were well aware of the district's violence but moved in anyway due to an errant belief that community afforded safety. He points out that "queer spaces are generally perceived as safe havens from this discrimination and violence, but they often serve as destinations of choice for 'gay bashers'" (p. 156). The concentration of LGBT people forms a target-rich environment in which predators attach like parasites (Felson 2006). Dupont Circle is no longer the haven it once was and the LGBT population today continues to disperse into several nearby neighborhoods (Castro 2008).

Wealth and LGBT People

In the 1990s at the height of the AIDS epidemic, there were many attempts by the LGBT community to facilitate acceptance of sexual minorities by characterizing the gay community as financially desirable to corporate advertisers. As corporations were beaten about the head with accusations of AIDS-phobia and employment discrimination, gay activists presented them with an attractive carrot: that LGBT people were an untapped source of revenue.

Marketing rhetoric included all sorts of exaggeration and misinformation (Badgett 2001). In part this served to help non-LGBT people to see the devastation of potential financial markets being brought about by HIV/AIDS. Gay men in particular were promoted as being highly affluent, educated, and brand loyal. This is not entirely true, however, since "overall, the more reliable household income figures suggest that gay households are not more affluent than heterosexual households" (p. 118). Recent incidents involving Target Corporation reveal that brand loyalty only holds so long as there is corporate integrity in alignment with LGBT politics. Target Corporation reportedly made financial contributions to a political candidate who "had praised a Christian rock band that condoned violence toward gays" (Kingser and Schmidt 2012, 28; Stassen-Berger 2010). Target had previously been a corporate sponsor of the Twin Cities Pride Festival. LGBT people are financially conservative when it comes to nonleisure, functional spending and quickly recognized how finances were linked to the promotion of anti-LGBT violence.

Wealth within the LGBT community has its own unique aspects. Bronski (1984) reports that the appearance of wealthiness and the identification of gay men with the upper class was a way to counter prejudice, saying, "The fact is that the upper class excepted themselves, with prestige and money, from the social proscriptions they had invented" (p. 141). Thus we find in gay culture, which spreads to the lesbian, bisexual, and transgender cultures as well, an emphasis on royalty and the *appearance* of wealth and frequent references to goddesses, queens, and high theater (Bronski 1984; Oswald 2003).

It is likely that many in our society have little understanding of finances—what Lucey and Giannangel (2006) call financial literacy. They warn that "in a capitalist society, financial literacy represents a basic life skill" (p. 269). For some LGBT people, the antigay barrier creates a distance between family and self that prevents the passing of financial know-how from parent to child. However, parents are considered the primary financial educators and most of our financial knowledge likely comes from them (Lucey and Guiannangel 2006). For most individuals, financial illiteracy probably has no bearing on sexual orientation but simply mirrors the incompetence of the rest of our society. LGBT people do have unique financial concerns and constraints with differing cultural sensibilities and different material values. What LGBT people want most from their money is political and social independence, as well as what everyone else wants and values. Amassing financial wealth is important to survival but also to ongoing political health of a marginalized and disenfranchised minority.

Wealth, in the form of economic power, is intrinsically linked to and helps build human rights. According to Farmer, "violence against individuals is usually embedded in entrenched 'Structural violence'" (Farmer 1999, 1488; Farmer 2005).

For instance, money helps win court cases by paying for good representation and allows for more expert consultations and witnesses. Money pays for research reports that can serve as foundational evidence to support an argument for rights legislation to be passed. Funds can pay for lobbyists and donations to various campaigns and projects, and can help buy influence with legislators and win passage for their bill or statute. Wealth alters how others view petitioners, and citizens are perceived by representatives of the courts on the basis of how they look and what kind of clothes they wear (Bradshaw n.d.). At a very base level, money can help build the social capital that is so necessary to political organizing.

Economic power affects social participation and membership activities (Schlozman, Verba, and Brady 2012). For example, the production of social events such as golf tournaments or the offering of dining banquets is conducive to education, discussion, political networking, and fundraising. An integral part of participating in these events is the building of social capital by those involved. According to criminologists Messner, Baumer, and Rosenfeld, "social capital facilitates the achievement of collective purposes" (2004, 883) by "greasing the wheels" of social interaction (Putnam 2000, 288).

People are kept out of the cycle of criminality, as defined by the dominant group, through economic responsibilities. It is a form of social control. Higher status people are busy managing their money and serving the community in various ways. Much of criminality is a result of too much free time. While organized leisure activities can provide social control, most leisure time facilitates the development of risk factors that are conducive to crime and therefore crime itself. For this reason, probation and parole functions focus heavily on encouraging school or employment for convicted clients (Simon 1993). The mantra of "get a job, get a job, get a job" is a useful one because employment prevents criminal recidivism (Smith, Bechtel, Patrick, and Smith 2006).

Wealth is necessary for a broad range of issues that can lead to healthier communities. It is required for educating LGBT community members about the political issues and about how best to counter opposing claims. Wealth helps determine where you will live and the degree of mobility you will have to be able to advocate on your own behalf. It impacts your exposure to crime and, perhaps to a lesser degree, the kind and level of police response you might have once a crime occurs.

Accumulation of wealth depends in part on how revenue is trapped within the minority community revenue stream. The means of retaining wealth is somewhat limited in LGBT culture due to antimarriage laws. Marriage is a fundamental vehicle to allow the systematic transfer of wealth (Cain 1991). Finding ways to retain and circulate money within a community is a means of asset building that reduces the slippage of money out to non-LGBT entities. Often LGBT people limit their spending only to gay-friendly businesses, which has spurred the production of LGBT business directories (Biagi and Kern-Foxworth 1997). Another effort has been to prevent the funneling of wealth into perceived antigay or faith-based agencies, such as The Salvation Army,* especially when they potentially benefit from the LGBT poverty resulting from violence and social injustice.

Wealth and LGBT Homicide Victimization

A central issue in the discussion of LGBT homicide victimization and economic power dynamics is whether wealth will actually serve to protect anyone from becoming a victim and, if so, how that will occur. It is important to say here that being wealthy will not necessarily protect you. It seems that a disproportionate number (18.8%) of LGBT homicide victims are wealthy.† Because nearly 16% of LGBT homicide deaths are victims targeted by hate-crime predators, wealth may actually be a strong lure rather than a protective factor. For example, spree-killer Andrew Cunanan purposefully targeted at least two of his five victims who were men of great means including Gianni Versace in Florida (Fisher 1997; Ryan 1997). Wealthy heterosexual people seldom suffer a comparable predation to their homosexual counterparts and even more rarely is that predation based on their heterosexuality.

Although most criminologists likely agree that poverty increases crime, homicide itself is a unique form of crime. Messner and Rosenfeld (1999) propose that although some theories predict that the wealth power dynamic should actually create homicide offending by wealthy actors against the poor, it does not. Society produces few wealthy homicide offenders. Messner and Rosenfeld explain that feminist theory supposes that men aggress against women because they hold all the power. LGBT intimate-partner homicides do showcase liberal examples of women assaulting or killing women (NCAVP Report 2012), which also are problematic to the feminist hypothesis. If power holders cannot help themselves, then why are there not more racist killings of blacks by whites? Why do not wealthy offenders kill the poor? It seems instead that the upper and lower classes are somehow both victimized, leaving the middle mainly untouched. Once again, the answer lies embedded in economic differences.

---

* Blackwell, Christopher W., and Sophia F. Dziegielewski. 2005. "The Privatization of Social Services from Public to Sectarian: Negative Consequences for America's Gays and Lesbians." *Journal of Human Behavior in the Social Environment* 11(2): 25–41. See also Rachel Gordon, 2001. "Salvation Army OKs, Partner Benefits." *San Francisco Chronicle*, Final Edition, November 2, A21. Clearly antigay prejudice, though occasionally moderating, is part of this religious organization. SDGLN Staff. 2012. "America's Shame: 40% of Homeless Youth are LGBT kids." *San Diego Gay Lesbian News*, July 13, accessed, December 26, 2012, http://www.sdgln.com/news/2012/07/13/americas-shame-40-percent-lgbt-youth-homeless. According to the LGBT Homeless Youth Provider Survey, 40% of homeless young people are LGBT.

† National Database of LGBT Homicide 1969-Present. Accessed December 21, 2012, Minneapolis, MN: Center for Homicide Research.

Economics Dynamics of Three Types of LGBT Homicide

Although the foregoing discussions were a bit more overarching, we now turn to inspect the micro level context and dynamics of LGBT homicides. Although many types of homosexual homicides occur, only three main varieties will be considered here. They are intimate-partner homicide, sexual homicide, and hate-crime homicide. The incidence of LGBT homicide is largely accounted for by these three types.

Intimate-partner homicides account for 14% of all homicides in the United States (Catalano 2009, 2). Intimate-partner homicides have been defined as those killings that involve the intentional death of "current or former dating, cohabiting, common-law, and formally married heterosexual couples" (Browne, Williams, and Dutton 1999). Much has changed since that definition was first written for both heterosexual and LGBT people. The term *intimate* is a euphemism for sex. Less commonly it can refer to sexless coupled relations. The concept, when applied to LGBT people, is even more problematic due to differing sexual values and norms and the uneven legal, civil, and religious ability to marry. Therefore, the following descriptors have been employed by researchers at the Center for Homicide Research to describe LGBT intimate relations. They include wife, husband, cohabitating partner, ex-cohabitating partner, boyfriend, girlfriend, and intimate acquaintance. Intimate acquaintance accounts for sexual relations with lesser-known individuals, some of whom are occasionally reoccurring, while other sexual encounters may occur only once.

Economic strain on relationships can lead to decreased coping skills and increased frustration. Lack of resources is one of the often-cited exacerbations in intimate-partner violence (Michalski 2004). The resources to provide for daily needs such as food, clothing, or shelter are stretched thin, which causes friction as the couple navigates their day and negotiate their relations. Financial stress can be used to manipulate one partner into supporting the other partner to keep them from leaving the home or relationship (Leventhal and Lundy 1999). This sense of relational entrapment could lead to killing as a form of self-help (Black 1983).

Economics can also lead to detrimental coping techniques and an inability to leave the relationship to become independent. Alcohol use, found in up to 88.2% of homicide offenders (Smith, Branas, and Miller 1999), increases in individuals struggling with troubled relationships (Greenfield 1998). Alcohol abuse among LGBT people has been estimated to be nearly double that of their heterosexual counterparts* (Drake 2004a; Schilit, Lie, and Montagne 1990). Lack of material resources can also bring on mental illness, brought on by strain in the forms of emotional

* Center for American Progress. 2012. "Why the Gay and Transgender Population Experiences Higher Rates of Substance Use." Accessed December 31, 2012, http://www.americanprogress.org/issues/lgbt/report/2012/03/09/11228/why-the-gay-and-transgender-population-experiences-higher-rates-of-substance-use/. According to the Center for American Progress, "Twenty-five percent of gay and transgender people abuse alcohol, compared to 5 to 10 percent of the general population."

instability and depression. Making matters worse, financial hardship can make it difficult to obtain care for these mental health services. Services for LGBT people experiencing intimate-partner violence are often quite limited. In more rural states, these programs are typically integrated into mainstream domestic violence services where little is known about the unique aspects of LGBT relationships (Leitenberg 1999). For instance, sometimes perpetrators of intimate-partner violence will threaten to *out* their partner to an employer as a means of controlling their behavior. The fear is often well founded since many disempowered states do not provide protection against discrimination in employment, and there is a plethora of accounts of job discrimination bias. Difficulty in gaining or maintaining employment leads some LGBT people to seek out a *sugar daddy* who will financially support them, thus leading to resentment by the usually older provider. In alternate scenarios, the younger partner kills the more financially secure one to obtain insurance money or property.

The second type of homicide is sexual homicide. Although there are many types of sexual homicide, typically it refers to killings that include a sexual component, whether or not it is sexually motivated (Geberth 1996; Schleshinger 2004). Some sexual homicides start out with consensual sex and evolve into nonconsensual sex and murder. According to data from the National Database of LGBT Homicide,* 28% of LGBT homicides are overt sexual homicides.† Covert sexual homicides, where there is no obvious evidence of sexual activity, can be virtually undetectable but must be presumed to exist (Schlesinger 2004). A subset of these intentional murders is sexually sadistic, predatory homicides. This means that the offender psychologically benefits from observing the "pain, humiliation, and suffering" of the victim and, furthermore, that it heightens their degree of sexual gratification (Frances and Wollert 2012, 414). Offenders who engage in this kind of killing are regarded as serial offenders due to the repetitive quality of sexual motivation.

Economics as a Homicide Risk

Several factors can increase the vulnerability of victims thus putting them at higher risk of being murdered. These risk factors include participating in lower-class illicit occupations such as prostitution or drug selling, which put victims in contact with other criminals. They also are occupations that limit access to legitimate help due to their own criminal involvement.

For example, in the LGBT community the killing of prostitution clients by their prostitutes is grounded in economics. Male prostitutes are more likely to kill their older, wealthy clients (Drake 2004a). Lesbians, when they participate

---

* National Database of LGBT Homicide 1969–Present. Accessed December 17, 2012, Minneapolis, MN: Center for Homicide Research.

† These do not include simple claims of an alleged sexual advance but instead appear to be inherently sexually motivated.

in prostitution, kill only serving heterosexual clients. Thirty-five percent of these female prostitutes are reportedly bisexual (Weinberg, Shaver, and Williams 1999, 507). Savitz and Rosen (1988, 205) put female (nonprostitution) same-sex encounters as high as 33%.* Although female prostitutes will routinely roll or rob their customers, it is nearly always the female prostitute who ends up dead, not the client (Brewer et al. 2006). In gay male homicide, we see the opposite dynamic in 91% of cases.† Young male street prostitutes typically kill their wealthy clients in what can best be described as motivated by relative deprivation (Fisher 1997; Van Gemert 1994). These hustlers are sometimes resentful of the wealth of their clients when they themselves are just trying to make enough money to survive the night. Domination of the poor prostitute‡ leads to objectification through the act of sexual purchasing, thereby antagonizing the eventual offender. Whereas income inequality may have provided the poor or powerless with a sense of moral obligation not to kill, the constraint is overpowered by the perceived harm; therefore a homicide is the result. This is a homicide motivated by relative deprivation, or a difference in the disparity of wealth between the offender and the victim.

Also included is the development of social isolation. Healthy social networks ward off predation by demonstrating to predators that their target will be noticed by others (what Cohen and Felson, 1979, label as guardianship). When these guardians (friends or family) are absent, it is unlikely vigorous advocacy will occur to locate or apprehend the killer. The problem is highlighted in that murdered victims in LGBT homicides are delayed 24 hours of more before police are notified in nearly 40% of the time. This is because few friends or relatives were in regular contact with the victim. In 6.8% of cases, the remains are never found, also leading to a delayed discovery. A large number of LGBT victims are qualitatively described as loners in the National LGBT Homicide Database.§ Throughout the 1970s, more than 30 of abducted LGBT victims were hitchhiking.

---

* Savitz and Rosen (1988) indicate that these women have sex with other women but do not identify as lesbian.

† Block, Carolyn Rebecca, Richard L. Block, and Illinois Criminal Justice Information Authority. Homicides in Chicago, 1965–1995. ICPSR06399-v5. Ann Arbor, MI: Inter-University Consortium for Political and Social Research (distributor), 2005-07-06. doi:10.3886/ICPSR06399.v5. Analysis used gender of the victim as correlated to prostitute or client.

‡ Crooks, Robert, and Karla Bauer. 1987. *Our Sexuality* (3rd ed.). Menlo Park, CA: Benjamin/Cummings Publishing. Streetwalkers, as opposed to call girls, are described as often being "from lower economic backgrounds" (p. 701). In recent years fewer prostitutes are considered streetwalkers due to the advent of cell phones and Internet social media. Marcia Cohen (1987) also points out in "Juvenile Prostitution," published by the National Association of Counties Research, Inc., that males nearly always attribute their prostitution to the financial benefit it provides.

§ National Database of LGBT Homicide 1969–Present. Accessed December 17, 2012, Minneapolis, MN: Center for Homicide Research. Details about social status are revealed in narratives about the homicide incident. This variable is only filled out in approximately 30% of homicides, as they are not yet fully coded.

Another risk factor is alcohol use, which can also be a symptom of financial strain, or a strain from prejudice or discrimination (Gay & Lesbian Equality Network 1995; Mays and Cochran 2001). Lack of social resources is also a form of social isolation. A survey focusing on violence among intimates administered at the Twin Cities Pride Festival in 2012 shows that although 84.4% of LGBT people are aware of social resources, few people indicate actually using them.*

When resources are scarce, victims can participate in nonfinancial forms of power seeking through status building. Agreeing to go with a photographer who promises fame (Ressler, Burgess, and Douglas 1988) or having sex with many partners to demonstrate sexual prowess can put one in a position to be victimized. Many of the victims of sex murders come from the lower class. They are the hitchhikers, prostitutes, street hustlers, and the destitute (Geberth, 1996; McClellan 2008). Serial sexual predators prefer trolling the dark side of society where the social constraints are fewer and the victim pool is more easily accessible and controllable.

Hate-crime homicides are another distinct variety of homicide (McDevitt, Levin, and Bennett 2004). These are cases where the victim was selected "due to their perceived membership in a 'class' of people" (Petersen 2006, 10) as outlined in state or federal law. Though little is known about the class status of hate-crime *homicide* victims, victims of anti-gay *violence* often come from the lower class (Mason and Palmer 1996). Hate crime is considered a symbolic attack (Jenness 1999) in that selection of the victim is not based on that victim per se but rather which group that victim represents. Individual offenders often come from a lower class status (Comstock 1991) along with its incumbent alcohol use[†,‡] and lower levels of educational attainment. Offenders operating in groups, however, are more likely to be middle class (1991). Less education can lead to lower verbal skills and therefore an increase in visual and symbolic displays that are so characteristic of hate-crime attacks. Levin and McDevitt (2002) argue that hate crimes occur in impoverished environments where offenders use class status to belittle gay victims in an attempt to raise their own lower class self-esteem.

The location of hate-crime attacks is more typically street based—29% for lesbians and 26% for gay males (Comstock 1991, 49)—due to their predatory nature. Often they occur around visible gay bars or clubs, which are usually relegated to the

* "Twin Cities Pride Festival Attendees Surveyed on Intimate-Relations." Center for Homicide Research. Accessed December 21, 2012, http://homicidecenter.org/twin-cities-pride-festival-attendees-surveyed-on-intimate-relations/.

† Dunbar, Edward. 2003. "Symbolic, Relational, and Ideological Signifiers of Bias-Motivated Offenders: Toward a Strategy of Assessment." *American Journal of Orthopsychiatry* 73(2): 203–211. Research on 58 hate-crime offenders shows that 36.2% of hate-crime offenders were intoxicated during the attack.

‡ Hamm, Mark. 1994. *American Skinheads: The Criminology and Control of Hate Crime.* Westport, CT: Praeger. Nearly all attacks by skinheads involve intense amounts of beer consumption.

poorer districts of a community. For instance, in Salt Lake City, Utah, most gay clubs are literally across the tracks from the main downtown area. Hate-crime offenders seek out this visible setting as a means of locating gay people for predation.* Many LGBT community institutions are still situated in these poorer districts due to their proximity to residential housing patterns, that is, the gay ghetto. The participation in routine activities (Cohen and Felson 1979) such as frequenting gay bars, walking to the store, shopping or going to movies in marginal areas of an urban landscape puts young and vulnerable LGBT victims at an even greater risk.

The act of hate-crime predation necessarily places an offender in power over the victim. While not explicitly, nor necessarily premeditated, this often recreational form of violence uniformly targets people who have victim-like qualities (De Becker 1997; Wolfgang 1958). Being victimized by hate crime can be disempowering and lead to long-term psychological deficits for gay males and lesbian females (Herek, Gillis, and Cogin 1999). Paul Farmer, a human rights worker, says that crimes against gay men and women are felt largely among the poor (2005, 381). Huge costs are associated with homicides (DeLisi et al. 2010), which can disempower any group experiencing repetitive victimizations.

Economic factors strongly play into each of these three types or syndromes of homicide. The three aforementioned examples are just the beginning of a discussion of these power dynamics, as there are many, many types of homicide. The taking of a human life is perhaps the ultimate power and, therefore, all types of killing contain aspects central to any economic discussion.

The Emergent LGBT Community

The advent of a community of LGBT people is a relatively new development (Drake 2004c). It was marked by the historical event of the Stonewall riots in Greenwich Village, New York, in 1969, and the subsequent organizing and community building that quickly followed. While many minority groups have advocated for their civil and human rights, a major difference is that their communities already existed as a cultural group. This was not the case for the LGBT people. Although people with same-sex attractions have always existed, their accompanying organizations and institutions did not, and the culture itself was extremely muted (Bronski 1984).

The development and maintenance of organizations within the LGBT community is complicated by the character of an emergent community (Nwankwo and Regis 1983) that is heavily impacted by crime. To address issues of community-level social disorganization, institutions are formed. Performance within an organization must be to a certain degree efficient to be effective. Lack of efficiency creates

* McFarland, Sheena. 2011. "Gay Man Attacked Outside Downtown Salt Lake City Club," *Salt Lake Tribune*, September 3.

unguarded social space allowing an opportunity for crime to take place both within and outside the organization (Drake 2004c).

The nature of this emergence affects the character and quality of organizations in the community and, in turn, their organizational capacity. The institutions that make up this emergent community are motivated in part by crime itself. LGBT organizations have become targets of crime and also contribute to its production through their own disorganization (Swan and Drake 2004). These components impede organizational capacity, which impacts their functionalism and prevents them from carrying out their missions, goals, and objectives. In the case of anti-violence agencies, it prevents them from reducing crime or restricts their ability to mediate crime's impact on secondary victims (Drake 2004c).

Disorder is related to social change (Faris 1955). Lack of a pattern map or lack of cultural patterns may facilitate this disorder since order is generally maintained through the adherence to cultural patterns. Anomic conditions, combined with a crime-based antagonism, for example hate crime, are instrumentally related to community disorder and disempowerment. When an organization develops outside the traditional or dominant cultural pattern, the potential for faulty cultural patterns to develop always exists.

The LGBT movement experienced a fundamental setback with the development of the HIV/AIDS pandemic. Although this was not the only one, it has drained resources and energy. When the dominant culture refused to respond to HIV/AIDS, LGBT people worked to build their own infrastructure and in the process developed an "AIDS Economy" (Escoffier 1997, 124). Although this did help train new leaders and give higher visibility to LGBT organizing, many of these same people died as the result of the pandemic. Issues such as crime and violence began to take a backseat to AIDS as the pandemic intensified (Magnus 2002). This led to further hate-crime attacks, not just on LGBT people but now HIV-positive people as well. Somewhat the same thing has happened with the advent of "marriage amendments," which have the effect of draining limited resources away from existing LGBT infrastructure; while directing money toward pro same-sex marriage organizations.

The community-building attempt at resolving this decades-old problem of antigay violence continues to permeate our culture. Resolution can only come by addressing the economic conditions that underlie it as a complex condition requiring a multidimensional solution.

Collective Social Organizing to Prevent Hate Violence

Over the years the LGBT community pulled together in an effort to address violence in the community (Jenness 1995). Most of this organizing has been targeted at violence committed against the community from outside, in other words, hate-crimes. Later on it began to focus, perhaps haltingly and only sporadically, on intimate-partner violence.* What has been missing, however, is any unified attempt to specifically address *homicide* and all types or syndromes of LGBT homicide, not just hate-crime homicides (Drake 2004a).

The character of the mission of these organizations has been greatly impacted by how the organizations initially developed. They were started by poor street activists and funded in the beginning almost exclusively by lesbian, gay, and bisexual people (Jenness 1995). All organizations required community investment and buy-in by key stakeholders but that presented a problem of mission bias. They often focused only on certain aspects of the problem, such as hate-crime attacks. Another issue is that the founding ideology was to focus on victim advocacy and victim services (Jenness and Broad 1994). This evolved out of the women's movement as part of a *care economy*, which largely benefited women (Folbre 2006) and did not focus as much on actually solving the root problem. There was little recognition of the structural nature of economics in creating the LGBT homicide problem.

At times, antiviolence programs have benefited from statewide funding for victim services through block grants. Considerable organizing had to occur to develop their structures internally so they were in a position to accept funding and, even more important, for the state to trust the organizations. With lack of funding, organizations often turn to the use of volunteers (Jenness 1995) or student interns to augment the staffing shortages (Drake and Shulka 2007). The Center for Homicide Research incorporates a well-developed internship program. This has been an important part of funding this independent research center, which focuses heavily on LGBT homicide. But internships bring with them their own challenges such as a heavy investment in training, high turnover, and lack of continuity. It also requires a lot of administration and supervision that would not be needed for full-time staff. Clearly the full funding of these organizations could have profound effects on the homicide problem.†

Social organizing can bring empowerment to many people living in a "culture of victimhood" (Billing 2009). These are people who might not otherwise have access to the development of social capital. When various minorities, sexual, racial, disabled, and immigrants, all work together in solving mutual problems, this diversity can strengthen everyone involved and create a better work product. The prevailing ideology, however, is problematic. Inherent in it is the idea that LGBT people are only victims and not offenders. This was part of the challenge in drawing attention to LGBT intimate-partner violence. LGBT people rejected the idea of LGBT offending.

---

* Even today, few organizations exist whose specific mission is to address LGBT domestic violence. One such organization is Communities United Against Violence (www.cuav.org) located in San Francisco.

† NCAVP Report. 1999. "Anti-Lesbian, Gay, Bisexual and Transgender Violence in 1998." New York, NY: National Coalition of Anti-Violence Programs. Their 2008 annual report (issued in 2009) cites "lack of funding" as an impediment to successful resolution of the violence problem (p. 4).

Ideologies can lead to negative outcomes in confronting the violence problem by constructing and emphasizing the *other* or the *outsider* as the aggressor in antigay attacks (Merton 1972; Porter 2005). Perhaps offenders are not heterosexual after all but rather homosexuals with internalized homophobia leading to self-loathing. The inability to perceive this makes the problem nearly unsolvable. Instead, antiviolence organizations are cluttered with politicized research reports (the kind of which we criticize the opposition for as using pseudoscience), the pursuing of temporary fixes and the misusing of murder victims' stories to push a misguided agenda. All of the information is created within an information bubble with little if any input from other experts in the field. What is needed is greater participation by academics working in the field of violence and aggression; researchers who deal specifically with homicide; and lawyers, judges, and violent crime investigators.

Organizing brings empowerment. The proper approach to dealing with homicide and violent crimes can help put LGBT people at ease, both at home and in the community, by reducing levels of victimization. Safety and security of citizens can boost worker productivity and help lift people up out of poverty to improve the economy.

Intransigence of the LGBT Homicide Problem

In spite of all the progress made in advocating for LGBT rights and changing mores of society, homicide in the LGBT communities has not declined much over the many decades and may actually be increasing. Although it is duly noted that the monitoring of these killings is poor at best, the FBI hate-crimes data collection is skeptically labeled the "book of zeros" (McPhail 2002, 5). The question remains: Where is the reduction in LGBT homicides? And why is it not getting any better?

The answer is perhaps as complex as homicide itself and is multifaceted. Connections of homicide to poverty in a minority community—a community made up of people from varying minorities—is certain to be a considerable part of the answer. Poorly funded antiviolence agencies and community organizations contribute to a lack of "capable guardianship" (Cohen and Felson 1979). Personal agency at the individual level will be facilitated by laws that protect employment and tax rights that will enable LGBT people to earn a livable wage income to put them on par with their heterosexual counterparts. This in turn will allow better funding of antiviolence research and crime victim advocacy.

Research by the Center for Homicide Research has also shown that an integral part of the homicide problem is that an us-versus-them or insider–outsider ideology prevents us from correctly perceiving the LGBT homicide problem. Ultimately gay homicide is not an externally based attack. It is instead, in most instances (84.2%), an attack on nonheterosexual individuals operating within the LGBT community or in the fringe of society who do not embrace the standard LGBT identity. As a result, they lash out to mitigate their own internalized homophobia by attacking their own people within a vulnerable, resource-deprived environment.

Conclusion

Researchers at the Center for Homicide Research computed the homicide rate of LGBT homicide for each of the 50 states using present-day population estimates provided by the Disaster Center.* They then computed the average for empowered versus disempowered states, which revealed .38 per 100,000 homicides in empowered states and .25 homicides per 100,000 in disempowered states. The top five states with the greatest prevalence of LGBT homicides were California, Wisconsin, Florida, South Dakota, and Nebraska. The lowest states included Arkansas, Kansas, South Carolina, New Hampshire, and Delaware. Cases were drawn only from coded cases within the database, and therefore, many cases were excluded from this analysis. The more that people are *out* and protected by human rights laws, the lower the incidence of LGBT homicide. Thus we need more resources directed toward building protective infrastructure in those states without protections.

References

Alsop, Zoe. 2009. "Uganda's Anti-Gay Bill: Inspired by the U.S.," *Time*, December 10, http://www.time.com/time/world/article/0,8599,1946645,00.html.

Badgett, M. V. Lee. 2001. "Income Inflation: The Myth of Affluence Among Gay, Lesbian, and Bisexual Americans." Washington, D.C.: The Policy Institute, National Gay and Lesbian Task Force, and the Institute for Gay and Lesbian Strategic Studies.

Baker, Donald E. 1990. "Anti-Homeless Legislation: Unconstitutional Efforts to Punish the Homeless." *University of Miami Law Review 45*, 417.

Beckett, Katherine. 1999. *Making Crime Pay: Law & Order in Contemporary American Politics*. Oxford: Oxford University Press.

Beeghley, Leonard. 2003. *Homicide: A Sociological Explanation*. Lanham, MA: Rowman & Littlefield.

Bérubé, Allan. 2001. "How Gay Stays White, and What Kind of White It Stays." In *The Making and Unmaking of Whiteness*, edited by Birgit Brander Rasmussen, Eric Klinenberg, Irene J. Nexica, and Matt Wray, 253–283. Durham, NC: Duke University Press. http://web.pdx.edu/~matg/Sociology/Gender_&_Sexualities_files/how%20gay%20satys%20white.pdf.

* Disaster Center, The. 2012. Accessed December 18, 2012, http://www.disastercenter.com/crime/uscrime.htm. See the hyperlinks for each state. The Disaster Center uses Uniform Crime Report data from the Federal Bureau of Investigation to compute these figures.

Biagi, Shirley, and Marilyn Kern-Foxworth. 1997. *Facing Difference: Race, Gender, and Mass Media*. Newbury Park, CA: Pine Forge Press.
Billing, Pelle. 2009. "Culture of Victimhood." Pelle Billing.com. Accessed December 30, 2012, http://www.pellebilling.com/2009/02/the-culture-of-victimhood/.
Black, Dan, Gary Gates, Seth Sanders, and Lowell Taylor. 2000. "Demographics of the Gay and Lesbian Population in the United States: Evidence from Available Systematic Data Sources." *Demography* 37(2): 139–154.
Black, Donald. 1983. "Crime as Social Control." *American Sociological Review* 48(1): 34–45.
Block, Richard, and Carolyn Rebecca Block. 1992. "Homicide Syndromes and Vulnerability: Violence in Chicago Community Areas Over 25 Years." *Studies on Crime and Crime Prevention* 1(1): 61–87.
Blumstein, Alfred, Frederick P. Rivara, and Richard Rosenfeld. 2000. The Rise and Decline of Homicide—and Why. *Annual Review of Public Health 21*: 505–541.
Bradshaw, Brad. n.d. "Advising Witnesses Regarding Courtroom Attire." Nashville, TN: Bradshaw & Associates Trial Consulting, LLC. Accessed December 27, 2012, http://www.litcounsel.org/may/Bradshaw.pdf.
Brewer, Devon D., Jonathan A. Dudek, John J. Potterat, Stephen Q. Muth, John M. Roberts Jr., and Donald E. Woodhouse. 2006. "Extent, Trends, and Perpetrators of Prostitution-Related Homicide in the United States." *Journal of Forensic Science* 51(5): 1101–1108. doi:10.1111/j.1556-4029.2006.00206.x.
Bromley, David G., and Anson Shupe. 1990. "Rebottling the Elixir: The Gospel of Prosperity in America's Religioeconomic Corporations." In *Gods We Trust: New Patterns of Religious Pluralism in America*, edited by Thomas Robbins and Dick Anthony, 233–254. Piscataway, NJ: Transaction Publishers.
Bronski, Michael. 1984. *Culture Clash: The Making of Gay Sensibility*. Boston, MA: South End Press.
Browne, Angela, Kirk R. Williams, and Donald G. Dutton. 1999. "Homicide Between Intimate Partners." In *Homicide: A Sourcebook of Social Research*, edited by M. Dwayne Smith, and Margaret A. Zahn, 149–164. Thousand Oaks, CA: Sage.
Burke, Marc. 1994. "Homosexuality as Deviance: The Case of the Gay Police Officer." *British Journal of Criminology 34*(2): 192–203.
Cain, Patricia A. 1991. "Same-Sex Couples and the Federal Tax Laws." *Law & Sexuality: Review: Lesbian & Gay Legal Issues* 1: 97–131.
Castro, Melissa. 2008. "After Gay Migration, 17th Street Seeks a New Identity." *Washington Business Journal,* July 28. Accessed December 26, 2012, http://www.bizjournals.com/washington/stories/2008/07/28/story3.html?page = all.
Catalano, Shannon M., Michael R. Rand, Erica L. Smith, and Howard Snyder. 2009. *Female Victims of Violence*. Bureau of Justice Statistics. Accessed December 13, 2012 from: http://bjs.ojp.usdoj.gov/index.cfm?ty = pbdetail&iid = 2020.
Christian, Darrell, Sally A. Jacobsen, and David Minthorn, eds. 2012. *Associated Press Stylebook, 2012*. New York: The Associated Press.
Ciarlo, James A. 1997. "Focusing on 'Frontier': Isolated Rural America." *American Journal of Community Psychology* 14: 457–458.
Cohen, Lawrence E., and Marcus Felson. 1979. "Social Change and Crime Rate Trends: A Routine Activity Approach." *American Sociological Review 44*(4): 588–608.
Collins, Patricia Hill. 1990. *Black Feminist Thought, Knowledge, Consciousness, and the Politics of Empowerment*. London: Unwin Hyman.

Comstock, Gary D. 1991. *Violence Against Lesbians and Gay Men.* New York: Columbia University Press.

Cooney, Mark, ed. 1998. *Warriors and Peacemakers: How Third Parties Shape Violence.* New York: New York University Press.

Crist, Dawn R. 1997. "The Failure to Utilize Mental Health Services in the American West: Case Study of the Lite Day Treatment Program in Big Horn County, Wyoming." Unpublished undergraduate thesis. Kalamazoo College, Kalamazoo, Michigan.

Daly, Martin, and Margo Wilson. 1988. *Homicide.* New York: Aldine De Gruyter.

De Becker, Gavin. 1997. *The Gift of Fear.* New York: Dell Publishing.

Declercq, Frédéric, Jochem Willemsen, Kurt Audenaert, and Paul Verhaeghe. 2012. "Psychopathy and Predatory Violence in Homicide, Violent, and Sexual Offences: Factor and Facet Relations." *Legal and Criminological Psychology* 17(1): 59–74.

DeLisi, Matt, Anna Kosloski, Molly Sween, Emily Hachmeister, Matt Moore, and Alan Drury. 2010. "Murder by Numbers: Monetary Costs Imposed by a Sample of Homicide Offenders." *The Journal of Forensic Psychiatry & Psychology* 21(4): 501–513.

Disaster Center. 2012. "Maryland Crime Index Rates Per 100,000 Inhabitants." Accessed December 16, 2012, http://www.disastercenter.com/crime/mdcrime.htm.

Douglas, John E., Ann W. Burgess, Allen G. Burgess, and Robert Ressler. 1992. *Crime Classification Manual.* San Francisco, CA: Jossey-Bass.

Drake, Dallas S. 2003. "Data-Set Construction in Homosexual Homicide Cases: Shedding the Political Issue of Motive." In *New Directions in Homicide Research: Proceedings of the 2001 Annual Meeting of the Homicide Research Working Group,* edited by M. Dwayne Smith, Paul H. Blackman, and John P. Jarvis, 197–204. Washington, DC: Federal Bureau of Investigation.

Drake, Dallas S. 2004a. "Confronting and Managing GLBT Homicide and Its Associated Phenomena." In *Handbook of Gay, Lesbian, Bisexual, and Transgender Administration and Policy,* edited by Wallace Swan, 311–348. New York: Marcel Dekker.

Drake, Dallas. 2004b. *Recognizing Gay Homicide* (research brief). Minneapolis, MN: Center for Homicide Research.

Drake, Dallas S. 2004c. "Crime in an Emergent Community: A Study in GLBT Social Disorganization." Paper presented at the Annual Meeting of the American Society of Criminology, November.

Drake, Dallas S. 2011. "Homicide Free: Exploring the Intervals Between Killings." Paper presented at the Summer Meeting of the Homicide Research Working Group, New Orleans, Louisiana, June.

Drake, Dallas, Jessica Proskin, and Charles Crain. 2010. *Homicide Analysis of Flint, Michigan* (research report). Minneapolis, MN: Center for Homicide Research.

Drake, Dallas S., and Shulka, Joseph E. 2007. "The Center for Homicide Research: Solving and Preventing Homicide." In *Homicide Studies: Ten Years After Its Inception. Proceedings of the 2007 Meeting of the Homicide Research Working Group,* edited by Lin Huff-Corzine, Katharina Gruenberg, and Gabrielle Salfati, 86–90. Chicago: Homicide Research Working Group.

Ellis, Lee. 2008. *Sex Differences: Summarizing More Than a Century of Scientific Research.* Boca Raton, FL: CRC Press.

Erdkamp, Paul. 1998. *Hunger and the Sword: Warfare and Food Supply in Roman Republican Wars (264–30 BC).* Amsterdam: Gieben.

Escoffier, Jeffrey. 1997. "The Political Economy of the Closet." In *Homo Economics: Capitalism, Community, and Lesbian and Gay Life*, edited by Amy Gluckman and Betsy Reed, 123–134. New York: Routledge.

Faris, Robert E. L. 1955. *Social Disorganization*. New York: Ronald Press Company.

Farmer, Paul. 1999. "Pathologies of Power: Rethinking Health and Human Rights." *American Journal of Public Health 89*(10): 1486–1496.

Farmer, Paul. 2005. "Suffering and Structural Violence." In *Beyond Borders: Thinking Critically About Global Issues*, edited by Paula S. Rothenberg, 368–393. New York: MacMillan.

Federal Bureau of Investigation (FBI). 2011. *Crime in the United States by Metropolitan Statistical Area, 2011*. Crime in the United States 2011. http://www.fbi.gov/about-us/cjis/ucr/crime-in-the-u.s/2011/crime-in-the-u.s.-2011/tables/table 6.

Federal Bureau of Investigation, Uniform Crime Reporting Statistics (FBI UCR). 2010. *State and National Crime Estimates by Year*. http://www.ucrdatatool.gov/Search/Crime/State/StateCrime.cfm.

Felson, Marcus. 2006. *Crime and Nature*. Thousand Oaks, CA: Sage.

Fine, Gary Alan, and Tim Hallett. 2003. "Dust." *The Sociological Quarterly 44*(1): 1–15.

Fischer, Nancy L. 2006. "Sex as a Moral Discourse." *Handbook New Sexuality Studies*, 56–63.

Fisher, Marc. 1997. "The Life of a Trophy Boy." *Washington Post*, July 25, D01.

Folbre, Nancy. 2006. "Measuring Care: Gender, Empowerment, and the Care Economy." *Journal of Human Development* 7(2): 183–199.

Fox, James Alan. 2000. Uniform Crime Reports [United States]: Supplementary Homicide Reports, 1976-1997 [Computer file]. ICPSR version. Boston, MA: Northeastern University, College of Criminal Justice [producer], 1997. Ann Arbor, MI: Inter-university Consortium for Political and Social Research [distributor].

Frances, Allen, and Richard Wollert. 2012. "Sexual Sadism: Avoiding Its Misuse in Sexually Violent Predator Evaluations." *Journal of the American Academy of Psychiatry and the Law 40*(3): 409-416.

Frayssinet, Fabiana. 2012. "Rights-Brazil: Gay-Bashing Murders Up 55 Percent." Inter Press Service News Agency, December 26. Accessed December 26, 2012, http://www.ipsnews.net/2009/04/rights-brazil-gay-bashing-murders-up-55-percent/.

Friend of God. (Ed. & trans. C. F. Kelley). 1954. *Review of, The Book of the Poor in Spirit By a Friend of God (A Guide to Rhineland Mysticism)*. New York: Harper and Brothers.

Gale, Lewis R., Will Carrington Heath, and Rand W. Ressler. 2002. "An Economic Analysis of Hate Crime." *Eastern Economic Journal 28*(2): 203–216.

Gates, Gary J., and Jason Ost. 2004. *The Gay and Lesbian Atlas*. Washington, D.C.: The Urban Institute Press.

Gay & Lesbian Equality Network. 1995. *Poverty: Lesbians and Gay Men—The Economic & Social Effects of Discrimination*. Dublin, Ireland: Combat Poverty Agency.

Geberth, Vernon J. 1996. *Practical Homicide Investigation* (3rd ed). Boca Raton, FL: CRC Press.

Gettleman, Jeffrey. 2011. "Remembering David Kato, a Gay Ugandan and a Marked Man," *New York Times*, January 29. http://www.nytimes.com/2011/01/30/weekinreview/30gettleman.html.

Glaser, Daniel. 1971. *Social Deviance*. Chicago: Markham.

Gluckman, Amy, and Betsy Reed, eds. 1997. *Homo Economics: Capitalism, Community, and Lesbian and Gay Life*. New York: Routledge.

Greenfield, Lawrence A. 1998. "Alcohol and Crime: An Analysis of National Data on the Prevalence of Alcohol Involvement in Crime." Washington, D.C.: Bureau of Justice Statistics.

Halfhill, Robert. 1986. "Loring's Gay and Lesbian Communities." In *Reflections in Loring Pond: A Minneapolis Neighborhood Examines its First Century*, edited by Bert Berlowe, 156–157. Minneapolis, MN: Citizens for a Loring Park Community.

Hamermesh, Daniel S., and Neal M. Soss. 1974. "An Economic Theory of Suicide." *Journal of Political Economy 82*(1): 83–98.

Hamm, Mark. 1994. *American Skinheads: The Criminology and Control of Hate Crime.* Westport, CT: Praeger.

Hannon, Lance E. 2005. "Extremely Poor Neighborhoods and Homicide." *Social Science Quarterly* 86: 1418–1434.

Harries, Keith. 1997. *Serious Violence: Patterns of Homicide and Assault in America* (2nd ed.). Springfield, IL: Charles C. Thomas.

Harris, Anthony R., Stephen H. Thomas, Gene A. Fisher, and David J. Hirsch. 2002. "Murder and Medicine: The Lethality of Criminal Assault 1960–1999." *Homicide Studies 6*(2): 128–166.

Harry, Joseph. 1974. "Urbanization and the Gay Life." *Journal of Sex Research 10*(3): 238–247.

Harry, Joseph. 1992. "Conceptualizing Anti-Gay Violence." In *Hate Crimes: Confronting Violence against Lesbians and Gay Men*, 113–122. Thousand Oaks, CA: Sage.

Herdt, Gilbert, ed. 1992. *Gay Culture in America: Essays from the Field.* Boston: Beacon Press.

Herek, Gregory M., J. Roy Gillis, and Jeanine C. Cogan. 1999. "Psychological Sequelae of Hate-Crime Victimization Among Lesbian, Gay, and Bisexual Adults." *Journal of Consulting and Clinical Psychology* 67(6): 945–951. doi:10.1037/0022-006X.67.6.945.

Hirsch, Jameson K. 2006. "A Review of the Literature on Rural Suicide: Risk and Protective Factors, Incidence, and Prevention." *The Journal of Crisis Intervention and Suicide Prevention 27*(4): 189–199.

Iraq Body Count. 2012a. "Iraqi Deaths from Violence 2003–2011." Accessed, http://www.iraqbodycount.org/analysis/numbers/2011/.

Iraq Body Count. 2012b. http://www.iraqbodycount.org/database/.

Ireland, Doug. 2009. "Iraqi Gay Murders Surge; World Finally Takes Note." *LGBT Asylum News* [Blog], April 17. Accessed December 26, 2012, http://madikazemi.blogspot.com/2009/04/iraqi-gay-murders-surge-world-finally.html.

Institute for War & Peace Reporting (IWPR). 2009. "New Wave of Violence Against Iraqi Gays." Accessed December 26, 2012, http://iwpr.net/report-news/new-wave-violence-against-iraqi-gays.

Jay, Karla. 1992. *Out of the Closets: Voice of Gay Liberation.* New York: New York University Press.

Jebsen, Kristian. 2012. "Brazil's Surge in Violence Against Gays Is Just Getting Worse." *The Daily Beast,* April 8. Accessed December 26, 2012, http://www.thedailybeast.com/articles/2012/04/08/brazil-s-surge-in-violence-against-gays-is-just-getting-worse.html.

Jenness, Valerie. 1995. "Social Movement Growth, Domain Expansion, and Framing Processes: The Gay/Lesbian Movement and Violence Against Gays and Lesbians as a Social Problem." *Social Problems 42*(1): 145–170.

Jenness, Valerie. 1999. "Making Sense of Hatred." *The Women's Review of Books 16*(5): 18–20.

Jenness, V., and K. L. Broad. 1994. "Antiviolence Activism and the (In)Visibility of Gender in the Gay/Lesbian and Women's Movements." *Gender and Society* 8: 402–423.

Johnson, Michael P., and Kathleen J. Ferraro. 2000. "Research on Domestic Violence in the 1990s: Making Distinctions." *Journal of Marriage and Family 62*(4): 948–963.

Jones, Adam. 2010. *Genocide: A Comprehensive Introduction* (2nd ed.). New York: Routledge/Taylor & Francis.

Karmen, Andrew. 2013. *Crime Victims: An Introduction to Victimology.* Belmont. CA: Wadsworth.

Kingser, Taren, and Patrick Schmidt. 2012. "Business in the Bulls-Eye? Target Corp. and the Limits of Campaign Finance Disclosure." *Election Law Journal 11*(1): 21–35.

Kubrin, Charis E., and Ronald Weitzer. 2003. "Retaliatory Homicide: Concentrated Disadvantage and Neighborhood Culture." *Social Problems 50*(2): 157–180.

Land, Kenneth C., Patricia L. McCall, and Lawrence E. Cohen. 1990. "Structural Covariates of Homicide Rates: Are There Any Invariances Across Time and Social Space?" *American Journal of Sociology* 95: 922–963.

Leahy, Samantha, Brian J. Francis, and N. Miller. 2004. "Gay Homicide Victims in England and Wales: Helping the Police With Their Enquiries." Discussion paper. London, UK: Home Office.

Leitenberg, Barbara, ed. 1999. "Domestic Violence is a Rural Health Issue." In *Research and Policy Brief*, Maine Rural Health Research Center, Institute for Health Policy, July.

Leventahl, Beth, and Sandra E. Lundy (eds.). 1999. *Same-Sex Domestic Violence: Strategies for Change*. Thousand Oaks, CA: Sage.

Levin, Jack, and Jack McDevitt. 2002. *Hate Crimes: America's War on Those Who Are Different*. Boulder, CO: Westview Press.

Loftin, Colin. 1986. "The Validity of Robbery Murder Classifications in Baltimore." *Violence and Victims 1*(3): 191–202.

Lucey, Thomas A., and Duane M. Giannangleo. 2006. "Short Changed: The Importance of Facilitating Equitable Financial Education in Urban Society." *Education and Urban Society 38*(3): 268–287.

Magnus, Stephen A. 2002. "Barriers to Foundation Funding of Gay Organizations." *Journal of Homosexuality 42*(2): 125–145.

Mason, Angela, and Anya Palmer. 1996. *Queer Bashing: A National Survey of Hate Crimes Against Lesbians and Gay Men*. London: Stonewall.

Mays, Vickie M., and Susan D. Cochran. 2001. "Mental Health Correlates of Perceived Discrimination Among Lesbian, Gay, and Bisexual Adults in the United States." *Journal Information 91*(11): 1869–1876.

McChesney, Chris. 2005. "Cultural Displacement: Is the GLBT Community Gentrifying African-American Neighborhoods in Washington, DC?" *The Modern American 1*(1): 24–27.

McClellan, Janet. 2008. "Delivery Drivers and Long-Haul Truckers: Traveling Serial Murderers." *Journal of Applied Security Research 3*(2): 171–190.

McDevitt, Jack, Jack Levin, and Susan Bennett. 2004. "Hate Crime Offenders: An Expanded Typology." In *Crimes of Hate: Selected Readings*, edited by Phyllis B. Gerstenfeld and Diana R. Grant, 107–117. Thousand Oaks, CA: Sage.

McPhail, Beverly Anne. 2002. "Constructing Justice: Prosecutorial Decision Making in Hate Crime Enhancements and a Grounded Theory of Justice Construction." Dissertation, University of Texas, Austin.

Merton, Robert K. 1972. "Insiders and Outsiders: A Chapter in the Sociology of Knowledge." *American Journal of Sociology* 77: 9–47.

Messer, Ellen. 1990. "Food Wars: Hunger as a Weapon of War." The Hunger Report, Alan Shawn Feinstein World Hunger Program, 27–37.

Messner, Steven F., Eric P. Baumer, and Richard Rosenfeld. 2004. "Dimensions of Social Capital and Rates of Criminal Homicide." *American Sociological Review* 69: 882–903.

Messner, Steven F., and Richard Rosenfeld. 1999. "Social Structure and Homicide: Theory and Research." In *Homicide: A Sourcebook of Social Research*, edited by M. Dwayne Smith, and Margaret A. Zahn, 27–41. Thousand Oaks, CA: Sage.

MGHS Database. 2000. Minnesota Gay Homicide Study Database 1970–2000 [Electronic file]. Center for Homicide Research. Accessed December 1, 2012.
Michaelski, Joseph. 2004. "Making Sociological Sense Out of Trends in Intimate Partner Violence: The Social Structure of Violence Against Women." *Violence Against Women* 10(6): 652–675. doi:10.1177/1077801204265018.
Morris, William, and Mary Morris. 1988. *Morris Dictionary of Word and Phrase Origins*. New York: HarperCollins.
Mosedale, Mike. 2006. "Panic in Loring Park: A Spate of Violent Robberies Near Loring Park Awakens Memories of a Four-year-old Killing in the Cold Case File." *City Pages* [Minneapolis], November 22.
Murphy, Ryan, and Alex Urquhart. 2010. *Queer Twin Cities: Twin Cities GLBT Oral History Project*. Minneapolis, MN: University of Minnesota Press.
Myslik, Wayne. 1996. Gay Communities as Safe Havens or Sites of Resistance? Bodyspace: Destabilizing Geographies of Gender and Sexuality. London: Routledge.
Nanda, Serena, and Richard L. Warms. 2004. *Cultural Anthropology* (8th ed.). Belmont, CA: Wadsworth/Thompson Publishing.
Nash, Paul. 1963. "Corporal Punishment in an Age of Violence." *Educational Theory 13*(4): 295-308.
National Coalition of Anti-Violence Programs (NCAVP) Report. 1999. "Anti-Lesbian, Gay, Bisexual and Transgender Violence in 1998." New York: National Coalition of Anti-Violence Programs.
National Coalition of Anti-Violence Programs (NCAVP) Report. 2012. "Lesbian, Gay, Bisexual, Transgender, Queer and HIV-Affected Intimate Partner Violence–2011." New York: National Coalition of Anti-Violence Programs.
Nwankwo, Robert L., and Humphrey Regis. 1983. "The Perception of Transcendent Interest: Communication and Identification in an Emergent Community." *International Journal of Intercultural Relations 7*: 361–375.
O'Connor, T. 2011. "Social Disorganization Theories of Crime." Megalinks in Criminal Justice. Accessed December 20, 2012, http://www.drtomoconnor.com/1060/1060lect05a.htm.
Osteen, Joel. 2004. *Your Best Life Now*. New York, NY: Faith Words.
Oswald, Ramona Faith (ed.). 2003. *Lesbian Rites: Symbolic Acts and the Power of Community.* (Copublished simultaneously as *Journal of Lesbian Studies 7*(2): 1–135.) New York: Harrington Park Press.
Patterson, Orlando. 1982. *Slavery and Social Death: A Comparative Study*. Cambridge, MA: Harvard University Press.
Paulsen, Derek J., and Matthew B. Robinson. 2004. *Spatial Aspects of Crime: Theory and Practice*. Boston: Pearson.
Petersen, Jennifer Anne. 2006. "Feeling in the Public Sphere: A Study of Emotion, Public Discourse, and the Law in the Murders of James Byrd Jr. and Matthew Shepard." Dissertation, University of Texas, Austin. Accessed December 30, 2012, https://www.lib.utexas.edu/etd/d/2006/petersend46798/petersend46798.pdf.
Porter, Elisabeth J. 2005. *Researching Conflict in Africa: Insights and Experiences*. Tokyo, Japan: United Nations University Press.
Putnam, Robert D. 2000. *Bowling Alone: The Collapse and Revival of American Community*. New York: Simon & Schuster.
Rapaport, Elizabeth. 1991. "The Death Penalty and Gender Discrimination." *Law & Society Review 25*(2): 367–383.

Reed, Wornie L. 1991. "Trends in Homicide Among African-Americans." *Trotter Review* *5*(3): 11–17.

Ressler, Robert K., Ann W. Burgess, and John E. Douglas. 1988. *Sexual Homicide: Patterns and Motives*. New York: The Free Press.

Reuters. 2012. "Fear as Death Squads Hunt Iraq's Gays and 'Emos.'" *Daily News* (New Zealand), March 13. Accessed December 27, 2012, http://www.iol.co.za/dailynews/news/fear-as-death-squads-hunt-iraq-s-gays-and-emos-1.1254979#.UL0b2IZwyH0.

Rosenblum, Darren. 1995. "Overcoming 'Stigmas': Lesbian and Gay Districts and Black Electoral Empowerment." Pace Law Faculty Publications, Paper 209. Accessed December 29, 2012, http://digitalcommons.pace.edu/lawfaculty/209.

Rubin, Gayle. 1999. "Thinking Sex: Notes for a Radical Theory of the Politics of Sexuality." In *Culture, Society and Sexuality: A Reader*, edited by peter Aggleton and Richard Parker, 143–179. London: UCL Press.

Ryan, Joan. 1997. "Cunanan a Chameleon Who Fed on Rich Gays," *San Francisco Chronicle*, July 17, Final Edition, A1.

Savitz, Leonard, and Lawrence Rosen. 1988. "The Sexuality of Prostitutes: Sexual Enjoyment Reported by 'Streetwalkers.'" *Journal of Sex Research 24*(1): 200–208.

Schilit, Rebecca, Gwat-Yong Lie, and Marilyn Montagne. 1990. "Substance Use as a Correlate of Violence: In Intimate Lesbian Relationships." *Journal of Homosexuality* 19(3): 51–65.

Schleshinger, Louis B. 2004. *Sexual Murder: Catathymic and Compulsive Homicides*. Boca Raton, FL: CRC Press.

Schlozman, Kay Lehman, Sidney Verba, and Henry E. Brady. 2012. *The Unheavenly Chorus: Unequal Political Voice and the Broken Promise of American Democracy*. Princeton, NJ: Princeton University Press.

Schneider, Beth E. 1997. "Owning an Epidemic: The Impact of AIDS on Small-City Lesbian and Gay Communities." In *Changing Times: Gay Men and Lesbians Encounter HIV/AIDS*, edited by Martin P. Levine, Peter M. Nardi, and John H. Gagnon, 145–170. Chicago: University of Chicago Press.

Shaw, Clifford R., and Henry D. McKay. 1942. *Juvenile Delinquency in Urban Areas*. Chicago: University of Chicago Press.

Shilts, Randy. 1988. *The Mayor of Castro Street*. New York: St. Martin's Press.

Simon, Jonathan. 1993. *Poor Discipline: Parole and the Social Control of the Underclass: 1890–1990*. Chicago: University of Chicago Press.

Smith, Cindy J., Jennifer Bechtel, Angie Patrick, and Richard R. Smith. 2006. "Correctional Industries Preparing Inmates for Re-Entry: Recidivism & Post-Release Employment." U.S. Department of Justice.

Smith, G. S., Branas, C. C., and Miller, T. R. 1999. "Fatal nontraffic injuries involving alcohol: A metaanalysis." *Annals of Emergency Medicine*, *33*(6), 659–668.

Stassen-Berger, Rachel. 2010. "A Possible Campaign Finance Violation—or not—Connects Emmer to Controversial Group." *Minneapolis Star Tribune*, Hot Dish Blog, May 25. http://www.startribune.com/politics/blogs/94874784.html.

Stevenson, Michael R., and Barbara R. Medler. 1995. Is Homophobia a Weapon of Sexism? *The Journal of Men's Studies 4*(1): 1–8.

Stewart-Winter, Timothy. 2009. "The Castro Origins to the Age of Milk." *The Gay & Lesbian Review*, January/February, 12–15.

Stoner, Madeline. 1995. *The Civil Rights of Homeless People*. New York: Eldine De Gruyter.

Straus, Murray A., Richard J. Gelles, and Suzanne k. Steinmetz. 1980. *Behind Closed Doors: Violence in the American Family*. Garden City, NY: Doubleday, Anchor Press.

Surgenor, Robert R. 2012. "Liberalism vs. God." Family Defense Network of Ohio. Accessed December 27, 2012, http://www.fdno.org/articles/liberalism.html.

Swan, Wallace, and Dallas S. Drake. 2004. "Criminal Justice Administration: A Survey of the Issues." In *Handbook of Gay, Lesbian, Bisexual and Transgender Administration and Policy*, edited by Wallace Swan, 285–310. New York: Marcel Dekker.

Tatchell, Peter. 2008. "Sexual Cleansing in Iraq." *The Guardian* (UK), September 25. Accessed December 21, 2012, http://www.guardian.co.uk/commentisfree/2008/sep/25/iraq.humanrights.

Tirellas, Joseph V. 1996. "Police Sweep LA in the Wake of Shakur Murder." *Rolling Stone* 747, 32.

Turvey, Brent E. 2003. "Criminal Motivation," In *Criminal Profiling: An Introduction to Behavioral Evidence Analysis* (2nd ed.), edited by Brent E. Turvey, 305–333. San Diego, CA: Academic Press.

U.S. Census Bureau. 2012. "Median Income of Households by State Using Three-Year Moving Averages: 1984 to 2011." Accessed December 21, 2012, http://www.census.gov/hhes/www/income/data/historical/household/2011/H08B_2011.xls.

Van Biema, David, and Jeff Chu. 2006. "Does God Want You To Be Rich?" *Time*, September 10, pp. 48–57. Accessed December 26, 2012, http://www.time.com/time/magazine/article/0,9171,1533448,00.html.

Van Gemert, Frank. 1994. "Chicken Kills Hawk: Gay Murders During the Eighties in Amsterdam." *Journal of Homosexuality 26*(4): 149–174.

Verghese, Abraham. 1994. *Soundings: A Doctor's Life in the Age of AIDS*. London: Orion Publishing Group.

Waddington, Peter A. J. 1999. "Police (Canteen) Sub-Culture: An Appreciation." *British Journal of Criminology 39*(2): 287–309.

Wagner, David. 2005. *The Poorhouse: America's Forgotten Institution*. Lanham, MD: Rowman & Littlefield.

Walling, Carrie Booth. 2000. "The History and Politics of Ethnic Cleansing." *The International Journal of Human Rights 4*(3-4): 47–66. doi:10.1080/13642980008406892.

Weinberg, Martin S., Frances M. Shaver, and Colin J. Williams. 1999. "Gendered Sex Work in the San Francisco Tenderloin." *Archives of Sexual Behavior 28*(6): 503–521.

Wilson, James Q. 2011. "Crime and the Great Recession" (blog). *City Journal*. Accessed May 14, 2014, http://www.city-journal.org/2011/21_3_crime-decline.html.

Winegar, Karin. 1990. "Nonwhites Say Racism Exists in Gay and Lesbian Community." *Star Tribune* (Minneapolis), November 12.

Wolfgang, Marvin E. 1958. *Patterns in Criminal Homicide*. Philadelphia, PA: University of Pennsylvania.

Wolfgang, Marvin E., and Ferracutti, Franco. 2007. The Subculture of Violence. In *Crime Readings* (3rd ed.), edited by Charis E. Kubrin, George S. Bridges, Joseph G. Weis, and Robert D. Crutchfield, 252–260. Thousand Oaks, CA: Sage.

Zorza, J. 1991. "Woman Battering: A Major Cause of Homelessness." *Clearinghouse Review 25*, 420–429.

Chapter 21

Incarcerated Lesbian, Gay, Bisexual, and Transgender People

Wallace Swan

Another "Great Divide" in our country involves the separation between people in the broader society and those who have become part of what some have called the prison industrial complex. "Federal and state corrections facilities held over 1.6 million prisoners at the end of 2010—approximately one of every 201 U.S. residents" ("Fact Sheet: Re-Entry" 2012). Certain racial and ethnic groups have been identified as having disproportionately large percentages of incarceration. However, no one knows how many lesbian, gay, bisexual, and transgender (LGBT) people are incarcerated in this country: A national survey would seem to be called for, because policy decisions are driven by data. Although we do not know how many such people are incarcerated, we can identify what some of the issues are that might face incarcerated LGBT people, based upon relatively limited literature on the subject.

A study by The Equity Project, titled "Hidden Injustice: Lesbian, Gay, Bisexual and Transgender Youth in Juvenile Courts," discusses the way in which bias determines the way in which LGBT youth are treated, the manner by which system professionals try to redirect LGBT sexual orientation, the role that rejection by their families and harassment within school systems plays in effecting the youth, the lack of placements and social services that could serve their needs, longer periods of pretrial detention, lack of protection of due process, and inappropriate confinement (Majd, Marksamer, and Reyes 2009). The study also makes recommendations about how to change these situations.

Zachary Wolfe (2014), in "Gay and Lesbian Prisoners: Recent Developments and a Call for More Research" identifies three major issues for prisons. They are spousal visitation rights (whether prisoners may have the right to visit their partners), the right to receive information (whether prisoners may receive information that a prison authority might consider problematic enough to cause difficult situations), and protective custody (whether it is appropriate for authorities to place certain prisoners in a custodial arrangement to protect them from other prisoners). Chapter 17 of this book discusses what the deleterious results may be when undocumented people are placed in 8-month detention to "protect" them from other undocumented people.

In an article titled "Protecting the LGBT Incarcerated," Katti Gray discusses the finding that studies by the National Institute of Corrections (NIC) "show lesbian, gay, bisexual and transgender inmates are 13 to 20 times more likely to be raped than incarcerated heterosexuals" (Gray 2012). According to Gray, the 2003 Prison Rape Elimination Act was added to by mandates that were put in place in May 2012. These mandates call for a reduction of 5% in federal dollars unless provisions designed to protect LGBT incarcerated people are not implemented within 3 years. The provisions include a range of options such as prevention of sexual abuse as well as an antirape policy. Gray notes that "juvenile and disabled inmates are also covered under the May 2012 provisions, ... addressed in the Institute's publication, entitled 'Managing Lesbian, Gay, Bisexual, Transgender and Intersex Inmates: Is Your Jail Ready?'"

The issue of health concerns in prison is also an issue that drives this effort. According to an article (which cites the findings of the 2002 National Commission on Correctional Health Care) titled "Collaborative Research to Prevent HIV among Prisoners and Their Families," "Rates of HIV are 8 to 10 times higher for incarcerated persons than for the general U.S. population, hepatitis C rates are 9 to 10 times higher, and sexually transmitted disease (STD) rates among men entering jails are as high as 35%" (Science to Community 2004).

Then, of course, there are the issues affecting the broader incarcerated population that also could reasonably be expected to impact the LGBT incarcerated population: (1) serious mental illness is 2 to 4 times more prevalent among incarcerated people; (2) a history of substance abuse is present in three quarters of the people who come out of prisons; (3) among the people who enter prisons; 10% were homeless before they were admitted, and for those who were mentally ill, the rate is 20%; and (4) 20% of people in prison do not have a high school diploma ("Fact Sheet: Re-Entry" 2012).

In conclusion, the issues of incarcerated lesbian, gay, bisexual, and transgender people are both many and severe. The author has only begun to identify some of the key issues that need to be addressed. Hopefully, others will begin to research these issues and recommend solutions to them.

References

"Fact Sheet: Reentry." 2012. Christians Working Together in Correctional Ministry (CMCA International). http://www.cmcainternational.org/wp-content/uploads/2012/01/Reentry-Fact-Sheet.pdf.

Gray, Katti. 2012. "Protecting the LGBT Incarcerated." The Crime Report: Your Complete Criminal Justice Resource, September 20, http://www.thecrimereport.org/news/inside-criminal-justice/2012-09-protecting-the-incarcerated.

Majd, Katayoon, Jody Marksamer, and Carolyn Reyes. 2009. "Hidden Injustice: Lesbian, Gay, Bisexual and Transgender Youth in Juvenile Courts." The Equity Project.

Science to Community. 2004. "Collaborative Research to Prevent HIV Among Prisoners and Their Families." Center for AIDS Prevention Studies. December 20. http://caps.ucsf.edu/uploads/pubs/reports/pdf/CenterforceS2C.pdf.

Wolfe, Zachary. 2014. "Gay and Lesbian Prisoners: Recent Developments and a Call for More Research." Prison Legal News, January 15. https://www.prisonlegalnews.org/(X(1)S(q4vvyl55paw2re55j12dic2l))/displayArticle.aspx?articleid=20578&AspxAutoDetectCookieSupport=1.

Chapter 22

LGBT Elected Officials and Their Roles in Changing America

Jane Laine

Contents

On November 6, 2012, a tidal wave swept through the United States in the form of democratic victories over fundamental civil rights issues. In Minnesota, a marriage amendment that would include in the state's constitution the definition of marriage as being between a man and a woman was defeated. On the same day in Maine, Washington, and Maryland same-sex marriage was legalized. As if these events were not historic enough, in Wisconsin, the home of the very conservative Paul Ryan, the Republican vice presidential candidate Tammy Baldwin was elected to the United States Congress. The people have spoken and a new day is on the horizon for equality and civil rights.

To be openly gay and a politician means living your private life in the public eye. Some may say that in order to be a public figure, one must expect a certain loss of privacy as part of the job description. However, heterosexual politicians, historically, have only been expected to discuss aspects of their private lives when it comes to the exposure of a scandal. This very idea sets up the notion that we as a society deem anything other than heterosexuality as scandalous. Let us take into consideration the recent example of General David Petraeus, former director of the Central Intelligence Agency. No one questioned his sexuality or ability to lead, or even had concerns one way or another regarding his private life until it was discovered that he was having an affair with his biographer. Even after all is said and done, he will probably emerge from the scandal some years down the line with little harm done to his career. Another example from recent years is Bill Clinton. People knew that he had a wife and daughter, no one questioned the background his marriage with Hillary was until it was discovered that he was having a relationship with an intern. Today, he is a well-respected politician and Hillary has become a highly regarded and respected politician in her own right.

For a politician that has not started their political career as "out" publicly, there can be very scary and harsh consequences if opposition discovers that one is opting to try and keep this part of their life private. Neil Giuliano discusses how scary this can truly be in his autobiography *The Campaign Within* (2012). Giuliano started out as a city council member in Tempe, Arizona, and was the mayor of Tempe from 1994 to 2004, but did not publicly come out until 1996. Giuliano discusses in his autobiography the threats he received when constituents started to suspect that he might be gay. He started being publicly ridiculed at city council meetings by constituents who suspected he might be hiding his sexuality. As if that were not enough, he also received threatening phone calls. Eventually, Giuliano felt like he had no other choice but to come out in order to avoid continued harassment and threats. What he did not realize at the time was how rewarding this experience would become for him. From that point forward, he was able to run as a publicly out candidate with the support of the Gay and Lesbian Victory Fund, an organization that has made a monumental difference in the lives of many politicians, as well as lesbian, gay, bisexual, and transgender (LGBT) people, the world over.

The Gay and Lesbian Victory Fund is a political action fund that works to organize and energize around electing openly LGBT people to office. The organization's mission is "to change (the) face and voice of America's politics and achieve equality for LGBT Americans by increasing the number of openly LGBT officials at all levels of government" (Gay and Lesbian Victory Fund 2013). Founded in 1991, the Victory Fund works on local, state, and federal levels to help channel money into candidate's campaigns to help finance campaigns, and also gives endorsements for candidates. This support is huge for candidates and can make all the difference for their campaigns. The inspiration for Victory Fund came from a similar organization, Early Money Is Like Yeast, or EMILY's List, as it is more commonly known. EMILY's List was an idea that started with 25 women and their Rolodexes and the idea to elect pro-choice, democratic women to political office. The idea was that if one could funnel monetary support into the campaign in the early stages, then the candidates would have a better chance of winning. After seeing this strategy work successfully for EMILY's List, William Waybourn, a leading gay activist, approached other leaders in the community and the idea for the Victory Fund was born. The Victory Fund has been extremely successful in training and endorsing LGBT candidates, including Senator Tammy Baldwin. There is one commonality between all of the candidates that the Victory Fund endorses beyond their sexuality: they are all trailblazers.

At the Gay and Lesbian Victory Fund's December 2013 LGBT Leadership Conference, it was noted that every state that now has a same-sex marriage law is one that also has an openly LGBT elected official. Additionally, Professor Andrew Reynolds presented at that conference a rigorously scientific paper titled "Out In Office," which indicates that the presence of LGBT elected officials dramatically affects the level of social tolerance and equality around the world.

According to a Gallup Poll conducted in October 2012, 3.4% of the adult population of the United States identify as LGBT. If we consider that the total number of people serving in a role as an elected official in the United States at last census is around 511,000 (Lewis 2012), then in order for an accurate representation of the LGBT community, there would need to be roughly 15,300 elected officials that identified as LGBT. In 1997, the total number of openly gay elected officials was 124 (Yeager 1999), which is far less than even 1% of the populous of elected officials, and today, 16 years later, that number has only grown to 346, which is still a statistically insignificant number. On a more hopeful front, the number of out officials currently serving in public office numbers today at 990: This is for both elected positions and appointed positions. This number is still not nearly close enough to where one should be to show true progress, but it is at least a start.

According to the Victory Fund's website, there are 91 state-level elected officials in the United States and only 4 at the federal level (Victory Institute 2013). These 95 elected officials have had to endure death threats, public outcry over their private lives, ridicule, hate mail, and other threats just for being who they are, and yet, they still act in service of the people every day as they have been elected to do so. This bravery that they show is something to be truly honored and admired, which is why instead of sharing a lot of information on many of these individuals,

I have opted instead to highlight a small amount of information about each of them. Additionally, because change begins with us, it is imperative that we stop focusing only on the sexuality of these brave politicians who must live the most private aspects of their lives publicly and we must start focusing on the amazing work they are doing for their constituents as well. In the chapter we will highlight 16 vignettes about the work of sixteen of these trailblazers. We have not included all of the openly LGBT elected officials, but hopefully these mini biographies will help to explain the powerful way in which these courageous LGBT elected officials have changed the face of America.

Tammy Baldwin

United States Senator, Wisconsin. Tammy Baldwin made history when she was elected on the historic day in November 2012 becoming the first Wisconsin woman and the first openly gay person to be elected to Congress (Grinberg 2012). Baldwin's election in 2012 was an interesting battle to watch for many reasons, especially because of the state she was running in and who she was running against. Coming from Wisconsin, a very conservative state, where the governor had recently cut collective bargaining rights for unions, it would have appeared to an outsider that Baldwin would have been fighting an uphill battle. Her opponent, Tommy Thompson, served as the governor of Wisconsin for 14 years and then served as the secretary for Health and Human Services under George W. Bush (Nocera 2012).

Making history is not new for Baldwin, because in 1998 when she was first elected to Wisconsin state Congress she became the state's first female member of Congress. She also became the "nation's first openly gay challenger sent to Congress" (Tammy Baldwin 2013). Prior to her election in 2012, Baldwin did an interview for Sirius XM OUtQ radio, where she discussed the impact that her being elected could have, and what she said was: "We have substantive impact as leaders and we have a symbolic impact as leaders … Substantively, we bring our life experiences to our jobs, and they inform our decisions and choices and votes. And so, having a seat at the table matters" (Signorile 2012). She then goes on to discuss the symbolic importance of being a leader. She then notes that the significance of that is not just being present at the table, but being welcome at the table and showing the impact that your seat has, creating a "ripple effect," as Baldwin puts it. This enables LGBT youth to envision themselves achieving goals they before did not see possible.

Tom Ammiano

California State Assemblyman, District 17, Sacramento, California. Tom Ammiano has served on the San Francisco Board of Education as well as being the assemblyman for the 13th district prior to moving to the 17th district. Ammiano has also worked as an educator, and most notably, "In 1975, he became the first public school teacher in San Francisco to make his sexual orientation a matter of public knowledge. In 1977, Ammiano founded the movement (No on 6) against the Briggs Initiative, an effort to ban all gay people from teaching in California, with activists Hank Wilson and Harvey Milk" (California LGBT Legislature 2013). Ammiano also notably authored a bill that passed the assembly floor in May 2013, AB 1266, which allows transgender students to have "equal and full access to programs and facilities on the basis of their gender identity" (California State Assembly Democratic Caucus 2013). In addition to helping author this bill, Ammiano also fights for domestic worker rights, protections for homeless youth, and prisoners' rights (California Legislative Lesbian, Gay, Bisexual, and Transgender Caucus 2013a).

Mark Ferrandino

Colorado State Representative, District 2, Denver County, Colorado. Mark Ferrandino is the first openly gay man to be elected Speaker of the House in Colorado. Additionally, upon being elected to the legislature in 2008, he became the first openly gay lawmaker in Colorado's history (Bartles 2008). Ferrandino began his childhood overcoming adversity and challenges having struggled with several learning disabilities and went to a school specializing in special education through fourth grade (Hoover 2011), which has enabled him to help tackle many adversities in his life. He recently made headlines when a reporter for *The Denver Post* ran a photo of Ferrandino and his partner, Greg Wertsch, kissing in Ferrandino's office. When asked about the photo, Ferrandino said: "This wasn't a choice. This is who I am. This is who we are," he told *The Denver Post*. "We need to make laws in our society that respect everyone equally" (*Huffington Post* 2013).

Simone Bell

State Representative, District 58, serving Atlanta, Georgia. Simone Bell is "the first openly lesbian African-American elected to a state legislative office in the country" (Bagby 2010). Bell did considerable work as a community organizer prior to becoming involved in politics and continues to connect to this work through the committees she is involved in (Simone Bell 2013).

Greg Harris

State Representative, District 13, Chicago, Illinois. Greg Harris is openly living with HIV and has won multiple awards for the work that he has done, including the Susan G. Komen Champion for the Cure Award, the Chicago House Public Service Award, and the Equality Illinois' Freedom Award (Greg Harris 2013). Harris is the sponsor of Illinois Marriage Equality bill, which was not put to a vote in the 2012–2013 legislative sessions. Harris received national attention for his tearful and heartfelt speech on the House floor when he announced that he would not put the bill to a vote, respecting his colleagues' request for more time to consider the issue (Erbentraut 2013). The bill was passed in the next session.

Matt McCoy

State Senator, District 31, Des Moines, Iowa. Matt McCoy was first elected in 1997 and is serving his fifth term in the Iowa senate. He is the first openly gay member of the Iowa Senate and was publically outed on the Senate floor by a Republican leader in 2004 (Clayworth 2006). He has won several awards including the John F. Kennedy Award for Outstanding Leadership for Democratic Elected Officials, the Distinguished Service Award from the Iowa Federation of the Blind, and the Association of General Contractors Legislator of the Year Award (Matt McCoy 2013). McCoy sponsored 23 bills in the 2012–2013 legislative sessions, including one that would allow individuals with foreign-born parents to attend college in Iowa at in-state tuition costs (Iowa Legislature 2013).

Liz Malia

Representative, 11th Suffolk District, in Jamaica Plains, Massachusetts: Liz Malia has been in office since 1998. In June 2012, Malia was arrested for trying to block the eviction of one of her constituents who had been locked into a high-interest mortgage loan by a bank. Malia and about 90 other protestors gathered to support the constituent who was being evicted due to her high interest rate. When questioned about the incident following her arrest, Malia said she thought it was the right thing to do (Kronenberg 2012).

Susan Allen

State Representative, District 62B, Minneapolis, Minnesota. Susan Allen is currently serving her second term in office in the Minnesota House of Representatives. She is the vice chair of the Civil Law Committee and sits on three other committees (State of Minnesota 2013). She is the first Native American lesbian in the United States to serve on a state legislature (*Huffington Post* 2012). When discussing her historic win, in an article in the *Twin Cities Daily Planet*, Allen said "It's about integration, it's not about assimilation … I think it's important that I reflect the diversity of our community in south Minneapolis. ... I realize how important or historic this is in the sense that ... young children ... will see somebody who looks like them" (Cook 2012).

Matt Titone

Assemblyman, District 61, Staten Island, New York. Matt Titone has been a member of the New York State Assembly since 2007. Prior to his political involvement, Titone garnered national attention when he represented a family in a lawsuit against the New York state adoption industry. The family had unknowingly adopted a child born with the AIDS virus and this issue, having not been disclosed to them, prevented the child from receiving treatment for several years after the adoption was completed. After the successful completion of the court case, Titone helped establish the Justin LiGreci HIV/AIDS Foundation for Children and Teens, which provides education to youth in the Staten Island, New York area (State of New York 2013).

Kate Brown

Secretary of State, Portland, Oregon. As Oregon's Secretary of State, Kate Brown, who is bisexual, is the country's highest ranking "out" political figure (Coleman 2010). Before becoming secretary of state in 2008, Brown served two terms in the Oregon House of Representatives and two terms in the Oregon Senate. She has received several awards including one for Outstanding Achievement by the Oregon Family Support Network, the Marilyn Epstein Pro Choice Champion Award from Planned Parenthood Advocates of Oregon, and the "Profiles in Courage" Award from Basic Rights Oregon (Kate Brown 2012). In her role as secretary of state, Brown has made history by moving Oregon to online voter registration and providing tablet technology to voters (*Oregon Blue Book* 2013). This has reportedly reduced the cost of voter registration to less than $1 per person from around $8 per person and made voting more accessible to vulnerable populations like the elderly and disabled (Foden-Vencil 2011).

Gordon Fox

Representative, District 4, Providence, Rhode Island. Gordon Fox was first elected to the Rhode Island House of Representatives in 1992. In 2010 he was elected the Speaker of the House (Gordon Fox 2012), making history becoming not only the first openly gay Speaker of the House in the state but also the first black Speaker of the House (Winter 2010).

Angie Buhl O'Donnell

Senator, District 15, Sioux Falls, South Dakota. Angie Buhl O'Donnell was first elected to the South Dakota Senate in 2010 at the age of 25, becoming the youngest member of the state's Senate (Angie Buhl 2012). Buhl O'Donnell is an "out" bisexual and is the first out legislator in the state of South Dakota (Reese 2012). She is a progressive activist serving in what is generally seen as a conservative state.

Victoria Kolakowski and Stu Rasmussen

Victoria Kolakowski is an Alameda County California Superior Court Judge and Stu Rasmussen is the mayor of Silverton, Oregon. They are both leaders in their jurisdictions as well as in the transgender community.

Jared Polis

United States House of Representatives, Colorado, District 2. Jared Polis was first elected to the United States House of Representatives in 2008. His political career began in 2000 when he joined the Colorado State Board of Education. Polis is currently serving on three committees: the Rules Committee, the Education and Workforce Committee, and the House Democratic Steering and Policy Committee (United States House of Representatives 2013).

Karen Clark

Representative, District 62A, Minneapolis, Minnesota. Karen Clark is currently serving her 17th term in the Minnesota House of Representatives, having been first elected in 1980. She is the "the longest-serving openly Lesbian State Legislator in the U.S." (Karen Clark 2012). She is an active and respected member of her community, and was one of the legislative leaders, along with Minnesota Senator Scott Dibble, who made it possible to stop the "One Man/One Woman" marriage law and to pass the same-sex marriage law in Minnesota.

Conclusion

These 16 vignettes represent only some of the trailblazers that represent the LGBT population as our elected officials in the United States. They have bravely put themselves forward as active members in our democracy by representing us all. As Aristotle said in *Politics*, "If liberty and equality, as is thought by some are chiefly to be found in democracy, they will be best attained when all persons alike share in the government to the utmost" (*The Telegraph* 2007).

The strategy of ensuring that there are openly LGBTQIA elected officials throughout the country has been a highly effective method of seeing to it that voters around the nation have the opportunity to become familiar with what would otherwise be an unknown and unpopular sexual orientation and gender identity minority. The courage of the elected officials who have made it their job to perform a public service and normalize a minority group is extraordinary.

Resources and Recommended Readings

Adam Ebbin for Congress. 2012. "About." Accessed January 19, 2013, http://www.adamebbin.com/about.

Alabama House of Representatives. "Representative Patricia Todd." 2013. Accessed January 12, 2013, http://www.legislature.state.al.us/house/representatives/housebios/hd054.html.

Angie Buhl. 2012. Accessed January 19, 2013, http://angiebuhl.com/about.

Anne Kaiser. 2013. Accessed January 15, 2013, http://annekaiser.com/?page_id = 2.

Arizona State Legislature. 2013a. Accessed January 13, 2013, http://www.azleg.gov/MembersPage.asp?Member_ID = 31&Legislature = 49&Session_ID = 87.

Arizona State Legislature. 2013b. Accessed January 12, 2013, http://www.azleg.gov/MembersPage.asp?Member_ID = 14&Legislature = 50&Session_ID = 107.

Atkins for Assembly. 2013. "Biography." Accessed January 12, 2013, http://www.atkinsforassembly.com/about/biography?_c = 1156yczs26wtyvu.

Baer, S. 2012. "Richard Madaleno: Showing the Way on Marriage Equality." *Washingtonian*, February 7. Accessed January 15, 2013, http://www.washingtonian.com/articles/people/richard-madaleno-showing-the-way-on-marriage-equality/index.php.

Bagby, D. 2010. "Georgia Lesbian Lawmaker Brings Power to the People from within the Gold Dome." *Georgia Voice*, March 17. Accessed January 14, 2013, http://www.thegavoice.com/index.php/news/georgia-news/47-georgia-lesbian-lawmaker-brings-power-to-the-people-from-within-the-gold-dome.

Bagby, D. 2013. "Jane Morrison Sworn in as Fulton County State Court Judge." *The Georgia Voice*, January 4. Accessed January 14, 2013, http://www.thegavoice.com/news/georgia-news/5685-jane-morrison-sworn-is-as-fulton-county-state-judge.

Bartles, L. 2008. "Citizen Legislator, March 20." *Rocky Mountain News*, March 20. Accessed January 14, 2013, http://www.rockymountainnews.com/news/2008/mar/20/citizen-legislator-march-20/.

Biskupic, J. 2006. "Amid Debate Over Rights, Number of Gay Judges Rising." *USA Today*, October 17. Accessed January 17, 2013, http://usatoday30.usatoday.com/news/washington/2006-10-17-gay-judges_x.htm.

Broverman, N. 2012. "Meet America's (Shockingly Small) Pool of Trans Elected Officials." November 14, http://www.advocate.com/politics/transgender/2012/11/14/meet-shockingly-small-pool-trans-elected-officials.

California Legislative Lesbian, Gay, Bisexual, and Transgender Caucus. 2013a. "Assemblymember Tom Ammiano." Accessed January 12, 2013, http://lgbtcaucus.legislature.ca.gov/assemblymember-tom-ammiano.

California Legislative Lesbian, Gay, Bisexual, and Transgender Caucus. 2013b. "Assemblymember Richard S. Gordon." Accessed January 13, 2013, http://lgbtcaucus.legislature.ca.gov/assemblymember-richard-s-gordon.

California State Assembly Democratic Caucus. 2013c. "Assemblymember Tom Ammiano." Accessed July 11, 2013, http://www.asmdc.org/members/a17/.

California Legislative Lesbian, Gay, Bisexual, and Transgender Caucus. 2013d. "Assemblyspeaker John Perez." Accessed January 13, 2013, http://lgbtcaucus.legislature.ca.gov/assembly-speaker-john-perez.

California State Assembly Democratic Caucus. 2013. "Assembly Passes Bill to Protect Transgender Students." May 9. Accessed July 11, 2013, http://www.asmdc.org/members/a17/press-releases/assembly-passes-bill-to-protect-transgender-students.

Committee to Elect Carl Sciortino. 2012. "About Carl." Accessed January 15, 2013, http://www.electcarl.org/carl.html.

Cathleen Galgiani for Senate. 2012. Accessed January 13, 2013, http://www.cathleengalgiani.com/.

City of Tacoma, Washington. 2012. Accessed January 19, 2013, http://www.cityoftacoma.org/Page.aspx?nid = 400.

Clayworth, J. 2006. "Contenders Talk Up Plans For Education, Avoid Sexuality." *Des Moines Register*, October 18. Accessed January 15, 2013, http://www.desmoinesregister.com/apps/pbcs.dll/article?AID =/20061018/NEWS09/610180393/1056.

Coleman, P. A. 2010. "Walking Bi Dancing Outside the Big Gay Party." *Portland and Mercury*, June 17. Accessed January 17, 2013, http://www.portlandmercury.com/portland/walking-bi/Content?oid = 2610445.

Congressman David Cicilline. 2013. "Full Biography." Accessed January 19, 2013, http://cicilline.house.gov/about-me/full-biography.

Congressman Jared Polis. 2013. "Biography." Accessed January 19, 2013, http://polis.house.gov/biography/.

Connecticut Mirror. 2013. "Maynard, Andrew M." Accessed January 14, 2013, http://www.ctmirror.org/node/286.

Connecticut State Democrats. 2012. "State Senator Beth Bye." Accessed January 14, 2013, http://www.senatedems.ct.gov/bye.php.

Cook, M. 2012. "Rep. Susan Allen: Always Looking to Help Others." *Twin Cities Daily Planet*, January 31. Accessed July 16, 2013, http://www.tcdailyplanet.net/news/2012/01/31/rep-susan-allen-always-looking-help-others.

Representative Deb Ruggiero District 74 Jamestown/Middletown. 2013. "About." Accessed January 19, 2013, http://debruggiero.com/index.php/about/.

Deborah Mell. 2012. Accessed January 15, 2013, debmell.org/about-deb/.

Donna Nesselbush. 2013. Accessed January 19, 2013, http://www.donnanesselbush.com/DefaultPermissions/Home/tabid/36/Default.aspx.

Douglas-Brown, L. 2012. "Election Results: Keisha Waites to Become Fourth Openly Gay Ga. State Legislator." *The Georgia Voice*, February 7. Accessed January 14, 2013, http://www.thegavoice.com/news/georgia-news/4157-election-results-keisha-waites-to-become-fourth-openly-gay-ga-state-legislator/.

Equality California. 2012. "Equality California Congratulates Cathleen Galgiani on Historic Win" (news release). *Equality California*, November 27. Accessed January 13, 2013, http://www.eqca.org/site/apps/nlnet/content2.aspx?c = kuLRJ9MRKrH&b = 4990109&ct = 12509481.

Erbentraut, J. 2013. "Illinois Gay Marriage: House Fails To Vote On Same-Sex Marriage Bill Friday, Bill Delayed Until Fall." *Huffington Post*, May 31. Accessed July 12, 2013, http://www.huffingtonpost.com/2013/05/31/illinois-gay-marriage-hou_0_n_3367329.html.

Foden-Vencil, K. 2011. "Online Voter Registration Celebrates First Anniversary." *Oregon Public Broadcasting*, February 27. Accessed July 16, 2013, http://www.opb.org/news/article/online-voter-registration-celebrates-first-anniversary/.

Gates, Gary J., and Frank Newport. 2012. "Special Report: 3.4% of U.S. Adults Identify as LGBT." *Gallup*, October 18. Accessed July 11, 2013, http://www.gallup.com/poll/158066/special-report-adults-identify-lgbt.aspx.

Garcia, M. 2011. "Lesbian Activist Named to Far North Side House Seat." *Chicago Tribune News Blog*, April 18. Accessed January 14, 2013, http://newsblogs.chicagotribune.com/clout_st/2011/04/states-attorney-administrator-named-to-far-north-side-house-seat.html.

Gay and Lesbian Victory Fund. 2013. "Mission." Accessed July 11, 2013, http://www.victoryfund.org/our_story/mission.

Gay and Lesbian Victory Fund. 2013. "The Victory Fund: A Brief Hisotry." Accessed July 11, 2013, http://www.victoryfund.org/our_story/history.

Gay Voices. 2012. "Al McAffrey, Oklahoma State Representative, Becomes State's First Openly Gay Senator." *The Huffington Post*, February 15. Accessed January 17, 2013, http://www.huffingtonpost.com/2012/02/15/al-mcaffrey-oklahoma-senator-gay_n_1279556.html.

Georgia Government. 2012. *Georgia House*. Accessed January 14, 2013, http://www.house.ga.gov/Documents/Biographies/drennerKarla.pdf.

Giuliano, N. 2012. *The Campaign Within*. New York: Magnus Books.

Gordon Fox. 2012. "Biography of Speaker Gordon D. Fox." Accessed January 19, 2013, http://www.gordonfox.com/bio.html.

Greg Harris. 2013. "Biography." Accessed January 15, 2013, http://www.gregharris.org/wp/biography/.

Grinberg, E. 2012. "Wisconsin's Tammy Baldwin Is First Openly Gay Person Elected to Senate." *CNN*. November 7. Accessed January 19, 2013, http://www.cnn.com/2012/11/07/politics/wisconsin-tammy-baldwin-senate/index.html.

Grodzins Romm, E. 2009. "Profiles: Micah Kellner: Harvey Milk Lives- in Albany." *The Huffington Post*, March 15. Accessed January 17, 2013, http://stewardshipreport.com/harvey-milk-lives-in-albany/.

Heather Mizeur. 2013. "About Heather." Accessed January 15, 2013, http://www.heathermizeur.com/content/about-heather.

Hoover, T. 2011. "Mark Ferrandino, New Colorado House Minority Leader, Overcame Challenging Childhood." *Denver Post*, November 24. Accessed July 12, 2013, http://www.denverpost.com/legislature/ci_19403803.

Huffington Post. 2012. "Susan Allen, Minnesota Democrat, Becomes First Native American Lesbian to Serve on a State Legislature." January 11. Accessed January 15, 2013, http://www.huffingtonpost.com/2012/01/11/susan-allen-minneapolis-democrat-native-american-lesbian_n_1199647.html.

Huffington Post. 2013. "Mark Ferrandino, Colorado House Speaker, Shown Kissing Partner in Denver Post Photograph." March 14. Accessed July 12, 2013, http://www.huffingtonpost.com/2013/03/14/mark-ferrandino-colorado-house-speaker-kiss-photo_n_2879086.html.

Iowa Legislature. 2013. Accessed July 12, 2013, http://coolice.legis.iowa.gov/Cool-ICE/default.asp?category = billinfo&service = dspldata&var = sspo&cfid = 134&GA = 85.

JoCasta Zamarripa. 2012. "Vote JoCasta." Accessed January 19, 2013, http://www.votejocasta.com/bio.html.

Karen Clark. 2012. "Vote Karen." Accessed January 15, 2013, http://www.votekaren.org/node/29.

Kate Brown. 2012. Accessed January 17, 2013, http://www.katebrownfororegon.com/about/.

Kate Hogan. 2012. Accessed January 15, 2013, http://katehogan.net/pages/about_kate.html.

Kronenberg, J. 2012. "State Rep. Elizabeth Malia Arrested in JP Eviction." *Boston Herald,* June 15. Accessed January 15, 2013, http://bostonherald.com/business/real_estate/2012/06/state_rep_elizabeth_malia_arrested_jp_eviction.

LA Law Library. 2012. Accessed January 13, 2013, http://www.lalawlibrary.org/about/board/default.aspx.

Lavers, M. 2012. "Gay N.H. Lawmaker Seeks to Become First Out Candidate Elected to State Senate." *Washington Blade,* October 25. Accessed January 16, 2013, http://www.washingtonblade.com/2012/10/25/gay-n-h-lawmaker-seeks-to-become-first-out-candidate-elected-to-state-senate/.

Lee, R. 2012. "The Bittersweet Saga of Karla Drenner: Politician, Pioneer." *The Georgia Voice,* July 20. Accessed January 14, 2013, http://www.thegavoice.com/news/georgia-news/4947-the-bittersweet-saga-of-karla-drenner-politician-pioneer.

Lewis, R. D. 2012. "Local Officials Must Remain in Control." New York *Times,* November 9. Accessed July 11, 2013, http://www.nytimes.com/roomfordebate/2012/11/08/does-our-voting-system-need-to-be-fixed/local-officials-must-remain-in-control-of-elections.

Lovett, I. 2011. "California to Require Gay History in Schools." *New York Times,* July 14. Accessed January 13, 2013, http://www.nytimes.com/2011/07/15/us/15gay.html?_r = 0.

Maggie McIntosh. 2012. Accessed January 15, 2013, http://www.delmaggie.com/?page_id=167.

Maine Senate Democrats. 2013. "Bartlett." Accessed January 15, 2013, http://senatedems.maine.gov/bartlett/index.htm.

Mapes, J. 2013. "For Oregon House, More Adventures With the New as Tina Kotek Becomes Fourth Speaker in as Many Terms." *Oregon Live,* January 14. Accessed January 17, 2013, http://www.oregonlive.com/mapes/index.ssf/2013/01/for_oregon_house_more_adventur.html.

Marcus Brandon. 2012. "Biography." Accessed January 17, 2013, http://www.marcusbrandon.com/biography.

Mark Leno. 2013. "2012 Legislation." Accessed January 13, 2013, http://sd11.senate.ca.gov/legislation/2012.

Mata, L. 2012. "Senator Ricardo Lara Sworn-in Today, Becomes California's First Openly Gay Senator of Color in State History." State of California. December 3. Accessed January 13, 2013, http://sd33.senate.ca.gov/news/2012-12-03-senator-ricardo-lara-sworn-today-becomes-california-s-first-openly-gay-senator-color.

Matt McCoy. 2013. Accessed January 15, 2013, http://www.matt-mccoy.com/matt-mccoy/profile.html.

Meyer, L. 2009. "Out in the Equality State." *Seattle Gay News,* March 6. Accessed January 19, 2013, http://www.sgn.org/sgnnews37_10/page12.cfm.

Multnomah Bar Association. 2012. "Justice Virginia Linder." Accessed January 17, 2013, http://www.mbabar.org/Resources/VirginiaLinder.html.

New York Court System. 2013. Accessed January 17, 2013, http://www.nycourtsystem.com/Applications/JudicialDirectory/Bio.php?ID = 7025190.

New York State Assembly. 2013. "Biography." Accessed January 17, 2013, http://assembly.state.ny.us/mem/Matthew-Titone/bio/.
Nocera, K. 2012. "Tammy Baldwin Tops Tommy Thompson in Wisconsin." *Politico*, November 7. Accessed July 29, 2013, http://www.politico.com/news/stories/1112/83453.html.
Open States. 2013. "Herb A. Font-Russell." Accessed January 19, 2013, http://openstates.org/vt/legislators/VTL000196/herb-a-font-russell/.
Oregon Blue Book. 2013. "Secretary of State Kate Brown." Accessed July 16, 2013, http://bluebook.state.or.us/state/executive/secretary_of_state/secbio.htm.
People for Pedersen. 2013. Accessed January 19, 2013, http://www.peopleforpedersen.org/.
Pocan for Congress. 2013. "Meet Mark Pocan." Accessed January 18, 2013, http://pocanforcongress.com/about/.
Rashad Taylor. 2012–2013. Accessed January 14, 2013, http://www.rashadtaylor.com/About.html.
Reese, P. 2012. "2012 Proving Busy Year for Victory Fund." *Washington Blade*, April 28. Accessed January 19, 2013, http://www.washingtonblade.com/2012/04/26/2012-proving-busy-year-for-victory-fund/.
Rice, S. 2010. "SGN Exlusive Interview: Openly Gay Bryce Bennett Runs for Montana Office." *Seattle Gay News*, April 30. Accessed January 15, 2013, http://www.sgn.org/sgnnews38_18/mobile/page3.cfm.
Sarah Peake. 2013. "Bio." Accessed January 15, 2013, http://www.sarahpeake.org/bio/.
Sarver, A. 2010. "Marcus Brandon Elected to House District 60, Becomes Second Openly Gay Member in N.C. General Assembly History." *The American Independent*, November 3. Accessed January 17, 2013, http://americanindependent.com/154273/marcus-brandon-elected-to-house-district-60-becomes-second-openly-gay-member-in-n-c-general-assembly-history.
Signorile, M. 2012. "Tammy Baldwin, Wisconsin's Lesbian Congresswoman, Talks Senate Candidacy, LGBT Issues at DNC." *Huffington Post*, September 11. Accessed http://www.huffingtonpost.com/2012/09/11/tammy-baldwin-wisconsin-lesbian-congresswoman-dnc_n_1873812.html.
Simone Bell. 2013. "Representative Simone Bell." Accessed January 14, 2013, http://www.simonebell.com/more/index.cfm?Fuseaction = more_57711&section = more_57711.
Stan Rosenberg. 2010. "Biography." Accessed January 15, 2013, http://stanrosenberg.com/index.php?filename=stan-rosenberg-biography.html.
State of Maryland. 2012. Accessed January 15, 2013, http://msa.maryland.gov/msa/mdmanual/06hse/html/msa15461.html.
State of Maryland. 2012. Accessed January 15, 2013, http://msa.maryland.gov/msa/mdmanual/06hse/html/msa14628.html.
State of Maryland. 2013. Accessed January 15, 2013, http://msa.maryland.gov/msa/mdmanual/06hse/html/msa15452.html.
State of Maryland. 2013. Accessed January 15, 2013, http://msa.maryland.gov/msa/mdmanual/06hse/html/msa15349.html.
State of Massachusetts. 2013. Accessed January 15, 2013, http://www.malegislature.gov/people/profile/car1.
State of Massachusetts. 2013. Accessed January 15, 2013, http://www.malegislature.gov/People/Profile/scr0.
State of Minnesota. 2013. Accessed January 15, 2013, http://www.senate.leg.state.mn.us/members/member_bio.php?leg_id = 10142.

State of Minnesota. 2013. Accessed January 15, 2013, http://www.house.leg.state.mn.us/members/members.asp?id = 15377.

State of Missouri. 2013. Missouri House of Representatives. Accessed January 15, 2013, http://www.house.mo.gov/member.aspx?year = 2013&district = 080.

State of Missouri. 2013. Missouri State Senate. Accessed January 15, 2013, http://www.senate.mo.gov/13info/Members/D10/bio.htm.

State of Montana. 2013. Accessed January 15, 2013, http://leg.mt.gov/css/Sessions/63rd/leg_info.asp?HouseID = 0&SessionID = 107&LAWSID = 13032.

State of Montana. 2013. Accessed January 15, 2013, http://leg.mt.gov/css/Sessions/63rd/leg_info.asp?HouseID = 2&SessionID = 107&LAWSID = 14470.

State of Montana. 2013. Accessed January 15, 2013, http://leg.mt.gov/css/Sessions/62nd/leg_info.asp?HouseID = 0&SessionID = 105&LAWSID = 13941.

State of New Hampshire. n.d. *New Hampshire State Senate*. Accessed January 16, 2013, http://www.gencourt.state.nh.us/Senate/members/webpages/district05.aspx.

State of New York. 2013. New York State Assembly. Accessed January 17, 2013, http://assembly.state.ny.us/mem/Deborah-J-Glick/bio/.

State of New York. 2013. New York State Assembly. Accessed January 17, 2013, http://assembly.state.ny.us/mem/?ad = 069&sh = bio.

State of Ohio. 2013. *Ohio House of Representatives*. Accessed January 17, 2013, http://www.ohiohouse.gov/nickie-j-antonio/biography.

State of Oregon. 2013. *Oregon State Legislature*. Accessed January 17, 2013, http://www.leg.state.or.us/kotek/.

State of Oregon. 2013. Accessed January 17, 2013, http://courts.oregon.gov/Supreme/pages/biokistler.aspx.

State of Rhode Island. 2013. *Rhode Island House of Representatives*. Accessed January 19, 2013, http://webserver.rilin.state.ri.us/Ferri/Biography.html.

State of Rhode Island. 2013. Accessed January 19, 2013, http://webserver.rilin.state.ri.us/Nesselbush/Biography.html.

State of Rhode Island. 2013. Accessed January 19, 2013, http://webserver.rilin.state.ri.us/ruggiero/Biography.html.

State of Vermont. 2013. Accessed January 19, 2013, http://www.suziwizowaty.com/bio.htm.

State of Wisconsin. 2013. Accessed January 19, 2013, http://legis.wisconsin.gov/senate/carpenter/Pages/Biography.aspx.

State of Wyoming. 2013. Accessed January 19, 2013, http://legisweb.state.wy.us/legislatorsummary/LegDetail.aspx?LegID = 1258.

Sue Schafer. 2013. Accessed January 14, 2013, http://www.sueschafer.com/aboutsue/experience.html.

Tammy Baldwin. 2013. "About Tammy." Accessed July 29, 2013, from http://www.tammybaldwin.com/about/.

Terry Morrison. 2013. Accessed January 15, 2013, http://www.terrymorrison.org/values/.

The Telegraph. 2007, July 12. Accessed August 7, 2013, http://www.telegraph.co.uk/culture/3673945/Famous-quotes-about-democracy.html.

Unified Courts of Guam. 2013. "The Hon. Benjamin J.F. Cruz." Accessed January 19, 2013, http://www.guamsupremecourt.com/Justices/cruz.html.

Victory Institute. 2013. Accessed January 19, 2013, http://www.victoryinstitute.org/out_officials/search.

Vote Smart. 2012. Accessed January 19, 2013, http://votesmart.org/candidate/biography/123607/brian-campion#.UPr64SKfvIU.

Vote Smart. 2012. Accessed January 19, 2013, http://votesmart.org/candidate/biography/5333/bill-lippert-jr#.UPr97SKfvIU.

Vote Smart. 2013. Accessed January 12, 2013, http://votesmart.org/candidate/biography/28338/kyrsten-sinema#.UPI4qyKfvIU.

Washington House Democrats. 2013. Accessed January 19, 2013, http://housedemocrats.wa.gov/roster/rep-marko-liias/biography/.

Washington House Democrats. 2013. Accessed January 19, 2013, http://housedemocrats.wa.gov/roster/rep-jim-moeller/biography/.

Washington House Democrats. 2013. Accessed January 19, 2013, http://housedemocrats.wa.gov/roster/rep-dave-upthegrove/.

Washington Senate Democrats. 2013. "David Parks Still Faces Many Hurdles." Accessed January 19, 2013, http://www.senatedemocrats.wa.gov/senators/murray/biography.htm.

Willis, S. 2010. *Las Vegas Sun,* January 30. Accessed January 17, 2013, http://www.lasvegassun.com/news/2010/jan/30/david-parks-still-faces-many-hurdles-nevada/.

Winter, M. 2010. "Rhode Island Gets Its First Black Gay House Speaker." *USA Today,* February 11. Accessed January 19, 2013, http://content.usatoday.com/communities/ondeadline/post/2010/02/rhode-island-gets-its-first-black-gay-house-speaker/1#.UPruHSKfvIU.

Yeager, K. 1999. *Trailblazers: Profiles of America's Gay and Lesbian Elected Officials.* Binghamton: The Haworth Press.

Chapter 23

Federalism, Incrementalism, and the Public Administration Infrastructure

Kristen Norman-Major

Contents

Introduction

The framers of the constitution had several goals in mind when constructing the system of government in the United States. Many of the arguments about the proper form of government expounded in the Federalist Papers revolved around concerns that power be dispersed, factions controlled, policy making be deliberate, and the people's needs, at least as defined by the founders, be heard. The framers' efforts resulted in our federalist system of government with republican representation and a policy-making process that requires deliberation by many. While these systems help control tyranny by the majority, in certain cases they can also make the public policy process less effective, efficient, and equitable than desired. This chapter considers the effects of federalism and incrementalism in building and supporting the public administration infrastructure necessary to support lesbian, gay, bisexual, and transgender (LGBT) rights.

Federalism

The federal system of government in the United States divides power between the central, federal government, and state and local governments. As written in Federalist Paper 51:

> It is of great importance in a republic not only to guard the society against oppression of its rulers, but to guard one part of society against the injustice of the other part. Different interests necessarily exist in different classes of citizens. If a majority be united by a common interest, the rights of the minority will be insecure.

According to the author(s) of Federalist Number 51, establishing a federal model would create a proper balance of interests that would in turn provide justice for citizens because, as they state, "justice is the end of government. It is the end of civil society."

At its core, the purpose of a federal system is to limit the power of the central government to only those things deemed so universal as to warrant national power while leaving other issues up to states and localities to determine based on local needs and available resources. The question arises as to which issues are deemed universal enough to warrant national policy versus being left to local policy development. As has been illustrated in several other chapters in this volume, the federal system of policy making and implementation has led to great inequities across states and localities in relation to LGBT rights. "The 1964 Civil Rights Act provides national protections against discrimination based on race, color, religion, sex or national origin but does not include protections for discrimination based on sexual orientation or gender identity" (Badgett 1995, 726); instead such protections have been mainly left to states and localities to determine. At odds here is the treatment of civil rights for different groups. Protections based on race, color, religion, sex, or national origin have been deemed central enough to warrant national policy. This has not been the case for protections based on sexual orientation or gender identity.

Advocates for LGBT rights have attempted to pass national legislation to provide protections to the LGBT community since at least 1974 when the Employment Non-Discrimination Act (ENDA) was first introduced in Congress (National Gay and Lesbian Task Force [NGLTF] 2013b). The bill has had several hearings over the years but has not been passed. It was reintroduced in the spring of 2013 and there is some belief that the increased support for LGBT equality across the United States may lead to more action on the legislation (Human Rights Campaign [HRC] 2013). The legislation has the support of the AFL-CIO (Johnson 2013) as well as over 90 major companies that are part of The Business Coalition for Workplace Fairness (HRC 2013). The question for policymakers at this point is whether they feel this is an issue that deserves attention at the federal level or if actions will continue to be left to state and local governments.

Incrementalism and Infrastructure

Along with understanding the system of government in which U.S. policymakers operate, students of public policy and administration must also consider models of decision making. In the case of LGBT rights, the model of decision making that best reflects policy development is incrementalism. Based on Charles Lindblom's (1959, 1979) argument that in most cases public policy change is gradual or evolutionary instead of radical or revolutionary, incrementalism reflects slow development of policy change with most changes coming in the form of adjustments at the margins. A criticism sometimes raised of this model is that is does not account for major policy changes like the passage of the Civil Rights Act of 1964 or the Patriot Act. However, it does seem to accurately reflect the path of policy development for LGBT rights that has not included major national legislation but instead consists mostly of piecemeal policy changes that have evolved over time.

Policies, implementation, and enforcement mechanisms make up the public administration infrastructure that supports LGBT rights. Agencies at the state, local, and national levels have various roles to play. The strength of the infrastructure depends on the policies, systems, and resources in place. The following examples serve to examine some aspects of the public administration infrastructure in support of LGBT rights at both the national and state level as well as how federalism and incrementalism have shaped the policies and systems in place.

Federal Policies and Actions

As noted earlier, there is no national legislation protecting rights based on sexual orientation or gender identity. Federal policies that included some protections have developed incrementally and in a very piecemeal fashion. Many changes have come as a result of the July 2013 Supreme Court ruling that struck down section 3 of the Defense of Marriage Act (DOMA) (Lambdalegal.org 2013). Others have developed in reaction to discrimination cases brought before federal agencies. The following are some highlights.

Expansion of Equal Employment Opportunity Commission (EEOC) Protections

Title VII of the 1964 Civil Rights Act prohibits discrimination in employment based on race, color, religion, sex, or national origin (EEOC 2009). The U.S. Equal Employment Opportunity Commission (EEOC) was established to enforce these rules (Huetteman 2013). The EEOC partners with state civil/human rights commissions or other enforcement agencies to prevent discrimination and investigate claims. Although Title VII does not include specific provisions to protect against discrimination based on sexual orientation or gender identity, two rulings in the past few years have virtually expanded coverage to these cases in employment.

In *Veretto* v. *Donohoe* the EEOC ruled in July 2011 that Title VII's protections against sex discrimination included discrimination based on sexual stereotypes that assume heterosexual behaviors. Thus, discrimination based on sexual orientation is prohibited on the basis that it assumes homosexuality goes against a sexual stereotype. In this case, the discrimination occurred when a postal worker's announcement of his engagement to his same-sex partner appeared in the local paper. "The EEOC ruled that the harassment he faced was due to the sexual stereotype that assumes men should only marry women, not other men, thus is covered under Title VII" (FEDManager 2011). In *Macy* v. *Holder,* similar protections were extended to those claiming discrimination based on gender identity. This case has been particularly important to expanding the employment rights of transgender individuals (EEOC 2012; Mottet 2012).

Social Security: Gender Change

In June 2013, the Social Security Administration (SSA) changed its policy to simplify the process of changing one's gender identity in their Social Security record. This was a particularly important change for transgender individuals. Although Social Security cards do not include a gender marker, Social Security records are used by many organizations to verify identity (National Center for Transgender Equality 2013). Under previous policy, transgender individuals wanting to change their gender ID on their Social Security record were required to submit proof of sex reassignment surgery. Under the new policy individuals can use any of the following as evidence of gender change:

- Amended passport showing lived gender
- Amended birth certificate showing lived gender
- Court order directing legal recognition of change of sex
- Medical certification of "appropriate clinical treatment for gender transition" (U.S. Social Security Administration 2013a; American Civil Liberties Union 2013)

These changes make it much easier for transgender individuals to have their records changed and reflect a growing understanding of the complexity of gender identity.

Social Security: Benefits

Under the provisions of the DOMA, surviving or disabled married same-sex couples could not apply for disability or survivor benefits through the SSA. After the repeal of section 3 of DOMA, the SSA began encouraging same-sex couples to file claims if they felt they were eligible for benefits. As of August 29, 2013, the SSA was still working with the Justice Department to finalize the policy and processing instructions for such claims (U.S. Social Security Administration 2013b). Thus, the infrastructure for implementing these changes is still in development as of this writing, but a process is expected to be developed to implement this policy change.

Immigration Policy

The Supreme Court ruling striking down section 3 of DOMA also led to a change in immigration policy regarding visa applications for same-sex spouses. The U.S. State Department recognizes the validity of a marriage based on where it takes place, not current place of residence. Thus those same-sex couples who were legally married in a marriage-equality state or other country will now have their visa applications for spouses processed the same as for opposite-gender spouses (U.S. Department of State 2013).

Taxes

In August 2013, the U.S. Department of Treasury announced that as a result of the Supreme Court ruling on DOMA, legally married same-sex couples "will be treated as married for federal tax purposes" including income, estate, and gift taxes (U.S. Treasury 2013). The ruling allows legally married couples to file amended returns for up to three years prior (2010, 2011, and 2012). The ruling applies regardless of whether the couple lives in a state that currently recognizes their marriage.

This is illustrative of the challenges of a federal system when state and national policy do not align. State Departments of Revenue will need to develop systems to aid couples who must file different state and federal tax forms based on marital status.

Retirement Policy and Family and Medical Leave Act (FMLA)

In the wake of the Supreme Court's DOMA ruling, the Office of Personnel Management (OPM) announced that it would "extend benefits to Federal employees and annuitants who are legally married to spouses of the same sex, regardless of the employee's or annuitants' states of residency" (Yoder 2013). This change means that same sex-spouses and the couple's children will be eligible to be added to health insurance and other insurance policies.

Human resources experts are also informing states with marriage-equality laws that they will need to extend benefits under the Family and Medical Leave Act (FMLA) to allow for leaves to care for same-sex spouses or their children. Even though the FMLA is a federal law, the standing of section 2 of the DOMA means that states without marriage equality do not have to apply the leave benefits to same-sex couples and their families (Smith 2013). This is another example of the challenge of treating individuals differently at the state and federal level. The interpretation and implementation of policy changes may lead to complex systems of enforcement to assure people's rights are being protected.

Military Benefits

Similar to the OPM policy expanding federal employment benefits to same-sex couples in federal civil service positions, the Department of Defense changed its policy to offer benefits to same-sex spouses of military personnel and other employees. These benefits include health care, housing, and survivor benefits (Huetteman 2013). The challenge in this instance is that the definition of spouse as a member of the opposite-sex is part of a separate federal law on military benefits, not DOMA, so was not directly affected by the Supreme Court ruling striking down section 3. Instead, as a response to both the DOMA rulings and a separate ruling by a U.S. district judge on the unconstitutionality of the military policy if enforced in states with marriage equality, the Obama administration decided to stop enforcing the provision and expand military benefits to legally married same-sex couples regardless of their state of residency (McCarty 2013; "Same Sex Spouses" 2013).

In a reflection of the challenges of federalism when trying to support and enforce LGBT rights, state-run National Guard offices in two states—Texas and Mississippi—refused to issue applications for benefits to same-sex couples (Reynolds 2013). The head of the Texas Army and Air National Guards and State

Guard announced that Texas would not comply because same-sex marriage is unconstitutional in the state (Reynolds 2013). Military personnel in Texas thus need to go to a federal military installation to apply for benefits. Although Texas is the only state as a whole to refuse to offer benefits to same-sex couples, some state-run offices in Mississippi also refused to issue applications (Reynolds 2013). As of December 2013, Georgia and Mississippi were the only states resisting the federal ruling by refusing to offer benefits to same-sex couples. [*Editor's note*: All states are now providing same-sex benefits to National Guard members.]

All of these changes at the federal level reflect an incremental approach to developing policies that protect and enforce LGBT rights. Each is an example of a change at the margin to existing policy, not a major overhaul or broad-based expansion of rights. The differences in treatment of couples at the state and federal level also raise challenges for the public administration infrastructure. It is difficult to implement and enforce policies when they apply differently depending on the level of government. This leads to inefficiency, ineffectiveness, and inequity in policy implementation.

State-Level Activities

Marriage

As of this writing, 18 states (plus District of Columbia [2010]) have implemented marriage equality. These are California (June 2013), Connecticut (2008), Delaware (July 2013), District of Columbia (2010), Hawaii (2013), Illinois (2014), Iowa (2009), Maine (2012), Maryland (2013), Massachusetts (2004), Minnesota (August, 2013), New Hampshire (2010), New York (2011), New Jersey (2013), New Mexico (2013), Rhode Island (August 2013), Vermont (2009), and Washington (2013) (Human Rights Campaign 2013a). [*Editor's note*: For a complete listing of all marriage cases pending in various courts around the country, go to the Lambda Legal Defense website and click on the individual states: http://www.lambdalegal.org/pending-marriage-equality-cases.]

Although a number of states have adopted marriage equality in the last five years, the majority of states had banned same sex marriage. A number of these bans have been successfully challenged in state and federal courts. [*Editor's note*: A number of these bans are now being challenged in court.] There are 28 states with statutory prohibitions against same-sex marriage, 10 constitutional amendments banning same-sex marriage, 7 statutes with broader prohibitions against same-sex marriage, and 19 constitutional amendments with broader prohibitions against same-sex marriage (NGLTF, 2014).

For couples in heterosexual marriages, the Full Faith and Credit clause of the U.S. Constitution allows their marriage to be recognized in any state, regardless of where the marriage license was issued. However, section 2 of DOMA allows states to not recognize same-sex marriages that were legally conducted in other jurisdictions if their states ban such marriages. Because this provision of DOMA was not covered in the Supreme Court rulings in July 2013, states without marriage equality do not have to recognize same-sex marriages, even though the federal government does (Lambdalegal.org 2013). Marriage is an area where the effects of federalism and incrementalism stand out. Policies differ across states and even across jurisdictions within states and at the federal level. These differences in policy add complexity to public administration systems that must determine who is eligible for what benefits, which laws apply to whom, and who has jurisdiction over disputes. This is particularly highlighted by the aforementioned examples of federal policies related to taxes, social security, and military benefits for legally married same-sex couples regardless of their current place of residence.

Discrimination

As noted earlier, because there is not overarching federal protection against discrimination based on sexual orientation or gender identity, much of the activity related to building protections has taken place at the state and local level. As noted in other places in this volume, 17 states and the District of Columbia currently prohibit discrimination based on sexual orientation and/or gender identity. States that prohibit discrimination based on both sexual orientation and gender identity are California, Colorado, Connecticut, Delaware, Hawaii, Illinois, Iowa, Massachusetts, Maine, Minnesota, New Jersey, New Mexico, Nevada, Oregon, Rhode Island, Vermont, and Washington (HRC 2013b). Maryland, New Hampshire, New York, and Wisconsin prohibit discrimination based on sexual orientation only (HRC 2013b). Twenty-nine states offer no protections against discrimination based on either sexual orientation or gender identity.

In states that do provide protections against discrimination for the LGBT community, education about and enforcement of antidiscrimination laws usually falls on a state Commission on Human or Civil Rights. "Review of the annual reports from several of these agencies shows that the number of discrimination cases filed based on sexual orientation or gender identity are consistently a low percentage of total cases filed usually running between 2% and 5%" (Government Accountability Office 2009). The discrimination complaint process can be long and complex, and requires clear evidence to support the claim. These factors may affect the number of people willing to initiate the process. However, given the much higher numbers of claims for discrimination based on other factors such as race, age, sex, and disability, it is likely there are other factors that inhibit LGBT individuals from filing complaints. A closer look at the process and potential repercussions for those making the complaint is worthy of further study.

The specific activities of the offices responsible for education and enforcement of antidiscrimination policy varies from state to state. A closer look at the annual reports from two states illustrates the extreme variation across jurisdictions.

Massachusetts

The Massachusetts Commission Against Discrimination (MCAD) was established in 1946 with the charge to enforce "the anti-discrimination laws by investigating, prosecuting, and adjudicating cases of discrimination, harassment and retaliation in employment, housing, place of public accommodation, credit and education" (MCAD 2011, 1). The commission also "fulfills its mission by reaching out to communities protected under Chapter 151B with education and training and prioritizes enforcement efforts to reflect the needs of Massachusetts' most vulnerable populations" (MCAD 2011, 1). According to MCAD's 2011 Annual Report, there were a total of 3,195 discrimination complaints filed that year. Also 130 cases or 2.5% of the total number were filed for discrimination based on sexual orientation (MCAD 2009).

Noteworthy in the case of Massachusetts is the fact that in November 2011 a law adding gender identity as "a protected characteristic to Massachusetts' employment, housing, credit and public education anti-discrimination laws and to Massachusetts' hate crimes law" was passed (Boston.com 2012, 1). The law defines gender identity as "a person's gender-related identity, appearance or behavior, whether or not that gender-related identity or behavior is different from that traditionally associated with the person's physiology or assigned sex at birth" (Boston.com 2012, 1). According to the 2011–12 MCAD Annual Report, one of its main activities for 2011 was "working with the Legislature in advancing civil rights bills, including the newly enacted Gender Identity law" and one of its objectives for 2012 would be "developing an enforcement and educational outreach plan under the new Gender Identity law" (MCAD 2011, 2). The Massachusetts' Commission Against Discrimination is an example of a state commission that actively works on education about and enforcement of antidiscrimination laws, including those encompassing LGBT rights. As is the case with other such agencies, however, these activities have not led to a higher percentage of claims filed. The low rate of discrimination claims based on sexual orientation or gender identity is worthy of more study to try to help determine what factors might play a role in preventing possible victims from bringing a formal complaint.

Hawaii

In Hawaii, the state where the same-sex marriage debate began, education and enforcement activities related to LGBT rights are governed by the Hawaii Civil Rights Commission (HCRC), which began operations in 1991 (HCRC 2010). The mission of the HCRC is "to eliminate discrimination by protecting civil rights and promoting diversity through enforcement of anti-discrimination laws and education" (HCRC 2011–12, 3). According to the HCRC, prior to its establishment, "jurisdiction over state anti-discrimination laws was split among several state departments. Enforcement was limited and sporadic. State prosecution of discrimination complaints was virtually non-existent" (HCRC 2010, 4). The goal in establishing the HCRC was "to establish a strong and viable commission with sufficient ... enforcement powers to effectuate the State's commitment to preserving the civil rights of all individuals" (HCRC 2010, 4). Similar to Massachusetts, discrimination claims based on sexual orientation make up approximately 2.5% of cases filed annually in Hawaii (HCRC 2010, 2011, 2012).

In its 2011–2012 annual report, the HCRC lists "restoring civil rights law enforcement capacity and effectiveness" as its highest priority (HCRC 2012, 3). According to the report, all state agencies were required to make major reductions starting in 2008 due to the economic downturn. While discrimination complaints for the year increased, the staff of the HCRC decreased by 27%, thus reducing its capacity to maintain enforcement efforts (HCRC 2012). This reduction in capacity has meant delays in investigating claims often making it more difficult to gather evidence necessary to support a claim of discrimination.

In contrast to the expanding activities of the MCAD, the reduction in funding to the HCRC has limited its ability to enforce civil rights in Hawaii. These cases show two extremes of activities in state agencies charged with the enforcement of LGBT rights. Regardless of the level of efforts across agencies, however, the number of discrimination cases filed based on sexual orientation or gender identity remains small. As noted earlier, the process is often cumbersome and cases can take years to settle. It is likely that the true amount of discrimination against the LGBT community is not reflected in the number of discrimination cases filed. A question for future research would be to determine if the process is a barrier to claims or what other factors may be at play in preventing the filing of formal complaints. These agencies are an important component of the public administration infrastructure designed to implement and enforce LGBT rights, but they appear to have limited impact on facilitating the enforcement of antidiscrimination laws directed at sexual orientation and gender identity.

Hate Crimes

Hate crime is another area where federal and state levels coordinate. Hate crime policy development, implementation, and enforcement mostly occur at the state and local level, but federal policies also play a role. Fifteen states and the District of Columbia have laws that address hate or bias crimes based on sexual orientation and gender identity (California, Colorado, Connecticut, Delaware, DC, Hawaii, Maryland, Massachusetts, Minnesota, Missouri, Nevada, New Jersey, New Mexico, Oregon, Washington, and Vermont). Fifteen other states have laws covering hate crime based on sexual orientation only (Arizona, Florida, Illinois, Iowa,

Kansas, Kentucky, Louisiana, Maine, Nebraska, New Hampshire, New York, Rhode Island, Tennessee, Texas, and Wisconsin). Fifteen other states have hate crime and bias laws that do not address sexual orientation or gender identity (Alabama, Alaska, Idaho, Indiana, Mississippi, Montana, North Carolina, North Dakota, Ohio, Oklahoma, Pennsylvania, South Dakota, Utah, Virginia, and West Virginia) (NGLTF 2013a). Five states have no hate crime laws.

In 2009, Congress passed the Matthew Shepard and James Byrd Jr. Hate Crimes Prevention Act. Effective in 2010, the law "provides funding and technical assistance to state, local and tribal jurisdictions to help them to more effectively investigate and prosecute hate crimes" (Department of Justice 2013). The law makes criminal the willful causing of bodily injury when

> the crime was committed because of the actual or perceived race, color, religion, national origin of any person or (2) the crime was committed because of the actual or perceived religion, national origin, gender, sexual orientation, gender identity, or disability of any person and the crime affected interstate or foreign commerce or occurred within federal special maritime and territorial jurisdiction. (Department of Justice 2013)

The act also calls for the Federal Bureau of Investigation (FBI) to expand its data collection in hate crimes to include those based on gender identity (Guequierre 2012).

The 2009 FBI Hate Crimes Report showed a decrease from the previous year in the total number of hate crimes nationwide as well as a decrease in hate crimes specifically directed at gays and lesbians (Anti-Defamation League 2013). However, the 2011 FBI report showed a reverse trend. While the number of hate crimes was down overall, the number of crimes against gays and lesbians increased from 1,277 in 2010 to 1,293 in 2011 (Guequierre 2012). Similar trends occurred at the local level. In Orange County, California, the County Human Relations Committee reported that while overall hate crimes were down 21% in 2012, those based on sexual orientation nearly doubled (Anton 2013). According to the commission, the most common targets were blacks and those "perceived to be gay, lesbian, bisexual or transgender" (Anton 2013).

New York City saw a similar trend in 2012 and 2013 with the most visible case being the shooting death of Mark Carson, an openly gay man who was killed after a struggle with a man who was shouting antigay slurs (Santora and Goldstein 2013). After two other antigay attacks in Manhattan in late May 2013, police reported that antigay crimes in the city were at 29 for the year, compared to 14 for the same time period in 2012 (Goodman 2013). These cases raise questions as to whether the increased attention to LGBT rights and the increased openness of same-sex couples also raised the hatred of those who would commit hate crimes directed at LGBT individuals. The partnership of federal and state authorities brings more resources to investigating and punishing the crimes, but the increase in the number of crimes also reflects a weakness in the ability of the local public administration infrastructure to prevent hate crimes aimed at the LGBT community.

As with the policy changes at the federal level, the aforementioned examples illustrate the effects of incrementalism and federalism on the public administration infrastructure at the state level. Differences in policies and enforcement efforts at the state level create difficulties for public administrators charged with enforcement. Inconsistencies lead to a public administration infrastructure that does not provide efficient, effective, economical, or equitable public service.

Conclusion

This chapter has provided a brief overview of policies at the state and federal level that are designed to protect the rights of LGBT individuals. The federalist system of government and incremental nature of policy making has meant that rights and protections for the LGBT population in the United States are piecemeal and unevenly distributed. Although federalism is designed to protect the minority against the majority, in the case of LGBT rights this has not been the case. An important comparison for further study would be to look at the development of the Civil Rights Act of 1964 and the establishment of national protections based on race, color, religion, sex, and national origin versus the development of protections based on sexual orientation and gender identity. The question is what makes a society decide what should be legislated at the national level versus what is left to the state and local level to determine. Have protections of LGBT rights followed a similar or different path than other civil rights protections?

Public administration scholars often argue that the four pillars of public administration are efficiency, effectiveness, economy and equity (Frederickson 2010; Norman-Major 2011). The current patchwork of policies that has developed, incrementally and unevenly at the state and federal levels, and the limited infrastructure to implement them means that policies and programs protecting LGBT rights are often none of these four things. While federalism allows for local control and limits the power of the central government, in this case, the lack of uniform federal protections has meant inequitable treatment and cross-jurisdictional inconsistencies. It has created a complex set of rules and systems that may inhibit public administrators from properly serving the public. An incremental approach to policy making assures more careful consideration of policy and prevents major upheavals in policy without proper analysis of options. In the case of LGBT rights, however, it has led to inconsistent policy and slow decision making that limits the rights of a sector of the population.

Another area of future research would be to conduct an inventory of policies related to LGBT rights at the local level. This chapter has focused on policies at the state and federal level but cities, counties, school districts, and other local forms of government are also part of the public administration infrastructure and thus play a critical role in the implementation of LGBT rights. Even within states with laws that provide marriage equality and protect against discrimination and hate crimes based on sexual orientation and gender identity, it is important to assess how well local governments work to enforce these laws.

This chapter has only touched the surface of public policies and administrations that affect LGBT rights. A deeper analysis of the development of these policies may help determine which factors of the policy-making process have had the largest influence on the outcomes and thus provide recommendations for how to most effectively, efficiently, economically and equitably protect the rights of LGBT individuals in a federalist system dominated by incremental policy making.

References

American Civil Liberties Union. 2013. "Victory! Social Security Administration Drops Surgery Requirement for Gender Change." Accessed September 11, 2013, https://www.aclu.org/blog/lgbt-rights/victory-social-security-administration-drops-surgery-requirement-gender-change.

Anti-Defamation League. 2013. "Matthew Shepard and James Byrd, Jr. Hate Crimes Prevention Act (HCPA): What You Need To Know." Accessed September 13, 2013, http://www.adl.org/assets/pdf/combating-hate/What-you-need-to-know-about-HCPA.pdf.

Anton, Mike. 2013. "O.C. Hate Crimes Fall; Attacks Based on Sexual Orientation Rise." *Los Angeles Times*, May 23. Accessed September 13, 2011, http://articles.latimes.com/2013/may/23/local/la-me-orange-county-hate-crimes-20130523.

Badgett, M. L. 1995. "The Wage Effects of Sexual Orientation Discrimination." *Industrial and Labor Relations Review*, 726–739.

Boston.com. 2012. "Gender Identity Protections Become Law in Massachusetts July 1." AccessedSeptember13,2013,http://www.boston.com/yourtown/news/allston_brighton/2012/07/gender_identity_protections_be.html.

Department of Justice. 2013. "Matthew Shepard and James Byrd, Jr. Hate Crimes Prevention Act of 2009." Accessed September 17, 2013, http://www.justice.gov/crt/about/crm/matthewshepard.php.

Equal Employment Opportunity Commission (EEOC). 2009. "Federal Laws Prohibiting Job Discrimination Questions and Answers." Accessed August 16, 2012, http://www.eeoc.gov/facts/qanda.html.

Equal Employment Opportunity Commission (EEOC). 2012. "Mia Macy v. Eric Holder. Appeal No. 0120120821." Accessed August 15, 2012, http://eeoc.gov/decisions/0120120821%Macy%20%v%20DOJ%20ATF.txt.

FEDManager. 2011. "Fed Can Sue for Hostile Work Environment Based on Sex Stereotyping." Accessed August 15, 2012, http://www.fedmanager.com/columnswhats-happening/case-law-update/235-fed-can-sue-for-hostile-work-environment-based-on-sex-stereotyping.

Frederickson, H. George. 2010. *Social Equity and Public Administration: Origins, Developments, and Applications.* Armonk, NY: M.E. Sharpe.

Government Accountability Office. 2009. "B-318502: Sexual Orientation and Gender Identity Employment Discrimination: Overview of State Statutes and Complaint Data." Washington DC: Government Accountability Office.

Goodman, J. David. 2013. "2 More Antigay Attacks Are Reported in Manhattan." *New York Times*, May 21. Accessed September 13, 2013, http://www.nytimes.com/2013/05/22/nyregion/2-more-antigay-attacks-are-reported-in-manhattan.html.

Guequierre, Paul. 2012. "FBI: Reported Hate Crime Based on Sexual Orientation on the Rise." *Human Rights Campaign* (blog). Accessed September 13, 2013, http://www.hrc.org/blog/entry/fbi-reported-hate-crimes-based-on-sexual-orientation-on-the-rise.

Hawaii Civil Rights Commission (HCRC). 2010. "2009–2010 Annual Report." Accessed September 1, 2013, http://labor.hawaii.gov/wp-content/uploads/2012/12/HCRC-Annual-Report-FY2009-10.pdf.

Hawaii Civil Rights Commission (HCRC). 2011. "2010–2011 Annual Report." Accessed September 1, 2013, http://labor.hawaii.gov/wp-content/uploads/2012/12/HCRC-Annual-Report-FY2010-11.pdf.

Hawaii Civil Rights Commission (HCRC). 2012. "2011–2012 Annual Report." Accessed September 1, 2013, http://labor.hawaii.gov/wp-content/uploads/2012/12/HCRC-Annual-Report-FY2011-2012.pdf.

Huetteman, Emmarie. 2013. "Gay Spouses of Members of Military Get Benefits." *New York Times*, August 14. Accessed September 11, 2013, http://www.nytimes.com/2013/08/15/us/politics/gay-spouses-of-members-of-military-get-benefits.html?_r=0.

Human Rights Campaign (HRC). 2013a. "Marriage Equality and Other Relationship Recognition Laws." Accessed September 22, 2013, http://www.hrc.org/files/assets/resources/marriage_equality_082013.pdf.

Human Rights Campaign (HRC). 2013b. "Statewide Employment Laws and Policies." Accessed September 22, 2013, http://www.hrc.org/files/assets/resources/employment_laws_072013.pdf.

Human Rights Campaign (HRC). 2013c. "State Hate Crime Laws." Accessed September 22, 2013, http://www.hrc.org/files/assets/resources/hate_crimes_laws_062013.pdf.

Human Rights Campaign (HRC). 2013d. "5 Myths About ENDA." Equality. Spring 2013, p. 19.

Johnson, Chris. 2013. "AFL-CIO Pledges to 'Redouble' Efforts to Pass ENDA." *Washington Blade*. Accessed September 13, 2013, http://www.washingtonblade.com/2013/09/11/afl-cio-pledges-redouble-efforts-pass-enda.

"Judge: State Must Allow Gay Marriage." 2013. *Star Tribune* (Minneapolis), September 28. p. A6.

Lambdalegal.org. 2013. "LGBT Organizations Fact Sheet Series: After DOMA What It Means for You." Accessed September 11, 2013, www.lambdalegal.org.

Lindblom, Charles E. 1959. "The Science of Muddling Through." *Public Administration Review, 19*, 79–88.

Lindblom, Charles E. 1979. "Still Muddling, Not Yet Through." *Public Administration Review, 39*, 517–529.

Massachusetts Commission Against Discrimination (MCAD). 2011, 2009. "Annual Report." Accessed August 7, 2012, http://www.mass.gov/mcad/forms.html.

McCarty, Maureen. 2013. "Federal Judge Rules VA Must Offer Benefits to Same-Sex Couples in Marriage Equality States." Human Rights Campaign.Accessed September 11, 2013, http://www.hrc.org/blog/entry/federal-judge-rules-va-must-offer-benefits-to-same-sex-couples-in-marriage.

Mottet, Lisa. 2012. "EEOC Affirms Expanded Definition of Sex Discrimination." American Constitution Society (ACSBlog). Accessed August 15, 2012, http://www.acslaw.org/acsblog/eeoc-affirms-expanded-definitions-of-sex-discrimination.

National Center for Transgender Equality. 2013. "Transgender People and the Social Security Administration." Accessed September 11, 2013, www.transequality.org/resources/SSAR-June2013.pdf.

National Gay and Lesbian Task Force (NGLTF). 2013a. "Hate Crime Laws in the U.S." Accessed June 21, 2013, http://www.thetaskforce.org/downloads/reports/issue_maps/hate_crimes_06_13_color.pdf.

National Gay and Lesbian Task Force (NGLTF). 2013b. "Nondiscrimination Legislation Historical Narrative." Accessed July 12, 2012, http://thetaskforce.org/issues/nondiscrimination/narrative.

National Gay and Lesbian Task Force (NGLTF). 2014. "State Nondiscrimination Laws in the U.S." May 21, 2014, http://www.thetaskforce.org/downloads/reports/issue_maps/non_discrimination_5_14color.pdf.

Norman-Major, Kristen. 2011. "Balancing the Four E's; or Can We Achieve Equity for Social Equity in Public Administration?" *Journal of Public Affairs Education, 17*(2), 233–252.

ProCon.org. 2013. "Gay Marriage." Accessed September 28, 2013, http://gaymarriage.procon.org/view.resource.php?resourceID=004857.

Reynolds, Daniel. 2013. "Texas Military Forces Refuse to Process Same-Sex Couples' Benefits." The Advocate.com. Accessed September 11, 2013, http://www.advocate.com/politics/military/2013/09/03/texas-military-forces-refuse-process-same-sex-couples-benefits.

"Same Sex Spouses in the Military Will Receive Full Benefits Despite Federal Law." 2013. *The Guardian*, Sept. 4. Accessed September 11, 2013, http://www.theguardian.com/world/2013/sep/04/gay-military-veterans-will-receive-benefits.

Santora, Marc, and Joseph Goldstein. 2013. "In Shadow of the Stonewall Inn, a Gay Man Is Killed." *New York Times,* May 18. Accessed September 13, 2013, http://www.nytimes.com/2013/05/19/nyregion/killing-in-greenwich-village-looks like-hate-crime-police-say.html?_r=0.

Smith, Allen. 2013. "DOMA Ruling Will Change FMLA Administration." Society for Human Resource Management. Accessed September 11, 2013, http://www.shrm.org/LegalIssues/FederalResources/Pages/DOMA-FMLA.aspx.

The Federalist Papers. 1788. "No. 51: The Structure of the Government Must Furnish the Proper Checks and Balances Between the Different Departments." Accessed September 9, 2013, http://thomas.loc.gov/home/histdox/fed_51.html.

U.S. Department of State. 2013. "U.S. Visas for Same-Sex Spouses." Accessed September 11, 2013, http://travel.state.gov/visa/frvi/frvi_6036.html.

U.S. Department of the Treasury. 2013. "All Legal Same-Sex Marriages Will Be Recognized for Federal Tax Purposes." Accessed September 11, 2013, http://www.irs.gov/uac/Newsroom/Treasury-and-IRS-Announce-That-All-Legal-Same-Sex-Marriages-Will-Be-Recognized-For-Federal-Tax-Purposes;-Ruling-Provides-Certainty,-Benefits-and-Protections-Under-Federal-Tax-Law-for-Same-Sex-Married-Couples.

U.S. Social Security Administration. 2013a. "Changing Gender on Social Security's Records." Accessed September 11, 2013, http://ssa-custhelp.ssa.gov/app/answers/detail/a_id/1667/~/changing-gender-on-social-security%27s-records.

U.S. Social Security Administration. 2013b. "Processing Claims for Same-Sex Couples." Accessed September 11, 2013, http://ssa-custhelp.ssa.gov/app/answers/detail/a_id/2492/~/processing-claims-for-same-sex-couples.

Yoder, Eric. 2013. "DOMA Decision Triggers Federal Retirement Policy Changes." *Washington Post,* August 5. Accessed September 11, 2013, http://www.washingtonpost.com/blogs/federal-eye/wp/2013/08/05/doma-decision-triggers-federal-retirement-policy-changes/.

Chapter 24

Conclusion: New Directions Following the Same-Sex Marriage Decisions by the U.S. Supreme Court

Wallace Swan

To many people, it has seemed that the U.S. Supreme Court cases *Hollingsworth* v. *Perry* and *United States Petitioner* v. *Edith Schlain Windsor, in her Capacity as Executor of the Estate of Thea Clara Spyer, et al.* are the ultimate decisions in American lesbian, gay, bisexual, and transgender (LGBT) life. For many of those in the 18 states with LGBT marriage rights guaranteed, it would appear that there are no other protections needed. However, there are several ways to look at this.

First, in the states that have most, if not all rights and protections, it must be recognized that following the battles with the right wing, LGBT activists as well as donors are exhausted from the efforts to obtain legal redress for years of discrimination. The effects have been especially significant for nonprofit LGBT organizations that have found their fund-raising efforts diminished. Within these states, we also will find niches of discrimination that still need to be addressed; for example, racial, religious, and ethnic groups.

Second, in those states that have most, if not all rights and protections, there remain many things left to do. As we have seen Chapter 13, "Data-Driven Health

Services and Senior Services," there are enormous health disparities within the LGBT community. The extremely high prevalence of alcohol and drug addiction, obesity, homelessness for adults and youth, and mental health issues, among many other health concerns, lead one to the conclusion that LGBT organizations may want to readdress their resources to deal with these concerns. Similarly, the issues of low income and isolation of LGBT seniors are truly major problems to overcome. Now it would appear likely that LGBT nonprofits can work with traditional non-profits in addressing problems of all seniors, while bringing to such coalitions a special knowledge of the issues of the LGBT senior community.

Third, in the states where there are no protections for LGBT people, the issues are not just the lack of same-sex marriage provisions. Needs include the lack of gender identity protection, the need for employment protection, the need for hate crimes legislation and effective antiviolence programs, the need for enumerated state protections against bullying in the schools as well as the workplace, the need for protections against harassment of LGBT people, and the need to have LGBT elected officials in office to ensure cultural change. There is clear empirical evidence that such human rights protections can be correlated with the presence of "out" elected officials, since these officials are able to humanize the experience of LGBT singles and couples. Building a safety net of protections was what was necessary in the empowered states (e.g., Minnesota) before they obtained full marital rights.

Fourth, the legal battles are not yet concluded for same-sex marriage. There may well be many lawsuits (more than 77 cases as of July 2014) pending in the dis-empowered states, as well as U.S. District Court decisions. If we win a substantial number of those cases we may well reach the threshold of 25 states, which would make it possible that the U.S. Supreme Court would again rule on the marriage issue in the near future, thereby bringing equal marital rights to all citizens of the United States.

Fifth, we need to develop a strategy that allows us to win the hearts and minds of the whole citizenry. As usual, individual "coming out" and building collaborative networks with supportive organizations is what it will take to win full human rights in these states. The Human Rights Campaign has recently launched Project One America, which will cost about $8.5 million (funded by Tim Gill) to ensure that people in Arkansas, Alabama, and Mississippi have equal access to all anti-discrimination protections. And the Gill Foundation is putting approximately $25 million into efforts to improve the legal status of LGBT people in the South and West. These are two of the regions that our book addresses; and hopefully the Rustbelt and Plains states will receive equal attention at some point in time (Mark Kellner, "Same-Sex Marriage Advocates Launch 'Southern Strategy,'' April 29, 2014, http://www.deseretnews.com/article/865601985/Same-sex-marriage-advocates-launch-southern-strategy-with-NC-lawsuit.html).

Sixth, we need to ally ourselves with groups that are willing to support common objectives. For example, we need to deal with the gerrymandering of seats, which allows people from the Democratic and Republicans parties to hold onto seats for an extended period of time. This gerrymandering has the effect of keeping key districts safely within the control of the Republican Party; and it thereby prevents consideration of a whole list of important agenda items (e.g., the Employment Non-Discrimination Act and Comprehensive Immigration Reform).

Seventh, we need to extend the range of federal rights to include the ability to ensure divorce as a right for LGBT people nationwide; and we need to eliminate the section of the Defense of Marriage Act that the U.S. Supreme Court left in place, namely the provision that allows disempowered states the capability to not recognize marriages that were granted in the empowered states.

Eighth, I have been surprised that no one has yet proposed reparations for those many injustices against LGBT people that were based purely upon discrimination. Maybe we are just too nice. Over 13,000 military personnel were discharged in the period from 1994 through 2010: At least they have recently been granted severance benefits but they were not reimbursed for the pay they lost; 1.3 million people in coupled relationships did not receive the marital benefits received by other couples for many years; and there are too many people to count who have been imprisoned or who have lost jobs, promotions, education, and housing opportunities.

Ninth, the *Burwell* v. *Hobby Lobby* case has led to the potential of closely held corporations refusing to serve or employ LGBT people on the basis of religious belief (especially in 29 states where there are no anti-discrimination protections).

Finally, the presence of protection in some (if not all American jurisdictions) may help provide some role modeling for the remainder of the world, many parts of which are still struggling with this issue. Africa, Asia, and Eastern Europe are three areas of especial importance in this regard: More than 76 countries make homosexual activity illegal (plus significant portions of 6 other countries), and of those countries 10 make homosexual activity punishable by death. Although the United States is certainly not the leader of the worldwide LGBT movement (because so many other nations have surpassed us in this regard) what we do accomplish is brought to the attention of lesbians, gay, bisexual, and transgender people around the world. It is truly noble human rights work that we are engaged in and our work needs to be shared with other countries, but we need to absorb the experience of other countries with full human rights (e.g., Argentina), since they have previously dealt with issues like the ones we continue to grapple with.

Appendix: State by State Listing of Rights

Heather Posthumus

State by State Listing of Rights

State	*Law Banning Discrimination Based on Both Gender Identity and Sexual Orientation (1)*	*Law Banning Discrimination Based on Sexual Orientation Only (1)*	*Law Banning Foster Care or Adoption for Same-Sex Parents (2)*	*Hate Crimes Based on Sexual Orientation Only (3)*	*Hate Crimes Based on Sexual Orientation and Gender Identity (3)*	*Same-Sex Relationship Recognition*	*Same-Sex Relationships*	*State Protects Students Against Bullying (2)*	*State Prohibits Antigay Harassment and/or Discrimination in Schools*	*States Voted Republican in 2012*
Alabama	No	No	There is no explicit ban.	No	No	No	"Alabama Marriage Protection Act" Ala.Code §30-1-19. (b) (1998). "Marriage is inherently a unique relationship between a man and a woman."	There are anti-bullying laws, but no specific groups are defined.	No	Yes
Alaska	No	No	There is no explicit ban.	No	No	No	ALASKA CONST. Art. I § 25, adopted 1998. "To be valid or recognized in this State, a marriage may exist only between one man and one woman."	There are anti-bullying laws, but no specific groups are defined.	No	Yes

Arizona	No	No	There is no explicit ban, however Ariz. Rev. Stat. § 8-103 (c) (2011) states: "If all relevant factors are equal and the choice is between a married man and woman certified to adopt and a single adult certified to adopt, placement preference shall be with a married man and woman."[a]	Yes	No	No statewide recognition, but some local domestic partnership registries are available.[a]	Ariz. Rev. Stat. §25-101(c) (2008). "Only a union of one man and one woman shall be valid or recognized as a marriage in this state."	There are anti-bullying laws, but no specific groups are defined.	No	Yes
Arkansas	No	No	A.C.A. § 9-9-204 (2)(3) (2013) The following individuals may adopt: "(2) An unmarried adult; (3) The unmarried father or mother of the individual to be adopted."[b]	No	No	Pulaski County Circuit Judge Christopher Piazza said that the state's 2004 voter-approved constitutional amendment that defined marriage as between a man and a woman violates[kk] the constitution. The state Supreme Court has put a moratorium on issuing marriage licenses to same-sex couples while it reviews a state appeal.	Ark. Const. Amend. 83. §1 (2004). "Marriage consists only of the union of one man and one woman."[d]	There are anti-bullying laws with sexual orientation and gender identity protections.[e]	Yes	Yes

Continued

State by State Listing of Rights

State	*Law Banning Discrimination Based on Both Gender Identity and Sexual Orientation (1)*	*Law Banning Discrimination Based on Sexual Orientation Only (1)*	*Law Banning Foster Care or Adoption for Same-Sex Parents (2)*	*Hate Crimes Based on Sexual Orientation Only (3)*	*Hate Crimes Based on Sexual Orientation and Gender Identity (3)*	*Same-Sex Relationship Recognition*	*Same-Sex Relationships*	*State Protects Students Against Bullying (2)*	*State Prohibits Antigay Harassment and/or Discrimination in Schools*	*States Voted Republican in 2012*
California	Yes	No	CAL. FAM. CODE § 9000(b)) (2003). "A domestic partner, as defined in Section 297, desiring to adopt a child of his or her domestic partner may for that purpose file a petition in the county in which the petitioner resides."	No, hate crimes cover both gender identity and sexual orientation.	Yes	Full marriage equality: and. Cal. Fam. Code §308(b) (2008). "A marriage between two persons of the same sex contracted outside this state that would be valid by the laws of the jurisdiction in which the marriage was contracted is valid in this state if the marriage was contracted prior to November 5, 2008."	Full marriage equality: Proposition 8 directed against same-sex marriage ruled unconstitutional by U.S. Supreme Court.	There are anti-bullying laws with sexual orientation and gender identity protections.[f]	Yes	No

Colorado	Yes	No	There is no explicit ban.	No hate crimes cover both gender identity and sexual orientation.	Yes	In effect May 1, 2013, Senate Bill 13-011 14-15-103. Defines Civil Unions: "As used in this article, unless the context otherwise requires: (1) "civil union" means a relationship established by two eligible persons pursuant to this article that entitles them to receive the benefits and protections and be subject to the responsibilities of spouses."[g]	In July 2014, Judge Raymond P. Moore ruled that Colorado's ban on gay marriage was unconstitutional. State officials are currently appealing the decision in the 10th Circuit Court of Appeals.[ll]	There are anti-bullying laws with both sexual orientation and gender identity protections.	Yes	No
Connecticut	Yes	No	There is no explicit ban and Conn Gen. Stat. § 45a-726a (2011) "Commissioner of Children and Families or a child-placing agency may consider the sexual orientation of the prospective adoptive or foster parent or parents when placing a child for adoption or in foster care."	No, hate crimes cover both gender identity and sexual orientation.	Yes	Full marriage equality	Full marriage equality	There are anti-bullying laws with both sexual orientation and gender identity protections.[h]	Yes	No

Continued

State by State Listing of Rights

State	*Law Banning Discrimination Based on Both Gender Identity and Sexual Orientation (1)*	*Law Banning Discrimination Based on Sexual Orientation Only (1)*	*Law Banning Foster Care or Adoption for Same-Sex Parents (2)*	*Hate Crimes Based on Sexual Orientation Only (3)*	*Hate Crimes Based on Sexual Orientation and Gender Identity (3)*	*Same-Sex Relationship Recognition*	*Same-Sex Relationships*	*State Protects Students Against Bullying (2)*	*State Prohibits Antigay Harassment and/or Discrimination in Schools*	*States Voted Republican in 2012*
Delaware	Yes	No	There is no explicit ban.	Yes	Yes	Full marriage equality	Full marriage equality	There are anti-bullying laws with both sexual orientation and gender identity protections.[i]	Yes	No
District of Columbia	Yes	No	There is no explicit ban.	No, hate crimes cover both gender identity and sexual orientation.	Yes	Full marriage equality	Full marriage equality	There are anti-bullying laws with both sexual orientation and gender identity protections.	Yes	No

Florida	No	No	In September 2010, the explicit ban on homosexuals being able to adopt was lifted, but Florida statute still states: "No person eligible to adopt under this statue may adopt if that person is a homosexual." Fla. Stat. §63.042 (3) (2008).[j]	Yes	No	No	In July 2014, Florida Monroe County Circuit Judge Luis Garcia wrote this opinion regarding his decision to overturn Florida's ban on same-sex marriages: "The court is aware that the majority of voters oppose same-sex marriage, but it is our country's proud history to protect the rights of the individual, the rights of the unpopular, and rights of the powerless, even at the cost of offending the majority."[qq]	There are anti-bullying laws but there are no protections against sexual orientation or gender identity bullying.	No	No
Georgia	No	No	There is no explicit ban.	No	No	No	O.C.G.A. § 19-3-3.1 (a) (LexisNexis 2012). "It is declared to be the public policy of this state to recognize the union only of man and woman. Marriages between persons of the same sex are prohibited in this state."	There are anti-bullying laws, but no specific groups are defined.	No	Yes
Hawaii	Yes	No	There is no explicit ban.	No, hate crimes cover both gender identity and sexual orientation.	Yes	Yes	Full marriage equality	There are anti-bullying laws, but there are no protections against sexual orientation or gender identity bullying.	No	No

Continued

State by State Listing of Rights

State	*Law Banning Discrimination Based on Both Gender Identity and Sexual Orientation (1)*	*Law Banning Discrimination Based on Sexual Orientation Only (1)*	*Law Banning Foster Care or Adoption for Same-Sex Parents (2)*	*Hate Crimes Based on Sexual Orientation Only (3)*	*Hate Crimes Based on Sexual Orientation and Gender Identity (3)*	*Same-Sex Relationship Recognition*	*Same-Sex Relationships*	*State Protects Students Against Bullying (2)*	*State Prohibits Antigay Harassment and/or Discrimination in Schools*	*States Voted Republican in 2012*
Idaho	No	No	There is no explicit ban.	No	No	No	"U.S. District Magistrate Judge Candy Dale wrote in her decision Tuesday evening that Idaho's laws barring same-sex marriage unconstitutionally deny gay and lesbian citizens their fundamental right to marry. Ten other federal district courts have issued similar rulings supporting gay marriage rights."[mm] As of May 19, 2014, it is under appeal.	There are anti-bullying laws, but no specific groups are defined.	No	Yes

Illinois	Yes	No	There is no explicit ban.	Yes	No	"Amend Senate Bill 10 by replacing everything after the enacting clause with the following: Section 10. Equal access to marriage. (a) All laws of this State applicable to marriage, whether they derive from statute, administrative or court rule, policy, common law, or any other source of civil or criminal law, shall apply equally to marriages of same-sex and different-sex couples and their children."[l]	Full marriage equality. In June 2014, District Court Chief Judge Richard Young ruled that Indiana's ban on same-sex marriage "violated the 14th Amendment's due process and equal-protection clauses." State officials are appealing the ruling at the 7th Circuit Court of Appeals.[m]	There are anti-bullying laws with both sexual orientation and gender identity protections.	Yes	No
Indiana	No	No	There is no explicit ban.	No	No	No	IND. CODE ANN. § 31-11-1-1 (1997). (b) "A marriage between persons of the same gender is void in Indiana even if the marriage is lawful in the place where it is solemnized."	There are anti-bullying laws, but no specific groups are defined.	No	Yes
Iowa	Yes	Yes	Yes	Yes	No	Full marriage equality	Full marriage equality	There are anti-bullying laws with both sexual orientation and gender identity protections.	Yes	No

Continued

State by State Listing of Rights

State	*Law Banning Discrimination Based on Both Gender Identity and Sexual Orientation (1)*	*Law Banning Discrimination Based on Sexual Orientation Only (1)*	*Law Banning Foster Care or Adoption for Same-Sex Parents (2)*	*Hate Crimes Based on Sexual Orientation Only (3)*	*Hate Crimes Based on Sexual Orientation and Gender Identity (3)*	*Same-Sex Relationship Recognition*	*Same-Sex Relationships*	*State Protects Students Against Bullying (2)*	*State Prohibits Antigay Harassment and/or Discrimination in Schools*	*States Voted Republican in 2012*
Kansas	No	No	There is no explicit ban.	Yes	No	No	"(a) Marriage shall be constituted by one man and one woman only. All other marriages are declared to be contrary to public policy of this state and are void. (b) No relationship, other than a marriage, shall be recognized by the state as entitling the parties to the rights or incidents of marriage." See Kansas Constitution Article 15, §16.[m]	There are anti-bullying laws, but no specific groups are defined.	No	Yes

Kentucky	No	No	There is no explicit ban.	Yes	No	No	Kentucky Constitution § 233A (2004). "Only a marriage between one man and one woman shall be valid or recognized as legal in Kentucky." In July 2014, Federal Judge John G. Heyburn overturned Kentucky's ban on same-sex marriages and the case is currently under appeal at the 6th U.S. Circuit Court of Appeals.[ss]	There are anti-bullying laws, but no specific groups are defined.	No	Yes
Louisiana	No	No	Children's Code Art. 1198 (1992) "A single person, eighteen years or older, or a married couple jointly may petition to adopt a child through an agency." Two single adults cannot petition for adoption together.	Yes	No	No	Louisiana Constitution Article XII, § 15 (2004). "Marriage in the state of Louisiana shall consist only of the union of one man and one woman."	There are anti-bullying laws, but no specific groups are defined.	No	Yes
Maine	Yes	No	There is no explicit ban.	Yes	No	Full marriage equality	Full marriage equality	There are anti-bullying laws with both sexual orientation and gender identity protections.[n]	Yes	No

Continued

State by State Listing of Rights

State	*Law Banning Discrimination Based on Both Gender Identity and Sexual Orientation (1)*	*Law Banning Discrimination Based on Sexual Orientation Only (1)*	*Law Banning Foster Care or Adoption for Same-Sex Parents (2)*	*Hate Crimes Based on Sexual Orientation Only (3)*	*Hate Crimes Based on Sexual Orientation and Gender Identity (3)*	*Same-Sex Relationship Recognition*	*Same-Sex Relationships*	*State Protects Students Against Bullying (2)*	*State Prohibits Antigay Harassment and/or Discrimination in Schools*	*States Voted Republican in 2012*
Maryland	No	Yes	MD CODE REGS. 07.05.03.09(A)(2)) (1998). "The agency may not deny an individual's application to be an adoptive parent because: Of the applicant's or adoptive child's race, color, culture, national origin, sexual orientation, or ethnic heritage."	Yes	Yes	Full marriage equality	Full marriage equality	There are anti-bullying laws with both sexual orientation and gender identity protections.	Yes	No
Massachusetts	Yes	No	There is no explicit ban.	No, hate crimes cover both gender identity and sexual orientation.	Yes	Full marriage equality	Full marriage equality.	There are anti-bullying laws with both sexual orientation and gender identity protections.[o]	Yes	No

Michigan	No	No	MICH. COMP. LAWS ANN. § 710.24 (2004). "Michigan law allows any adult or married couple to petition to adopt" and they ban adoption for same-sex couples married in other jurisdictions.	No	No	Currently no, but it is under appeal as of May 19, 2014.	Mich. Constitution, Article I § 25 (2004). "To secure and preserve the benefits of marriage for our society and for future generations of children, the union of one man and one woman in marriage shall be the only agreement recognized as a marriage or similar union for any purpose."	There are anti-bullying laws, but no specific groups are defined.	No	No
Minnesota	Yes	No	There is no explicit ban.	No, hate crimes cover both gender identity and sexual orientation.	Yes	Full marriage equality	Full marriage equality	There are anti-bullying laws with both sexual orientation and gender identity protections.[p]	Yes	No
Mississippi	No	No	Couples of the same gender may not adopt MISS. CODE ANN. § 93-17-3.[q]	No	No	No	Mississippi law states: "Any marriage between persons of the same gender is prohibited and null and void from the beginning. Any marriage between persons of the same gender that is valid in another jurisdiction does not constitute a legal or valid marriage in Mississippi. Any attempt to evade section 93-1-1 by marrying out of this state and returning to it shall be within the prohibitions of said section."[r]	Yes anti-bullying, but no specific group identified.	No	Yes

Continued

State by State Listing of Rights

State	*Law Banning Discrimination Based on Both Gender Identity and Sexual Orientation (1)*	*Law Banning Discrimination Based on Sexual Orientation Only (1)*	*Law Banning Foster Care or Adoption for Same-Sex Parents (2)*	*Hate Crimes Based on Sexual Orientation Only (3)*	*Hate Crimes Based on Sexual Orientation and Gender Identity (3)*	*Same-Sex Relationship Recognition*	*Same-Sex Relationships*	*State Protects Students Against Bullying (2)*	*State Prohibits Antigay Harassment and/or Discrimination in Schools*	*States Voted Republican in 2012*
Missouri	No	No	There is no explicit ban.	No, hate crimes cover both gender identity and sexual orientation.	Yes	No	MO. CONST., Art. I, Sect. 33 (2012). "That to be valid and recognized in this state, a marriage shall exist only between a man and a woman."	There are anti-bullying laws, but no specific groups are defined.	No	Yes
Montana	No	No	There is no explicit ban.	No	No	No	The state constitution prohibits marriage between same-sex couples. Amended in 2004 to read: "Only a marriage between one man and one woman shall be valid or recognized as a marriage in this state". Montana Constitution, Article XIII § 7.[s]	No laws, just policy. sexual orientation and gender identity are not protected.	No	Yes

Nebraska	No	No	NEB. REV. STAT. § 43-101 (2002) "Any adult person or persons. However, a same-sex partner cannot adopt the partner's child without terminating the other partner's parental rights." In 1995 Nebraska's Dept. of Soc. Services enacted an Administrative Memorandum that prohibits adoption by gay individuals and unmarried co-habiting individuals.[t] It is unclear whether the directive is currently enforced.	Yes	No	No	NEB. CONST. art. I, sec. 29 (2006). "Only marriage between a man and a woman shall be valid or recognized in Nebraska. The uniting of two persons of the same sex in a civil union, domestic partnership or other similar same-sex relationship shall not be valid or recognized in Nebraska."[u]	There are anti-bullying laws, but no specific groups are defined.	No	Yes
Nevada	Yes	No	There is no explicit ban.	No	Yes	"Yes, domestic partnerships. See Nevada Revised Statutes §§ 122A.010 et seq."[v]	NEV. CONST. art I, Sec. 21; Senate Bill 283 (2002). "Only a marriage between a male and female person shall be recognized and given effect in this state." "The 9th U.S. Circuit Court of Appeals in San Francisco has scheduled arguments for Sept. 8 (2014). Nevada Attorney General Catherine Cortez Masto is refusing to defend the ban."[tt]	There are anti-bullying laws, but no specific groups are defined.	No	No

Continued

State by State Listing of Rights

State	Law Banning Discrimination Based on Both Gender Identity and Sexual Orientation (1)	Law Banning Discrimination Based on Sexual Orientation Only (1)	Law Banning Foster Care or Adoption for Same-Sex Parents (2)	Hate Crimes Based on Sexual Orientation Only (3)	Hate Crimes Based on Sexual Orientation and Gender Identity (3)	Same-Sex Relationship Recognition	Same-Sex Relationships	State Protects Students Against Bullying (2)	State Prohibits Antigay Harassment and/or Discrimination in Schools	States Voted Republican in 2012
New Hampshire	No	Yes	There is no explicit ban, and some lower courts have allowed second-parent adoptions to proceed.	Yes	No	Full marriage equality	Full marriage equality	There are anti-bullying laws with both sexual orientation and gender identity protections.	Yes	No
New Jersey	Yes	No	N.J. ADMIN. CODE 10:121C-2.6 (1995). Specifically required to allow any adult to petition to adopt, regardless of sexual orientation.[w]	No, hate crimes cover both gender identity and sexual orientation.	Yes	In October 2013, a New Jersey Superior Court Judge overturned a ban on same-sex marriage. In December 2013, "Key Senate Democrats are moving forward with a plan to turn a court decision legalizing gay marriage into state law, saying they want to protect same-sex couples from having this right removed by a future court."[x]	Full marriage equality	There are anti-bullying laws with both sexual orientation and gender identity protections.	Yes	No

New Mexico	Yes	No	There is no explicit ban.	No, Hate Crimes cover both gender identity and sexual orientation.	Yes	In December 2013, New Mexico's High court said, "Prohibiting same-gender marriages is not substantially related to the governmental interests advanced by the parties opposing same-gender marriage or to the purposes we have identified. Therefore, barring individuals from marrying and depriving them of the rights, protections, and responsibilities of civil marriage solely because of their sexual orientation violates the Equal Protection Clause under Article II, Section 18 of the New Mexico Constitution."[y]	Full marriage equality	There are anti-bullying laws with sexual orientation protections, but gender identity not included.	No	No
New York	No	Yes	New York law permits an adult or a married couple to petition to adopt. The state regulation reads, "[a]pplicants shall not be rejected solely on the basis of homosexuality" N.Y. COMP. CODES R. & REGS. tit. 18, § 421.16(h)(2) (1995).[aa]	Yes, the law addresses only hate crimes related to sexual orientation.	No	Full marriage equality	Full marriage equality	There are anti-bullying laws with both sexual orientation and gender identity protections.[bb]	Yes	No

Continued

State by State Listing of Rights

State	*Law Banning Discrimination Based on Both Gender Identity and Sexual Orientation (1)*	*Law Banning Discrimination Based on Sexual Orientation Only (1)*	*Law Banning Foster Care or Adoption for Same-Sex Parents (2)*	*Hate Crimes Based on Sexual Orientation Only (3)*	*Hate Crimes Based on Sexual Orientation and Gender Identity (3)*	*Same-Sex Relationship Recognition*	*Same-Sex Relationships*	*State Protects Students Against Bullying (2)*	*State Prohibits Antigay Harassment and/or Discrimination in Schools*	*States Voted Republican in 2012*
North Carolina	No	No	N.C. GEN. STAT. § 48-2-301 (c) (2009). "If the individual who files the petition is unmarried, no other individual may join in the petition."	No	No	No	N.C. Const. Art. 14 §6 (2012). "Marriage between one man and one woman is the only domestic legal union that shall be valid or recognized in this State."	There are anti-bullying laws with both sexual orientation and gender identity protections.	Yes	Yes
North Dakota	No	No	There is no explicit ban, however, N.D. CENT. CODE § 50-12-07.1 states: "A child-placing agency is not required to perform, assist, counsel, recommend, facilitate, refer, or participate in a placement that violates the agency's written religious or moral convictions or policies."	No	No	No	N.D. Constitution, Article XI § 28 (2004). "Marriage consists only of the legal union between a man and a woman. No other domestic union, however denominated, may be recognized as a marriage or given the same or substantially equivalent legal effect."	There are anti-bullying laws, but no specific groups are defined.	No	Yes

Ohio	No	No	State law provides that a husband and wife may jointly petition to adopt, and does not explicitly provide for joint adoption by other couples.	No	No	In December 2013, "A federal judge Monday ordered Ohio authorities to recognize gay marriages on death certificates, saying the state's ban on such unions is unconstitutional and that states cannot discriminate against same-sex couples simply because some voters don't like homosexuality."[cc]	Ohio Constitution, Article XV § 11 (2004). "Only a union between one man and one woman may be a marriage valid in or recognized by this state and its political subdivisions. This state and its political subdivisions shall not create or recognize a legal status for relationships of unmarried individuals that intends to approximate the design, qualities, significance or effect of marriage."	There are anti-bullying laws, but no specific groups are defined.	No	No
Oklahoma	No	No	There is no explicit ban.	No	No	No	"The 10th Circuit Court of Appeals in Denver ruled on June 25 (2014) that Utah must allow gay couples to marry, finding the Constitution protects same-sex relationships. The court made the same ruling on Oklahoma's ban Friday."[nn]	There are anti-bullying laws, but no specific groups are defined.	No	Yes

Continued

State by State Listing of Rights

State	*Law Banning Discrimination Based on Both Gender Identity and Sexual Orientation (1)*	*Law Banning Discrimination Based on Sexual Orientation Only (1)*	*Law Banning Foster Care or Adoption for Same-Sex Parents (2)*	*Hate Crimes Based on Sexual Orientation Only (3)*	*Hate Crimes Based on Sexual Orientation and Gender Identity (3)*	*Same-Sex Relationship Recognition*	*Same-Sex Relationships*	*State Protects Students Against Bullying (2)*	*State Prohibits Antigay Harassment and/or Discrimination in Schools*	*States Voted Republican in 2012*
Oregon	Yes	No	There is no explicit ban.	No, hate crimes cover both gender identity and sexual orientation.	Yes	Yes. "Same-sex couples in Oregon can enter into domestic partnerships that provide the same rights, benefits, and responsibilities as marriage under state law, thanks to the Oregon Family Fairness Act, Public Law Number 99, (2007)."[dd]	Full marriage equality. On May 19, 2014, U.S. District Court Judge Michael McShane wrote, "the laws violate the equal protection clause of the Fourteenth Amendment to the United States."[oo] The state has no plans to appeal the decision.	There are anti-bullying laws with both sexual orientation and gender identity protections.[ee]	Yes	No
Pennsylvania	No	No	There is no explicit ban.	No	No	Yes. Justice Alito turned down an appeal by the state.	In May 2014, "Judge Jones did not issue a stay, writing, 'By virtue of this ruling, same-sex couples who seek to marry in Pennsylvania may do so, and already married same-sex couples will be recognized as such in the Commonwealth.'" The state does not plan to appeal the decision.[uu]	There are anti-bullying laws, but no specific groups are defined.	No	No

Rhode Island	Yes	No	There is no explicit ban.	Yes, the law addresses only hate crimes related to sexual orientation.	No	Full marriage equality	Full marriage equality	There are anti-bullying laws with both sexual orientation and gender identity protections.[ff]	Yes	No
South Carolina	No	No	There is no explicit ban.	No	No	No	S.C. CONST. Art. XVII, §15 (2007). "A marriage between one man and one woman is the only lawful domestic union that shall be valid or recognized in this State."	There are anti-bullying laws, but no specific groups are defined.	No	Yes
South Dakota	No	No	There is no explicit ban.	No	No	No	S.D. CONST Art. XX1; §9 (2006). Marriage. "Only marriage between a man and a woman shall be valid or recognized in South Dakota. The uniting of two or more persons in a civil union, domestic partnership, or other quasi-marital relationship shall not be valid or recognized in South Dakota."	There are anti-bullying laws, but no specific groups are defined.	No	Yes
Tennessee	No	No	There is no explicit ban.	Yes, the law addresses only hate crimes related to sexual orientation.	No	No	TENN. CONST. Art. XI, §18 (2004)."The historical institution and legal contract solemnizing the relationship of one man and one woman shall be the only legally recognized marital contract in this state."	There are anti-bullying laws, but no specific groups are defined.	No	Yes

Continued

State by State Listing of Rights

State	Law Banning Discrimination Based on Both Gender Identity and Sexual Orientation (1)	Law Banning Discrimination Based on Sexual Orientation Only (1)	Law Banning Foster Care or Adoption for Same-Sex Parents (2)	Hate Crimes Based on Sexual Orientation Only (3)	Hate Crimes Based on Sexual Orientation and Gender Identity (3)	Same-Sex Relationship Recognition	Same-Sex Relationships	State Protects Students Against Bullying (2)	State Prohibits Antigay Harassment and/or Discrimination in Schools	States Voted Republican in 2012
Texas	No	No	There is no explicit ban.	Yes, the law addresses only hate crimes related to sexual orientation.	No	No	In February 2014 it was U.S. District Judge Orlando L. Garcia who declared the ban to be "state–imposed inequality."[pp]	There are anti-bullying laws, but no specific groups are defined.	No	Yes
Utah	No	No	Utah Code § 78B-6-117 (3) (2008). "A child may not be adopted by a person who is cohabiting in a relationship that is not a legally valid and binding marriage under the laws of this state."	No	No	No	"The 10th Circuit Court of Appeals in Denver ruled on June 25 (2014) that Utah must allow gay couples to marry, finding the Constitution protects same-sex relationships."[tt]	There are anti-bullying laws, but no specific groups are defined.	No	Yes

Vermont	Yes	No	Same-sex couples who are joined by civil unions or marriage may petition to jointly adopt.	No, Hate Crimes cover both gender identity and sexual orientation.	Yes	Full marriage equality	Full marriage equality	There are anti-bullying laws with both sexual orientation and gender identity protections.	Yes	No
Virginia	No	No	There is no explicit ban, however, "Child-placing agency; shall not be required to participate in placement of child for foster care or adoption when it would violate agency's written religious or moral convictions or policies."[hh]	No	No	No	As of May 19, 2014, the ban is under appeal.	There are anti-bullying laws, but there are no protections against sexual orientation or gender identity bullying.	No	No
Washington	Yes	No	There is no explicit ban.	No, hate crimes cover both gender identity and sexual orientation.	Yes	Full marriage equality.	Full marriage equality.	There are anti-bullying laws with both sexual orientation and gender identity protections.[ii]	Yes	No

Continued

State by State Listing of Rights

State	*Law Banning Discrimination Based on Both Gender Identity and Sexual Orientation (1)*	*Law Banning Discrimination Based on Sexual Orientation Only (1)*	*Law Banning Foster Care or Adoption for Same-Sex Parents (2)*	*Hate Crimes Based on Sexual Orientation Only (3)*	*Hate Crimes Based on Sexual Orientation and Gender Identity (3)*	*Same-Sex Relationship Recognition*	*Same-Sex Relationships*	*State Protects Students Against Bullying (2)*	*State Prohibits Antigay Harassment and/or Discrimination in Schools*	*States Voted Republican in 2012*
West Virginia	No	No	State law provides that a husband and wife may jointly petition to adopt, and does not explicitly provide for joint adoption by other couples. There is no explicit ban.	No	No	No	W. Va. Code § 48-2-603 (Last Updated 2007). "A public act, record or judicial proceeding of any other state, territory, possession or tribe respecting a relationship between persons of the same sex that is treated as a marriage under the laws of the other state, territory, possession, or tribe, or a right or claim arising from such relationship, shall not be given effect by this state."	There are anti-bullying laws, but no specific groups are defined.	No	Yes

Wisconsin	No	Yes	Unclear. Wisconsin courts have never precisely decided the issue, though they have strongly suggested that joint adoptions by unmarried individuals are not available under the current statutes.	Yes, the law addresses only hate crimes related to sexual orientation.	No	Yes. "Same-sex couples can register as domestic partners and receive limited rights and responsibilities under state law (not all the rights and responsibilities available to spouses)."[ii]	WIS. STAT. §765.001(2) (Last Updated 2011). "Under the laws of this state, marriage is a legal relationship between 2 equal persons, a husband and wife, who owe to each other mutual responsibility and support." Currently under appeal.	There are anti-bullying laws with sexual orientation protections, but gender identity not included.	No	No
Wyoming	No	No	There is no explicit ban.	No	No	No	WYO. STAT. ANN. §20-1-101 (2003). "Marriage is a civil contract between a male and a female person to which the consent of the parties capable of contracting is essential."	There are anti-bullying laws, but no specific groups are defined.	No	Yes

(1) http://www.thetaskforce.org/downloads/reports/issue_maps/non_discrimination_6_13_color.pdf
(2) http://www.hrc.org/laws-and-legislation/state
(3) http://www.guardian.co.uk/world/interactive/2012/may/08/gay-rights-united-states?fb = native Last Updated May 8, 2012.
a http://www.azleg.state.az.us/FormatDocument.asp?inDoc=/ars/8/00103.htm&Title=8&DocType=ARS
b http://www.lexisnexis.com/hottopics/arcode/Default.asp
c http://www.hrc.org/laws-and-legislation/entry/arkansas-marriage-relationship-recognition-law
d http://www.hrc.org/laws-and-legislation/entry/arkansas-marriage-relationship-recognition-law
e http://www.lexisnexis.com/hottopics/arcode/Default.asp
f http://www.leginfo.ca.gov/cgi-bin/displaycode?section=edc&group=00001-01000&file=234-234.5
g http://www.leg.state.co.us/clics/clics2013a/csl.nsf/fsbillcont/35CE5FDC5F040FF487257A8C0050715D?Open&file=011_enr.pdf
h http://cga.ct.gov/2011/ACT/PA/2011PA-00232-R00SB-01138-PA.htm
i http://delcode.delaware.gov/sessionlaws/ga146/chp378.shtml
j http://www.flsenate.gov/Laws/Statutes/2012/63.042
k http://www.lambdalegal.org/states-regions/hawaii
l http://www.ilga.gov/legislation/fulltext.asp?DocName=09800SB0010sam001&GA=98&LegID=68375&SessionId=85&SpecSess=0&DocTypeId=SB&DocNum=0010&GAID=12&Session=
m http://www.lambdalegal.org/states-regions/kansas
n http://www.mainelegislature.org/legis/bills/bills_125th/billtexts/HP092807.asp
o http://lawlib.state.ma.us/subject/about/transgender.html Accessed 1/31/2013

p https://www.revisor.mn.gov/statutes/?id=148F.17&year=2012&keyword_type=all&keyword=gender+identity
q http://www.hrc.org/laws-and-legislation/entry/mississippi-adoption-law
r http://www.hrc.org/laws-and-legislation/entry/mississippi-marriage-relationship-recognition-law
s http://www.lambdalegal.org/states-regions/Montana
t dhhs.ne.gov/children_family_services/Documents/AM-1.pdf
u http://www.hrc.org/laws-and-legislation/entry/nebraska-marriage-relationship-recognition-law
v http://www.lambdalegal.org/states-regions/nevada
w http://www.hrc.org/laws-and-legislation/entry/new-jersey-adoption-law
x http://www.nj.com/politics/index.ssf/2013/12/nj_legislature_same-sex_marriage_bill.html
y http://blogs.wsj.com/law/2013/12/19/new-mexico-supreme-court-legalizes-same-sex-marriage/
z http://www.hrc.org/laws-and-legislation/entry/new-mexico-marriage-relationship-recognition-law
aa http://www.hrc.org/laws-and-legislation/entry/new-york-adoption-law
bb http://public.leginfo.state.ny.us/LAWSSEAF.cgi?QUERYTYPE=LAWS+&QUERYDATA=$$EDN13$$@TXEDN013+&LIST=LAW+&BROWSER=BROWSER+&TOKEN=13176117+&TARGET=VIEW
cc http://www.ohio.com/news/ohio-gay-marriage-ban-is-rejected-in-narrow-ruling-1.454593
dd http://www.hrc.org/laws-and-legislation/entry/oregon-marriage-relationship-recognition-law
ee http://www.leg.state.or.us/07reg/measures/sb0001.dir/sb0002.en.html
ff http://webserver.rilin.state.ri.us/statutes/title11/11-24/11-24-2.1.htm
gg http://www.latimes.com/nation/nationnow/la-na-nn-utah-gay-marriage-supreme-court-20131226,0,6677614.story#axzz2onsjkrrB
hh http://lis.virginia.gov/121/idx/noframes/help/0063.html
ii http://www.k12.wa.us/SafetyCenter/BullyingHarassment/default.aspx
jj http://www.hrc.org/laws-and-legislation/entry/wisconsin-marriage-relationship-recognition-law
kk http://www.npr.org/blogs/thetwo-way/2014/05/09/311143379/judge-strikes-down-arkansas-ban-on-gay-marriage
ll http://www.washingtonpost.com/national/judge-strikes-down-gay-marriage-ban-stays-ruling/2014/07/23/6416850c-12c9-11e4-ac56-773e54a65906_story.html
mm http://www.washingtonpost.com/news/volokh-conspiracy/wp/2014/05/14/federal-judge-strikes-down-idaho-law-banning-same-sex-marriage/
nn http://www.washingtonpost.com/national/gay-marriage-legal-challenges-where-things-stand/2014/07/18/94667af4-0ea1-11e4-b0dd-edc009ac1f9d_story.html
oo http://www.washingtonpost.com/blogs/govbeat/wp/2014/05/19/federal-judge-strikes-down-oregon-ban-on-same-sex-marriage/
pp http://www.washingtonpost.com/politics/judge-strikes-down-texas-gay-marriage-ban-paving-way-for-shift-in-conservative-bastion/2014/02/26/201d6cd0-9f1f-11e3-9ba6-800d1192d08b_story.html
qq http://www.npr.org/blogs/thetwo-way/2014/07/17/332331829/judge-overturns-floridas-same-sex-marriage-ban
rr http://www.washingtonpost.com/politics/appeals-court-puts-ruling-overturning-indianas-same-sex-marriage-ban-on-hold/2014/06/27/96348a1c-fe5a-11e3-932c-0a55b81f48ce_story.html
ss http://www.nytimes.com/2014/07/02/us/kentucky-gay-marriage-ban-rejected.html
tt http://www.washingtonpost.com/national/gay-marriage-legal-challenges-where-things-stand/2014/07/18/94667af4-0ea1-11e4-b0dd-edc009ac1f9d_story.html
uu http://www.nytimes.com/2014/05/21/us/judge-strikes-down-pennsylvania-ban-on-gay-marriage.html

References

Alabama State Constitution. "Alabama Marriage Protection Act". Accessed November 22, 2012. http://www.legislature.state.al.us/CodeofAlabama/1975/30-1-19.htm.

Alaska State Constitution. "Marriage." Accessed November 22, 2012. http://www.legis.state.ak.us/basis/folioproxy.asp?url=http://wwwjnu01.legis.state.ak.us/cgi-bin/folioisa.dll/acontxt/query=*/doc/{@3}?next.

Arizona State Legislature. "Who May Adopt." Accessed November 22, 2012. http://www.azleg.state.az.us/FormatDocument.asp?inDoc=/ars/8/00103.htm&Title=8&DocType=ARS.

Arizona State Constitution. "Marriage." Accessed November 22, 2012. http://www.azleg.gov/FormatDocument.asp?inDoc =/const/30/1.htm.

Arkansas Constitution. "Marriage Amendment." Accessed November 22, 2012. http://www.sos.arkansas.gov/ar-constitution/arcamend83/arcamend83-1.html.

California Family Code. Accessed November 22, 2012. http://www.leginfo.ca.gov/cgi-bin/displaycode?section=fam&group=08001-09000&file=9000-9007.

California Family Code. Accessed November 22, 2012. http://www.leginfo.ca.gov/cgi-bin/displaycode?section=fam&group=00001-01000&file=300-310.

Connecticut Marriage Statutes. Accessed November 22, 2012. http://search.cga.state.ct.us/dtsearch_pub_statutes.html.

Delaware Title Thirteen. "Adoption." Accessed November 22, 2012. http://delcode.delaware.gov/title13/c009/sc01/index.shtml.

Delaware Title Thirteen. "Civil Unions." Accessed November 22, 2012. http://delcode.delaware.gov/title13/c002/index.shtml.

Delaware Title Thirteen. "Marriage." Accessed November 22, 2012. http://delcode.delaware.gov/title13/c001/sc01/index.shtml.

Florida Civil Practice and Procedure. "Who May Adopt." Accessed November 22, 2012. http://www.leg.state.fl.us/statutes/index.cfm?mode=View%20Statutes&SubMenu=1&App_mode=Display_Statute&Search_String=63.042&URL=0000-0099/0063/Sections/0063.042.html.

Florida Statutes. "Marriages between Persons of the Same Sex." Accessed November 22, 2012. http://www.leg.state.fl.us/Statutes/index.cfm?App_mode=Display_Statute&URL=0700-0799/0741/Sections/0741.212.html.

Georgia Constitution. "Domestic Relations." Accessed November 22, 2012. http://www.lexisnexis.com/hottopics/gacode/Default.asp.

Hawaii State Legislature. "Who May Adopt." Accessed November 22, 2012. http://www.capitol.hawaii.gov/hrs2006/Vol12_Ch0501-0588/HRS0578/HRS_0578-0001.HTM.

Idaho Constitution. "Marriage." Accessed November 22, 2012. http://www.legislature.idaho.gov/idstat/IC/ArtIIISect28.htm.

Illinois Compiled Statutes. "Illinois Marriage and Dissolution of Marriage Act." Accessed November 22, 2012. http://www.ilga.gov/legislation/ilcs/ilcs4.asp?ActID=2086&ChapterID=59&SeqStart=900000&SeqEnd=3000000.

Indiana Code. "Who May Marry." Accessed November 22, 2012. http://www.in.gov/legislative/ic/code/title31/ar11/ch1.html.

Kentucky "Petition for Adoption of Child." Accessed November 22, 2012. http://www.lrc.ky.gov/krs/199-00/470.pdf.

Kentucky Constitution. "Valid or Recognized Marriage—Legal Status of Unmarried Individuals." Accessed November 23, 2012. http://www.lrc.ky.gov/Legresou/Constitu/233A.htm.

Louisiana Children's Code "Persons Who May Petition for Adoption." Accessed February 1, 2013. http://www.legis.state.la.us/lss/lss.asp?doc=72670.

Louisiana Constitution. "Defense of Marriage Law." Accessed November 23, 2012. http://senate.legis.state.la.us/Documents/Constitution/Article12.htm#%A715.%A0%A0Defense%20of%20Marriage.

Maryland Government Code. "Criteria for Consideration as an Adoptive Parent." Accessed November 23, 2012. http://www.dsd.state.md.us/comar/getfile.aspx?file=07.05.03.09.htm.

Michigan Probate Code. "Petition for Adoption; Filing; Jurisdiction; Verification; Contents." Accessed November 23, 2012. http://www.legislature.mi.gov/(S(nd0r4tewx3lhptvavqqru5bl))/mileg.aspx?page=getObject&objectName=mcl-710-24.

Michigan State Constitution. "Marriage." Accessed November 23, 2012. http://www.legislature.mi.gov/%28S%28qkimviqjlpl1zavzrt2bt5uh%29%29/mileg.aspx?page=getobject&objectname=mcl-Article-I-25&queryid=14962083.

Minnesota Statutes. "Prohibited Marriages." Accessed November 23, 2012. https://www.revisor.mn.gov/statutes/?id=517.03.

Missouri Constitution. "Marriage, Validity and Recognition." Accessed November 23, 2012. http://www.moga.mo.gov/const/a01033.htm.

Nebraska Revised Statute. "Children Eligible for Adoption." Accessed November 23, 2012. http://uniweb.legislature.ne.gov/laws/statutes.php?statute=43-101.

Nebraska State Constitution. "Marriage; Same-Sex Relationships Not Valid or Recognized." Accessed November 23, 2012. http://www.nebraskalegislature.gov/laws/articles.php?article=I-29.

Nevada State Constitution. "Limitation on Recognition of Marriage." Accessed November 23, 2012. http://www.leg.state.nv.us/Const/NVConst.html#Art1Sec21.

New Jersey. "Civil Union Act." Accessed February 2, 2013. http://www.njleg.state.nj.us/2006/Bills/PL06/103_.HTM.

North Carolina General Statute. "Petition for Adoption; Who May File." Accessed November 23, 2012. http://www.ncga.state.nc.us/gascripts/statutes/statutelookup.pl?statute=48-2-301.

North Carolina State Constitution. "Marriage." Accessed November 23, 2012. http://www.ncga.state.nc.us/Legislation/constitution/ncconstitution.html.

North Dakota Century Code. "Child-Placing Agency." Accessed February 2, 2013. http://www.legis.nd.gov/cencode/t50.html.

North Dakota Constitution. "General Provisions". Accessed December 2, 2012. http://www.legis.nd.gov/constitution.

Ohio State Constitution. "Marriage Amendment." Accessed December 2, 2012. http://www.legislature.state.oh.us/constitution.cfm?Part=15&Section=11.

Oklahoma State Constitution. "Marriage Defined—Construction of Law and Constitution—Recognition of out-of-State Marriages—Penalty." Accessed December 12, 2012. http://www.oscn.net/applications/oscn/DeliverDocument.asp?CiteID=441397.

Oregon State Constitution. "Policy Regarding Marriage." Accessed December 12, 2012. http://www.leg.state.or.us/orcons/orcons.html.

Pennsylvania Statute. "Marriage between Persons of the Same Sex." Accessed December 15, 2012. http://www.legis.state.pa.us/WU01/LI/LI/CT/HTM/23/00.017.004.000..HTM.

South Carolina Constitution. "Lawful Domestic Unions Recognizable in State; Domestic Unions Created in Another Jurisdiction." Accessed December 15, 2012. http://www.scstatehouse.gov/scconstitution/a17.php.

South Dakota Codified Laws. "Marriage." Accessed December 15, 2012. http://legis.state.sd.us/statutes/DisplayStatute.aspx?Statute=0N-21-9&Type=Statute.

Tennessee State Constitution. "Miscellaneous Provisions." Accessed December 15, 2012. http://www.capitol.tn.gov/about/docs/TN-Constitution.pdf.

Texas State Constitution. "Marriage." Accessed December 15, 2012. http://www.statutes.legis.state.tx.us/SOTWDocs/CN/htm/CN.1.htm.

Utah State Law. "Who may adopt." Accessed December 15, 2012. http://le.utah.gov/~code/TITLE78B/htm/78B06_011700.htm.

Utah State Constitution. Accessed December 15, 2012. http://le.utah.gov/code/CONST/htm/00I01_002900.htm.

Virginia State Constitution. "Marriage." Accessed December 15, 2012. http://constitution.legis.virginia.gov/ConstOfVa.pdf.

West Virginia State Law. "Certain Acts, Records, and Proceedings Not to be Given Effect in this State." Accessed December 15, 2012. http://www.legis.state.wv.us/legisdocs/code/48/WVC%2048%20%20-%20%202%20%20-%20603%20%20.htm.

Wisconsin State Law. "The Family Code." Accessed December 15, 2012. http://docs.legis.wisconsin.gov/statutes/statutes/765/30#/statutes/statutes/765/_4.

Wyoming State Law. "Marriage a Civil Contract." Accessed December 15, 2012. http://legisweb.state.wy.us/statutes/statutes.aspx?file=titles/Title20/Title20.htm.

Index

A

D

E

L

N